# Adva

"In one volume, *Mounting Evidence* provides the most important evidence accumulated over many years that calls into question the government's account of 9/11. Any citizen of conscience reading it will demand a new investigation."

—Mike Gravel, United States Senate, 1969-1981

"With breadth enough to engage readers new to 9/11 issues, yet depth of analysis enough to challenge those with more knowledge, *Mounting Evidence* has achieved a real coup. Moving beyond facile conspiracy theory and simplistic 'inside-job' interpretations, this book puts 9/11 in more complex contexts. Hats off to Dr. Rea for building a case for reexamination."

—Mickey Huff, Professor of History at Diablo Valley College and Director of Project Censored.

"*Mounting Evidence* offers a concise and readable analysis of what is concretely known about 9/11 and the inconsistencies in the US government's *9/11 Commission Report*. This is the book that fills in the gaps on 'why they hate us' and puts in context the historical and ongoing abuses of the Media Empire. Ten years of lies and deceit are enough; it's time to demand a complete and through public investigation into 9/11."

—Peter Phillips, Ph.D., Professor of Sociology, Sonoma State University and President of the Media Freedom Foundation/Project Censored.

"Paul Rea's book provides us with both meaningful contexts and a fresh, detailed analyses of the 9/11 evidence in a compelling, readable package. His work is indispensable for any real understanding of our twenty-first century world."

—Laurence H. Shoup, PhD, author of *Imperial Brain Trust* and *Rulers and Rebels*

# MOUNTING EVIDENCE

Also by Paul W. Rea . . .

*Canyon Interludes* (1995)
*Still Seeking the Truth about 9/11* (2005)

# Mounting Evidence

## Why We Need a New Investigation Into 9/11

Paul W. Rea, PhD

iUniverse, Inc.
Bloomington

**Mounting Evidence**
**Why We Need a New Investigation Into 9/11**

iUniverse books may be ordered through booksellers or by contacting:

iUniverse
1663 Liberty Drive
Bloomington, IN 47403
www.iuniverse.com
1-800-Authors (1-800-288-4677)

ISBN: 978-1-4620-0066-1 (sc)
ISBN: 978-1-4620-0068-5 (ebk)

Library of Congress Control Number: 2011911458

Printed in the United States of America

iUniverse rev. date: 09/11/2011

# Contents

# Acknowledgments

Special thanks to Victoria Ashley; Jeremy Baker; Russ Baker; Jane Bark; Lois Battuelo; Carol Brouillet; Byron Belitsos; Sue Byerley; Sandy Cashmark; Dana Carson; David Chandler; Gabriel Day; Matt Everett; Tom Ford; Joan Friedman; Richard Gage, AIA; Kyle Gardner; Brian Good; David Ray Griffin, PhD; Glenn Greenwald; Jim Hoffman; Robin Hordon; Mickey Huff; Ken Jenkins; Steven Jones, PhD; Frank Legge, PhD; Janette MacKinlay; Janice Matthews; Kai Middleton; Chuck Millar; Rowland Morgan; Scott Page; Lori Patotzka; Peter Phillips, PhD; Ed Rippy; Brian Romanoff; Lisa Ryan; Kevin Quick; Kevin Ryan; Gregg Roberts; Frank Runninghorse; Camille Sauvé; Peter Dale Scott, PhD; Ryan Shehee; Larry Shoup, PhD; Sandra Taylor; Paul Thompson; Chuck Thurston; Bill Veale; Elizabeth Woodworth; John Wright; and Mike Zimmer.

# Author's Preface

Early in life, I decided not to be a bystander. As a young man I sought knowledge and became involved in politics as ways to better the world. The former led me to become a professor of humanities, and the latter gave my work an activist edge. Propelled by a passion for peace and a love of nature, my life continues to feature peace work and environmental activism. In 1995, my reverence for the natural world led to a first book, *Canyon Interludes*.

More recently, passions for peace, justice, and better government have led me to write two books about 9/11. In 2005, these concerns came together in *Still Seeking the Truth about 9/11*, a short treatment of the issues. *Mounting Evidence* represents six additional years of research and analysis. More evidence was emerging all the time, and these findings needed to reach a wider audience. Many books have dealt with that tragic day, but most focus on limited areas. This one doesn't specialize; its breadth allows it to connect widely spaced dots. It draws on findings from many perspectives to illuminate different facts of 9/11 while also making connections to other important issues.

Although this rendering reflects serious sleuthing, what you'll find here is less a research treatise than a detective mystery in the spirit of Sherlock Holmes. The inquiry goes where the evidence leads it. And while this book doesn't solve the crime of our century, it does take us closer to that goal. In this journey of discovery, we'll learn much that's amazing, instructive, and restorative. As a window to see how the world works, a better understanding of 9/11 reveals new perspectives into American foreign policy, government agencies, and mainstream corporate media.

Designed for the inquisitive citizen, *Mounting Evidence* is reader friendly; I write hard so you read easy. More than one editor has remarked, "this will be a page turner, Paul." Citations appear right on the page, so you can immediately see where the findings were found. I've taken pains to cite solid sources, both establishment and alternative. A very complete Bibliography is available at www.mountingevidence.org.

Yes, there's a lot of information here, but you'll likely experience the evidence as significant, even stunning in its implications. I know I did.

Paul W. Rea, PhD
June 2011
Newark, California

# Acronyms & Abbreviations

AA – American Airlines

AFB – Air Force Base

AP – Associated Press

CBC – Canadian Broadcasting Corporation

*Christian Sci. Mon.* – *The Christian Science Monitor*

COG – Continuity of Government

*The Comm.* - *The* [9/11] *Commission* (Philip Shenon)

DOE – Department of Energy

DoD – Department of Defense

DOJ – Department of Justice

DOT – Department of Transportation

DPS – Defense Protective Services (Pentagon Police)

*For. Pol. Journ.* – *Foreign Policy Journal*

FAA – Federal Aviation Administration

FDNY – New York City Fire Department

IFE – In Flight (or "Air") Emergency

INS – Immigration and Naturalization Services

*J.* – generic abbreviation for *Journal*

*Jane's Intell. Rev.* - *Jane's Intelligence Review*

JCI – Joint Congressional Inquiry

*Minn. Star-Trib.* – *Minnesota Star-Tribune*

NEADS – NorthEast Air Defense Sector

NORAD – North American Aerospace Defense Command

NMCC – National Military Command Center

NRO – National Reconnaissance Office (CIA)

NSSE – National Special Security Event

NTSB – National Transportation Safety Board

*NYT* – *The New York Times*

NYPD – New York Police Department

OEM – Office of Emergency Management

OPEC – Organization of the Petroleum Exporting Countries

*OWH* – *Omaha World Herald*

PDB – President's Daily Briefing

PEOC – Presidential Emergency Operations Center

Pers. Correspond. – personal correspondence

PNAC – The Project for the New American Century

*Pop. Mech.* – *Popular Mechanics*

SCADs – State Crimes Against Democracy

*San Fran. Chron.* – *The San Francisco Chronicle*

SOF – Supervisor of Flying

SOP – Standard Operating Procedures

*Touch. Hist.* – *Touching History* (Lynn Spencer)

UAL – United Air Lines

UL – Underwriters Laboratories

UPI – United Press International

WMDs – weapons of mass destruction

*WS Journal* – *The Wall Street Journal*

*Wash. Post* – *The Washington Post*

# Prologue

*In fictional times, we need non-fiction.*
—Michael Moore

Most of us would agree that the 9/11 tragedy has defined our time, but how well do we actually understand it? Following such national debacles, it's all about stories—how they're told, who tells them, how they're reinforced, and what their meanings lead people to do. This is especially true when those who create the storylines benefit immensely from those they construct.

People around the world share indelible memories of 9/11. For many, recollections began when they casually turned on the radio or received an urgent phone call: "Turn on your TV right away!" Overwhelmed by images of death and destruction, many watched as history cracked open before their eyes.

Recoiling in disbelief, most of us peered through personal lenses. Novelist Martin Amis saw the second plane—streaking "low over the Statue of Liberty, galvanized with malice"—as foreshadowing a "clash of civilizations" (Amis *The Second Plane* p. 3). For linguist George Lakoff, the airliner shot through the South Tower like an assassin's bullet, its fireball composed of flesh and blood (Lakoff *Don't Think of an Elephant* p. 53). To Col. Robert Bowman, PhD, a former fighter pilot and air-defense specialist, the events made no sense: "Where are the interceptors? Hijacked airliners do not fly around for an hour and a half like that …" (www.youtube.com/watch?v=1weA6jsx-ok).

Observers near the Pentagon also experienced personal reactions. When Air Force Col. Karen Kwiatkowski saw the "surreal" fireball, she vowed to understand what had happened. Later, though, she found her "effort at self-education was marred by the insistent drumbeat of the 'one true path'

1

as broadcast by the administration, most of Congress, and the mainstream media" (Griffin and Scott *9/11 and the American Empire* p. 21). And from his apartment overlooking the Potomac, former senator Mike Gravel watched the smoke billowing from the Pentagon as he pondered "the damage to the American psyche," especially the specter of increased violence.

In the final reckoning, 2,973 people had died, thousands more were injured, and hundreds of thousands, especially in New York, were traumatized. Manhattan residents returned to homes choked with toxic dust. Along with the odor of death, huge holes in the skyline intensified the sense of loss. The symbols of global capitalism and American dominance were gone. What came to be called "the pile" smoldered for five months atop pools of molten steel (Knight Ridder 5/29/02).

To make matters worse, terrorists armed with box cutters had struck the headquarters of the world's most powerful military. Someone had wounded the world's sole remaining superpower: someone would have to pay.

Violence became the unchallenged response to violence. Just hours after the attacks, Secretary of Defense Rumsfeld ordered a search for evidence linking Osama bin Laden to Saddam Hussein. Three days later, Congress authorized the use of force against Afghanistan (*Wash. Post* 9/15/01). It was unpatriotic to suggest that the attacks were crimes—including mass murder— and that they might be addressed through non-violent legal means.

## A Story Assembled with Amazing Speed

New details were provided with unprecedented speed. That very day, the FBI somehow determined who was responsible and released its list of twenty hijackers, complete with their photos, just a few hours after the attacks (MSNBC 9/12/01). Considering later government insistence that these were surprise attacks, that "no one could have imagined" using airliners as missiles, this was exceptionally fast detective work.

Just moments after the Towers came thundering down, an Official Story continued taking shape. Live coverage cut to a "man on the street" near Ground Zero. A guy in a baseball cap explained that he'd "witnessed both Towers collapse ... mostly due to structural failure because the fire was just too intense" (Fox 9/11/01). Thus a passerby who couldn't possibly have known why the skyscrapers had fallen was allowed to introduce a central premise of the Official Story: that both Towers came down because of "structural failures" and "intense" fires.

With little additional information, scientific experts amplified the same pronouncement. A mere two days after the Towers fell, Northwestern math/structural engineering Professor Zdenek Bazant submitted an article entitled "Why did the World Trade Center Collapse?" Amazingly, the article appeared just a week later in the prestigious *Journal of Engineering Mechanics* (9/22/01). Setting a speed record for scientific analysis and scholarly publication, this paper emblazoned a recognized academic brand on a fast-emerging official account. This set the stage for numerous other reinforcing accounts from academics and scientists who uncritically advanced the Official Story (www.youtube.com/watch?v=DF4C6qtU_Fc&amp).

**Early News Coverage: Some Before the Fact, Some Too Candid To Repeat**
Much of the story spinning would have seemed almost comic had the situation not been so tragic. By making before-the-fact reports about the fall of WTC-7, CNN and BBC seemingly displayed foreknowledge that the building was coming down. BBC reported that WTC-7 had fallen, "weakened during this morning's attack" (CNN & BBC 9/11/01), while airing video of the skyscraper still standing over the reporter's shoulder. That's a novel way to score a "scoop."

On the news that evening, three network anchors reported an uncanny resemblance between the disintegration of the WTC buildings and controlled demolitions. Remarking on the unprecedented fall of *three* skyscrapers on a single day, Dan Rather commented on similarities to "when a building was deliberately destroyed by well-placed dynamite" (CBS 9/11/01). Yet no network and no government inquiry have ever followed up on the obvious resemblances. So began the censorship of anything that challenged the Official Story. As a result, many Americans still don't know that a *third* WTC building came down that day, one that was not hit by a plane, and that major news outlets reported its fall while it was still standing.

But these resemblances didn't keep the networks from running and re-running videos of the falling Towers, as most of us remember only too well. Over and over, viewers watched 110-story buildings explode at the top, drop and disintegrate (ABC 9/13/01). Beyond the shots of the Towers, the networks repeatedly rolled out heartbreaking images of office workers hanging out windows, of "jumpers," of crowds running in terror away from dust clouds, and of responders and iron workers working the hellish "pile." Never before had so many excruciating images reinforced a master narrative.

In stark contrast, since that terrible day the networks have rarely re-broadcast the straight-down fall of WTC-7, the building that wasn't hit by a plane. Since no steel-framed skyscraper had ever before come down because of fire, this disintegration alone would have raised questions about the emerging Official Story.

## Ongoing Reinforcement of the Master Narrative

The White House seized the moment to reinforce the new narrative with emotion and symbolism. Just days after the attacks, the country watched the president—bullhorn in hand, arm around a fireman—standing tall atop the rubble. Playing on the public's increased affection for firemen, this symbolism-laden image would become an icon of American resilience. The next day, Bush received religious blessings for his new crusade. At the National Cathedral, accompanied by "Onward Christian Soldiers" on a thunderous pipe organ, he solemnly condemned "the evildoers" (www.youtube.com/watch?v=lDcdpEBcta). From this high altar, surrounded by other high-ranking officials, the president declared his unholy War on Terror.

Considered over the years, never before has a master narrative received so much ongoing reinforcement. For Flight 93 alone, four movies have rendered the passenger revolt (R. Morgan *Flight 93 Revealed* pp. 31-36, 43-45). And each year since the attacks, the official account has received plenty of airtime, including "NOVA" or National Geographic specials. Anniversaries don't just provide journalists with "hooks"; they also offer opportunities to reinforce societally approved narratives. In considering 9/11 remembrances, it's well to recall that "the ghost at the banquet of all public commemoration is always politics"—above all, serving up another helping of the standard fare (*Harper's* 9/2011).

The 9/11 Commission's best-selling *Report* formalized the Official Story, providing more details. Hoping to make closure on the nightmare, most Americans accepted a superficially credible narrative. Few in the populace cared to deal with the strange stuff that didn't square with that account or even considered that the *Report* might be a slick cover-up. At that time, perhaps it was still too scary to go there. Perhaps the fireballs had seared the collective psyche, leaving many Americans to feel more vulnerable and more apt to accept government/media accounts. Simple stories of good versus evil—of heroes, victims, and villains—do offer psychological comfort. But they do so at a high cost.

## Official Story Ignores Inconvenient Facts

Although the attacks were undoubtedly shocking, they weren't necessarily surprising. In the summer of 2001, intelligence and counterterrorism officials were sounding urgent warnings. Counterterrorism "czar" Richard Clarke and his staffers were "running around with their hair on fire" (MSNBC 3/28/04). CIA Director George Tenet watched as "the system was blinking red" but couldn't get the White House to listen.

Just a month before the attacks, these concerns culminated in a now-famous president's daily briefing, "Bin Laden Determined to Strike in US." Although President Bush received this warning on August 6, he took no action other than to tell the CIA briefer, "All right, you've covered your ass." That afternoon, Bush went fishing at his Texas ranch (*Wash. Post* 8/7/01). But did these warnings go *completely* unnoticed? Hardly. As September 11th approached, prominent American officials had stopped flying the commercial airlines (*Newsweek* 9/24/01) and hundreds of inside traders were betting that airline stocks would plummet (M. Ruppert *Crossing the Rubicon* pp. 238-52).

Even before the Official Story was spun, a different reality emerged from eyewitness accounts on the ground. Hundreds of first responders reported hearing explosions both before and while the WTC buildings crumbled (D. R. Griffin *Mysterious Collapse of WTC-7* pp. 79-91). At the time of the impact at the Pentagon, hundreds of observers watched a strange white plane circling over the White House (CNN 9/11/01). Within *minutes* of the impact, the FBI arrived to confiscate videotapes from any surveillance cameras that could have filmed an incoming airliner (*Wash. Times* 9/21/01). That afternoon, hundreds of firefighters stood and watched as the 47-story World Trade Center Building 7 (WTC-7), which was never struck by a plane, dissolved neatly into a pile at near free-fall speed (CBS 9/11/01).

## Suppression by News Media

Information on 9/11 that didn't fit the Official Story has encountered near-complete blockages from American news media, both corporate and independent. For many years, both have effectively prevented most factual reportage and serious analysis of 9/11. Among the exceptions, those tidbits of information that have slipped by editorial filters, most remain unconnected. If meaningful connections aren't made, significant patterns can't emerge.

Facts that in isolation appear unrelated and insignificant take on new meaning when they're seen within a larger pattern. It's one thing to learn that human remains from the WTC were discovered on the roof of the Deutsche Bank Building (*USA Today* 4/13/06); but this discovery, along with other widely dispersed debris, raises an obvious question: If gravity alone pulled the Towers *down*, what hurled human bodies and huge steel girders hundreds of feet *laterally*? Similarly, it's one thing to acknowledge that a third skyscraper fell on 9/11; it's quite another to report on independent scientific inquiry into what caused such an unprecedented event. In the absence of a single "smoking gun," a challenge to the Official Story involves building a cumulative case based on a growing body of circumstantial evidence.

## The Aftermath of 9/11: Winners and Losers

The 9/11 Commission never asked a basic question posed by any crime investigator: *Cui bono*? "Who benefited?" By 2003, when the "blue-ribbon panel" finally began to convene, most of the big winners had already emerged: the Bush administration, the Pentagon, military contractors, intelligence agencies, and hard-liners in Israel. The administration's neoconservatives had already advanced their objective of two wars and, under the guise of "executive privilege," a still more dominant executive branch.

In fact, many of the winners emerged quite quickly. In the three days following the attacks, the president's ratings shot up to 86 percent. A week later, they'd reached 90 percent (A. Franken *The Truth, With Jokes* p. 34). Almost overnight, the Pentagon's inability to account for trillions of dollars (DoD 9/10/01) was forgotten. At the urging of Defense Secretary Rumsfeld, Congress appropriated additional vast sums: military spending rocketed (CBS 1/29/02). In the years following 9/11, the stock of Halliburton, Xe (Blackwater Worldwide), and other huge government contractors skyrocketed. Huge no-bid contracts enriched major corporations and their stockholders, including Dick and Lynne Cheney (CBS 9/26/03). Following the detective's logic of "who benefited?" our investigation will look at such persons of interest.

### The Big Losers: The American People

The broader consequences of the crimes on 9/11 are all about us. While fears impaired our vision, American democracy has decayed before our eyes. Individual liberties have atrophied while government control has become more and more ominous. Erosions of freedom have included blatant violations of the Bill of Rights—warrantless electronic surveillance and illegal searches of private homes—plus gross abuses of "executive privilege" and further politicalization of the federal judiciary. The Feds have justified these encroachments under the familiar banners of "fighting terrorism" or "national and homeland security" (Wolf *End of America* pp. 1-5). These pretexts exist mainly because of the official account about 9/11: if al Qaeda terrorism was not solely responsible for 9/11, then such extreme measures make even less sense.

### Hypotheses to Account for 9/11

Even a decade later, anyone who raises doubts about the Official Story risks dismissal as a "conspiracy theorist." Yet this standard narrative *itself* espouses a conspiracy theory—one in which al Qaeda operatives conspired against the United States. So it makes little sense to dismiss a hypothesis with "oh, that's conspiracy theory." Sure, conspiracy nuts are out there, those who believe flying saucers from Mars will invade the earth. But real conspiracies obviously do occur; conspirators do plan crimes. Shakespeare understood this scheming side of human nature: that's why his best plots involve plotters.

In the case of 9/11, thoughtful citizens face a conspiracy of silence: the news media haven't wanted to tell, and most of the public hasn't wanted to hear. So much hinges, however, on how Americans interpret the 9/11 tragedy, which is one reason why it's a taboo subject. Today, in light of constantly emerging new evidence, a range of possible explanations exists. Intellectually honest readers can consider a range of possibilities:

1. The US government didn't have a clue; the attackers struck like bolts from the blue.
2. The US government had many clues but didn't connect them.
3. Elements within the government had clues and even foreknowledge but deliberately "let it happen."
4. Elements within the government worked with perpetrators and helped make it happen.
5. Elements within the government took control of or even devised the plot and "made sure it would happen."

While the first and second hypotheses could, upon considering all the evidence, be the least probable, they're the only ones most people have entertained. Thankfully, this is changing. Skepticism about the Official Story is now spreading among former government and military officials— as well as among firefighters, academics, scientists, and other professionals. Over 1500 architects and engineers, for instance, have joined a call for a new investigation (AE911truth.org).

**Consequences of Continuing to Believe the Official Story**
Today, a decade after the Crime of the Century, some among us are still hoping the anomalies surrounding 9/11 will drop down the memory hole of collective amnesia. As Bill Moyers has remarked, "the struggle against power is the struggle of memory against forgetting." If we remain ignorant or forget about those cataclysmic events, we limit our ability to

understand their causes; they're more likely to happen again. With the country in moral, political, economic, and military decline, this is no time for tall tales.

As we've seen, the War on Terror depends upon the Official Story. Suppression of the truth buttresses a brittle structure built on the assumption that the US military was caught *entirely* by surprise, that Islamic terrorists were *entirely* responsible for the crimes, and that military action is the best response to terrorism. But once we deconstruct the Official Story—which is a central purpose of this book—the main rationale for the Patriot Act and the War on Terror also falls apart: a renewal of American democracy can finally dawn.

*Mounting Evidence* shines light into the dusky corners of American politics, exposing recognizable faces. It challenges conventional assumptions about the country's political system, intelligence agencies, and corporate mass media—plus the way it generates its master narratives and starts its wars. By understanding recent tragic experience, Americans can begin to end runaway militarism, restore their democracy, and take back personal freedoms they've lost.

Col. Bob Bowman has repeatedly declared that "the truth about 9/11 is that we don't *know* the truth about 9/11—and we need to" (www.youtube.com/watch?v=1weA6jsx-ok). This is why we need a truly independent investigation with grand jury powers.

# 1.  "The Eye Begins to See": 9/11 in Meaningful Contexts

*As nightfall does not come all at once, neither does oppression.*
*In both instances, there is a twilight when everything remains*
*seemingly unchanged. And it is in such a twilight that we all*
*must be most aware of change in the air—however slight—*
*lest we become unwitting victims of the darkness.*

—Justice William O. Douglas

The ancient Greek dramatist Aeschylus famously observed that "in war, truth is the first casualty." Today, however, this strikes us as an understatement: given so many wars, truth has died a thousand deaths. Generating war propaganda may be "the world's second oldest profession," and today its practitioners are very well paid.

Even when truth survives, it's often hidden within a thicket of distortions, half truths, and outright lies. Prof. Peter Phillips of Project Censored alerts us to a "truth emergency" in which "we're awash in a sea of information but left without contexts for real understanding" (M. Huff *Censored 2011* pp. 221-229). True, we live in the "information age," blessed by all the possibilities enabled by the internet, but we also live in a time of misinformation, disinformation, and just plain info overload. Confusing information with understanding, we face a crisis of meaning—of knowledge framed so we can act on it.

While today's shortage of readily available, accurate, meaningful knowledge has many causes, two stand out: secrecy and suppression. Many, even most government officials and corporate media outlets perceive sharing the truth as contrary to their interests. This said, certain "sensitive" areas are particularly prone to secrecy and suppression.

**Areas of Special Secrecy and Suppression**

All matters nuclear have long been shrouded in secrecy and subjected to suppression. Taking one example among many, How was it possible, when all of Europe was finding fallout from the Chernobyl disaster, that the French government could doggedly deny that radioactive dust had fallen on France? (DVD: *The Story of Chernobyl*). Even after all the media coverage devoted to the Fukushima disaster, how many of us understand how governments treat nuclear power?

Compounding the problem, many of our fellow citizens aren't paying much attention, and even fewer are demanding the truth. As American humorist Josh Billings quipped, "scarce as truth is, the supply has always exceeded the demand" (www.quotedb.com/quotes/1588). As a result, the public is fed—and too often swallows—readily available junk food for thought.

The 9/11 tragedy is another area of especially intense secrecy and suppression. Pulling together solid facts about 9/11 is like trying to solve a jigsaw puzzle with pieces missing, lost, or destroyed—and with still others impounded by government agencies. The picture that emerges is incomplete, riddled with holes.

More broadly, few areas are more beset by a lack of candor than national security and military matters. Because 9/11 lies at the intersection of these realms, and because this watershed event threatened to expose powerful interests, it's been a bastion of especially strong resistance to truth-telling. When the air-defense failures raised questions about the ability of the federal government to protect citizens, they activated the usual mechanisms for evasion: adoption of an Official Story, media spin, distortion, suppression, and denial.

# A Closer Look at the 9/11 Commission

Whatever its other failings, the 9/11 Commission didn't let facts get in the way of telling a good story. Comprised almost entirely of Washington insiders, the Commission—as we'll see later—was most interested in covering for both parties as well as for the federal agencies most implicated in the debacle. The Commission seemed especially keen on buffing the tarnished image of the Pentagon brass.

When the Commission finished its work in 2004, three months before George Bush and Dick Cheney were up for election, it seemed obvious to many that *it* didn't want to be held responsible for their defeat. Wanting to appear bipartisan, the Commission basically said, "Clinton was somewhat at fault, and Bush was somewhat at fault, but nobody was responsible." Early on, its *Report* made it clear that it would establish "no individual blame" *(Report* p. xiv). How could no one be held responsible for the biggest national-security failure in the nation's history?

Vietnam veteran and former senator Max Cleland resigned from the Commission in disgust, calling the charade a "national scandal." Citing dogged stonewalling at the White House, Sen. Cleland charged "the president ought to be ashamed" (Salon 11/21/03). Benjamin DeMott, Professor Emeritus at Amherst and an insightful cultural critic, described the *Report* as "a cheat and a fraud. . . . . a series of evasive maneuvers that infantilize the audience, transform candor into iniquity, and conceal realities that demand immediate inspection and confrontation" *(Harper's* 10/04).

In 2004, even before the 9/11 Commission came out with its *Report*, it had become obvious that its conclusions would be woefully inadequate. The commissioners were fully aware they'd been lied to: at a secret meeting, they even "debated referring the matter to the Justice Department for criminal investigation" *(Wash. Post* 8/2/04). Aside from being politically awkward, such a referral would have proved risky, because any fair investigation would have found the Commission lying every bit as much as the Pentagon.

Since that time, co-chairs Thomas Kean and Lee Hamilton have made significant admissions. They've acknowledged that they not only knew the CIA "made a conscious decision" to stonewall their requests for documents, but the Pentagon's initial timeline for its responses to the attacks "may have been part of a deliberate effort to mislead the Commission and the public" *(NYT* 12/22/07).

John Farmer, the Commission's own senior counsel, has revealed that "the official version ... is almost entirely untrue.... there was a decision not to tell the truth to the American people" (Farmer *Ground Truth* p. 4). Former commissioner and US Senator Bob Kerrey (D-Neb.) called 9/11 "a 30-year-old conspiracy," yet the Commission's probe seldom extended back beyond three or four years. Before it ever got underway, the inquiry was compromised by its narrow scope and lack of real independence.

Regardless of who was responsible for 9/11, the resulting cover-up was itself a State Crime Against Democracy (SCAD): offered a distorted account of a national tragedy. When one compares the Commission's standard narrative with the known facts, things don't add up. September 11 widow and activist Kristen Breitweiser, one of the "Jersey Girls" (the 9/11 widows who pushed for an investigation), has observed that "it's been said that terrorists only have to get it right once and defenders have to get it right every time; but those terrorists weren't just lucky once, they were lucky over and over again" (DVD "9/11: Press for Truth").

In the Official Story, the laws of probability don't seem to apply. Skeptics have pointed to the sheer number of facts that don't square with the standard accounts. While the Official Story presented the alleged hijackers as strict fundamentalist Muslims devoted to Allah, their personal habits included using alcohol, tobacco, and cocaine, and hiring prostitutes (A. Collins *My Jihad* p. 248). Inconsistencies and contradictions abound. The Pentagon issued three *different* official timelines attempting to explain its failure to intercept *any* of the four airliners, and Secretary of Defense Rumsfeld gave three different accounts of his whereabouts during the attacks (Griffin *9/11 Commission Report* pp. 141-43, 217-219). Cheney told one tale, but the Commission told another on his behalf. Such contradictory accounts inevitably compromise credibility. Yet the contradictions extend far beyond these. When one pulls on the loose fibers, the whole yarn unravels.

Today, a decade after the tragedy, the trail may look cold, the clues hard to find. Fortunately, though, the ensuing years haven't gone to waste. Researchers have made remarkable discoveries, and the prospects for better understanding have never looked more compelling.

## Imperatives for Seeking the Truth

Among the reasons for us to look more deeply into 9/11, five seem most apt to help restore American democracy:

- **To Honor the Victims and Ensure Them Justice**

On 9/11, nearly 3,000 Americans were killed; to honor them, we need to find out who, beyond nineteen hijackers and a few al Qaeda leaders, might have been involved in the largest national-security failure in American history. So far, no one has been held accountable. Insisting on accountability and justice is the highest form of respect Americans can pay to those victimized by the attacks.

- **To Promote Political Awareness and Critical Thinking**

It was Euripides, the sharpest skeptical thinker among the Greek playwrights, who concluded that "man's most valuable trait is a judicious sense of what not to believe." More recent political thinkers, from James Madison to Bill Moyers, have also understood that knowledge and the ability to use it are crucial in any democracy. That's why Thomas Jefferson furnished his amazing collection of books, the largest in the new republic, to help establish the Library of Congress (www.loc.gov/exhibits/jefferson/jefflib.html).

Unlike Jefferson, though, most of us don't have time to plow through Gibbon's three-volume *Rise and Fall of the Roman Empire*. We need history that's readily available, instructive, and useful. As the founders understood, knowledge of political history helps citizens curtail potential abuses of power. The moves of the tricksters are hardly new, and the ability to spot them is immensely empowering. Seeing patterns among past "trigger" and traumatic events promotes better understanding of current instances, including 9/11. If critical thinking involves questioning our most cherished assumptions, contrived provocations provide great opportunities to see how the real world works.

- **To Challenge the War on Terror** Americans may groan beneath the burden of a huge national debt, but they don't always consider the *full* costs of what G. W. Bush and Dick Cheney defined as "endless war" (*Wash. Post* 10/4/01). Like the Cold War, the Global War on Terror has helped obscure the underlying reasons for military action, which include resources, profits, power, and status—all "the privileges of empire." While many conscientious citizens have opposed individual wars, fewer challenge their underlying premise—what revered policy analyst Richard Falk called the Global Domination Project. This push for power, profit, and status, Dr. Falk explains, has long driven much of US foreign policy (PBS "Frontline" 4/12&25/03). While the Global Domination Project isn't the same as old-fashioned colonialism and world conquest, it does involve an ongoing attempt to use military, economic, and diplomatic power to grab the lion's share of the goodies.

Moreover, endless global war has extracted many unforeseen and hidden costs. Canadian researcher Elizabeth Woodworth has articulated what is little understood: "The September 11 attacks have done more to shape world conflict in this century than any other event. More resources are being committed to the resulting War on Terror than to the foundational issue of the survival of our ecosystem. Additionally, the War on Terror is being waged in the oil-rich Middle East, whose promise of vast oil supplies is delaying the development of alternative energy sources" (*Foreign Policy Journal* 10/24/10). If the United States can't afford "endless war," neither can our increasingly beleaguered planet.

The costs in money alone are staggering. When all the national-security-related expenses from other budgets are factored in, American taxpayers pay closer to a *trillion* dollars a year in military spending (Stockholm Intl. Peace Res. Inst.). By mid 2011, the astronomical costs for Afghanistan and Iraq had surpassed *four trllion* dollars (Pacifica "Democracy Now!" 6/2911). A few trillion here, a few trillion there; it can add up to real money.

Adding to the burden, taxpayers also subsidize the 737 US bases worldwide (www.alternet.org/story/47998). These, too, are manifestations of the Global Domination Project. While many of these serve no military purpose, they do provide protection and cover for espionage operatives, often as launching pads for "special operations," known in the trade as "black ops." In 2011, returning from a trip to Afghanistan, retired Army Col. Ann Wright tallied 400 bases in that country alone (*Maui Times* 1/23/11). At Super Bowl parties, fans still lift a Bud when announcers "proudly welcome members of America's armed forces viewing in 177 nations around the world" (Fox 2/6/11). They don't tout the 737 *bases*, however. Such an outlandish number is hardly something to cheer about.

Despite the cancellation of some new weapons, military spending has grown under Obama (*SF Chron.* 2/7/11). Today, the United States outspends the other top fifteen militaries together (www.costofwar.com). Given the burden of the national debt, the state of the economy, and the decline of democratic and social institutions at home, these massive expenditures are something the nation can now ill afford—if it ever could.

- **To Help Restore Civil Liberties**

If the War on Terror has provided pretexts for disastrous wars and ballooning military budgets, it's also supplied a "rationale" for the Department of Homeland Security and other stateside mechanisms of control. Since 9/11, Americans have seen extensive curtailment of their liberties, many of them constitutionally "guaranteed." Invasions of privacy have come from several directions—from warrantless wire tapping to airport security scanners to expanded no-fly lists. In an excellent piece of investigative journalism, Dana Priest and William Arkin have documented not just the expanding military but also the burgeoning "clandestine services." These overlapping spy agencies, their research demonstrated, are "growing beyond control" (*Wash. Post* 7/16/10).

Secret prisons, another feature of the War on Terror, can hardly be dismissed as "over there." In a passionate wakeup call, human rights activist Naomi Wolf has warned of encroachments on our freedoms, letting Guantánamo symbolize many other "dark sites": "We should worry about the men held at Guantánamo, because history shows that stripping prisoners of their rights is intoxicating not only to leaders but to functionaries. How easy it is for even decent people to become desensitized and act as instruments of evil" (Wolf *End of America* p. 48).

It's one thing to condemn extralegal incarceration; it's another to realize that policies conceived with limited application often come home to haunt us.

When foreigners are detained in solitary confinement without ever being charged, it becomes more likely that similar legal violations will happen to Americans at home. During the Bush years, most of the world cringed at the mistreatment of prisoners. More recently, however, Americans faced the equally outrageous mistreatment of Army Pvt. Bradley Manning Jr. Charged with unauthorized disclosure of information to Wikileaks, Private Manning was held at a Marine base in Virginia. Stripped to his underwear, Manning languished for many months in solitary confinement for 23 hours a day (Pacifica "Democracy Now!" 1/24/11) until public outcry forced a move to more humane conditions.

Similarly, the same "private contractors" who've killed civilians overseas have killed civilians at home. The disaster of Hurricane Katrina afforded opportunities to expand reliance on private security firms into domestic situations. In complete violation of law and morality, Blackwater Worldwide (Xe) gunned down a peaceful group of African-American "gangbangers" in New Orleans (J. Scahill *Blackwater* pp. 327-29). When a country has staged provocations for war, subverted elected governments, trained foreign armies in torture techniques (SOAW.org), and assassinated leaders abroad for many decades, should it surprise us when it applies these strategies at home?

## • To Let the Truth Help Heal Our Wounds

Ghosts haunt the national psyche; many Americans harbor suspicions from earlier unresolved national traumas. The public long ago came to doubt the Warren Commission's official account of the JFK assassination. Today, almost five decades later, how many of us believe Lee Harvey Oswald was a lone gunman? (*NY Mag.* 3/27/06). Our society still doesn't understand a crime that changed its history. Together with suspicions about other major crimes, these doubts have inflicted wounds. Beneath the scar tissue, the body politic needs restorative treatment. If the truth can hurt, it can also heal.

Painfully aware of their needs for healing, other societies have set up truth commissions. In the short run, sometimes the cure can seem more painful than the disease. But the healing process can yield great benefits. Led by Archbishop Desmond Tutu, South Africa has promoted public disclosure, accountability, and reconciliation (Huffington Post 5/14/10). More recently, Chile opened an investigation into the 1973 death of President Salvador Allende (BBC 1/27/11). Even more courageously, it has begun to exorcise the ghosts of its past under Gen. Augusto Pinochet's military junta. After years in comfortable denial, Chilean Judge Juan Guzmán came to realize that "a wounded country needs to know the truth" (Film: *The Judge and the General*). Similarly, Spain and Argentina have come to grips with their pasts. Seeking better futures, moving from toxic to tonic, these societies have found ways to face and process their collective experience.

In the case of 9/11, time may make it easier for Americans to take a hard second look. That's tough—it will require uncommon and unflinching courage—but well-conceived international truth commissions can help make it possible.

## Illuminating 9/11: Patterns Surrounding SCADs and Shock Events

Before we get into the particulars of 9/11, let's look at the larger patterns:

### "Blowback": When Your Own Poison Gas Blows Back in Your Face

One of these patterns is "blowback," a CIA term for the unintended consequences of exploitive policies and covert actions. Blowback occurs when one of the CIA's "greatest hits" starts hitting back—as, say, in the Iranian Revolution of 1979. Since World War II, American attempts at projecting power in the Middle East and southern Asia have commonly used Islamic militants for self-serving purposes, frequently as proxies or mercenaries. Al Qaeda, after all, emerged from the *mujahedeen* ("holy warriors") the CIA helped to recruit, train, and equip to fight the Soviets (A. Rashid *Taliban* p. 26).

Over time, this policy of proxy war has backfired. Some call it "the revenge of the *jihadi*." "What the press reports as the malign acts of 'terrorists' or 'drug lords' or 'illegal arms merchants,'" notes foreign-policy analyst Chalmers Johnson, "often turns out to be blowback from earlier American operations" (Johnson *Blowback* p. 8). Once the people obtain the means, those whom Western powers have long exploited or attacked will strike back. Is it coincidental that the great majority of Islamist attacks have targeted the US, UK, and other NATO countries involved in Afghanistan? However, "blowback" can't begin to fully explain 9/11, nor does it have to.

18

*"The Eye Begins to See": 9/11 in Meaningful Contexts*

## The Shock Doctrine: Domestic "Shock and Awe"

Today, informed by author and activist Naomi Klein's Shock Doctrine, we're more able to understand that disasters like 9/11 create conditions for changes that would otherwise be impossible. Without the story of a sneak attack on Pearl Harbor, would the US have gone to war against Japan, Germany, and Italy? Without 9/11, would the American public have accepted the huge changes that ensued?

The blasts of 9/11 didn't just blow away Americans' illusions of invincibility; they also enabled the Bush administration to execute its preexisting plans for Afghanistan, Iraq, and other "weak" countries well endowed with resources. The valuable minerals and metals in Afghanistan had been known since the mid-1990s, and at that time discoveries of the vast oil reserves in the Caspian Basin ignited intense interest in an oil pipeline across Afghanistan (P. D. Scott *Road to 9/11* pp. 166-71). Within days of the 9/11 tragedy, the administration was using the Official Story to justify its plans for an endless War on Terror; within a month it was bombing Afghanistan; and within a year, in time for the attack on Iraq, it was using the Story to justify the Bush Doctrine of "preemptive war" (*Wash. Post* 3/16/06). As Klein has demonstrated, the 9/11 shocks have also fomented domestic repression—to draconian measures that, only days before, would have seemed unthinkable. Later shocks made possible more changes (Klein *Shock Doctrine* pp. 4, 406-15).

## So Much Depends on the Official Story

Since the War on Terror relies on public acceptance of this Official Story—which tells of nineteen Arab terrorists who caught the world's only superpower by surprise—powerful forces initially exploited "shock-and-awe" events to "control the narrative" and "frame the issue" (Klein *Shock Doctrine* pp. 4-6). These forces are still heavily invested in reinforcing this standard account and quashing any alternatives. If the Official Story were shown to be even partially untrue, the War on Terror might collapse like a house of cards: the vast expenditures of life and treasure in Afghanistan, Iraq, Pakistan, Yemen, and elsewhere might seem (even more) misguided.

19

To understand the Official Story, it's important to see 9/11 in broader contexts.

## Recent State Crimes against Democracy (SCADs)

One of the most inclusive patterns is a notion articulated by Professor Lance deHaven-Smith at Florida State, "to move beyond the debilitating, slipshod, and scattershot speculation of conspiracy theories by focusing inquiry on patterns in elite political criminality ..." (*American Behavioral Scientist* 2/10). Granted, the English language hardly needs another acronym, but this one stands for a useful new concept. When we first encounter the idea of SCADs, we're likely to imagine assassinations of elected officials, tanks ousting protesters from a square, riot police pummeling demonstrators, or dictators dissolving parliaments.

These, however, are only the obvious kinds of SCADs. Here we'll look into the more subtle and secretive instances—the ones that may happen regularly, just beneath the radar, in established democracies. In part, they happen because so few citizens in those societies know what to look for. Or, if they do know, they're in dogged denial, thinking "that stuff can't happen here." For whatever reasons, those who grasp that something's amiss are often unwilling to speak about "the general problem of elite political criminality in the national security state" (deHaven-Smith *American Behavioral Scientist* 2/10).

SCADs, then, are crimes that government elites commit, sabotaging democratic processes to concentrate power in their own hands. Several types of SCADs are most relevant to the 9/11 attacks: contrived provocations or pretexts for war, "false-flag" operations, and staged "near-miss" domestic terrorist attacks. These tend to remain secret—or if they're publicly reported, aren't presented in contexts so they're widely understood. This concept allows us to see what might otherwise seem odd or improbable.

### Schemes for Provoking Wars with Weaker Countries

Since voters seldom approve plans for wars, governments violate democratic process when they connive to start them. In 1997, a top Clinton administration official discussed a plan to entice Iraq into shooting down an

American plane. A recent memoir by Gen. Hugh Shelton, then Chairman of the Joint Chiefs of Staff, revealed that a member of Clinton's cabinet proposed setting up the Iraqis to kill an American pilot. Gen. Shelton recalled that the cabinet member asked him, the top commander of the US military, to help trick Iraq into shooting down an American spy plane as a pretext for attacking the country (Salon 10/15/10).

As other attendees chatted over breakfast, one of the cabinet members reportedly leaned over to Gen. Shelton and said, "Hugh, I know I shouldn't even be asking you this, but what we really need in order to go in and take out Saddam is a precipitous event.... Could you have one of our U-2s fly low enough—and slow enough—so as to guarantee that Saddam could shoot it down?" (Salon 10/15/10).

The way Shelton told the story, this cabinet member was Madeleine Albright, then Secretary of State. Often called "Madame War," the nation's top diplomat infamously asked, "What's the point of having this superb military that you're always talking about if we can't use it?" (*LA Times* 12/17/00). The incident provides a revealing example of how diplomatic officials charged with promoting peaceful solutions commit SCADs in service of the Global Domination Project.

This was hardly the first, nor would it be the last time the US had considered using—or actually used—contrived pretexts for initiating military action.

## Bush Plans Another Shoot-Down Provocation

G. W. Bush, for instance, considered another contrived provocation against Iraq. According to the *New York Times*, Bush told Prime Minister Tony Blair that he was "determined to invade Iraq [even] without the second [UN] resolution ..." (*NYT* 3/27/06). Bush reportedly added that "the United States was thinking of flying a U-2 reconnaissance aircraft" painted in UN colors over Iraq, accompanied by US fighter jets. "If Saddam fired on them, he would be in breach" (of UN resolutions) (Huffington Post 10/15/10). The president would have his pretext for war. Like the scheme concocted by Clinton's cabinet member, this ploy involved committing a SCAD: it was, after all, conceived to subvert diplomatic and democratic processes—to manipulate the UN Security Council into violating its charter and to usurp the constitutionally defined right of Congress to declare war.

In the light of Washington's obsession with attacking Iraq, it's fair to ask, Was 9/11 just "blowback" from decades of bad foreign policies or strictly a national-security failure? Or did somebody possibly decide to permit a devastating terrorist attack so as to generate a pretext for "endless war"?

## "False Flag Operations": Another Type of SCAD

Provocations have long-served US war planners, and so have false-flag operations. More recently, the schemes have become even more risky. Seymour Hersh, the ace investigative journalist who broke both the My Lai Massacre and Abu Ghraib stories, once again delivered the details. This time, the beam of exposure fell on Cheney. In 2008, apparently desperate to attack Iran at all costs, the vice president's office came up with a novel scheme: it involved building some PT boats to resemble those of Iran, manning them with Navy Seals dressed as Iranians, and having them fire upon a US ship in the Straits of Hormuz (*New Yorker* 7/7/08). Video cameras would be set up to document the "attack." If carried out, the predictable consequences would have included the worst conflagration the Middle East had ever seen, a serious disruption of the world's oil supply, and an unprecedented eruption of terrorist acts against the US. These outcomes sound disastrous to us—but did they to Cheney?

Understanding the mentality behind SCADs is instructive. Peace activist and author David Swanson has rightly remarked that just because these plans weren't carried out "does not diminish their value as clues to the thinking of the people from whose brains they emerged" (Swanson *War Is a Lie* p. 70). When enough of us understand these schemes, false flags won't fly.

## Domestic Provocations of Fear and Loathing

While foreign contrived provocations are intended to arouse public outrage against another country, domestic provocations (SCADs) are used to arouse fear at home. This fear not only translates into anger and aggression against ethnic groups; it makes the population feel more dependent upon and more submissive to government. In many cases, the effect of government-generated internal terrorist events is to rekindle the sense of threat and to reinforce a perception—in this case, that "Islamic terrorism is a bigger threat than ever"—which might "justify" *both* oppression of the population at home and aggression against Muslims abroad.

Let's look at a widely publicized recent example: the Christmas-tree sting operation. On November 26, 2010, thousands attended a tree lighting ceremony in Portland, Oregon. At this event, the FBI claimed to have thwarted an Islamist terrorist attack. A young Somali-born Muslim, Mohamed Osman Mohamud, was immediately apprehended when the "dud" bomb the FBI had given him failed to detonate (*SF Chron.* 11/27/10).

Several strange features of the incident soon emerged. Author and talk-show host Thom Hartmann discovered that in this case, as well as others, the FBI actually sent undercover agents to mosques in order to recruit prospective terrorists (Air America Radio 1/5/11). According to the FBI, its undercover agents had pretended to be accomplices of a suspected Pakistani terrorist whom Mohamud had known. Unlike the Pakistani, however, the FBI actually supplied the nineteen-year-old with a bomb. On November 4, in a run-up to the staged event, agents reportedly detonated a "real device" with Mohamud (www.inewp.com/?p=5824). If you were truly dedicated to stopping terrorists, why would you first recruit them and then help them improve their skills?

The implications of FBI agents posing as terrorists and providing real explosives to them are deeply unsettling. Economist Paul Craig Roberts has asked, "Why does the FBI orchestrate fake terror plots?" (Global Research 11/30/10). Is it possible that federal authorities might have wanted to stage a scary "close call" with terrorism before a public becoming skeptical about the War on Terror? Or did someone especially want an incident to disrupt Christmas celebrations—much as the "underwear bomber" had done the previous year—in order to heighten public perceptions of a "clash of civilizations"?

Such provocations are hardly without precedents. Former head of Homeland Security Tom Ridge complained that the Bush administration spiked terrorist threat levels to raise sagging public support for the Patriot Act (*USA Today* 5/10/05). Probable provocations involving the FBI go much farther back, however. In fact, Portland's staged terror event seemed like a reprise of a similar FBI operation that actually "went wrong" in 1993 at the World Trade Center (WTC). This time, too, the FBI was in contact with Islamists, whom it helped to build a huge bomb. Inexplicably, however, the agents failed to substitute the inert powder for the real explosive (*NYT* 10/28/03).

When these Islamists detonated the huge bomb in the WTC parking garage, it killed six and injured more than a thousand people. If the bombers hadn't made a slight miscalculation in the placement, the blast could have toppled both Towers, possibly killing 50,000 people. The FBI's odd role in the bombing was made public after its own FBI informant, former Egyptian army officer Emad Salem, revealed his conversations with the FBI agents, establishing that the FBI knew about plans for the bombing but didn't intervene to stop it (P. Thompson *Terror Timeline* p. 11).

Was the FBI careless, or did it intend for the bomb to detonate? The 1993 WTC bombing had definitely delivered a "close call" in a highly visible setting: was it intended as another staged scare? We just don't know. Nor was the FBI the only agency to seemingly bear responsibility. The CIA admitted it was "partly culpable" for the attack because it had trained several of the bombers during its campaign against the Soviets during the 1980s (*Independent* [UK] 11/1/98).

But did the FBI or the CIA apply these lessons to prevent 9/11? The answer, tragically, is no: the very *same* group of Islamists went on to attack the exact *same* targets. Khalid Sheikh Mohammed (KSM), the uncle of the 1993 "master bomber," emerged to become the "mastermind" behind 9/11 (*LA Times* 9/1/02). So several of the *same individuals* were allegedly involved in 9/11, and all of them were well-known to US clandestine agencies.

Nor is this just an American problem. Any thorough examination of the world's intelligence and espionage agencies leads us to see that they typically don't act in the best interest of citizens in their country. Like the military, they're most often used to advance the internal or external agendas pursued by the governments that run them. Worse, they may pursue their *own* agendas, independent of any restraints. Pakistan's military spy agency, the ISI, provides one example of how such agencies can move beyond espionage into terrorism, drug trafficking, and even the black market in nuclear weapons (*New Yorker* 5/16/11).

## Prophetic Warnings from Neocons and al Qaeda Go Unheeded

In the late 1990s, Cheney, Rumsfeld, Paul Wolfowitz, and others formed the Project for the New American Century, a neoconservative pressure group. After pushing hard but unsuccessfully for "regime change" in Iraq, these ultra hawks became still more hawkish. In 2000, they concluded that "the desired transformation" (of the United States and the world, not just Iraq) would not be possible without a "great disruption." The increases in spending needed for more military interventions would require "some catastrophic and catalyzing event—like a new Pearl Harbor" (PNAC *Rebuilding America's Defenses* p. 51). These neocons were true believers in the Shock Doctrine; they believed that only after a *big* shock would the public accept their plans for war. After the catastrophe came, Rumsfeld even came out and called 9/11 "a blessing in disguise" (PBS "NewsHour" 9/11/02). Like so much else about 9/11, the blessings must have been well disguised.

During the 1990s, US authorities had received several explicit warnings in advance of the attacks. The 1993 World Trade Center bombers even revealed their future plans. One left a chilling admonition: "Next time, it will be very precise" (AP 9/30/01). Then, fewer than two years before 9/11, FBI agents overheard an al Qaeda arms dealer crowing that "those Towers are coming down." So as not to assume that such warnings remained in a dusty file cabinet, recall that several administration officials avoided commercial flights. In July, while publicly dismissing warnings of an imminent al Qaeda attack, Attorney General John Ashcroft began to fly only on "specifically chartered jets" (CBS 9/26/01 & 8/26/04). Other government officials received warnings not to fly commercial airlines on 9/11 (*Newsweek* 9/24/01).

This apparent foreknowledge of the attacks is only one among several areas of research into 9/11; others include the likely role of US intelligence agencies and the question of what actually brought down the *three* World Trade Center skyscrapers. All of these areas have engaged rigorous researchers, many of them drawing on professional and technical expertise. They're listed in Appendix A at www.mountingevidence.org.

Given government and media reluctance to look deeply into 9/11, independent researchers have led challenges to the Official Story. Two outstanding humanities scholars—David Ray Griffin from Claremont Graduate University and Peter Dale Scott from the University of California, Berkeley—came to a stark conclusion: "9/11 was not only the largest and least-investigated homicide in American history but perhaps also the largest hoax, with extremely fateful consequences for human civilization" (Griffin and Scott *9/11 and the American Empire* p. xiii).

Responsible debunking of the Official Story doesn't dismiss the ongoing threat of Islamic terrorism; after all, al Qaeda did assault the Twin Towers in 1993, bomb two US embassies in 1998, and attack the *USS Cole* in 2000. Since 9/11, al Qaeda has targeted the US Embassy in Yemen five times (NPR 9/18/08). Contrary to the official account, though, 9/11 didn't come like a bolt from the blue: it was the climax of a storm that was building for a long time, certainly since the first massive US intervention in Afghanistan began in 1979. Over several decades, a cluster of private and public actors—rich Saudis plus prominent neoconservatives plus elements within British, American, and Pakistani intelligence agencies—all contributed to the 9/11 tragedy (Scott *Road to 9/11* Chaps. 8-10).

For most 9/11 researchers, though, the issue isn't whether al Qaeda had help—it's about how much, from whom, for how long, and why it was offered. If elements in Washington hoped for a "great disruption" to inflame public opinion, did they pursue "let-it-happen" or "helped-it-happen" actions, or did some seek to "make-it-happen"? One of our tasks will to be to determine which of these hypotheses, if any, the evidence best supports.

On foreign and domestic fronts, the aftermath of the tragedy has left the citizens of many countries less safe, less free, and more impoverished. Untold numbers of people have already died in the War on Terror. Other means of dealing with Islamist extremism—especially abandoning a dominator mentality toward other countries—would better address the roots of the problem.

While such inquiry can lead to unsettling realizations, deeper understanding is crucial to healthy democracy and examining the "shadow stuff" need not lead to despair. It's better to face the bedrock reality, thereby averting the vulnerability we feel when we're completely in the dark, whistling by the graveyard. It's *safer* to know the truth.

To face the darkness is itself an act of hope. As American poet Theodore Roethke tells us, "In a dark time, the eye begins to see."

Let's take a look.

# 2.   How America Starts Its Wars

*No people can be both ignorant and free.*

—Thomas Jefferson

A s many of us have sensed for some time, American democracy remains in serious, even critical condition. Yet more than most of us have acknowledged, the cumulative symptoms of the malaise are deeply disturbing: the concentration of wealth and power in fewer and fewer hands; a bloated military-industrial complex; normalized torture; extraordinary renditions; secret prisons; military tribunals; detainments without legal recourse; increasing concentrations of media ownership; invalid or stolen elections; faulty voting machines; plus attacks on personal privacy, political expression, and other civil liberties. Many of these violate our Constitutional rights, and all degrade our democracy.

While most politicians and pundits remain in denial about the seriousness of the crisis, several of our most perceptive voices are speaking out. Legendary defenders of democracy Bill Moyers, Glenn Greenwald, Chris Hedges, and Thom Hartmann have pointed to the fragility of democracy and how easy it is to lose it (www.commondreams.org/views03/0316-08. htm). Similarly troubled by what's gone on since 9/11, social critic Naomi Wolf has turned to neglected American history for meaning and guidance: "I could no longer ignore the echoes between events of the past and forces at work today" (Wolf *End of America* p. xi).

## Why Pay Attention to Precedents?
Responding to these threats to American democracy, we'll examine precedents from its history. Though not well-known, these precedents have everything to do with understanding our present predicament. As

Mark Twain sagely noted, "history doesn't repeat itself, but it does rhyme" (www.quotedb.com/quotes/3038).

In these opening chapters, we'll look at patterns among historical precedents, at the crucial functions served by an awareness of history in a democracy, and at the role of media in the mythmaking that often follows traumatic events. As we'll see, historical ignorance and amnesia inhibit critical thinking, jeopardize democracy, and facilitate acceptance of war. It's a sure way for citizens to give away their power (www.pbs.org/moyers/journal/ btw/watch.html).

Fellow citizens often remark, "Hey, forget the history; it's a thing of the past. That was then, this is now." When they do, they're showing a naïveté that must amuse those in government who understand that knowledge is power—and who may prefer that citizens don't have much of either. The National Security Agency (NSA), for instance, has long resisted any declassification of materials on the Gulf of Tonkin "incident" of 1964, which led the United States into the Vietnam War. Despite repeated requests by the Senate Foreign Relations Committee for declassification, senior NSA officials continued, fully 44 years after the hoax, to block release of key information. Only persistent use of the Freedom of Information Act would finally drag the facts into the light of day (UPI 1/9/08).

Why should the Feds be so stubborn? Reporting on the blockage, *New York Times* reporter Scott Shane revealed that NSA higher-ups were "fearful that [declassification] might prompt uncomfortable comparisons with the flawed intelligence used to justify the war in Iraq" (*NYT* 10/31/05). History is threatening to those who don't want citizens making meaningful connections; that's one reason it's so often trivialized into lists of dates, kings, and battles.

**Information and Empowerment**

Now that concern might seem overblown, given that most Americans are already aware of the bogus justifications for the attack on Iraq. But if we look to more direct parallels, NSA's fears become more understandable. If we recall that the Gulf of Tonkin incident involved supposed attacks by North Vietnamese torpedo boats on US Navy vessels, we get a bingo.

What if, when Iranian swift boats supposedly buzzed navy ships in the Persian Gulf early in 2008, citizens (and even the news media) were empowered to ask, Is this another Gulf of Tonkin? Now *that*'s a question the Pentagon doesn't want us asking. However uncomfortable these precedents may make those in power, informed comparisons are crucial. They they encourage critical thinking, a key step in creating the possibility for a democratic process.

What if, while Washington and the mass media were flooding the airwaves with reports of events that never happened and weapons that didn't exist, more of us could have drawn on the many relevant precedents within American experience? Would a fully informed American public have been so easily suckered into the Vietnam quagmire or the Iraq fiasco? What if more of us were able to say, "Hey, that's war propaganda, just like …"?

To catch up on our relevant but forgotten history, let's take a brief look at some schemes that weren't highlighted in history textbooks: how the US precipitated its involvement in five major conflicts: the Mexican-American War, the Spanish-American War, World War I, World War II, and Vietnam. As we discover how and why the country got into these wars, the historical "rhymes" will ring loud and clear. This won't be pop history, full of bubbles and sweeteners. But armed with greater insight, wiser in the ways of the world, we'll become more empowered as citizens.

## 1846: The Mexican-American War Enables Major Land Grab

After annexing the Lone Star Republic of Texas, which pushed the US border with Mexico southward, President James Polk turned his sights toward Mexico's vast lands in the West. These included California, which Polk, an expansionist, had long wanted to "appropriate" (H. Zinn *People's History of the US* p. 150). To justify an invasion of Mexico, the president needed a pretext, an incident enabling the United States to invade a far weaker country and seize much of its land. To generate such an incident, he sent an army led by Gen. Zachary Taylor on maneuvers south of the Rio Grande. The provocation drew a predictable response. As the Mexicans tried to repel the foreign troops, they killed or captured American soldiers. Once the Mexicans fired the first shots, the war was on. Taylor wrote to Polk that "hostilities may now be considered as commenced." After claiming that an enemy had launched an aggressive attack that had to be avenged, the president waged the war he'd wanted (Zinn *People's History* pp. 150-51).

Although Polk was the one who'd initiated the deception, he nonetheless sent an indignant message to Congress demanding a declaration of war. (This was back when presidents still observed such Constitutional niceties.) The war found support among Americans propelled by a belief in Manifest Destiny. The war was short, but the gains were huge. As a price for halting its drive southward, the United States forced Mexico to sign over a vast area, which included all of what is now New Mexico, Arizona, Utah, Nevada, California, and part of Colorado (E. Foner *Give Me Liberty!* Vol. 1 pp. 402-405).

Extending the American tradition of protest, men of conscience dissented. Henry David Thoreau, who strenuously opposed war and oppression, sensed that an expansion of slavery lurked behind the quasi-religious justification for expansion. In a one-man protest, Thoreau went to jail rather than pay his War Tax (Thoreau "Civil Disobedience"). Just half a century after its founding, the young Republic was heading toward repeated provocations and pretexts for war.

## 1898: Sinking of the *Maine* Triggers Spanish-American War

On the night of February 15, 1898, the US Battleship *Maine* rested at anchor in Havana harbor, its white hull gleaming above the black water. A month before, as Cuban rebels renewed their fight for independence from Spain, President McKinley sent the warship on a "friendly visit" to demonstrate the American desire for order in Cuba and to "protect American interests" (D. M. Kennedy *Brief American Pageant* p. 382). To the Spanish, struggling to retain their colonies, the ship signified American support. To the independence-minded Cubans, however, it was a floating fortress intruding into their affairs.

As "taps" approached on the *Maine*, an explosion shattered the silence. Fires engulfed the vessel, casting an eerie glow on the rippled water. Although nearby Spanish ships rescued some survivors, 266 American seamen were dead with 59 more wounded (www.smplanet.com/imperialism/ remember.html). Four major inquiries into the disaster concluded that an explosion in the forward ammunition magazines caused the sinking. Exactly why those magazines exploded no one has determined. Little evidence has ever supported the widely trumpeted allegation of sabotage by the Spanish.

## First Journalists, Then Politicians Fan Flames of War

Back home, big-city and small-town newspapers were indulging in an orgy of patriotic bloodlust. For more than two years, backed by bankers, the "yellow" press had been beating the drums for war against Spain. The spectacular sinking of the *Maine* provided a new opportunity to wave the bloody flag. With war fever rising, a battle cry resounded: "Remember the Maine! To hell with Spain!" The sinking was immediately blamed on a mine detonated by the Spanish; it became unpatriotic to even question whether something else might have caused the explosion (hnn.us/articles/1009.html).

Beginning in 1896, two years before the *Maine* exploded, newspaper tycoon William Randolph Hearst employed an illustrator to supply drawings favorable to the Cuban insurrection against Spain. After a year on assignment in Cuba, the illustrator reported "there is no trouble here. There will be no war." Hearst shot back with a now-famous telegram, "You furnish the pictures, and I'll furnish the war" (www.smplanet.com/imperialism/ remember.html).

To its credit, Washington didn't initially jump at the prospect of the war. Though public sentiment increasingly ran in favor of the Cuban rebels, the administrations of Grover Cleveland and William McKinley remained steadfast in wanting to see the war in Cuba end. Despite hesitation at the White House, powerful interests combined to thrust the country into war—and into empire. Sensing Spain's weakness, expansionist banking, business, and military interests became increasingly keen to access additional resources (J. Combs *History of American Foreign Policy* pp. 142, 144-45).

With war-fever rising, the sinking of the *Maine* stirred passions that swept a republic toward empire. Major commercial interests intended to instigate a war that would allow the United States to seize Spain's empire. In *The Spanish-Cuban-American War and the Birth of American Imperialism,* prominent historian Philip S. Foner argued that from the outset, Washington's intention was to control the Philippines, which promised cheap labor, markets for manufactured goods, a rich array of resources, and an ideal location for a naval base. These amenities became available only after a long and bloody occupation.

But the *Maine* would hardly be the last time that an accidental or a contrived or staged event would serve to justify a major military action.

## 1915: The *Lusitania* Sinking, Another "Trigger Incident"

Because Americans remained largely ignorant of how their government had manipulated events to start earlier wars, few questioned official accounts about why their country entered World War I. If more Americans had understood how pretexts trigger military campaigns, more might have raised questions about the sinking of the luxury liner *Lusitania.*

In May 1915, before the United States entered World War I, the *Lusitania* set out from New York. When a German U-boat "lurking beneath the surface" sank the great Cunard liner, 1195 passengers and crew were lost. These included 112 Americans, "mostly women and children." In the ensuing months, public outrage at the German atrocity mounted, effectively propelling the US into World War I. Unbeknownst to its passengers, however, the liner was "secretly carrying munitions in its hold" (T. DiBacco *History of the United States* p. 486).

Although the official narrative mentions that the *Lusitania* carried munitions, the emphasis usually falls on how the "barbaric Huns" attacked and sank a defenseless passenger liner. What most histories don't say is that the British Admiralty had secretly installed several six-inch guns on the passenger ship. Nor do they inform readers that the Germans had learned, unbeknownst to passengers, that the *Lusitania* would sail with 4,200 cases of Remington rifle cartridges (at 1,000 rounds to a box) plus 1,250 cases of shrapnel shells (K. Allen *Lusitania Controversy* Part 4). Nor does history mention that these stowaway munitions—hundreds of tons of them—were expressly intended for English forces fighting the Germans (Zinn *People's History* p. 362).

Contrary to the official narrative, the stowaway cargo revealed a major effort to support the British, an attempt to deliver militarily significant quantities of munitions under cover of a passenger ship. When the German Embassy learned of this huge shipment, it attempted to place 50 newspaper ads warning passengers not to book passage on the *Lusitania*. However, the State Department blocked the ads. And when members of Congress tried to issue a public warning to avoid ships carrying military cargo, President Woodrow Wilson quickly quashed their plan. Since only one such warning slipped by the government agents, hundreds of unsuspecting passengers booked passage on the doomed liner.

These developments illustrate the power of government to suppress information that doesn't suit its purposes. It's still little known that to make sure the *Lusitania* would be a floating duck crossing an area infested with U-boats, lord of the British Admiralty Winston Churchill ordered the escort ship *Juno* back to port (J. Kenworthy and G. Young *Freedom of the Seas* p. 211). It's hardly common knowledge that American and British officials falsified the ship's packing list, omitting the secret munitions. Their intent was both to establish "plausible deniability" when the liner was torpedoed and to kindle the fiery passions of war. Although the US didn't immediately enter the conflict, the deliberate German sinking of a British ocean liner created a political climate that made war more likely. Above all, the official story doesn't let on that British and American governments together planned and helped orchestrate the attack on the *Lusitania*, that it was financed by major banking houses, or that Wilson and Churchill personally arranged for the luxury liner to carry weapons (www.teachpeace.com/teachpeacemoment9.htm).

The United States' entry into World War I provides an example of how insightful historical accounts are sometimes developed and actively applied to the present, only to eventually slip down the memory hole. During the 1930s, the (Gerald P.) Nye Committee (or Senate Munitions Investigating Committee) studied the causes of US involvement in World War I. After holding 93 hearings and questioning more than 200 witnesses, including J. P. Morgan and Pierre DuPont, the Committee found that bankers had pressured President Wilson to protect their loans abroad (http://en.wikipedia. org/wiki/Nye_Committee).

Bankers were deeply invested in the war. Between 1915 and April 1917, US banks had loaned the United Kingdom and its allies $2.3 *billion* (*Nye Report* 1933). The bankers couldn't allow the British to lose the war. The munitions industry also exerted "excessive influence on American foreign policy leading up to and during World War I." In short, the Committee concluded that the US entered the war largely because it was in bankers' and munitions makers' best interest for the Western allies to win—assuming there were any real winners in World War I. The mass carnage approached nine million dead (P. Fussell *Great War and Modern Memory* pp. 8, 18).

Although the Nye Committee didn't achieve its goal of nationalizing the arms industry, it did expose how the War was driven by banking and industrial interests.

### 1941: The "Sneak" Attack on Pearl Harbor

For most Americans, Pearl Harbor remains an emotionally charged event. Because of Japan's "Black Sunday" attack, 2,403 Americans lost their lives and another 1,178 were wounded. Moreover, Japan's gamble triggered "the Good War," which was fought to victory by "the Greatest Generation" and led by Franklin Delano Roosevelt, often revered as the greatest president of the twentieth century. Though layers of hallowed mythology have obscured many key facts, when they're finally presented they're very persuasive.

In his well-documented study *Day of Deceit: The Truth About FDR and Pearl Harbor*, historian Robert Stinnett demonstrated that the president provoked war with Japan (Stinnett *Day of Deceit* pp. 171ff). By enforcing an embargo on oil and steel, FDR ensured that Japan would attack the United States. In fact, FDR ordered "eight specific measures which amounted to acts of war, including an embargo on trade with Japan, the shipment of arms to Japan's adversaries, the prevention of Tokyo from securing raw materials essential for its economy, and the denial of port access, thus provoking a military confrontation" (www.globalresearch.ca/index.php?context=va&aid=9063).

### Pearl Harbor: Little-Known Events Leading to the Attack

- *May 1940-January 1941:* Seeking "secret entrance" into a war the public doesn't want, Roosevelt projects American naval power

5,000 miles westward, toward Japan. In this first of several provocations, he personally orders that Pearl Harbor become the new home port for the Pacific Fleet. By January 1941, Imperial Japan has taken the bait; the US learns of its plans to attack the huge new naval base. Over the next few months, the White House devises additional provocations and monitors Japan's responses to them (www.lewrockwell.com/orig/stinnett1.html).

- *May 24, 1941*: Washington announces it has sent "numerous fighting and bombing planes" to China, and "Bombing of Japanese Cities is Expected" (*NYT* 5/24/41).

- *June 26, 1941:* The Roosevelt administration freezes all Japanese assets, effectively cutting off the island nation's principal supply of steel and oil. This makes war virtually inevitable (D. Kennedy *Brief American Pageant* p. 496). FDR's advisor Harold Ickes assures the president that the embargo could "make it not only possible but easy to get into this war" (W. Thomas *Days of Deception: Ground Zero and Beyond* pp. 2, 4).

- *August 14, 1941:* At the Atlantic Conference, Prime Minister Winston Churchill remarks on the "astonishing depth of Roosevelt's intense desire for war" (www.wvwnews.net/story.php?id=6198).

- *September 24, 1941:* Having "cracked" the top-secret Japanese naval code, US intelligence knows that Japan has opted for war (Kennedy *Brief American Pageant* p. 496). However, top brass order the decoded warnings withheld from Adm. Husband Kimmel, commander of the Pacific Fleet at Pearl Harbor (Thomas *Days of Deception* p. 4).

- *October 16, 1941:* To conceal its intentions, Tokyo enters into prolonged negotiations with Washington (Kennedy *Brief American Pageant* p. 496). However, FDR deliberately humiliates Japan's ambassador and refuses to meet with its premier, outraging the Japanese public. The diplomatic slights help General Hideki Tojo's war party seize power (www.wvwnews.net/story.php?id=6198). Washington understands this development as meaning war could be imminent.

- *October 20, 1941:* When a Soviet spy informs the Kremlin that Japan will attack Pearl Harbor within 60 days, Moscow passes this information on to Washington (*NY Daily News* 5/17/51).

- *November 13, 1941:* William "Wild Bill" Donovan, head of the Office of Strategic Services (OSS, the predecessor of the CIA) describes to FDR the bind in which Japan finds itself: "If Japan waits, it will be comparatively easy for the United States to strangle Japan. Japan is therefore forced to strike now, whether she wishes to or not" (*NYT* 12/7/08).

- *November 19, 1941:* A Dutch submarine spots Admiral Yamamoto's mighty flotilla and alerts American intelligence. However, the Roosevelt administration never relays the sighting report to the Pacific Fleet command in Hawaii (Thomas *Days of Deception* p. 1).

- *November 21, 1941:* Admiral Kimmel, the Commander in Honolulu, becomes frantic to locate the Japanese aircraft carriers now heading east. When he launches a task force to locate the Japanese, he receives orders to terminate the mission. Adm. Kimmel is misinformed or otherwise prevented from taking action that could thwart the imminent Japanese attack (http://en.wikipedia. org/wiki/Husband_E._Kimmel).

- *November 25, 2001:* Exploiting their access to Japan's code, American cryptographers intercept Adm. Yamamoto's cable, which implies an imminent attack on Pearl Harbor. When British intelligence comes to the same conclusion, Churchill telexes an urgent warning to Roosevelt, who cables back: "Negotiations off. Services expect [military] action within two weeks" (Thomas *Days of Deception* p. 2).

- *November 26, 1941:* After a cabinet meeting dealing mainly with the Japanese, Secretary of War Henry Stimson remarks that "the question was how we should maneuver [the Japanese] into the position of firing the first shot without allowing too much danger to ourselves" (*Time* 4/1/46).

- *November 27, 1941:* Washington learns that a formidable Japanese fleet is steaming toward Hawaii. The next day, the Pentagon sends the *Enterprise* and the *Lexington,* its new aircraft carriers, out to sea and away from the Japanese. While the departure of these prime assets reduces the already inadequate fighter protection at the base, it also preserves them for the war that's sure to follow (www. chroniclesmagazine.org/2008/12/07/misallocated-infamy).

- *November 28, 1941*: After Roosevelt authorizes a warning, Admiral Royal Ingersoll sends a priority dispatch to naval commanders: "HOSTILE [Japanese] ACTION POSSIBLE AT ANY MOMENT. IF HOSTILITIES CANNOT REPEAT CANNOT BE AVOIDED THE UNITED STATES DESIRES THAT JAPAN COMMIT THE FIRST OVERT ACT ...." This warning leaves Pearl Harbor's command with few options because it's impossible to hide the aircraft involved in a massive search for the Japanese fleet (Stinnett *Day of Deceit* p. 171ff).

- *Dec. 1, 1941:* The Office of Naval Intelligence in San Francisco also locates the missing Japanese fleet (E. Layton *And I Was There* p. 261).

- *Dec. 4, 1941:* From Dutch Java, the US chief of counterintelligence sends four messages about an imminent attack on Pearl Harbor. Not only does Washington fail to heed his warnings, it even orders him to stop sending them (*NYT* 6/29/89). In the final ten days before the Day of Infamy, seven radio intercepts confirm Japanese plans to attack Pearl Harbor (Stinnett *Day of Deceit* p. 203).

- *Dec. 5, 1941*: At a cabinet meeting, Secretary of the Navy Frank Knox remarks, "'Well, you know, Mr. President, [that] we know where the Japanese fleet is?" "Yes, I know." A scowling FDR cuts him off and changes the subject (J. Toland *Infamy* Ch. 14 Sec. 5).

- *Dec. 7, 1941:* Roosevelt's wife, Eleanor, later recalls that after learning of the attack, the president became "in a way more serene" (E. Roosevelt *This I Remember* p. 233). When, later in the day, FDR meets with CBS reporter Edward R. Murrow, they speak about the tragic news from Pearl Harbor. Then, apparently testing or taunting the press, FDR asks, "Did this surprise you?" After Murrow nods, the president asks, "Maybe you think it didn't surprise *us*?" (www. independent.org/newsroom/article.asp?id=408).

- *Fall 1944:* A US Army board of inquiry confirms that, because of American access to the code, "everything the Japanese were planning to do was known to the United States" (Thomas *Days of Deception* p. 1).

Damning as all this might seem, some historians believe that subsequent events vindicate FDR's tough decisions and devious scheming. Some point out that US involvement in World War II did, after all, pull the country out of the Depression. Others contend that Roosevelt, foreseeing the enormous threats posed by Hitler and Mussolini, understood that the public and Congress nevertheless remained overwhelmingly against entering a war in Europe. The president, they argue, believed that events required the United States to suffer an attack that appeared sufficiently debilitating to entice European dictators into declaring war on the United States.

Whether FDR's decision is viewed as tactical or treasonous, it certainly extended an American tradition of using deception to foment public outrage and generate support for wars.

## 1962: Operation Northwoods: A "False-Flag" Operation against Cuba

As just shown, American history reveals instances in which Washington either treated an accident as a provocation or generated events intended to provoke public indignation. However, the history has also involved the deliberate staging of "false-flag" attacks in order to justify military actions. A "false flag" attack is perpetrated by one party but designed to be blamed on another.

### Backdrop: Fiasco at Bay of Pigs

In April of 1961, a new Kennedy administration had supported an abortive invasion of Cuba at the Bay of Pigs. This plan, secretly authorized by President Dwight Eisenhower and implemented by the Central Intelligence Agency (CIA), called for arming and training anti-Castro Cuban exiles. Though Kennedy was hesitant to commit American forces, he did approve the use of some unmarked warplanes. The plan was for the exiles to land and kindle a general uprising, but Castro's forces defeated the CIA-trained invaders in just three days (Zinn *People's History of the US* p. 440).

Ultraconservatives at the Pentagon were hardly chastened, however. In 1962, the Joint Chiefs of Staff, the generals commanding the entire US military, came up with Operation Northwoods, a much more ambitious scheme against Cuba. This new plan, which again involved the CIA, called for staged attacks that would "justify" a US invasion of Cuba. A "false-flag" operation, it featured several alternative schemes. The schemes ranged from having boatloads of Cuban émigrés "ruthlessly" sunk by "communist Cubans" to having a decoy passenger plane shot down by "Russian-made MiG fighters" and then telling the world that the empty drone had been full of "civilian victims" (J. Bamford *Body of Secrets* pp. 82-89).

The Joint Chiefs' ingenious plan for "provocations" reads like the script for a low-tech *Dr. Strangelove*. Its objective, as rendered in unusually clear "Pentagonese," was "to camouflage the ultimate objective and create the necessary impression of Cuban rashness ... to place the United States in the apparent position of suffering defensible grievances ... and to develop an international image of a Cuban threat to peace in the Western Hemisphere" (Joint Chiefs *Memorandum for the Secretary of Defense* 3/13/62 pp. 3, 5, 12). The intent then was to use a series of outrageous deceptions to generate a pretext for an unprovoked war on Cuba.

Operation Northwoods was plotted down to the most minute details. In one scenario, attacks led by the Cuban expatriates would be staged around Guantánamo Bay to give the "appearance of being done by hostile Cuban forces." Provocations were to "include starting rumors by clandestine radio, landing allied Cuban expatriates (in Cuban military uniforms) . . . , and burning aircraft inside the base. . . . A 'Remember the Maine' incident could be arranged. . . . We could blow up a US ship in Guantánamo Bay and blame Cuba." This initial deception was intended to "provoke Cuban reactions." At that very moment, American forces would be conducting "war games" in the area; if the Cubans fought back, the exercises would be changed into actual attacks (*Memo for Secy. of Def.* pp. 7-8).

Knowing what we do about the *Maine*, the plan to "blow up a ship" is particularly intriguing. On one hand, it suggests that military planners, unlike the general public, *do* recall the events that launched earlier campaigns. On the other hand, the plan illustrates a principle that informs much of this analysis: that tactics which have worked tend to stay in the bag of tricks, ready for Pentagon tricksters to use again. Informed citizens need to have some idea of what they're likely hiding in that bag.

## Staged Events at Home and Abroad

But the Guantánamo deception was just the beginning. Beyond staging events on foreign shores, the Joint Chiefs also planned provocations on US soil: "We could develop a Communist Cuban terror campaign in the Miami area, in other Florida cities and even in Washington.... We could foster attempts on lives of Cuban refugees in the United States even to the extent of wounding in instances to be widely publicized ..." (*Memo. to Secy. of Def.* pp. 7-8). The Joint Chiefs apparently anticipated no problems getting full cooperation from journalists.

But the electronic *coup de theatre* was still to come. The Joint Chiefs planned deceptions in the skies that involved substituting a drone aircraft for a commercial flight and then destroying it through remote control. The plan called for staging "an incident which will demonstrate convincingly that a Cuban aircraft has attacked and shot down a chartered civil airliner ...." With CIA agents posing as "passengers," an airliner was to head for Cuba. But the plane would secretly land at a CIA airfield; here it would receive a new tail number, making it seem like a different airliner. Then it was to take off, ready to veer off when a duplicate but unmanned airliner took its place in midair. The substitute drone airliner would be flown by remote control toward Cuba, sending back prerecorded calls for help.

Then came the climactic blowout of the plot. "When over Cuba," the generals proposed, "the drone will begin transmitting on the international distress frequency a 'MAYDAY' message stating he is under attack by Cuban MiG aircraft. The transmission will be interrupted by destruction of the aircraft, which will be triggered by radio signal. This will allow Latin American radio stations to tell the United States what's happened to the aircraft instead of the United States trying to 'sell' the incident" (*Memo. to Secy. of Def.* pp. 9ff). Having blamed Havana for the atrocity, Washington could proceed with the invasion it had longed to execute (*Harper's* 7/01).

"Buck Rogers" schemes aside, it's worth noting that the Northwoods plot reveals how, nearly 40 years before 9/11, Americans had seriously considered relying on high-tech deceptions.

*Civilians Assert Control, Planners Plot On* Admiral Lyman Lemnitzer, Chairman of the Joint Chiefs and the main proponent of the Northwoods plot, presented it to Defense Secretary McNamara and President Kennedy. After both rejected the scheme, Admiral Lemnitzer sought to destroy all evidence of the Northwoods plan (*Baltimore Sun* 4/24/01). Undeterred, the Pentagon continued to plan other "false flag" or "staged pretext" operations through 1963, when JFK was assassinated, and in 1964, its Gulf of Tonkin scheme "justified" a massive escalation of US bombing of North Vietnam. The JFK assassination itself enabled a sharp escalation of the Vietnam War and must be considered, along with 9/11, as a pivotal covert action or trigger event (P. D. Scott *American War Machine* pp. 22, 171).

## 1964: A Gulf of Tonkin "Incident" That Never Happened

Whereas the Mexicans had struck back at an American incursion, the North Vietnamese—whose leader, Ho Chi Minh, had studied American history—were more savvy. They didn't respond to provocative American attacks along their coast. As a result, American officials had to fabricate a Vietnamese response and then use it as the pretext for war.

Today, most historians believe that by the last few months of his life, Kennedy had decided to phase out of Vietnam. In October 1963, the president seemed to lean toward withdrawing US troops from Vietnam, a plan he didn't intend to implement until after the 1964 elections. That November, Kennedy made his fateful visit to Dallas. While President Johnson initially assured a stunned nation that he intended to carry out his predecessor's agenda, Johnson promptly rescinded Kennedy's order to have American troops start coming home. Just three days after the assassination, the new president met with Henry Cabot Lodge, US ambassador to Vietnam. Johnson told Lodge that "Saigon can count on us." Just four days after Kennedy's death, Johnson authorized plans to bomb North Vietnam, a drastic shift in policy (J. Galbraith *Boston Review* 10/03 & 11/03).

It seems unlikely, however, that LBJ had drawn up these plans by himself.

## Beginning a Full-Scale War in Vietnam

Trying to ready the public for war, Johnson, McNamara, and other top officials concluded that some flash point would be needed to trigger public outrage. American planners executed provocative raids along the North Vietnamese coast, but American ships took no return fire (www.globalresearch. ca/index.php?context=va&aid=9063).

Soon the nonevents flashed across the airwaves. On August 2, 1964, the destroyer *Maddox* was supposedly attacked by North Vietnamese torpedo boats but drove them off, sustaining only the slightest damage. "The destroyer maneuvered to avoid torpedoes and used her guns against her fast-moving opponents, hitting them all. In turn, she was struck … by a single 14.5-millimeter machine gun bullet." Two days later, the Pentagon announced the North Vietnamese had attacked a second American ship (US Naval Hist. Center *USS Maddox* 1944-1972). Although the Pentagon insisted that its warships were on "routine patrol," it's more likely that they entered the Gulf to provoke or spy on North Vietnam .

From the onset, military professionals in the field tried to tell the Pentagon brass that the attacks didn't occur. Capt. John J. Herrick, the task force commander in the Gulf, dismissed the reports as the work of an "overeager sonar man." Captain Herrick concluded that "torpedoes fired appear doubtful" and advised "complete evaluation before any further action." Years later, Herrick recalled that "our destroyers were just shooting at phantom targets—there were no PT boats there" (D. C. Hallin *Uncensored War* pp. 16-17).

But Washington didn't want the facts. Presenting the United States as the innocent victim, Johnson claimed that the United States had to "retaliate" against "communist aggression." McNamara rushed to Congress, charging that he had "unequivocal proof" of an "unprovoked attack." An officer at the Pentagon told Sen. Wayne Morse (D-Ore.) about the hoax, but Morse couldn't persuade his colleagues in Congress to halt the rush to war. Within hours, Congress passed the Tonkin Gulf Resolution, plunging the country into a disastrous "police action" that lasted a decade (S. Karnow *Vietnam: A History* p. 375).

Both the war's tactics and their effects proved genocidal. Even McNamara, architect of the massive "carpet" bombing campaigns, would acknowledge that two million Vietnamese were killed, most of them noncombatants (E. Morris film *Fog of War*). The actual toll probably ran closer to *three* million dead—including 58,000 Americans and hundreds of thousands of additional Asians, most of them killed by US bombs in Laos and Cambodia (D. Model *Lying for Empire* p. 138).

## Another Preplanned War

Were the results not so terribly tragic, it might seem comic for a superpower to make so much of so little—to launch a war over a single bullet, assuming there actually was a bullet (Bamford *Puzzle Palace* p. 294). Legendary independent journalist I. F. Stone characterized the Gulf of Tonkin incident as a "question not just of decision-making in a crisis, but of crisis-making to support a secretly prearranged decision ..." (*NY Review of Books* 3/28/68).

We've been looking at history here. Does that mean contrived provocations and false-flag operations are a thing of the past? Hardly. It's no secret that during the later years of the Bush regime, administration hawks were looking for a pretext to attack Iran. Never caught without a scheme, Dick Cheney did not disappoint. Pulitzer-prize-winning journalist Seymour Hersh and MSNBC both reported that Cheney had proposed to the Pentagon a plan to have the US Navy deploy fake Iranian patrol boats that would stage an "attack" on US destroyers in the Strait of Hormuz. This "act of aggression" was to be blamed on Iran and used as a pretext for war (*New Yorker* 7/7/08).

If the people understood the history of pretexts for war, would Cheney have been as likely to imagine that the US could get away with such a scheme?

Although this chronology of American foreign-policy malfeasance rests on solid historical facts, some readers may find it disturbing and difficult to accept. It's unsettling to realize that, with the exception of the Civil War, deception and trickery have helped the US to launch or enter every major war in its history. This is worked out in John Quigley's *The Ruses for War*—which, after examining the 25 most prominent US military actions since World War II, demonstrates how each was promoted by deception. Becoming more specific about the typical mechanism, political analyst Peter Dale Scott concludes that "nearly all of America's foreign wars since 1959" were "disguised as responses to unprovoked aggression" (Scott *American War Machine* p. 195). Even the "UN intervention" in Korea likely resulted from provocations; see I. F. Stone, *Hidden History of the Korean War*.

Presentation of these deceits can dent egos and undercut national pride; it also threatens the powers that be, who frequently denounce it as "unpatriotic." It's tempting to ignore the evidence or to dismiss this history as distortions by radicals who don't love their country. However, some of America's sharpest critics do so from a commitment to the core American value of facing and telling the truth. Examples include Mark Twain, legendary analyst Noam Chomsky, and widely published theologian David Ray Griffin, who offers a historical overview similar to this one (Griffin *Christian Faith and the Truth Behind 9/11* pp. 3-15).

## It's Hardly Unique to the United States

Following this survey of "trigger" events in American history, most of them state crimes against democracy (SCADs), let's look at other highly instructive precedents from recent history beyond the United States. Again, we'll find parallels to the present. These precedents include planned provocations, false-flag operations, "shock-and-awe" events, or simply traumas exploited for a political takeover. The famous Reichstag Fire falls in the latter category.

## Arson at the Reichstag: A Fiery Path to Power

In January of 1933, fires erupted at the Reichstag (German parliament), and the conflagration soon consumed the building. The actual perpetrators, beyond confessed Dutch communist Marinus van der Lubbe, remain uncertain. On this question, heavyweight historians have tilted both sides of the scale. In *The Rise and Fall of the Third Reich*, William L. Shirer believed that the Nazis *did* burn the building; yet in *Hitler: 1898-1936: Hubris*, British expert Ian Kershaw concluded that the Nazis didn't help the Dutch firebomber burn the Reichstag.

For now, it seems, we'll have to ride the paradox, accepting the ambiguity.

What is beyond dispute, though, is that the Reichstag fire provides a classic example of Klein's Shock Doctrine. The Nazis were amazingly quick to exploit a trauma that soon catapulted them into power. The day after the fire, as Berliners gazed at the smoldering ashes of a building that symbolized their democracy, the Nazis were busy drafting their

Reichstag Fire Decree. Immediately exploiting a weakness for authority in the German character, President Paul von Hindenburg and Chancellor Adolph Hitler invoked the Constitution to issue a decree permitting suspension of civil liberties in a "national emergency." With the public still in shock, the Nazis began to ruthlessly suppress all opposition (www. weyrich.com/political_issues/reichstag_fire.html).

Aided by the mainstream press, the Nazis were able to blame the fire on the Communists. The resulting backlash against opposing parties on the left allowed the fascists to assume totalitarian power in the elections of March 1933.

The causes behind the takeover hold implications for today. Ian Kershaw points out that Hitler rose to near-total power under a liberal constitution, albeit one that was never accepted by the Nazis' strongest supporters—the military, aristocracy, and big industry (*NYT Book Review* 2/3/08). To this list of contributing causes, one could add failures by the press, the churches, the courts, and many intellectuals to investigate or critique (www.alternet.org/story/71881). Ultimately, however, it was the apathy, conformity, dissipation, cowardice, and ignorance of history among most Germans that allowed the Nazis to seize power.

To what degree might the fears stirred by the 9/11 trauma and a similar lack of political sophistication have contributed to similarly uncritical public acquiescence?

It's difficult to ignore parallels to both the US Patriot Act, passed less than a month after 9/11, and to the immediate spike in popularity for President Bush. Regardless of whether political leaders played a part in a politically pivotal event, what they do after it occurs usually reveals prior intentions. This is the "priority principle," which states that the first things politicians do in office usually reveals their agendas. Solidifying their power by crippling competitors is typically a high priority. Ironically, soon enough the voters who elected the officials may also be seen as adversaries. Such attitudes suggest one motivation for officials to commit SCADs, which compromise the democratic process.

Parallels to the ascending corporate control in the United States indeed are deeply troubling. However, it's too glib just to say, "it's Germany in

1933 all over again." Historical analogies are never exact. When we note sobering parallels to the rise of fascism in Germany, we also need to recall that Americans enjoy one great advantage—a history of democracy and long exposure to its ideals—if only they will bring the best of their past to bear on the present.

### Fear Mongering: Conjuring "Barbarians at the Gate"

Another dependable power play is to conjure the "boogie man." Never ones to miss a trick that worked, the Nazis relied heavily on imagined, inflated, or contrived enemies. At the Nuremberg Trials, Luftwaffe Commander Hermann Göring explained how Nazi leaders exploited the fears they'd fabricated: "it is always a simple matter to drag the people along, whether it is a democracy, or a fascist dictatorship, or a parliament, or a communist dictatorship.… Voice or no voice, the people can always be brought to the bidding of the leaders. That is easy. All you have to do is to tell them they are being attacked, and denounce the pacifists for lack of patriotism and exposing the country to danger" (http://www.wisdomquotes.com/001993.html).

Could Göring's candid disclosure also characterize White House pronouncements during the leadup to recent wars?

In practice, the Nazis magnified *external* threats (England, France, and Soviet Union) and conjured *internal* threats (communists, socialists, and Jews), using these not just to control the population but to motivate external and internal aggression. Jews in general were seen as threats to Aryan racial purity, and "Jewish bankers" were scapegoated for the sins of bankers more broadly, blinding the public to the role of bankers in calamitous German militarism. The passivity and miseducation of the populace proved colossally costly: forty million people lost their lives.

How could this have happened in a highly cultured industrial democracy? If we pose this question, we rarely get much beyond stock footage of storm troopers goose-stepping through the Arc de Triumph. Rarely is Göring's revelation either taught or quoted, probably because powerful interests don't want us to wonder whether it might apply elsewhere.

Despite many Americans' ongoing fascination with their country's role in World War II, how many know that war began with a false-flag operation?

## Heinrich Himmler's Schemes: A Classic False-Flag Operation

Like many of the American administrations we've looked in on, the Third Reich also needed a pretext for an attack. In August 1939, German soldiers disguised as Polish troops staged an assault on a German radio station near the Polish border. Adding realism to the stagecraft, German political prisoners dressed in Polish uniforms were killed as they "attacked." After German SS personnel dressed as Polish troops "captured" the station, they delivered an anti-German broadcast in Polish. On the same day, other staged incidents provided additional pretexts for vengeance and war. Reacting to such "aggression" against the Fatherland, Hitler wasted no time; he ordered a "defensive" invasion of Poland to begin the very next day (B. Lightbody *Second World War* p. 39).

Governments and political groups use contrived events so frequently because they evoke powerful emotions. We've just seen that the dramatic nighttime conflagration at the Reichstag, whether or not deliberately set by the Nazis, left most Germans in shock, vulnerable to the ascendant fascists. Again, civil authority and order seemed to be going up in flames, and the Nazis promised a strong Father to fill the void.

But more than "allowed" or "assisted" events, carefully staged provocations are apt to evoke the strongest reactions, especially when combined with a psychological operation—a "PSYOP," or "psych-war"—designed for maximum impact. As Zwicker observes, "the false-flag op is the indispensable, most dependable device rulers use to mobilize their populations behind wars …" (Zwicker *Towers of Deception* pp. 260-61). Despite the great impact of such events, "shock and awe"—even when intensified by a PSYOP— usually isn't trusted to carry enough impact; it's immediately framed within narratives that spin the event and promote political agendas, usually those of the perpetrators. Thus such provocations are often followed by scary stories or shocking images, such as the propaganda newsreels of the Reichstag on fire.

Any parallels to the seemingly perpetual replays of the burning and disintegrating Twin Towers weren't coincidental, regardless of who was responsible for their destruction. Public outrage propelled the country toward a revenge attack on Afghanistan—which, as we'll see, was probably less involved with the attacks than Pakistan and Saudi Arabia. But Pakistan had nuclear weapons, and Saudi Arabia supplied much of America's oil, so the bombs fell on Afghanistan.

Even today, planned provocations, false-flag operations, and PSYOPs remain a mystery to most Americans. So why don't even educated people know more about these sinister schemes? Why aren't staged deceptions included in mainstream renderings of history, such as realistic war movies and TV documentaries? Why doesn't the public learn about these events in history classes, on the History Channel, or from *The War*, Ken Burns's thirteen-hour documentary about World War II? The answer may lie with other questions: If a documentarian had covered these false-flag operations or how Pearl Harbor had actually come about, would he retain his corporate sponsorship? Would his series have aired at all?

So there's a lot of information which should be common knowledge that just hasn't been readily available. Similarly, there's a lot of information about unsolved traumas that needs to come into the national conversation. That will be one of the subjects of the next chapter.

# 3.   The Power of Patterns and Precedents

*A popular government without popular information or the means of acquiring it is but a prologue to a farce or a tragedy … a people who mean to be their own governors, must arm themselves with the power knowledge gives.*

—James Madison

The last chapter revealed how historical precedents provide meaningful contexts for understanding more current developments, especially 9/11. When Americans seek to better comprehend 9/11, it's not only useful to know about past provocations for wars; it's also important to understand the national traumas that have haunted Americans over recent decades. Unfinished business can hang like a cloud over the present, damaging the quality of our lives.

## A Backlog of Unresolved National Traumas
Still unresolved traumas, especially unsolved political crimes, linger as scars on the political landscape. As noted earlier, South Africa, Spain, Chile and other countries have realized the importance of closure, and are struggling to heal the wounds of their pasts.

To illustrate the problem of unresolved national issues, the aftermath of the Vietnam War malaise is the obvious place to begin. During that prolonged national nightmare, repressed demons were unleashed with full fury: the racism, the addictions to power, indiscriminate killing, and high-tech slaughter (P. Slater *The Pursuit of Loneliness* pp. 38-61). Because of bitterness about the war and the cultural upheavals associated with it, Vietnam veterans didn't return to victory parades.

While the ghosts of 'Nam still haunt the American psyche, there have been few opportunities to exorcise them. Most of the returning vets, many dealing with PTSD, have had to bear their wounding privately or among themselves, sometimes in support groups. A recent Iraq-war veteran articulated the suffering endured by so many vets from so many wars: "I'm still fighting a war at home.... A war of anger and anxiety, fought within the recesses of my mind" *(San Fran. Chron.* 2/1/11). Yet while hundreds of thousands of vets have returned damaged by subsequent wars, many with the very same symptoms, Vietnam was where America began to crash and burn: it was the shocker, and still its malaise hangs over the land.

Although the country hasn't fully processed its Vietnam agony, creative artists have made some sense of the senseless tragedy. Films such as *The Deer Hunter, Platoon, Apocalypse Now, Coming Home,* and *Who'll Stop the Rain* have proved therapeutic to some vets; at their best, these powerful films were finally able to represent what veterans had experienced, representing their experience for noncombatants who didn't understand and who'd often turned away from the nightmare.

And Vietnam is hardly the only unresolved trauma lingering in the American psyche.

## The Still-Unsolved Murder of Martin Luther King Jr.

In 1967, after Dr. King saw graphic photos of atrocities in Vietnam, he began to openly oppose the war. In his famous Riverside Church address, he lamented that his government had become "the world's leading purveyor of violence" (Pacifica Radio "Democracy Now!" 4/4/03).

Dr. King's indictment of a major American military intervention and those promoting it signaled that he was no longer just challenging racism and poverty. He was now confronting the federal government plus the military, political, and economic interests deeply invested in the Cold War. Although FBI surveillance and wiretapping of the leader continued, his security protection was withdrawn, all but assuring his assassination (http://mlk-kpp01.stanford.edu). During his last year of life, King "talked about death all the time" (D. Garrow *Bearing the Cross* pp. 602-03). The advocate for Gandhian nonviolence was gunned down on April 4, 1968, exactly a year after his full emergence as an eloquent voice for peace in Vietnam.

Just days after King was assassinated, the FBI named James Earl Ray, supposedly a lone gunman motivated by racism, as the prime suspect. Faced with the death penalty, Ray pled guilty and received a life sentence. Like Kennedy assassin Lee Harvey Oswald, Ray was quickly moved "out of the way," never to speak in an open courtroom. But if Ray was the killer, did he act alone? To this day it remains little known that the King family had long believed that other conspirators, including the federal government, had helped kill Dr. King—and that Ray was likely just a "patsy" who was first framed and then offered a plea bargain.

Nor is it widely known that a congressional inquiry found a "likelihood" that James Earl Ray did *not* act alone (www.cnn.com/US/9804/23/ray.obit). Attorney William Pepper became convinced of Ray's innocence and spent years trying to get him a new trial. It didn't help Ray's case that he seemed to have every opportunity to inform on others, yet didn't (www.cnn.com/US/9804/23/ray.obit). Except for a shadowy shooter named "Raoul," he never named others—possibly because he couldn't. Ray's reticence responds to a common objection to allegations of conspiracy: "Over time, surely *someone* involved in that crime would have come forth." It's well to recall, though, that those participating in conspiracies often don't know who else is involved. Plotters don't circulate organizational flow charts.

Nor is it well known that in 1999, after Ray's death in prison, the King family won a wrongful death lawsuit against Lloyd Jowers (owner of the cafe in the rooming house where someone fired the fatal shot) and "other unknown coconspirators." Providing reams of evidence, attorney Pepper proved direct complicity in King's murder by the Memphis police, the Mafia, the FBI, and the CIA. After deliberating less than an hour, the jury found that a conspiracy to kill Dr. King *had* existed, and that "governmental agencies were parties" to the plot. The King family concluded that Ray was "not the shooter" but an "unknowing patsy" (www.thekingcenter.org/kingcenter/trial/transcript_info.aspx).

All this, of course, is not what we hear in retrospectives on Martin Luther King. Like 9/11, these findings are rarely mentioned—not on NPR, not even by progressive media that may revere Dr. King. When this media blackout is contrasted with the airtime devoted, say, to the O. J. Simpson trials, the disproportion boggles the mind. Like the Kennedy assassinations and 9/11, King's murder remains an unsolved mystery, one that also casts a shadow on government institutions and the public's confidence that real justice can and will be done.

### Similar Nagging Doubts about the Robert Kennedy Assassination

Just two months after Dr. King was killed, with much of the nation still grieving, Sen. Robert Kennedy was also assassinated in June of 1968. Once again, investigators blamed a lone gunman, this time an anti-Zionist Palestinian. However, suspicions about whether Sirhan Sirhan acted alone still linger. These suspicions have spawned book-length studies exploring a possible role by Israel, which benefited from the ensuing anti-Palestinian backlash (W. Turner *Assassination of Robert F. Kennedy*).

But whether or not Mossad was involved, Sen. Kennedy was widely feared and hated. He'd just won the California primary and seemed likely to win the presidency. Given his commitment to ending the war, Bobby, like his brother John, posed a threat to the military/intelligence establishment (J. Newman *JFK and Vietnam*). Again, those who control information, historical or contemporary, have hardly encouraged full public awareness about such "sensitive" political issues.

As tragic and traumatic as the loss of RFK was, especially for those who were young at the time, the earlier killing of a highly charismatic president probably delivered an even more enduring blow to the country's soul.

### JFK and 9/11: Traumas with Uncanny Parallels

Let's look at three striking similarities between two additional American traumas—the JFK assassination and the 9/11 attacks. By connecting the dots, we can see striking similarities between these tragic events. In both, the alleged perpetrators died while committing the crime or in the immediate aftermath. In both, the suspects were identified or apprehended with uncanny rapidity. Moreover, both traumas occasioned shifts in leadership or public opinion that enabled plans for wars to go forward. Concerned

Americans have tried to determine whether one or even both was another "act of state," a State Crime against Democracy (SCAD).

While everyone knows Lee Harvey Oswald was supposedly the lone assassin, few know the JFK assassination involved near-instant identification of Oswald. This was curious, since no one saw him commit the crime. Nevertheless, only fifteen minutes after the shooting, the Dallas Police were broadcasting a description: 5'10" and 165 lbs. (*Warren Comm. Report* pp. 614, 5). While these measurements didn't fit Oswald, the suspect apprehended in a movie theater, they did match the description of him in both CIA documents and his FBI file (Newman *Oswald and the CIA* p. 512). This broadcast, notes master researcher Peter Dale Scott, suggests "someone had already determined that Oswald would be the designated culprit before there was any evidence to connect him to the crime" (www.politicalassassinations.com/PeterDaleScott.html).

Here we note a pattern, also manifest right after 9/11, in which alleged perpetrators are immediately identified and an official narrative is rapidly released.

On 9/11, the speedy identifications were even more remarkable because the FBI immediately identified twenty perpetrators, not just one, and because White House officials fingered al Qaeda during the attacks (R. Clarke *Against All Enemies* p. 2). If 9/11 was a surprise suicide attack done by perpetrators who all died, how could the FBI so quickly determine who was responsible? Some might argue that the names came from the passenger lists, but even if we accept this hypothesis, we still have to explain the photos.

When the news media failed to ask questions about the information it received, the amazing speed of these accusations stirred suspicions among FBI professionals. "I don't buy the idea that we didn't know what was coming," remarked William Norman Grigg, a former official with years of experience in counterterrorism. "Within 24 hours [of the attacks], the Bureau had about 20 people identified, and photos were sent out to the news media. Obviously, this information was available in the files and somebody was sitting on it" (*New American* 3/11/02).

Nor were military professionals fooled. Army intelligence expert Col. Anthony Shaffer, who'd tracked al Qaeda operatives himself, had a similar reaction: "We were amazed at how quickly the FBI produced the names and photos of all nineteen hijackers. But then again, we were surprised at how quickly they'd made the arrests after the [1993] World Trade Center bombing. Only later did we find out that the FBI had been watching some of these people for months prior to both incidents" (P. Lance *Triple Cross* p. 383). In fact, the FBI had been tracking several of these *very same* operatives for the eight and a half *years* between 1993 and 2001 (P. Thompson *Terror Timeline* pp. 169-71, 186-87). This, too, does seem odd.

But when one looks into 9/11, these oddities are only a few among the many improbabilities, anomalies, coincidences, and contradictions within the Official Story. All of these can make us skeptical about instant attributions of responsibility in the wake of assassinations or other political crimes. Those in power may exploit the public's emotional need to reduce anxiety by immediately announcing the suspected perpetrators of a criminal act. They seem to understand that once a narrative is imprinted in the public mind, especially in situations of shock and trauma, most people don't want questions: they want answers. Moreover, those in power seem to understand that it's very difficult to alter, let alone erase, an imprinted story, despite a huge amount of information that may contradict it.

With this in mind, the instant construction and installation of a story by government and media will become a main focus of Chapter 4.

## Surmounting a Crisis of Confidence

The unsolved crimes and unresolved traumas may cost us more than we realize. Vietnam, Watergate, Iran/Contra, unresolved assassinations, two suspect presidential elections, debacles in Iraq and Afghanistan, and the massive deceit of recent governments have all contributed to a corrosion of public trust. This, in turn, leads to a decline in public participation so crucial to democracy.

When a major political crime remains unsolved, Peter Dale Scott has observed, one result is more mistrust of democratic institutions: "To leave 9/11 in the same state of unresolved suspicion would be an even greater shock to the conditions of democratic government" (Scott *Road To 9/11* p. 232). Can democratically elected officials be trusted to sustain democratic institutions? Many vow to support and defend the Constitution, but how many take their oaths seriously? More and more Americans are asking these questions.

Along with declining stature on the world stage and concerns about economic recovery, gnawing doubts about the Official Story of 9/11 may contribute to a growing national crisis of confidence. We need to know what really happened not only to help reverse the decline in public institutions but to help *revitalize* them.

Once we grasp this pattern of pretexts, contrived provocations, and false-flag operations, we're newly empowered. Viewed through well informed eyes, alternative hypotheses about 9/11 aren't strange anomalies; rather, some *fit the pattern* we encountered in Chapter 1—that of State Crimes Against Democracy (SCADs). These were deceptions designed to manipulate public opinion, enabling domestic repression and foreign wars.

Once you know the playbook, it's easier to spot the plays. Several of these patterns have continued because citizens just didn't know enough. In 1915, if more Americans had known the truth about the sinking of the *Maine*, would Woodrow Wilson have so easily deceived the public about the *Lusitania*? If more Americans had known about the *Maine* and the *Lusitania*, about Pearl Harbor and about Operation Northwoods, would they have allowed Lyndon Johnson to sell them a bogus "police action"? (J. Bamford *Puzzle Palace* p. 294). And if, in the confused, tumultuous days following 9/11, more Americans had known about how planned provocations have been exploited in the past, would they have so passively accepted what they were told?

I don't think so.

Most readers now know that during the 1980s, a conservative Reagan administration (working secretly through the CIA) sent massive support to the *mujahedeen* ("holy warriors") in Afghanistan. Yes, Congressman Charlie Wilson (D-Tx.) was a big promoter, but this was hardly "Charlie Wilson's War." After the Soviets withdrew, these "freedom fighters" (as Reagan called them) soon morphed into Islamist extremists, notably the Taliban and al Qaeda. The new leader of the latter group was a young

Saudi who spoke English well—Osama bin Laden. In a classic case of "blowback," al Qaeda arose from the massive American intervention (Scott *Road to 9/11* pp. 123-4, 161-63).

Yet this was only a small part of the largely forgotten past with a definite bearing on 9/11.

Also during the 1990s, the US had increasingly come into conflict with the Taliban ruling Afghanistan. Western powers desperately wanted approval to build an oil and gas pipeline, and the ruling Taliban fundamentalists resisted the corporate-driven plan. This meant they were impeding expansion for American firms like Halliburton, whose CEO was Dick Cheney (Scott *Road to 9/11* pp. 166-72). The stakes ran high, for without the cooperation of *both* Afghanistan and Pakistan, oil and gas pipelines might go through Russia. Worse, India and Pakistan had started to discuss a route through Iran that would bypass Afghanistan entirely (*Wall Street Journal* 6/27/01).

**Neocons Call for "Regime Change," Yearn for a "New Pearl Harbor"**
During the late 1990s, years before 9/11, key neoconservatives were organizing pressure groups to strategize interventions in Afghanistan and especially Iraq. In 1997, 25 prominent neocons formed the Project for the New American Century (PNAC). Founders included Dick Cheney, Donald Rumsfeld, Paul Wolfowitz, Richard Perle, Lewis "Scooter" Libby, William Bennett, Robert Kagan, Bill Kristol, Jeb Bush, Francis Fukayama, Eliot Abrams, Dan Quayle, and Steve Forbes.

By 1998, PNAC was calling for "regime change." It sent an "Open Letter to President Clinton" calling for an invasion of Iraq, where a militarily weak tyrant was controlling vast reserves of high-quality, easily accessible oil. Most of the group's leading members, including Cheney, Rumsfeld, Perle, and Wolfowitz would soon enough become primary proponents for Operation Iraqi Liberation (OIL). For reasons not terribly difficult to discern, they later changed the operation's name to Operation Iraqi Freedom. The neocon group had also entertained the prospect of a "new Pearl Harbor" (PNAC *Rebuilding America's Defenses* p. 51). The problem, the neocons believed, was that the public wouldn't want to pay the costs in dollars and lives. New enemies and big shocks would be necessary to build public support for military adventurism.

## Bush's Early Interest in Invading Iraq

About this same time, Gov. George W. Bush was getting ready to launch his campaign for president. He had not, however, worked out some personal issues. He made it clear that he saw many benefits to invading Iraq and overthrowing Saddam—completing the job his father had left unfinished: "If I have a chance to invade … I'm not going to waste it." This is what the soon-to-be president said, and not with a wink. "In aggressive military action," observed writer and researcher Russ Baker, Bush "saw the opportunity to emerge from the shadow of his father" (R. Baker *Family of Secrets* p. 423). Although G. W. Bush never formally joined the neocons, his psychological needs—plus his deep connections to both Eastern and Texas power elites—led him toward similarly militaristic outlooks.

In early 2001, Cheney, Rumsfeld, Perle, Wolfowitz, and other neocons came to power. Even if one were not familiar with their previous involvements in government, they'd made their objectives clear at the Project for the New American Century (PNAC). At the White House and the Pentagon, plans were discussed in the spring and summer of 2001— well before September 11—for "convincing the Taliban in Afghanistan to accept construction of an American (UNOCAL) pipeline" (K. Phillips *American Theocracy* p. 83). Well beyond concerns about increasing Islamist terrorism, then, the US had economic motives to threaten Afghanistan with war.

After neocons assumed prominent positions in the Bush administration, the saber rattling got louder. Former French intelligence officers have reported a stark ultimatum: that in talks with Afghan officials, the Bush administration demanded the Taliban choose between "carpets of bombs" or "carpets of gold" (J. C. Brisard and G. Dasquié *Forbidden Truth* p. 43). Washington's backup plan, made explicit three months before 9/11, involved possible use of Pakistan's ISI (secret military intelligence) "to change the Taliban leadership" (A. Rashid *Descent Into Chaos* pp. 59-60). This plan indicated ignorance about the actual loyalties of the ISI, which was helping to finance al Qaeda before 9/11 and later apparently helped harbor Osama bin Laden for several years (BBC 5/16/11). How many of us knew that the United States was seriously considering an attack on Afghanistan months *before* September 11?

## Questions We the Public Weren't Equipped to Raise

In July, the Taliban government had warned US officials that al Qaeda was planning an attack on the American homeland. Dismissing this friendly warning, senior administration officials responded that the United States was planning to attack the Taliban in October. A Pakistani diplomat told the BBC "it was doubtful that Washington would drop its plan even if bin Laden were to be surrendered immediately by the Taliban" (*For. Pol. Journ.* 9/20/10). We now know that well before 9/11—even before Bush took office, in fact—key players, particularly among the neocons, had also decided to invade Iraq. The decision was made; it was only a question of how to make the war: "How [to] start [it]?" Rumsfeld had asked in a memo (T. Hartmann Air America Radio 9/23/10).

This disclosure raises questions:

- Were other factors, such as gas, oil, and minerals, driving US plans?
- If so, How could the administration arouse public opinion to support an attack on a distant, defenseless country that posed no immediate threat to the US?
- And, most crucial to our concerns here, Did powerful political forces hijack 9/11 for their own predetermined purposes?

We'll grapple with these questions as our inquiry unfolds.

## Fomenting Vengeance and Violence

Although conventional wisdom says that "after 9/11, we just had to attack Afghanistan," the record tells us something more complex. Framed historically, the American-led attack on Afghanistan (launched only five weeks after 9/11) further illustrates the Shock Doctrine, the priority principle (how early actions are often revealing), the primacy of corporate concerns, and a wounded superpower's longings for revenge.

It's natural to feel like striking back when you've taken a hit. We don't, however, expect both a president and national magazines to enflame these feelings. As Bush would do later with his "axis of evil" speech, Bush evoked the Apocalypse, thundering about his commitment to lead "a monumental struggle of good against evil" (White House 9/12/01). Corporate journalists were just as bad, if not worse: a *Time* editorial written immediately after the attacks urged that "for once, let's have no fatuous rhetoric about 'healing' … a day cannot live in infamy without the nourishment of rage. What's needed is a … Pearl Harbor sort of purple American fury" (*Time* 9/11/01).

Mass media spread the story quickly and widely, saturating the airwaves to imprint it on the public mind before any others, and reinforcing the narrative. Too often, the instant legend is uncritically accepted because it meets the psychological needs of the shell-shocked population and the political priorities of those controlling government and media. As one example, one can recall the public's reaction to a president with the bullhorn, his arm around a firefighter, standing atop Ground Zero. At that time, that was a reassuring image to many viewers, though today it likely strikes most of us as calculated and loaded with symbolism. At that time, that newly minted Official Story met our needs; today we know a lot more, so it seems much less plausible. These tragic events have tended to be defined by a narrative rapidly constructed out of the smoking rubble. As we saw in chapter 1, visibility during the immediate aftermath was far less clear than it is today.

## Plans for Both Wars Advance Again

Early during Bush's first year, a sense of secrecy and urgency surrounded Cheney's Energy Task Force, which began to meet in the spring 2001. In the months before 9/11, Task Force participants, many of them oil and gas executives, often pored over maps of Iraq's oil fields (*Wash. Post* 7/18/07). While the Bush administration's main project was Iraq, it also had plans for "regime change" in Afghanistan.

The events of 9/11 provided the catalyst, making two wars planned well beforehand not just politically possible but virtually imperative, at least in the minds of the Bush administration's neocons. Immediately after 9/11, the administration declared its open-ended Global War on Terrorism, a significant departure from previously stated US policy (*Wash. Post* 9/16/01). Stretching the usual definitions of "war," this campaign was not aimed at a national state designated as "the enemy." Instead, an unprecedented War on Terror targeted "Islamic terrorism," a difficult-to-define abstraction, and promised near-perpetual warfare for generations. This concept was of tenuous application to Afghanistan and even less application to Iraq, which was a secular state. For his own reasons, Saddam Hussein was strongly opposed to Islamic fundamentalism. Nevertheless, in the aftermath of 9/11, the administration was quick to deploy its new conceptions of endless war against both countries (*New Yorker* 5/13/02).

In 2002, the administration unveiled the Bush Doctrine of "preemptive war," which legitimized "offensive first-strike" against anybody Washington deemed a threat, or even a potential *future* threat (*NYT* 9/22/02). Cheney's 1 percent dictum allowed the US to hit virtually any country; even if there was only the smallest chance of attack, that was sufficient grounds for a military strike. The double standard was striking: attacking America was a whole different matter from being attacked by America (*NYT Book Rev.* 1/30/11).

Strongly influenced by neocon ideology and the mentality of the Global Domination Project, the Bush Doctrine received strong support from Rumsfeld, Cheney, Wolfowitz, Richard Perle, Condoleezza Rice, and her friend Philip Zelikow, the main author of the doctrine. Zelikow, who'd served on the Bush transition team, would soon leave the White House to become executive director of the 9/11 Commission (*Report* p. 199). As our inquiry continues, this will become an important biographical detail.

To further explain its endorsement of an unprovoked first strike, the Bush Doctrine relied on traditional notions of American innocence of motive and the country's uniquely divine mission. In his State of the Union address, Bush told the country that "the liberty we prize is not [just] America's gift to the world, it is God's gift to humanity" (White House

1/28/03). Bush, Cheney, and Rumsfeld now had the emotional aftermath of 9/11 and an ideological justification for "shock and awe," starting with bombs over Baghdad.

To the public's detriment, the Commission decided not to look any further back than a few years so it could "focus on recommendations" for the future (*Report* p. xvi). As a result, the panel gave scant coverage to the 1993 bombing of the World Trade Center—which was masterminded by the same Islamists who later planned other terrorist attacks, including 9/11. Granted, the Commission's coverage on the CIA/mujahedeen genesis of Islamist extremism is some of the best in its book (*Report* pp. 54-57), it doesn't cover the role of the CIA, let alone that agency's extensive involvement in opium trafficking (Scott *Drugs, Oil, and War* pp. 39-52). And of course it made no mention of the neocons and their aspirations—the events we've just looked at.

When the Commission airbrushed so many details, it not only kept the public from viewing the complete picture, it created a vacuum that the commissioners, as august insider authorities, were all too ready to fill. This was nothing new.

Researcher Russ Baker places the Commission's Official Story in the pattern of other official narratives: "The common narrative on the most complex, disturbing events is usually generated by insiders—so-called investigative commissions made up of figures acceptable to the establishment, and by a handful of designated authorities.... For the rest of us, it is almost always easier ... to accept the most benign interpretation. If everything is tied up neatly, then we don't have to do anything" (Baker *Family of Secrets* p. 245).

For many of us, it's convenient to have a blue-ribbon commission endorse a superficially plausible Official Story. It's temptingly easy to "move on," no questions asked.

However, a few of our " best" have continued to question things that don't add up. All the anomalies led public intellectual and talk-show host Thom Hartmann to lament that "we still don't know what happened on 9/11" (Air America Radio 12/20/07). Hartmann understand that this is a big problem, for accurate knowledge is the oxygen that nourishes the lifeblood of a vibrant democracy.

Sometimes it's not easier to just accept an official narrative; it's that many of us today are deep into our diversions—music, movies, sports, gourmet delicacies, relationship dramas, video games, mind-altering substances, eye candy of various flavors—whatever gets us through the day or night. In moderation, diversion and entertainment aren't bad things. But when they become all-consuming, that's a problem. It's akin to the old question, How can we run a democracy when half the population doesn't inform itself and vote.

## The Costs of Apathy and Escapism

In the wake of these secret plans for wars, conscientious Americans have started to examine more closely the news media they've sometimes trusted far too uncritically. Veteran war correspondent Sydney Schanberg has pointed to "the apparent amnesia of the American public," noting that "we Americans are ... forever desperate to believe that this time the government is telling us the truth" (*Newsday* 2/8/91). This "desperate" desire to believe reflects a naive optimism, an avoidance of truths that, if accepted, would demand serious citizen involvement. But the opposite stance—a cynical rejection of *all* communications put out by the news media—is equally paralyzing. Skepticism is healthy; cynicism is toxic.

On the first day of World War II, with Hitler's armies poised to overrun Europe, British poet W. H. Auden ruminated on an unaware, escapist America in his poem "September 1, 1939." According to poet David Orr, the famous poem was "endlessly quoted on the internet after 9/11 to express grief over what had happened and foreboding about what was to come" (*NYT Book Review* 4/10/11).

But as times change, the parallels to the present may also strike us as uncanny:

> Faces along the bar
> Cling to their average day:
> The lights must never go out,
> The music must always play
> Lest we should see where we are,

Lost in a haunted wood,
Children afraid of the night
Who have never been happy or good.

Though Auden's poem is topical, written for a particular moment in history, it also speaks powerfully to today's malaise. As the *Wehrmacht* began marching across Europe, Auden deplored the public's apathy. Having spent time in Berlin around 1930, during the waning days of Weimar democracy, he was painfully aware of how apathy and escapism was contributing to that decline. The dissipated, zonked-out lifestyle so creatively rendered in Bob Fosse's classic *Cabaret* had indeed been rampant in Berlin. While it was delightful to see the Nazis mocked, the outcome was hardly a delight. At the end, as the camera pans around the club; red armbands, brown shirts, and black boots have infiltrated the last pleasure palace. When the champagne bubbles burst, there was no "away."

Clearly *Cabaret* was more than just a musical; like Auden's poem, it warned of how citizens can lose a democracy. Because most Americans don't pay much attention to history, they're apt to assume that their country's pioneering democracy, once established, runs on automatic pilot without much maintenance. Deaf to historical overtones, few Americans recall Ben Franklin's response when a woman on the street asked him what the Constitutional Convention had come up with: "A republic, madam, if you can keep it" (*American Historical Review* V. 11 p. 618). Franklin's prescient quip never did inform civics classes—and today, alas, civics is hardly taught at all.

Today, instead of AM radio and scratchy 78 rpm records delivering "music that must always play," electronic devices accompany us everywhere, allowing us to text the day away, oblivious to outside realities, encapsulated in our own little world. As the technology has improved, the private psychic numbing and public political paralysis have worsened. Many Americans, remarked media critic Neil Postman, have become addicted to entertainment technologies that diminish their abilities to see reality or think (Postman *Amusing Ourselves to Death* pp. 3, 34). Video games may come to mind—if the mind hasn't played too many.

## Surmounting Our Fears

Without some suggestive historical precedents in mind, it's tougher for people to imagine how "their" leaders might be hoodwinking them, how State Crimes Against Democracy are committed and then covered up. Granted, people watch deceit, intrigue, plots, and conspiracies all the time on the silver screen but tend to think, *It's only a movie.* To many of us, the prospect of "our" leaders purposefully attempting to start costly, divisive, disastrous wars based on a contrived event may not simply seem far-fetched; it may feel downright scary.

After all, if the deceptions were exposed, citizens would not only feel unprotected, they'd feel vulnerable to retribution by their "protectors." To avoid that anxiety, many fall back on evasions such as "I just can't believe they'd do something like that." Even those who *do* know more history may say, "Oh, but this is America; they wouldn't try to pull something like that *again*; the news media would expose it." Today, do we have the *watchdogs* the founders deemed so essential, do we have a trusted "Uncle Walter" Cronkite to tell us that a war can't be won? Today we can't depend on institutions to protect our democracy; we've got to do it for ourselves.

Now let's deepen our inquiry into how the Official Story was created by looking at the interplay of political power and the mass media that had so much to do with inscribing that narrative in the popular mind. As we focus on the Official Story of 9/11, we'll deal with the power of myth in contemporary contexts, especially 9/11. By political myths, we don't necessarily mean complete untruths but partial truths that pass themselves off as full truths—and that have become conventional commonplaces.

In this sense of the word, the Official Story is a public myth. If that seems like an extreme characterization, let's look at how it came about. There's a lot at stake in stories that purport to explain pivotal events. Much more than the public itself, those who control what the public believes seem to grasp a key insight from George Orwell: "He who controls the present, controls the past. He who controls the past, controls the future" (www. quotedb.com/quotes/3947). Orwell's insight underscores the need to examine master narratives, including the one for 9/11.

# 4. Media Mythmaking in the Wake of Catastrophe

*The great enemy of the truth is very often not the lie—deliberate, contrived, and dishonest—but the myth—persistent, persuasive, and unrealistic.*

—John F. Kennedy

Appropriately enough, America promised itself it would never forget. But it's a question of *what* the nation remembers; if it's only the stuff it received from the corporate mass media, then it's in trouble. While a country's population is stunned and confused following a shocking event, it's vulnerable to fakers and fabulists. Those in control have a special opportunity to fashion and spin out a story.

Right after 9/11, rapidly created myths began to define public perceptions. As in the JFK assassination, it involved a four-part process: a shocking event; near-instant imprinting of a narrative in the public memory; ongoing, relentless media reinforcement; and finally the endorsement of a official commission. From the outset, then, alternative narratives are marginalized, systematically suppressed, or derided as "conspiracy theories."

## The Uses of Political Myths

When most of us say "that's a myth," we mean a story that doesn't adhere to reality, one that's "make-believe," less fact than fantasy. But fewer of us recognize that myths also serve a multitude of social, political, or economic purposes—that, in short, widely believed cultural myths (or master narratives) carry big ideas that influence how millions of people think and act.

As a period of unprecedented national angst, loss, guilt, and humiliation, the Vietnam War provided unique opportunities for mythmaking. In response to a defeat they perceived as humiliating, some vets and many conservatives turned to evasive mythmaking. Blockbusters such as *Rambo: First Blood* and *Missing In Action* falsified the Vietnam experience. As media critic Michael Parenti observes, "these films not only refight the Vietnam War; they rewrite it" (Parenti *Make-Believe Media* p. 45). Instead of being the aggressors, American forces were presented as the victims of a fickle public, the peace movement, or "the liberal media."

Though conservatives complained about (relatively) graphic news coverage, many Americans had remained in denial about many dimensions of the war. Soon enough, a new and comforting myth emerged. Black POW/MIA banners accentuated the belief that Americans were the victims and not the aggressors in Vietnam. Despite the fact that a Congressional investigation had found "no Americans being held alive as prisoners of war in Indochina," 82 percent of Americans had been misled to believe that prisoners of war were still being held (*The Nation* 6/4/88). Public myths have less to do with what actually happened than with what powerful people want others to believe.

Like never before, today we're awash in a sea of misinformation, swept upon the rocks by treacherous crosscurrents of calculated falsehoods. Taken cumulatively, these falsehoods have supported broader fictions about Afghanistan, Iraq, Iran, al Qaeda, the Taliban, and other politically defined enemies. Again, the stories we tell ourselves—or that politicians and corporate media tell us—do have consequences.

**Features of the Official Conspiracy Narrative**
While much of this book will critique the Official Story as a cleverly contrived myth, the rest of this chapter will examine the origins of the conspiracy theory it has popularized. Forgetting that both history and everyday life teem with plots, many Americans reject conspiracy theories outright. They also forget that the Official Story, still accepted by many, itself involves a conspiracy—defined as "a secret plan by a group to do something unlawful or harmful." Unless we assume that one man flew all

four planes, then the standard account of 9/11 clearly involved a "group." So it's not a question of whether to accept a conspiracy theory, but of which one best fits the evidence.

The Official Story tells of nineteen Islamic terrorists, members of an al Qaeda network, who plotted the September 11 the suicide attacks against an unsuspecting United States. Osama bin Laden, the leader of the terrorist group, directed these attacks from Afghanistan (*Report* pp. 63-70). Under the direction of "ringleader" Mohamed Atta, hijackers seized control of four flights, killing pilots and some crew members. The first two airliners slammed into the Trade Center Towers, and the third struck the Pentagon. The fourth hijacked plane, UA Flight 93, crashed near Shanksville, Pennsylvania, after its passengers conspired to revolt against the hijackers (*Report* pp. 44-45). After suffering structural damage from aircraft impacts, both WTC Towers collapsed in fewer than two hours because aircraft impacts and resulting fires weakened their structural steel (NIST *Report* 2005). Though the 9/11 Commission would make minor changes to this master narrative, it remains essentially unchanged to this day.

The Official Story distracted attention from much more likely contributing factors. These include decades of American foreign policy in the Middle East, particularly its support for repressive regimes in Egypt, Pakistan, and Saudi Arabia—and above all its policies favoring Israel, whose "state terrorism" has stoked a "cauldron of animosities" (N. Chomsky *Hegemony or Survival* pp. 170-85). Literary journalist Lewis Lapham, longtime critic of US foreign policy, was among many observers pointing to these factors in the rise of Islamic terrorism (*Harper's* 3/02). Christopher Hitchens, an argumentative English intellectual, argued that Washington was too quick to blame al Qaeda and too slow to look at blowback from its own policies (*The Nation* 10/22/01).

Instead of these historically supported factors, the Official Story asks us to believe that al Qaeda's stealth attacks succeeded for several other reasons:

- Not recognizing the full extent of the al Qaeda threat, American intelligence agencies and armed forces didn't know enough soon enough to prevent the attacks and didn't communicate well enough to thwart them (*Report* pp. 407-418).

- Surprised by a sneak attack, hampered by both the small number of fighter jets on full alert and their outmoded configurations, America's formidable air defenses suddenly failed (*Report* pp. 17-18).

- Air defenders were slow to react because they questioned whether the calls for intervention were "real world or exercise" and were hampered because of the cumbersome length of NORAD's chain of command (D. R. Griffin *9/11 Comm. Report* pp. 157-58).

- The Federal Aviation Administration (FAA), the Commission contended, experienced great difficulty tracking airliners with their transponders turned off, thereby providing sketchy information to air defenders, and was slow to report the hijackings. Making it very clear who would be "the fall guys," the Commission referred to FAA staffers as "bunglers" (*Report* pp. 10, 17, 20-21, 323, 429).

- Slow reactions and communication problems between the FAA and NORAD combined to hobble air defenders (*Report* pp. 17-35).

As one skeptic quipped, "it sounds like everybody messed up that day except the hijackers."

The standard narrative does contain elements of truth, which is one reason it's been widely accepted. "Like virtually all propaganda systems," notes legendary analyst Chomsky, "this one contains elements of truth" (Chomsky *Fateful Triangle* p. 40). Contrary to popular belief, the "biggest" lies aren't always the most readily believed.

**Immediate Construction of an Official Story**

Although the standard narrative is well known, its genesis remains much less so. The aftermath of 9/11 provided a textbook case of instant government/media mythmaking. Immediately on 9/11, government officials and media outlets began to construct an account with unprecedented dispatch: surprising as it might seem, the Official Story had its genesis right on that fateful morning. Even before the attacks were over, the FBI's counterterrorism division was telling National Security Advisor Richard

Clarke it was al Qaeda operatives who'd attacked the World Trade Center (Clarke *Against All Enemies* pp. 2, 13-14). Within two days of the attacks, the FBI published its list of nineteen suicide hijackers and the Official Story took shape.

The emerging story held great emotional appeal. Cultural critic Susan Faludi has observed that "by September 12, our culture was already reworking a national tragedy into a national fantasy of virtuous might and triumph. No doubt, the fantasy consoled many." But rather than make the country any safer, the story misled it into danger, "damaging the very security the myth was supposed to bolster" (Faludi *Terror Dream* p. 289).

Equally early on, though, the contradictions began to emerge. On one hand, top officials were claiming that these were sneak attacks, that defenders had been caught completely off-guard, their pants around their ankles. On the other, as we noted earlier, by 11:00 a.m. on 9/11, the FBI had started releasing the names, nationalities, and photos of the suspected hijackers. It published a complete list just two days later (*NYT* 9/13/01). But if the federal establishment knew so little as to be taken completely by surprise, how could it so rapidly come up with a complete list of those responsible?

## New Media Jump to Conclusions

If the rapidity of the initial identifications was amazing, the instant involvement of the news media was equally so. Before either Twin Tower had fallen, Fox News informed its viewers: "the FBI have roped this area off. They were taking photographs and securing this area just prior to that huge explosion that we all heard and felt" (www.youtube.com/watch?v=PWgSaBT9hNU). Was this assignment of personnel a reasonable priority during such an extreme emergency? As we'll see, it *is* odd how here and elsewhere on 9/11, FBI agents arrived so *very* fast, sometimes even before first responders. What might the Bureau have known that could have helped *avert* the tragedy? Neither Fox nor any other corporate outlet revisited the question of what might have caused "that huge explosion."

In the first hours following the attacks, strange reports from several major news outlets contributed to instant mythmaking. While both Towers were still standing, MSNBC ran a surprisingly detailed biographical program on Osama bin Laden emphasizing his anti-US philosophy (MSNBC 9/11/01). Immediately after the North Tower had fallen, Fox had implicated bin Laden (Fox 9/11/01). At four o'clock that afternoon, CNN also blamed bin Laden "based on new and specific information developed since the attacks" (Thompson *Terror Timeline* p. 465). What, one has to wonder, were CNN's sources for this "new and specific information"—and just seven hours after the impacts, how solid could they have been?

Again, if these were surprise attacks, then how, in a few hours, could two networks accuse those responsible and then broadcast special coverage of them? How could the networks have so decisively determined that bin Laden was the lead perpetrator? Are we to believe NBC and Fox both had these programs completed, all ready to air? Granted, the networks could have planned to do a program on al Qaeda, which had already committed several attacks against US interests (*Wash. Post* 3/20/07). It's true that bin Laden wasn't an unknown—not at all—but still, the rush to judgment often resembled a stampede.

## Immediate Political Exploitation of the Emerging Narrative

Calls for military action came just as quickly. L. Paul Bremer III, who later governed Iraq immediately after the US-led invasion, provides an example of how carefully selected experts often advance agendas which exhibit conflicts of interest. On 9/11, Bremer was CEO of Marsh Crisis Consulting, a risk and insurance services subsidiary of Marsh & McLennan Companies, Inc. Just three hours after the attacks, Bremer appeared on NBC television. As a counterterrorism expert, Bremer not only stated authoritatively that Osama bin Laden was responsible but also that quite possibly Iraq and Iran were also involved. Long associated with hawkish neoconservatives, Bremer immediately called for aggressive military responses to the 9/11 attacks (NBC 09/11/01).

But Bremer not only made accusations that he had no way of verifying; he also called for military interventions that would later profit him and his clients. In 2003, after the Bush administration (while also attempting to link bin Laden to Saddam Hussein) spearheaded the invasion of Iraq,

Bremer left Marsh Crisis Consulting to head the Provisional Authority in Iraq. As governor, Bremer was generous to foreign firms like Bechtel and Halliburton but stingy with Iraqi contractors. He's best remembered for issuing directives that guaranteed American and British oil companies access to Iraq's oil (www.informationclearinghouse.info/article5692.htm).

### Ignoring First-Responders' Testimony

With one hand, the corporate media were glorifying firefighters as national heroes; with the other, they enabled suppression of the first responders' testimonials. Anticipating the historical importance of eyewitness observations, dozens of first responders recounted experiences forever etched in their memories. Dozens spoke of hearing explosions, particularly "boom, boom, boom" sounds just as the Towers began to come down (WTC Task Force Interview 1/17/02). Shortly after the attacks, the City of New York impounded the tapes and the Fire Department forbade discussion of their contents, because, it claimed, the tapes might later become evidence in court trials.

This suppression of evidence continued under both Mayors Giuliani and Bloomberg. It was not until nearly four years later, after ongoing pressure from families of the victims and a successful lawsuit by the *New York Times*, that the City finally released the oral histories (S. Faludi *Terror Dream* p. 67). Although the paper did make these FDNY testimonials publicly available, it did little to promote public discussion of their implications.

A few months later, very similar reports of explosions emerged in interviews with other firefighters. Thomas Turilli recalled that it "sounded like bombs going off, like boom, boom, boom, like seven or eight, and then just a huge wind gust just came ..." (WTC Task Force Interview 1/17/02). As we'll see in Chapter 21, this is only one of literally dozens of similar first-responder testimonials making reference to explosions.

### Networks Initially Report Explosions, Resemblance to Demolitions

On 9/11, two major newsrooms inferred that the Towers had not simply "collapsed." CBS News anchor Dan Rather observed that the collapse was "reminiscent of ... when a building was deliberately destroyed by well-placed dynamite to knock it down" (www.youtube.com/watch?v=Nvx904dAw0o). ABC News anchor Peter Jennings also reported this resemblance to a planned demolition (www.archive.org/details/abc200109110954-1036). Since that day, however, no one in the corporate media has dared make that comparison again.

Moments after the buildings came down, Fox News interviewed an anonymous "man on the street" wearing a ball cap who explained that the Towers had fallen "mostly due to structural failure because the heat was so intense" (Film *911 Mysteries*). Rather than describing the catastrophic destruction around him, the man began speculating on the cause for the buildings' demise. He foreshadowed what very soon became the official interpretation: that heat from the fires was the main cause of the "collapses." So although alternative narratives were offered on the first day, they were crowded out by a speculative hypothesis, born on streets engulfed by clouds of dust, that would become the official account.

All this seems odd. Granted, one could argue that the fellow was excited to be an eyewitness to history and delighted to appear on TV. Or that under the circumstances, his conclusion that fires caused structural failures was reasonable: planes hit the buildings but the buildings didn't immediately fall; therefore, fires must have weakened their steel frames, causing a collapse. But why did Fox choose *this* fellow? A great many police and firemen, similarly reeling in shock after watching two 110-story skyscrapers disintegrate and crumble into dust, were exclaiming about explosions they'd heard as the Towers came down. Was Fox just rushing to get something on the air, as journalists do? Or did network executives possibly perceive that the cause for the disintegrations could become a major controversy, and that explosions would contradict the emerging master narrative?

## Jumping toward Unscientific Conclusions

If Fox were alone in apparently rushing to promote the weakened-by-fire theory of collapse, these questions about immediate mythmaking might spark less interest. However, the issue takes on additional significance when one considers three facts: that no steel-framed skyscraper had ever before come down mainly because of fire; that three came down allegedly because of fire on one day; and that a scientific paper explaining these disintegrations was submitted just two days later.

Prestigious engineering professors were involved. Representing the American Society of Civil Engineers, they presented the "weakened-steel" theory fewer than 48 hours after the Towers came down (*Journal of Engineering Mechanics*: in press 9/13, expanded 9/22/01). The fact that the nation's premier civil engineering organization would, without any forensic analysis, publish one theory for three different and unprecedented occurrences had to stretch credibility. Scientists and engineers don't rush into print.

This relentless reinforcement of a single hypothesis curtailed discussion of others. As we've seen, scores of first responders reported explosions. Yet when newsrooms covered first responders' impressions, they focused on acts of heroism or the unforgettable horror of the experience. After the first few hours, American news coverage made no mention of explosions. And as firefighters were becoming national heroes, those who mentioned explosions or faulty radios didn't get on TV.

Along with Jay Rosen, New York University's pioneer of citizen journalism, one can understand that the corporate press corps "wants to run things down the rails they've laid down" so stories can be more readily assimilated (PBS "Bill Moyers Journal" 2/6/09). But who lays the rails? This narrow, channeled focus wasn't just a case of following conventional patterns; this was a corporate media blackout. A later revelation gave credence to Professor Rosen's characterization of his profession as a monolith. Reacting to the kidnapping of a *New York Times* reporter, editor Bill Keller disclosed that the paper had decided not to report on the crime and "asked other news organizations to do likewise. Almost without exception," said Keller "they supported us" (PBS "NewsHour" 6/22/09). Clearly most corporate journalists do fall in line.

## Premature Reports on Fall of WTC Building 7

A similar pattern of odd initial coverage followed by a blackout appeared again with a third skyscraper, World Trade Center 7 (WTC-7). For starters, a Fox News Channel 5 crew was all set up to film before the 47-story building ever began to drop and disintegrate (Fox 9/11/01). Since no plane hit this skyscraper, and since its fires were smaller than those in the Towers, why would anyone anticipate its fall? Even more amazing, however, was CNN's story about the "collapse" of WTC-7 an hour *before* it happened (www.youtube.com/watch?v=58h0LjdMry0). BBC's coverage followed, fully 23 minutes *before* the building actually came down (BBC 9/11/01).

Also known as the Salomon Brothers Building, WTC-7 was still standing in the background when BBC reporter Jane Standley described its demise: "You might have heard ... about the Salomon Brothers building collapsing ... this was not a result of a new attack; it was because the building had been weakened during this morning's attacks" (BBC 9/11/01). The structural-damage hypothesis was imprinted before the building had come down. CNN and BBC "got the story" literally before it happened.

Despite the egg on its face, BBC didn't eat humble pie. Instead, the network not only withheld a transcript of its premature report but had the footage pulled from the internet. Apparently attempting to cover its tracks, BBC claimed that *all* its 9/11 archives disappeared because of a "cock-up"! Richard Porter, head of news at BBC World, offered a comically evasive explanation: Ms. Standley, he claimed, "doesn't remember minute-by-minute what she said" (www.bbc.co.uk/blogs/theeditors/2007/02/part_of_the_conspiracy.html). Even if Porter's statement were true, it skirted the obvious questions: If its reporter was filmed against a stock image of the WTC, why not just say so? If an honest error was made, why didn't BBC simply issue a correction?

Was it just coincidental that these news stories, obviously based on no investigative research at all, appeared so quickly on major news networks to establish the Official Story? Perhaps. But in the entire history of journalism, how often has something like this happened? How likely is it that two major networks would make the *same* mistake while covering the *same* event? Espionage professionals use a rule of thumb that may apply here: "once is happenstance, twice is coincidence, but three times is enemy action." Here we have *multiple* instances that seem either highly improbable or completely incredible. Is it mere "happenstance" that all these bizarre behavior aberrations occurred on 9/11?

## The Heroic Myth of "America's Mayor"

When one thinks about legendary 9/11 heroes, none looms larger than Mayor Rudy Giuliani. While Bush and Cheney were nowhere to be seen, Giuliani was everywhere, visible on the street barking commands at confused crowds. By giving the sense that someone forceful was in charge, the mayor comforted a traumatized city and nation. On that day and during the ensuing ones, media coverage of Giuliani reached an intensity rarely bestowed on any leader, local or national, domestic or foreign. The result was a rapid elevation from cunning local politician to "America's Mayor." Bullhorn in hand, striking a pose of resilient optimism, Giuliani seemed to embody what Americans most wanted to believe about themselves in the aftermath of the trauma (Shenon *The Commission* pp. 347-48).

Accepting Giuliani in this new role required forgetting about the mayor's record. In its rush to fashion a national hero, the new media rarely reported on how ill-prepared for the attacks New York City actually was. Firefighters ascended the Trade Center Towers carrying fifteen-year-old radios that, especially after they'd proved useless in the 1993 bombing of the Towers, had become notorious for dysfunction inside Manhattan's tall buildings (Shenon *The Comm.* pp. 348-49).

These failures embittered many of the very firefighters the mayor was fashioning into "his" heroes (S. Faludi *Terror Dream* p. 67). One complained, "there was no command structure.... Nobody can get on the radio. The fucking radio was useless" ("Sept. 11 Records" p. 12). The firefighter was referring to the fact that Giuliani knew for years that the police and fire radios were dysfunctional but had done nothing to replace them. Giuliani's inattention to this problem probably cost many hundreds of lives. It's not surprising, then, that the Mayor's office suppressed the firefighters' testimonials for almost four years, refusing to make their oral histories public until court ordered to do so.

The news media also gave Giuliani an undeserved pass on the failure of his brand-new, ultra-high-tech $15 million Emergency Command Center. In pushing this project through (which consumed funds that might have purchased new radios), the mayor had stubbornly disregarded advice from all parties. He insisted on building the command center in—of all places—the World Trade Center Complex, the locus for one previous major terrorist attack and a prime target for others. Built on the twenty-third floor of WTC-7, the bunker in the sky had been derided as "Rudy's Nuclear Winter Palace" (Shenon *The Comm.* p. 347).

The WTC-7 location was a script for disaster, and the dysfunction on 9/11 was predictable enough. Caught in the chaos of the attacks that morning, Giuliani never even reached his command center. By about 9:00 am, everyone in the command center was ordered to evacuate because of concerns that more hijacked aircraft were heading for lower Manhattan. "The crisis center was shut down because there was a crisis," Shenon observes with wry irony. With the Command Center shut down, Giuliani and his aides had nowhere to go but the street. It was here that Giuliani was photographed for the iconic image of the soot-covered mayor braving clouds of smoke, dust, and debris as he led Trade Center workers to safety (Shenon *The Comm.* p. 347).

While the corporate news media bear much of the responsibility for elevating "America's Mayor" to iconic status, Giuliani himself helped script the scenario. He wasn't above mythologizing by matching iconic images as he sought to link himself to heroic first responders: "When I saw the picture of the firefighters who put the flag up at ground zero, [it looked] just like the marines at Iwo Jima, many years before ..." (*Newsday/* AP 12/16/07). Giuliani declared that "our firefighters helped save more than twenty-five thousand lives that day—the greatest single rescue mission in America's history" (*Wash. Post* 9/20/01). "That was a claim," remarked media analyst Susan Faludi, "that the firefighters themselves would regard as preposterous" (Faludi *Terror Dream* p. 66).

Although many among the families of the victims and the first responders came to see through the charade, much of the public, indelibly imprinted by the echo-chamber effect from Giuliani's talk-show appearances, were slow to perceive the contradictions. In good part, this ignorance has resulted from the unwillingness of the news media to report on the contradictions documented in their own archives. How often, for instance, is the public reminded that Giuliani had ordered evacuation of his own command post, stated that he'd heard the WTC buildings were going to come down (ABC News 9/11/01), and done little to help evacuate the thousands of workers still inside the Towers?

### "If They Didn't Have a bin Laden, They Would Invent Him"

If the public needed someone to epitomize its hopes, it also needed someone to embody its fears. If Giuliani became the hero of the melodrama, Osama bin Laden became the villain. At the time, few understood how bin Laden and al Qaeda, however much they were actually responsible for 9/11, would amply serve the interests of the White House, the Pentagon, Wall Street, and the corporate media.

Media demonization of bin Laden, which conveniently ignored his two-decade-long CIA connections, was nearly as out of touch with reality as its idolization of Giuliani. In Washington's long tradition of magnifying national-security threats, bin Laden was soon made to fill oversized shoes once worn by Hitler and Stalin, Mao, and Fidel Castro. The fact that bin Laden commanded no military machine—in fact, ruled no country—didn't deter the threat mongers. Early on, though, perceptive insights slipped through the media filters. Sharp observers lifted the curtain, exposing the wizard. Milton Bearden, gruff-talking former CIA director of operations in Afghanistan, told Dan Rather "look, if they didn't have a bin Laden, they would invent him." Given "the scale of the attacks, blame should not be automatically laid on bin Laden." Instead, Bearden elaborated, "it is more likely that a far more 'sophisticated' intelligence operation was behind these precise [and] coordinated attacks" (CBS 9/12/01).

But someone killed nearly 3,000 Americans, so a foreign Arch Villain was required. Just a week after the tragedy, Bush reached into the mythology of the Wild West to define bin Laden: "There's an old poster out West, as I recall, that said 'Wanted, Dead or Alive'.... We're goin' to find him" (*NYT* 9/18/01). As a final touch on the "wanted" poster, Washington placed a $25 million bounty on the Saudi's head (Cable News Network 2/6/02). Little attention was paid to missed opportunities during the late 1990s and again in 2000 when Washington had failed to kill or capture the al Qaeda leader (www.msnbc.msn.com/id/4540958). This will receive thorough examination in Chapter 17.

The next year, the US missed another opportunity to kill bin Laden. Commanders held back air strikes on night convoys comprised of hundreds of vehicles, allowed special Taliban flights to sail right through air patrols, and failed to send troops to search the caves (J. Risen *State of War* pp. 185-87). All this was odd, since bringing back bin Laden "dead or alive" was supposedly one of the main reasons for the attack on Afghanistan.

## Washington Loses Interest in Public Enemy Number One

By January of 2002, though, bin Laden had dropped off the radar. Though Bush inveighed against the "Axis of Evil" in his State of the Union speech, the president made no mention of the al Qaeda leader. Days later, when asked about America's Arch Enemy, Secretary of Defense Rumsfeld waxed lackadaisical when asked about bin Laden: "We'll find him one day. And we'll know what's happened" (Cable News Network 2/6/02). Could the fact that bin Laden probably *did* know what happened be one reason he was never captured alive? Or were there other reasons *not* to get bin Laden? In a moment of candor, former CIA Executive Director A. B. "Buzzy" Krongard indicated that it might be better not to kill or capture bin Laden. Other American officials felt it might be better to "keep bin Laden pinned down on the border of Afghanistan and Pakistan rather than make him a martyr or put him on trial" (*London Times* 1/9/05).

And the incongruities went on and on. Although the FBI had put a $25 million bounty on bin Laden's head, it never charged him for the crimes of 9/11. In 2006, the Bureau dropped him from its Most Wanted List. According to Chief of Investigative Publicity Rex Tomb, the FBI had "no hard evidence" connecting bin Laden to 9/11 (*Wash. Post* 8/28/06). Later in 2006, the CIA closed Alec Station, its elite special unit devoted to al Qaeda (*NYT* 7/4/06). Such contradictions, together with the government's regular releases of amateurish bin Laden videos, played well on Comedy Central.

## Bin Laden, Terror Mongering, and the Media

As a threat of larger-than-life mythical stature, bin Laden has also served an internal political purpose: the personification of Islamic terrorism resulting in a reason for the War on Terror. His video pronouncements often triggered Homeland Security orange-alerts, warnings of "clear and present danger." By evoking the threat of bin Laden, Washington had won a double victory. Right after 9/11 it gained a degree of control over news content that it had long coveted and wouldn't soon relinquish. Later, when the administration began to exploit bin Laden's potential to intimidate the public and promote its War on Terror, it could count on the networks to give his tapes the broadest possible exposure. Bin Laden, the administration, and the networks became the big winners; American democracy became the big loser.

In the months following 9/11, corporate news media responded to and helped promote a climate of aggressive patriotism. Speaking for Fox, super-magnate Rupert Murdoch promised to do his patriotic duty. A slightly more liberal outlet pledged that "in deciding what to air, CNN will consider guidance from appropriate authorities" (*Miami Herald* 10/11/01). Among the few exceptions was MSNBC's Phil Donahue, once the godfather of daytime television. When Donahue raised fair questions about the impending war on Iraq, his patriotism was questioned and he was summarily marginalized. After the network canceled his talk show in 2003, Donahue was forced to "wander through the outskirts of the American media" (*NY Observer* 6/19/07). MSNBC's bosses had made Donahue an example for any other media personalities who might consider raising "unpatriotic" questions or otherwise stepping out of line. When corporate censors clamped down on dissent, they did so with a vengeance.

In the days, weeks, and months after the tragedy, Secretary of Defense Rumsfeld, National Security Advisor Condoleezza Rice, and White House filmmakers continued to spin the story, linking it to their plans to launch a War on Terror.

In a frenzy of classic "agenda setting," Rumsfeld worked feverishly to get his message out. His director of public relations, Victoria ("Torie") Clarke, indicated that the secretary intended to dominate the public conversation. Like her boss, Ms. Clarke was keenly interested in "flooding the zone," leaving "no vacuum available for other sources of information to fill" (A. Cockburn *Rumsfeld* p. 120). The saturation included the use of retired military officers described as "media message force multipliers" to deliver Pentagon propaganda. The result, according to one of these "independent experts," was "PSYOPS on steroids" (*NYT* 4/20/08).

Rumsfeld and the Pentagon weren't just spinning the 9/11 narrative; they were manufacturing consent for their plans to attack Afghanistan and Iraq. The long-standing calls by neocons (including Rumsfeld, Wolfowitz, and Cheney) for an attack on Iraq are well known; the similar statements by George Bush less so. In 1999, the future president stunned reporters with a blunt pronouncement about attacking Iraq: "'I'd take 'em out,' [Bush] grinned cavalierly, 'take out the weapons of mass destruction ...'" (*Houston Chronicle* 11/01/04). While the Official Story tells us that the administration decided to invade Afghanistan and Iraq after 9/11, mounting evidence indicates that both decisions were well in the works not only before 9/11 but before Bush ever took office. As we'll see, these were about controlling gas and oil and the pipelines needed to deliver them. Ace analyst Peter Dale Scott has concluded that "the Bush agenda, in other words, depended on 9/11, or something like it" (Scott *Road to 9/11* pp. 170-71, 191-93).

In tracking the frenzy of mythmaking after 9/11, one mustn't overlook less-visible master players. Philip Zelikow served on the Bush administration's transition team, sat on the National Security Council, and authored the administration's notorious policy document on "preemptive war" (Shenon *The Comm.* p. 128). Nevertheless, Zelikow got himself appointed executive director of the 9/11 Commission; this positioned him to both control the Commission's agenda and author its *Report*.

In ironic ways, Zelikow's academic specialties qualified him for the job. As a historian of the presidency, Zelikow had written about how presidents manipulate the presentation of recent events to muster public support for their policies (http://hnn.us/articles/5280.html). Even more relevant was specialization in "the construction and maintenance of public myths." Following his studies of public mythmaking, Zelikow argued that "contemporary" history is "defined functionally by those critical people and events that go into forming the public's presumptions about its immediate past" (Zelikow *Thinking About Political History* p. 5). This was his way of saying that key people in power should attend to how they frame events.

To maximize control and impact, Zelikow advised that renditions of events be anchored to individuals: "A history's narrative power is typically linked to how readers relate to the actions of individuals in the history; if readers cannot make a connection to their own lives, then a history may fail to engage them at all" (Zelikow *Thinking About Political History* p. 5).

This show-don't-tell approach informed many early, strongly formative presentations of 9/11, though most of it could not be linked to Zelikow. In the immediate aftermath, the mass media gave maximum exposure to "the actions of individuals" such as Mayor Giuliani leading dazed crowds and President Bush, bullhorn in hand, putting his arm around firefighters at Ground Zero. Media outlets repeatedly featured the poignant faces of victims, survivors, and first responders. While this approach "put a human face on tragedy," it also drew attention away from questions about the *institutional factors* behind the tragic events.

## Government Heroes in Glossy Mags and TV Movies

Arresting imagery also helped elevate Bush administration regulars from clever politicians to mythical figures, the "good guys" in the melodrama. Again, cartoon-like figures evoked the Wild West. One cover story and photo layout featured Bush as a flinty, cowboy-in-chief sporting a Texas-sized belt buckle and also referred to all the president's men in superhero superlatives: Cheney on these glossy pages became "The Rock," Attorney General John Ashcroft "The Heat," and Homeland Security Chief Tom Ridge "The Protector" (*Vanity Fair* 2/02). The message came across as clear as a Wyoming sky: terrorist outlaws would face some mighty tough hombres guarding the OK Corral.

As the White House extended its preoccupation with public perceptions, magazines seemed to pale beside the power of movies. In the first year after 9/11, networks rushed to produce two very different docudramas presenting administration leaders in the most flattering light. Around the two-month anniversary of 9/11, chief advisor Karl Rove summoned top film and TV executives to discuss America's motives and depict the president's valor during the tragic events. The White House granted filmmakers full access to Bush, Rice, Rove, Cheney, Rumsfeld and other top officials (www.alternet. org/mediaculture/66823).

The first of these docudramas, *The Spirit of America,* was rushed into production. Featuring a new pantheon of heroes, it sought to rally the public behind the administration's "war against evil." This blockbuster was directed by Chuck Workman, whose previous credits included *Playboy: The Story of X,* a pastiche of pornography. Predictably, the film's production and distribution were amply financed: enough prints were struck to show on 10,000 movie screens, fully a quarter of those available throughout the country (Faludi *Terror Dream* pp. 49, 6-7). Deep in the long, mythic shadow cast by Reagan, the movie portrayed top officials as "reluctant revenge takers" and "cowboy-code-of-honor types" to suggest their idealistic nature as patriotic American heroes. Again fitting new mythology into the old, the film included scenes of valorous vengeance deep in the American grain: from *Birth of a Nation* to *Shane* to *Dirty Harry*—plus, inevitably, clips from Westerns starring John Wayne. Again the message was clear and simple: righteous revenge was as American as Tombstone, Arizona. As mass-audience mythmaking and propaganda, *The Spirit of America* had few equals.

But even this wasn't enough for the White House. Not to be overshadowed by mythic Hollywood avengers, the president's handlers decided to make *DC 9/11: Time of Crisis,* a second TV movie championing Bush's valor. The film purported to depict the president's actions during and just after the tragedy, especially how he "tended to the needs of a wounded country." It aired on Showtime and starred Timothy Bottoms as George Bush (http:// imdb.com/title/tt0353042/plotsummary). This rendering of the president as a man of action, noted 9/11 widow and activist Kristen Breitweiser, was largely the product of "Karl Rove's art direction." Alluding to Bush's well-known inaction at the Booker elementary school, Breitweiser mocked the president as "an action hero except when it really counts" (Salon 9/8/03).

Though only a made-for-TV movie, *DC 9/11: Time of Crisis* was masterful mythmaking: to ensure a rightward ideological slant, the film was scripted by several neocons. The team leader was Lionel Chetwynd, who'd also scripted *Kissinger and Nixon* and went on to write a vitriolic rebuttal to Michael Moore's *Fahrenheit 911*. The involvement of neocons in the project suggested not only their strong presence within the administration but their characteristic interest in expanding the power of the executive branch. To neocon scriptwriters committed to an imperial presidency, redemption of the president's actual lackluster performance on 9/11 must have seemed like an ideological imperative.

If the administration felt a pressing need to imprint its account of the president's performance, it apparently experienced a similarly urgent need to explain the demise of United Flight 93, which went down in Pennsylvania.

## More Media Mythmaking: Networks Script Saga of Flight 93

A famous story of passenger heroism began to come together the afternoon following the attacks. In this account, the passengers either took back the cockpit and/or caused the hijackers to lose control of the plane: in doing so, they became patriotic heroes. Regular American civilians had not only fought back but also, according to the networks and the Commission, actually prevented another attack on Washington (*Report* p. 45). This passenger-revolt story immediately became an inspirational symbol of a bloodied nation's ability to fight back against terrorism. While the Flight 93 revolt probably did happen, it was shamelessly exploited for political purposes.

The rapid release of the narrative also suggests active media involvement in constructing an inspirational story of heroism. In the first few days after the attacks, limited evidence of a revolt was available. Nevertheless, several networks rushed a story of heroic uprising on the air, devoting enormous amounts of time to family members and friends who had reportedly received calls from the doomed flight (Fox, NBC, ABC 9/12/01).

### "Let's Roll": Overlooked Factors Surrounding Todd Beamer's Call

Software salesman Todd Beamer's famous battle cry, "Are you guys ready? Okay. Let's roll," reportedly started the passenger revolt (*Report* pp. 12-13). Beamer had not talked to his wife but spoke instead with GTE Airfone/ Verizon supervising operator Lisa Jefferson, who reportedly overheard Beamer's outcry at the end of their fifteen-minute conversation. As the two talked, Ms. Jefferson had promised to call Todd's wife, Lisa, "if he didn't make it home" (*Newsweek* 12/3/01).

This didn't happen. Though Jefferson was a supervisor, she failed to follow GTE company protocol: she didn't record a passenger's emergency call, so there was no record of her conversation with Beamer. Nor was Ms. Jefferson *allowed* to convey the message to Mrs. Beamer, for the matter was removed from her hands. Verizon's management and the FBI held the information for three and a half days before finally allowing Beamer's message to reach Lisa, his bereaved widow (CBS 9/14/01). Moreover, it was not Verizon but United Airlines that relayed the message, informing Lisa that "the FBI has been keeping the information private until they had the opportunity to review the material" (R. Morgan *Flight 93 Revealed* p. 19).

## Widows Provide Emotional Impact

Working from fragmentary shards of evidence, the media insisted on running single-source feature pieces based almost entirely on statements from bereaved family members. Mythmaking researcher Susan Faludi has pointed out that such recollections were "treated by correspondents like hard news leads" (Faludi *Terror Dream* p. 57).

Intensive coverage of Flight 93 widows allowed networks to present emotionally supercharged interpretations of events that comforted the public, insured high ratings, pleased the powers that be, and helped flesh out the Official Story. In addition, key media personalities appeared to actively pursue mythmaking agendas. Like several other celebrity broadcasters, NBC's Jane Pauley brought together grieving wives who often touted the personal attributes and athletic exploits of their husbands (NBC 10/2/01). Some TV personalities sometimes all but told guests what to say. Before an audience of millions, CBS host Diane Sawyer prompted Flight 93 widows with one leading statement after another: "You really believe in your hearts you know what happened.... So you feel maybe they got control, got into the cockpit, but they weren't pilots, they didn't know how to fly the plane" (CBS 9/18/01).

Did this pattern of disregard for journalistic professionalism stem from pressures to get high ratings, from playing to a shaken public's need for heroes, or did other factors drive this mythmaking? Immediately after 9/11, the networks seemingly catered to audiences seeking heroes and trafficked in the sensational to garner ratings. While pressures to improve ratings by playing to public sentiments might explain much of this programming, they don't fully explain a host's insistence on a tale not just of heroic acts but also of conscientious self-sacrifice. Whose idea was *that*?

If this critique sounds too tough, recall that Katie Couric, who would later anchor the "CBS Evening News," has acknowledged she "had felt pressure from government officials and corporate executives to cast the [Iraq] war in a positive light." Couric has also disclosed that she's felt pressure from "the corporations who own where we work and from the government itself to really squash any kind of dissent or any kind of questioning of it" (*NYT* 5/30/08). At the time of 9/11, Couric co-hosted the "Today" show for NBC. If Katie Couric experienced those government pressures in 2003, did Diane Sawyer, her counterpart at CBS, acquiesce to them in 2001? These are among the many questions a new investigation of 9/11 needs to pursue.

Even more importantly, the focus on the passengers and their bereaved families diverted attention from many unresolved issues. Clearly the media-driven obsession with what happened *in* the airliner eclipsed coverage of what happened *to* it, distracting attention from questions about a possible stand down or shoot down. After the first few days, media coverage of the plane's widely scattered debris fields and its curiously small impact crater would receive little media exposure beyond Pennsylvania.

Yet among the issues surrounding the military's performance that morning, none have produced more contradictory statements than the final moments of Flight 93. Based on these statements, it seems possible, even probable, that *both* an uprising *and* a shoot down occurred. Considerable forensic evidence from the debris fields—one fully eight miles from the crash site—points to a shoot down (Griffin *New Pearl Harbor* pp. 52-53). Several individuals, from local observers to fighter pilots to top Pentagon officials, reported that Flight 93 *was* shot down. Some of the eyewitnesses changed their initial statements, often under pressure from the FBI (Morgan *Flight 93 Revealed* pp. 134-146).

Among those affirming a shoot down were military professionals in positions to know. Major Daniel Nash, one of the F-15 pilots sent toward New York City on 9/11, reported that when he landed, he was told that an F-16 had shot down an airliner over Pennsylvania (*Cape Cod Times* 8/21/02). Another Air Force aviator confirmed a shoot down (*Aviation Week* 6/3/02). The Pentagon's initial releases on Flight 93 disclosed that F-16 fighters were tracking the troubled flight and were positioned to take it out (PBS "NewsHour" 9/14/01). Similar statements were made by top Pentagon officials: Rumsfeld, Deputy Secretary of Defense Paul Wolfowitz, and Chairman of the Joint Chiefs Gen. Richard Myers (Griffin *New Pearl Harbor* p. 53).

As master myths gain widespread acceptance, they marginalize alternative narratives. Even though belief in a shoot down could never eradicate the heroism, the passenger-revolt story has seemingly inhibited a full and fair examination of the shoot-down scenario. The shoot-down question will receive full analysis in Chapter 20.

### "The Path to 9/11": Alteration in the Name of Commemoration

Since Hollywood has a long history of promoting popular mythology, it's not surprising that four TV or movie reenactments were produced in the years following 9/11: *Let's Roll: The Story of Flight 93* (2002), *The Flight That Fought Back* (2005), *Flight 93: The Movie* (2006), and *United 93* (2006) (Morgan *Flight 93 Revealed* pp. 31-36, 43-45). Reenactments of the revolt reinforced the official narrative and didn't include details that would challenge it. A docudrama can also reshape public perceptions—in this case placing blame for the disaster upon the Clinton administration—and, by extension, onto the Democrats.

The result, baldly stated, was pseudo "history" as partisan propaganda. A five-hour, two-part ABC/Disney docudrama *The Path To 9/11* generated controversy behind the scenes. Promoted by full-page ads that depicted dark eyes peering through a slash in an American flag, this TV special caused a loud flap. It was co-produced by former Commission chairman Tom Kean who, it became apparent, was eager to revise an Official Story he'd helped write.

The docudrama's director, David Cunningham, also helped define its slant and substance (PBS "NewsHour" 9/13/06). David Cunningham and his wife were known for their efforts to plant evangelical Christian perspectives in the mass media. They led an association "called" to the communications industry to "both influence the Hollywood film industry and produce major motion pictures that would carry a Biblical, values-based message." When Cunningham spoke about making the 9/11 film, he titled his talk "Christ-like Witness in the Film Industry" (*Guardian* [UK] 9/13/06).

## Blaming the Previous Administration

Although the Bush administration had never borne much responsibility—let alone any blame—for the most devastating air-defense failures in American history, *The Path To 9/11* attempted to shift responsibility for the attacks. When former Clinton administration officials learned about the script, they went ballistic.

Although the Clintonistas demanded corrections, *The Path To 9/11* aired without many changes. When the program showed Clinton officials refusing to approve missile strikes against al Qaeda, it implied that Clinton and his advisors weren't just preoccupied by a sex scandal; they were overly inhibited by legal niceties and ethical restraints (PBS "NewsHour" 9/13/06). In this way, the filmmakers could reinforce a widely held perception: that Democrats are soft on terrorism. Just two months before the 2006 elections, then, the docudrama promoted a supposed Republican superiority on national defense.

When partisan squabbling began to completely subsume historical truth, Democrats finally got interested in the history leading up to 9/11. Former Clinton administration officials who hadn't uttered a peep of protest about the 9/11 Commission's omissions and distortions suddenly fumed with righteous indignation. Referring to a scene in which Clinton aide Sandy Berger was shown hanging up on the CIA, Tom Kean dodged the issue of falsification: "My memory is that it could have happened any number of ways" (*NY Post* 7/28/06).

Though the historical record supported the Clinton officials' objections, Kean offered no apologies. Even though the docudrama was intended for high school classes, the former Commission chair saw no problem with inventing new scenes. Sad to say, Kean's cynical disregard for the truth accords only too well with what we know about the Commission he led.

**Shock Jocks Discover History**

Smelling blood, AM radio shouters suddenly discovered recent history. Immediately after the ABC/Disney docudrama aired, Republican spokespersons and conservative shock jocks began to circle, hungry for an easy kill. Sounding like a study guide for the movie, they suddenly spotlighted what US intelligence agencies had known and what the White House hadn't done about al Qaeda—but only during the *Clinton* years (PBS "NewsHour" 9/13/06). While many regard right-wing radio as a dungeon of arrogant ignorance, someone down there grasped the uses of selective history. Suddenly the pundits were discussing significant issues the Commission hadn't covered—and which, of course, they too had never before mentioned. An otherwise non-historical Rush Limbaugh started citing al Qaeda's Bojinka Plots of 1994 as evidence that the Clinton administration could have stopped the 9/11 attacks (Morgan *Flight 93 Revealed* p. 38). As the History Commons Terror Timelines show, there's some truth to this contention, however disreputable its source (www.historycommons.org).

**Convenient Doctrines, Old and New**

Much as the White House had chosen the term "Axis of Evil" to evoke the enemy Axis powers of World War II, Condoleezza Rice tried to frame al Qaeda within the myth of the cosmic struggle with evil, the biblical battle of the Apocalypse. Reviewing the history of al Qaeda, Rice recalled the "dark day" in 1998 when al Qaeda attacked two American embassies. These attacks, Rice suggested, initiated "the start of a campaign of terror" that culminated on 9/11, setting off the ultimate battle of the Final Days (AP 8/8/08).

To validate their distortions, mythmakers usually seek sacred texts. By evoking biblical language and myth, by pouring new wine into a very old bottle, Rice could imply that the War on Terror is a divinely sanctioned struggle in which good (Christian America) will eventually triumph over evil (radical Islam). In the aftermath of 9/11, Samuel Huntington's *Clash of Civilizations* acquired a near-prophetic authority that valorized the Bush administration's war on political Islam.

## Moving Beyond Simplistic Stories

Since the full truth is always complex, the news media must not promote a single narrative to the exclusion of all others. Media critic Bill Moyers was deeply troubled by a situation in which "the press as a whole remains in denial about its complicity in passing on the government's unverified claims as facts, while 'blocking out any other narrative.'" The great danger, Moyers believed, is "not simply that the dominant media see the world as the powerful see it; [it's that] they don't allow alternative and competing narratives to emerge that would enable us to measure the claims of the official view of reality" (www.freepress.net/node/41601).

As received wisdom, even as hallowed myth, the Official Story has not only crowded out other hypotheses, its adherents and enforcers have often opposed revisions, disdained alternative narratives, and squelched more nuanced analyses.

These are what the world needs, and what *Mounting Evidence* intends to provide.

# 5. "It Did Not Fit with the Story We Wanted to Tell"

*The public has been seriously misled about what occurred during the morning of the attacks, for at some level of the government ... there was an agreement not to tell the truth about what happened.... I was shocked at how different the truth was from the way it was described ... a radically different story from what had been told to us and the public for two years.*

—John J. Farmer, Senior Legal Counsel
for the 9/11 Commission

Before focusing on the 9/11 Commission, it's important to sketch the big picture about how it handled the officials, witnesses, and evidence. To examine the Official Story, it makes sense to start with the stories given by those at the top. However, clarity regarding who did what and when soon disappears into a thicket of contradictions. Those government officials most responsible for the defense of the country—President Bush, Vice President Cheney, Secretary of Defense Rumsfeld, and Acting Chairman of the Joint Chiefs of Staff Gen. Richard Myers—each gave contradictory accounts of his actions on that fateful morning. The big players just didn't get their stories straight.

The conflicting versions cast shadows of doubt. This left it to the Commission, officially tasked with articulating an Official Story, to fashion narratives that fit together. In at least three of these four instances, the Commission came up with a new variant, different from any version told by these officials before.

### Different Versions of the President's Stories

President Bush's behavior on 9/11 was strange, and his accounts don't add up. About 8:30 a.m., before the presidential party departed from its lodgings, a press corps reporter asked the president whether he knew about a hijacking—about "what's going on in New York?" Bush had apparently not been informed that a hijacking was in progress. As Flight 11 slammed into the North Tower at 8:46 a.m., Bush's motorcade was on the way to Booker Elementary School (*Wash. Times* 10/8/02). About 8:50, while riding in a motorcade vehicle, Press Secretary Ari Fleischer took a call, and he blurted out, "Oh my God, I don't believe it. A plane just hit the World Trade Center" (*Christian Sci. Mon.* 9/17/01). Reporters waiting for Bush at the school also learned of the crash just minutes after it happened (CBS 9/11/02).

Surely someone would have notified the president about the crash. After all, the presidential limousine sported five antennae that gave Bush "the best mobile communications money could buy" (B. Sammon *Fighting Back* p. 38). Yet Bush and his closest associates contended that he was *not* informed en route. Just before 9:00, as soon as the president arrived at Booker Elementary School in Sarasota, trusted advisor Karl Rove "rushed to the president, took him aside in a hallway, and told him about the plane crash" (C. Unger *House of Bush, House of Saud* p. 248).

To this day, the Official Story remains that Bush wasn't told about the first crash until he arrived at the school. Information analyst James Bamford commented wryly that despite having an entire national security staff and a secure phone in the limo, "it appears that the president of the United States knew less than tens of millions of other people in every part of the country who were watching the attack as it unfolded" (J. Bamford *Pretext for War* p. 17).

As Bush entered the school, he made another decision that likely delayed possible intervention in the rapidly unfolding attacks. In spite of having just received urgent reports of the first crash, the president was in no hurry to take an urgent call from his national security advisor, Condoleezza Rice. Finally Andy Card was forced to intrude: "Mr. President, you need to take this call right now" (*St. Petersburg Times* 9/8/02).

Rice later claimed that at this time—about 9:00—she was unaware that NORAD had already scrambled interceptors about fifteen minutes earlier in response to the hijacking of American Flight 11—and that she continued with her national security staff meeting (*Newsweek* 12/31/01). Bamford found it difficult to believe that the national security advisor wasn't aware "that the United States had gone to 'battle-stations' alert and had scrambled fighter jets ... to intercept and possibly take hostile action against multiple hijacked airliners . . ." *(Bamford Pretext for War p. 17).*

## Delays in the Classroom

The classroom became the scene of both more delays in notification and of consequent inaction. After the second impact, Andy Card whispered to the president that "America's under attack" (*NYT* 9/16/01). Bush sat, looking stressed, and did nothing. A few minutes later, Ari Fleischer held up a sign with instructions for Bush: "Don't Say Anything Yet" (*Wash. Times* 10/7/02).

As director Michael Moore documented so memorably in his film *Fahrenheit 9/11*, Bush sat for at least seven minutes while children read "My Pet Goat." Unhurried greetings consumed a couple minutes more. The commander-in-chief wasted precious minutes more as he drafted a short speech to the public, which he delivered at 9:29 (Sammon *Fighting Back* p. 94). Again and again, this pattern of delay and inaction—both actual and alleged—would become a theme in the narratives of 9/11.

Establishing a pattern of lying about his involvement, Bush claimed later in the day that "immediately following the first attack, I implemented our government's emergency response plans"; in fact, it was lower-level officials, not the president, who activated CONPLAN (Interagency Domestic Terrorism Concept of Operations Plan) in response to a possible crisis. Later on, Bush admitted he didn't give any orders responding to the attack until after 9:55 a.m. (*Wall Street Journal* 3/22/04).

Almost as though Bush was trying to compensate for his slow reactions and leadership failures, he told a tale that could not possibly be true. Contradicting published reports from his staff, Bush twice claimed that he saw the first plane crash live on TV. This was impossible for two reasons: Bush was riding in a limo that didn't have a TV, and the first impact was not broadcast live. In fact, no footage of Flight 11 became available until that evening (CNN 9/11/01). Nor could Bush have confused the first and second impacts because at 9:03, the time of the second, he was just entering the classroom. There he sat with the children for at least seven crucial minutes after Andy Card had *told* him of the attack (A. Fleischer *Taking Heat* pp. 139-140).

Though this delay meant that the second and third planes continued to streak toward their targets, the president, unlike Richard Clarke, neither acknowledged that "your government failed you" nor owned his part in the tragic drama. Instead, Bush drawled "I'm glad I took the time" with the kids (Film: *911: Press for Truth*). Since then, both the president and the first lady have proclaimed that Bush "kept the American people safe" (White House 9/20/08).

## Different Accounts of Cheney's Comings and Goings

Because of the conflicting accounts, much confusion has surrounded the activities of the vice president that morning.

Just five days after 9/11, Cheney talked about his time of arrival at the Presidential Emergency Operations Center (PEOC), or White House command bunker. Appearing on NBC's "Meet the Press," Cheney (now sporting a red, white, and blue ribbon) told Tim Russert he'd "arrived in the PEOC before the Pentagon was hit" at 9:37 (NBC 9/16/01). According to Cheney, Secret Service agents burst into his office, lifted him right out of his chair, and whisked him into the tunnel leading to the PEOC (*Newsweek* 12/31/01). If true, this time of arrival would have made it impossible for Cheney, as reported by Transportation Secretary Norman Mineta, to have ordered a "stand down" of air defenses about 9:26 as a suspicious plane raced toward the White House. Eleven minutes later, Flight 77 hit the Pentagon (BBC 9/1/02).

When Cheney told Tim Russert that he'd arrived at the PEOC before the Pentagon was hit, he wasn't lying outright. But he probably wasn't telling the full truth either. Secretary Mineta indicated that when he'd arrived at the PEOC just after 9:20, Cheney was *already there* (MSNBC 9/11/02). National Security Advisor Richard Clarke, who was running a parallel emergency teleconference, also affirmed this *earlier* time of arrival, not the one given by Cheney (Clarke *Against All Enemies* pp. 2, 5).

Air traffic controllers also corroborated the earlier time of arrival. Five weeks after the tragedy, controllers at Dulles recalled how they had tracked an incoming, unidentified aircraft heading for the White House. In response, said the controllers, "Vice President Cheney was rushed to a special basement bunker" and White House staff members were told to run away from the building (ABC 10/24/01). Although the controllers didn't give an exact time when they first spotted the incoming plane, their report accorded with others. The NORAD tapes showed that NEADS fighter defenses were triggered by an incoming, unidentified plane which controllers at Dulles first detected at 9:21 (*Vanity Fair* 8/06).

This raised an obvious question directed toward government authorities: If you knew about Flight 77 at 9:21, and the airliner struck the Pentagon at 9:37, what happened during those sixteen minutes that you didn't take effective action? This is one of the big questions.

## Mineta's Unwelcome Revelation

It was Transportation Secretary Mineta who addressed this question and provided corroboration for Cheney's earlier arrival time. Mineta recounted how a naval aide, Douglas F. Cochrane, had burst into the PEOC three times. The first time, the "young lieutenant" announced an unidentified incoming aircraft "50 miles out." The second time, the "young man" announced that it was "30 miles out." The third time, he announced with greater urgency that "it was 10 miles out" and asked the vice president, "Do the orders still stand?" To which Cheney allegedly retorted, "Of course they still stand; have you heard anything to the contrary?" (Hearing 5/23/03).

This was a telltale moment, a disclosure crucial to understanding 9/11. Though Lee Hamilton, who'd questioned Mineta, had framed the questioning around "a shoot-down order approved by the president" and tried to make Mineta's startling disclosure apply to Flight 93, which went down in Pennsylvania 40 minutes later. Although Mineta made it clear he was talking about Flight 77, neither he nor Cochrane have clarified whether Cheney had issued a shoot-down or a *stand-down* order.

Nevertheless, Cheney's gruff the-order-still-stands affirmation has become one of the most troubling challenges to the Official Story. It clearly wasn't something the Commission wanted the public to know about: it not only excised Mineta's testimony from its *Report,* but also suppressed the video version from its archives.

Secretary Mineta has given the time of the lieutenant's first warning as "about 9:25 or 9:26," but the NORAD tapes, as just mentioned, put the first discovery of Flight 77 at 9:21 (Scott *Road to 9/11* pp. 198-204). Thus we're looking at a narrow window in which Cheney entered the PEOC, learned of the incoming airliner, issued a stand-down order, and refused to rescind it. Why would Cheney have apparently allowed an erratically flown rogue airliner to strike its target, killing 125 people?

## Commission Further Changes the Story

Other typically reliable sources, notably counterterrorism "czar" Richard Clarke, have also placed Cheney inside the PEOC starting about 9:20, and Cheney placed himself there starting about 9:37. The Commission, however, stated that Cheney didn't arrive until 9:58 (*Report* p. 40). Since this later arrival time seems to contradict so much else, it raises all sorts of questions. When the Commission said "arrived," did it mean for the *first* time that morning? If Cheney left his office at either 9:21 or 9:37, and if he arrived at the PEOC but left, then what was the vice president doing during these twenty minutes of intense danger? By having Cheney arrive so late, these are questions the Commission made sure it didn't have to answer.

The Secret Service logs have Cheney entering the tunnel at 9:36, though not necessarily for the *first* time or coming from his office. Might Cheney have stepped out of PEOC bunker into the tunnel after the hit on the Pentagon? In a late 2001 interview, the vice president had implied a fifteen-minute delay in the tunnel for a call to the president "advising [Bush] that three planes were missing and one had hit the Pentagon" (*Newsweek* 12/31/01). Although the White House and Pentagon wouldn't allow the Commission to interview military or Secret Service phone operators, other sources confirmed that this crucial call between Cheney and Bush ran from about 9:45 to 9:55, just before AF-1 rocketed off at Sarasota (Gellman *Angler* pp. 121-23).

So if Cheney sought secrecy in the tunnel, what did he and Bush talk about? Although apparently no record exists of the call to Bush, it seems highly likely, based on other evidence, that Cheney asked for and received permission to give two orders of crucial importance: to issue both a shoot-down directive and an order for partial Continuity of Government (COG) (Scott *Road to 9/11* pp. 200-201).

Since the Commission's *Report* never mentioned the order to implement partial COG on 9/11, apparently this wasn't a development it wanted to reveal. This isn't surprising, for COG (discussed more fully later) has remained a well-kept state secret since its inception in the 1980s (Scott *Road to 9/11* pp. 183-87, 209-10). But the Commission apparently had particular problems with Cheney's order, issued following his conversation with Bush, to shoot down any hijacked aircraft. Its solution was simple: question whether there was a Bush/Cheney call before 10:00. Rather than calling attention to the blockages it encountered in obtaining phone records, the Commission's co-chairs, Thomas Kean (R-NJ) and Lee Hamilton (D-Ind.), assumed that because they saw "no documentary evidence," there was "no event" (Kean and Hamilton *Without Precedent* p. 112). Relying on such sleight of hand, the 9/11 Commission was able to implicitly deny any stand-down order from Cheney, any shoot-down order from Bush to Cheney before 10:00, and, therefore, any shoot down of Flight 93 (D. R. Griffin *9/11 Commission Report* pp. 237-43). The changes made by Cheney and the Commission will receive further coverage in later discussions.

Three objectives seem to explain these alterations of the record—i.e., the delayed times of arrival given first by Cheney and then later by the Commission. One was to avoid any appearance of involvement in the military stand-down order reported by Mineta. Another was to delay the perceived issuance of a shoot-down order from Bush to Cheney until after Flight 93 had gone down, thereby making it seem impossible that Cheney could have ordered this last flight shot down. A third was to have Cheney receive permission from Bush to issue a shoot-down order, rather than give the appearance of Cheney issuing one without approval from Bush, which could have led to major political or legal consequences not only to Cheney but to his boss.

It's more clear, though, how Cheney pressured the Commission to make time changes. When drafts of the *Report* began to circulate around the White House in June 2004, Cheney and his neocon counsel, David Addington, were outraged by the Commission's timeline on Cheney's actions that morning. They particularly objected to the implication that Cheney had issued an unconstitutional shoot-down order without Bush's approval (P. Shenon *The Comm.* p. 411). One would also surmise that the vice president and his cunning lawyer wouldn't have much liked the suggestion that the order could have led to the shooting down of an airliner. Like Rumsfeld, Cheney was attentive to covering his tracks; on his last day in office he strained his back as he personally carried out boxes of records (*Wash. Post* 1/20/09).

In his biography of Cheney, Barton Gellman concludes that the Commission didn't believe the stories they'd heard from Bush and Cheney but didn't dare expose top officials. "The president and vice president of the United States ... staved off that verdict by daring a bipartisan commission to call them liars" (Gellman *Angler* p. 125). Unfortunately, the gambit worked. Both the Commission and the press corps failed to ask the tough questions, especially before the presidential election of 2004.

Since the Commission's *Report* emerged, establishment figures, some of them academics, have validated its skewed version of events. Richard Posner, a widely respected judge on the US Court of Appeals, was overwhelmingly laudatory (*NYT Book Review* 7/31/05). Columbia historian Alan Brinkley concluded that "quickly and instinctively," "within hours of the attack on the World Trade Center and the Pentagon on September 11, 2001, Dick Cheney in effect took command of the national security operations of the federal government." Brinkley did, however, point to the neocon ideological basis of Cheney's actions: "he began to act in response to two long-standing beliefs: that the great dangers facing the United States justified almost any response, legal or otherwise; and that the presidency needed to expand its authority, which had been unjustifiably and dangerously weakened in the post-Vietnam, post-Watergate years" (*NYT Book Review* 8/3/08).

## Rumsfeld's Equally Varied Accounts

Like Cheney's, Rumsfeld's actions and reactions are complex—even convoluted—and contradictory. They're further complicated and often contradicted by other accounts, particularly those of Richard Clarke, which contradict the stories the secretary told or approved.

Let's start with Rumsfeld on Rumsfeld. On different occasions the secretary of defense himself told very different stories about what he, the man entrusted with defending the nation, was doing that morning.

## Version I: Under Reaction and Limited Emergency Involvement

About 8:30, at a breakfast with congresspersons including Rep. Christopher Cox (R-Ca.), Rumsfeld invoked the threat of terrorism to push for more "defense" (military) spending: "there will be another event—I don't know when, I don't know how, but it'll be bad—and you won't want to have been on the wrong side of this issue'" (AP 9/16/01). At 8:46, NORAD launched F-16s to intercept a hijacked airliner; since all such launches had to go through the secretary, it's difficult to imagine that he wouldn't have known something was up. Yet at 9:04, the secretary was informed of the *second* plane hitting the Towers—showing everyone that the nation was under attack—but the secretary of defense still took no decisive action other than to "make a few calls" (AP 9/16/01).

In similarly cavalier fashion, Rumsfeld's neocon crony Paul Wolfowitz, the deputy secretary of defense, later recalled "we were having a meeting in my office. Someone said a plane had hit the World Trade Center. Then we turned on the television and we started seeing the shots of the second plane hitting, and this is the way I remember it. It's a little fuzzy.... There didn't seem to be much to do about it immediately, and we went on with whatever the meeting was about" (*Vanity Fair* 5/9/03). In contrast to the big bosses at the DoD, when Sgt. Jose Rojas Jr. of the Pentagon police saw the burning WTC buildings on TV, he thought, logically enough, "we're next" (*NYT* 4/12/06). It would figure.

Yet in none of their accounts did Rumsfeld or Wolfowitz suggest they drew any such conclusion. Instead, the defense secretary continued the briefing, claiming he was as surprised as everyone else when half an hour later, Flight 77 slammed into the Pentagon. When the building was hit at 9:37, he continued with his briefing for several minutes. Next, he claimed, he walked downstairs, helped place the wounded on stretchers, and went "[to the parking lot] for a while," about a "half hour," and returned to his office about 10:20 to figure out what to do (*Minneapolis Star Tribune* 9/12/01). In a self-indicting popular magazine interview, Rumsfeld recalled that "at some moment I decided I should be in here figuring out what to do" (*Parade* 10/12/01). Recall that all of this was going on while the Pentagon was burning and Flight 93 was roaring toward the nation's capital at 500 mph (J. Longman *Among the Heroes* p. 208).

This version of events appeared on the DoD website and in numerous news stories. One is struck that Rumsfeld makes no mention of either his inaction following the second impact in New York (after which he sat in his office for 34 minutes) or his absence from command centers and video conferences that were desperately seeking direction from the secretary of defense. Incredulous, ABC's John McWethy asked Rumsfeld, "after the second building had been hit in New York, you did not alter your routine. You continued your intelligence briefing?" (ABC 8/12/02). A few members of the press often asked the right questions but seldom received adequate answers.

**Version 2: Rumsfeld's Account to the 9/11 Commission**

In this account (Hearing 3/23/04), Rumsfeld recounted how he was in his office "with a CIA briefer … when at 9:38 the Pentagon shook with an explosion…. I went outside to determine what had happened…. I was back in the Pentagon with a crisis action team shortly before or after 10:00" (P. Thompson *Terror Timeline* pp. 424, 426). Note that in this version, Rumsfeld started his story late, after much had already happened. He made no mention of his noninvolvement in the scrambling of interceptor jets, his inaction following the second attack in New York, or his participation in rescue efforts, which are recorded on video. (It's a bit comic to see the secretary of defense helping carry a stretcher while the Pentagon burns in the background and Washington is bracing for another attack.) Note too that the time when he finally returned to his office (not when he reported for duty at the command center) was around 10:00, rather than 10:20. Given a walking time of ten minutes each way, he clearly didn't remain outside for a "half hour."

Different as Rumsfeld's stories were, they shared what seemed to be a cavalier dereliction of duty. Moreover, the accounts simply had to involve lies. Both accounts could not be true, notes David Ray Griffin: "either Rumsfeld was not telling the truth to the Commission or else he and other people put untruths on the Department of Defense website" (Griffin *9/11 Comm. Report* p. 218). Either the story Rumsfeld told the commissioners wasn't credible to them, or they, for their own purposes, set the time of Rumsfeld's arrival in the National Military Command Center (NMCC) at 10:30. This raised the question of why the secretary was a no-show at the NMCC for an hour and a half while the nation was under attack. For once, the Commission provided some revealing answers, though the revelations clearly weren't intended.

## The Commission's Version

Apparently putting more stock in Rumsfeld's original story, the Commission affirmed that the secretary went to "the parking lot to assist with rescue efforts" and that during this time, military commanders were unable to reach or locate him (*Report* pp. 37-38). Then the Commission moved toward some startling statements: "He went from the parking lot to his office [where he spoke to the president shortly after 10:00] and then to the Executive Support Center, where he participated in the White House video teleconference. He moved to the NMCC shortly before 10:30, in order to join Vice Chairman [Gen. Richard] Myers" (*Report* pp. 43-44). Thus the Commission attempted to save Rumsfeld from himself—by having him speak with Bush, participate in Richard Clarke's video conference, and report to the Pentagon's "war room," they managed to make him look somewhat more responsible.

Different as they are, both Rumsfeld's and "Torie" Clark's accounts place the secretary back in the NMCC about 10:00, just before Flight 93 plowed into the ground in Pennsylvania. But even this was apparently too close to reality for the Commission. It stated that Rumsfeld finally entered "the NMCC shortly before 10:30…" and "was gaining situational awareness when he spoke with the vice president at 10:39" (*Report* pp. 43-44).

In all three versions, Rumsfeld remained oddly out of the loop. In still another implausibility, the secretary accepted that he didn't report to the Pentagon's "war room" until 10:30, fully 53 minutes after Flight 77 hit his own headquarters (CNN 9/4/02). Now that's a stretch. If we accept this account, obvious questions arise: How could a secretary of defense, presiding over a military establishment frantically launching fighters to intercept airliners, not be more engaged? Why didn't the secretary reach a war room, located about 300 feet from his office, for nearly an hour after the Pentagon had been struck?

Ignoring the obvious, the mainstream press has never questioned Rumsfeld about why he was so slow to react. Why, as secretary of defense, wasn't Rumsfeld doing his main job: directing the nation's defenses? By his own accounts, Rumsfeld makes no effort to execute the duties that both his oath and military protocol require of him—i.e., to take charge of the command loop, which was led by Cheney instead.

Others on the scene told stories quite different from any of those told by Rumsfeld. His close associate, Assistant Secretary of Defense Victoria "Torie" Clarke, gave a still different account of events.

### Torie Clarke's Tale of Heroism

In her book *Lipstick on a Pig: Winning in the No-Spin Era by Someone Who Knows the Game*, "Torie" Clarke presented an account in which she and Larry Di Rita, the secretary's "right-hand man," dashed up to Rumsfeld's office; the secretary told them to go down to the Pentagon's Executive Support Center (ESC), which was "spinning up into operation" following the second impact, and wait for him there. "In the meantime," Clarke recalled, "he would get his daily intelligence briefing, which was already scheduled for nine thirty" (Clarke *Lipstick* pp. 218-19).

At the ESC, according to Clarke, aides apparently tried to cover for Rumsfeld. When someone asked where Rumsfeld was, someone answered, "he's out of the building … helping emergency workers load victims onto stretchers." Inflating matters further, even waxing grandiose, Clarke declared that around 10:15, Rumsfeld "walked into the command center, his suit jacket over his shoulder and his face and clothes smeared with ash, dirt, and sweat" (Clarke *Lipstick* pp. 219-223).

## Another "Heroic" Tale of Outdoor Rescue

Whereas Torie Clarke promoted Rumsfeld as a paragon of openness and transparency, *Washington Post* journalist Andrew Cockburn painted a very different picture in *Rumsfeld: His Rise, His Fall, His Catastrophic Legacy.* "Just after 9:37 a.m. ... Rumsfeld, though aware that the World Trade Center Towers in New York had already been hit, was proceeding with his regularly scheduled CIA briefing" (Cockburn *Rumsfeld* p. 1). After a plane hit the Pentagon, Rumsfeld set off with scarcely a word to anyone to inspect the damage; soon his phone and those of his aides were erupting with urgent calls: "Where's Rumsfeld?" (Pacifica "Democracy Now!" 3/7/07).

When Rumsfeld arrived, the Pentagon crash site was strewn with fragments of aircraft wreckage and debris. A Pentagon police officer recalled "the secretary picked up one of the pieces of metal. I was telling him he shouldn't be interfering with a crime scene, when he looked at some inscription on it and said, 'American Airlines.'" The officer's radio was "crackling with frantic pleas ... regarding Rumsfeld's whereabouts." Nevertheless, the heroic legend grew. One of Rumsfeld's staffers even claimed that Rumsfeld had "'torn his shirt into strips to make bandages for the wounded" (Cockburn *Rumsfeld* pp. 2-3).

## Clarke and Others Contradict Rumsfeld's Stories

Even more challenging to the Rumsfeld legend is the account provided by Richard Clarke, the country's counterterrorism "czar." Since by all accounts Clarke had done his job in the crisis, he didn't need diversionary tales. Clarke reported that by 9:15 a.m., just minutes after the second WTC attack, he'd convened a teleconference in the White House Executive Support Center (ESC) near the Situation Room. He listed other participants as Rumsfeld, Gen. Richard Myers, CIA Director George Tenet, National Security Advisor Condoleezza Rice, FBI Director Robert Mueller, and FAA Director Jane Garvey. Even before the Pentagon was hit,

Clarke recalled that he could "see Rumsfeld on the screen" (Clarke *Against All Enemies* pp. 1-7). Whereas Rumsfeld's own account placed him in his own office when the Pentagon was hit, Clarke placed him in the Pentagon's secure teleconferencing studio (Griffin *9/11 Contradictions* p. 59).

To head outside after the crash, Rumsfeld must have left the teleconference, abandoning his post in a crisis. Perhaps a senior official in the Situation Room summed up matters best: "What was Rumsfeld doing on 9/11? He deserted his post.... The country was under attack. Where was the guy who controls America's defense?" (Cockburn *Rumsfeld* pp. 3-4).

Nor does Rumsfeld's story square with the testimony of Secretary of the Treasury Norman Mineta. As Cheney's main story goes, Rumsfeld didn't speak with Bush or Cheney until after 10:00 a.m., just before the final plane crashed in Pennsylvania (*Village Voice* 12/5/05). According to Mineta and others, however, the president issued a shoot-down order to the vice president *before* 10:00; this makes one wonder why they didn't consult the secretary of defense, as protocol required.

Why would Bush have discussed the use of deadly force with Cheney but not Rumsfeld? Why was the vice president calling the shots when the accepted protocol assigns "national command authority" to the president and the secretary of defense? Rumsfeld's apparent dereliction is particularly outrageous, not simply because he failed to execute his duties, but because he'd recently issued a directive that—for the first time—*required* approval of the secretary of defense for dealing with hijacked planes (DoD CJCSI 3610.01A). Rumsfeld had made himself responsible for fighter responses, but on that morning, according to the tales he told, he evaded that responsibility.

Three years later, Rumsfeld's behavior suggested he was still worried about being held responsible for the air-defense failures. Utterly contradicting common sense, Rumsfeld tried to alter his job description. In 2004, he told the 9/11 Commission that "the Department of Defense did not have responsibility for the borders. It did not have responsibility for the airports … civilian aircraft was a law enforcement matter...." (Hearing 3/23/04). If the US military is not tasked with defending the country's borders, why are so many of its air bases positioned so near them?

## Readily Identified Scapegoats

Bush and Rumsfeld shared a common obsession with immediately blaming Iraq for the attacks. Just hours after the attacks, Bush reportedly pulled counterterrorism expert Richard Clarke aside and said, "I want you to find that Iraq did this." Later the president got more testy, demanding that Clarke "look into Iraq, Saddam" (*Wash. Post* 3/22/04). Within hours of the colossal air-defense failures that took place on his watch, Rumsfeld was riding the same warpath: he dictated his infamous "best-info-fast" memo to initiate a "fishing expedition" for all available "dirt" on Saddam's Iraq (CBS 9/4/02). A few days later, Rumsfeld established his new Office of Special Plans, headed by neoconservative Abram Shulsky (www.alternet.org/story/15935/). "Special plans," it turns out, was a Pentagon euphemism for "preparations to attack Afghanistan and Iraq." The fact that no one could have known for sure that foreign actors were responsible didn't dampen Rumsfeld's fervor for fingering the Taliban and the Iraqis.

Both incidents accord with documented expressions of intent to attack Iraq not only by Bush and Rumsfeld but also by Cheney and other neocons. All this accords with the priority principle, which states that what politicians do first often reveals their real priorities.

## More Contradictions: Gen. Richard Myers

General Myers, the nation's top commander that day, claimed he was visiting Sen. Max Cleland (D-Ga.) at the Capitol prior to his Senate confirmation hearing as chairman of the Joint Chiefs of Staff. Before entering Senator Cleland's office at about 8:50, Myers claimed, he glanced at a TV report on a plane hitting the World Trade Center. Assuming, he said, it was only "a small plane," Myers went ahead with his plans to visit Senator Cleland (MSNBC 9/11/02).

Pleading ignorance of everything going on, General Myers further claimed that "nobody informed us" about the second plane crash. Myers went on to say that only when he and Senator Cleland emerged from their meeting—fully 50 minutes later at 9:40—did he see a news report that a second plane had hit the other Tower. Then somebody told him "the Pentagon has been hit." After that, according to Myers, "someone handed me a cell phone" connecting him with Gen. Ralph Eberhart at NORAD headquarters. Immediately after talking to General Eberhart, Myers said that he "jumped in the car, [and] ran back to the Pentagon" (Armed Forces Radio and Television 10/17/01). Although, according to this version, Myers had just spoken on a cell phone, he apparently didn't think about using one to help command the nation's air defenses while he was in the car. Myers said nothing about additional conversations during the ride, which would have taken at least twenty minutes.

This is quite a tale. Are we to believe, David Ray Griffin has asked, "[even] after the second strike, which everyone reportedly took as evidence that the country was under attack, neither Cleland's secretary nor anyone from the Pentagon ... called him, even after it was struck? As acting chairman, Myers was the highest-ranking military officer at the Pentagon. Dozens of people ... would surely know where he was that morning (Griffin *9/11 Contradictions* p. 47). Clearly someone knew, for how else could Gen. Myers have received the call from General Eberhart? And are we to believe that the commander in charge of the nation's defenses wouldn't carry a cell phone?

It's not even certain Gen. Myers was on Capitol Hill. Counterterrorism expert Richard Clarke and Assistant Secretary of Defense Torie Clarke placed him elsewhere at this key moment. At 9:15, while Gen. Myers was supposedly sequestered in Sen. Cleland's office, Clarke included him among the big players on the screen as he entered the White House Video Teleconference Center: "Air force four-star Gen. Dick Myers was filling in for the chairman of the Joint Chiefs, Hugh Shelton...." Clarke placed Myers at the Pentagon *throughout* the attacks, with "generals and colonels around him." Clarke even quoted Myers as asking, regarding Cheney's shoot-down order at about 9:50, "'Okay, what are the ROE [Rules of Engagement]?'" (Clarke *Against All Enemies* pp. 3-4, 8).

About 9:45, Clarke recalled himself asking about possible air-defense responses, for which Myers offered an update: "Not a pretty picture, Dick. We are in the middle of ... a NORAD exercise, but ... Otis [AFB] has launched two birds toward New York. We have three F-16s from Langley over the Pentagon. Andrews [Air Base] is launching fighters from the

DC Air National Guard. We have fighters aloft from the Michigan Air National Guard moving east toward a potentially hostile [plane] over Pennsylvania" (Clarke *Against All Enemies* pp. 4-5, 12). Thus Myers, the military's top commander, told Clarke, the nation's terrorism expert, that his "birds" might be slow to scramble because NORAD was in the middle of an exercise. This statement also implied that Andrews AFB *was* actively involved, contrary to the Commission's claim. Like Rumsfeld, Myers may not have been as out of the loop as his narrative would indicate. If not, both men may have preferred to look remiss or even incompetent than to be held responsible for making decisions.

Although Gen. Myers made no mention of any other efforts to participate in decisions about the country's defenses, and although the most devastating air-defense failures in US history had taken place on his watch, two days later the Senate confirmed Gen. Myers as nation's top military commander. No matter that, by his own account, Myers had remained incommunicado as he was apparently lobbying for a job that, at the same exact moment, he was failing to do. This was the first but hardly the last instance in which those officials most responsible for a catastrophe were *promoted*, not demoted, disciplined, or fired. As columnist Robert Scheer quips, we not only live in a culture of non-accountability but one in which "failure has its lush rewards" (*San Fran. Chron.* 12/10/08). A more complete list of those promoted or otherwise rewarded appears in Appendix B at www. mountingevidence.org.

Since the next few chapters will deal with two investigations into 9/11, and especially the 9/11 Commission, it's a good idea to sketch a few of the issues they should have resolved. Unfortunately, neither came anywhere close to doing that. The Commission never questioned, for instance, why the Secret Service had first allowed the presidential entourage to linger casually at the school but then required that the president spend the rest of the day either in the air at 35,000 feet or in an ultra-safe bunker at Offutt Air Force Base (P. Thompson *Terror Timeline* p. 464).

Another example—only one among many—of the Commission's selectivity is that it made no mention of Operation Able Danger, the military intelligence program that had gathered masses of information on the al Qaeda operatives, often within the US, only to see it all dumped just before 9/11 (http://en.wikipedia.org/wiki/Able_Danger). The decorated officers who ran this data-mining program made repeated attempts to share their experience but were thwarted at every turn (*NYT* 9/21/05).

When a Congressional staffer asked Chris Kojm, a spokesman for the commissioners, why they didn't put anything about the Able Danger intelligence program in their final *Report*, Kojm's answer was surprisingly candid: "It did not fit with the story we wanted to tell" (www.abledangerblog. com/2006/02/it-did-not-fit-with-story-we-wanted-to.html). This is a damning self-indictment, for it reveals how the Commission suppressed anything, far beyond Secretary Mineta's testimony or Able Danger's findings, that didn't fit its political agenda.

Skeptical wits often quip that the Commission "made it up as they went along." In fact, though, the staffers on the Commission, notably its Executive Director Philip Zelikow, had begun to sketch out a draft of the Official Story even before the Commission's hearings had ever begun. This wasn't about finding the evidence and following it where it led: instead, the Commission knew the story it wanted to tell, and cherry-picked evidence to flesh that narrative (Shenon *The Comm.* pp. 387-89).

## Surprising Admissions by the Commission's Leaders

Several of those who'd led the Commission have since critiqued their own *Report*. In 2006, former leaders of the Commission cast doubts on the stories told by Pentagon officials. In their book *Without Precedent*, former Commission Chair Thomas Kean and Vice Chair Lee Hamilton admitted they'd suspected NORAD and the FAA of lying to them about the air-defense failures on 9/11 but secretly decided to keep these lies from the American people, thereby protecting those who had told them (AP 8/5/06).

According to Chairmen Kean and Hamilton, the Commission understood that "the Pentagon's initial story of how it reacted to the terrorist attacks may have been part of a deliberate effort to mislead the Commission and the public." In fact, "suspicion of wrongdoing ran so deep that the ten-member Commission, in a secret meeting ... debated referring the matter to the Justice Department for criminal investigation." Serious legal issues arose when the Commission discovered that, in the words of Kean and Hamilton, "military and aviation officials violated the law by making false statements to Congress and to the Commission" (*Wash. Post* 8/2/06). These, plus the Commission's own alterations to accepted air-defense notification and response times, will receive full coverage in Chapter 11.

However, the Commission didn't refer to the individuals who covered up their failures to the Justice Department, nor did it mention this huge credibility problem in its official *Report*. Instead, as we'll see, the Commission often validated the lies it heard, thereby deceiving the public. Why didn't the Commission give the public any indication of its deep "suspicion of wrongdoing"? If this back-room conspiracy of silence wasn't a betrayal of public trust, what is?

When one looks at factors contributing to the widespread misunderstanding of 9/11, many of them are connected with government stonewalling. Here again the Commission was culpable; it ignored the information that had already been suppressed, made no mention of the fact that suppression had gone on, and suppressed still more information.

### Destruction and Suppression of Evidence: A Cover-Up?

As we lift the shroud of secrecy that's covered many troubling questions about 9/11, let's look at a few startling instances beyond those in the Preface. A much longer catalogue of destroyed, suppressed, or impounded evidence also appears on the MountingEvidence.org website.

*Impounding FAA Tapes* Just hours after the attacks, sixteen employees at New York's Air Traffic Control Center, including six who'd dealt directly with the hijacked flights, made an audio recording to capture what they'd experienced that day. That afternoon, an FAA "quality assurance manager" shredded the tape into small pieces and stuffed them into different trash cans (*Wash. Post* 5/6/04). The next day, the FAA refused to discuss its procedures or the sequence of events, claiming that they're "part of the FBI's inquiry" (*NYT* 9/15/01). Since 9/11, the FBI has ordered airline employees, air traffic controllers, firefighters, eyewitnesses, and victims' relatives not to discuss what they saw or heard on 9/11. Truth has suffocated under a national-security blanket.

***Strange Seizure of "Black Boxes"*** The 9/11 Commission's official account claimed that the flight data recorder ("black boxes") from the planes that struck the Twin Towers were either not recovered or contained no useful information. If this were true, it was certainly odd. A National Transportation Safety Board (NTSB) spokesperson commented that "it's extremely rare that we don't get the recorders back." According to the NTSB, the boxes are designed to be "nearly indestructible" (ABC 9/17/01). Moreover, two men who worked in the wreckage reported that they'd helped federal agents locate the "black boxes," but the agents immediately carted them off, never to be seen again (*Phila. Daily News* 10/28/04).

For years, government officials made public neither the contents of these black boxes nor of the four others (two per plane) they admitted recovering. When questioned about Flight 77, which apparently struck the Pentagon, FBI Director Robert Mueller III claimed that the boxes contained no useful information (CBS 2/23/02). If that were the case, why would the public be denied access to the boxes?

***Illegal Disposal of Wreckage and Rubble*** Despite being the sites of mass murders, the WTC buildings weren't treated as crime scenes, nor was the crash site for Flight 93 subjected to an NTSB investigation as mandated by federal law. Rather, the twisted wreckage of *three* WTC buildings was rapidly removed from the crime scenes and mostly shipped to Asia, making it virtually impossible for anyone to study the wreckage and rubble (*Fire Engineering* 1/02). The need to look for survivors or bodies under innumerable tons of glass, concrete, and steel was sacrificed as heavy machinery was deployed to remove the rubble (*NYT* 9/15/01).

Forensic professionalism disintegrated along with the buildings. The *New York Times* complained that the rapid removal of the evidence "means that definitive answers may never be known" (*NYT* 12/25/01). Although it's a federal offense to remove evidence from a crime scene, the FBI not only allowed the removal but actually supervised it, barring observers, journalists, and photographers from much of lower Manhattan. Even structural engineers working with FEMA's investigation were allowed only late and limited access (*NYT* 12/25/01). Usual investigative procedures were also violated at the crash site of Flight 93 in Pennsylvania (J. Longman *Among the Heroes* pp. 262-63).

***Avoiding and Delaying Trials*** Since 9/11, the Bush administration avoided trying terrorist suspects in open court, where it couldn't control who defense lawyers might subpoena or what information might be exposed in court records. Instead, the administration preferred to incarcerate suspects indefinitely in secret prisons, or if trials are held, to try detainees in military "commissions," otherwise known as tribunals (*NYT* 12/11/05 & 7/9/06). Since open trials make a lot of politically "sensitive" information available to journalists, researchers, and attentive citizens, governments seeking to control information try to preclude them.

When reporters have asked about prisoners, suspects, and trials, they've met with blockages. Administration officials have informed them "it's our policy not to discuss sensitive matters pertaining to an ongoing investigation or impending prosecution." Or, even years after the detainee was captured, they claim that any disclosures about prisoners "could expose our intelligence assets in the field." In those rare instances when al Qaeda operatives have come to trial, information has been suppressed. While court proceedings don't often become fully available, when they do, it can occasion a bonanza for researchers. Following the trial of al Qaeda operative Zacarias Moussaoui, detailed lists of objects found in the rubble and lists of phone calls made from the hijacked planes have been made public (US v. Moussaoui 7/31/06). This outpouring of information suggests why *this* has remained the only open trial of someone charged with aiding or abetting the perpetrators of the attacks.

To get a sense of how far the US has deviated from democratic legal traditions, consider since the attacks of 2001, the United States had tried only this *one* defendant in a regular court. That's one in ten years, plus a few others in military tribunals at Guantánamo, sequestered from public view. In sharp contrast, Spain has tried 29 suspects in the first *five* years since the Madrid bombing of 2003. And in the first year after the United Kingdom experienced its July 7, 2005, suicide attacks, authorities initiated proceedings against 41 terrorism suspects (NPR 7/7/06).

And only reluctantly did the US government undertake investigations into 9/11.

## Narrowing the Scope of Both Inquiries

The Joint Congressional Inquiry (JCI), the first official investigation of the tragedy, confined itself to failures within various intelligence-gathering agencies. This meant it would look at only "one leg of the elephant" in the room, and that many of its findings could easily be cloaked beneath the blanket of "state secrets." Similarly, the 9/11 Commission placed many crucial issues out-of-bounds, beyond the pale. By its own admission, the panel avoided "listing US support for Israel as a root cause of al Qaeda's opposition" because to do so would indicate that "the United States should reassess that policy" (AP 8/5/06). Since unidentified Commission members didn't want that reassessment, there was precious little discussion of the policies inflaming Islamist militancy—and therefore underlying the attacks. This is only one among a myriad of instances where the Commission apparently paid far more attention to the political effects of its findings than it did to finding and telling the truth.

## Five-Year Cutoff Eliminates Troubling Precedents

The Commission also drew a boundary at 1996, thereby eliminating consideration of a huge amount of relevant information. Casting their nets narrowly allowed the commissioners to avoid catching fish they didn't want to fry. The five-year rule and historical myopia permitted the Commission and the Bush administration to avoid the implications of not one but two stark previews to the 9/11 attacks: the deadly "near-miss" WTC bombing of 1993, and the thwarted Bojinka plots of 1994. Both were the work of al Qaeda, and both targeted iconic buildings, but the similarities go far beyond these. Had both received more scrutiny, it would have become obvious that these earlier terrorist schemes were plotted by the *same individuals* from the *same group,* using the *same means*—aircraft—to strike the *same targets*. The iconic Trade Towers had always topped the group's list, and al Qaeda's operatives had taken flying lessons for at least five years prior to 9/11.

Unaware of this history, the public and the press weren't able to see these startling parallels, so the administration could avoid an embarrassing question: How could the same terrorists have planned two shots at the Towers and still be given a third?

According to their later revelations, the commissioners were nervous about holding hearings in New York, since they didn't want to be seen as puncturing myths of heroic response to the attacks and ensuing devastation (Kean and Hamilton *Without Precedent* pp. 212-17). When they did allow public testimony from former Mayor Rudi Giuliani—most of it occurred behind closed doors—they ignored repeated, often vociferous public calls to address crucial issues. These weren't limited to the mayor's failure to replace the long-dysfunctional radios used by first responders. They also included Giuliani's statement to ABC News that he'd received advanced notice that the Twin Towers would come down (ABC 9/11/01). When Giuliani left office, he had the archives for his stint as mayor sealed for 25 years (W. Barrett and D. Collins *Grand Illusion* p. 363).

Because of the Commission's timidity, Giuliani was allowed to look much better than he actually was. After abandoning his new command center on the twenty-third floor of WTC-7, Giuliani claimed he had directed responses from an alternative command post: "Pier 92 was selected as the command center because on the next day, on Sept. 12 … It had hundreds of people there … from the State Emergency Management Office, and they were getting ready for a drill for biochemical attack" (Hearing 5/19/04). The fact is, Giuliani provided limited direction—and not from Pier 92 but from an emergency command bus—spent much of the time on the streets in front of TV cameras, and made limited use of the emergency personnel he was assembling (B. M. Jenkins *Lessons Learned* p. 20).

Let's look more closely at the reasons why these attempts at investigation failed, which are most instructive.

# 6. The Joint Congressional Inquiry: "There Are Some Bombshells Out There"

*Something happened in that briefing that produced almost a necessity to deliver a story that's different from what actually happened ....*

–Sen. Bob Kerrey, member of the 9/11 Commission, after NORAD's White House briefing, 9/17/01

Afer the toxic fumes in New York lifted, dread and denial continued to discolor the nation's skies. Seizing the moment of shock, the political class in Washington immediately sought to force a twenty-first-century situation into a twentieth-century worldview. Shocked by a new sense of vulnerability, prompted by administration officials and media pundits, many Americans reverted to familiar patterns of us/them thinking. Islamic fundamentalism became the new communism: declared just days after the tragic attacks, the Global War on Terror became the new Cold War.

As part of this reversion, the nation tolerated a resurgence of government secrecy, intrusion, and non-accountability. This chapter will use the first investigation into 9/11 as a springboard into these larger issues, which have become still larger concerns today.

## Unprecedented Resistance to Real Investigation

Looking back on the dark aftermath, PBS legend Bill Moyers remarked "the highest officials in government didn't want us to know the truth." The Official Story crowded out troubling doubts, implying that "the atrocities were inevitable, the plot so diabolical, and its execution so precise that only a super hero could have prevented it" (www.pbs.org/moyers/journal/blog/2007/09). The subscript was, if "only a superhero" could have stopped the attacks, then why would anyone need to ask why mere mortals had failed? Clearly the establishment didn't want anyone questioning its official narrative; its resistance to investigating 9/11 was unprecedented. Nor was most of the public in a hurry to investigate the debacle. After all, government and mass media had already inculcated a narrative that, if not examined too closely, seemed to make sense.

Ironically though, top-secret investigations had actually begun right after the 9/11 attacks. Behind closed doors, in closed sessions, the FBI, CIA, and other arms of the law-enforcement/intelligence complex had conducted investigations into possible accomplices. As they generated long lists of Islamic names, these meetings abetted mass roundups of Arabic- or Islamic-Americans in the weeks that followed (Film: *Divided We Fall*). These FBI/CIA sessions did not, however, consider the possibility that some of their own leaders or field personnel might have functioned as enablers or accomplices (P. Lance *Triple Cross* pp. 299-318).

Secret sessions were one thing, but a *public* investigation into what went on and what went wrong was a whole different matter. Never before had American citizens seen such a delayed inquiry into a national calamity. By way of comparison, it took the US government *six days* to open an investigation of the *Titanic* sinking, *seven days* each for the JFK assassination and NASA's *Challenger* disaster, and *nine days* for Pearl Harbor. Why, if it had nothing to hide, did it take this administration *months,* not weeks, to accept even a drastically limited Joint Congressional Inquiry—and fully *422* days to finally agree to a slightly more "full and independent" investigation? On the second anniversary of the attacks, a major newspaper would ask: "Why, after 730 days, do we know so little about what really happened that day?" (*Phila. Daily News* online 9/11/03).

Hoping questions about 9/11 would go away, the White House stalled and stonewalled. Demanding that Congress *not* mandate an inquiry, both Bush and especially Cheney personally lobbied Senate Majority Leader Tom Daschle (D-SD) (*San Fran. Chron.* 4/12/02). Both "expressed concern that a review of what happened on September 11 would take resources and personnel away from the war on terrorism" (*Wash. Post* 1/30/02). At a time when flag lapel pins were mandatory for public figures, both threatened the Congressional leaders: "you wouldn't want to appear unpatriotic right now, would you?" Members of the families of the 9/11 victims also commented on fierce resistance from the White House. "From the beginning it was clear," charged 9/11 activist and Family Steering Committee leader Sally Regenhard, "that this administration was going to fight this tooth and nail" (http://en.wikipedia.org/wiki/Sally_Regenhard).

A compromise envisioned a "fallback" plan. While both the White House and Congressional Republicans had resisted a full fact-finding investigation, pressures from a few courageous members of Congress, from a few progressive or independent news sources, and especially from the families of victims finally prevailed. The Bush administration eventually approved a Joint Congressional Inquiry (JCI) strictly limited to the House and Senate Intelligence Committees (P. Lance *Cover Up* p. 135). This meant that the investigators would be members of Congress who were psychologically and politically invested in espionage agencies. Since the proceedings of these two committees typically remain secret, assigning the investigation to them promised to limit public access to their findings. In this way, the intelligence apparatus could be both protected and expanded.

## The Joint Congressional Inquiry: Shackled from the Start

Although White House pressure on the leaders of Congress to *not* investigate remained intense (*Wash. Post* 1/30/02), Congress finally acted. In February 2002, Congress began investigating the biggest homeland disaster in American history.

The Joint Congressional Inquiry (JCI), which began many months after 9/11, was hobbled from the outset. News media "watchdogs" failed to bark about the lack of open process. Historian Howard Zinn observed that when the first defense mechanisms of denial, stalling, and stonewalling fail politicians, a backup defense "is to investigate, but not too much; the press will publicize, but will not get to the heart of the matter" (Zinn *People's History the United States* p. 586).

Clearly this wouldn't be a full and free inquiry into the failures of intelligence agencies to predict and prevent the attacks. Instead, in the immortal words of Richard Nixon, the probe would deliver "a limited hangout." It would involve just a few members of Congress, and it would be drastically limited in scope. The Senate Select Committee on Intelligence and the House Permanent Select Committee on Intelligence would conduct the inquiry, but *only* into American espionage or investigative agencies, the CIA and the FBI. All other areas of concern—including White House failures to heed a blizzard of warnings, the odd paralysis of multi-trillion-dollar air defenses, or the strange fall of three skyscrapers in a single day—lay beyond the purview of the inquiry. The forces of resistance deployed the classic device of reductionism, narrowing the range of vision and discouraging investigators from "connecting the dots."

## A Long List of Impediments

The JCI was inherently compromised, starting with its makeup. The chairs of the two intelligence committees, Sen. Bob Graham (D-Fla.) and Rep. Porter Goss (R-Fla.) were not overtly in conflict, but Rep. Goss was much more likely to compromise the mission. A former CIA agent, Goss was a ten-year veteran of the Agency's clandestine operations division (*Wash. Post* 5/18/02). He was also a primary author of the USA PATRIOT ACT and had strenuously resisted *any* investigation into 9/11. As the Republican co-chair of the JCI, Rep. Goss acquiesced to blockages imposed by the White House and the intelligence apparatus. In 2004, Bush appointed him as director of the CIA, where Goss impeded both release of the spy agency's reports on its role in 9/11 and its report on CIA's abductions of suspected terrorists (*Time* 12/19/05). Yet Goss would shamelessly tell the world that "we don't torture" (Reuters 3/18/05). While such lying was hardly new, never before had Americans suffered such thick shrouds of government secrecy, not even from the CIA.

Far beyond Porter Goss, other insider politicians conducted the investigation. Since the JCI was comprised wholly of senators and representatives on intelligence committees, it was rife with conflicts of interest. While the JCI included Republicans unlikely to scrutinize an administration from their own party, the Democrats faced inhibitions of their own. Trying to avoid appearing unpatriotic, most of the Democrats saw little to gain from casting a still-popular president in a bad light. Furthermore, the members of Congress comprising the inquiry included a high percentage of insiders with long-term connections to the very intelligence apparatus they'd be investigating. Protective of both their party and the agencies, these members of the House and Senate Intelligence Committees weren't used to asking tough questions—and certainly not doing so in open forums. After years of conducting public business behind closed-doors, secrecy had become their *modus operandi*.

Moreover—and even more significantly—the JCI was shackled by unreasonable limits. The inquiry could only look into "intelligence failures preceding the terrorist attacks" (*Wash. Post* 1/30/02). Here the government dealt the public a joker it would play again several times, right through the 9/11 Commission and the National Institute for Standards and Technology (NIST) *Report* on the Towers: limiting the scope to circumscribe what could be discovered. In addition, the time allotted was unreasonably short. Since the JCI had only six months to probe many years of intelligence malfeasance, and since its requests for documents were often stymied, its Report was predictably sketchy. Even so, the White House harassed the investigators and censored their Report.

Finally, members of the JCI were not only limited in what they could see but in what they could share with the public. The JCI received only a small portion of the documents it had requested from the White House (*WS Journal* 7/8/03). More documents than ever before were classified. Furthermore, members of the panel were only able to review, not release, documents, and the White House decided which ones they'd get to review. Reporting that only those JCI briefings "that the White House deemed relevant" would be provided to the press, the *New York Times* complained about the "substantial limits on access" (*NYT* 11/3/03).

### Cheney's Intense Intimidation of JCI Leaders

As a further impediment to its independence, the JCI faced significant, even unprecedented intimidation from the executive branch, led by the

White House. The Justice Department, FBI, and CIA were also consistently antagonistic to investigators (*NYT* 10/5/02).

The administration pounced on one incident as a pretext for ongoing harassment. In a closed-door hearing, National Security Agency (NSA) Director Michael Hayden, made an unsettling disclosure. He told the JCI that although phone calls intercepted by NSA the day before 9/11 warned of an imminent attack, the agency failed to translate these intercepts until the day after the 9/11 attacks. These calls had al Qaeda operatives saying "the match is about to begin" and "tomorrow is zero hour." Sen. Richard Shelby (R-Ala.), the ranking Republican on the Senate Intelligence Committee, leaked this highly classified information to Fox News. Fox didn't run the story, but CNN did (CNN 9/19/02).

Although electronic surveillance experts indicated that the information about the NSA intercepts contained nothing harmful to national security, the White House went ballistic. Administration and intelligence agency officials were quick to claim the leak showed how Congress couldn't be trusted with classified information (*Wash. Post* 8/5/04). The next day, an enraged Dick Cheney called Senate Intelligence Committee chair Bob Graham.

Eager to exploit the situation, Cheney threatened to terminate the (already tenuous) White House cooperation with the investigation unless Sen. Graham and his House Intelligence Committee counterpart, Porter Goss, immediately investigated the leak (*National Journal* 2/15/07). Neither classified records nor administration witnesses would be available to the inquiry, Cheney threatened. Furthermore, unless the JCI ensured that such leaks would never happen again, Bush would tell the country that Congress couldn't be trusted with national-security information. Perhaps the vice president felt his best defense was a strong offense—that if he intimidated the investigators, he wouldn't be cited as a witness or considered a suspect.

Whatever the motives, the intimidation worked. Sen. Graham called a special meeting of the JCI leaders plus Nancy Pelosi (D-Ca.). Making a hasty decision under pressure, almost in panic, they went along. To placate Cheney, they "requested" the Justice Department conduct a criminal inquiry into whether anyone leaked the information. But even this concession didn't chill Cheney or mollify the White House. Upping the ante, Press Secretary Ari Fleischer told reporters "the president [has] very deep concerns about anything that would … harm our ability to maintain sources and methods and anything else that could interfere with America's ability to fight the War on Terrorism" (White House 6/20/02).

This was only the beginning; the intimidation got much worse.

### FBI Also Intimidates Members of JCI

Descending on Capitol Hill, FBI agents questioned members of the JCI. The FBI even asked these members of Congress to submit to lie-detector tests. Blessedly, most refused, expressing "grave concern" over this unprecedented intrusion. But the intrusion allowed the FBI to build dossiers on members and staffers, putting a chill on any who might be critical of the Bureau (*Wash. Post* 8/2/02). Like the others, this was a move from the neocon playbook about how to concentrate power in the executive branch and marginalize its legislative counterpart.

The FBI's conflicts of interest and hypocrisies were blatant. Breaking with the administration, Sen. John McCain (R-Az.) blustered, "What you have here is an organization compiling dossiers on people who are investigating the same organization. The administration bitterly complains about some leaks out of a committee, but meanwhile, leaks abound about secret war plans for fighting a war against Saddam Hussein.… There's a bit of a contradiction here . . ." (*Wash. Post* 8/2/02).

Later, the hunt for the leaker intensified to unprecedented levels when the FBI asked seventeen senators to turn over any records that would reveal possible contacts with reporters (*Wash. Post* 8/2/02). Most turned over their records, while some complained the FBI was "trying to put a damper on our activities" (AP 8/29/02). That had to be the understatement of the year. In effect, the JCI had squandered a lot of resources investigating itself.

However, congressional investigators and the White House agreed on one outcome: a huge expansion of the intelligence apparatus. Wanting both to contain the embarrassing linkages between a "friendly" Pakistan and the alleged hijackers and to cover for NSA, the JCI claimed NSA's 30,000 employees and $5 billion budget weren't sufficient—that NSA didn't have the resources to share its intercepts with other intelligence agencies (Knight Ridder 6/06/02). Bigger budgets were the goal, but money was no object. This marked one of several instances where members of intelligence committees, colluding with the intelligence-gathering agencies they were supposed to oversee, took the opportunity to lobby their colleagues for increased intelligence budgets.

## That Stormy First Hearing

Formed in February 2002, the JCI had suffered months of delays. After a summer of FBI harassment, the JCI finally held its first public hearing. This was its chance to question the intelligence agencies they were supposed to investigate. Committee members from both parties decried the Bush administration's lack of cooperation with their inquiry, and some threatened to renew efforts to establish an independent Commission (*Wash. Post* 9/19/02).

The day's testimony focused on intelligence warnings that should have led officials to grasp that airplanes might be used as missiles (US Congress 9/18/02). Predictably, the layers of secrecy proved impenetrable, occasionally evoking the Seven Seals from the Book of Revelations. Eleanor Hill, the JCI's staff director, argued that "the American public has a compelling interest in this information and that public disclosure would not harm national security." However, CIA Director Tenet countered that "the president's knowledge of intelligence information relevant to this inquiry remains classified even when the substance of that intelligence information has been declassified" (*Wash. Post* 9/19/02). Relying on such Catch-22 logic, Tenet all but said, "not only is that information classified, but so is your question."

Things got testy when Ms. Hill communicated the Committee's interest in "a particular al Qaeda leader [who] may have been instrumental in the attacks" and whom US intelligence has known about since 1995. Tenet refused to declassify the information "on the grounds that it could compromise intelligence sources and methods and that this consideration supersedes the American public's interest in this particular area" (US Congress

9/18/02). It later emerged that this leader was Khalid Shaikh Mohammed (KSM), the alleged "mastermind" of the attacks (*NYT* 9/22/02). Small wonder that Tenet had clammed up: US intelligence had known of KSM since *1993*, not 1995, and had also known of his 1994 Bojinka "airplane plot."

## White House "Sets Up" the Congressional Inquiry

After his retirement from politics, Sen. Graham revealed much more. He concluded that "we were clearly set up by Dick Cheney and the White House…. they wanted to shut down a legitimate Congressional inquiry that might raise questions about whether their own people had aggressively pursued al Qaeda in the days prior to the September 11 attacks" (*National Journal* 2/15/07). "The leak was intended to sabotage [the JCI's] efforts," Graham surmised. "I am not by nature a conspiracy theorist, but the fact that we were hit with this disclosure at the moment we began to make things uncomfortable for the Bush administration has stuck with me" (Graham and J. Nussbaum *Intelligence Matters* p. 140).

Sen. Graham believed that the NSA phone-tap leak was done not only by a member of the inquiry but also by someone at the White House. He based this inference on newspaper stories containing information *not* disclosed during the JCI hearing. "That would lead a reasonable person to infer the administration leaked as well," Graham noted, so they were "trying to set us up … to make this an issue which they could come after us with" (Graham and Nussbaum *Intelligence Matters* p. 140).

Graham concluded that Cheney had " attempted to manipulate us …. if his goal was to get us to back off, he was unsuccessful" (*National Journal* 2/15/07). Yet Philip Shenon, an expert on the 9/11 Commission, concluded that the tactic of intimidation *did* work, for "members of the Joint Committee and their staffs were frightened into silence about the investigation" (Shenon *The Comm.* p. 55). It has since become a Beltway commonplace that Cheney and others at the White House seized "an opportunity to undercut Congressional oversight and possibly restrict the flow of classified information to Capitol Hill" (*Natl. Journ.* 2/15/07).

The intensity of White House, FBI, and CIA opposition only increased suspicions about their possible roles in 9/11. What could have been so threatening that the FBI directorate would run the risk of antagonizing members of Congress who supposedly oversee its operations and determine the Bureau's budgets? For the FBI to be *that* aggressive and run *that* degree of risk, something must have looked pretty scary.

## Additional Suppression and Censorship

The administration kept the JCI on a short leash, choking off the flow of information coming in and going out. When even a highly restricted probe began to bring in the "wrong" findings—and the trail of evidence began to lead toward the White House—the gates slammed shut. Access to documents was often blocked—but when blockage failed, much of the JCI's *Report* was classified, de facto censored. The *Report*'s ponderous "Foreword" told the public "where necessary, information that the Intelligence Community has identified as classified for national security purposes has been deleted" (www.gpoaccess.gov/serialset/creports/911.html). In short, the espionage agencies under investigation were not only allowed to determine what investigators could see but what they could share with the public.

## White House Redactions to the Report

Even the compromised, sometimes self-censored coverage proved too much for the Bush administration. Exercising the option announced in the *Report*'s "Preface," White House redacted much of the JCI's *Report*. In 2003, with White House backing, the CIA, NSA, and FBI blacked out a famous 27-page section of the JCI's *Report* (D. R. Griffin *911 Commission Report* p. 67). The pretext was predictable enough: "national security." It's little wonder the Bush people didn't want those pages to see the light of day. But it's equally dismaying, if not surprising, that the news media wouldn't press for full disclosure.

Similarly blatant conflicts of interest would later compromise the 9/11 Commission's inquiry. The corporate media—even the seasoned observers of Beltway games—did little to expose these travesties of good government. Aware of how little information the public was getting and how much the JCI had not been able to uncover, Sen. Richard Shelby, the ranking Republican, groused "we've just scratched the surface.... There is explosive information that has not been publicly released.... There are some bombshells out there" (*Wash. Post* 5/17/02).

## Sen. Graham Unveils White House Redactions

In addition to exposing the White House setup, Sen. Graham made three important disclosures after the investigation was over. In his exposé *Intelligence Matters*, Graham divulged the contents of the redacted 27-page section; tellingly, much of it dealt with the Saudis. It exposed links between the US government, notably the Bush family, and Saudi elites, particularly the bin Laden family. While one can readily see how this information would threaten the White House, one has to wonder how it could jeopardize "national security."

Equally importantly, Graham revealed that of the four and a half pages devoted to al Qaeda leader Khalid Shaikh Mohammed (KSM), more than half were "redacted for security reasons." Why wouldn't the public want to know as much as possible about KSM, who came up with the master plan for the attacks in 1994? As future chapters will reveal, the 9/11 Commission also played down the crucial role of the "mastermind" (Lance *Cover Up* pp. 45, 134).

These acts of avoidance take on additional significance when one becomes aware that federal officials did a low-intensity search for the "mastermind" at the same time they ran a high-visibility campaign for his nephew, "master bomber" Ramzi Yousef. According to political analyst Peter Lance, Yousef, the al Qaeda perpetrator of the 1993 World Trade Center bombing, was likely responsible for the crash of TWA Flight 800 off Long Island in 1996. In the latter crime, however, he had help from his uncle, though KSM was never charged. Moreover, Lance's *1000 Years For Revenge: International Terrorism and the FBI—the Untold Story* recounts how the Justice Department limited the scope of its trial for those behind the Bojinka Plot, again focusing of Yousef rather than its primary planner, KSM (www.readersread.com/features/peterlance.htm). The obvious question—and one the JCI never asked—was why did the feds place more attention on convicting the "master bomber," deadly as he was, than on getting the "mastermind"?

Equally importantly, Graham exposed the strange treatment given to two notorious al Qaeda operatives, alleged hijackers Nawaf al Hazmi and Khalid al Mihdhar. Both had been under surveillance by the CIA, which had tracked them to the al Qaeda summit in January 2000 that finalized plans for 9/11 (Graham and Nussbaum *Intelligence Matters* pp. 160-166). Since the CIA had been spying on al Hazmi and al Mihdhar, why was the deadly duo allowed to enter the country?

Why, researchers have persistently asked, didn't the CIA alert domestic agencies? Researching the matter deeply, espionage expert James Bamford has argued that Gen. Michael Hayden (then head of NSA, later director of CIA) failed to seize the moment to monitor the operatives in the US, even though he had a legal mandate to do so (J. Bamford *Shadow Factory* p. 177). In addition, CIA officer Clark Shannon sketched his role in the failed communication. Although Shannon attended a meeting where the CIA and FBI discussed the investigation into the bombing of the *USS Cole,* he failed to mention al Hazmi and al Mihdhar to investigators. Shannon told the staff that yes, he was aware that al Hazmi had already traveled within the country and that al Mihdhar held a US visa, but he didn't disclose this to the FBI. Despite the threat posed by the pair, Shannon claimed he couldn't share CIA information unless authorized to do so (*NYT* 10/17/02).

While the Official Story attributes such failures to share information to "bureaucratic rivalries," "turf protection," and the different missions among the agencies, other analysts will raise questions about whether the CIA and later the FBI were possibly protecting the pair. Were they possibly getting information from them or otherwise using them to advance American foreign policy? After all, attempts to use Islamic extremists stretch back to the 1980s, when the CIA funded and armed al Qaeda fighters, including Osama bin Laden (P. D. Scott *Road to 9/11* pp. 117-22, 166-67).

Sen. Graham also chronicled a strange case in which the FBI and the White House blocked attempts to interview an FBI counterterrorism informant who'd actually rented an apartment for al Hazmi and al Mihdhar. The story is a stunner.

## The FBI and al Qaeda: Up Close and Personal in San Diego

When the two alleged 9/11 hijackers entered the US in 2000, they made contact with Abdussattar Shaikh, a Muslim FBI undercover asset in San Diego. Shaikh worked in close contact with his handler, agent Steven Butler (Lance *Triple Cross* pp. 350-51). Not only did Shaikh watch the new arrivals; he also reported to agent Butler on four other al Qaeda militants. It's difficult to grasp how the FBI could have watched the two that closely and not suspected sinister intentions.

Sen. Graham also revealed that during early 2000, al Qaeda supporter Omar al Bayoumi not only helped Hazmi and Mihdhar find the apartment but also helped them locate flight schools. Al Bayoumi made an "unusually large number of telephone calls with Saudi government officials in both Los Angeles and Washington," Graham revealed, which led the FBI to consider him a Saudi spy. Adding to suspicions, Graham indicated that this increased communication corresponded with the arrival of alleged hijackers al Hazmi and al Mihdhar in California. Along with other evidence, this spike in phone calls suggested Saudi government involvement with these operatives (Graham and Nussbaum *Intelligence Matters* pp. 168-169).

A long-secret 2002 FBI report supported these conclusions. It specified that from January through May 2000, al Bayoumi called the Saudi embassy in Washington 32 times, the Cultural Mission in Washington 37 times, and the consulate in Los Angeles 24 times. Al Bayoumi made particularly regular contact with Fahad al Thumairy, a fellow Islamist radical working at the LA consulate (Intelwire.com 2008). And this was not all. After 9/11, FBI agents tracked Bayoumi to England, where he'd moved just two months before the attacks. But the FBI let the Saudi go, saying it believed his story about meeting al Hazmi and al Mihdhar by chance (*Newsweek* 9/24/02).

When all this had started to surface in the JCI inquest, the FBI attempted to block Abdussattar Shaikh and Steve Butler from testifying. Nevertheless, the JCI concluded that if the FBI had seized this remarkable opportunity to intervene, it could have capitalized on "the intelligence community's best chance to unravel the 9/11 plot" (P. Thompson *Terror Timeline* p. 171). Why, one reasonably asks, wouldn't a Congressional inquiry looking into intelligence failures be allowed to interrogate either a "mole" who'd spied on two hijackers or his FBI handler? And matters got even worse than this. Members of Congress on the JCI panel weren't just denied access to the informant; they were "summoned to meet with FBI top brass on a 'very sensitive issue'" (J. Ridgeway *Five Unanswered Questions* p. 166). Can the intensity of the resistance be explained simply by the FBI's fears of being fingered for "blowing" it? Or did the Bureau also fear being seen as coddling or sheltering al Qaeda operatives?

Speculating on why the FBI would once again resort to such intimidation, Graham concluded that the informant must know something that, if more broadly known, could threaten those in power. When it became evident that the FBI was implementing orders from the highest levels, Graham remarked on what "we had suspected for some time: the White House was directing the cover-up" (Graham and Nussbaum *Intelligence Matters* pp. 160-66).

Working from the belief that "what gets most actively suppressed may hold the most significance," we'll pay special attention to what the official investigations sought to suppress or ignore.

### The Big Money: A Self-Censored Financing Connection

Graham didn't tell all, for he had some suspicious connections in his own past. In August 2001, along with Porter Goss and Sen. John Kyl (R-Az.), Graham flew to Islamabad to meet with Pakistan's President Pervez Musharraf and Gen. Mahmoud Ahmad, director of Pakistan's notorious military intelligence agency, the ISI. Since Gen. Ahmad had ordered $100,000 sent to al Qaeda "ringleader" Mohamed Atta (*Times of India* 10/11/01), this linked the JCI's leaders to both a major funder for the alleged attackers and also to the president of a country that had long condoned Islamist terrorism.

Raising still more questions, Graham and Goss were meeting with Gen. Ahmad in Washington when the attacks began that morning (*Wash. Post* 5/18/02). And making matters even more interesting, Peter Rodman, assistant secretary of defense and member of the Project for a New American Century, also hosted meetings with the ISI leader just days before 9/11 (www.911blogger.com/node/21978). These were wrinkles within the riddle which the FBI didn't have to block and the White House didn't have to censor: the chairs of the JCI made sure they didn't see the light of day.

Though Sen. Graham made useful revelations about the JCI, he was disingenuous, it would surely seem, when he claimed he'd been "surprised at the evidence that there were foreign governments involved in facilitating the activities of at least some of the terrorists ... that is an extremely important issue and most of the information is classified ... the American people should know the extent of ... foreign government involvement" (PBS "NewsHour" 12/11/02).

Professional analysts in other countries were less circumspect about their suspicions. British General Dr. Mahmoud Khalaf, a member of the Royal College, stressed that the 9/11 attacks involved "a technical operation of extremely great dimensions." He further added, "we estimate that planning for this operation must have consisted of at least 100 specialized technicians, who needed one year for planning.... The high level of the operation does not match the level of the evidence presented.... Now the puzzling question is the preparation and training of these people.... There is no proportionality between the performance of the operation and the performance of bin Laden and his followers" (N. M. Ahmed *War on Truth* p. 361).

While someone might object to a prejudicial assumption that "Islamists couldn't have pulled all that off by themselves," the fact that Gen. Khalaf comes from a Muslim background may mitigate that perception. And Khalaf's judgment, as Chapter 16 will demonstrate, underestimates the brilliance of "master bomber" Ramzi Yousef, "mastermind" KSM, and triple agent Ali Mohammed, "the American." But that's not to say they didn't get help.

Nor was this British analyst alone in expressing doubts raised by the disconnect between a simplistic Official Story and the sophistication of the attacks. Dr. Andreas von Bülow, former state secretary for the German State Defense Ministry, agreed that "the planning of the attack was technically and organizationally a master achievement. To hijack four huge airplanes within a few minutes and ... to drive them into their targets, with complicated flight maneuvers! This is unthinkable without years-long support from secret apparatuses of the state and industry" (*Tagesspiegel* 1/13/02).

When von Bülow spoke of "secret apparatuses," he probably meant the espionage agencies of several countries, especially those of the United States, Saudi Arabia, Israel, and Pakistan. And when the defense ministry official spoke about "industry," he probably referred to the point, made elsewhere, that Boeing airliners came equipped with remote override devices which allowed someone outside the cockpit to override the pilot and fly the plane. Or he may have referred to the fact that at least one high-ranking official at the Pentagon had held a prominent role in a company specializing in remote control (www.cbsnews.com/sections/home/main100.shtml). These contentions will be explored later.

## Failure to Act at the Airlines

There was indeed serious negligence within the airline industry. In the case of American Airlines, Betty Ong, one of the flight attendants on AA Flight 11, had phoned in vivid, real-time accounts of the first hijacking. As her frantic pleas for help got relayed to American Airlines managers, however, they met with disbelief and then with warnings from AA managers to "keep this quiet" and "keep this among ourselves." In Fort Worth, two managers at Systems Operations Control agreed: "Do not pass this along.... Keep it among the five of us.'" Astoundingly, the corporate managers did not immediately alert the FAA, the FBI, NORAD, or even its own personnel at airports, let alone those in the air. This decision not to share Ong's reportage prevented spreading the alarm early in the crisis (*NY Observer* 2/25/04 & 6/20/04).

Since these delays occurred before the other planes were hijacked, even before any had left the tarmac, this stalling led to deadly consequences. Had AA's managers immediately spread Ms. Ong's alarm, workers in the South Tower could have evacuated before the second crash; city officials would not have initially told these workers that they faced no danger following an "accidental" plane crash at the other Tower. "How many hundreds or thousands of lives might have been saved," asks journalist James Ridgeway, "if the airline had quickly passed on the information provided by these courageous flight attendants?" (www.buzzflash.com/contributors/05/11/con05439.html).

One could also wonder why the airline industry, after receiving ample warning about terrorism in the months leading up to 9/11, hadn't taken more action to prevent or manage hijackings. The 9/11 Commission made thorough inquiries into what had happened at American and other airlines, but the results were relegated to the *Report*'s footnotes. In fact, Ridgeway notes, "the full contents of these staff inquiries were classified and will not be made public for years" (www.buzzflash.com/contributors/05/11/con05439.html).

Nevertheless, the JCI findings challenged the myth of the "intelligence failures." In addition, the JCI learned that in April 2001, US intelligence sources learned that "bin Laden was interested in commercial pilots as potential terrorists" (CBS 5/16/02). A few progressive news outlets came to conclude that the problem was much less a failure to gather intelligence than an unwillingness to act on it. When one ponders how much was known and how little action was taken, the *Guardian* notes, "'conspiracy' begins to take over from 'incompetence' as a likely explanation for the failure to heed—and to inform the public about—warnings that might have averted the worst disaster in the nation's history" (*Guardian* [UK] 5/19/02). Typically, though, the corporate press didn't pay close attention, and the progressive or alternative press, fearing loss of its limited readership and credibility, remained hostile to anything resembling a conspiracy.

## The "Failure-of-Imagination" Defense

In 2002, trying to tamp down questions the JCI's findings evoked, Condoleezza Rice uttered the first of her self-indicting denials: "I don't think anybody could have predicted they would try to use an airplane as a missile" (CBS 12/17/03). The following year, the Commission also overstated the importance of a "failure of imagination": "The threat of terrorists hijacking commercial airliners ... and using them as guided missiles ... was not recognized by NORAD on 9/11" (Hearing 6/17/04). Yet the Commission's internal documents told a different story: investigative reporter Eric Lichtblau discovered that "American aviation officials were warned as early as 1998 that al Qaeda could 'seek to hijack a commercial jet and slam it into a U.S. landmark'" (*NYT* 9/14/05). Nevertheless, the Commission's myth of a "failure of imagination" allowing for a surprise attack was more reassuring than the facts—which suggested that rogue elements in government or industry could have contributed to the catastrophe.

Even in areas where the JCI had unearthed significant evidence (such as the failures of intelligence and the apparent involvement of Saudi, Pakistani, and American intelligence agencies with al Qaeda), the 9/11 Commission had little to add. Though the 9/11 Commission's mandate was to move forward the investigation initially launched by the JCI, the 800-page unclassified *Report* remained unavailable to the Commission until a late date (Lance *Cover Up* p. 137). This allowed the Commission to postpone dealing with explosive issues—especially funding from the Saudis, supposedly the great friends of America and the Bush family. All this becomes clear in Chapter 8.

## The Sleuth's Questions

Without jumping to conclusions, one is reminded of the detective's adage that those persons most actively thwarting an investigation often include those who feel most threatened by it. Why, if it had nothing to hide, would the executive branch have gone through all those contortions? Why would it have so doggedly opposed any real investigation into the tragedy?

If the Joint Inquiry's *Report* wasn't nearly superficial enough to suit the White House, it was far too superficial for the civil-rights community, including a few gutsy Democrats (mostly from the Black and Progressive Caucuses) and for the disappointed families of the victims. Public pressure once again forced the White House to accept an inquiry—this time one independent of Congress and broader in scope—though, it would turn out, hardly more "independent" from the entrenched political class.

Unfortunately for American democracy, the 9/11 Commission would exhibit the same telltale signs of another cover-up. In every area of concern, it too dodged the tough questions:

- What did government officials and intelligence agencies know, and when did they know it?
- Why were many of the warnings provided by intelligence agencies from several countries so consistently ignored?

- Had American intelligence agencies put the country at risk by trying to use Islamist extremists for ulterior purposes, such as fighting against Serbia?
- If the president knew as little as he claimed, why was he allowed to remain so ignorant?
- Why did FBI higher-ups actively block requests from field agents to apprehend suspicious Muslim men attending American flight schools?

So many questions, so few answers.

From one viewpoint, the JCI was a botched first try that demanded a reprise; from another, though, it did bring more to light than one might have predicted—especially given the limits of scope and time, the pre-compromised congressional investigators, and the stiff resistance.

But from still another more important perspective, the Joint Congressional Inquiry was bad for good government. By allowing the integrity of it proceedings to be violated by an invasive FBI "fishing expedition," it set a most unfortunate precedent. The result, as discussed, was a chill that may not warm for a long time. And when secret branches of government are allowed to function with less and less oversight, they're much more liable to get out of control. Moreover, when the JCI members increased the budget for the intelligence apparatus, they contributed to a bloat that's grown beyond anyone's comprehension, let alone oversight. On this score, readers are referred to one of the best pieces of investigative journalism to appear in recent years: Dana Priest and William Arkin's "A Hidden World, Growing Beyond Control" (*Wash. Post* 7/19/10).

In chapters to follow, the ways of the 9/11 Commission will become clear, including the selection of the commissioners and the staff plus the ways the Commission evaded issues and covered the failings —or even the complicity—of prominent politicians.

# 7.   Selecting the Cover-Up Squad

*Perhaps it should come as little surprise that the 9/11 Commission Report failed to assign any real blame or demand any real accountability for the terrorist attacks. After all, the formation of the Commission itself was more or less a political accommodation, taken up reluctantly and only after the tireless lobbying by the families of 9/11 victims. And the chosen commissioners, Republicans and Democrats, were political insiders, unlikely to ask questions that might seriously threaten the White House or any other political or economic institution.*

—James Ridgeway, *Five Unanswered Questions about 9/11*


The 9/11 Commission was far more about insiders with agendas than most people realize. So while this chapter and the next won't read like memoirs featuring family secrets, they will bring out surprising facts about the players and their records.

After sixteen months of stonewalling, the Bush administration finally accepted the inevitability of a national commission. Once again, though, the sniffer dogs would be kept on short leashes. Like the Joint Congressional Investigation, 9/11 Commission was tightly circumscribed. For starters, the time allotted was very limited. Although the families of the victims and Sen. John McCain had pushed for a two-year inquiry, the White House demanded that the investigation be completed in just one. Although the parties finally settled on eighteen months, in practical terms the Commission wouldn't have even that long. And although the

Families Steering Committee had helped force the inquiry into existence, the Commission soon came under the thumb of far more powerful forces. The Families Steering Committee wasn't even represented.

Nor, as we've seen, were the vast majority of the Families' questions and concerns ever raised, let alone answered. These included:

- How could *all* levels of a trillion-dollar air defense system fail simultaneously?
- How could both Twin Towers, which were designed to take a hit from an airliner, come down in such a very short time?
- How could a *third* skyscraper, World Trade Center Building 7, have fallen down without sustaining damage from a plane? (www. ae911truth.org/wtc7.php).

When the Commission's *Report* emerged, activists from the Families expressed disillusionment with an investigation they'd pushed so hard to initiate. One among them, Patty Casazza, would express a common disillusionment: "They lied. They all lied" (Film: *9/11: Press for Truth*).

## White House Makes the Rules

The Commission promised "to provide the fullest possible account of the events surrounding 9/11" (*Report* p. xvi). From the outset, however, it became obvious that political forces were making sure the Commission couldn't deliver a full and accurate account. Congress, which created the Commission, hobbled any real investigation by granting many concessions to the White House. It allowed the administration to choose five of the ten commissioners, including the chair and the executive director, and also granted it the power to approve all appointments. Congress simply gave away its power: it, too, didn't want much revealed.

Hopes dimmed further when the White House dictated still more conditions, including criteria for membership. The Commission, it insisted, would be comprised of "prominent citizens," which turned out to mean "trusted Washington insiders." The only apparent exception was James Thompson, tough-guy federal prosecutor and former Republican governor of Illinois. Yet even he was well connected to the political class in Washington. For years, Thompson had remained a close friend of core insider House Speaker Dennis Hastert (R-Ill.). Gov. Thompson missed many of the Commission's meetings because he was consumed with extricating himself from the scandals surrounding Conrad Black, former owner of several newspapers (P. Shenon *The Commission* pp. 27, 92, 284).

## Minders and Bureaucratic Blockages

White House rules restricting testimony also limited chances for getting at the truth. When personnel from intelligence agencies were interviewed, "minders" from the agencies would be present. Because of their presence, Chairman Kean later complained about "intimidation" of witnesses (*NYT* 7/9/03). "How much candor can you expect from an FAA flight controller when his boss is breathing down his neck?" remarked one Commission staffer. "It was a joke" (P. Lance *Cover Up* p.137). Recall that Saddam Hussein also insisted that his "minders" be present when UN inspectors interviewed Iraqi scientists about weapons production. In that case, American journalists identified the practice for what it was—an obvious ploy to control information.

At every turn, the Bush administration sought to hobble the Commission. Not only would the commissioners not interrogate suspected terrorists, they would seldom take sworn testimony (Lance *Cover Up* p. 139). To make it more difficult to ferret out facts, issuing subpoenas would require approval of both chairs or at least six members (*NYT* 11/15/02). Predictably, few subpoenas were issued. One was required, though, to get New York Mayor Michael Bloomberg to finally release the records of emergency calls made on 9/11. While the Commission claimed that the city's stonewalling had "significantly impeded" its investigation (*NYT* 12/4/03), it rarely enlisted the press to help bring pressure on recalcitrant parties—whether the stonewalling came from a mayor's office or a White House obsessed with controlling information.

By creating so many hurdles, the administration kept essential information from the Commission. All requests for documents had to clear a Justice Department headed by Attorney General John Ashcroft.

The White House demanded the right to review all requested documents so it could invoke "executive privilege" on potentially incriminating information. Its gatekeeper was Alberto Gonzales, the White House counsel (www.achievement.org/autodoc/page/gon0bio-1). Neither man was known for his commitment to transparency.

Thus while Bush gave speeches about wanting to get to the bottom of 9/11, his personal attorney ensured that the Commission didn't peer too deeply into the shadows. To limit the investigation, intelligence specialist James Bamford noted, Bush tried "to throw up every roadblock possible" (*NYT Book Review* 8/20/06). When requests for documents were actually granted, the documents sometimes arrived unsorted in piles of boxes.

## Media Inattention to an Unfolding Cover-Up

"White House resistance became so acute," remarked terrorism analyst Peter Lance, "that the Commission investigators were denied access to the fully declassified 800-plus-page report of the Joint Inquiry." The delicious irony was that when a Commission created by Congress requested a report from a Congressional inquiry on the same subject, it was denied access on the odd basis of "Congressional privilege" (Lance *Cover Up* p. 137). Despite these obstacles, the Commission rarely invoked its subpoena powers. Nor did the news media, which are often so crucial to prying information out of governments, pay much attention to the interminably slow release of documents. Only a few observers seemed to perceive that the White House, after negotiating a shorter time frame, released information at a glacial pace to run out the clock.

The media's lack of attention allowed the Bush administration to pay a low political price for stonewalling. When a hearing was called in New Jersey, neither a single major paper nor a single New York TV station crossed the Hudson to cover it. According to one member of the Families Steering Committee, "the networks went AWOL." The "Jersey Girls," a group of courageous 9/11 widows, also presented the Commission with several hundred questions that the press should have raised. In one instance, "Jersey Girl" Kristen Breitweiser put her finger on a key issue: "How did the FBI get the names and pictures of the hijackers so soon after the event?" (Lance *Cover Up* pp. 140, 136).

Had the press done its job, it would have pointed out the Commission's increasingly apparent deviation from its legal mandate. The language of the law was clear: the 9/11 Commission was supposed to "examine and report upon the facts and causes relating to the terrorist attacks" (Public Law 107-306). From the start, though, a heavily compromised Commission seemed most dedicated to posturing before TV cameras, covering for those individuals most responsible, doing damage control for the military/intelligence establishments, and, above all, reinforcing the Official Story. The mandated probing of "facts and causes" never happened.

## Additional Acts of Contempt and Control

In another final attempt at control, the Bush administration initially allotted the Commission only $3 million. To make matters worse, the White House delayed $11 million of additional funding necessary for the Commission to progress toward its completion date. Though the administration finally would increase the Commission's budget to $14 million, this was still less than the $16 million and three years that NIST was given to investigate just the disintegrations at the World Trade Center (*NYT* 10/17/05). And these paltry amounts pale in comparison with the $49 million spent to probe Bill Clinton's sexual escapades and the $50 million spent to investigate the *Challenger* disaster (*Wash. Post* 10/27/05).

Beyond the time and money allotted, one can learn a great deal about the Commission by scrutinizing its members.

## Kissinger Initially Selected to Chair Commission

Hopes plummeted still further when Bush appointed Henry Kissinger to chair the Commission (*NYT* 11/28/02). The consummate New York/Washington insider, Kissinger had impressive experience in cover-ups and evasions. Kissinger had served as President Nixon's National Security Advisor and Secretary of State during the Watergate and Vietnam period; he was hardly inexperienced in dealing with "sensitive" situations. He'd managed, after all, to extricate himself from several scandals— including the CIA-assisted overthrow of democracy in Chile (H. Zinn *People's History* pp. 548-554).

Not surprisingly, Kissinger brought a reputation for secrecy incompatible with an open investigation. In addition, Kissinger was cozy with Bush and Cheney. According to journalist Bob Woodward, Kissinger became "a frequent visitor" to the White House, where he was "almost like a member of the family" (CBS 10/1/06). Despite the failure of many of Kissinger's policies, and despite his being sought for war crimes by foreign governments (*Harper's* 3/01), the networks (including NPR and PBS) present Nixon's former confidant as an elder statesman.

## Saudi Connections Do In Henry K.

But the deal breaker for Kissinger was that his clients included families and countries associated with Islamic terrorism. He'd long run a consulting firm well known to advise foreign governments and corporations. Since Kissinger was so well connected to people in power, his "advice" came at a dear price. Moreover, for many years, Kissinger had profited lavishly by representing prominent Saudis. In addition, he'd done consulting for Unocal, the oil giant that sought to build the pipeline across Afghanistan but met with resistance from the Taliban (*Newsweek* 9/22/02). Kissinger, it surely seemed, could be trusted to avoid looking into areas so crucial to the cover-up.

When 9/11 activists, not the press, questioned Kissinger, the business connections that had made him rich proved to be his undoing. Undaunted by Kissinger's fortune and fame, 9/11 widow Kristen Breitweiser, a recent graduate of Seton Hall Law School, had done her homework. When she and fellow "Jersey Girl" Lorie van Auken asked the prospective Commission chair, "Do you happen to have a client by the name of bin Laden?" the usually unflappable Kissinger "nearly fell off his chair" (Lance *Cover Up* p. 136). Rather than disclose either his list of clients or the financial ties of Kissinger Associates, the consummate insider declined the chair (*NYT* 12/14/02).

This time the news media hounds *did* howl—and Kissinger had to run, tail between his legs. While the *Wall Street Journal* continued to defend the appointment, the *New York Times* cited Kissinger's blatant conflicts of interest and characterized his selection as "a clever maneuver by the White House to contain an investigation the administration has long opposed" (*NYT* 11/29/02).

A second, seemingly better choice for chair, former Sen. George Mitchell (D-Me.), also resigned because of widely reported controversies over his links to Saudi power brokers (N. M. Ahmed *War on Truth* p. 351). In late 2003, trying to "spin" the forced resignations of the two original candidates for Commission chair, Vice Chair Lee Hamilton remarked, without apparent irony, that "all of us on the Commission will have to [recuse ourselves] in relation to some issues" (*NYT* 12/17/03). While this would prove to be a telling statement, seldom did any commissioner recuse himself or herself.

Since Kissinger and Mitchell were so different, these appointments invited obvious questions: Did Bush select Kissinger and Mitchell in part because they *did* have these connections to rich Saudis? If so, did he assume that, if accepted, both would follow self-interest and play down links to the Saudis? From the onset, the 9/11 Commission was really about story reinforcement, damage control, and "covering tracks."

Even without Kissinger and Mitchell, the Commission was rife with conflicts of interest. After the initial selections for chair backfired, administration and Congressional leaders agreed upon lower-profile insiders: former Governor Tom Kean (R-NJ) and former Congressman Lee Hamilton (D-NY) would serve as chairman and vice chairman respectively. Since the White House didn't want another embarrassment, Bush himself called Kean, urging him to take the job (T. Kean and L. Hamilton *Without Precedent* pp. 115-16).

## Tom Kean: An Outside-the-Beltway Insider

Gov. Kean's long association with illicit and regressive causes should have hoisted a warning flag. At the time of his appointment, Kean sat on the Board of the National Endowment for Democracy. In the 1980s, the Endowment had sponsored a guerrilla operation run by Col. Oliver North against the elected government of Nicaragua (*Wash. Post* 2/16/87). By 2003, the Endowment had become better known for doling out "millions of dollars to groups that fight labor unions" (S. Hicks *Big Wedding* p. 76).

Gov. Kean's business, oil, and banking connections also should have arched eyebrows. Kean was a member of the board of directors and a significant investor in Amerada-Hess, a company in secret partnership with Delta Oil of Saudi Arabia. Delta was owned by Khalid bin Mahfouz, the Saudi mega-banker who did business with both Bush family enterprises (the Carlisle Investment Group) and the bin Laden family. Bin Mahfouz was also closely associated with the Bank of Credit and Commercial International (BCCI), best known for laundering drug and terrorism money as well as for brokering the sale of US arms from Israel to Iran (P. D. Scott *Road To 9/11* pp. 93-99).

Like Kissinger, Kean was well-connected to multinational oil and drug interests that would benefit from a long occupation of Afghanistan and the planned trans-Afghan oil pipeline—a covert objective of the initial attack in the War on Terror (M. Ruppert *Crossing the Rubicon* pp. 127, 69-75). Thus, Kean's business dealings positioned him to face financial consequences if Saudis, Afghans, or Pakistanis were implicated in 9/11. The simple fact that Kean's company had been doing business with al Amoudi, Osama bin Laden's brother-in-law (*Boston Herald* 12/10/01), should have disqualified Kean from the Commission.

Although Kean served as a board director of the CIT Group, he didn't disclose this involvement to the Commission or the public. Kean sat on the board of a company that financed airlines. Just months before the 9/11 attacks, CIT Group faced billions of dollars in potential risk if anything should happen to American or United Airlines. In June 2001, just three months before the attacks, CIT sold a controlling interest to the corporate giant Tyco. As it accepted this friendly takeover, a company that stood to lose billions if anything happened to key airlines suddenly ended its exposure to potentially catastrophic losses (SEC docs: Tyco's acquisition of CIT).

### Lee Hamilton: Consummate Insider with the Right Résumé
During many of his 34-years in Congress, Rep. Lee Hamilton (D-Ind.) had chaired the Foreign Affairs Committee and the Permanent Select Committee on Intelligence. These involvements meant that Hamilton had been deeply involved with the foreign-policy establishment and the

espionage apparatus. He'd known Rumsfeld since the 1960s and Cheney since the 1970s, developing a close relationship with Cheney's powerful neocon lawyer, David Addington (Shenon *The Comm.* p. 33).

Vice Chair Lee Hamilton brought considerable experience with "blue-ribbon" investigations which had come to naught. In protecting various powerful interests during several major scandals, Hamilton had proved himself a master of nonpartisan "damage control" (Ahmed *War on Truth* pp. 352-53).

Hamilton was best remembered for the Iran-Contra Scandal. In 1986, as chair of the House Intelligence Committee, Hamilton failed to follow up on reports that the Reagan administration was illegally selling arms to Iran and using the CIA to funnel funds to the Nicaraguan Contras. Hamilton took Reagan at his word that there was nothing illegal going on—and then, when the truth came out, admitted he'd been "gullible" (Shenon *The Comm.* p. 33). Moreover, Hamilton failed to investigate several key administration officials, including Vice President George H. W. Bush.

Working closely with Rep. Dick Cheney, the vice-chairman also cast a blind eye on the involvements of Gen. Colin Powell and Richard Armitage, both of whom would later lead G. W. Bush's state department (Ahmed *War on Truth* p. 353). When it came out that hostages were traded for arms in Iran, and the profits from illicit arms sales had financed Contra attacks on Nicaragua, Hamilton again allowed Vice President Bush to deny involvement (Zinn *People's History* pp. 586-88). Though much of the Iran-Contra operation was run out of Bush's office, Hamilton managed to hide this complicity (J. Vankin & J. Whalen *80 Greatest Conspiracies* pp. 178-181, 230-38).

Later, Rep. Hamilton chaired the Congressional Task Force investigating the 1980 Republican "October Counter-Surprise." In this cynical scheme, candidates Ronald Reagan and George H. W. Bush learned that President Jimmy Carter was arranging a release of American hostages as an "October Surprise." To sabotage the release, their supporters (mostly neoconservatives) cut a secret deal with Iran's Islamic revolutionaries to delay release of American hostages until after the election, thus humiliating Carter (Scott *Road To 9/11* p. 110). Before that investigation even began, Hamilton held a press conference to clear Vice President Bush (*Global Outlook*

Sum. 04). Disregarding abundant evidence to the contrary, Hamilton's Task Force exonerated the administration.

All this "damage-control" experience made Hamilton a "safe" Democrat; after all, he'd served on *four* investigative commissions, all of which had covered up serious wrongdoing. More recently, Hamilton had been invited to join the G. W. Bush administration to advise a Pentagon National Security Study Group and a CIA Advisory Panel (AP/*Mercury Times* 3/28/03). Since any inquiry into 9/11 had to explain the major military and intelligence failures that occurred on the Bush administration's watch, was it appropriate for someone involved with *this same* administration in *these key areas* to cochair the investigation? Any conflicts of interest here?

However legendary Hamilton's failures when it came to finding any wrongdoing, they didn't deter Senate Majority leader Tom Daschle (D-SD) from inviting him aboard (Shenon *The Comm.* pp. 32-33). Once Hamilton became vice chair, he and Kean worked together to project a "public face" conveying an impression of bipartisanship (Kean and Hamilton *Without Precedent* p. 24). The pair—and the Commission more broadly—played to a common tendency to confuse "bipartisan," meaning supported by both major parties, with "independent," meaning free of interference from all parties and committed to serving the public.

## Jamie Gorelick: Equally Compromised by Her Record

Commissioners weren't just "distinguished citizens"; many brought closets stuffed with personal and professional baggage. Gorelick, a conservative Democrat, was compromised by both her current affiliations and by actions she'd taken in the 1990s. At the time she joined the Commission, Gorelick was serving the Bush administration on the CIA's National Security Advisory Panel and on the President's Review of Intelligence (www.9-11commission.gov/about/bio_gorelick.htm). Gorelick also was a close associate of CIA Director George Tenet, a prime "person of interest" in the Commission's investigation.

Previously a Pentagon lawyer, Jamie Gorelick became deputy attorney general in 1993. At the Justice Department, she was involved with high-profile trials of alleged Islamic terrorists. Deputy Attorney General Gorelick issued a memo regulating prosecutors' access to intelligence information generated in the 1993 WTC bombing cases. Gorelick's new procedures thickened the "wall" between FBI information gathered for immediate law enforcement from that gathered for long-range espionage (DOJ *Review* p. 28). Her "Wall Memo" produced unsettling consequences. Since much of the Justice Department's knowledge of Islamist operatives resided in the files of agents doing either counterintelligence or law enforcement, Gorelick's memo in effect divided the Justice Department's counterterrorism efforts (Lance *Triple Cross* pp. 167-69).

Oddly, it might seem, conservatives called for Gorelick's removal from the Commission. They hoped to shift the blame to the Clinton administration and believed, probably rightly, that Gorelick would find ways to suppress actions taken under Clinton that enabled the rise of Islamist terrorism. As the debate grew heated, one conservative commentator contended "Gorelick belongs in the witness chair, not on the Commission's bench" (*Natl. Rev. Online* 4/19/04). When the Bush Justice Department made preparations to issue reports exposing Gorelick, the president intervened personally to halt their release (*NYT* 10/9/09). In doing this, Bush gained something to hold over her head.

The Commission's *Report* made no mention of the Wall Memo, nor did the Commission's narrative mention the failed prosecutions of the 1990s. But the question of someone on a panel steering the investigation away from relevant past issues is hardly moot. It had happened before, reported ex CIA agent Ray McGovern: "As the de facto head of the Warren Commission, [ex-CIA Director Allen] Dulles was perfectly positioned to exculpate himself and any of his associates, were any commissioners or investigators—or journalists—tempted to question whether the killing in Dallas might have been a CIA covert action" (www.commondreams.org/view/2009/12/29-8).

### More Major Conflicts of Interest

Although Gorelick had no experience in finance, she ran Fannie Mae from 1998 to 2003. Soon after claiming the company was doing well (*Bus. Week* 3/25/02), Gorelick left the firm just as it was coming under scrutiny for a

$10 billion accounting scandal (*WS Journal* 6/11/08). Later Fannie Mae had to be rescued by the government as part of a $200 billion bailout deal (*NYT* 10/9/09).

Nor was this all. Gorelick also sat on the Board of United Technologies, a major military contractor and a primary supplier of engines to Boeing and other aircraft manufacturers. She was earning $100,000 a year from this involvement alone (AP/*Mercury Times* 3/28/02). But the topper was that shortly after she accepted her post on the Commission, Ms. Gorelick joined the large Washington law office of Wilmer, Cutler & Pickering. Only a few months earlier, the firm had decided to defend Saudi Prince Mohammed al Faisal, that country's third in command against "the billion-dollar lawsuits brought on by the families of victims of 9/11" (Hicks *Big Wedding* pp. 77-78). Thus not only was Gorelick deeply embedded in the military/intelligence/technology complex; she was linked through the law firm to prominent Saudis.

Gorelick and Executive Director Philip Zelikow were the only representatives from the Commission (beyond the co-chairs) to receive full access to the classified documents made available (www.readersread.com/features/peterlance.htm). After looking at a document, Gorelick and Zelikow would write a report and Kean and Hamilton would review it; then Gorelick and Zelikow would edit the already-twice-edited draft before the other commissioners—let alone the press or the public—ever got to see it (Lance *Cover Up* pp. 138-39). Along with Kean and Hamilton, Gorelick and Zelikow possessed the enormous power to suppress information.

## Slade Gorton, the New "Senator from Boeing"

Other commissioners also carried heavy political or ethical baggage, as well as serious conflicts of interest in the very matters under investigation.

In many ways, Sen. Slade Gorton (R-Wa.) had served as a replacement for a predecessor, Sen. Henry Jackson (D-Wa.), "the senator from Boeing." Gorton also abused his influence to benefit Boeing, one of his major contributors. Predictably, Sen. Gorton cultivated other close connections to the airline industry. He consulted for airlines seeking federal loan guarantees, and his own law firm represented several carriers, including

Delta (Ahmed *War on Truth* p. 354). Since the Commission was tasked with investigating aviation-security and air-defense failures, these connections should have glared off Gorton's résumé. As things turned out, his presence on the panel likely lessened the chances that the airline industry would be implicated.

Prior to his appointment, commissioner and former US senator Gorton made statements that would have disqualified him from serving on a jury. Just days after 9/11, Sen. Gorton informed a TV audience that his mind was made up: there was nothing government agencies could have done to avert the 9/11 attacks. Later, Gorton expressed doubts that "we can get much inside information no matter what we do" (Ruppert *Crossing the Rubicon* p. 465). These aren't the utterances of someone who's likely to undertake a thorough investigation.

### John Lehman: Connections to Pentagon, NSC, and Kissinger

Since all commissioners required White House approval, they also needed to be "known commodities." Former Secretary of the Navy John Lehman, a Republican, was nominated by Senators Trent Lott (R-Miss.) and John McCain (R-Az.) (Kean and Hamilton *Without Precedent* p. 32). More important, though, were Lehman's previous associations and endeavors as a New York financier. A prominent neocon and member of the Project for the New American Century, Lehman was known for his militaristic outlooks (*The Nation* 3/16/09). As one might expect from the author of *On Seas of Glory: Heroic Men, Great Ships, and Epic Battles of the American Navy*, Lehman was psychologically invested in the military, a major focus of the 9/11 investigation.

After heading the Navy during the Reagan administration, the former secretary became a special council and senior staff member to Henry Kissinger on the National Security Council, a prestigious and powerful group of insiders. Lehman also joined the board of directors of the Ball Corporation. Since Ball was a major supplier for the military and aerospace industry, once again one notes a preference for commissioners with the right connections (Ahmed *War on Truth* pp. 355-56).

As a commissioner, Lehman's links and loyalties became clear. By 2004, it had become clear that several top Pentagon officials had delivered false testimony to the Commission (*Vanity Fair* 9/1/06). When the Commissioners realized they'd received "misstatements" from top Pentagon officials, the former Navy secretary sought to protect the military establishment he'd once helped run. Lehman argued that the Commission shouldn't refer the matter of false testimony to the Justice Department. He dismissed the falsehoods as the work of incompetent bureaucrats: "whether it was willful or just the fog of stupid bureaucracy, I don't know. But ... going after bureaucrats because they misled the Commission didn't seem to make sense to me" (*Wash. Post* 8/2/06). Note Lehman's assumption that it was lowly "bureaucrats"—never top brass—who had made "misstatements" to the panel.

### Fred Fielding: Another Well Seasoned, Much Compromised Insider

Another holdover from earlier Republican administrations was Fred Fielding, a White House Counsel under presidents Nixon and Reagan. Rather than appointing someone with skill at *doing* investigations, the White House brought aboard a smooth but tough attorney whose experience lay in *blocking* them. A slick, white-haired establishment lawyer, Fielding was, in the words of the Commission's own chairmen, "a widely connected figure in Washington" (Kean and Hamilton *Without Precedent* p. 31). Should this fact have been touted as a qualification, or should it alone have *dis*qualified Fielding?

Like nearly all the other commissioners, Fielding brought major conflicts of interest. When he joined the Commission, Fielding was a senior partner at Wiley, Rein & Fielding, a law firm that lobbied for several airlines—including United, which had had two planes hijacked on 9/11 (AP/*Mercury Times* 3/28/03). If these weren't compromising enough, Fielding had also worked for the Bush-Cheney Presidential Transition Team (Ahmed *War on Truth* p. 354). Fielding went on to represent Blackwater International (now Xe), a private military contractor with a reputation for wanton violence against civilians (*The Nation* 4/2/07). Blackwater has often needed heavyweight legal help—and given the billions it's made from government contracts, can well afford it.

In 2007, Fielding became the president's lawyer again. Described as a "smooth, soft-spoken yet battle-hardened" veteran, Fielding was hired "in preparation for any forthcoming struggle with a new Democratic Congress eager to investigate the administration" (*Wash. Post* 1/9/07). He was invited back aboard to defend the primary neocon project, so dear to Dick Cheney and others, of regaining "the executive power that was lost after Watergate" (*NYT* 1/21/07).

## A Well-Mixed Bag: Cleland, Ben-Veniste, Roemer, and Kerrey

Of the commissioners who might have remained more independent, only one actually did—and then only for a short while. Early on, former Sen. Max Cleland (D-Ga.) spoke out against the White House stalls and stonewalls, commenting that they "should be a national scandal" (Salon. com 11/21/03). Unfortunately, Sen. Cleland didn't stay long. Frustrated by the administration's resistance, Cleland resigned from the Commission in disgust. His main concern was lack of access to documents, especially within the tight time frame (*NYT* 10/16/03).

### Ben-Veniste: Hero of Watergate, Defender of Underworld Figures

Since Richard Ben-Veniste had served as a pugnacious Watergate Special Prosecutor, his appointment as a commissioner initially inspired high hopes.

On the rare occasions when the Commission finally seemed to get tough, Ben-Veniste was usually the star of the show. Although the tough, no-nonsense prosecutor said he didn't care about being famous, he did seem to revel in the spotlight (Shenon *The Comm.* p. 236). As we'll see, Ben-Veniste did ask tough, even pointed questions of NORAD's generals and Bush's National Security Advisor Condi Rice. After Rice claimed that the August 6, 2001, Presidential Daily Briefing focused mainly on threats from *outside* the country, it was Ben-Veniste who confronted her with the fact that the CIA's warning was titled "OBL [Osama bin Laden] Determined to Strike *Within* the US" (Italics mine) (Film: *9/11: Press for Truth*).

More than any other commissioner, Ben-Veniste was perceived as a threat. His name, often followed by expletives, frequently flew from the lips of Andy Card, Karl Rove, and others at the White House. It wasn't just that Ben-Veniste was sharp and could be confrontational that rattled

Bush's aides; it was also likely that they recalled how he'd damaged an earlier Republican president. Most politicos have far better recollections of history than most of the public.

But Ben-Veniste lugged heavy baggage. In the 30 years since Watergate, he'd represented Boeing and United Airlines, two major corporate interests in the events of 9/11 (CBS 3/5/03). The former special prosecutor had also worked for underworld characters. One of Ben-Veniste's clients was Barry Seal, a drug-running CIA asset. Ben-Veniste defended Seal, the operative who, in order to finance the Nicaraguan Contras, smuggled cocaine from Central America to Arkansas (Hicks *Big Wedding* p. 68). Although Barry Seal was arguably the biggest drug smuggler in US history, Ben-Veniste boasted "I did my part by launching [Seal] into the arms of Vice President Bush, who embraced him as an undercover operative" (Ruppert *Crossing the Rubicon* p. 460).

Ben-Veniste did some tough questioning, but Commission hearings were much briefer than those of Watergate. Time was tightly controlled, encouraging witnesses to stall. Time often ran out on the former prosecutor just when he was getting someone on the grill. Fellow commissioners seldom pursued his line of questioning, which might have turned up the heat. In the end, not only did Ben-Veniste contribute little to the outcome of the Commission's investigation, but his direct, forthright manner probably helped put a better face on its betrayal of the public trust.

### Tim Roemer: Spy Links and Airline Associations

Of the other two potentially more independent commissioners, one blocked key challenges to the Official Story. Rep. Tim Roemer (D-Ind.) had served on the House Permanent Select Committee on Intelligence. He therefore became a member of the Joint Congressional Inquiry, the first failed attempt to investigate 9/11. After the JCI turned in its censored *Report*, Roemer became a member of the Intelligence Committee's Task Force on Security and Terrorism. To his credit, he also supported the legislation creating a 9/11 Commission.

Like Lehman and Fielding, Tim Roemer largely stayed true to his affiliations. True, Rep. Roemer was well versed on Islamist terrorism and espionage agencies, but he was also likely invested in protecting these agencies from unfavorable exposure. This became evident in the fact that he neither furnished the JCI's full *Report* nor called for its release to the Commission. (The 27 redacted pages contained revelations about the Saudi funders and US espionage agencies.) In addition, Roemer's law firm had represented Boeing and Lockheed Martin, both major contractors for the military and airline industries (Ahmed *War on Truth* pp. 355-56). The bio didn't bode well.

Roemer's most telling moment came during the testimony of Transportation Secretary Norman Mineta. As Mineta began to recall Cheney's role in the final moments of Flight 77 before it slammed into the Pentagon, he implied that Cheney had blocked activation of anti-aircraft batteries to stop the incoming aircraft. At this key point, Roemer first attempted to put words in Mineta's mouth and then changed the subject, taking up some of Mineta's time. Once suppressed, Secretary Mineta's testimony is now available (www.9-11commission.gov/archive/hearing2/9-11Commission_Hearing_2003-05-23.htm).

## Senator Bob Kerrey: Good Intentions Buckle under Baggage

Another potential maverick, Sen. Bob Kerrey (D-Neb.) on occasion raised some important issues, but these had little effect on the final *Report*. On one occasion, Senator Kerrey drew the Commission's attention to a crucial Pentagon briefing he attended at the White House just days after 9/11. He told the Commission "something happened in that briefing that produced almost a necessity to deliver a story that's different than what actually happened [on 9/11]" (P. Thompson *Terror Timeline* p. 498). While Sen. Kerrey implied that since September 17, 2001, the Pentagon and the White House had operated in cover-up mode, he didn't elaborate nor did the news media ask him to. The day after this briefing (9/18/01), the military released its second timeline of events—the one the Commission later overrode in its *Report*. In 2004, however, neither Kerrey nor the rest of the Commission communicated much awareness that the Pentagon had fudged its figures.

Though Kerrey was billed as a fair and honest broker, his involvements and loyalties made that difficult. In the 1980s, while Governor of Nebraska, Kerrey became instrumental in the cover-up of the White House "callboys" scandal (Film: *Conspiracy of Silence*). Like Gorelick and Roemer, Kerrey had ties to the clandestine world. When Sen. Kerrey joined the Commission, the *Washington Post* described him as "an influential figure in intelligence circles who has also been a strong supporter of CIA Director George Tenet," a logical subject of the inquiry. In fact, just before joining the Commission, Kerrey was involved with a CIA science panel (*Wash. Post* 12/10/03). Even more startling was Kerrey's involvement with the Committee for the Liberation of Iraq, a hawkish front for that neocon think tank, the Project for the New American Century (Ahmed *War on Truth* pp. 355-56).

A former military hero, Bob Kerrey helped the Commission take NORAD off the hook for the air-defense failures. In the Commission's hearings, Kerry was an especially tough questioner of the FAA officials Laura Brown and Monte Belger, wrongly charging that a "plane was headed to Washington. FAA Headquarters knew it and didn't let the military know" (www.911truth.org/article.php?story=2006091418303369).

**Political, Economic, and Military Establishments Investigate Themselves**
While some commentators at the time protested individual conflicts of interest, far fewer looked at the clear patterns among them. CBS, however, presented the big picture. Its exposé featured Terry Brunner, a former federal judge then heading the Aviation Integrity Project: "here we've got the most important event in America in the past 50 years ... yet we pick a bunch of people who are connected to the very people who are at the center of the question of who's at fault" (CBS 3/5/03).

When one lays out the full array of connections, two impressions become impossible to ignore. One is the sheer *number* of conflicts of interest, with almost every commissioner's résumé sporting at least one conflict that would disqualify a potential juror. The other is the definite *pattern* among the interconnections. These people didn't just bring individual issues, such as the ill-advised legal decisions made by Jamie Gorelick; beyond those, the commissioners' compromising connections often paralleled or complemented one another, with several of the appointees firmly tied to the military, the intelligence apparatus, or to the airline industry.

Finally, profession and wealth were factors. The Commission's leanings and limitations become especially apparent when one looks not simply at personal histories, but also at professions: seven of the ten voting members were prominent lawyers. The Commission, notes retired Air Force Lt. Col. Karen Kwiatkowski, brought "no thinkers, no scientists, no engineers, and no intelligence analysts to the official task of assessing what happened on 9/11." Instead, Washington insiders and the Bush administration apparently believed that their interests, if not the country's, were "best served by legal tacticians, politicians, political theorists, and political supporters" (Griffin and P. D. Scott *9/11 and the American Empire* p. 25).

Since the Commission was radically under funded, and since its members were accustomed to large incomes, they were unlikely to put their professions on hold while they worked for far less. Not having full-time commissioners led to predictable results. While much is made of the fact that most of the testimony was received behind closed doors, with no witnesses and transcripts immediately classified, less noticed is the fact that typically only one or two commissioners were present, if any (hnn. us/articles/11972.html). The staff did most of the interviews, and most of the Commissioners never read the transcripts.

Led by Kean and Hamilton, the Commission successfully conveyed an illusion of objectivity. The fact that it was bipartisan served mainly to intensify its tendency to become "political" in the sense of protecting those in power or formerly in power: the Bush and Clinton administrations. Since members came from both parties, the tacit agreement on assigning blame for 9/11 seemed to be, "Hey, exposure of this stuff could damage both of us; it's a can of worms, and we're not liftin' the lid." Judging by what the Commission delivered, it's difficult to conclude that it was motivated by anything resembling a commitment to telling the truth.

When the Commission's "prominent citizens" served government, partisan, and personal interests, they rendered a gross disservice to the country. If a vibrant democracy needs viable institutions, the Commission did real damage. The commissioners provided strong representation for federal military, intelligence, and law-enforcement establishments, each of them closely tied to corporate interests. But the FAA, on which the public depends for safety, wasn't well defended. When the FAA became the fall guy, it allowed the other institutions to escape the scrutiny they need.

# 8.   The Commission's Troubling Staff Appointments

*This is a very, very important part of history and we've got to tell it right.*

—Commission Chair Thomas Kean

I f the commissioners were compromised, the core staffers were even more so. The previous chapter showed how most of the commissioners were compromised by conflicts of interest, as well as—in some cases—their need to cover past misdeeds. But the Commission's staff was less in the public eye; its appointments could be even more fraught with conflicts of interest and, in some cases, even more ideologically skewed. One cannot underestimate the power of a former top Bush administration official and neoconservative, Philip Zelikow.

## Staff Leanings toward Intelligence Agencies

Even more than the commissioners' conflicts of interest, those among the staffers leaned toward the intelligence agencies. Of the 50-odd professional (as opposed to administrative) staffers, at least half had intelligence-agency backgrounds (http://hnn.us/articles/11972.html). In fact, an astonishing 32 of the Commission's 75 staff members had either worked for the same agencies they were charged with investigating—the FBI, CIA, or NSA—or had worked for the congressional intelligence committees that, as Chapter 6 showed, were often cozy with the intelligence agencies they were supposed to oversee (www.readersread.com/features/peterlance.htm). Were these staffers likely to come up with findings that would embarrass the entities they'd worked for?

According to Harvard professor Ernest May, a key consultant, "the urgent reporting deadline made it advantageous if a potential member of the staff already had high-level security clearances.... That meant preference for people who could be detailed from national security agencies or who had been on the staff of one of the congressional intelligence oversight committees" (http://hnn.us/articles/11972.html). One might surmise that these connections would have ensured better access to the requisite documents, starting with the *full* Joint Congressional Inquiry Report, not just the publicly available redacted version. But the supposed advantages didn't materialize.

Prof. May's characterization of the hiring raised several questions. Did the short time frame really require a constricted, mostly local pool of applicants who already had clearances, or was it simply assumed government offices would be slow in processing them? Did fully half the Commission's staff really *need* security clearances? Or was the alleged necessity for clearances a pretext for hiring an inordinate number of associates from the "clandestine services"?

The question of personal and professional loyalties of these staffers from the national security/intelligence agencies can't be avoided. Prof. May acknowledged that many on the staff who'd worked in these agencies "felt loyal to them, and some of them expected to return to work there." Careers and connections were often at stake. Prof. May, who did a good bit of the drafting of both the outline and the final *Report*, has revealed that staff teams worked out of offices provided by the CIA. That may be a telling detail. May also revealed that "collective drafting [of the *Report*] led to the introduction of passages that offset criticism of an agency with words of praise. Not all these words were deserved" (http://hnn.us/articles/11972.html).

Like loyalties to a branch of the military, affinities for home agencies were apt to prevail. Because of staffers' split loyalties and career concerns, the Commission's *Report* deliberately muted its criticism of most government agencies. Is it surprising, then, that when the CIA refused the Commission access to interview al Qaeda prisoners, most of those on the Commission didn't push for it? They certainly didn't call in the news media, as they did when the White House tried to block sworn testimony by Condoleezza Rice (www.thedailyshow.com/watch/thu-april-8-2004/condoleezza-rice).

Some staffers did thorough and dedicated research, even hand copying or even memorizing classified documents which the White House wouldn't allow them to photocopy. Many interviews done by staffers contain useful information, especially regarding (alleged) hijacker-training or air-defense failures. Many of these interviews are finally accessible in the National Archives under "Memoranda for the Record" (www.archives.gov/legislative/research/9-11/commission-memoranda.html).

These national-security/intelligence pros exerted considerable influence over what the Commission found and eventually published—or didn't. Sometimes, though, these research teams seemed to come up with astoundingly little. One, for instance, was charged with investigating terrorist financing. Yet after assigning a team to work on this key issue for many months, the Commission dismissed the money trail. In one of the most astounding statements in its whole *Report*, the Commission claimed "the US government has not been able to determine the origin of the money used for the 9/11 attacks. Ultimately, the question is of little practical importance" (*Report* p. 172).

Can the public believe that a Commission freighted with intelligence professionals was unable to enlist the espionage establishment to follow the money? What about the rich Saudis? Or Pakistan's ISI? Or the ledgers of corrupt banks like BCCI? Are we to believe that knowing who paid for the al Qaeda flight training is "of little practical importance"?

Not only did the Commission hire inordinate numbers from espionage agencies, but some of these staffers had held high positions within them. Harvard's Prof. May already held a security clearance because of his work with the CIA's Intelligence Science Board, which focuses on applied science, technology, and interrogation techniques (www.nndb.com/gov/019/000172500). The CIA involves a culture of great secrecy and the highly selective release of information; the mission of the Commission was just the opposite: to let the public see what its government had been doing.

### Another Likely Conflict of Interest: "Dieter" Snell

Much as Commissioner Jamie Gorelick likely brought personal concerns surrounding her Wall Memo, staffer Dietrich "Dieter" Snell also carried baggage—some of it, in fact, shared with Gorelick. In 1996, as a Department of Justice prosecutor working for then Deputy Attorney General Gorelick, "Dieter" Snell failed to fully prosecute the 1993 WTC bombers or the terrorists behind the 1994 Bojinka scheme. Several of the same al Qaeda plotters were involved with both plots: yet seasoned terrorists were allowed to walk away, free to make more plans. Khalid Sheikh Mohammed (KSM), the master planner of the 1994 Bojinka "airplane plot," went on to become the alleged "mastermind" of 9/11. Since these failures to prosecute may have helped 9/11 occur, surely the Commission should have investigated them. Thanks in part to Gorelick and Snell, this didn't happen (P. Lance *Triple Cross* p. 342). For several years, these failures to prosecute had gone unnoticed by the increasingly insular corporate media. When the Fourth Estate becomes a gated community, citizens seeking information are shut out.

Early in 2000, however, a secret military intelligence program called Able Danger exposed failures to prosecute key al Qaeda operatives—in fact, several of the very al Qaeda operatives who apparently plotted and executed much of 9/11. In a hasty response, Gorelick, Snell, and other prominent Justice Department officials intervened to quash the Able Danger program and, worse, to dump its massive amounts of data (P. Lance *Triple Cross* pp. 342-44, 570-71). The Pentagon, apparently fearful that the sweeping breadth of its "data mining" was gathering information might prove politically embarrassing, agreed to dump the data. The *quantity* of data dumped—which was truly staggering—shouldn't obscure its potential *significance*. Even if its revelations about "ringleader" Mohamed Atta weren't accurate, as some have claimed, Able Danger had bought in valuable information.

**Denial of Trashing Data from Able Danger**

Equally important, Snell blocked information about the dumping of the highly pertinent military intelligence. Several military officers formerly involved with the program urged the Commission to investigate their findings about al Qaeda and the Pentagon's trashing of massive amounts of data. The Pentagon had ditched about 2.5 terabytes, equal to one-fourth of the printed materials in the Library of Congress (AP 9/15/05). The officers who'd run Able Danger hoped to present a chart summarizing their findings, but Snell rebuffed them several times. As a result, the *Report* makes no mention of Able Danger—neither of its relevant findings nor the flushing of its data. Yet several staffers, Shenon has reported, remained convinced "that the other vital intelligence about the 9/11 attacks and about al Qaeda did remain in government files after the Commission had shut its doors" (Shenon *The Comm.* p. 417).

Though the dumping of Able Danger's data was later exposed in Congress, in the press, and on TV talk shows, Snell's intervention to dispose of its evidence had gone unnoticed—at least until 2006, when investigative journalist Peter Lance finally got his *Triple Cross* past the censors and into print. Lance showed that Snell had personal motives to limit the scope of the 9/11 investigation: to avoid any exposure of the failures to prosecute terrorists who went on to commit the crimes of 9/11, and to excise not only the findings of the intelligence program but his involvement in ditching its findings. Even after Able Danger had finally grabbed the attention of politicians and the media, Snell refused to testify before Congress about his role in preventing discussion of the spy program in the *Report* (Lance *Triple Cross* pp. 342-51).

As a prominent staff member on the Commission, Dieter Snell helped ensure that the "wrong" information didn't get into the *Report*. For starters, Snell blocked any mention of Saudi cash transfers—including one by the wife of Saudi Ambassador Prince Bandar—to the alleged hijackers (Shenon *The Comm.* p. 398). Readers will recall that the prince was a close friend of presidents Bush, both father and son. "Prince Bandar lives at the crest of Washington diplomatic and political society," remarked former FBI Director Louis Freeh. "Bandar practically has his own key to the Oval Office" (Freeh *My FBI* p. 8).

The Saudis were delighted with the bland, sanitized coverage they received in the *Report*. They ran a public relations campaign quoting the Commission's conclusion, which stated that it "found no evidence that the Saudi government as an institution or senior Saudi officials individually funded [al Qaeda]" (Griffin *911 Comm. Report* p. 66). This language doesn't rule out Prince Bandar's wife, wealthy bankers, oil sheiks, or the bin Laden family, all of whom were demonstrable sources of cash. It also contradicts the redacted section of the JCI *Report*, which had pointed to "the Saudi government and the assistance that government gave to some and possibly all of the September 11 terrorists" (B. Graham and J. Nussbaum *Intelligence Matters* p. 215). No doubt relieved, Prince Bandar liked the Commission's *Report* so well that he posted parts of it on the Saudi embassy's website (www.saudiembassy.net).

**Possible Motives for Involvement**

To the detriment of the nation, Gorelick and Snell succeeded in suppressing these crucial issues. Commentators have contended that Gorelick and Snell were interested in joining the Commission, at least in part, so they could investigate, rather than *be* investigated. If so, did Gorelick and Snell sense what might come out if they *weren't* sitting at the table? Since the Commission was all about control of information, it would be interesting to know who picked Gorelick and Zelikow to become the only members (beyond the chairs) to see *all* of the secret documents—that is, to control what documents others would see.

Sometimes, these questions evoked righteous indignation. British researcher Nafeez Mosaddeq Ahmed has pointed out that new documentation showed how the Commission was "utterly co-opted by a significant net of powerful, vested political, military, and economic interests connected not only to the US government but also to those suspected of supporting international terrorism" (Ahmed *War on Truth* p. 356).

**Erasing "Errors" from the Historical Record**

To help avoid the problem of FBI and Justice Department failures to prosecute key plotters (Lance *Triple Cross* pp. 405-6), Gorelick and Snell established a cutoff point beyond which the Commission couldn't search for clues. As already noted, they drew this line at five years before the attacks, which kept their problematic prosecutions safely out of sight.

Snell ran the Commission's team that wrote Staff Statement #16, which supposedly established the "the date of origin" for the 9/11 plot. In it, the staffers claimed that "mad bomber" Ramzi Yousef and "mastermind" Khalid Shaikh Mohammed (KSM) didn't hatch the 9/11 plot in 1994. Rather, the statement claimed, KSM did so by himself in *1996*, a year after Bojinka was foiled (Lance *Triple Cross* pp. 405-07). This was a convenient falsehood, for it minimized the importance of the Justice Department's failure to apprehend and prosecute KSM.

The revisions of history in Snell's Statement would be amplified in the Commission's final *Report*; only a few readers would raise an important question: If you really wanted to understand an attack by Islamic fundamentalists, why—rather than looking no further back than the origin of a specific plan for 9/11—wouldn't you examine the root causes of Islamic fundamentalism? But doing that, of course, would have brought in American foreign policy, another verboten topic.

By maintaining that KSM alone conceived the 9/11 plot and keeping his nephew Ramzi Yousef out of it—even by claiming that KSM wasn't a member of al Qaeda at the time—Snell also shielded the Justice Department from questions about partial responsibility for the 9/11 attacks. The sharp contrast in approach was indeed puzzling. The feds distributed worldwide a "wanted" poster for Yousef, complete with a mug shot on matchbook covers. All this visibility led to his capture in 1996. Strangely, though, the Justice Department kept KSM's identity quiet. This lowered visibility no doubt helped him evade capture (www.readersread.com/features/peterlance.htm). Why the Justice Department made such decisions will be a key question for a real investigation into 9/11.

If anybody knew why those decisions were made, Lance has surmised, it would be Dieter Snell, the prosecutor for the case. From this viewpoint, Snell should have been a *witness* before the Commission, not a staffer. Accordingly, when Lance himself appeared as a witness to give closed-door "testimony," the bold journalist took the opportunity to ask Snell pointed questions on these issues. Taken aback, Snell reportedly replied "that's classified," and "I can't discuss that" (www.readersread.com/features/peterlance. htm). With Snell and Gorelick, one observes a pattern that pervaded the 9/11 Commission's hearings—that the people who should have *answered* questions were asking them.

## Another Conflicted Top Appointment

Nor was this tilt at the top of the pyramid atypical, for other conflicts of interest ran rampant throughout the staff. Its deputy executive director, Chris Kojm, illustrated an obstacle that had hobbled the Joint Congressional Inquiry: political and emotional investments with the subjects of the investigation—especially the intelligence apparatus.

Chris Kojm had been a close disciple of "damage-control specialist" Lee Hamilton. After serving as a staffer in Rep. Hamilton's office from 1984 to 1992, Kojm worked under the congressman's supervision in other positions (Ahmed *War on Truth* p. 356). Since Hamilton chaired the House Select Committee on Intelligence for many years, and Kojm worked for the Bureau of Intelligence and Research at the State Department (www.9-11pdp.org/about/bio_kojm.htm), Kojm was well acquainted with institutional cultures of deep secrecy.

A Beltway insider, Kojm had held senior intelligence-network positions in the Clinton and Bush administrations. He'd worked in the State Department's Bureau of Intelligence and Research until February 2003—right up to when the Commission began to select its staff. Thus we have a key player going directly from the Bush administration to a Commission tasked with investigating that administration. This intelligence-apparatus experience deepened when Kojm joined the new renditions branch at the CIA's counterterrorism center. Looking back on his time there, Kojm told the Commission that "70 terrorists were rendered and brought to justice before 9/11" (Hearing 3/24/04). This meant that the number-two staff executive for the Commission had supervised a secret program of "extraordinary renditions," otherwise known as "kidnappings with a high chance of torture."

Important as May and Kojn were, the most dominant figure, by far, was the Commission's Executive Director, Philip Zelikow. Another Washington insider, high-ranking Republican, and leading neocon, Zelikow was hardly an impartial party conducting an independent inquiry. Given his active links to the White House, Zelikow wielded far more control than any of the commissioners, including Kean and Hamilton. (Griffin *9/11 Comm. Report* p. 8).

A glance at the Philip Zelikow's résumé would have shown several items that should have jumped off the page. In 1997, Zelikow had become founding member of the Project for the New American Century (PNAC), whose other founders included Dick Cheney and Donald Rumsfeld (www. newamericancentury.org). Less than a year before 9/11, at the behest of his friend Condoleezza Rice, Zelikow joined the Bush/Cheney transition team. Just months before 9/11, Zelikow took a seat at the National Security Council (NSC), an enclave for a powerful elite. There he joined Rice, Bush's national security adviser at the time (http://hnn.us/articles/11972.html).

These were only a few among many red flags.

Prior to 2001, as a professor of history at Harvard and the University of Virginia, Zelikow had coauthored, with Condoleezza Rice, a scholarly book on the reunification of Germany. A stylishly suited Ivy Leaguer, Dr. Zelikow was a well-known historian of the presidency and the national security services (Kean and Hamilton *Without Precedent* p. 28). Like many academics with this specialization, he'd apparently become fascinated with tactics used by power brokers.

Even more so than the commissioners, Snell, or Kojm, Zelikow revealed attitudes that would seemingly have disqualified him from wielding a powerful position on a board of inquiry. Like many neocons, Zelikow believed that governments must lie to their citizens. He wrote a scholarly paper endorsing politically advantageous public myths—"beliefs thought to be true" as formulated "by those critical people and events that go into forming the public's presumptions about its immediate past" (Zelikow *Thinking About Political History* p. 5). On the Commission, Zelikow received the opportunity to put theory into practice: he oversaw mythmaking intended to shape public opinion.

**An Article of Contention**

In 1998, as project director of the Catastrophic Terrorism Group, Zelikow was a lead author of an article in *Foreign Affairs*, the flagship journal of the prestigious Council of Foreign Relations. His coauthors were fellow neocons: Ashton Carter, another Harvard academic whom President Obama placed in charge of arms procurement at the Pentagon, and John

Deutch, former director of the CIA who'd resigned two years before. Along with other neocons, Zelikow had written about the far-ranging consequences of another catastrophic event like Pearl Harbor (*Foreign Affairs* Nov./Dec. 1998).

The article, "Catastrophic Terrorism: Elements of a National Policy," proved prophetic and unsettling. It speculated that if the 1993 bombing of the World Trade Center had succeeded, "the resulting horror and chaos would have exceeded our ability to describe it. Such an act of catastrophic terrorism would be a watershed event in American history. It could involve loss of life and property unprecedented in peacetime and undermine America's fundamental sense of security ... the event would divide our past and future into a before and after" (*Foreign Affairs* Nov./Dec. 98).

This sure sounded a lot like 9/11.

Such statements are wide open to interpretation, of course, and they've had no shortage of interpreters. Some have argued that the article parallels the statement made by the neocon group Project for the New American Century (PNAC), of which Zelikow was a founding member. It was PNAC, readers will recall, that infamously affirmed the need for "a new Pearl Harbor" (PNAC *Rebuilding America's Defenses* p. 51).

Others have seen parallels to statements made the previous year by foreign-policy hawk Zbigniew Brzezinski, who believed that pursuit of "the global domination project" required a catastrophic event:

Never before has a populist democracy attained international supremacy. But the pursuit of power is not a goal that commands popular passion, except in conditions of a sudden threat or challenge to the public's sense of domestic well being. The economic self-denial (that is, defense spending) and the human sacrifice (casualties, even among professional soldiers) required in the effort are uncongenial to democratic instincts. Democracy is inimical to imperial mobilization (Z. Brzezinski *Grand Chessboard* p. 35).

Written fewer than five years before 9/11, this revealing statement suggests the ambivalence and even satisfaction some neocons expressed privately when the 9/11 attacks produced "conditions of a sudden threat."

## Anticipating the Shock Doctrine

It's true that the article Zelikow coauthored doesn't ruminate on how a democracy requires catastrophic events in order to run an empire. It does, however, anticipate many of the most problematic legacies of 9/11: "Constitutional liberties would be challenged as the United States sought to protect itself from further attacks by pressing against allowable limits in surveillance of citizens, detention of suspects, and the use of deadly force" (*Foreign Affairs* Nov./Dec. 98). Given what has actually happened, this is deeply disturbing.

But rather than seeming to exult at the prospect of erosions to American democracy, the authors seemingly sought to convince other opinion leaders that the threat of terrorism was real and should be taken more seriously. Some would argue that this was still fear mongering, and perhaps it was. But given the hits the US had been taking from al Qaeda, and the *fatwa* (or decree from an Islamic religious leader) bin Laden had issued about launching still more attacks (*The Nation* 2/15/99), this wasn't a totally inappropriate concern. Others see the article as preparing the public, starting with the influential readership of *Foreign Affairs*, to accept the prospect of diminished civil liberties if and when a domestic terrorist attack did occur.

This said, still other items in Zelikow's background make him a highly dubious choice for executive director. For example, he joined the International Institute for Strategic Studies, a think tank associated with British intelligence agencies (S. Hicks *Big Wedding* p. 76). He'd also directed the Aspen Strategy Group, which included neocons such as Dick Cheney, Paul Wolfowitz, and Condoleezza Rice (Griffin *9/11 Comm. Report* p. 8).

## Power Positions within the Bush Administration

In 2000, on the likely recommendation of Dick Cheney, Donald Rumsfeld, and Condoleezza Rice, President-elect Bush made Philip Zelikow part of his Transition Team. Soon after taking office, Bush appointed Zelikow to his Intelligence Advisory Board, where he assisted Stephen Hadley, an immediate subordinate to Condi Rice and another prominent hawk in the White House. Clearly Zelikow was at home with the neocons in the G. W. Bush administration.

But after 9/11, Zelikow's troublesome sides soon surfaced. When Rice wanted to launch a "a whole new order," she asked Zelikow to articulate a foreign policy calling for "preemptive interventions" and "preventive warfare"—i.e., for first strikes against any country or organization deemed even remotely threatening to the US. Obliging his boss, Zelikow became a lead author of "The National Security Strategy of the United States" (J. Mann *Rise of the Vulcans* p. 316).

## Zelikow on Iraq, Israel, and Preemptive War

In plain English, Zelikow articulated the Bush Doctrine, an endorsement of preemptive war. Never content just to theorize, Zelikow played a key role in planning its first application: a preemptive war of choice on Iraq. As Zelikow rose to prominence at the White House, his connections to the intelligence, national security, and military establishments became increasingly apparent (*Wash. Post* 3/13/02). These alone should have disqualified him to lead an investigation into the military and intelligence failures leading up to 9/11.

In attempting to blunt objections that Saddam Hussein posed no real threat to the US, Zelikow made a statement that, if true, should have received wide reportage. During his stint on the Foreign Intelligence Advisory Board, Zelikow apparently made the controversial claim that the real threat posed by Iraq was not to America at all: "Why would Iraq attack America or use nuclear weapons against us? ... the real threat [is] and actually has been since 1990—it's the threat against Israel" (http://hnn.us/articles/5280.html). This surprisingly candid remark reflected the thinking of many in the Washington establishment; it implied that the US should start a major war to protect Israel, which already possessed about 200 nuclear weapons and had a record of being more than able to protect itself (BBC 9/23/00). It also raised another question with far-reaching implications: Will officials who hold two passports give their primary loyalty to the United States? This is not a question one asks at Georgetown dinner parties.

It was the White House, not Congress, that appointed Zelikow to become the Commission's powerful executive director. The Harvard historian was hardly an unknown around Washington. Somehow, though, the White

House eased him into the driver's seat, beneath the media radar. Somehow, he was appointed to run a Commission charged with investigating the administration that had appointed him. Clearly there were conflicts of interest involved with having someone who'd been a close friend of Rice, a primary object of the investigation, suddenly leave to investigate her. Some journalists protested, but not nearly enough or loud enough.

Zelikow's appointment involved a practice Americans see with increasing frequency: people in power investigating themselves—or their friends, associates, ideological cronies, and home institutions. And the media watchdogs—snoozing, scared, overfed, or gone bad in the teeth—typically fail to howl. As executive director, Zelikow controlled all the key dimensions of the investigation—who would be interviewed, which documents the commissioners would see, and what would be included in the Commission's much-critiqued *Report*. Just to be sure, he wrote much of it himself.

## Zelikow Preconceives the Commission's *Report*

Soon after Zelikow left the White House to head the Commission's staff, he hired his mentor at Harvard, historian Prof. Ernest May, also a specialist in the applied history of national security. In March 2003, before the Commission's staff had ever met, May arrived in Washington to help Zelikow sketch out a sixteen-chapter narrative. Together the two historians prepared a detailed outline.

When Zelikow shared the outline with Kean and Hamilton, the co-chairs wondered whether people outside the Commission would see the executive director's early outline as predetermining the content of the *Report*. Worried, they insisted that Zelikow keep the document secret from the rest of the staff. Apparently sensing that his professional reputation could be seriously smudged, Prof. May agreed that the outline should be "treated as if it were the most classified document the Commission possessed." Hamilton demanded that the Commission's *Report* avoid the impression that judgments had been made. "Go for the facts," he directed, apparently unaware that Zelikow had already made the big decisions (Shenon *The Comm.* pp. 386-88).

Despite the secrecy, some the staffers got a look at the outline, including Zelikow's proposed chapter entitled "the Blinding Effects of Hindsight." They inferred, probably correctly, that Zelikow, a historian, was intending to dismiss the value of hindsight in order to diminish any assignment of responsibility to the Bush administration. Soon the staffers circulated a parody of Zelikow's draft: "The Warren Commission Report—Preemptive Outline." Its chapter headings included "Single Bullet: We Haven't Seen the Evidence Yet. But Really. We're Sure" (Shenon *The Comm.* p. 389). The two Harvard historians obviously should have known how irresponsible and unprofessional it was to write history before they'd gathered the facts. But it took staffers, most of them lacking Ivy League pedigrees, to point this out.

Given this controversy, it's not surprising that spokesman Chris Kojm would say the Commission excluded information because "it did not fit with the story we wanted to tell" (www.abledangerblog.com/2006/02/it-did-not-fit-with-story-we-wanted-to.html).

## Avoiding the Historical Roots of Islamic Terrorism

Zelikow initially planned to present the whole history of Islam; if he still has an outline around, it would no doubt make instructive reading. Although he and Kean both held a doctorate in history, both ended up helping ensure that the Commission's approach—and above all its *Report*—would remain essentially non-historical.

In the case of al Qaeda, Zelikow promoted the same distortions of history promulgated by Dieter Snell (Lance *Triple Cross* p. 406). This non-historical approach also meant that they wouldn't consider the 9/11 attacks in the full contexts of Euro-American colonialism; the long-term mistreatment of Palestinians; ongoing Israeli expansion and militarism; American support for repressive regimes in Libya, Saudi Arabia, Bahrain, Egypt, and Pakistan; the rise of Islamic fundamentalism; or other possible consequences of American foreign policy.

## Zelikow the Zealot: The First Abuses of Power

What's most astonishing, though, is that from the start, Zelikow made no attempt to cover his sympathies for White House obsessions with containment of information and justifications for preventive war against Iraq.

To the amazement of many, Zelikow broadcast his connections to the White House by using the Commission as a platform to trumpet the doctrine of preemptive attack and rally support for the Iraq War. For the Commission's first expert witness, Zelikow called in Abraham Sofaer, formerly an advisor to the Reagan administration and then a fellow at the Hoover Institution, a conservative think tank. Like Zelikow, Sofaer was closely associated with the "preemptive war" doctrine—which both espoused openly before the Commission (Shenon *The Comm.* pp. 103-04).

Nor did Zelikow's ideological intrusions end here. Despite staff protests, Zelikow also brought in Laurie Myroie from the American Enterprise Institute, an even more conservative think tank. Myroie was also a special favorite of neocon Paul Wolfowitz, the Deputy Secretary of Defense. True to her recent book, *Revenge*, the "intellectual godmother" of the Iraq War contended that, even if no weapons of mass destruction were found, Saddam deserved his fate for helping with the 9/11 attacks. Myroie's polemic began by thanking Wolfowitz, his wife Clare, and Lewis "Scooter" Libby for their help (Shenon *The Comm.* pp. 130-31). Under the misguidance of Zelikow, a Commission supposedly seeking unbiased truth listened to ideologically slanted lies.

Once in power, Zelikow made no effort to conceal his previous involvements and political predilections. Zelikow acknowledged working for Rice, an object of the inquiry, but he'd lied about other items on his résumé. He listed nothing about his role in the Bush Transition Team, nothing about his authorship of the "preemptive war" document, and nothing about his critique of terrorism expert Richard Clarke, another "person of interest" in the investigation. Other staffers, shocked when they found out, surmised that Zelikow had lied because he feared that Kean and Hamilton wouldn't have hired him if they'd known. But when the co-chairs were informed about the lies, they seemed surprised but not perturbed, certainly not enough to ask Zelikow to resign (Shenon *The Comm.* pp. 170-71). The press, too, largely ignored these omissions from the résumé and the challenges they posed to the Executive Director's integrity.

But for many others, the lies weren't the main problem: it was concerns about who Zelikow was and what he was doing with the Commission. In 2003, Commissioner Bob Kerrey confronted Chair Tom Kean and threatened to quit in protest against Zelikow's conflicts of interest (AP 2/4/08). Several public interest groups, including the "Jersey Girls," the 9/11 Families Steering Committee, and 9/11 Citizens Watch, perceived such serious conflicts of interest that they demanded Zelikow's resignation (http://hnn.us/articles/5280.html). Especially incensed by the conflict of interest posed by Zelikow's appointment to the National Security Council (NSC), Mindy Kleinberg of the Jersey Girls remarked "if he's looking into the NSC, that means he's investigating himself.... When we found out who Zelikow was, we hit the ceiling" (Lance *Cover Up* pp. 138, 137). Observing his covert Republican-insider bias, the Families Steering Committee repeatedly called for Zelikow's removal, but their pleas fell on muted ears (Griffin *9/11 Comm. Report* p. 8).

Further exasperated with both the secrecy and a lack of testimonials under oath, members of the Families Steering Committee asked Zelikow not just to resign but to "take your place on the other side of the table, as a witness to be questioned in the investigation, in public and under oath" (www.911independentcommission.org/mar202004.html). Despite his major conflicts of interest, and despite these calls for resignation, Kean and Hamilton allowed Zelikow not only to stay on but also to control the Commission's agenda and who would author its *Report*. One has to wonder why the chairs didn't keep Zelikow under control. As it was, they came to resemble boys with toy steering wheels who imagine they're driving the car.

What Zelikow didn't anticipate, though, was that counterterrorism "czar" Richard Clarke would publish *Against All Enemies*, a best-selling book that presented a very different account. If Clarke didn't tell all, he told far too much for Zelikow and the commissioners' liking. Clarke's account, for instance, gave different narratives for Donald Rumsfeld and Gen. Richard Myers, and this meant that the Commission had less freedom to simply accept or adapt the stories they told (Clarke *Against All Enemies* pp. 2-9). In addition, Clarke drew on his three decades in national security work to cite the Bush administration for not doing all it could to combat terrorism. These disclosures not only made the Commission's work more difficult, they provoked fierce attempts by the White House and Republican commissioners to destroy Clarke's credibility (Slate 3/24/04).

While conflicts did arise, together the commissioners managed to cover the "sensitive" bases. As we've seen, Jamie Gorelick and Dieter Snell, both former high-ranking officials at the Justice Department, helped ensure that its irregularities weren't looked into; John Lehman, former secretary of the Navy, made sure the Pentagon didn't get blamed; Slade Gorton, the new "Senator from Boeing," could look out for the airline industry; Lee Hamilton and Tim Roemer, longtime members of the House Intelligence Committee, were positioned to guide flashlights away from the CIA and FBI; and Fred Fielding and Philip Zelikow had worked for the White House, whose interests they ably represented.

They all seemed to concur that looking at foreign policy and holding individuals responsible weren't any of the Commission's business. The FAA, the one major entity that wasn't represented on the Commission, ended up "taking the blame" to the extent that responsibility was assigned to any *institution*. Even at the FAA, though, no one was disciplined for mistakes.

With its high concentration of well-established Beltway insiders, especially lawyers and government functionaries, the 9/11 Commission was notably inbred and exclusive. Few regular citizens were allowed meaningful involvement. Often operating behind closed doors, the Commission ducked not only concerned citizens and the press but nearly all of the most troubling questions. These are among the issues that a new investigation will need to address.

To deepen our understanding, next we'll examine how the 9/11 Commission performed—for it was indeed political theater.

# 9.  The Commission: How the Process Went Wrong

*Two things must be said about knowledge deniers.*
*Their rationale is always political.*
*And more often than not, they hold in their*
*hand a sacred text for certification.*

—E. L. Doctorow

After twenty months of evasions from the White House, the Pentagon, and Congress, many Americans longed for an official account—one that provided meaningful explanations for a national tragedy. Much of the public longed for closure to the nightmare. Finally, in July 2004, an impressive-looking red, white, and blue volume rolled off the presses. Running 816 pages, more than a hundred for footnotes, it looked like the real item.

Granted, the Commission got some things right. Its coverage of the passenger revolt on Flight 93 was vivid and memorable (*Report* pp. 10-14). As government reports go, its style was remarkably readable. However, a focus on air-defense responses diverted attention away from systemic air-defense failures—especially the mysterious inability to activate the fighter and anti-aircraft defenses that so amply surround Washington.

In both corporate and alternative news media, the *9/11 Commission Report* received a warm reception. Most of officialdom, Republican as well as Democrat, sang its praises. After having opposed *any* investigation and impeded the investigation at every turn, Bush and Cheney lauded the *Report* as "very constructive." Applause from politicians, pundits, and the press, plus the public's need for closure, led most Americans to overlook its flaws.

**Ominous Beginnings**

Since Congress provided the Commission with no office space of its own, it initially had to operate out of Executive Director Philip Zelikow's hotel room. Drawing on personal connections, Vice Chair Lee Hamilton persuaded the CIA to lend the Commission a secure facility in downtown Washington. Thus the Commission had to beg a favor from the CIA, which should have been a subject of its investigation (http://hnn.us/articles/11972.html). All this didn't bode well.

Before the Commission ever began its deliberations, the Families Steering Committee, comprised mainly of 9/11 widows, provided several hundred thoughtful questions. Despite the fact that the Families group had proved so instrumental in forming a commission, the vast majority of their questions were never addressed, let alone satisfactorily answered. After reading the Commission's *Report*, the widows were aghast. They found that 200 of their questions had been completely ignored, 73 inadequately answered, and only 27 answered fully (www.justicefor911.org/ Appendices_111904.php). They were incredulous to find that even their most heartfelt questions—such as why buildings weren't effectively evacuated— were never addressed.

The Commission began to look more and more like a cover-up, a sham. Lori van Auken, one of the Jersey Girls, rightly concluded that the commissioners "decided early on what they wanted the public to know and then geared the hearings to fit this preconceived script" (P. Lance *Cover Up* p. 3). Subsequent disclosures of Zelikow's secret outline corroborated Van Auken's sense that preconceived conclusions had steered the inquiry. It became clear that when information "did not fit with the story we were trying to tell," the Commission didn't want to hear it. The official narrative couldn't be true. Even John Farmer, the Commission's senior legal counsel, later stated "there was an agreement not to tell the truth about what happened" (Farmer *Ground Truth* p. 4).

**Commission Evades Questions about Names of Alleged Hijackers**

Within hours of the attacks, government officials claimed they'd identified the hijackers, and just two days later the FBI published a list of the nineteen attackers, fifteen of them Saudis (CNN 9/13/01). Two weeks later, though, the identities of at least six the FBI had named were becoming confused. Young men in Arabic countries with the same names, photographs, personal histories, and even the same date-of-birth began to protest that they were not only alive but innocent of any allegations. On September 20, responding to their objections, FBI director Robert Mueller had to acknowledge that the identities of several hijackers were now in doubt (BBC 9/23/01). Since the passenger manifests for the flights allegedly listed no Arabic names, questions surrounding the identity of the alleged hijackers still persist (D. R. Griffin *Cognitive Infiltration* p.128). However, the Commission refused to deal with this issue because it undercut the claim that al Qaeda was solely responsible for the attacks.

In the first year following the release of its *Report*, Commission spokespersons tried to minimize the obstacles that had compromised the inquiry (*New Republic* 5/23/05). However, the record said otherwise. When the Commission sought access to documents, it repeatedly faced blockages. To block the release of documents, the White House relied on the obscure doctrine of "state secrets privilege." If these impediments weren't restrictive enough, the White House reserved the right to designate documents as "classified" (*NYT* 2/9/04). In effect, the Bush administration controlled the information available to the inquiry investigating it. Frustrated with months of evasions and blockages, Commission staffers complained about "maddening restrictions by White House lawyers on their access to key documents ..." (*Newsweek* 2/16/04).

**Different Standards for "Safe" Journalists** On several occasions, the White House invoked different rules for different researchers, giving leads and insider scoops to "trusted" journalists. After Bob Woodward's *Bush at War* and *Plan of Attack* had cast the Bush administration in a favorable light, the consummate "insider" journalist was granted access to documents denied to a national commission. Some observers wondered why Woodward didn't do more reporting on the documents the Commission wasn't allowed to see—instead of forcing it, as a last resort, to request that the *Washington Post* legend open his notebook (*Newsweek* 1/18/04). The favored access granted to insiders like Woodward spoke to the much broader problem of a careerist press corps which may place access to "government sources," "leaks," and "scoops" ahead of telling the public what it needs to know.

In another instance, this one better publicized, the White House blocked access to nearly 10,000 pages of Clinton-era documents requested by the Commission. Looking for a way around the blockages so he could defend his administration's record, former President Clinton asked his former National Security Advisor Samuel "Sandy" Berger to locate documents pertinent to the inquiry. When the former advisor got caught removing documents from the National Archives, however, he had to plead guilty to stealing government property (*Wash. Post* 3/31/05). Unlike hundreds of government and military personnel involved with the failures of 9/11, at least Berger *did* face consequences.

## Chairman Kean Cuts Deal to Shield Bush and Cheney

Special arrangements compromised the *Report*'s credibility and the nation's ability to understand its history. In a sweetheart deal, first Kean agreed to review only edited extracts of the daily intelligence briefings Bush received before 9/11. Then the Chairman allowed the president to define the terms of his own appearance before the Commission, which were unprecedented. Bush would not testify under oath, no reporters would be present, no recordings would be made, no transcripts would be released, and Dick Cheney would be present (*Wash. Post* 4/28/04). Though being "present" did not include taking questions, Cheney probably answered many of them.

This time the press raised a ruckus. The *New York Times* complained that "the White House has given no sensible reason for why Mr. Bush is unwilling to appear alone" (*NYT* 4/29/04). Journalist James Ridgeway reported "the public was prevented from even hearing the questions some commissioners might have asked—questions so explosive that they were themselves dangerous" (Ridgeway *Five Unanswered Questions* p. 167). Even worse, the public was kept from watching the slow-pitched softballs the Commission typically lobbed at prominent officials. "Because of the insistence on secrecy," notes intelligence expert James Bamford, "whatever was said in the room was largely lost to history" (*NYT Book Review* 8/20/06).

No one asked an even more important question: Why didn't the Commission insist on a special interview with Dick Cheney?

**Completely Blocked Access to Detainees**

While limited access to documents was a significant impediment, blocked access to key suspects and witnesses soon became an even greater one. Powerful resistance came from far beyond the White House, for the entire executive branch threw up imposing obstacles. In early 2004, Defense Secretary Rumsfeld, Attorney General Ashcroft, and CIA Director Tenet warned the Commission about "a line commissioners should not cross—the line separating the Commission's proper inquiry ... from interference with the government's ability to safeguard the national security.... The staff's proposed participation in questioning of detainees would cross that line" (CIA Doc. 4-0002 p. 26).

By the time the Commission had begun its work, two alleged major leaders of the 9/11 plot were in US custody: Ali Mohamed "the American" (MTA) and Khalid Shaikh Mohammed (KSM). However, neither was interviewed by the Commission, nor did it demand videotapes of FBI or CIA interviews. The closest it came was when co-chair Lee Hamilton requested access to alleged "mastermind" KSM. Hamilton met CIA Director George Tenet over breakfast, but before he'd finished the pleasantries, Tenet blurted out "Lee, you're not going to get access to them. It's not going to happen. Meeting adjourned" (Shenon *The Comm.* p. 181). Was this simply an expression of the Agency's characteristic obsession with secrecy, or did Tenet fear what the captives might say?

Without exception, the Bush administration and the CIA denied access to captured terrorism suspects whose statements, often extracted in multiple torture sessions, had already contributed to the official narrative. Even when suspects were available (and not imprisoned at Guantánamo or CIA "black sites" in foreign countries), they weren't allowed to respond to the Commission's inquiries because they "might disrupt the sensitive interrogation process" (*Report* p. 146). In effect, the administration and the CIA played the national security card, which trumped all others.

Absent tapes or transcripts of interviews, the Commission's access was "limited to the review of intelligence reports based on communications received from the locations where the actual interrogations took place" (*Report* p. 146). Although it's widely believed that Pakistan's military intelligence (ISI) had long-protected KSM, the Commission never so much as hinted at a connection—and never pressed the CIA to interview him, settling instead for third-hand information (Griffin *9/11 Comm. Report* pp. 112-13).

This inability to question suspects and detainees in American custody—some of whom probably played key roles in the plot—marked another major failure of the Commission. It was a bit like the FBI keeping the Warren Commission from interviewing Lee Harvey Oswald, had he been around to talk. As researcher on intelligence agencies James Bamford astutely noted, "talking to the detainees was especially important because the Commission was charged with explaining not only what happened, but also why it happened" (*NYT Book Review* 8/20/06). But in reality, getting the "what" and the "why" right were hardly the Commission's concerns.

## Commission Skirts Issues Surrounding Suspects

Even if the Commission couldn't interview al Qaeda operatives, it could have at least provided a more realistic account of what was known. Of the three central planners of 9/11—Ali Mohamed "the American" (MTA), Khalid Sheikh Mohammed (KSM), and Mohamed Atta—the Commission discussed only one in any detail—and that discussion avoided several crucial issues.

The *Report* devoted just one paragraph to MTA, the brilliant Egyptian-born strategist with a 23-year career in terrorism (*Report* p. 68). By almost any metric, MTA was one of the most important figures for understanding 9/11. A former Special Forces trainer, MTA was the hardened operator who penetrated American intelligence, becoming a "double agent," and also trained the Islamists who bombed the World Trade Center in 1993 (L. Wright *Looming Tower* pp. 204-07). After avoiding indictments for several heinous crimes, MTA went on to help commit many others, including the 1998 embassy bombings and the 2001 airliner attacks.

Investigating MTA, like interviewing KSM, would have involved shining a light into dark corners of the military/intelligence complex. Especially when they've been "assets" or "double agents," these master operatives simply knew too much: Who could predict what they might say—or whom they might expose as a collaborator? Chapter 16 will show how that one paragraph on MTA spoke volumes about what the Commission didn't want to investigate.

While the Commission did cover Khalid Sheikh Mohammed (KSM), it presented a short biography (*Report* pp. 145-48, 276-77) but skipped the alleged "mastermind's" more disturbing connections, especially those with American espionage agencies and Saudi funders. Moreover, the Commission's coverage of KSM skirts his most important contributions to the 9/11 attacks (Wright *Looming Tower* pp. 267, 347-8).

## No Discussion of KSM's Virtual Blueprint for 9/11 Attacks

Ignoring the connections between earlier plans for attacks and those carried out on 9/11, the Commission's *Report* discussed only the first two phases of al Qaeda's 1994 Bojinka Plot. The first called for assassinations of famous figures (Bill Clinton and the pope) and the second for blowing up twelve airliners over the Pacific (*Report* pp. 147-48).

However, the Commission made little mention of the far more prophetic *third* phase of the Bojinka Plot, conceived mainly by KSM. The Commission made it seem that KSM was only "contemplating" a third phase of the Plot that closely resembled 9/11, one that involved flying into iconic tall buildings. Actually, the third phase of the Plot was not just "contemplated"; it was on its way to execution. Pilots were already in training. In this third phase, KSM and his co-conspirator Ramzi Yousef envisioned *hijacking ten airliners* for simultaneous suicide hijackings against *several of the same targets* as those struck on 9/11. The Bojinka planners had targeted the World Trade Center, the Pentagon, CIA headquarters, the Sears Tower in Chicago, the Transamerica Tower in San Francisco, and a nuclear power plant. This ultimate phase of Bojinka, observed investigative journalist Peter Lance, represented "a virtual blueprint of the 9/11 attacks" (Lance *1000 Years for Revenge* pp. 278-80). The similarities are startling, to be sure. Though several of the specific Bojinka targets were different, all but one came from the same categories as the 9/11 targets: centers of US military or economic power and iconic tall buildings.

Nor did the Commission mention that KSM later proposed to hijack ten airliners, flying the last of them himself. After killing all the men aboard, alerting the media, landing the airliner, and setting the women and children free, KSM proposed to deliver a speech excoriating US support of Israel, the Philippines, and repressive governments in the Arab world (Wright *Looming Tower* p. 347). By performing these feats before a world audience, a grandiose KSM could become the prophetic martyr he apparently sought to become.

Somehow, though, the Commission airbrushed all this out of the picture and insisted that the Bojinka plotters "did not yet consider using hijacked aircraft as weapons" (*Report* pp. 149, 154). Had the Commission covered this third phase of Bojinka, it would have inevitably faced troubling questions: If, for more than six years, US intelligence had known about plotters' plans to hijack airliners and crash them into iconic buildings (*Guardian* [UK] 8/26/98). Why weren't officials able to prevent 9/11? How was KSM, one of these same plotters, allowed to mastermind similar attacks? By making the hijacked-planes-as-weapons scheme seem to be an idea that entered KSM's mind after the Bojinka Plot, the Commission could avoid mentioning that his scheme had been known to US intelligence agencies. It could thus evade questions about failures to act.

Nor did the Commission delineate KSM's ongoing involvement with Saudi funders, with the CIA and FBI, and with Pakistan's military intelligence, the ISI. The Commission also failed to mention that the CIA had reportedly waterboarded KSM 183 times in March 2003, an average of six times a day (BBC 10/6/10), and that much of its information came from this notoriously unreliable method.

**Simplistic Analyses of Terrorism**

Oversimplification was another of the Commission's favorite tactics. By stereotyping the hijackers as religious fanatics, it diverted attention from the hijackers' political motives: that deep resentment over American foreign policy, especially in the Middle East, was a significant factor in the rise of Islamist extremism. FBI Special Supervisory Agent James Fitzgerald, who'd studied the hijackers closely, drew the logical conclusions: "they feel a sense of outrage.... They identify with people who oppose repressive regimes and ... tend to focus their anger on the United States" (*NYT Book Review* 8/20/06).

As noted, though, the Commission decided to truncate any investigation into the past, so it wasn't much interested in establishing historical causes and consequences. This Commission was a cover-up, after all, and providing less historical background offered more opportunities to tell the story it wanted told.

## White House Cuts Deal to Make Rice Testify Before Commission

Much as the White House and other agencies had impeded requests for documents and detainees, they also blocked access to key government and military witnesses. The White House did everything in its power to keep witnesses—not to mention suspects within the executive mansion—beyond the reach of questioners. Particularly memorable was its foot-dragging on the Commission's request to interview Condoleezza Rice, Bush's friend and national security advisor. Only when the news media kept the spotlight on its refusals did the White House relent, forcing Rice to appear before the Commission and testify under oath (*Independent* [UK] 4/3/04). The White House extracted a price for access to Rice, however. It cut another deal with the Commission, forcing Rice to appear so it could avoid public appearances by Bush and Cheney (*NYT* 3/31/04). The administration fell back on the oldest trick in the political playbook: throw underlings to the wolves while the top dogs hide behind the ramparts.

### "No One Could Have Imagined..."

When Condi Rice finally appeared, she told several "whoppers." Oblivious to the prospect of perjury, Rice claimed (referring to government officials) that "no one could have imagined using airliners as missiles." Then, waffling a bit, she recalled, "there were some reports done in '98 and '99. I think it was—I was certainly not aware of them" (*Wash. Post* 4/8/04). A few days later, Bush delivered his similar, now-classic denial: "If I had any inkling whatsoever that people were going to fly airplanes into buildings, we would have moved heaven and Earth to save the country" (AP 4/13/04).

What's astounding here is not that the national security advisor and the president would lie, but that they would so easily get away with lying—that no one on the Commission, few in the mainstream media, and even fewer in Congress rose to challenge their "misstatements." Their "nobody-told-us" defense didn't jibe with a huge number of documented warnings, both foreign and domestic, about terrorists commandeering aircraft as weapons of mass destruction (P. Thompson *Terror Timeline* pp. 18-33).

Rice claimed, again falsely, that "almost all of the reports [before 9/11] focused on al Qaeda activities outside the United States." Yet when Rice was asked whether she had told Bush of the existence of al Qaeda cells *within* the United States before August 2001, she said she didn't remember whether she'd "discussed it with the president" (*Wash. Post* 4/8/04). Rice's claims to have lacked knowledge about al Qaeda in the US also flew in the face of a vast assemblage of evidence, all of it accessible to officials with security clearances. Rice had to be negligent, incompetent, or lying.

The year before, the Joint Congressional Inquiry (JCI) had concluded "that before Sept. 11, the intelligence community received at least twelve reports over a seven-year period suggesting that terrorists might use airplanes as weapons" (Reuters 7/24/03). It was hardly a state secret that the CIA had tracked "ringleader" Atta from Germany to the United States, where he joined an existing al Qaeda cell (*Die Zeit* 10/03/02). It was also well known that the Pentagon's Project Able Danger had amassed data on al Qaeda operatives in several countries, including the US (*NYT* 8/9/05).

By summer of 2003, understanding that its credibility was at risk, the Commission became desperate to see Presidential Daily Briefings (PDBs). Kean and Hamilton were aware that the Commission must get them—or at least be *seen* as trying to get them—to maintain any credibility. According to reporter Philip Shenon, "the PDBs were becoming the 'holy grail' for the 9/11 families and for the press corps." Some commissioners probably recalled the uproar when the public learned the Warren Commission hadn't seen files on Operation Mongoose, the Kennedy administration's plan for the CIA to assassinate Fidel Castro (Shenon *The Comm.* pp. 214-15, 75).

## Rice Changes Her Story, Lies Under Oath
Through the pleas of ignorance made by Rice and others, the White House positioned itself to minimize what was known immediately before the

attacks. But the famous Presidential Daily Briefing (PDB) of August 6, 2001 posed a problem. In 2004 Rice again falsely claimed that the long memo contained only "historical" information from 1998 and before, "not threat reporting … not a warning." Yet when the White House finally had to release the PDB, it was seen to contain considerably more than just historical background. Instead, it clearly *was* an "alert." Titled "Bin Laden Determined to Strike in US," the PDB was difficult to construe as anything other than an urgent warning about an *imminent* al Qaeda threat from *within* the country. Yet Rice denied the dire warnings in the memo and lied under oath before several 9/11 widows, the Commission, and the world (www.youtube.com/watch?v=CcrgeuLb3dQ).

Among themselves, Democratic commissioners groused that Rice had crossed the "threshold" between spin and perjury, but they never went public with their concerns (Shenon *The Comm.* pp. 237-38). While the Commission got more assertive in demanding to see the August 6 PDB, redactions not only allowed the administration to dodge the major contradictions raised by the memo; they helped Bush's national security adviser evade the consequences of lying about it.

Reversing course, Rice had to tacitly admit that yes, warnings had been received; and yes, they were passed on to the FBI, which had 70 ongoing investigations into terrorism. She also admitted that "for more than 20 years, the terrorist threat gathered and America's response across several administrations of both parties was insufficient." At the same time, however, she contended that there was "nothing in particular the Bush administration itself could have done differently that would have prevented the attacks" (*Wash. Post* 4/9/04).

Yet even if Rice had somehow misread the PDB as simply "historical" and "not a warning," counterterrorism expert Richard Clarke *had* warned her about impending attacks—and in no uncertain terms. Just two days before, on August 4, he'd written his boss, asking her, "are we serious about dealing with the al Qaeda threat?" (Shenon *The Comm.* pp. 148, 64-65).

Commission Executive Director Zelikow consistently defended the administration's decision to release only edited versions of PDBs and adamantly opposed demands for interviews with the CIA analysts who wrote them (*Sunday Herald* [Scotland] 3/24/03). He claimed that the CIA was opposed to the idea "since the career people involved in preparing and presenting PDBs would be intimidated, disrupting the sense of confidentiality and candor they considered essential" (Shenon *The Comm.* pp. 376-77). This is the standard excuse used by intelligence agencies: "if you force us to give testimony, you'll hamper our work." In many cases, this might not be a bad thing.

### Suppressed Interviews: Muzzling or Marginalizing Key Witnesses

As we've just seen, the Commission blocked many interviews, such as those repeatedly requested by the military officers who ran Project Able Danger. Less known until recently, however, is that Commission staffers conducted other interviews that, unfiltered, were often quite revealing. Although some of these were mentioned or partially summarized in the *Report,* many others weren't mentioned at all. Notes from the interviews were locked away in the National Archives until 2009.

Eyewitness William Rodriguez, FBI whistleblower Sibel Edmonds, and military intelligence expert Col. Anthony Shaffer all found themselves muzzled, marginalized, and deliberately silenced.

William Rodriguez, for twenty years a custodian at the North Tower, provided one example. While the Bush administration had initially wined and dined Rodriguez as a hero, the Commission didn't like his talk of explosions at the WTC. So when it came time for Rodriguez to testify, the Commission insisted that he do so behind closed doors. Sequestered away from the news media, Rodriguez told investigators about hearing explosions in the WTC basement and then observing dramatic evidence of their destructive power (www.911blogger.com/node/19439). The Commission, however, never called the other eyewitnesses he recommended, including several first responders.

In a more actively aggressive way, the Commission also squelched Sibel Edmonds, the former FBI translator-turned-whistleblower who'd seen documents connecting prominent officials to the crimes of 9/11. In her work with the Bureau, Edmonds discovered and reported serious security breaches, cover-ups, and intentional blocking of intelligence with national security implications. After 9/11, the former translator charged the FBI with knowing that terrorists planned to fly planes into the WTC yet did nothing to stop them (www.prisonplanet.com/Pages/230904_edmonds.html).

Though Ms. Edmonds also gave several hours of closed-door testimony, she, too, wasn't mentioned in the *Report*. Her detailed depositions apparently threatened not just the Commission but also the FBI. Over several years Edmonds has faced the longest-standing gag order ever issued by the Justice Department (www.alternet.org/mediaculture/66823). But even this hasn't silenced this courageous truth teller. Much as she had spoken out about the FBI's mishandling of information, Edmonds also exposed a black market for nuclear materials (allegedly known to the FBI) that included high officials at the Pentagon and in Congress (*London Times* 1/20/08).

The Commission also stifled several other whistleblowers, including FBI informant Randy Glass, whom a Pakistani intelligence agent had warned in 1999 that "those towers are coming down" (*Palm Beach Post* 10/17/02). These people had tales to tell, to be sure, but their narratives didn't sync with Zelikow's outline.

In other prominent cases, the commissioners refused to hear testimony from highly relevant sources. Three of the officers who'd led Able Danger, the Pentagon's huge "data-mining" program, made repeated attempts to communicate what they knew to the Commission—including that Able Danger had pre-identified two of the three cells responsible for 9/11— but the panel's staffers rebuffed their overtures and didn't include this information in the final *Report* (CNN 8/17/05).

The Commission's lack of interest in finding out what actually happened was becoming fully evident.

## Undercutting Clarke, Suppressing Mineta's Revelations

During the investigation, Richard Clarke contradicted Rice's testimony, pointing out that al Qaeda wasn't a high priority for the new Bush administration. Clarke had presented ample evidence to document White House inattention to terrorism. Though he didn't tell all—and at times lied about what he must have known—Clarke disclosed far too much for the Commission's leaders. In so doing, he became the arch nemesis of

Zelikow. Clarke corroborated the testimony of witnesses Zelikow sought to discredit—among them Transportation Secretary Norman Mineta, who'd reported hearing Cheney give what he believed was a shoot-down order. This was by far the most revealing moment in the public hearings (www.youtube.com/watch?v=bDfdOwt2v3Y).

It wasn't just a matter of canning interviews that staffers conducted; the Commission also excised highly relevant disclosures made at its hearings. Although these were part of the record, they often didn't appear in its *Report*. This was especially apt to occur when the testimony cast shadows on the Pentagon or the White House. The Commission's deletions included testimony from Secretary Mineta, who'd worked alongside Cheney in the bunker where the latter was calling the shots that morning. Readers will recall that Mineta was indiscreet enough to suggest that the vice president never received a shoot-down order from the president (*Newsweek* 2/27/06). Worse, Mineta's testimony implied that Cheney actually *allowed* a hijacked airliner to enter the highly restricted, well-defended airspace over the nation's capital. By implication, Mineta's narrative of Cheney's reaction to news of incoming Flight 77 accused the vice president of issuing a stand-down order.

This wouldn't do. It's hardly surprising that the Commission chose to suppress the Secretary Mineta's testimony—even to the point of initially scrubbing the videotape from its archives. Coverage of important issues before the Commission—notably White House inattention to al Qaeda and disregard of multiple warnings—were deliberately blipped from the screen. As even Prof. Ernest May, one of the lead writers, had to admit, "the *Report* veils all this" (*New Republic* 5/23/05).

### The "Late-Notification" Defense

But even the deletion wasn't enough, so the Commission resorted to its forte—time warps. To make sure that Mineta's revelation "couldn't possibly be true," the Commission moved the time of the FAA's identification for incoming Flight 77 to 9:34, about eight minutes later than Mineta had reported (Comm. Staff Statement #17). Its *Report* made no mention that fully 38 minutes earlier, FAA controllers had determined that Flight 77 was way off course, out of radio contact, and emitting no transponder signal.

This much later time of 9:34 had the airliner a mere three miles from its target, ready to swoop down at 500 mph (NTSB 2/19/02). In this scenario, reaction time was short, so if air defenders attempted to take the plane out, they'd have had less chance of success. Therefore, if it were shown that Cheney had given a stand-down order allowing an incoming aircraft to reach the Pentagon, it could be "justified." This time shift typifies the tactics of a Commission that relied on a key principle: those who control the perceived times of events also control the narrative that connects them. This extensive reliance on time shifts will be the focus of Chapter 11.

The 9/11 Commission distorted what it included and dismissed much that was pertinent to understanding the "what" and "why" of 9/11. Its omissions surrounding the World Trade Center, for instance, were particularly amazing. In discussing the WTC, it provided little analysis of the "collapses" and denied that the airliners' "black boxes" were recovered, contradicting workers who reported finding two in the debris and turning them over to the FBI (*Phila. Daily News* 10/28/04). The Commission failed to even mention the fall of WTC-7, the 47-story skyscraper that mysteriously came down without taking a hit from a plane.

## New York's Mayors: Big Time Suppression, Evasion, and Denial

After the Commission disbanded, former chairs Tom Kean and Lee Hamilton revealed that the hearings in New York were hampered by fears of "criticism that might accompany a comprehensive assessment of the emergency response on the morning of September 11" (Kean and Hamilton *Without Precedent* pp. 213-17). Simply put, the chairs were scared about seeming to challenge the heroic myth of Rudy Giuliani and the exalted stature of first responders.

### "America's Mayor" Gets an Intentional Pass

First the Commission interviewed Giuliani behind closed doors; then it released only a censored version of the former mayor's testimony. In the public meeting, the Commission lobbed whiffleball questions at Giuliani. By Kean and Hamilton's own admission, "there were no questions posed to him about communication problems between police and firefighters in the

Towers, or why NYC had built its emergency response command center in the WTC after the complex had been the target of the 1993 terrorist attack" (Kean and Hamilton *Without Precedent* pp. 213-17).

Outspoken first responders and members of the affected families were well aware that Giuliani had refused to adequately replace the emergency radios that had malfunctioned back in 1993 (J. Joyce and B. Bowen *Radio Silence F.D.N.Y.* pp. 138, 169). At one public hearing, members of these groups shouted "the radios, the radios," but Chairman Kean ignored their pleas to have Giuliani address this issue. Yes, one can ask, along with Philip Shenon, "would the Commission be willing to take on the most popular political figure in the country—the president-in-waiting, it seemed...? [Giuliani] was a hero, the embodiment of everything Americans wanted to believe about themselves on 9/11" (Shenon *The Comm.* pp. 349-50). But such an inhibition doesn't excuse the unwillingness to address Giuliani's failure to replace the radios. The firefighters and the surviving family members deserved far better not just from the mayor but from the Commissioners.

## Mayor Bloomberg Turns Defensive, Blocks Investigation

Though Giuliani was no longer mayor, his successor was quick to parry any challenges. When the Commission came to New York, the office of billionaire Mayor Michael Bloomberg demanded to know "what are you doing here?" Oblivious to the Commission's (seldom used) powers of subpoena, Bloomberg first refused to appear; then he refused to take questions. After that, the mayor himself blasted the Commission, claiming "it had no mandate to investigate New York." Later, ex-chairs Kean and Hamilton admitted they were intimidated by the mayor's bellicose posturing and the prospect of angry crowds at hearings (Kean and Hamilton *Without Precedent* pp. 27, 50, 213-17).

It did seem odd that a local official would try to dictate conditions to a national inquiry. Was Bloomberg trying to garner political support from the Fire Department by protecting its top brass from unfavorable exposure? What, one has to wonder, did Bloomberg and Giuliani fear a real investigation might uncover? Could it have involved the rapidity and secrecy of the cleanup at Ground Zero—or the epidemic of health problems that had already begun to plague many brave souls who'd worked there?

The Commission's own co-chairs later expressed their concerns about criticism from powerful New Yorkers protective of "America's mayor," especially those who "saw the 9/11 response as the cornerstone of the mayor's legacy" and the key to his candidacy for president (Kean and Hamilton *Without Precedent* pp. 213-17, 229, 231). Not surprisingly, the Commission made no mention of other persistent questions for which we still have no answers, such as why Giuliani spoke of hearing that the Twin Towers were coming down—yet while vacating his own command center in WTC-7, failed to order a full evacuation of the Twin Towers (Griffin *9/11 Comm. Report* pp. 30-31).

While the Commission's deferential treatment allowed Giuliani to retain his laurels as "the hero of 9/11," the evidence suggests just the opposite. According to one recent analysis, "Giuliani had revised his own history, casting himself as a prescient hawk on terrorism when in fact he ran his administration as if terrorist attacks simply did not exist, too distracted by pet projects and turf wars to attend to vital precautions" (W. Barrett and D. Collins *Grand Illusion: The Untold Story of Rudy Giuliani and 9/11* p. 28).

## What the Commission Evaded or Distorted Is Instructive

Perspectives that "did not fit with the story we wanted to tell" simply got ignored or suppressed. Such omissions illustrate that what is distorted, denied, suppressed, or omitted often indicates how "sensitive" the information is—and that such matters should be of special interest to us, the citizen investigators who want to find out the truth.

Here we're talking about protection for administration insiders—especially at the White House, the Pentagon, and the intelligence agencies—combined with suppression of other perspectives. This wasn't just about lack of access documents and to KSM, MTA, and other key al Qaeda planners.

While these blockages no doubt compromised the Commission's *Report*, they were mainly the doing of the White House and the CIA. But it was the Commission itself that squelched Secretary Mineta, Sibel

Edmonds, and other FBI whistleblowers plus the officers who wanted to report on findings from Project Able Danger (Lance *Triple Cross* pp. 327-331).

These are among literally hundreds of significant omissions, distortions, and evasions that, taken together, helped to fashion a national myth. The Commission's *Report* became a "sacred text," to be treated as holy writ by millions; the next chapter examines key themes within the narrative the Commission told.

# 10. The Commission's Report: "Not Bad for Government Work"

*If the Bush administration was innocent of involvement,*
*why did they feel a need to cover up so much?*

—USAF Col. Robert Bowman, PhD

This part of our overview will examine how the Commission refused to look at evidence challenging its outline, changed the times for key events to cover for top officials, and utterly failed to hold individuals responsible. Not surprisingly, the Commission also completely ignored questionable relationships between the government agencies and Islamist operatives. Although the Commissioners rewrote parts of the narrative, they largely reinforced preconceptions about what happened on 9/11. Ready to believe a comforting Official Story, the public paid it little mind. The *Report* is a well-crafted artifact whose veneer gleamed with Beltway polish.

## Shallow Scope/Lack of Historical Depth

Before the Commission ever got underway, it made decisions to limit the scope of its investigation in ways that would affect its conclusions. In order *not* to look at several embarrassing US intelligence lapses, law-enforcement failures, and close associations with Islamist groups, the commissioners agreed to look only five years back, to 1996. Commissioner Jamie Gorelick, who pushed for this time limitation, seemed pleased to report that "the vast preponderance of our work ... focused on the period of 1998 forward" (*NYT* 4/14/04). As we've seen, however, the 1996 date in effect eliminated highly relevant events that would have allowed readers to better understand the attacks. If you wanted to get to the bottom of things, why would you deliberately skim the surface?

While the Commission described its task as "looking backward in order to look forward" (*Report* p. xvi), it offered more surface history than cause-and-effect analysis. It was a given that US policies and interventions widely perceived as skewed toward Israel and Saudi Arabia and against the Palestinians wouldn't be discussed, let alone related to Islamist extremism.

When it came to the Middle East, the Commission avoided even the most basic considerations. When, for instance, President G. H. W. Bush decided to drive the Iraqis out of Kuwait, he extended a tradition of armed intervention against Islamic nations that intensified Islamist rage against the US. And when Bush established and Clinton expanded bases in Saudi Arabia, the Muslim Holy Land, they further enraged many Muslim fundamentalists (N. M. Ahmed *War on Truth* pp. 12-13). In 1993, just two years later, Islamist militants delivered their first strike against America: they bombed the World Trade Center. Were these actions possibly a contributing cause? The Commission never asked.

Because of these failures to make connections, the Commission's conclusion that "the terrorists exploited deep institutional failings in our government" seems simplistic at best. The Commission offered no evidence that the perpetrators studied, understood, and then exploited the failings of agencies within the US government. True, brilliant operatives like KSM and MTA did study their enemies: since MTA served in the Army Special Forces and worked as an informant for the CIA and FBI, he was very well positioned to do so (P. Lance *Triple Cross* pp. 6-7, 292-93). While there's some evidence that the alleged hijackers flew on airliners to better understand airport security protocol, there's no evidence that they studied air-defense configurations, radar capabilities, fighter scramble times, or the frequency of military exercises.

While the *Report* overplayed *some* actual factors, it underplayed or ignored *many* others of crucial significance—including the extensive insider trading on the stock market and the disruption caused by at least six military exercises or "war games" running on 9/11. The Commission's hearings touched upon past exercises but entirely avoided the issue of the exercises being conducted on 9/11 (M. Ruppert *Crossing the Rubicon* pp. 238ff, 333ff). Thus the Commission was able to skirt key questions: Who planned and approved so many exercises for the morning of September 11? How many of them went through Secretary of Defense Rumsfeld? Why would so many be scheduled on the same day?

Many thoughtful observers have raised questions about the Commission's oversimplified Official Story, in which vast military and intelligence establishments were caught napping by nineteen terrorists commanded by a religious fanatic in Afghanistan. This is quite a tale. Especially when we consider that most air-defense agencies were running war games that morning, putting many personnel on alert, it's tough to believe that the White House, the Pentagon, the FBI, the CIA, and the FAA were all caught off guard, snoozing at their desks or asleep in the control tower.

### Issues the Public Wasn't Supposed to Recall

Apparently, the Commission expected the public and the press would forget several key facts. One is that air-defense commanders had been trained to "scramble" fighter jets and routinely *intercept*—not shoot down—errant aircraft. This was standard operating procedure for many years; Air Force pilots intercepted planes all the time—up to a hundred of them a year—and they needed no permission beyond that of base commanders (CBS 8/14/04). These procedures, which had worked admirably for years, were suddenly changed just three months before 9/11. Under this new directive, all requests for help with hijackings had to go through the National Military Command Center at the Pentagon and then through the Secretary of Defense (DoD Directive CJCSI 3610.01A). This meant that if the secretary wasn't immediately available, the military responses to hijackings might be significantly slowed.

As we've so often seen, the Commission frequently relied on limiting assumptions to avoid issues, so it's not surprising that it would rely on them in its analysis of air defenses. The Commission's approach to explaining air-defense failures tended to assume that jet interceptors were the only means of defense. Actually, interceptor aircraft were only *one* wing of US air defenses; the other included anti-aircraft guns and surface-to-air missiles. This isn't a stunning revelation, but the press allowed the Commission—which was loaded with Washington insiders connected to national security, military, and intelligence agencies—to get away with acting as though fighter aircraft were the only way to defend the nation's capital.

The assumption that fighters were the only line of defense flew in the face of well-known recent history. During the first Gulf War, a battery of surface-to-air missiles was installed on the roof of the White House and that installation has remained there ever since (*Daily Telegraph* [UK] 9/16/01). Moreover, portable surface-to-air missiles had protected President Bush on trips, including one to the July 2001 Economic Summit in Genoa, Italy. In fact, portable missiles were deployed at Bush's hotel in Florida on the night before 9/11 (http://tinyurl.com/zv8dt).

Why would anyone simply *assume*, without providing any rationale, that such missiles protected the country's president but not its sprawling military complex? If, on the contrary, one more logically infers that the Pentagon, headquarters for the world's largest military establishment, was protected by similar defensive systems (www.fas.org/man/dod-101/sys/missile/rim-7.htm), then why weren't either anti-aircraft guns or missiles activated to defend it?

If one accepts Transportation Secretary Mineta's testimony implying that Cheney refused to approve a shoot down of Flight 77 as it zeroed in on the Pentagon, then one has to wonder, What mode (or modes) of interception did Cheney feel he needed to stand down?

### The "Caught-by-Surprise" Defense

Throughout its *Report*, the Commission returned to its favored excuse for the spectacular air-defense failures: unpreparedness, exacerbated by bureaucratic bungling and poor communication. It asked the country to believe that the hijackers were able to surprise both the world's premier intelligence-gathering network and "a military unprepared for the transformation of commercial aircraft into weapons of mass destruction." According to the Commission, "the threat of terrorists hijacking commercial airliners within the United States and using them as guided missiles was not recognized by NORAD before 9/11" (*Report* pp. 31, 17).

But the public record, as the commissioners must have known, indicated quite the opposite. In fact, the North American Aerospace Defense Command (NORAD) and the Pentagon *had* conducted drills which "gamed" that very tactic of using airliners as missiles (Ruppert *Crossing the Rubicon* pp. 333ff). The Commission apparently assumed that its readers had very short memories. It apparently figured that the public and the press had forgotten that, just two months before its *Report* came out, a mass-audience newspaper article had reported a military drill planned in July of 2001 which "posed hijacked airliners, originating in the United States, used as weapons to crash into targets including the World Trade Center" (*USA Today* 4/18/04). And this was only one of several exercises which, before 9/11, had simulated attacks using commercial or private aircraft as missiles. These and other military drills will receive our scrutiny in Chapter 14.

Attempting to protect its "caught-by-surprise" thesis, the Commission chose to exclude a vast amount of information. Though the Pentagon and the CIA had "gamed" suicide hijackings, the Commission preferred not to have this known. Similarly, it was surely relevant that "since 1996, the FBI had been developing evidence that international terrorists were using US flight schools to learn to fly jumbo jets" (*Wash. Post* 9/23/01). This, too, the Commission failed to discuss. In characteristic fashion, it went to great lengths to protect the military/intelligence establishment.

### The Incompetence Defense

Why would the Commission, apparently with the approval of the national security apparatus, want to make the military establishment and the intelligence agencies look ignorant, even inept? Perceptive political analyst Michael Parenti offers an insightful hypothesis: policy makers and military leaders, he points out, frequently "seize on incompetence as a cover," a way of denying responsibility for, let alone involvement in, a catastrophic event. Soon enough, the admission of incompetence was "eagerly embraced by various commentators" and the public, who preferred to see their leaders as incompetent "than to see deliberate deception" (Parenti *Terrorism Trap* pp. 93-94).

In addition, Griffin has noted, institutional actors are usually relieved because "a mere charge of incompetence does not bring with it a threat of prosecution for, among other things, mass murder" (Griffin *9/11 Comm. Report* p. 263). When we understand this psychological need to believe that those supposedly protecting us are trustworthy, even if sometimes incompetent, we understand a great deal about public resistance to looking deeply into 9/11.

## Excuses Made by Intelligence, Air-Safety and Military Officials

The Commission not only accepted the excuses but actively promulgated them, embellishing several for mass public consumption.

- **"In a classic case of 'stove piping,' American intelligence agencies didn't talk to each other; the CIA and the FBI failed to communicate."** While it was appropriate for the Commission to point out "structural barriers to performing joint intelligence work," it was surely inappropriate for it to ignore several key moments when agencies, according to existing structures, could have communicated but did not, allowing the alleged hijackers to enter the country (*Report* pp. 407ff, 181-2, 353-57).

- **"American intelligence didn't know enough to grasp the seriousness of the threat."** By largely limiting its scope to the five years before the attacks, the Commission tended to make it appear that only in the last few months beforehand did the intelligence apparatus start to bring in alarming information (*Report* Chapt. 8). The Commission allowed the CIA and FBI to minimize or classify the information they'd gathered over many years about al Qaeda and Islamist terrorism (N. M. Ahmed *War on Truth* pp. 157-200). Thus while press accounts, court records, and spy-agency files teemed with information about al Qaeda operatives, the public was asked to believe that little was known before the attackers struck.

- **"America's defenders experienced a 'failure of imagination.'"**
Citing "a failure of imagination" to explain the Pentagon's supposed
inability to imagine how a hijacked airliner could become a weapon of
mass destruction, the Commission attempted to excuse the failure of
air defenses (*Report* p. 335). But NORAD had been conducting exercises
based on exactly this scenario for several years beforehand. In fact, one
of the war games running on 9/11 called for this type of attack (Ruppert
*Crossing the Rubicon* pp. 333ff).

- **"Turning off the planes' transponders caught the FAA by surprise
and made the airliners invisible to radar."** The FAA claimed that it
was caught by surprise when the hijackers turned off the transponders
(electronic signal senders). When this was done, some FAA officials
claimed, airliners "disappeared" from its radar screens. Ignoring the
attention that civilian and military agencies had devoted to hijackings,
the Commission contended that US air defenses were "improvised by
civilians who had never handled a hijacked aircraft that attempted
to disappear" (*Report* p. 31). These claims were not true; planes without
transponder signals don't "disappear" from radar screens; when the
transponder goes off, the plane's identity tag disappears and its altitude
is no longer indicated. A plane without a transponder signal stands out:
that why the FAA's own manual listed a switched off transponder as one
of the *signs* that a plane is hijacked (D. R. Griffin *9/11 Comm. Report* p. 259).

- **"Late notification from the FAA was the main reason NORAD
wasn't able to launch planes in time to stop the airliners."** The
Commission adopted most of the military's timeline, especially its
consistent implication that the FAA was tardy in asking for military
intervention. But it also altered the timeline so that NORAD was
seemingly notified too late. Citing one puzzling example, scholar/
analyst David Ray Griffin asked how the Commission could claim
the military received no notification about Flight 175 (which hit the
South Tower at 9:03)—when "NORAD had maintained for almost
three years that it had" (Griffin *9/11 Comm. Report* p. 255).

- **"NORAD's defenses were configured outward, so it was difficult to track those hijacked planes."** The Commission promoted the Pentagon's claim of an outward orientation of American air defenses. It tried to explain this orientation as a holdover from the Cold War, when NORAD's defenses were configured outward to intercept against Soviet bombers (*Report* p. 16). By 2001, however, the Soviet threat was long defunct. Why, a decade later, would defenses still be configured against a nonexistent threat?

- **"Defending the interior of the country wasn't the military's responsibility."** Not only were defenses configured outward, high-ranking Pentagon brass claimed, but the military assumed no responsibility for "internal" hijackings. This, they argued, was because the Constitution prohibits *Posse Comitatus*—i.e., the use of the military for domestic law enforcement. Echoing these spokespersons, the Commission (in a moment of exceptional absurdity) echoed the claim that NORAD's mission involved only "defending against external attacks" (*Report* p. 16). If the Commission's contention were true, why had the Air Force been intercepting dozens of errant planes each year over US territory? This logic would deserve red ink on a sophomore midterm.

- **"Beyond the fighters from two bases, one in Massachusetts and one in Virginia, no other interceptors were available."** The Commission made no mention of the fact that other fighters apparently *were* available and that some were already in the air. Two F-16s from Andrews Air National Guard Base, for instance, were training about 200 miles from Washington. Commanders could have ordered them back immediately to protect the nation's capital. But they didn't, and the Commission never asked why. These F-16s finally arrived over Washington nearly two hours after the Pentagon was hit (*Aviation Week* 9/9/02).

- **"Because of base closings in the 1990s, NORAD had only two bases in the northeast sector with fighters on alert that morning"** (Griffin *9/11 Comm. Report* p. 258). While some bases had been closed or taken off "on-alert" status, this contention overlooked the fact that other bases run by the Air National Guard (thus not part of NORAD) *did* have fighter jets on active alert or training status.

Andrews AFB was (and is) home to the 113th Wing of the DC National Guard, whose mission is to protect the nation's capital (www.globalsecurity.org/military/facility/andrews.htm). Since Andrews is home to Air Force One, it's also closely linked to the Secret Service—which, commanded by Cheney, was issuing military orders on 9/11. The secretary of defense was supposed to be in charge of the nation's defenses, but Rumsfeld kept himself scarce during the attacks. Once again, the Commission never got around to questioning this role reversal and breach of protocol.

The Commission also ignored the full range of air-defense alternatives. Skeptics have questioned why NORAD sent the first scramble order to Otis Air National Guard Base, 180 miles from Manhattan, rather than to McGuire AFB in New Jersey, just 70 miles away, and why the second order went to Langley AFB, more than 100 miles from Washington, but not to Andrews Air Base, located only ten miles away. If you weren't sure where hijacked airliners might strike, why not send up interceptors from all four bases?

Although these excuses for the air failures were obviously inadequate, they did divert attention from a myriad of other questions that were never asked, let alone addressed.

## A Culture of Non-Accountability

The Commission had stated early on that "our aim has been to provide the fullest possible account of the events," "what happened and why" but, oddly, without assigning "individual blame" (*Report* p. xiv). It's impossible, of course, to have it both ways: providing "the fullest possible account," which implies determining the actions or inactions of government officials and military personnel, necessarily involves holding individuals responsible. When the Commission turned away from assigning *individual* responsibility, it limited itself to identifying *institutional* mistakes, malfeasance, or dysfunction.

If 9/11 was the crime of the new century, why would no one beyond al Qaeda's leaders and suicide bombers be held accountable—not even chastised, censored, or demoted, let alone brought to justice? Two years after their *Report* had come out, Commission chair Tom Kean remained unapologetic about failing to hold anyone accountable, adopting a defensive tone: he dismissed the panel's many failures, conflating "establishing responsibility" with "pointing fingers" (Kean and L. Hamilton *Without Precedent* p. 49). However, Philip Shenon saw through the ruse: "When government fails to act in situations in which it has a legal authority to do so," he pointed out, "it is almost always because specific and identifiable officials made a decision, formally or informally, not to act" (Shenon *The Comm.* p. 392).

As it blamed everybody equally—that is, nobody at all—the Commission focused its attentions on future recommendations for problems located within institutions. The Commission asked the world to believe that only government institutions and agencies had failed, not individuals within them. Thus it cited "systemic breakdowns," "intelligence failures," "communication snafus," "bureaucratic walls," or "turf wars between agencies." Tellingly, when the Commission pointed to "failure of imagination," it characteristically placed the failure within an institutional context: "Imagination is not a gift usually associated with bureaucracies" (*Report* p. 344-45). No kidding.

Three years still later, a new Obama administration used similar abstractions to avoid holding individuals or institutions responsible for the banking/Wall Street meltdown. "A culture of irresponsibility took root, from Wall Street to Washington to Main Street," Obama intoned. "A regulatory regime basically crafted in the wake of a twentieth century … was overwhelmed by the speed, scope, and sophistication of a twenty-first-century global economy." In other words, we can blame it on runaway technology, on machines but not on people.

### Officials Invited Only as Witnesses and Experts
When the Commission, out of necessity, focused on prominent individuals, it often worked from unfounded assumptions. It assumed that officials in charge at the FAA, the White House, and the Pentagon should not be

interrogated as "persons of interest"—that they could be treated as witnesses or even consulted as authorities. In short, the Commission *assumed* the competence, integrity, and innocence of key officials—some of whom were seemingly involved—actively or passively—with unprecedented national security failures.

When the Commission blamed al Qaeda operatives, it also assumed they alone were responsible. Top officials and commanders surely bore some responsibility. Cheney, who apparently issued a stand-down order allowing an airliner to enter highly restricted air space, was one example. Rumsfeld, who allegedly remained incommunicado throughout much of the crisis, was another. Four-star General Richard Myers, the commander in charge of the nation's defenses, was by his own accounts also out of the loop (P. Thompson *Terror Timeline* p. 456). And Gen. Ralph Eberhart, NORAD's top commander, had left his post and jumped in a car, going incommunicado for 40 minutes during the crisis (*Colo. Springs Gazette* 6/16/06).

Given such behavior among top officials, the Commission's singular focus was especially astounding. Widely published theologian and leading 9/11 scholar Griffin points out that a *truly* independent Commission would have proceeded on the assumption that "Rumsfeld, [Gen. Richard] Myers, and [Gen. Ralph] Eberhart had to be regarded as possible suspects. After all, these were the individuals in charge of agencies that had not only failed but had deviated from their standard operating procedures. Instead, the testimonies of these men were treated as unquestionable sources of truth despite the contradictions in their stories" (Griffin *9/11 Comm. Report* p. 122). Rather than questioning Bush and Cheney separately, under oath, on the record, in a public forum, the Commission interviewed Bush and Cheney together, behind closed doors. This joint session, Bush told reporters, "was just a good discussion" (MSNBC 4/29/04).

None of the officials in charge on 9/11 were cited, not even for negligence. Even the conservative *Wall Street Journal* characterized the operating assumptions—especially that individual government personnel and authorities bore no responsibility—as a "theory that dare not speak its name" (*WS Journal* 9/29/03). In addition, Sen. Max Cleland, who eventually resigned from the Commission in disgust, challenged the Commission's decision to assume that there was no official wrongdoing: "That decision compromised the mission of the 9/11 Commission, period" (Global Research 6/27/04). If there were no mistakes made, no bad judgments rendered, no wrongs committed, then why would air defense officials have fudged their official timelines? (Griffin *9/11 Comm. Report* pp. 141-46). And if no one was at fault, why would the Commission have further fudged the times for events? The chairmen of the Commission later disclosed that they knew many officials were lying but decided not to call them out or take meaningful action (Kean and Hamilton *Without Precedent* p. 16).

Much as the Commission dodged hot-button questions, it allowed individuals holding high office to evade responsibility for their mishandling of national security and even possible collusion with the perpetrators. When the Commission evaded questions of individual responsibility, it broke with long traditions in American life. After Pearl Harbor, Adm. Husband Kimmel, the Navy fleet commander in the Pacific, was relieved of his command, reduced in rank, and disgraced (Shenon *The Comm.* p. 388). More recently, when careless Air Force personnel allowed nuclear-armed missiles to be flown around the country, those responsible faced punishments (AP 10/23/07). Whatever happened to accountability for 9/11?

**Startling Revisions to Official Timelines**
Since the beginning, the failure of multilayered, multi-trillion-dollar air defenses had proved particularly difficult to explain. As we've seen, when the Pentagon's two initial timelines failed to resolve these questions, the Commission's response was simple: revise the Pentagon's account for all of the hijacked planes. Even the Pentagon's final version, a timeline that had essentially gone unchallenged and become "official," wasn't enough for the Commission. Without providing any rationale, its *Report* further altered the accepted times for many events, delaying both the times when air traffic controllers realized that planes were hijacked and those when air defenders received calls for help (*Report* pp. 285-315).

The Commission's specific motives for making most of these alterations, noted Griffin, boiled down to four: to make it seem impossible for air defenders to have intercepted the rogue flights, to have defended the Pentagon, or to have shot down Flight 93—and, at the same time, to make the FAA "take the fall" for the air defense failures (Griffin *9/11 Comm. Report* pp. 256, 139-54). When evidence impeded these objectives, the Commission consistently found ways to ignore or sidestep it (www.twf.org/News/Y2007/0507-United93.html).

### Cheney Attempts to Blunt Suspicions of a Shoot Down

The demise of United 93, the flight with the much-publicized passenger revolt, posed special problems for the Commission. Not only did the public recall the revolt from the extensive publicity it had received in various media, including prime-time talk shows, but Dick Cheney made memorable statements. Cheney's less-scripted interviews posed special problems.

On NBC's "Meet the Press" just five days after the tragedy, Tim Russert asked Cheney what the most difficult decision he made during the course of the day had been. Though Cheney was a former secretary of defense, he somehow conflated intercepting a plane with shooting it down:

**Cheney:** I suppose the toughest decision was this question of whether or not we would intercept incoming commercial aircraft.

**Russert:** And you decided…?

**Cheney:** We decided to do it. We'd, in effect, put a flying combat air patrol…. It doesn't do any good to put up a combat air patrol if you don't give them instructions to act, if, in fact, they feel it's appropriate.

**Russert:** So if the United States government became aware that a hijacked commercial airliner was destined for the White House or the Capitol, we would take the plane down?

**Cheney:** Yes. The president made the decision … that if the plane would not divert, as a last resort our pilots were authorized to take them out. … It's a presidential-level decision, and the president made, I think, exactly the right call …" (NBC 9/16/01).

Much has been said about this famous, unintentionally revealing interview. Some skeptics have pointed to the contradiction between Cheney's assertion, on the one hand, that commanders gave pilots "instructions to act, if, in fact, they feel it's appropriate" and his statement, just seconds later, that shoot downs are "a presidential-level decision." Others have noted that Cheney's narrative shifts the time frame until after the hit on the Pentagon, thereby avoiding the question of whether he barked out a *stand-down* order about 9:25, as described by Secretary Mineta (www.911truth.org/article.php?story=20080618131336892). Note, too, that in addition to making it seem like Bush gave all the important orders, Cheney also reinforced the assumption that interceptors were the only line of defense drawn around Washington

## Reports of a Shoot Down from People in the Know

Beyond Cheney's interview with Russert, several reports stated that prior to crashing, Flight 93 was being tailed by military fighters. Reports came from a flight controller who'd ignored an order not to talk to the media and from Maj. Daniel Nash, one of the F-15 pilots sent toward New York City on 9/11, who reported hearing that another pilot had shot down an airliner in Pennsylvania (*Cape Cod Times* 9/21/02). Bush has since indicated that he too believed that his order had led to the shoot down of Flight 93 (*Guardian* [UK] 10/29/10). Another such report came from Senate Armed Services Committee Chairman Carl Levin, who spoke of hearing "statements that the aircraft that crashed in Pennsylvania was shot down"; still another even came from Deputy Secretary of Defense Paul Wolfowitz (http://mujca. com/flighttales.htm); and yet another came from Rumsfeld, who spoke about how the air force had "shot down the plane over Pennsylvania" (CNN 12/27/01). Immediately afterward, of course, the staffers sought to correct the secretary's "misstatement."

Although in the short run Cheney's appearance on "Meet the Press" soothed some frayed nerves, in the long run it left the Commission three problems that needed attention:

- That reputable public testimony by Secretary Mineta had Cheney giving a stand-down order;
- That several sources, including Cheney, Rumsfeld, and Paul Wolfowitz, had alluded to a shoot down;

- And that persistent reports of a shoot down had continued to surface, many from people in positions to know.

## The Commission's Stroke of Propaganda Genius

It took some very creative writing for the Commission to generate an account that bagged two birds with one shot. Cleverly precluding both a stand-down and a shoot down, the new narrative "solved" the problems listed above. It also anticipated the fact that Secretary Norman Mineta's account, which the Commission attempted to completely suppress, would become something of an underground classic among skeptics following the 9/11 issues closely.

For starters, this new narrative diverted attention from the *third* hijacking, Flight 77, for which Secretary Mineta had recounted Cheney's stand-down order. To clear Cheney of the charge, the Commission made it seem like Mineta was talking about the *fourth* airliner, Flight 93, which in this substitute scenario seemed to have already crashed in Pennsylvania:

> At 10:02, the communicators in the shelter began receiving reports from the Secret Service of an inbound aircraft.... At some time between 10:10 and 10:15, a military aide told the vice president and others that the aircraft was 80 miles out. Vice President Cheney was asked for authority to engage the aircraft.... The vice president authorized fighter aircraft to engage the inbound plane.... The military aide returned a few minutes later, probably between 10:12 and 10:18, and said the aircraft was 60 miles out. He again asked for authorization to engage. The vice president again said yes (*Report* p. 41).

This mythic account raised some mathematical questions, such as how could the incoming plane have been "60 miles out" when Flight 93 crashed about 125 miles from Washington?

While this story shares elements in common with Secretary's Mineta's, it also differs in major respects, Griffin has observed: "It makes clear that Cheney issued a shoot-down, not a stand-down order. And it came far too late to have had any relevance to the Pentagon attack ... by coming so late, it also—and this provides a second possible motive for the revised timeline— could have had no relevance to another controversial issue: Whether the US military had shot down United Flight 93 over Pennsylvania ..." (www. globalresearch.ca/index.php?context=va&aid=9368).

### Zelikow Agitated about Challenges to Official Story

It's now clear that while counterterrorism expert Richard Clarke didn't spill all he knew, he had become a credible primary source of information that contradicted the Commission. For years, bad blood had been brewing between Clarke and Philip Zelikow, the powerful executive director of the Commission. When Clarke learned that the Commission had hired Zelikow for the position, he muttered, prophetically, "the fix is in." Clarke was outraged that the Commission had hired someone so close to the Bush administration—especially National Security Adviser Condoleezza Rice—to investigate his own close associates (Shenon *The Comm.* pp. 63-65).

Come March 2004, with Clarke slated to appear before the Commission and his book *Against All Enemies* scheduled to come out just days before, matters heated up. When Zelikow learned that Clarke's book would be available to the public and the press earlier than expected, he "went ballistic" and "wanted to subpoena [the book]." Rightly suspecting that Clarke would challenge the story he'd been trying to fabricate, Zelikow didn't want new information surfacing close to an appearance that would become a major media event. Desperate to control information, Zelikow demanded that the Commission subpoena the book from the publisher. The Commission's legal counsel, however, pointed out that since the Commission hadn't used its subpoena power to pry information out of government agencies, relying on it to commandeer one book would make it look bad (Shenon *The Comm.* pp. 70-71).

### Sound and Fury from the White House

Readers will recall that in the summer of 2004, when sections of the Commission's *Report* began arriving at the White House, they set off rumblings heard all the way to the panel's vault-like chambers on K Street.

The loudest thunder and lightning came from Cheney and his famously assertive counsel, David Addington. Both were outraged by the draft of the Commission's timeline covering Cheney's actions on September 11 (Shenon *The Comm.* p. 411).

When the Commission altered times in consistent directions, it invited questions about its intentions. Its changes to the timeline of events followed three characteristic patterns: to *lengthen* the time that it supposedly took the FAA to report the hijackings to the military, to *push ahead* (with the exception of the 8:52 first fighter launch) the times when the Air Force scrambled interceptors, and, in one case, to *move up* the time of impact, again seeming to shorten the time available for effective action. In the latter instance, the Commission had Flight 93 crashing in Pennsylvania at 10:03—even though, according to local seismic records, the plane actually hit the ground at 10:06 (*London Daily Mirror* 9/13/02).

The end result of these revisions to the timeline for events was to shorten the perceived reaction times available to air defenders, making it seem impossible for them to have prevented the devastating attacks. Nor, the Commission apparently wanted the public to conclude, could air defenders have possibly shot down a plane. As they fit the pattern, sometimes the time shifts were dramatic—and also incredible. In one instance, government agencies initially established that an Air Force base had received notification about a hijacking at 9:16 a.m., but the Commission changed the time to 10:07, a stunning *51 minutes* later (*Minneapolis Star Trib.* 7/31/04). Surely this radical change required some explanation, but the Commission didn't offer any, nor did the press demand one. Both notification times—the Pentagon's and the Commission's—were in all probability incorrect. The fact that the Commission would arbitrarily override the Pentagon's notification time by 51 minutes not only revealed considerable chutzpah; it also suggested that the Commission wanted to squelch suspicions of a shoot down.

These changes reveal more about the intent of the Commission than they elucidate the events of 9/11. Were these alterations, particularly those involving significant changes in notification times, intended to release the Pentagon from responsibility and heap still more blame upon the FAA?

From start to finish, everything about the Commission's conduct would answer "yes."

## Uncritical Acceptance in Corporate Mass Media

After wresting a two-month extension from a resistant White House and an even more intransigent Republican-dominated House, the Commission issued its final *Report* in July 2004. Packaged in a red, white, and blue dust jacket sporting the nation's insignia on the spine, *The 9/11 Commission Report* ran 816 pages. An initial printing of 600,000 copies sold at the government-subsidized price of $9.95 for the hefty hardback. (The cost to taxpayers was not disclosed.) The *Report* was a book the Feds wanted people to read. It had stories to tell, and it told them well. If only more were true.

Operating under the thumb of the White House and under the nose of the Washington press corps, the "independent" Commission offered the nation a simplistic product, one the pubic was all too willing to buy. Offering precious little commentary, the American corporate media helped to sell the Official Story. Although journalists' files bulged with evidence contradicting the *Report*, few seemed interested in whether the Commission had delivered a credible account.

One after one, the major outlets chimed in. *Newsday* typified media commentary when it called this election-year bipartisanship "miraculous" but failed to ask, "At what price?" *Time* called the *Report* one of "the most riveting, disturbing, and revealing accounts of crime, espionage, and the inner workings of government ever written." Both ABC and NBC announced plans for TV miniseries based on the *Report* (Shenon *The Comm.* p. 415). The book not only rose to the top of the *New York Times* Bestseller list, it was even nominated for a National Book Award. The *Times'* review was doubly telling. The reviewer, US Court of Appeals judge Richard Posner, lavished the highest praise on the *Report*, calling it "an uncommonly lucid, even riveting, narrative ..." (*NYT* 7/31/05). Confusing style with substance, Posner attempted to explain away the news media's lack of critical analysis, saying, in effect, "analysis doesn't sell newspapers; so that's the way they have to do business these days."

While several major figures in US journalism (Dan Rather, Bob Woodward) have lamented their failures to ask more questions in the run-up to the Iraq War, few have made any similar apologies for their validation of a Commission whose leaders are now talking about the falsehoods it perpetrated on the public.

## Overwhelmingly Favorable Reactions to the *Report*

Among establishment figures, it was applause all around. The Commission issued its unanimous report to broad, bipartisan acclaim. The kudos from political and intellectual luminaries was almost breathtaking. Forgetting that novels are fiction, Bush's aide Andy Card told the president "it reads like a novel" (Shenon *The Comm.* p. 415).

Among the establishment intelligentsia, reactions bordered on group think. Arthur Schlesinger Jr., once a close confidante to JFK and the dean of the Harvard historians, called the *Report* "a tour de force" (*San Fran. Chron.* 11/12/04). Schlesinger's literary counterpart, the urbane novelist and celebrated stylist John Updike, hit the highest notes of all. Prior to the *Report*, intoned Updike, the King James *Bible* had been "our language's lone masterpiece produced by committee" (*New Yorker* 11/1/04). While the Report did carry near-scriptural authority, a "masterpiece" is surely more than an appealingly told exercise in propagandistic mythmaking.

## Lonely Voices of Protest and Dissent

The families who'd pushed so hard for a Commission were among the first to speak out in disappointment and disbelief. Patty Casazza, whose husband died in the South Tower, was deeply disillusioned by the Commission's process: "They lied. They all lied." A strong activist, Casazza was one of the Jersey Girls and a member of the Families Steering Committee (http://en.wikipedia.org/wiki/Jersey_Girls). Master researcher Paul Thompson was among the first to call attention to how the *Report* betrayed the public trust. In his book *The Terror Timeline*, Thompson revealed how much was actually known prior to 9/11, showed how foreign-policy blowback likely helped to propel the attacks, and exposed the links between Islamist militants and American, Pakistani, and Israeli spy agencies.

## A Lone Outcry from the Senate

Amid a sea of acquiescent faces, Sen. Mark Dayton (D-Minn.) became a lone voice of dissent. In a blistering critique of the Commission's *Report*, Sen. Dayton exposed the changes to the timeline, stressing both the unreliability of its primary sources and the Commission's collaboration with the White House.

Standing nearly alone in the Senate, Dayton charged that Pentagon officials had "lied to the American people, they lied to Congress and they lied to your 9/11 Commission to create a false impression of competence, communication, coordination and protection of the American people." Barely avoiding the term "whitewash," Sen. Dayton cited a gross failure of accountability: "we can set up all the oversight possible at great additional cost to the American taxpayers and it won't be worth an Enron pension if the people responsible lie to us; if they take the records and doctor them into falsehoods, and if they get away with it. For almost three years now NORAD and FAA officials have been able to hide their critical failures that left this country defenseless during two of the worst hours in our history" (www.youtube.com/watch?v=VNQ-HywKG5Q).

Sen. Dayton was not only eloquent; he also provided particulars.

## Exposing the Commission's Shenanigans

While Senator Dayton pointed out several contradictions, none was more central than the Commission's changing the times assigned communications between Bush and Rumsfeld. Senator Dayton noted that two of Washington's best-known reporters had investigated top administration officials' actions on 9/11. Their story reported that just after the Pentagon was struck at 9:37, Rumsfeld had "taken up his post at the National Military Command Center." Here, according to this reporting, "Bush then talked to Rumsfeld to clarify the procedures military pilots should follow before firing on attack planes. With Bush's approval Rumsfeld passed the order down the chain of command" (*Wash. Post* 2/27/02). Highlighting the Commission's alterations, Dayton pointed out that according to the *Report*, Bush spoke to Rumsfeld "for the first time that morning shortly after 10:00 a.m." (*Minneapolis Star Trib.* 7/31/04). Dayton asked, "Which is it, guys? Both can't be true." However, Senator Dayton's cogent critique wasn't a story with "legs." Even journalists who thrive on conflict apparently avoided this one. The networks had an account they wanted to report and much of the nation wanted to hear.

After Dayton's words fell silent, Rep. Cynthia McKinney (D/Green-Ga.) became one of the very few in government or mainstream media who seriously challenged the Commission's politically motivated alterations. Held in 2005, Representative McKinney's Congressional hearings featured "Jersey Girl" widow/activist Lorie Van Auken and scholars John Cooley and Peter Dale Scott; skeptics confronted Rumsfeld and other Pentagon officials about the "war games" taking place on 9/11 (http://portland.indymedia. org/en/2005/07/321991.shtml).

**Intelligence Professionals Also Damn the *Report*** Other credentialed critics included Michael Scheuer, who'd headed the CIA's bin Laden unit. Scheuer had provided more than 400 pages of documents detailing intelligence failures before 9/11. After Zelikow and the Commission ignored this evidence, Scheuer dismissed its *Report* as "a whitewash, and a lie from top to bottom" (*Dissident Voice* 10/10). But it was Ray McGovern, PhD, a 27-year CIA veteran and former Chairman of the Agency's National Intelligence Estimates (NIE), who was most perceptive: "In the simplest terms, there's a cover-up. The 9/11 *Report* is a joke." Then McGovern inquired, "So the Commission was a cover-up—the question is, What was it trying to cover up?" (http:patriotsquestion911.com). Above all others, this is the core question we're still trying to answer.

### Bronner and the Newly Released NORAD Tapes

Two years after the Commission published its *Report*, the Pentagon finally released 30 hours of audiotapes. These allegedly documented the conversations among NORAD personnel on the morning of September 11. Oddly, the Pentagon released them not to the public or the press but to Michael Bronner, associate producer of *Flight 93* (2006), which dramatized the Official Story, and later producer of *Green Zone* (2009), a thriller about CIA agents on the trail of terrorists. Why did it take the Pentagon more than five years to release these tapes, and why did it release them to someone in the entertainment industry rather than to someone with special expertise?

Working from these tapes, Bronner published "9/11 Live: The NORAD Tapes" (*Vanity Fair* 8/06). The article repeated familiar positions: that NORAD was still configured outward to intercept Soviet bombers, that this "hollow-donut" configuration left the country's interior airspace unguarded, and that air bases had been "mothballed" in the 1990s. These were claims the Pentagon brass had made three years after 9/11: they surely didn't appear on the tapes recorded during the attacks. And since the Pentagon had provided the tapes to Bronner alone, it was difficult for researchers to check his citations.

These tapes from NORAD, Bronner claimed, also showed that air defenses had failed because of "confusion and miscommunication." Thousands of commercial and private aircraft had overloaded the FAA's radar screens, which were even more antiquated than those of NORAD, and once-active air bases were closed, requiring that commanders "jump start a dormant military machine." Worse, according to Bronner, air defenders had chased a "phantom Flight 11." This was a nonexistent airliner streaking south toward Washington after the real Flight 11 had slammed into the South Tower. Confused, interceptors supposedly chased a ghost instead of hijacked planes actually heading for Washington (*Vanity Fair* 8/06).

Since the Commission hadn't made much of these ostensible problems, Bronner's presentation was received as additional evidence in support of the Official Story. They raised an obvious question, however: If this radar overload and ambiguity plus a phantom flight were such significant factors, why wouldn't air controllers and military commanders have said so all along? It would have been in their institutional self-interest, if not that of the nation, to make such an excuse (www.911truth.org/article.php?story=2006091418303369). The fact that the fragmentary excerpts made available didn't affirm all of Bronner's contentions aroused additional suspicions.

## So Many Unanswered Questions

As we've seen, the Commission's *Report* failed to investigate the often-strange actions of the four officials most responsible for the nation's defense on 9/11.

It made no attempt to account for why the president, the secretary of defense, and two top commanders remained out of the loop for so long that morning (P. D. Scott *Road To 9/11* pp. 220-26). Nor, as we've seen, was there any explanation as to why Bush and his aides told different stories about how the president had learned of the first WTC impact (*Boston Herald* 10/22/02).

Since the Commission didn't attempt to explain the fall of the WTC buildings, its narrative was obviously incomplete. The Commission left it to the National Institute for Standards and Technology (NIST) to analyze the World Trade Center disintegrations. These analyses, to be examined thoroughly later, proved just as unconvincing. The Commission's postponement of them suggests that it understood that the buildings, particularly the fall of WTC-7, were additional weak points of the government narrative.

The Commission told and legitimized an Official Story, the master narrative that still inhabits the minds of millions. As the real story of events is being uncovered, it's proving far more intriguing. Although there's some truth to the Commission's findings—perhaps just enough to lend them credibility to inattentive or uninformed minds—much of its Official Story is clever contrivance. As the *Report's* omissions, distortions, and evasions are exposed, it's becoming the *Warren Commission Report* of our time.

It's often remarked that governments get caught for the cover-up, not for the crime. Although the Commission's lies were designed to conceal, they may eventually help expose those involved or implicated. Even if a real investigation were to conclude that no conspiracy occurred (other than the one implied by the Official Story), the Commission's cover-up was itself a conspiracy to obscure the truth. Its short-term objectives will become obvious: to ensure that nothing would surface that could harm the Bush administration's prospects for reelection. Its broader, long-term objectives appear to lie with rationalizing attacks that made possible military interventions in Afghanistan, Iraq, Yemen, and probably elsewhere.

In doing so, however, the Commission falsified American history, adding to the unreality of a culture already awash in misinformation, mythology and distrust. Truth decay. Given this decline and the importance of getting it right, these falsifications were serious crimes against the country.

# 11. The Politics of Time: Commission Shifts Times for Key Events

*For almost three years now, NORAD and FAA officials have been able to hide their critical failures that left this country defenseless during two of the worst hours in its history.*

—Sen. Mark Dayton, July 2004

As the Commission attempted to cover for air-defense failures, its main device was to alter established times for events. Earlier reports had differed about the times, but the Commission came up with its own, oblivious to the information it had received. The main source was the North American Aerospace Defense Command (NORAD). Providing no rationale for its changes, the commissioners drastically altered NORAD's already-revised, widely accepted timeline, itself an attempt at self-exoneration.

While NORAD and the Commission made changes in similar directions, the commissioners took additional liberties with the truth. In its *Report*, postponement of notification times and insistence on *formal* notification became blatant. Their intent was hard to miss: to cover for the military, make the FAA look inept, and make interception of the hijacked airliners seem impossible. As the Commission did all this, it raised still more doubts about the evolving Official Story. This final version, observed Dr. David Ray Griffin, "implies that the military's earlier story, which it had been telling for almost three years, was almost entirely false" (Griffin and P. D. Scott *9/11 and the American Empire* pp. 8-9).

## The Politics of Time: Three Untenable Timetables

For many months, from September 2001 to early 2004, government officials from a range of agencies had told contradictory tales. In the six days following 9/11 NORAD issued two timelines. Then, almost three years later, the 9/11 Commission came out with a third and very different revision of NORAD's revision. All three versions sought to explain why NORAD (specifically NEADS, NORAD's North East Air Defense Sector) experienced so much difficulty getting its interceptors in the air.

These timelines dealt with significant issues that the Commission wove into its *Report*:

- The times the FAA first detected the hijackings and *formally* notified NORAD about them;
- The "loss" of Flight 77 to both FAA and NORAD radar for half an hour;
- The problems caused when interceptor jets allegedly tried to locate a "phantom" Flight 11;
- The supposed ineffectuality of both the interagency conference calls and the government teleconferences running on 9/11.

These issues and others were involved in finessing the Official Story. Rising to the occasion, the Commission relied on strategic omissions and superficially plausible distortions to tel an appealing story on a new timetable. It gave creative writing a new fictional form: the readable government report.

Here's how the institutional timelines evolved, starting with NORAD's original version. Like Amtrak schedules, these timetables proved "subject to alteration without notice."

# I. NORAD's First Timeline (9/11-13/01)

The initial account, which the Department of Defense began to release on the very day of the attacks, coalesced from September 11 through 14. In this version, NORAD explained that "the fighters were not scrambled for more than an hour after the first hijacking was reported." NORAD didn't immediately scramble fighters, said Maj. Mike Snyder, "even though it was alerted to a hijacking ten minutes before the first plane ... slammed into the first World Trade Center [at 8:46]." In fact, "the fighters remained on the ground until after the Pentagon was hit ..." (*Boston Globe* 9/15/01).

When this first story also claimed that no interceptors left the ground until after the Pentagon was hit at 9:37—that is, after three hijacked planes had already hit their targets—it made an embarrassing admission; it implied that air defenders remained on the ground for 95 minutes after FAA air traffic controllers had first detected signs of a hijacking at 8:13, for 83 minutes after the first hijacking had become certain at 8:25, and for 58 minutes after the first formal notification of NORAD, allegedly at 8:40 (*Wash. Post* 9/12/01). What happened to the fabled fighter jets?

This initial timeline made NORAD look bad, but the FAA hardly looked any better. If one believed this initial account, then FAA controllers, instead of immediately reporting Flight 11 to NORAD around 8:15, had waited fully 25 minutes after the first three clear signs of a hijacking and sixteen minutes after they'd heard the first Arabic-inflected announcement from the cockpit.

Given these numbers, both NORAD and the FAA had some explaining to do. But rather than explain, NORAD changed its story.

## II. NORAD'S Second Account Makes Telling Changes

On September 18, NORAD released a second, significantly altered timeline. Not surprisingly, this new version changed both the times the FAA had notified NORAD about hijackings and the times NORAD scrambled planes. In this version, the FAA's notification times were typically later—in one case drastically so—but this time NORAD presented itself as having scrambled planes well before the third impact, into the Pentagon at 9:37. According to this second timeline, NORAD's interceptor jets got airborne at 8:53. This was still ten minutes before the second airliner, Flight 175, hit the second Tower, so that takeoff time had to arch some eyebrows (Griffin *9/11 Comm. Report* pp. 144-45).

Thus, NORAD's new story raised more questions than it answered. If NORAD did launch twin-tailed, F-15 Eagles eleven minutes before the second impact, why didn't the supersonic interceptors cover the 180 miles from Cape Cod to New York and intercept Flight 175? Obvious as these questions might seem, few in Congress, academia, or the news media raised them. And few have asked since.

## Patterns Emerge in NORAD's Altered Version of Events

• ***The Fighters Get Airborne Earlier*** Whereas the first version had NORAD fighters in the air only *after* the country had taken three hits—i.e., for only the last hijacked plane—NORAD's second version had fighters aloft before three of the four airliners crashed. In this later version, air defenders "looked better": at least they got more interceptors aloft more quickly.

• ***The Airliners Crash Earlier*** In its second version, NORAD seemed intent on *shortening the duration* of the last three flights—and therefore on reducing the perceived possibility for its fighters to have intercepted them.

• ***Formal Notification Becomes Mandatory*** A third pattern was that NORAD now claimed the FAA had given notification *later* than it had originally acknowledged. The first hijacking, American Airlines Flight 11, provided one example. In NORAD's second version, the time of the FAA's first notification for Flight 11 changed drastically. It jumped from 8:25, when controllers notified other flight control centers, to 8:40, when the military claimed that controllers had given *formal* notification (CNN 9/17/01).

Looking for a technicality, NORAD characteristically defined "notification" in the most *formal* sense. It omitted the fact that just after 8:30, FAA controllers at Boston Center had made direct calls to two air bases, desperately seeking interceptors (L. Filson *Air War Over America* p. 47). When NORAD insisted on formal notification, the FAA not only came off as delaying military response to Flight 11 by fifteen crucial minutes, but also as putting NORAD "behind the curve" in responding to the other hijackings. In the case of Flight 175, the other airliner which took off from Boston, NORAD also failed to mention that since about 8:50 its personnel were participating in conference calls with their FAA counterparts, discussing how to handle the hijackings (www.911truth.org/article.php?story=2004081200421797).

However, NORAD was reluctant to acknowledge that its personnel were involved in phone-bridge conversations. The obvious response to what NORAD personnel were hearing about hijackings would have been to order interceptors in the air, pronto. The FAA's policy had long been, "If you are in doubt ... handle it as though it were an emergency" (FAA Order 7110.65M). Neither NORAD nor the Commission emphasized this key facet of FAA protocol; instead, both implied that controllers must be *certain* before they report a hijacking to NORAD.

In NORAD's rendition of American Flight 77, the third hijacking, the FAA didn't receive credit for notification until 9:24—not at 8:56, when FAA controllers noticed the plane was in big trouble and declared it "lost" (*NYT* 10/16/01). Moreover, NORAD quibbled, the FAA had only reported that Flight 77 "*may*" have been hijacked and "*appeared* to be heading back towards Washington" (AP 9/18/01). NORAD's revision, then, alleged that although Flight 77 was suspected of being hijacked by 8:56, controllers waited another 28 minutes before *formally* notifying NORAD (Griffin *9/11 Comm. Report* p. 147). Once more NORAD played the formality card, its favored ace in the hole.

Nor was this the only alteration for Flight 77. NORAD had originally claimed that in response to notification, it immediately ordered fighters scrambled from Langley AFB. These fighters, it had said, got into the air at 9:30 but couldn't reach Washington by 9:37, when Flight 77 hit the Pentagon. However, NORAD's new timeline explained neither why its F-16s didn't cover the 130 miles in the seven minutes nor why the Pentagon wasn't evacuated, which would have saved 125 lives (Griffin *9/11 Comm. Report* pp. 189-90, 171).

**Strategically Shifting the Blame**

If we assume that government agencies are apt to put out information (or misinformation) making themselves look good, we can understand how an embarrassed American military, its vaunted technology temporarily impotent and its superpower image tarnished, would try to save face by shifting the blame. Although NORAD seems to have revised its timeline with these concerns in mind, it also, as we'll see in subsequent chapters, may have sought to cover up intentional systemic slowdowns.

Thus NORAD's second version held the FAA to strict standards of formal notification, making no mention of other sources of real-time information. How could FAA controllers have observed so many signs of hijackings and informed NORAD via "open phone bridges" yet not receive credit for having given notification?

### Altering Times to Quash Questions

Besides the insistence on formal notification, another pattern characterized NORAD's revision of September 18. Its second timeline was all about closing the window of opportunity for the military to intervene. Right from the start, the air defense command's strategy had been to delay the times when it received calls for help. Griffin has observed that NORAD's second version essentially asserted that "although the military did order planes scrambled, they were too late because the FAA had not notified the military in time" (Griffin *9/11 Comm. Report* p.173).

Most of the public had no idea that NORAD changed its story during the first week after the attacks, or that the Commission changed NORAD's account in drastic ways.

## III. The Commission Comes Up a Whole Different Version

NORAD's second timeline reigned for two and a half years until, in June 2004, the Commission revised NORAD's revision. In retelling the tale, the Commission acted as though NORAD's second timeline had never become the standard account. Examined flight by flight, these new stories flew smack into a mountain of facts. Especially when considered together, they defy belief.

### The Commission's Amazing New Story for Flight 11

Although the Commission had received times from the FAA and NORAD, it introduced completely new ones. Exploiting these contradictions, the

Commission introduced new excuses for NORAD's delays in launching its fighters: late notification, lack of a destination, and lack of a target.

Though initial reports had Flight 11's transponder going dead around 8:13, the air traffic controller handling the flight had later placed it at 8:20 (MSNBC 9/11/02). Col. Robert Marr, NORAD's battle commander for NEADS, had moved the turnoff time later yet, claiming the transponder was turned off after 8:30 (ABC 9/11/02). In the revision, the telltale signs of a hijacking came at least seven minutes *later* than in the original timeline. The 8:13 time was likely correct, but it raised troubling questions. It had to be changed, and a later time was better.

Neither the FAA nor NORAD nor the Commission wanted to explain why it took so long to determine that a hijacking was going on. The controller, the colonel, and the Commission shared a need to have the transponder turnoff—the most telltale sign of a terrorist hijacking— seem to have occurred later. All wanted to shorten the time available to determine that Flight 11 was hijacked, request military intervention, scramble fighters, and intercept the airliner.

## Why the Interceptors Failed to Intercept

Whereas NORAD's timeline for Flight 11 had notification coming to NEADS at 8:40, NEADS ordering a scramble at 8:46, and interceptors taking off at 8:53, the Commission again revised the story; it moved the time when the jets at Otis AFB received scramble orders from 8:46 to 8:53. Because the FAA failed to provide directions to a target, the Commission claimed, the F-15s from Otis sat on the tarmac for seven minutes because they supposedly lacked a "destination"; once aloft, they were told to "hold as needed" in " military-controlled airspace off the Long Island Coast" (*Report* p. 20).

The Commission claimed that the Otis jets remained on the runway until 8:53 and then stayed in a holding pattern until 9:13—fully ten minutes after the second impact on the Twin Towers—mostly because "NEADS didn't know where to send its fighter aircraft" (*Report* p. 20). Again, the FAA was allegedly at fault because it hadn't provided enough information.

Surely, though, the immediate mission for the Otis fighters should have been obvious. FAA controllers in Boston had already told NEADS "we have a hijacked aircraft (Flight 175) headed toward New York" (*Report* p. 20). After NEADS in upstate New York realized it needed to deal with a second hijacking heading for New York, why would it fail to indicate what to intercept and where to find it? The new version also ignored the narratives that the F-15 pilots had originally provided. Fighter pilots Daniel Nash and Timothy Duffy spoke of learning that "your contact's over Kennedy." With those instructions, Nash and Duffy reported streaking for New York "full blower [1,800 mph, or 30 miles a minute] all the way" (ABC 9/11/02). If the Otis jets had lacked a mission, why would they have roared "full blower all the way"?

Yet the Commission asked readers to believe that even after the second impact, these F-15s continued to fly a holding pattern while they could see both Trade Towers going up in smoke. It's hard to imagine that protecting New York wouldn't have become an urgent priority, as in fact it was. Several NORAD officials reportedly urged immediate implementation of a Combat Air Patrol (CAP) over New York (*Aviation Week* 6/3/02).

Somehow, the Commission's revision asked the nation to believe that NORAD received before-crash notification for only the *first* hijacking, Flight 11; to make this claim, the Commission had to ignore extensive evidence strongly suggesting that NORAD knew about Flights 175, 77, and 93 before they'd crashed.

Sorry, no sale. The evidence says otherwise.

## Flight 175: Additional Amazing Revisions

For the second hijacking, the Commission made additional changes, most of them equally damaging to the FAA. At 9:03, Flight 175 struck the South Tower, exploding into a huge fireball. But even this horrific image, the Commission claimed, didn't rouse the FAA from its alleged torpor. It claimed that not until 9:15, twelve minutes after this second impact, did the FAA finally notify NORAD about the crash (*Report* p. 32). Since the FAA had been tracking that plane as it zeroed in on its target, and since its fireball was dominating TV screens, are we to imagine that the FAA wouldn't have reported it—or, for that matter, that NORAD would have needed—a formal report?

If an element of surprise can be factored into the FAA's allegedly negligent or incompetent handling of Flight 11, it shouldn't have been a factor with Flight 175. After 8:40, when NORAD staffers received notification about Flight 11, they'd stayed in close touch with controllers at Boston Center. For the second hijacking, then, NORAD already "had their headsets linked to the FAA in Boston" (*Press Gazette* 4/15/02). Within just a few minutes, Flight 175 was the second airliner coming out of Boston to act strangely. When its transponder faltered and its radio went dead, flight controllers notified NORAD immediately (CNN 9/17/01). By 8:43, NORAD had learned that a second plane "also was not responding. It, too, was moving to[ward] New York" (Newhouse News 1/25/02).

All these reports didn't faze the Commission, however. It played down the heightened alertness that must have carried over from Flight 11 and played up an alleged tendency of controllers to remain preoccupied with that first hijacking (*Report* p. 22). However, a voice from within NORAD itself challenged the credibility of the Commission's interpretation. Capt. Michael Jellinek, a Canadian overseeing NORAD's headquarters in Colorado, was connected to NEADS. After seeing the second plane crash into the Trade Center, Jellinek asked, "Was that the hijacked aircraft you were dealing with?" NEADS told him that "unfortunately it was" (*Toronto Star* 12/9/01). Thus NORAD in Colorado had known about a second hijacking, and so did NEADS in upstate New York. So if NEADS knew before the crash that Flight 175 was another hijack, how could anyone claim the military hadn't received notification?

The Commission simply ignored information that "didn't fit with the story it wanted to tell." Shortly after 8:46, as Capt. Charles Leidig at the National Military Command Center (NMCC) saw the TV feed, he notified the chairman of the joint chiefs, the secretary of defense, and the FAA Operations Center. Capt. Leidig also recalled "a second round of notifications after the second impact." In these recollections, which were suppressed by the Commission, the NMCC, NORAD, and the secretary of defense's office were all notified about a second hijacking as early as 8:50-8:55 (Memorandum for the Record MFR04020719).

## Ongoing Conference Calls

The FAA, the White House, and the Pentagon each initiated these emergency conference calls, though the Pentagon's began significantly later. In addition, the first of the FAA's conference calls began about 8:50. Since NORAD was a key link in these calls, by 8:55 it too must have been receiving updates on the location of Flight 175, which the FAA first reported hijacked at 8:43. From this, Griffin draws the inescapable conclusion: "if NORAD had two F-15s circling off Long Island, it could have had Flight 175 intercepted before 9:03" (Griffin *9/11 Comm. Report* p. 186).

To avoid challenges like this, the Commission moved the FAA's notification time to 9:05 (Thompson *Terror Timeline* p. 392), two minutes *after* the airliner had crashed into the South Tower. Once again, the Commission first shortened NEADS's reaction time and then eliminated it altogether for the last three flights. Once again, too, it discounted the ongoing flow of information and held out for a single formality. Thus the Commission provided the military with an ostensibly valid excuse for not intercepting Flight 175: it could say, "Sorry, but we just didn't hear about it in time."

## Flight 77, "Lost" and "Missing": Another Imaginative Fiction

The Commission's account of Flight 77 was even more far-fetched. Although the "loss" of Flight 77 was a minor feature in NORAD's timelines, it ballooned into a prominent feature in the Commission's narrative (*Report* pp. 12-13, 28-31, 33, 624-25). As we'll see, it had its reasons.

As the Commission crafted this episode in its Official Story, it echoed its mantra, claiming that NORAD "didn't hear about it in time." Early reports stated that at 8:46, Flight 77 was reported going off course for several minutes (*USA Today* 8/13/02). Yet in the Commission's revised narrative, the airliner first deviated from its flight path at 8:54—*eight minutes later* than the FAA and NORAD had previously announced. Providing no rationale, the panel simply stated that at 8:56, the air controller working the flight noted a loss not only of radio contact and transponder signal, but also of radar tracking. Even more oddly, he drew the strange conclusion that "American 77 had experienced serious electrical or mechanical failure, or both, and was gone" (*Report* p. 24).

If Flight 77 had faltered, disappeared, or crashed, why didn't the unnamed controller follow the protocol for handling an "in-flight emergency" (IFE)? Apparently anticipating that the "lost" theory might be hard for the public to accept, the Commission emphasized that the controller "did not know that other aircraft had been hijacked" (*Report* p. 24).

This, too, is tough to accept. Even before the first hijacking, September 11 was no average day for air security personnel. Because of the several military exercises starting early that morning, the FAA and NORAD were already on alert (M. Ruppert *Crossing the Rubicon* pp. 336-37). And after the first hijackings, civilian and military personnel moved rapidly to high alert. Moreover, reports appearing just after 9/11 reported that about 8:25 Boston Center had notified other regional centers about the hijacking of Flight 11. One of them, in fact, was Indianapolis (*Guardian* [UK] 10/17/01). Is it likely, then, that a controller in Indianapolis wouldn't have heard about earlier hijackings from concerned colleagues, or from radio conversations with pilots, many of whom were receiving advisories from their airlines? (*Report* p. 24).

## Flight 77's "Lost" U-Turn and Return Flight

In similar fashion, the Commission airbrushed another inconvenient detail from the picture. NORAD's timeline had noted that just before Flight 77 allegedly disappeared from FAA radar, it made a U-turn and headed back eastward toward Washington. This was well known, but that too didn't inhibit the Commission. It denied that anyone had seen such a move: "Indianapolis Center never saw Flight 77 turn around...." As a result, the commissioners said, "American 77 traveled undetected for 36 minutes ..." (*Report* p. 25).

Now that's also a real stretch. After the alleged disappearance from the controller's scope, the Commission contended, the flight went "missing" and remained "lost" to all radar tracking for over a half hour. For this to be true, the FAA would have to lack radar coverage over southern Ohio, most of West Virginia, western Maryland, and northern Virginia. Why, after that telltale turn, were other flight controllers allegedly unable to track a Boeing 767 as it streaked eastward? Especially with the skies starting to clear of aircraft, is it credible that an airliner flying erratically—radically off course, at high speeds, and at unauthorized altitudes—wouldn't be noticed for 36 minutes? Commercial flights follow consistent flight paths; when they stray off course, increase speed, change altitude, or turn off their transponders, they attract attention.

To accept NORAD's claim that it was only informed that Flight 77 was reported "missing"—not hijacked—at 9:24, the Commission had to ignore substantiated testimony from FAA officials, tapes of air-security conversations, documented teleconferences in which the NORAD participated, and salient facts about NORAD and FAA radar. The Commission's scenario was possible, yes, but highly improbable—and the improbabilities were mounting.

On the issue of *formal* notification for Flight 77, the Commission brazenly overrode NORAD. In its second timeline, NORAD said it received notification at 9:24, thirteen minutes before Flight 77 reportedly slammed into the Pentagon. But whereas NORAD said it received formal notification at 9:24 that a "possible hijack appeared to be heading toward Washington" (AP 9/18/01), the Commission pushed notification still later, to 9:*34*—and then insisted that notification was only for a "missing" airliner, not a hijacking (*Report* pp. 32-33).

### Solid Sources Contradict *Both* NORAD and the Commission

At 9:20, air traffic controllers at Dulles Airport outside Washington spotted an unidentified aircraft about 50 miles away coming toward the capital at "a high rate of speed." The controllers notified the Secret Service, NORAD/NEADS, and the FBI. NORAD's own tapes captured reactions at NEADS headquarters in Rome, N.Y. The time was 9:21:

> Sgt. Maureen Dooley: "Another hijack! It's headed toward Washington!"
> Maj. Kevin Nasypany: "Shit! Give me a location!" (MSNBC 9/3/06).

Gotcha! So NORAD/NEADS *did* learn of the hijacked flight at 9:21; they knew where it was, and they did know where it was heading. They had sixteen minutes to intercept the airliner as it meandered over Arlington, Virginia. The Commission's claim of non-notification for Flight 77 was demonstrably false.

Controllers at Dulles also notified the FBI's Washington Office that the incoming plane (Flight 77) was another hijacking. The FBI dispatched a team of 50 agents to Dulles to provide additional security to prevent another hijacking there; it also sent another team to Reagan National Airport as a precaution (Dept. of Health and Human Safety, Arlington Co. *After Action Report* p. C-55). Most significantly, they alerted the White House bunker, where, according to Secretary Mineta, the young man kept apprising Cheney about how far out it was, only to be waved away (Hearing 5/23/03). Since Cheney was controlling possible military intervention against the airliner, it's disingenuous to claim that the military had no notification.

For all these reasons, the Commission not only failed to support its changes; it suppressed the FAA or NORAD audio tapes that it claimed supported its "lost" or "missing" interpretation, failed to identify the controller working Flight 77 in Indianapolis, and failed to document the civilian and military radar capabilities that, it claimed, were unable to track the Boeing 757.

## Commission Twice Precludes any Possibility of Interception

By radically reducing the notification time, the Commission's changes slammed shut NORAD's window of opportunity to intercept before impact. The 9:34 notification for a "missing" airliner, said the Commission, meant that NORAD had no chance to intercept Flight 77. Three minutes later, after coming out of its famous steep 270° descent, the "lost" Flight 77 swooped low over traffic, knocked down light posts, and slammed into the Pentagon (*Wash. Post* 9/15/01).

Understandably, the FAA begged to differ. According to one top administrator, Laura Brown, NORAD logs indicated "that the FAA made formal notification about American 77 at 9:24 a.m., but information about the flight was conveyed continuously during phone bridges before formal notification." Ms. Brown stressed that formal notification was primarily just that—a formality that didn't define when the military actually knew that a given airliner was hijacked (Hearing 5/23/03). Important as Brown was to both real-time communication and the later investigation, her name doesn't appear in the Commission's *Report.*

If the FAA was communicating continuously about Flight 77, then the plane obviously wasn't simply "lost." A *New York Times* story corroborated Brown's assertion that the FAA was feeding information to NORAD starting well before 9:24, allowing the Pentagon to track the rogue airliner: "During the hour or so that American Airlines Flight 77 was under the control of hijackers, up to the moment it struck the west side of the Pentagon, military officials in a command center on the east side of the building were urgently talking to law enforcement and air traffic controllers about what to do" (*NYT* 9/15/01). If this report is accurate, then the claims of "lost 77," like the rumors of Mark Twain's death, were "greatly exaggerated."

## Flight 93: Another Supposed Failure to Intercept—Yet a Possible Shoot Down

The Flight 93 of myth and legend flew west for at least 35 minutes without incident. As hijackers barged into the cockpit, air traffic controllers overheard sounds of struggle. A hijacking became fully evident at 9:30, when the plane's transponder went dead and controllers heard an accented voice announce, "Here is the captain, please sit down. Keep remaining sitting. There is a bomb aboard" (*Newsweek* 9/22/01).

Tasked with monitoring the flight, the FAA in Cleveland reportedly felt little sense of urgency and didn't call for help. This time the signs were even harder to miss. Even before the airliner turned, leaving its scheduled course about 9:30, the hijackers had called air traffic control to file new flight data for Washington (ABC 9/13/01). Why, unless the hijackers were fairly confident that they wouldn't face military intervention, would they risk revealing their identity, that of the plane they'd commandeered, and the city they intended to attack?

## Flight 93: More Alleged Non-Notification

Like Flights 175 and 77, the Commission claimed, the FAA didn't formally notify NORAD about Flight 93. At 9:34, Cleveland Center did alert the FAA in Washington about the hijacking of United 93, but FAA headquarters allegedly dawdled and didn't notify NORAD about the problem until 10:07. This was 33 minutes later and four minutes after the plane had reportedly crashed at 10:03. Furthermore, the FAA's Washington headquarters supposedly didn't notify NORAD about the hijacking until 10:07 and didn't report the crash to NORAD until 10:15 (*Report* pp. 28-31, 33).

Are we really to believe that the military didn't know about Flight 93 until it crashed? Three planes had already been flown into buildings, a fourth was known to be hijacked. As told by the Commission, Flight 93 (unlike Flight 77) was supposedly tracked by radar after it made its U-turn over north central Ohio. Exactly why one plane approaching Washington from the west would be found "missing" for 36 minutes and another could be tracked for almost exactly the same number of minutes, the Commission didn't say (*Report* pp. 29-30).

## No Fighters Going After Flight 93?

Above all, the Commission claimed that, lacking any notification, NORAD couldn't scramble any fighters to intercept the airliner before it crashed in Pennsylvania. Even though NORAD's top commanders would later contend that the fighters *were* positioned to intercept Flight 93, the claim that NORAD didn't scramble fighters for Flight 93 would also become an insistent drumbeat in the Commission's *Report*. Just to be sure that everyone got the point, the Commission repeated it *four* times (*Report* pp. 31, 34, 38, 44).

For Flight 93, the Commission was interested in promoting four perceptions: the apparent unprofessionalism of the FAA; the heroic passenger revolt with its demonstrable potential for drama and impact; the absence of response time and fighter intervention; and the flight's final plunge into the earth, allegedly caused by the revolt, not a shoot down. These priorities no doubt influenced the Commission's decision to place "The Battle for Flight 93" near the front of its narrative (*Report* pp. 10-14).

In another unexplained change, the Commission altered the original time when the FAA notified NORAD of the last hijacking by fully 51 minutes, from 9:16 to 10:07 (*Report* pp. 30-33). Since 10:07 was after the airliner had buried itself in the earth, this change completely eliminated any response time for NORAD. In doing so, it also conveniently allowed the air-defense establishment to evade a squadron of embarrassing questions about its tardy responses.

As evidence mounts, the Official Story's claims about non-notification for Flights 77 and 93 stretch credulity way beyond belief. To believe the Commission's stunning changes, one would have to discount reports from three generally reputable sources: Col. Robert Marr, counterterrorism "czar" Richard Clarke, and Secretary of Transportation Norman Mineta. Several NORAD officials, including Col. Marr, affirmed that NORAD knew Flight 93 was hijacked by 9:16 (Hearing 5/23/03). Moreover, one would have to forget that Clarke provided a detailed chronology of how his teleconference received information about Flights 77 and 93 (Clarke *Against All Enemies* pp. 5-7). One would also have to forget that, judging by the testimony given by Secretary Mineta, for at least ten minutes Secret Service (FAA) radar had been tracking an incoming, unidentified flight which turned out to be Flight 77 (Hearing 5/23/03). All this belies the Commission's claim that NORAD had no warning about Flight 93. For if the FAA's radar was able to track one airliner bearing down on Washington from the west, then why, just a half hour later, would it fail to detect a second?

The issue of radar coverage will be treated more fully in Chapter 13.

### "Phantom" Flight 11: A Useful Fiction

Like "lost" Flight 77, "phantom" Flight 11 would become a key episode in the Official Story. In it, the Commission claimed, the Langley jets were scrambled in response not to "an actual hijacked aircraft," but "a phantom aircraft" (*Report* p. 34). It was a "phantom" because it never existed.

Although Flight 11 had crashed at 8:46 and American Airlines was aware of its loss, the Commission claimed that Boston FAA had erroneously informed NEADS that Flight 11 hadn't crashed but was still in the air, heading for Washington (*Report* pp. 32, 594-95). As a result of this confusion, the Commission contended, NEADS scrambled fighters from Langley AFB to go after a "phantom" Flight 11. While some FAA and NORAD staffers apparently did believe that Flight 11 wasn't the plane that hit the North Tower, it didn't follow that they launched fighters to go after it. The ostensible pursuit of a "phantom" flight would serve to "explain" several key air-defense failures.

The Commission needed answers to several questions, one of which was, Why had supersonic interceptors stationed only 130 miles from Washington failed to provide air cover for the nation's capital? NORAD's interceptors, the Commission stated and restated, were wild-goose-chasing a "phantom," an airliner that supposedly flew by the WTC and continued southward. The Commission claimed that at 9:21 an unnamed individual at the FAA's Boston Center told a NEADS technician that "American 11 is still in the air, and it's on its way towards—heading towards Washington." The Commission had to acknowledge "we have been unable to identify the source of this mistaken FAA information" (*Report* p. 26). When it constructed its "phantom" story, the Commission built its edifice on a shaky foundation.

## Ignored Evidence and Mounting Contradictions

Once again, the Commission ignored evidence that challenged its contentions. Much as it had done with the Indianapolis controller, it based its interpretation on a single shred of hearsay evidence. Apparently not keeping its story straight, the Commission itself stated that "shortly after 8:50, while NEADS personnel were trying to locate the flight (AA 11), word reached them that a plane had hit the World Trade Center" (*Report* p. 20). The Commission also contradicted authorities it had typically treated with reverence. One of these, Gen. Richard Myers, indicated that the White House Situation Room (Clarke's teleconference) called him at 9:16 "to confirm that American Airlines Flight 11 … had hit the North World Trade Center Tower" (R. Myers *Eyes on the Horizon* p. 9). At the highest levels of command, then, it was known that Flight 11 had *already* impacted—and therefore was *not* continuing toward Washington.

Nor did the Commission deal with the fact that its "phantom" idea contradicted the testimony of several controllers at Boston Center, all of whom said they'd never lost sight of Flight 11. About 8:38, the FAA was tracking Flight 11 over Albany as it streaked southward at more than 500 mph (FAA "Summary of Air Traffic Hijack Events"). Flight controller Mark Hodgkins "watched the target [radar image] of American 11 all the way down" (ABC 9/6/02). Watching in helpless horror, several controllers had tracked the doomed airliner for a half hour until it dropped under their radar (*Christian Sci. Mon.* 9/13/01). When Boston controllers heard that a plane had hit the North Tower, they knew in the pit of their stomachs that it had to be Flight 11 (*NYT* 9/13/08).

Nor did the "phantom" Flight 11 story address the host of related questions it raised. Who among the NORAD commanders approved the deployment of resources to go after the "phantom"? Was this the same NORAD which had so often refused informal requests, especially those that hadn't gone up the chain of command? The ultimate irony, underscored by Griffin, was that, according to the Commission, nothing *else* got the military to act with dispatch that morning: NORAD (supposedly) didn't launch interceptors to go after Flights 11, 175, 77, or 93 while they were in the air: "The only time fighters were scrambled on this day, they were sent after a phantom" (Griffin *9/11 Comm. Report* p. 195).

Since it was supposedly based on NORAD's tapes, the new story needed support from NORAD commanders who had never mentioned chasing a "phantom." Known as a masterful interrogator, Commissioner Richard Ben-Veniste was apparently selected for the task.

When Gen. Larry Arnold made a second appearance before the Commission, Ben-Veniste had one main item on the docket—getting NORAD's continental commander to endorse the chase after the "phantom." He began by putting Arnold on the defensive by implying that the general had lied to the Commission in his previous testimony. As though scripted, Gen. Arnold acknowledged that since his previous appearance, the Commission's staff had unearthed information not available at that time. Somehow, staffers had found evidence in NORAD's 9/11 audiotapes that Pentagon experts had apparently been unable to access.

But instead of affirming the full story that the Langley F-16s were sent northward toward Baltimore to intercept the "phantom" flight, Gen. Arnold clung to the position (very likely correct) that "we scrambled those aircraft to get them over Washington...." Ben-Veniste also praised the staff's "painstaking work" to establish that someone had indeed made a false report about a "phantom" Flight 11. Slowly, the lawyer got the general to change his testimony. Hinting that the Commission had new information that could prove embarrassing, Ben-Veniste cajoled the former commander into expressing acceptance of the "phantom" story: "I take it you have no disagreement with the facts put forward in the Staff Statement" (Hearing 6/17/04). By assenting, Arnold in effect admitted that much of what NORAD had told the world for two and a half years was false.

## Clincher Critiques of the "Phantom" Story

Though tactically impressive, Ben-Veniste's manipulation of the witness raised intriguing issues. Given that NORAD had over two years to study its tapes, how could it have missed something so major as sending its interceptors after a "phantom"? If such a big mistake did occur, why did it only surface in 2004? Much earlier on, NORAD had every motive to say, "Hey, we were misinformed, so, yeah, we chased a phantom." But NORAD had never made that claim. Instead the fog rolled in, out of the blue.

To make the "phantom" story fly, one had to assume impaired visibility: that on 9/11 the thousands of aircraft in the air above the continental US were tracked on a *single* radar screen. Stepping up to the task, *Popular Mechanics* ignored the existence of *regional* radar in order to grossly exaggerate the overload on the FAA screens: "When the hijackers turned off the planes' transponders, which broadcast identifying signals, [air traffic controllers] had to search 4,500 identical radar blips crisscrossing some of the country's busiest air corridors" (*Pop. Mech.* 3/05). Not content to distort the FAA's problems with radar tracking, the reputedly "scientific" journal even upped the estimated number of aircraft by 500.

Insightfully, former Boston Center flight controller Robin Hordon has contended that the whole Phantom Flight 11 story diverted attention from a more fundamental question: Why weren't the Otis fighters launched more promptly, and why did they fail to intercept the airliners that hammered New York? Hordon has pointed out that if the FAA had treated the hijackings as the in-flight emergencies (IFEs) they were, the fighters at

Otis would have received priority getting off the ground, FAA controllers would have cleared other planes out of the fighters' way so they'd have been able to intercept one or possibly both of the airliners before they hit the Towers (M. Gaffney *9/11 Mystery Plane* p. 7). If this had happened as standard procedures required, Phantom Flight 11 would have become impossible, whether in fact or fiction.

### Commission Overrides NORAD's Statements about Flight 93

To preclude any suspicion of a shoot down, the Commission once again had to ignore additional evidence. It also disregarded statements from senior officials who claimed NORAD was tracking Flight 93 as it raced toward Washington and, if necessary, was prepared to shoot it down. Three top commanders concurred that Flight 93 was in their sights. Gen. Montague Winfield, for example, stated that the Pentagon's Command Center (NMCC) had "received a report from the FAA that Flight 93 … was now heading towards Washington." At that point, he said, "the decision was made to try to go intercept Flight 93." In addition, General Arnold and Deputy Defense Secretary Paul Wolfowitz had also spoken of interceptors positioned to take out Flight 93 (ABC 9/11/02).

Why would the Commission completely contradict the testimony of high-ranking officers and officials well positioned to know what happened? Obviously, it sought to dispel lingering suspicions that the Air Force had shot down an airliner. It went out of its way to emphasize that Air Force pilots had "negative clearance to shoot" and was consistently adamant in its denial that NORAD had even *known* about Flight 93 before it crashed.

The Commission also seemed keenly interested in reinforcing the patriotic account of a passenger revolt widely regarded as the first battle in the War on Terror. It was quick to remind readers that the heroic sacrifices by the passengers "saved the lives of countless others, and may have saved either the Capitol or the White House from destruction" (*Report* pp. 44-45). To reinforce the full significance—saving lives in Washington—it had to invalidate NORAD's claim that if the passengers hadn't brought the plane down, fighter jets could have done so. To reduce the time available for a shoot down, the Commission had the plane crash at 10:03—even though a seismic study placed the impact at 10:06 (Md. Dept. of Nat. Res. 2002). No one was supposed to notice, and few have.

## Commission Plays Down Importance of Conference Calls

Accepting the teleconference in the White House bunker (PEOC) as the real deal, the Commission invalidated the other "phone bridges." Since these teleconferences eroded the Commission's claims of delayed or non-notification, they had to be debunked. The FAA's teleconference, the Commission claimed, began at 9:20; in fact, it had started a half hour earlier. Laura Brown, Deputy Director of Public Affairs at FAA headquarters, explained that "within minutes after the first aircraft hit" at 8:46, she established open phone bridges not only to other FAA offices but also to NORAD, the NMCC at the Pentagon, and the Secret Service in the White House (PEOC) (Hearing 5/23/03). Since this teleconference was directly wired to the FAA's controllers, this was information central, the hub.

The Commission, however, contended that at the Pentagon, the FAA's input line "was monitored only periodically because the information was sporadic, it was of little value, and there were other important tasks" (*Report* p. 36). Now *that* doesn't just defy belief; it takes the breath away. Since the FAA had the better radar, and the challenge was to locate rogue aircraft before they hit targets, how could the information on the FAA's line have been "of little value"?

The Pentagon's NMCC teleconference, according to the Commission, began much later at 9:29. Considering that airliners had struck the WTC at 8:46 and 9:03, this was very late indeed. However, the Commission asked no questions about either the tardy inception, about the fact that it began as a mere "significant event" conference, or about the fact that, astonishingly, the FAA "had not been added to the call." Only after the Pentagon was hit at 9:37, did NORAD upgrade its phone bridge to an "air threat" teleconference.

This time the "phone bridge" did include the FAA, but the NMCC supposedly "had equipment problems and difficulty finding secure phone numbers" (*Report* p. 37). As Griffin remarked, the Commission was asking us to believe that "the NMCC had problems getting connected only with the FAA—the primary organization that regularly, by means of secure telephones, informs the NMCC about potential crises involving airplanes (Griffin *9/11 Comm. Report* p. 231). It was telling that the Commission apparently wanted to make it seem that the FAA and NORAD were hardly connected, when in fact they were in constant communication.

As if the Commission's mischaracterizations of these teleconferences weren't bad enough, its treatment of the videoconference in the White House Situation Room seriously eroded its own credibility. Run by counterterrorism expert Richard Clarke, this was arguably the most professional of the teleconferences. It convened fairly early, starting about 9:15, and was wired to the FAA, the PEOC, and the NMCC. The Commission, however, presented this teleconference as worthless: "none of the information conveyed in the White House teleconference, at least during the first hour, was being passed on to the NMCC" (*Report* p. 36). This, too, hardly passes the sniff test.

In contrast to the Commission's dismissal, Clarke's widely accepted rendition of events included warnings about incoming unidentified aircraft (Clarke *Against All Enemies* p. 7). Small wonder that Bush administration officials undertook an aggressive campaign to discredit Clarke. Philip Zelikow, the Commission's Executive Secretary, went "ballistic" and Dick Cheney ranted on Rush Limbaugh's show (P. Shenon *The Comm.* pp. 275-79). Had Clarke not been made to seem so controversial, the explosive revelations in his best-selling book would have made it more difficult for the Commission to get away with many of its fabrications.

### The Commission's Credibility Crumbles

It doesn't take a scholar to see that most of the Commission's claims were nowhere near believable. After hijackers seized planes and crashed them into targets, obviously putting controllers on alert and occasioning "phone bridges" between the FAA and NORAD, how could the Commission claim non-notification? Were all *three* teleconferences—those initiated by NORAD, the FAA, and Richard Clarke—of no use at all?

Clarke's videoconference also implicated Cheney. Clarke listened to updates from Jane Garvey, "honcha" of the FAA, about hijacked aircraft still in the air: Garvey listed "United 93 over Pennsylvania...." Participants heard her warn that "radar shows aircraft headed this way." And, underscoring the quality of Garvey's information, Clarke pointed out that the Secret Service used a system allowing it to see what FAA's radar was seeing (Clarke *Against All Enemies* p. 7). Since Cheney was running the Secret Service's command post (PEOC), he too must have known about incoming airliners. About 9:45, Cheney reportedly received permission from Bush to issue a shoot-down order. Why didn't he call for fighter protection, initiate interception procedures, or activate anti-aircraft missiles? At 9:49, FAA headquarters learned that Flight 93 was "twenty-nine minutes out of Washington" but, the Commission claimed, for the second time in an hour the FAA had lost track of a rogue airliner (*Report* pp. 29-30).

## Changing the Rules of the Blame Game

Clearly the Commission had cast the FAA to take the fall. Recall that a half hour earlier, before 9:00, the FAA had observed several highly suspicious signs—Flight 77 was way off course, flying erratically, out of radio contact, and emitting no transponder signal. These were flaming flags, and the FAA *did* alert NORAD about them. Nevertheless, the Commission contended that the FAA had provided no notification: that "no one at FAA Command Center or headquarters ever asked for military assistance with American 77" (Hearing 6/17/04). In the case of Flight 93, said the Commission, the FAA languished amid "uh" moments and couldn't decide whether to request a scramble (*Report* pp. 29-30). The Commission left the impression that only a few individuals at the FAA knew about the hijacked aircraft and those few failed to act. In fact, dozens of air safety professionals knew and many were discussing them laterally with their NORAD counterparts.

In making its claims, the Commission played games with semantics. When it stated that no one had "asked" for assistance, it implied that telling military personnel about an air emergency wasn't enough—the FAA had to explicitly *ask* for help. This is like reporting a blaze to the fire department's dispatcher and then, when the engines don't appear, having the chief shrug and say, "Hey, you didn't *ask* for them." The Commission's insistence on up-the-chain-of-command formal notification generated a diversion from the fact that NORAD, up and down its chain, was hearing about the attacks as they unfolded.

## A Split-Screen View of Reality

The commissioners' altered timeline disregarded not only information from FAA administrators, but also voice recordings of the "phone bridges"; both supported a very different sequence of events. In the Commission's coverage of all four hijacked planes, the FAA came out looking even more inept than in NORAD's previous versions. And we've noted how the "NORAD tapes," which the Commission cited but didn't release, differed from the recollections of several reliable witnesses.

The Official Story of 9/11, then, presents a deeply schizoid take on the FAA; the incongruity is staggering. When it came to landing thousands of aircraft for a "national ground stop" the FAA had never before attempted, its performance was stellar, nearly flawless. Despite overcrowded skies and runways at many airports, all 4,000 aircraft in the air above the continental United States landed safely (*NYT* 9/12/01). But when it came to following air-emergency (IFE) procedures it *had* practiced and *had* executed hundreds of times—or to tracking errant planes like it does every day—FAA personnel were portrayed as inattentive bunglers.

## Why the Commission Made the Time Changes

Since the Commission provided no rationale for either its changes to an established historical record or its omissions of likely causal factors, we have to raise the obvious question: Why did it do so? If the Commission was trying to make NORAD look better and the FAA look worse, why would it make changes that made the secretary of defense look inept, even derelict, in his duty?

To provide tentative answers to these questions, we draw inferences from patterns in the changes. Such choices suggested that when desirables came into conflict, the Commission's priority was to cover tracks at the top. Better to look inept that complicit. As already noted, the Commission's changes almost always had the consequence of making it seem temporally impossible for NORAD to intercept any of the airliners or for Bush,

Cheney, or Rumsfeld to have issued an order that resulted in a shoot down of Flight 93.

As the Commission came up with its new timelines, it was especially attentive to Cheney. The vice president, after all, was not only the most powerful person in Washington; he was also up for reelection. Cheney had always presented himself as arriving at the White House bunker (PEOC) later than anyone else recalled his arrival there. This included not only Richard Clarke, who was in close contact with both the PEOC and Cheney, but also Karl Rove at the White House and Secretary of Transportation Mineta, who recalled that Cheney was already present in the bunker when he arrived just after 9:20 (NBC 9/2/02). The Secret Service provided 9:33 as the time of arrival, which would still have allowed time for the vice president to tell the young lieutenant that his order (not to take action against the incoming airliner) still stood (Hearing 5/23/03).

The Commission was not only careful but also especially creative in crafting a story for Cheney. The vice president had always put his arrival closer to 9:40, seemingly too late to issue this stand-down order but not too late to issue a shoot-down order for Flight 93. Apparently this was seen as a problem. To resolve it, the Commission had Cheney only entering the *tunnel* leading to the PEOC at 9:37, the very minute when the Pentagon was hit. By assigning this time of arrival *in the tunnel* to the bunker, the commissioners made sure that Secretary Mineta's account (Hearing 5/23/03)—in which he implied that Cheney issued a stand-down order for Flight 77—would seem impossible. The Commission then had Cheney actually enter the PEOC about 9:55, just after he'd completed a call with Bush (*Report* pp. 39-40). The key piece was that Cheney didn't have time to issue a shoot-down order and NORAD didn't have time to execute one before Flight 93 crashed at 10:03.

While the Commission slammed the FAA (*Report* p. 30), and its chairs later implied that Pentagon personnel had lied, the panel consistently protected the Bush administration's top officials. In spite of their blatant failures to defend the nation, Myers, Rumsfeld, Cheney, and Rice come off looking far better than they actually were.

## Getting Bush and Cheney Reelected

Arousing suspicions wouldn't do, especially just months before the elections. As already noted, Cheney could become furious and aggressive in his attempts to suppress information about 9/11. As recounted earlier, he threatened to terminate the Joint Congressional Investigation after someone made a troubling leak: that the day before the attacks the NSA had intercepted phone calls in which al Qaeda discussed its plans (*National Journal* 2/15/07).

Apparently those running the Commission felt they could count on the news media to remain quiescent, providing minimal and sometimes demeaning coverage of the citizens' and survivors' groups that were raising far tougher questions. In its *Report,* the Commission hoped the loose ends of the 9/11 narrative would be tied together in a neat bow for posterity, avoiding the puzzling anomalies surrounding 9/11. They did so, however, at the exorbitant cost of distorting the historical record and leaving the odor of something fishy beneath the shiny surfaces.

If some FAA personnel didn't perform optimally, the performance of many others in the military was far worse, especially at the top of the command structure. We've noted that Vice President Cheney was supposedly late to arrive in the White House bunker, but other key commanders—President Bush, Secretary Rumsfeld, Gen. Richard Myers, Gen. Ralph Eberhart, Gen. Mike Canavan, and others—either absented themselves or claimed they were out of the loop. In at least two key cases, this left "newbies" at the controls that morning.

Once aware of the many distortions, contradictions and omissions, thoughtful citizens have to wonder, What happens to someone's credibility when he replaces his first story with a second and even comes up with a third? Who would believe *any* of these stories? If this were the only challenge the Official Story faced, it might have retained some credibility. But this was the least of its problems.

# 12. Paralysis: Strangely Dysfunctional Air Defenses

*If our government had merely done nothing—and I say that as an old interceptor pilot ... I know what the procedures are, I know what they were, and I know what they changed them to—if our government had merely done nothing and allowed normal procedure to happen on the morning of 9/11, the twin towers would still be standing and thousands of dead Americans would still be alive.*

—Col. Robert M. Bowman, PhD, former fighter pilot and Director of Advanced Space Programs Development, US Air Force

The Commission faced a daunting challenge: to explain an unprecedented paralysis of air defenses, both civilian and military. It claimed that "the defense of U.S. airspace on 9/11 was not conducted in according with existing training and protocols" (*Report* p. 31); but it never explained why standard procedures were not implemented. Hence it evaded a central question it was charged with answering: How could such low-tech attackers have foiled such high-tech defenses?

This chapter will point to other factors likely contributing to the unprecedented air-defense failures. It will look at how the traditional (slow-response) hijacking protocol, recently reemphasized by Defense Secretary Rumsfeld's Directive, contributed to delays; at how key commanding officers (including Secretary Rumsfeld and Gen. Myers) were supposedly absent, strangely "out of the loop"; at how inexperienced substitutes or neophytes at the FAA and NORAD may have contributed to compromised responses; and at how runway delays and in-flight confusion further hampered fighter pilots.

While some of these factors possibly contributed to the outcome, even taken together they don't explain the stunning air-defense failures on 9/11.

### Clarity Regarding Standard Operating Procedures (SOP)

For the 9/11 attacks to succeed, air-security personnel must have breached Standard Operating Procedures (SOP). At the time, reports former Boston Center air traffic controller Robin Hordon, protocols called for interceptors to scramble fighters in three situations: attacks on the United States, aircraft experiencing in-flight emergencies (IFEs), and hijackings. In the first two cases, protocols called for *immediate* scrambling of interceptors; in the third, the scrambles did not have to be immediate, assuming the hijackings were "traditional" and not "terrorist" ("Affidavit of Robin D. Hordon").

The FAA's standard procedures were straightforward: if an air traffic controller noticed telltale signs which indicated a flight was having problems or posed a danger, he was required to report the flight immediately. The signs included loss of radio contact, failure to emit transponder signal, and divergence from assigned route or altitude. If these problems weren't resolved, then the FAA had to ask NORAD to scramble aircraft and intercept the plane (FAA Orders JO7110.65S, 10-1-3, 10-2-5F, 7610.4Jf). On 9/11, each of the four airliners showed these signs, which indicated "in-flight emergencies" (IFEs). When each of the airliners manifested not one but several characteristics of an IFE, the FAA should have sounded the alarm and called for help.

But in all four instances, the Commission claimed, this didn't happen in time.

### Traditional Procedures for Handling Different Types of Hijackings

Traditionally, different types of hijackings required different protocols. If the situation was a "traditional" hijacking, one in which someone commandeered an aircraft and told pilots where to land, an immediate scramble of fighters wasn't deemed necessary. If, however, the situation involved a "terrorist" hijacking, one posing imminent danger to life and property, then IFE procedures applied; fighters were scrambled immediately.

On 9/11, oddly enough, the FAA and NORAD dithered, treating the airliners under attack as *traditional*, not as *terrorist* hijackings—and not as the IFEs they clearly were. Since the Commission never referred to these procedures, few Americans had any idea how far the FAA and NORAD deviated from their own Standard Operating Procedures.

Nor do most have any idea how, a mere three months before the attacks, traditional procedures were altered. This changed everything.

## Rumsfeld's Directive: Small Changes with Big Consequences

On June 1, 2001, Rumsfeld and the Joint Chiefs of Staff released a directive on aircraft piracy requiring that the Secretary of Defense approve all scrambles for hijackings of either sort. These new Department of Defense (DoD) guidelines changed air defenders' responses to hijackings: they discouraged personnel from applying long-routine procedures for intercepting aircraft in distress.

Rumsfeld's new air defense directive blurred a crucial distinction. Standard procedures suddenly changed when the DoD released its new protocols (DoD CJCSI 3610.01A). According to Canadian researcher Elizabeth Woodworth, the 1997 hijacking scramble protocol had distinguished *emergency* situations (those requiring immediate action) from *non-emergency* situations, which could be handed more slowly (Woodworth *Global Outlook* 2009 p. 86).

The new Directive, titled "Destruction of Derelict Flying Objects," conflated different types of hijackings: the "traditional," in which hijackers seek to extort money, effect the release of prisoners, or gain political asylum; and the "terrorist," in which hijackers seek to use the plane as a weapon. The procedure for traditional hijackings had been to vector other aircraft away from the errant plane and order fighters to trail it until it landed. Since traditional hijackings had never been treated as emergencies or threats to national security, responses could be slower: interceptor aircraft were *launched* promptly but not *scrambled* immediately (Woodworth *Global Outlook* 2009 p. 86).

## Directive Encouraged a Throwback to Old Conceptions

Judging by statements made just after the attacks, many of those involved in airline safety and air defense may have reverted to traditional notions about hijackings (L. Spencer *Touching History* p. 39). While the Directive was hardly the source of this antiquated attitude, it did insist that air defenders work from an assumption which DoD knew to be false: "after all, a hijacking is a hijacking." Thus Rumsfeld's Directive implied that a *terrorist* hijacking wouldn't constitute an In Flight Emergency requiring immediate intervention.

### "If It's a Hijacking, Run the Request through Me"

With the exception of "immediate emergency responses," fighter "scrambles" now had to go through the secretary's office (*NY Observer* 6/17/04). If, as the procedure had been for so long, routine scrambles involved nonviolent investigation or interception, then why would a defense secretary place strict controls on them? When the Directive concentrated more authority with the secretary of defense, it made an auspicious change: as we'll see, the secretary isn't always available, even when he's right in his office (Spencer *Touching History* p. 22). By conflating traditional and terrorist hijackings, the Directive encouraged air defenders to react with agonizing slowness to an emergency.

When Rumsfeld issued his Directive, he had to have known that a slow-track response was completely inappropriate for *terrorist* hijackings. The FAA had just issued its 52 warnings about al Qaeda's interest in aircraft, including an advisory about bombs or hijackings (FAA 4/18/01). On several recent occasions, Rumsfeld himself had warned of increasing terrorist threats (*Wash. Post* 4/24/01). Furthermore, well before he took office, the Pentagon had been "gaming" suicide hijackings that involved flights carrying WMDs or crashing into buildings (AP 8/21/03). In fact, Rumsfeld and Cheney had personally involved themselves with the Pentagon's "war games" (J. Mann *Rise of the Vulcans* pp. 138-45). So by 2001, when NORAD subsumed "terrorist" hijackings into its "traditional" protocol, it was running more and more exercises that involved terrorist attacks using airplanes.

The results of the new Directive were immediate and dramatic. For many years, the FAA had routinely requested military interventions. A 1994 GAO report revealed that over four years, NORAD scrambled jets 1,518 times to intercept unidentified, off-course, or distressed aircraft (www.fas.org/man/gao/gao9476.htm). This averaged out to nearly 400 interceptions a year. In 2000, the number had declined but was still significant; NORAD scrambled fighters 129 times (*Calgary Herald* 10/13/01). Between September 2000 and June 2001, the FAA had asked NORAD to launch fighters 67 times (FAA News Release 9/9/02). This averaged out to 100 scrambles a year, two a week.

Rumsfeld's Directive changed all this. During the three months prior to 9/11, the number of fighter scrambles and interceptions dropped from the previous average of two a week under the old protocol to *none at all* under the new one (Woodworth *Global Outlook* 2009 p. 86). Later in 2001, after the old protocol was inexplicably restored, scrambles and interceptions once again became common (Griffin *Debunking 9/11 Debunking* pp. 39-41).

## How Did the New Directive Affect Outcomes on 9/11?

The consequences of handling all hijackings under the "slow" protocol almost certainly contributed to the air-defense failures on 9/11. By making all requests for hijack interventions go through one person, the secretary seemingly made it more likely that terrorist hijackings could *not* be intercepted. Intentionally or not, Rumsfeld revised regulations in ways that produced an air-defense *slow down*—one that could, given the right conditions, effect a temporary *stand down*. When Capt. Leidig at the Pentagon contacted Col. Robert Marr, commander of the North East Air Defense Sector (NEADS), Marr initially followed the slow-track protocol: he ordered fighter pilots at Otis Air Base to their "battle stations" but rejected (the FAA) Boston Center's urgent requests for a fast-track scramble (www.cooperativeresearch.org/entity.jsp?entity=robert_marr).

## Slow-Track Protocol Delays Responses

By 9:20, alarm lights should have been flashing. Four airliners had cut radio contact and either shut off or reset their transponder beacons; they'd also altered both their flight paths and their altitudes. In addition, three of the four had inadvertently sent radio data indicating cockpit violence or takeover. Any *one* of these aberrations should have signaled an in-flight emergency (IFE) and triggered an immediate scramble. When *several* aircraft manifested these warning signs within less than an hour, surely the system should have been urgently flashing red.

Somehow, though, appropriate action didn't follow. Both the FAA and NORAD treated these situations as traditional hijackings in which pilots fly the plane to a destination. In these situations, the standard procedure was to warn pilots and launch fighters to trail the plane (www. cooperativeresearch.org/entity.jsp?entity=robert_marr). Following Rumsfeld's Directive, most of the responders construed the hijackings as traditional and followed *slow-track* protocols rather than the *fast-track* ones applicable to In Flight Emergencies.

But it wasn't just new procedures that caused the delays; it was also the performance of individuals.

## Absentees Contribute to Air-Defense Paralysis

As hijacked airliners slammed into buildings, many senior decision-makers were preoccupied, absent, incommunicado, or otherwise out of the loop. Bush's dawdling is well documented, but the dysfunction caused by Rumsfeld, Gen. Richard Myers, Gen. John Jumper, Gen. James Roche, Gen. Ralph Eberhart, Gen. Mike Canavan, and Gen. Montague Winfield are less widely known.

Rumsfeld's own accounts place him in his office at the Pentagon but incommunicado; Gen. Myers and Gen. Eberhart were also inaccessible, one in a meeting and the other in a car (P. Thompson *Terror Timeline* pp. 424, 426, 376-77); Air Force generals Jumper and Roche lingered in a meeting; Army Gen. Canavan, hijacking coordinator for the FAA, was not only unreachable by phone but had failed to appoint a required substitute (*Wash. Post* 1/27/02); and Army Gen. Winfield ordered a rookie substitute to take over the Pentagon's Command Center yet didn't relieve him, even though the general remained in the Center (CNN 9/4/02). Among these seven key players within the command structure, some apparently wanted to be *seen* as out of the loop, while others actually *went* incommunicado. With key commanders absent or incommunicado, three inexperienced managers—two at the FAA and one at the Pentagon—were forced to improvise responses to the unprecedented crisis.

As noted earlier, Rumsfeld told different stories about his actions that morning. In each, the defense secretary placed himself not at the Pentagon's National Military Command Center (NMCC)-where he belonged in a crisis-but in his office just down the hall. According to his accounts, when the Pentagon was hit he reacted, but not by reporting to the NMCC. In one version Rumsfeld strode through the corridors and out to the Pentagon's parking lot, where he helped place victims on stretchers; in another, he simply stepped outside to see what had happened and then returned to his office by 10:00 (Thompson *Terror Timeline* pp. 424, 426). Richard Clarke, a more dependable source, placed Rumsfeld at the NMCC starting around 9:30 (Clarke *Against All Enemies* p. 7). What would have led Rumsfeld to prefer being seen as away from his post to being seen as doing his duty, or even taking command?

The Commission, however, came up with a *fourth* story, one that no one had ever told before. When it combined Rumsfeld's two stories, it perpetuated another apparent contradiction (Griffin *9/11 Comm. Report* p. 218). Its new version had Rumsfeld going outside and assisting with rescues yet arriving back to his office by 10:00 a.m. Given the vast size of the Pentagon, the fact that the impact area was on the side opposite the secretary's office, and the fact that the building was filling with smoke, an obvious question had to arise: Was it plausible that the oldest defense secretary in American history, wearing a suit and dress shoes, could cover that distance, render aid outside the building, and return to his office in just over twenty minutes?

**The Story Gets Stranger Yet**

The Commission also added two astonishing details to this story: that during the crisis, NORAD commanders had been looking for "Rummy," and that he finally arrived at the NMCC "shortly before 10:30" (*Report* pp. 37-38, 43-44). Since the NMCC was so close to the secretary's office, this account implied that Rumsfeld arrived scandalously late—that, oblivious to dozens of urgent calls, the secretary of defense had lingered in his office for nearly a half hour. If this were true, then what was Rumsfeld doing there? Why didn't he report immediately to the NMCC, where he belonged as the second in command?

But these were minor dings compared to the major dents the Commission filled in and painted over. Whatever its shortcomings, the Commission's story averted a potentially explosive revelation: that Rumsfeld had first issued a Directive requiring that requests for a military response to any hijacking go though him and then, in just such a moment of crisis, remained intentionally unreachable for a key hour and a half.

The Commission made no mention of other narratives, certainly not that of Clarke, who placed Rumsfeld in the NMCC about 9:30, in time to participate in making life-and-death decisions. Yet as Griffin pointed out, "the Commission was surely aware that these mutually inconsistent versions of Rumsfeld's activities exist[ed].... It would appear, therefore, that the Commission deliberately covered up the fact that Rumsfeld had lied ..." (Griffin *9/11 Comm. Report* p. 219). Rumsfeld didn't protest these alterations to his narratives, at least not publicly. Perhaps he felt relieved when the Commission quietly resolved contradictions, no questions asked.

## Gen. Myers Also Takes Himself out of the Loop

As indicated in Chapter 5, Rumsfeld was hardly the only top-ranked member of the command structure who told three different stories, each of which implied dereliction of duty. Gen. Richard Myers, the acting Chairman of the Joint Chiefs of Staff, recalled spending most of the crucial time in the office of Sen. Max Cleland (D-Ga.). In one account, claiming "no one informed us," Gen. Myers made no mention of either making or receiving any phone calls during the 40-minute meeting (Armed Forces Press Service 10/23/01).

In another version, Gen. Myers stated that "after the second tower was hit, I talked to the Commander of NORAD." In a third story, the one he told the Commission, Myers said he received a call from the Commander just before the Pentagon was hit (Thompson *Terror Timeline* pp. 376-77). All three versions imply a detachment that had to seem peculiar; after all, Gen. Myers was not only charged with overseeing all US forces that day but also directly involved with the military exercises the Pentagon was conducting (Clarke *Against All Enemies* p. 5).

All of Myers's accounts seem highly improbable. Referring to his "courtesy-call" meeting with Sen. Cleland and his absence from the

Pentagon's Command Center (NMCC), intelligence analyst James Bamford has quipped that while Myers was "self promoting his talents to lead the military," he was remaining incommunicado (Bamford *Pretext for War* pp. 38-39). Although credible sources had placed Myers at the NMCC before 9:30, these didn't keep the Commission from reverting to Myers's earlier tale about remaining incommunicado and not arriving there until 10:00 (*Report* pp. 38, 463n). The *Report's* uncritical repetition of this story, Griffin has remarked, "makes it hard not to conclude that the Commission was deliberately attempting to protect Myers ..." (Griffin *9/11 Comm. Report* p. 216). "Protect," yes, in the sense of reducing the perception that Gen. Myers was involved with making decisions about Flights 77 or 93.

Just two days after 9/11 Gen. Richard Myers, the Vice Chair of the Joint Chiefs, was confirmed as chairman, the top position in the US military. Despite the unprecedented air-defense failure that occurred on his watch, Gen. Myers was overwhelmingly confirmed by the Senate as though nothing had happened. President Bush bestowed the Medal of Freedom on the four-star general in 2005 (AP 11/9/05).

Beyond Rumsfeld and Myers, *five* other key players were either missing or slow to respond during the rapidly developing emergency. In fact, the tardy responses of several Air Force generals more than matched those the Commission attributed to FAA personnel.

### USAF Top Brass: Slow to Show

At the Pentagon, air force commanders Gen. John Jumper (Air Force Chief of Staff) and Gen. James Roche (Secretary of the Air Force) ignored calls for help and remained ensconced in a meeting even after news of the WTC attacks started coming in (A. Goldberg *Pentagon 9/11* p. 136).

Both Gen. Jumper and Gen. Roche were prominent members of the elite USAF Crisis Action Team. Having watched the second impact on TV, Jumper and Roche were both aware of the attacks in New York. Just after 9:03, someone called the commanders down to the Air Force Operations Center. However, according to the Defense Department's own history of events, Gen. Jumper did not respond; he watched televised news "for about eight minutes," resumed his meeting, and returned to his office (A. Goldberg *Pentagon 9/11* p. 136).

If the leaders of the Crisis Action Team were slow to draw a logical conclusion from what they'd seen on TV, officers at the Pentagon's "Ground Zero" snack bar were quick to get the point: "When the second plane deliberately dove into the Tower, someone said, 'The World Trade Center is one of the most recognizable symbols of America. We're sitting in a close second'" (Defenselink News 9/13/01). Many other Pentagon personnel reported similar forebodings. Is it credible that neither Jumper nor Roche nor the Pentagon's other commanders had any inkling that another airliner might be headed their way? (*Newsday* 9/23/01).

Much like Rumsfeld, Generals Jumper and Roche didn't respond for a half an hour and didn't arrive at the Air Force's Operations Center until something clobbered their own headquarters (CNN 10/10/01). With the Center's designated leaders away, a subordinate had taken charge of emergency operations (*Prospectus* 9/06 pp. 3-6). When the pair finally arrived at the Operations Center, it wasn't yet in the loop. Three airliners had struck iconic targets, killing thousands of American citizens, yet the Air Force Operations Center still hadn't established an open line to NORAD (*Dover Post* 9/19/01).

When the generals did "hook up with the North American Air Defense Command," it was "to stand by and start to think of how we, the Air Force, could support any casualties or any other things that might develop" (*Dover Post* 9/19/01). Only later in the day did the Crisis Action Team reportedly "become the eyes and ears of the Air Force," working with the FAA to monitor flight activity and coordinating with NORAD to put fighters on alert (CNN 10/10/01).

## Jumper and Roche Had Called for Dismantling NORAD's "On-Alert" Sites

While the generals' nonchalance itself merits investigation, additional factors make it even more suspicious. During the summer of 2001, task forces assigned by Defense Secretary Rumsfeld had recommended unprecedented reductions in air defenses (*LA Times* 9/15/01). Discussions at the highest levels called for dismantling NORAD's seven "on-alert" sites plus its command and control structure. Generals Roche and Jumper had favored discontinuance of funding for domestic air defense (Spencer *Touch. Hist.* pp. 149, 289).

Were top commanders simply considering the main mission of the Air Force to lie less with protecting the homeland than with supporting overseas campaigns that would require purchase of new aircraft, such as Predator drones? Gen. Roche did have links to military contractors. As a vice president of Northrop Grumman Aircraft, a major military supplier, Roche had sat on the board at the Center for Security Policy (CSP), a conservative advocacy group headed by neocon and Fox News commentator Frank Gaffney. In the months leading up to 9/11, more than two dozen of the Center's neocon advisors had received powerful positions in the Bush administration; these included Richard Perle, Elliott Abrams, Douglas Feith, and Dov Zakheim (www.rightweb.irc-online.org/profile/Roche_James#_edn6).

### Gen. Eberhart: NORAD's Commander Jumps in a Car

The temporary absence of Gen. Ralph Eberhart, NORAD's top Commander, was particularly curious. As the crisis worsened, Gen. Eberhart had become actively involved with decision-making at the highest level. About 9:15, calling from Colorado Springs, Gen. Eberhart told Gen. Myers he was "working with the FAA to order all aircraft in the national airspace" to land at the nearest airport (R. Myers *Eyes on the Horizon* p. 9). About twenty minutes later, Eberhart phoned Myers from NORAD's headquarters in Colorado. Myers recalled that this was about 9:37, when the Pentagon was hit (Armed Forces Radio/TV 10/17/01). Until this time, Eberhart was actively in the command loop.

But then, instead of continuing to direct NORAD's efforts, Gen. Eberhart decided to move from NORAD's headquarters at Patterson AFB to NORAD's operations center at heavily fortified Cheyenne Mountain, a dozen miles away (*Legion Mag.* 11/04). This was about 9:40, after airliners had struck the Towers and the Pentagon—hardly a good time for a continental commander to leave his post. Making matters worse, Eberhart took 45 minutes to make the 12-mile drive, missing several important phone calls, including one from Cheney (*Colo. Springs Gazette* 6/16/06). Are we to believe that the NORAD's commander wasn't equipped with a mobile phone so he could communicate in a national emergency?

Although Gen. Eberhart reportedly made the drive to access the "better communications capabilities available at Cheyenne Mountain," it did seem strange that, in the midst of a national emergency, NORAD's commander would make a choice initially involving *worse* communications capabilities: why would Eberhart jump in a car, taking himself away from secure phones? (*Denver Post* 7/28/06). Eberhart's disappearance from the command loop extends a perplexing pattern in which many of those in command were, in one way or another, oddly "unavailable" during that crucial hour and a half.

Did Gen. Ralph Eberhart face disciplinary action or even questions about his actions? To the contrary, he received a promotion and prestigious awards. The governor general of Canada awarded him the Meritorious Service Cross, and President Bush picked Eberhart to head the new "Northern Command" (www.defenselink.mil 5/8/02).

### Gen. Canavan, FAA Hijack Coordinator, Also Goes Incommunicado

In late 2000, Army Gen. Mike Canavan became director of the FAA's Office of Civil Aviation Security. As director, Gen. Canavan became the hijack coordinator responsible for military responses (*LA Times* 10/13/01).

While visiting an airport in Puerto Rico that morning, Gen. Canavan remained oddly incommunicado. Regulations required that FAA requests for help with a hijacking go through "the FAA hijack coordinator in direct contact with the National Military Command Center (NMCC)" (FAA 11/3/98). And although Gen. Canavan was supposed to appoint someone to stand watch in his absence (*Report* pp. 17-18), he apparently didn't. As the crisis worsened, Canavan's absence as hijack coordinator became a serious problem: "an [unnamed] FAA security person" had to run the "hijack net" open communication system during the crisis (Hearing 6/17/04). Did Canavan's absence, intentional or otherwise, contribute to delays that allowed the attacks to go forth?

A few months later, Canavan left the FAA after only ten months on the job, reportedly because of a dispute with FAA officials, and ended his military career that same year (*LA Times* 10/13/01). In 2003, Gen. Canavan became group senior vice president for Homeland Security at Anteon Corporation. A major military contractor, Anteon provided information technology to federal agencies until it was purchased by General Dynamics, an even larger military contractor (www.usfalcon.com/SiteCollectionDocuments/ Leaders/MCanavan.pdf). In 2006, Canavan joined the Board of US Falcon, another military supplier (www.linkedin.com/companies/usfalcon).

### Gen. Winfield Assigns Rookie, Fails to Relieve Him in Crisis

In addition to the FAA, NORAD also experienced problems with an inexperienced substitute in a key slot. On September 10, NORAD's director, Gen. Montague Winfield, ordered his neophyte deputy, Capt. Charles Leidig Jr. to "stand a portion of his duty" as deputy for Command Center Operations at the Pentagon (NMCC). Capt. Leidig had started to train as Deputy for Command Center Operations only two months earlier; he'd qualified for the position just the month before. Leidig's assignment ran from 8:30 to 10:30, the time frame of the attacks.

On the next morning, September 11, the inexperienced substitute took over the communications hub. Suddenly in charge of the Pentagon's "war room" at a crucial moment, Capt. Leidig had difficulty handling a crisis he wasn't prepared for. When Gen. Winfield learned of the hijackings, he neither returned to his watch nor came to the aid of his distressed deputy. Winfield was absent from his post and didn't intervene until about 10:30, when the crisis was over (Thompson *Terror Timeline* pp. 431-32, 364). Yes, it's possible Gen. Winfield supervised Captain Leidig, who perhaps sat in the chair so Gen. Winfield could "put out fires." On the other hand, not replacing his substitute could have provided "plausible deniability" so Winfield couldn't be held responsible because he wasn't in command.

When the 9/11 Commission interviewed Capt. Leidig, illuminating information emerged. Leidig recalled that Gen. Winfield was attending a meeting down the hall and that "such meetings are generally not disturbed unless the reason is significant." (Were several hijacked airliners not "significant"?) Although Leidig was "certain that Gen. Winfield returned after the Pentagon was hit," he did not indicate that Winfield took over at the NMCC when he did return (Memo for the Record MFR04020719).

The general's self-presentations served him well. When Winfield appeared in *Attack on the Pentagon*, a Discovery-Times documentary, he glossed over his absence on 9/11. He claimed that the "national leadership" was called to the NMCC "after the World Trade Center was struck." Winfield talked about "resolving" problems with Flight 93, the final hijacking, as though he'd been right at his post all along (www.911truth.org/article.php?story=20050830185334880). Winfield's official Web entry claims he "was present as the general officer-in-charge during the terrorist attacks of 9/11," not that he'd arranged for a less-qualified substitute and didn't resume his duties, even when a whirlwind nearly blew the guy off his feet.

By 2003, Gen. Winfield had been promoted to major general and joined the Council on Foreign Relations (CFR) (www.defense.gov/releases/ release.aspx?released=3817). The council is widely regarded as a nexus of elite power committed to the "Global Domination Project" driving US foreign policy. Despite their obvious pertinence to tragic outcomes on 9/11, neither Winfield nor Leidig was even mentioned in the Commission's *Report*.

## A Pattern of Staying "out of the Loop"?

When we place these "anomalies" side-by-side, staring at the number of high officials who remained incommunicado, or "out-of-the-loop," at key moments, the picture is perplexing. Starting with President Bush, is there a pattern among those who topped the chain of command and were most responsible for protecting the nation? If we consider mathematical probabilities, can we conclude that these key absences were simply coincidental? At what point do "coincidences" cease to be coincidental?

On 9/11, Secretary Rumsfeld, generals Myers, Jumper, Roche, Eberhart, Canavan, and Winfield became the largest cluster of top brass in the country's history to turn up temporarily missing-in-action. Yet however much their absences compromised the country's defenses, their substitutes—some appointed, some improvised—may have done even more damage.

When senior managers of an organization are absent, incommunicado, or removed from the loop, someone with less experience or less clout usually has to take over. As any supervisor knows, "newbies" on a job are prone to mistakes. In a crisis, rookies and substitutes can put the FU in SNAFU. On 9/11, three key players were doing crucial jobs for the first time, and one was substituting, working with one of the "newbies." Capt. Leidig, an inexperienced replacement, was assigned to the demanding watch commander position at the Pentagon's National Military Command Center (NMCC).

### Replacement Junior Officer Commands "War Room" at Pentagon

Deputy director for operations at the NMCC is a challenging position. According to espionage/military tech expert James Bamford, doing the watch commander job "would require supervision and operation of all necessary communication" (Bamford *Pretext for War* p. 65). Since the deputy director of operations job carries enormous responsibility, one wonders why Gen. Winfield, knowing that Captain Leidig had only recently met training requirements, would assign him to run the controls at the NMCC (M. Ruppert *Crossing the Rubicon* pp. 388-9).

Due to his inexperience, the rookie initially launched a "significant-event" conference, not a full-emergency response to the crisis (*Report* p. 37). As a result, the much-needed "emergency response" conference began later than it could have. When Leidig didn't recall when the conference began, the Commission pegged it at 9:39 (Hearing 6/17/04)—which, if accurate, was already very late indeed. While this tardiness suggested bungling by a novice, other factors, including Rumsfeld's reported absence and Winfield's reluctance to resume his duties, may have contributed to the delay. Despite his likely contribution to slowed air-defense responses on 9/11, Capt. Leidig received a prestigious appointment at the Naval Academy and a promotion to admiral (*Baltimore Sun* 8/29/03). If it hadn't become so typical, this might seem peculiar.

Another newbie, Ben Sliney, was working his first morning on a new job as the FAA Command Center's National Operations Manager. Coordinating the "shout-line" phones at the FAA's Command Center (Spencer *Touching History* pp. 1-2, 19-20), including the links to NORAD, Sliney had suddenly become "the chess master of the air traffic system" (*USA Today* 8/13/02).

On his first day, Sliney faced a challenging reception. When he showed up in a suit, his colleagues snickered and ribbed, "Do we need to address you as 'Your Honor?'" "No," the new operations manager shot back, but "henceforth you may not approach me without permission." Later in the day, after the neophyte had helped successfully complete a "national ground stop," Sliney went from confident to arrogant. When a plane ostensibly carrying Attorney General Ashcroft asked for an exception so it could land in Washington, Sliney retorted that if he couldn't be sure Ashcroft was aboard, someone should "get him out of my sky" (Spencer *Touch. Hist.* pp. 2-3, 258).

Sliney's problems started with difficulty establishing a secure phone link with the PEOC (Hearing 9/11/04). Sliney was also frustrated that Gen. Canavan, the FAA's hijack coordinator, was absent and incommunicado. "There's only *one* person?" Sliney complained. "There must be someone designated or someone who will assume the responsibility of issuing an order, you know" (Hearing 6/17/04). With more experience, Ben Sliney might have perceived the unfolding events as *in-flight emergencies* requiring urgent action. In such extreme situations, FAA personnel were authorized to call the military *directly* to request an immediate scramble and possible interception (Hordon "Affidavit").

### FAA's National Operations Manager Also Runs "Slow" Protocol

Seemingly unaware of the full threats posed by *terrorist* hijackings, Sliney followed the "slow" protocol for dealing with *traditional* hijackings (Spencer *Touching History* pp. 20-21). Sliney seemed somehow unaware of either the precautions taken by the Secret Service (and FBI) or the military exercises that NORAD had been running, several of which anticipated terrorist suicide hijackings (Hearing 4/13/04). The FAA was fully involved in many of NORAD's "war games"; in fact, it had been alerted about an exercise involving a hijacking running that very day (Spencer *Touching History* p. 24).

When Sliney took the job, he was told that his authority was "unlimited" (*USA Today* 8/13/02). Yet so far as we know, Sliney didn't request military assistance for Flight 11. In fact, historian Lynn Spencer has concluded that "the higher echelons at headquarters in Washington will make the determination as to the necessity of military assistance in dealing with the hijacking." Despite Sliney's significant shortcomings in responding to the hijacked airliners themselves, he was promoted before leaving the FAA to establish a law practice (Spencer *Touch. Hist.* pp. 21, 1-2). In 2006, Sliney appeared as himself in the movie *Flight 93* (CBS 4/25/06).

Linda Schuessler, deputy director of system operations at the FAA's Command Center was yet another substitute that day. Schuessler filled in as manager of tactical operations because the regular manager, Jack Kies, was also absent (P. Freni *Ground Stop* pp. 65-66). Since Ms. Schuessler had only worked previously at FAA administrative headquarters, she lacked operations-level experience (Spencer *Touch. Hist.* p. 81).

After staff members at the command center watched the second attack on TV, Schuessler ordered all non-FAA personnel to leave and had the center's doors locked (*Aviation Week* 12/17/01). Whether because of inexperience or temperament, she had difficulty "thinking the unthinkable." The substitute deputy director later recalled "something that seemed so bizarre as flying a hijacked plane full of people into a skyscraper didn't seem possible" (Spencer *Touching History* pp. 1, 19-21).

Decisive, effective action was rare. Schuessler's account emphasized "gathering together information," not taking rapid steps toward notification of the military: "Every few minutes," she recalled, "we would ... discuss what ... we needed to be doing." Rather than taking direct action, she assigned staff members to take notes on all the decisions made, consuming precious time (Freni *Ground Stop* pp. 64- 65).

Finally, Col. Matt Swanson had to substitute for a more-experienced superior during the crisis. In the absence of the air force's Crisis Action Team's unnamed "usual leader," its less-experienced second-in-command had to take charge of air force emergency operations. Starting right after the second strike on the WTC, Swanson had to cover the post in the absence of top generals Jumper and Roche (*Air Force Mag.* 10/01).

**Military Makes False Claims about Radar**

While the FAA was able to track Flight 11 all the way to New York, NEADS worked with inferior radar, the Commission emphasized. After NEADS was told about the hijacked plane about 8:35, military radar allegedly couldn't locate it: NEADS had to phone the FAA and, according to its after-the-fact narrative, eventually focused on a radar blip its personnel believed was Flight 11 (*Aviation Week* 6/3/02). "Weak radar coverage" became the alibi of choice. Although NORAD's early statements made little mention of problems with its radar, over time these supposed shortcomings would become a mantra for both the military and the Commission.

The Pentagon even claimed, that "NORAD's radar system was never intended to monitor commercial jets over the United States. That job belongs to the FAA.... America's air defense forces were trying to down a hijacked airliner they could not see" (Fox 9/8/02). The US Air Force can't track aircraft over the country it's charged with protecting?

**Overstating the Outward-Orientation of NORAD's Radar**

Readers may recall that another of NORAD's characteristic claims, readily adopted by the Commission, was that its radar was oriented outward, supposedly leaving it barely able to track aircraft over the interior of the country. Among several other commanders, NORAD's Gen. Arnold characterized US air defenses as still "looking outward" in a Cold War mode (Hearing 5/23/03). The Commission underscored this claim (*Report* pp. 16-18). Arnold even implied that NORAD's internal radar was so hopelessly outmoded and ineffectual that "we had to hook up to FAA radars throughout the country ..." (Spencer *Touching History* p. 290).

Granted, the basically outward orientation of NORAD's radar was rightly asserted by military professionals. Historically, the Air Force has scanned the horizons from bases on the periphery of the continental US. But the Air Force and Air National Guard also maintain dozens of bases in the interior that deploy primary surveillance radar (PSR). Although the Air Force had long invested far more of its huge budget on projecting power overseas than on protecting the homeland, the evidence doesn't support the claim that NORAD's radar was anywhere near as archaic as its leaders claimed (www.DNotice.org NORAD Papers III-VI).

Like NORAD, the Commission typically downplayed the power of military radars, both external and internal. To believe the Commission's "lost-for-36-minutes" story about Flight 77 and the "no-military-response-was-possible" account for Flight 93, one has to underestimate the *combined* coverage offered by the Pentagon's internal capabilities and the FAA's regional radars. While NORAD deployed more of its long-range radar towers along the East Coast, the FAA deployed its short-range radar in a greater variety of locales (M. Gaffney *9/11 Mystery Plane* p. 11).

### "The Layperson's Guide to Aeronautical Technologies"

Primary surveillance radar (PSR) sends out signals that strike a distant object such as an airplane and bounce back to a receptor or antenna. These "returns" provide information about the size, direction, and velocity of the object but not its identify or altitude. The military advantage of PSR is that it operates independently of the target aircraft: no transponder signal from the aircraft is required to provide a radar return. Most, though not all of NORAD's radar was primary.

In contrast, secondary surveillance radar (SSR) does rely on signals from a plane's transponder beacon; therefore, it's able to both identify the plane and indicate its altitude. Because air safety requires keeping planes on planned flight paths at designated altitudes, nearly all civil (FAA) radar is SSR. However, secondary radar also offers military applications. As early as the 1960s, it became the basis of the Identification Friend or Foe (IFF) system developed as a means of distinguishing friendly from enemy aircraft (www.airwaysmuseum.com/Surveillance.htm).

Far from being an academic exercise in Electronics 101, the distinction between primary and secondary surveillance capacity is important because the Official Story falsely claimed that once the airliners' transponders went dead, they became invisible to military radar (*Report* pp. 25, 32-33). Not so. On the civilian side, loss of transponder signal removes the characters from the blip on secondary radar screens, those which identify the aircraft and indicate its altitude. Not only does the icon itself remain, it suddenly becomes more distinguishable from others, which still provide full information. On the military side, loss of transponder signal doesn't change much. After all, military radar has to meet exactly this challenge, since attacking aircraft don't beam signals to reveal their identity and altitude. However, aircraft flying erratically and/or at unusually high speeds do stand out from others on the screens.

All this holds particular pertinence for Flight 77, which was supposedly "lost" to civilian and military radars as it approached Washington. Planes approaching the capital must be careful as they enter highly restricted "Class-B air space," which encompasses much of the metropolitan area surrounding the capital. No one is supposed to enter this air space without both a transponder code and permission from a controller (*NYT* 9/29/01). Planes approaching Washington's even more highly restricted P-56 air space must "squawk" a military transponder code that identifies them as a "friend." If they don't, they're taken for a "foe" and can be shot down. In 2004, we recall, this fate nearly befell a plane carrying Kentucky Gov. Ernie Fletcher (http://governor.ky.gov/biography.htm).

Way beyond NORAD's primary radar, the military enjoys other powerful options that neither the Pentagon nor the Commission cared to discuss. Among them are at least five other radar modalities offering varying degrees of internal coverage: Ground Control Intercept (GCI), E-3 Airborne Warning and Control Systems (AWACS), E-4B flying electronic platforms, surveillance satellites, and special links between the FAA radar and the Secret Service. Neither NORAD nor the Commission made mention of these.

The first two of these systems were revealed by Capt. Brandon Rasmussen, one of the pilots who flew an F-16 on 9/11: "we're used to working with AWACS [Airborne Warning and Control System] weapons controllers or GCI [ground control intercept]." GCI, he explained, can "give you the tactical air picture; control and coordinate who is targeting what aircraft," so you "run the air war that way" (Filson *Air War* p. 84). Deployed since the 1970s, the E-3 AWACS put state-of-the-art electronics high above the earth. Built with a radar scanning "tower" on their tops, these militarized Boeing 707-320s can see hundreds of miles out, as far the earth's horizon (www.boeing.com/defense-space/ic/awacs/index.html).

## Ultra-High-Tech E-4B Flying Radar Platforms

Larger and even more impressive in their capabilities were the E-4Bs, converted Boeing 747s packed with an amazing array of communications equipment. Four of these flying radar/communications platforms were in the air on the morning of 9/11. In fact, one E-4B was circling above Washington just as Flight 77 was bearing down on the city and Flight 93 was completing its U-turn about 350 miles out (www.informationclearinghouse. info/article19413.htm). Given the astonishing capabilities of E-4Bs to see for many hundreds of miles, it seems unlikely that military radar could not have spotted both incoming airliners. Even more than the E-3s, E-4Bs carry advanced command and control equipment. These capabilities may help explain why the Pentagon so doggedly denied that it had an E-4B over Washington, even though the media aired footage of this flying communications center and Cheney spoke of ordering one over the capital (MSNBC 9/16/01).

In addition, the Secret Service could access the FAA's advanced air-surveillance capabilities, and as we'll soon see, it was calling many of the shots on 9/11. For starters, the capabilities included a system called Tigerwall, which provided "early warning of airborne threats" and "a geographic display of aircraft activity." According to Barbara Riggs, an administrator at Secret Service headquarters that day, the agency was also "able to receive real time information about other hijacked aircraft" through "activating an open line with the FAA" (US Dept. of the Navy *Brief 2000* p. 28). Since Cheney was commanding the Secret Service that morning, it's not surprising that he started to state that "the Secret Service has an arrangement with the FAA" but caught himself and broke off, mid-sentence (MSNBC 9/16/01).

Everything considered, NORAD was hardly blind inside the country. All NORAD's talk about outward-oriented radar doesn't square with many of its own disclosures. If military radar scopes didn't show actual aircraft, then why, during exercises over North America, would NORAD inject simulated blips onto its radar screens? If the FAA's internal radar was superior to NORAD's, it doesn't follow that NORAD's delivered no coverage *at all*.

Here again, the half truth tried to pass for the whole. If we don't count E-3 AWACS and the E-4Bs, it's true that the FAA had better internal radar than NORAD. It's also true that NORAD's radar showed all aircraft aloft, so its technicians had to deal with dozens of blips around New York or Washington. Without assistance, it might have become mayhem, with too many blips in too little space (*Vanity Fair* 8/06). On 9/11, however, NORAD *did* have guidance; the FAA did provide information regarding direction, speed, and type of aircraft. If NORAD had relayed this info to its fighter pilots, it might have saved countless lives.

Dismissing NORAD's long-established mission, however, several Pentagon officials rejected NORAD's responsibility for US airspace. Forsaking his sworn constitutional duties, Rumsfeld claimed "the Department of Defense, of course, is oriented to external threats. This was a domestic airplane that was operated by people who were in the United States, against a US target, which makes it historically a law enforcement issue ..." (PBS 3/5/04). If the 9/11 attacks were just a "law-enforcement issue," then why did the US, egged on by Rumsfeld himself, attack two Islamic countries that allegedly supported the attacks?

When Gen. Richard Myers sang this same refrain, telling the Commission "we did not have situational awareness inward because we did not have radar coverage," his fraudulent claim was publicly exposed. Commissioner Jamie Gorelick, who'd worked for the DoD, quoted NORAD's charter, which called for "control of the airpace about the United States." In a moment of absurd humor, the former chair of the Joint Chiefs tried to wriggle out by citing the *Posse Comitatus* Act. Swallowing none of this nonsense, Gorelick interrupted the Air Force general and blew him out of the sky: "Posse Comitatus means you can't arrest people. It doesn't mean the military has no authority, obligation, or ability to defend the United States from attacks that happen ... in the domestic United States" (Hearing 6/17/04).

### A Long Chain of Command?

The early calls to NORAD and Otis AFB challenged conventional assumptions, strongly reinforced by the Commission, that all requests for assistance had to ascend the FAA's chain of command, move across to NORAD's top commanders, and then descend to base commanders. As the hijacking protocols existed on 9/11, the Commission claimed, air defenders had to go through "multiple layers of notification" to receive "approval at the highest levels of government" (*Report* p. 17).

Like the Commission, the military pointed to cumbersome protocols. According to NORAD, its calls to Tyndall Air Force Base in Florida and Cheyenne Mountain in Colorado resulted in delayed responses. Seeking permission to launch aircraft, regional NORAD commander Col. Marr called his superior, continental commander Gen. Arnold. Eight minutes into the call, Arnold finally approved Marr's call for action: "go ahead and scramble them. We'll get authorities [sic] later" (*NYT* 9/12/01). This was action that Col. Marr, if he'd treated the terrorist hijackings as in-flight emergencies, already had the authority to order. As noted, regulations provided that in cases of emergency, NORAD's regional commanders did have this authority (Orders JO7110.65S, 10-1-3, & 7610.4J). Yet the military brass, high Bush administration officials, and the commissioners all left the impression that the president (but interestingly not Rumsfeld) had to approve all interventions. And, as everybody also knows, Bush lingered in an elementary classroom, incommunicado, until about 9:20 (*Wash. Post* 9/12/01).

The "cumbersome-chain-of-command" legend enabled the Commission to rationalize how America's vaunted air defenses failed, leaving the nation defenseless for an hour and a half. The Commission needed to account for the lost time, and going up and down a chain of command consumed lots of it. By first postponing the times when the military brass received notifications from the FAA and then exaggerating the time required to go up the chain of command, the Commission could limit the response opportunities available to NORAD. As noted in the last chapter, when notifications allegedly came later and possibilities for response seemed to wane, it became easier to impart the impression that "we just didn't have time."

The evidence, however, demonstrates that actual channels of communication were less hierarchical than advertised. News reports indicated that Boston Center first contacted NEADS around 8:31 and then contacted its Cape Cod facility at 8:34 to request that Otis prepare to scramble aircraft (ABC 9/11/02). The FAA's direct call to Otis was also significant because it disproved a key tenet of the Official Story. While this lateral communication disproved the Commission's claim that vertical protocols held sway, the FAA's request didn't initiate an actual scramble at Otis, which only took orders for action from NEADS. But in emergencies, base commanders still had the prerogative to launch and intercept errant aircraft (N. M. Ahmed *War on Truth* pp. 269-70).

The core contradiction within NORAD's insistence on formal and vertical protocol was also exposed when it received a mistaken report on a "phantom" Flight 11 and allegedly ordered the Langley jets in futile pursuit (Griffin *9/11 Comm. Report* p. 199). The Commission not only failed to ask how the FAA could have made the false report, but also how NORAD came to breach its stated policy of going up the chain of command, even to the secretary of defense.

## A Puzzling Litany of Delays

All the discussion about telltale signs and late notification times has often obscured delays within the air-defense establishment. These three instances were only the first of many odd delays; others were equally puzzling and costly.

When the official order to scramble finally reached Otis at 8:46, the F-15s had already been waiting for six minutes, "cocked and loaded," fueled up and armed with missiles. At this very instant, the Boeing 767 carrying 10,000 gallons of jet fuel slammed into the North Tower, engulfing the colossus in a massive ball of fire and smoke. "Even after the FAA had concluded that it was American Airlines Flight 11 that struck the skyscraper," James Bamford remarked, "NORAD still didn't move with much greater dispatch. At Otis, it took six more minutes before the alarm sounded, mechanics freed up the wheels, and a red light turned green" (Bamford *Pretext for War* p. 14). By then it was 8:53. Why the additional delay? Because these F-15s weren't responding to an in-flight emergency, they had to wait their turn on the runway. According to BBC, at least twelve precious minutes were lost while the F-15s idled on the tarmac and runway (BBC 9/1/02). While they sat idle, Flight 175 was closing in on the South Tower.

In another equally odd occurrence, the Otis F-15s received little direction about what to do once they were finally off the ground (*Vanity Fair* 8/06). According to the Commission, they lacked a target so they "were vectored toward military controlled airspace off Long Island." To avoid New York's air traffic, the fighters remained in the holding pattern (*Report* p. 20). These accounts didn't mention NORAD's emergency option—to declare AFIO (Agreement for Fighter Interceptor Operations), which allowed NORAD to take control of the skies and appropriate responsibility for keeping aircraft separated, a duty normally performed by the FAA (Spencer *Touching History* pp. 111-13).

## Slow-Protocol Runway Delays at Langley

As events spun out of control, then, both the FAA and NEADS implemented traditional *slow-track* procedures. At 9:09, Col. Marr called Gen. Arnold back to discuss launching F-16s from Langley AFB in Hampton City, Virginia. Again following the "slow-track" hijacking protocol, Arnold and Marr ordered the Langley jets to "battle stations," poised on the runway with their engines off (Spencer *Touch. Hist.* pp. 112-13). Why didn't Arnold and Marr scramble first and ask questions later?

On the runway, the Langley jets faced still more delays. According to military historian Lynn Spencer, the three pilots had to sit on the runway to "hold for an air traffic delay" because the FAA in Washington hadn't cleared air traffic out of the way. However, the Langley jets were apparently *not*, as NORAD had told the world, launched to protect Washington—and definitely didn't head for the capital. The three F-16s flew eastward, 60 miles out to sea, more than 150 miles from Washington (Spencer *Touch. Hist.* p. 143). These delays, remarked British analyst Nafeez Mosaddeq Ahmed, remain "inexplicable, indefensible, and in breach of standard procedures" (Ahmed *War on Truth* p. 279).

Langley AFB *did* scramble fighters more promptly, but in so doing it breached Air Force regulations that called for keeping a supervisor of flying (SOF) on the ground to guide fighter pilots. Moreover, it did so on order from a mysterious source who apparently *didn't* occupy a high rung on the ladder (Filson *Air War* pp. 63-66). Unfortunately, this scramble (which also experienced runway delays) took these Langley interceptors out of the game, insuring that the F-16s could neither intercept Flight 93 nor protect Washington. This ironic oddity will be examined in Chapter 13.

Inaction by both civilian and military personnel proved especially significant because it delayed responses to the other hijackings. This fact did not escape media outlets like ABC News, which commented "there doesn't seem to have been alarm bells going off.... There's a gap there that will have to be investigated" (ABC 9/14/01). Unfortunately, there's been no thorough investigation of these delays, nor has anyone been held responsible, let alone disciplined for them.

Few Americans noticed that no one from either the FAA or NORAD has had to account for the obvious departures from protocols and derelictions of duty. Even conservative Sen. Charles Grassley (R-Ia.) remarked that not only has no one in government been fired or disciplined for 9/11, many have actually received awards, promotions, or opportunities for lucrative careers in industry (Salon 3/3/03). Aside from blaming the entire FAA, NORAD has never singled out scapegoats in its own ranks—probably because to do so would have implied that it screwed up, big time. And, despite evidence suggesting multiple derelictions of duty and a conspiracy to cover-up, not a single government official was reprimanded, rebuked, charged, demoted, court martialed or otherwise held accountable. Conversely, across-the-board promotions and awards implied that everybody had performed well, beyond expectations. And the Commission, we all recall, announced at the outset that it would not assign "individual blame" (*Report* p. xiv)—so if everyone was responsible, then no one was responsible.

On the contrary, the government officials who were specifically assigned to defend the country and failed to do so on 9/11 were, astonishingly enough, actually honored with promotions. The list includes most of the prominent players:

- Gen. Richard Myers, who was in charge of all US military forces on 9/11, was promoted to Chairman of the Joint Chiefs just three days later (*Wash. Post* 9/14/01);

- Gen. Ralph Eberhart, NORAD commander-in-chief who disappeared into a car, was promoted to chief of the whole northern command (*Legion Mag.* 11/04);
- Capt. Charles Leidig, who substituted as director of operations at the National Military Command Center on 9/11, was promoted to rear admiral (*Baltimore Sun* 8/29/03);
- Gen. Montague Winfield, who ordered Captain Leidig to replace him as director of the NMCC, was promoted to major general (www.defense.gov/releases/release.aspx?released=3817);
- Ben Sliney, who worked his first day on the job as FAA national operations manager on 9/11, was also promoted (Spencer *Touch. Hist.* pp. 1-2);

A fuller list of the rewards and promotions appears in Appendix B at www.mountingevidence.org.

As revealed in Chapter 11, close inspection lays bare the Commission's preconceptions. Whenever it came to faulting NORAD or the FAA, the blame invariably fell on the FAA. Following this pre-established bias, the Commission manipulated times of key events, highlighted failings at the FAA while it played down those of NORAD, and allowed several Pentagon and administration officials to promote self-serving distortions. Although the image of a president posing with a firefighter comes readily to mind, the manipulative distortions were often much more subtle. These range from conflating *interception* of a flight with *shooting it down* to claiming that military radar was completely inadequate. It's difficult to see the Commission's active promotion of these deceptions as anything other than a deliberate attempt to confuse, mislead, and pacify the American public and the world.

Chapter 13 will look at other factors in the dysfunction of air defenses: the failure to use the resources, some already in the air, some at other air bases—and, in particular, the failure to activate Andrews, the Air Force base specifically tasked with protecting the nation's capital.

# 13. Untapped Resources: Atlantic City, Andrews, and Beyond

*What the hell went on here…? How were they able to fly around and no one go after them?*

—Air Traffic Controller at Miami International Airport

Whereas the last chapter emphasized problems centered in Boston and New York, this chapter will focus on the failures to defend Washington. How could the world's premier air defenses have failed to defend the nation's capital?

Here we'll look at:

- The failure to enlist airborne fighter jets on training missions;
- The failure of both the Atlantic City and Andrews AFB squadrons to launch jets in time;
- Failures to defend the highly restricted airspace above the nation's capital;
- The mysterious call that ordered a communications officer away from his post and into the air;
- Two military exercises running at bases near the Pentagon.

Along with those that follow, this chapter moves us closer toward answering the broader questions: Why, for more than an hour and a half, didn't a single interceptor reach any of the hijacked airliners? Even if we accept the much-altered timeline presented by the Commission, we still have to face the fact that NORAD received the first of several notifications at 8:38 yet still had not, by the time of the last crash at 10:06, intercepted any of the four airliners.

## NORAD's Questionable Configurations

Official explanations for the unprecedented failure of multi-trillion-dollar air defenses demand scrutiny. NORAD had divided US airspace into three sectors. One of them, running from Maine west to North Dakota and south to Virginia, was the Northeast Air Defense Sector (NEADS). According to NORAD spokespersons, only fourteen fighters were maintained on alert, armed and ready to protect all of US continental air space (*Report* p. 17). Had the Pentagon cost cutters gone too far, or were other factors involved here?

A vast area of more than a half million square miles, NORAD's Northeast sector is not just the most densely populated: it also sees the most air traffic and presents the greatest number of potential terrorist targets (D. R. Griffin *9/11 Comm. Report* p. 159). Despite the sector's importance and vulnerability, at the time NEADS kept only four fighters on ready alert (*Report* p. 17). When military leaders assigned only four armed, "on-alert" fighters to protect the whole northeastern part of the country, they obviously left it woefully under protected (J. Bamford *Pretext for War* pp. 60-61).

Granting these limitations, we still have to wonder why other, closer bases weren't also tasked to cope with an unprecedented emergency on 9/11.

## Closer Bases Don't Get the Scramble Orders

It's especially difficult to believe that planners wouldn't have stationed "on-alert" fighters much closer to New York and Washington, the most obvious targets for attacks. Because of this odd arrangement, the Official Story told us, the calls for help had gone to more distant bases: Otis Air National Guard Base (ANGB) on Cape Cod, 188 miles from New York, and Langley Air Force Base (AFB) on the Virginia coast, 130 miles from Washington.

When NORAD finally gave orders to intercept planes, the first scramble order went to Otis, the second order to Langley. In contrast, the

Air National Guard installation at Pomona near Atlantic City is about 100 miles south of New York (www.177fw.ang.af.mil) and Andrews AFB in Maryland is situated only ten miles from Washington. True, Otis and Langley were official NORAD "on-alert" sites while Atlantic City/Pomona and Andrews were not. But why wouldn't NORAD have *also* tasked these closer bases, especially when both already had fighters (on training missions) in the air? (L. Spencer *Touching History* pp. 183-84).

At the time of the attacks, the New Jersey Air National Guard and the DC Air National Guard had training fighters in the air. Two F-16s from Atlantic City/Pomona were training over southern New Jersey, just minutes' flying time from New York. Simultaneously, three F-16s from Andrews AFB were flying a practice-bombing mission over North Carolina. All five jets were ordered back to base, but only one was put into immediate action.

A few minutes after the FAA's Boston Center notified NEADS at 8:38, its personnel noticed that fighter jets hadn't yet launched from Otis ANGB. Desperate for military assistance with Flight 11, Boston Center called Atlantic City, home to the New Jersey Air National Guard (Spencer *Touching History* pp. 32-34). NORAD made it seem that if a base wasn't designated as "on alert," it could offer no help at all. Atlantic City wasn't an "on-alert" site, but it was an *active* site; later in the day, it launched eight more F-16s armed with missiles (*Code One Mag.* 10/02).

Besides the F-16s in the air, Atlantic City had two others idling on the runway, ready for training missions. They too carried potentially effective munitions. Neither pair, however, was sent immediately to protect Manhattan (*Code One Mag.* 10/02). And neither pair was tasked with intercepting "phantom" Flight 11, which was supposedly flying along the Jersey coast. How strange that airborne and flight-ready F-16s were so near New York yet not sent to protect it (*Bergen* [Co.] *Record* 12/5/03).

Delays became the demons of the hour. In typical NORAD fashion, dubious decisions at Atlantic City reduced possibilities for intervention. Rather than immediately reassigning the airborne fighters to help protect New York, commanders ordered them to land so their training munitions could be replaced with air-to-air missiles (Spencer *Touching History* p. 120).

But were missiles *essential* for the interceptors to offer at least *some* protection? For optimal effectiveness, fighters would be armed with Sidewinder heat-seeking missiles. But they also could have been effective with explosive bullets or even non-explosive but still potent training rounds. The two pairs of planes on training missions weren't unarmed; they were armed with real 20 mm bullets, just not the type that explode when they hit. F-16 Fighting Falcons carry a M-61 Vulcan rotating cannon that can fire up to 7,000 rounds a minute (www.fas.org/man/dod-101/sys/ac/equip/m61.htm).

Or, at a last resort, the fighters could have flown unarmed yet still been able to intercept, deflect, and, as a very last recourse, ram a rogue airliner. Military professionals, including NEADS commander Robert Marr, considered such options, including ramming (*Wash. Post* 9/14/01).

### Atlantic City Commander Makes Decisions, Causes Delays

Once the two pairs of fighters were on the ground at Atlantic City, Acting Wing Commander Col. Brian Webster demanded that missiles replace the live practice munitions. Since missiles weren't stored near the aircraft, these changeovers took time. Under the best of circumstances, loading missiles would take an hour—but on 9/11 it took even longer. Col. Webster also insisted on the "authenticator" slips used by pilots to verify the code before executing an order to fire. But since Atlantic City was no longer an "on-alert" base, it reportedly had no authenticators on hand. This caused additional delays (Spencer *Touch. Hist.* pp. 121-22). Surely something was askew when a mission to defend the country languished on the ground, lacking a slip of paper.

As a result of this unfunny comedy of errors, Atlantic City made no response until 11:15, an hour and a half after the Pentagon was hit and more than an hour after Flight 93 had crashed. All this had to raise additional questions. If, according to the protocol, fighters were mainly needed to identify, intercept, trail, or escort errant aircraft, how could NORAD claim it absolutely had to arm its fighters with missiles? Might it have been better to get interceptors in the air, even if not fully armed, than to have them sit on the tarmac?

**Interceptors Available over New Jersey Are Never Mentioned**

Despite the crucial role the two pairs of Atlantic City/Pomona fighters could have played, the Commission's *Report* made no mention of them. None. The Commission indicated only that the FAA's Boston Center had called the base in Atlantic City (*Report* p. 20); since it failed to mention the planes in the air and on the runway, it eliminated any need to explain why the FAA's call for help wasn't conveyed to the fighter pilots.

Events in New Jersey were hardly beyond the Commission's purview. Former New Jersey governor Thomas Kean and former state attorney general John Farmer, both prominent members of the Commission, surely knew of this oddly untapped resource. Amazingly though, neither showed any interest in finding out why these already-airborne fighters weren't alerted for emergency intervention.

This omission has puzzled several observers. Emmy Award-winning journalist Peter Lance wondered "how could the Commission leave out an act of negligence by the FAA and NORAD in not contacting two airborne fighters who were close enough to have interdicted the UA flight before it struck the South Tower?" "Jersey Girl" activist Lorie van Auken, who lost her husband in the North Tower, was more pointed: "If two fighters were only eight minutes away, the Commission should have done an exhaustive study on why they didn't get called" (Lance *Cover Up* pp. 230-31). Why, with black smoke from the Towers visible on the horizon, would commanders send armed, flight-ready fighters to the hangar for better armaments?

## Andrews AFB: "Capital Defenders" Fail to Defend the Capital

Another little-discussed oddity of 9/11 involved Andrews Air Force Base near Washington. Situated just a few minutes' flying time from the White House, Andrews was home to Air Force One. Although Andrews wasn't a designated "on-alert" site, it served as home base for two formidable, combat-ready forces: the 321st Marine Fighter Attack Squadron and the 113th Wing of the District of Columbia Air National Guard. Tasked with protecting the nation's capital, the Air National Guard squadron is called the Capital Defenders (www.andrews.af.mil/units/index.asp).

So how could Andrews have failed to defend the capital? Why, once more, did the Commission have so little to say about this failure? Like so many other aspects of 9/11, different stories attempted to explain the failure of Andrews to fulfill its mission. As in other instances, several of these variants have proved more revealing than their tellers intended.

F-16s already in the air were not immediately asked to assist. At 8:36, three F-16 fighters took off from Andrews and flew to North Carolina for a routine training mission. This placed them about 200 miles and 20 minutes away from Washington when the attacks in New York occurred (*Aviation Week* 9/9/02). These three F-16s were slated to return to Andrews at 10:45. Despite the crisis, the three jets weren't immediately asked to respond, and didn't arrive back until between 10:14 and 10:36 (*Aviation Week* 9/9/02). By this time, the attacks were over.

### Early On, Andrews Gets the Call

Shortly after 9:04, the Secret Service notified FAA headquarters that it wanted "F-16s to cap the airspace over Washington." At this moment Flight 77 was over West Virginia, about 200 miles from Washington. In about 15 minutes, controllers at Dulles will first spot Flight 77 just 50 miles out (P. D. Scott *Road to 9/11* p. 202).

Back at the base, personnel did react. About 9:05, a few minutes after the second impact on the WTC, Maj. Daniel "Raisin" Caine called the Secret Service to offer assistance; unbelievably, he was told they didn't need help—which was strange, since they'd just asked for it. How could the Secret Service decline air cover after New York had already taken two hits and Washington was the next logical target? It wasn't until 9:33, when the White House bunker learned of a suspicious aircraft bearing down on Washington, that the Secret Service changed its mind. One of its agents called on Andrews to launch armed fighters for a Combat Air Patrol (CAP) over the city (Spencer *Touch. Hist.* p. 184). If Andrews was not ordinarily involved in defending Washington, why would the Secret Service have called the base in an emergency?

Maj. Caine, who took the call, could hear Dick Cheney: "I could hear plain as day the vice president talking in the background. That's basically where we got the 'execute' order" (Filson *Air War* p. 76). This too was odd: after all, Cheney had just stood down anti-aircraft defenses against this very incoming plane (Hearing 5/23/03). Had Cheney also delayed activation of fighters at Andrews?

Moments later, just after the Pentagon was struck at 9:37, the situation got much more serious. One of Maj. Caine's colleagues recalled that after the Pentagon was hit "the squadron leadership went into action." With that news, Maj. Caine ordered missiles and his superior, Col. Marc Sasseville, readied fighters for launch, pending permission from the commander (Spencer *Touch. Hist.* pp. 124, 156-58). The Pentagon impact gave Gen. David Wherley, commander of the DC Air National Guard, his "first inkling that the attacks would go beyond New York...." Why the general had assumed they would not—especially when hundreds of other people at the Pentagon were thinking "God, we're next"—is still puzzling (Defenselink News 9/13/01).

Before Gen. Wherley would approve a scramble, however, he too insisted on authorizations. Unlike other Air National Guard units which reported to the governors of their states, the DC unit reported to the president or those protecting him. Gen. Wherley must have understood this. Because the Secret Service provided protection for the commander in chief, it necessarily exercised considerable authority over the DC National Guard (*Wash. Post* 4/8/02). Nevertheless, Gen. Wherley initially insisted on senior *military* approval. About 9:40, Wherley declined an urgent request to launch fighters "while watching TV footage of employees evacuating the White House complex" (Filson *Air War* p . 79).

Yet even the sight of staffers running from the presidential mansion didn't weaken Gen. Wherley's resolve. Agent Kenneth Beauchamp implored the commander to launch: "We need some fighters *now*." However, Wherley was still "not very comfortable taking orders from a Secret Service agent" (Spencer *Touch. Hist.* p. 185). Although Cheney was directing a teleconference closely linked to the Secret Service, the vice president apparently never assured the reluctant commander at Andrews.

Although Wherley knew the Secret Service had asked Andrews to provide a Combat Air Patrol (CAP) over Washington, he continued to demand military authorization and more explicit instructions before launching aircraft (S. Vogel *The Pentagon* pp. 445-446). Finally, after at least a half hour of quibbling and wrangling, the chief of safety for the Guard unit told Wherley that the Secret Service was in a near-panic: they "want us to launch anything we've got" (Filson *Air War* p. 81). Sensing the urgency, Wherley relented: "What exactly do they want me to do?" (Spencer *Touch. Hist.* p. 184-85).

Gen. Wherley's dogged adherence to formal protocols paralleled Col. Webster's bureaucratic hesitations. Both commanders seemed to forget that, for decades, scrambles and interceptions had been *routine* and that the most urgent concern was obvious: get fighters in the air to protect passengers. Like the commander's holdout for authenticators at Atlantic City, the drama at Andrews seemed like something out of *Dr. Strangelove*. In this classic film, many readers will recall, nuclear-armed runaway B-52s streaked toward targets in the Soviet Union while Capt. Mandrake (Peter Sellers) lacked a dime to phone the White House and couldn't get Col. Bat Guano (Keenan Wynn) to execute his order to liberate one from a Coke machine. Sometimes life imitates art.

When Gen. Wherley arrived at squadron headquarters, Maj. Caine was holding a phone to each ear. Passing a call from the Secret Service to Gen. Wherley, Maj. Caine blustered, "Boss ... here, you take this one!" Pulling rank on the other pilots, Maj. Caine decided *he* was going to fly; a subordinate would replace him as the unit's supervisor of flying (SOF) (*Aviation Week* 9/9/02). About 10:15, fully 38 minutes after the Pentagon strike and at least 15 minutes after Cheney received shoot-down approval ("you bet") from Bush (*Newsday* 9/23/01), Andrews finally received permission to launch fighters and use "whatever force is necessary" to prevent aircraft from striking "buildings downtown" (Vogel *Pentagon* p. 446).

## Denials that Instructions Came from Cheney

Gen. Wherley later claimed that Special Agent Becky Ediger was "standing next to the vice president" during their call (Filson *Air War* p. 79). Although Secret Service officials confirmed that Cheney gave its agents shoot-down clearance, the White House claimed the Secret Service acted on its own.

Speaking for Cheney, one staffer claimed he didn't know whether the vice president directed the agents and, furthermore, wouldn't be able to find out (*WS Journal* 3/22/04).

The Commission told a different tale, one that not only contradicted the Secret Service but also contradicted itself. It first spoke of how Wherley received instructions from a Secret Service agent who "was getting [it] from the vice president." Yet a few sentences later the Commission claimed that Cheney and Bush had "indicated to us they had not been aware that fighters had been scrambled out of Andrews at the request of the Secret Service and outside the military chain of command" (*Report* p. 44). Again the Commission went out of its way to exonerate the White House.

Significant issues of command and control do arise. The vice president was giving commands in the absence of the president, even though traditional protocol assigns that responsibility to the secretary of defense; Cheney was literally calling the shots—even invoking Continuity of Government (COG)—which involved suspension of the Constitution in order to empower a shadow government-in-waiting (P. D. Scott *Road to 9/11* p. 210). This move could be seen as the culmination of many years of planning, in which Cheney was a prominent planner.

## Ongoing Neocon Involvement with Shadow-Government Plan

To this day, how many Americans know that the United States moved into a partial secret-government, suspend-the-constitution mode on the morning of September 11? To this day, few journalists, not even progressive ones, have reported on this plan; they neither mention its partial implementation on 9/11 nor track it back to those who originated a scheme right out of *Dr. Strangelove*. This shouldn't have come as a surprise in 2001—let alone now, a decade later. Yet for many of us, it does come as a surprise—and not a pleasant one.

In the 1980s, a little-known plan for Continuity of Government (COG) was developed by Cheney and Rumsfeld along with Col. Oliver North; it anticipated a situation in which the Constitution would be suspended, martial law imposed, dissidents rounded up, and a "shadow government" would rule from a remote location. No one warned of the possibility that those who thought up the plan and now had everything to gain from its implementation might contrive a pretext for declaring COG. Yet lo and behold, Cheney *did* declare COG—and did so before 10:00 on the morning of September 11, 2001 (Scott *American Military Machine* pp. 205-13). Cheney was a busy guy that morning: Did someone have the paperwork ready, or wasn't any needed to start sending top officials out of Washington to a remote underground bunker?

The public was told only that Cheney was in contact with the White House "from an undisclosed location"; it wasn't told that the vice president was giving orders from Site R, "the underground Pentagon," as part of the COG plan he'd implemented on 9/11 (Knight Ridder 7/20/04).

### Andrews Finally Gets Fighters over Washington

Between 10:14 and 10:36, the first of the F-16s recalled from training finally returned to Andrews (*Aviation Week* 9/9/02). Since the jet could cover the 200 miles in fewer than twenty minutes and midair refueling took fifteen, max, this arrival time implied that these planes weren't ordered to abort and return before 9:40—and possibly as late as 10:00. So why didn't Andrews recall its fighters earlier so they'd be available to defend Washington? Moreover, Andrews had fifteen additional fighters and four additional pilots right on site, so those on the training mission were hardly the only ones its commanders could have ordered to fly (Spencer *Touching History* p. 156).

Once back at Andrews, the three F-16s were more effectively deployed, though some darkly comic touches remained. For starters, Captain Hutchison landed but didn't take on fuel or munitions before taking off. When his F-16 streaked down the runway at 10:38, it had enough fuel for just ten minutes in the air (Spencer *Touch. Hist.* pp. 216-217). His mission was "to intercept an aircraft coming toward DC," though Flight 93, the last of the four hijackings, had already gone down a half hour before. The other two returning F-16s, rapidly refueled and rearmed with training ammunition, roared off at 10:42. Two additional Andrews fighters carrying heat-seeking missiles finally got airborne at 11:11 (Filson *Air War* pp. 79-84), an hour and five minutes too late for Flight 93.

## Timeline Discrepancies for the First Launch

Journalistic accounts reported that Andrews had fighters in the air "within minutes of the attack [on the Pentagon]" (*Telegraph* [UK] 9/16/01). They implied a fairly high state of readiness at Andrews. In one later version, the Secret Service called Andrews at 9:03, right after the second impact at the WTC, ordering the base to get F-16s armed and ready to scramble. Yet when the Pentagon was hit at 9:37, Andrews was still loading missiles. Immediately after the impact, the Secret Service bellowed: "Get in the air now!" (*Aviation Week* 9/16/02). If the Secret Service didn't believe Andrews had combat-capable aircraft to launch, why would it have issued these orders? If Andrews was unable to help, why, about 9:05, would Major Caine have offered it?

Once again, justice was not served. Gen. David Wherley, the Guard commander at Andrews, was promoted to major general (*Wash. Post* 6/23/09).

## Tracks Lead Toward Cheney

While the post-Pentagon-impact scramble order did not, in itself, imply that the Andrews jets were armed or on full alert, it did make other revelations. Despite the DoD Directive of 6/01 (DoD CJCSI 3610.01A), all orders to scramble apparently did *not* go through Rumsfeld or even through NORAD's top brass. Independent of Rumsfeld, Gen. Larry Arnold had issued a scramble order; even earlier, counterterrorism expert Richard Clarke had ordered a "Combat Air Patrol over every major city in this country" (Clarke *Against All Enemies* pp. 5, 8).

Arnold's order also raised a crucial question: Why would Secret Service agents have waited until after a *third* impact to activate a scramble at Andrews, when by several accounts they'd been tracking the rogue aircraft as it raced toward Washington? To answer this question, readers will recall that Cheney was running the bunker at the White House—and that he had waived off a young staffer trying to take action against this imminent threat (Hearing 5/23/03).

## Andrews Was More "Alert" Than Acknowledged

Even testimony by NORAD officials cast serious doubts on claims that Andrews had no planes it could have launched. Some initial reports indicated that Andrews, only a minute's flying time from the Pentagon, had actually scrambled fighter jets *before* the airliner hit the building (NBC 9/11/01). In one early news account, the wording is suggestive: "It was after the attack on the Pentagon that the Air Force then *decided* to scramble F-16s out of the DC National Guard at Andrews …" (ABC 9/11/01 *Emphasis added*). The implication was that the military had planes at Andrews and *could* have scrambled them earlier, but for some reason had "decided" to wait.

Indeed, after two devastating terrorist attacks had already activated air defenses, already putting the Secret Service on high alert, and already prompting the White House (Richard Clarke) to call for a Combat Air Patrol (CAP) over DC, why weren't fighters from Andrews scrambled *earlier*, possibly enabling them to intercept Flight 77? The official answer was initially that fighters weren't available, later that they had to be armed, and still later that it took time to install the missiles. If you buy all this, I've got a bridge I'd like to sell you.

As so often occurs in crime situations, initial statements—those made before authorities have time to "get their stories synchronized"—frequently come closest to the truth. Especially when early accounts are altered or deleted from later narratives (such as those we've just heard), those changes are themselves instructive. Detectives ask, What facts did they alter, delete, or ignore? What seemed to be the most sensitive issue? *Who* wanted *what* played down or even deleted?

## All the While, Andrews Is Launching Other Aircraft

It's not just that Andrews failed to get fighters in the air for an hour after the strike on the Pentagon; it's that Andrews was launching other aircraft between 9:26 and 9:44. Three other military planes of relevance to the attacks did leave Andrews. At 9:26, a military Boeing 747 lifted off. This huge plane, the first of two E-4B flying intelligence platforms, set out for Offutt AFB near Omaha, Neb. Then at 9:32, a C-130 transport lifted off, also heading for Offutt. Immediately following takeoff, however, this C-130 was asked to identify and the track Flight 77 as the latter descended into its sweeping downward arc. And at 9:44, a second E-4B took flight from Andrews and flew some loops in the Washington area. These moves are of particular interest because an E-4B was spotted circling above the White House at about this time. Could this have been the *second* E-4B? (M. Gaffney *9/11 Mystery Plane* pp. 94-96, 82, 92-94).

In short, while the Secret Service was urging and pleading that Andrews provide air cover over Washington, Andrews was launching other aircraft of no use in the unfolding emergency. How was it that Andrews could launch these lumbering behemoths but not the supersonic fighters needed to secure the skies?

For decades, Andrews had been tasked with guarding Washington. Amply provisioned for its mission, Andrews housed Marine and Air National Guard fighter squadrons (Griffin and P. D. Scott *9/11 and the American Empire* p. 9). Well-known in aviation and military circles, Andrews's mission was articulated by an Air National Guard spokesman the day after the tragedy: "Air defense around Washington is provided mainly by fighter planes from Andrews Air Force Base in Maryland" (*San Diego Union-Tribune* 9/12/01). The phrase "*mainly* by fighter planes" is intriguing, for it suggests that other defensive means such as anti-aircraft batteries could also have defended the city.

In the realm of fighter interception, Andrews was scarcely the only air show in town: Washington had other response-capable options for its defense. In other of those candid "day-of" statements, former Defense Secretary Caspar Weinberger told Fox that "the city is ringed with Air Force bases and Navy bases, and the ability to get defensive planes in the air is very, very high" (Fox 9/11/01).

**Andrews Alters Mission Statement**

Following the attacks, however, Andrews's official mission statement was altered on its website. According to the pre-9/11 mission statement, the base was ready "to provide combat units in the highest possible state of readiness" to protect the nation's capital (N. M. Ahmed *War on Freedom* pp. 154-55). Some time before September 13, however, someone changed the website's language. The altered version stated that Andrews's "vision," not its "mission," was "to provide *peacetime* command and control and administrative mission oversight to *support customers* … in achieving the highest levels of readiness." (*Italics* added.) The phrase "in the highest possible state of readiness" no longer described the base's own mission, just that of its "customers," whomever they might be (Griffin *9/11 Comm. Report* pp. 163-64).

If Andrews was tasked with only "peacetime command and control," then who was charged with defending the nation's capital? Did Andrews's altered language and lower profile indicate that its interceptors weren't "on alert" that day, or did it imply that the Pentagon didn't want to admit some were supposed to have been—and quite likely were?

## Pronouncements Rely on Falsehoods and Technicalities

From the get-go, official versions of events have not only contradicted one another; they've also affronted common sense. During the first week, the news media broadcast the Pentagon's excuses for its failures to protect Washington. One even claimed that Andrews "had no fighters assigned to it" (*USA Today* 9/17/01). The Pentagon made it seem that Andrews, though explicitly charged with protecting the nation's capital, was somehow of no use in preventing an attack that day. NORAD's official line about Andrews was misleading. Its commander, Gen. Larry Arnold, claimed "we [didn't] have any aircraft on alert at Andrews" (MSNBC 11/23/01). Here the operative word is "we," which would logically mean "the US military" but could technically refer only to fighters under NORAD's own command.

Technicality is an old trick, often tried but seldom true. Though technically accurate, Gen. Arnold's statement conveniently left out the fighters under the DC Air National Guard, with its separate chain of command. Though not under NORAD's command, the Air National Guard (Andrews) did answer directly to the Secret Service—and thus to the White House—which rightly, especially after the second and third impacts, believed itself to be a primary target. By 9:15 its staff had started heading for bunkers or begun to evacuate—and by 9:30 Richard Clarke had even ordered the speaker of the House removed from the Capitol (Clarke *Against All Enemies* pp. 2, 5-9). This act began to implement Continuity of Government (COG). Not surprisingly, the order to initiate COG came from Cheney (Scott *Road to 9/11* p. 237).

Traditionally celebrated for protecting the president and nation's capital, Andrews became the object of evasion, spin and "damage control." The Commission evaded questions about why Andrews wasn't more effective. It showed no interest in explaining why, in the 34 minutes between the second impact at the WTC and the impact at the Pentagon, air defenders failed to take the two obvious steps: activating anti-aircraft batteries and ordering Andrews to launch fighters. The Commission reverted to reports claiming that Andrews wasn't keeping any fighters "on alert" (*Report* p. 44). How was it that Andrews, home to the president's plane, wouldn't remain active, alert, and armed? "Are we to expected to believe," asked Griffin, "that the presidential plane would no longer be protected by alert fighters at Andrews, so that the Secret Service ... would need to rely on fighters sent up from Langley?" (Griffin *9/11 Comm. Report* p. 160).

### "Hot Guns," Unarmed Interceptors, and Extreme Measures

While the Official Story tells us that NORAD faced a shortage of fuel and armed interceptors, other fighter pilots were more than ready to engage. As the attacks were going on, "calls from fighter units ... started pouring into NORAD and sector operating centers, asking 'what can we do to help?' ... 'Give me ten minutes and I'll give you hot guns'" (*Aviation Week* 6/3/02). The Commission made no mention of these offers, nor did it reveal that several NORAD pilots expressed willingness to ram the hijacked airliners, risking their own lives if extreme measures were necessary to save others.

If the ramming scenario sounds far-fetched, consider that highly respected intelligence analyst James Bamford quoted NEADS's Col. Marr as saying "the only solution would be for one of the fighter pilots to give up his own life" (Bamford *Pretext for War* p. 67). As we've just seen, fighter pilots themselves proposed this extreme intervention (ABC 9/11/02). Since calls from pilots, many of them in the air, started to pour in right after the second impact, why were none of these pilots ordered to defend Washington against Flights 77 and 93? "If such offers were indeed declined, and then NORAD later claimed that the Pentagon was struck because no fighters were available to protect Washington ..." Griffin has remarked, then it would seem that "NORAD had deliberately left the nation's capital unprotected" (Griffin *9/11 Comm. Report* p. 224).

## Anti-Aircraft Missiles at the Pentagon?

The immediacy of the Pentagon's equivocations and its denials casts doubts on their credibility. Before anyone had even asked about anti-aircraft capabilities, one Pentagon spokesman had explained that the building didn't have such a system because it deemed surface-to-air missiles "too costly and too dangerous to surrounding residential areas" (WorldNet Daily 9/11/01). How often does the Pentagon volunteer information about its weapons systems, and since when has it made cost or collateral damage a deciding consideration, especially when the survival of its own personnel are at stake?

Claims that surface-to-air missiles were "too dangerous" is also suspect. After all, the White House sits in a much more populated area than the Pentagon, yet missiles have reportedly guarded it since 1994. Secret Service personnel armed with portable surface-to-air missile launchers have been stationed on the roof of the presidential mansion, which is "protected by specialist Stinger teams in case of an aerial attack by terrorist organizations" (*Jane's Land-Based Air Defence* 10/13/00). With a range of five miles, Stingers offer close-in defense against low-altitude targets such as aircraft, helicopters, and cruise missiles (Federation of American Scientists 8/9/00).

## The P-56: Washington's Highly Restricted Air Space

The nation's capital has the most restricted air space on the planet. The Prohibited Area (P-56) zone, which included the entire District of Columbia, was closely monitored day and night by FAA radar. Other than approved flights, no aircraft were allowed to enter this air space. If not identified by a military transponder code, an unauthorized intruder would have activated formidable air defenses.

Since scrambling aircraft takes time, possibly allowing an intruder to strike, surface-to-air missiles provide an effective additional means to enforce the policy requiring a military transponder signal. This highly restricted area had long come under the scrutiny of a special air controller who can launch surface-to-air missiles. On one occasion when a commercial flight accidentally overflew the White House, the FAA issued a stern warning: "treat this area as a Granite Mountain to be avoided in every possible way" (www.informationclearinghouse.info/article17162.htm).

Nor was this the only situation in which FAA security personnel almost pushed the button. During the Reagan funeral in 2004, a private jet bringing Kentucky Gov. Ernie Fletcher strayed into the P-56 airspace. Like Flight 77, the governor's plane was not emitting the required military transponder code. As reported by Brian Ross of ABC News, a controller at Washington's Dulles Airport "came within a minute of shooting down that plane carrying the governor" (PBS "Charlie Rose" 6/19/04). Did this near-calamity possibly result from another overreaction to 9/11? Perhaps, at least in part. Yet the fact that it almost happened implied that beyond the missiles protecting individual buildings, the capital is also guarded by anti-aircraft batteries. When Secret Service personnel with Stingers weren't on the White House roof, other weapons must have enforced the no-fly ban. So how could Flight 77, its transponder turned off, not emitting the required signal, have entered or skirted highly restricted airspace—especially at a time of heightened vigilance following two devastating attacks?

## Flight 77 Somehow Evades Defenses

Most accounts have Flight 77 meandering over Arlington, Va., flying along the Potomac past the Pentagon, and looping back to strike massive building (NTSB Flight Path Study 2006). Other reports have it approaching coming within four miles of the White House before veering off (ABC 10/24/01). One major British paper reported that "if the airliner had approached much nearer to the White House it might have been shot down by the Secret Service, who are believed to have a battery of ground-to-air Stinger missiles ready to defend the president's home" (*Daily Telegraph* [UK] 9/16/01). If, as seems likely, Flight 77 entered or skirted the P-56 zone, that would only intensify questions about what allowed an airliner to evade the zone's deadly defenses.

Even if the flight never crossed the Potomac, entering the P-56 zone, note that the area immediately west of the Potomac near the Pentagon is Class B Restricted Air Space, which also requires that a plane be "squawking" a transponder signal (www.avweb.com/news/avtraining/183284-1. html). If a plane doesn't, its green blip immediately glares in the eyes of controllers—who'd been tracking a rogue airliner since it was (at the very minimum) 22 miles out (Spencer *Touch. Hist.* pp. 145-46).

## Were Anti-Aircraft Defenses Available near the Pentagon?

Right after the second WTC impact, the head of defense and security at the Pentagon warned that the building wasn't equipped to defend against attack by an airplane. John Jester, the chief of the Defense Protective Service (DPS) that guards the Pentagon, indicated that he knew of nothing that could protect against an air attack. The Pentagon's official history concluded that the huge edifice "did not have an antiaircraft system on the roof of the building or on the grounds. Even if DPS had received word of an inbound plane, it had no plan to counter a suicide air attack" (A. Goldberg *Pentagon 9/11* p. 152). Similarly, corporate journalistic outlets reported that the Pentagon had "no anti-aircraft guns posted on its roof, nor any radars of its own for tracking local air traffic" (*Wash. Post* 9/16/01). Perhaps so, but these statements don't rule out offsite anti-aircraft defenses.

Such statements may be factual, but they're certainly counterintuitive. How could the Pentagon, headquarters for the world's largest military, *not* be defended beyond fighter jets that, after all, are useless against missiles? If we're going to accept that Andrews, the base tasked with defending Washington, was not an "on-alert" site, this would seem to make it all the more imperative that the Pentagon, like the White House, be equipped to defend itself against attack (*NYT* 9/13/94). It's also reasonable to conclude, along with Griffin, that the Pentagon was very likely ringed by anti-aircraft installations "programmed to destroy any aircraft entering the Pentagon's airspace, except for an aircraft with a US military transponder" (Griffin and Scott *9/11 and the American Empire* pp. 204, 9). How then could such an incoming flight have escaped both the anti-aircraft batteries very likely surrounding the nation's capital and the supersonic jets definitely stationed at Andrews and other air bases?

Among several factors that the Official Story doesn't mention, three stand out.

***New Facility Designed to Improve Communication*** Official investigators made no mention of the Air Traffic Services cell created by the FAA and the DoD to coordinate aircraft movements during emergencies. Only a few weeks before 9/11, the communication and command center had received a secure terminal, "greatly enhancing the movement of vital information" (*Aviation Week* 12/17/01 & 6/10/02). Despite the potential significance of this new center to understanding the confused responses to the attacks, the Commission failed to even mention it. Instead, it spent a lot of time representing communications between the FAA and NORAD as unprofessional, even incompetent (P. Thompson *Terror Timeline* pp. 389-90).

***NORAD Already on Alert for Exercises*** Military exercises or "war games" going on that day became another factor affecting air defenders' responses. Starting at 6:30 a.m., personnel at the NEADS headquarters in Rome, New York, had resumed the fully staffed, high-alert posture required by ongoing military exercises. Two of these, code named Northern Vigilance and Vigilant Guardian, demanded that the entire chain of command become involved (ABC 9/11/02). Even more interesting is the fact that Vigilant Guardian was designed to create a fictional crisis and test the nation's radar and was actually "gamed" to include notification of the Air National Guard in Atlantic City (Bamford *Pretext for War* p. 4). Still another exercise, one conducted by the National Reconnaissance Center in Washington, simulated the use of a hijacked airplane as a weapon of mass destruction (UPI 8/22/02).

While these exercises may have raised defenders' state of alertness, other war games and training exercise were not helpful on 9/11.

***Military Exercises Near Pentagon Reduce Defenses*** That morning, two Army bases near the Pentagon were conducting training exercises, and both drills simulated terrorist attacks or plane crashes. At Ft. Myer, an Army base a mile and a half northwest of the Pentagon, firefighters were attending an "aircraft crash refresher class" (*Pentagram* 11/2/01). This drill extended others, which, in the months before the actual attacks, had "gamed" strikes on the Pentagon from the air, many of them involving hijacked aircraft (www.911truth.org/article.php?story=20060718232126585).

As the airliners were bearing down on their targets, another exercise was going on at Ft. Belvoir, twelve miles south of the Pentagon. Here an Army Aviation support unit for the Washington area was doing weapons training; it didn't return to base until later in the day (Army Center of Mil. Hist. 11/14/01). Stationed at Davison Army Airfield within Ft. Belvoir, the Twelfth Aviation Battalion provided aviation support. Davison Airfield's stated mission included maintaining "a readiness posture" and exercising "operational control" of Washington's airspace (*Pentagram* 5/7/99). After hearing of the crash at the Pentagon, the chief warrant officer remarked ruefully that protecting the building was "basically one of our missions. So we just pretty much packed up and came back … " (*Fort Belvoir News* 1/18/02).

## An Odd Fiasco at Langley

Military exercises had more immediate negative effects at Langley AFB, one of the two on-alert sites. Starting in late August 2001, personnel and fighter planes from Langley AFB's Seventy-First Fighter Squadron had participated in Operation RED FLAG, a regular exercise held at Nellis AFB in Nevada. The unit's 25 pilots were training in preparation for an expected deployment over Iraq (*Milwaukee Journal Sentinel* 10/19/01). Although this Red Flag exercise began on August 11 and ended on September 7, the unit's F-15s didn't return to Langley until September 17 (*Virginian-Pilot* 9/24/01). The Squadron commander complained that "we had most of our F-15s at Nellis" for the exercise (Langley AFB 9/15/06).

Nor was this the only unit that had been drawn away from Langley: the 94th Fighter Squadron was deployed in Saudi Arabia (BBC 12/29/98). These distant deployments, especially the squadron returning late from the Red Flag exercise, left the base "under resourced." Although Langley was one of the two "alert sites" NEADS could call upon for quick launches, its three fighters were parked across the runway, not at the central facilities (Spencer *Touching History* p. 114).

These were only four of the many drills going on that day that arguably affected outcomes. In the next chapter, we'll delve into the effects of the six major exercises going on—into civilian drills that closely simulated actual events and military exercises that affected the country's air defenses.

Although Langley had received early warnings, it didn't make much use of them. About 8:50, Capt. Craig "Borgy" Borgstrom, operations and communications manager for his small unit, took a call from his fiancé. She asked him whether he'd heard that "some airplane had run into the World Trade Center." When "Borgy" replied that it was "probably some idiot trying to commit suicide in a Cessna 172," she informed him "it's a pretty big fire for a small airplane" (*Tampa Tribune* 6/8/08).

## Mysterious Caller Renders the Mission Impossible

Moments later, after the second impact at 9:03, Capt. Borgstrom got another call. NEADS ordered fighters to "battle stations," on the tarmac with pilots in the cockpits. The response was swift. As the Klaxon horn sounded, two pilots suited up and climbed into their sleek, shiny F-16s. By 9:09, Langley had planes poised near the runway, ready to roar. However, its interceptors wouldn't get into the air for another twenty-one minutes (J. Longman *Among the Heroes* pp. 63-64).

On-alert units such as the Fighter Wing at Langley maintain a supervisor of flying (SOF) who both communicates with commanders and directs interceptor pilots in the air (Spencer *Touch. Hist.* pp. 114, 116). On 9/11, Capt. Borgstrom was the SOF or communications manager at Langley. About 9:15, someone from NEADS called Borgstrom demanding to know, "How many total aircraft can you launch?" When Borgstrom replied "I have two F-16s at battle stations right now," the unidentified caller retorted: "That's *not* what I asked! How many *total* aircraft can you launch?" Borgstrom responded that "the only other pilot here is me—I can fly. I can give you three!" Then the caller instructed him: "Suit up and go fly!" (*Christian Sci. Mon.* 4/16/02).

## Communications Coordinator Flies Away, Leaving His Post

Despite this broad breach of protocol, Borgstrom did fly a third jet, though not without consequences. When, following the highly irregular order, Capt. Borgstrom roared off, he left his unit without a SOF to communicate with NEADS and convey information to pilots. One historian of the air-defense failures found this order "almost unthinkable" (Spencer *Touch. Hist.*

pp. 118-19). When Borgy flew off, not only was there no SOF, there was no officer left at the desk. It's hard to imagine a military professional issuing such an order, a base commander approving one, or a seasoned officer following one, even in an emergency. While military personnel are trained to follow orders, they're also trained not to leave their posts, especially without designating a substitute. What was going on here? Was the caller someone in high enough position to occasion an override of protocol?

Dysfunction was quick to follow. As the three jets lifted off at 9:30, NEADS called to tell Langley that the mission was to set up a combat air patrol (CAP) over Washington and intercept any rogue airliners. But with Borgstrom absent from his post, the phone flashed and rang, unattended. A colleague who finally answered indicated that the unit's SOF was in the air. Aware that on-alert units kept an SOF on duty 24/7, NEADS's Sgt. Jeremy Powell was dumbfounded. Because of Borgstrom's absence, the three pilots couldn't receive current or detailed information about their mission. They flew 60 miles east, away from the capital (Spencer *Touch Hist* p. 148). Due in part to these communication problems, the three F-16s didn't appear over Washington until about 10:30, almost an hour after an airliner struck the Pentagon.

Additional breaches of protocol added to the confusion. Capt. Borgstrom recalled "we were getting orders from a lot of different people" (Filson *Air War* p. 66). Soon the squadron received another order that represented yet another serious breach of protocol. Breaking with NORAD's command structure, someone from the Secret Service ordered the pilots "to protect the White House at all costs" (*NYT* 10/16/01). From deep within the White House bunker, Cheney was directing the Secret Service. It was one thing for the Secret Service to give orders to the Air National Guard at Andrews, it was quite another to issue one to NORAD's jets. All these departures from standard procedure may have compromised defenders' attempts to intercept Flights 77 and 93 (Longman *Among the Heroes* pp. 67, 222).

The source of the order for the third F-16 remains one of the great mysteries of 9/11. When Sgt. Powell found out that Capt. Borgstrom had flown a third jet, he exclaimed, "*Three?* I only scrambled *two!*" Still baffled as to who gave a command that sabotaged Langley's response, Borgstrom has indicated that "to this day, I don't know who made that call" (Filson Interview w/Borgstrom). This seems like an obvious question to pursue, yet it's rarely even been raised. Neither NORAD nor the Commission showed any interest in finding out. In fact, the Commission omitted any discussion of this or *any* out-of-protocol orders (Spencer *Touch Hist.* pp. 118-19).

These oddities make no sense unless one wonders whether someone possibly compromised air defenses by arranging for many little delays—in this case by ordering "small" deviations from standard operating procedures that threw air defenses into disarray. This lens offers one way to see the many drills and exercises scheduled for 9/11. Although none of these decided the outcome, the cumulative effect of many cannot be ignored.

### Air-Defense Failures: Who Was in Charge?

The failures of multi-trillion-dollar air defenses remain one of the key anomalies surrounding 9/11. Questions about who was ultimately responsible for them remain unanswered. In keeping with its avoidance of assigning responsibility, the Commission, in its final public hearing (6/17/04), waffled once again on the question of who had operational control of the country's air defenses. At this last hearing, Commissioner John Lehman, a former Secretary of the Navy, questioned Gen. Richard Myers, Chairman of the Joint Chiefs of Staff, about who was in charge of the nation's defenses on 9/11.

The commissioner's superficial questions and the top military commander's evasive answers were classic—and telling:

> **Lehman**: I think what disturbs us most with regard to NORAD is … the problem of command and control—let's start at the top. Who was in charge on 9/11? Was it [a] NORAD commander? Was it you? Was it NMCC? Was it SecDef? Was it FAA? [Note that Cheney's name does not appear among the list of choices.] With all the [drills and] exercising that had been done in the past, clearly somebody should have been in charge…. I'm talking about *operationally*, the minute-by-minute . . ."

**Myers**: And operationally, General Eberhart was on duty and at his duty station, as was General Arnold.... So as you know, I'm not in the chain of command. I'm a military adviser to the chain of command and to the National Security Council. So I went back to my duty station, and what we started doing at that time was to say, "Okay, we've had these attacks ..." (www.npr.org/911hearings).

Knowing what we do, we can see Gen. Myers covering for Rumsfeld, who was incommunicado much of the time, and also for Gen. Eberhart, the NORAD commander who deliberately left his post—and was neither "on duty" nor "at his duty station" (*Colo. Springs Gazette* 6/16/06). Myers also covered for himself. Recall that one of the stories he'd told placed him in senator's office and then in a car, not at his duty station (MSNBC 9/11/02). As if to underscore his condescension, even contempt, Gen. Myers left the hearing early, telling everyone that he had "another commitment" (Hearing 6/17/04). It was revealing, too, that no one in the room seemed surprised about the chairman's abrupt departure.

If the interview went nowhere and produced nothing, it did illustrate a truth most pertinent to what happened on 9/11. What some in the room may have secretly sensed is that the power to make things *not* happen is indeed daunting. Col. Fletcher Prouty, a former Pentagon liaison to the CIA, has remarked that "the power to see to it that regular government operations don't occur is one of the greatest controls over power you can wield in a government" (www.oilempire.us/standdown.html).

From this viewpoint, all indicators pointed toward a couple of neocons with an appetite for power: Cheney and Rumsfeld. The commissioners had to know that in the months before the attacks, both had taken active steps to increase their control of key functions. Cheney had increased his control not only over energy policy and military exercises, but also over FEMA's emergency responses—including preparations for declaring Continuity of Government, or COG (Scott *Road to 9/11* pp. 183-85, 210). As we've also seen, Rumsfeld had extended his control over hijacking scramble procedures. The commissioners had also heard testimony that Cheney occupied the epicenter—that he was positioned to stand down air defenders who were tracking an incoming Flight 77, and that Rumsfeld, by remaining incommunicado for so long, had likely retarded responses at the Pentagon's Command Center (NMCC).

However, this is not to conclude that "Cheney and Rumsfeld were behind 9/11." That would be a premature conclusion—and besides, other factors likely contributed to the debacle. These include the many war games that the US military had been conducting, and especially those it was running right on 9/11. They're the subject of the next chapter.

# 14. How Drills Helped Paralyze Air Defenses

*"Is this real world or exercise?"*

—FAA Air Flight Controller on 9/11

To finish our coverage of air-defense failures, this chapter surveys the preparations made before 9/11 to avert plane-as-missile attacks, examines six military exercises running that day, focuses on how the exercises slowed defenders, and explores Dick Cheney's possible role in compromised military responses. These exercises, or "war games," became an important impediment to the performance of the world's premier air defenses.

Somewhere around the world, armed forces conduct drills nearly every day. Militaries routinely conduct war games to dispel boredom, maintain combat readiness, intimidate or provoke adversaries, and reinforce images of predefined enemies. Exercises also prepare personnel for new threats such as hijacked airliners used for simultaneous suicide attacks. In the years preceding 9/11, the number of exercises had been scaled back to at most one each week (L. Spencer *Touching History* pp. 4-5).

On 9/11, however, at least *six* drills were running. The Pentagon hasn't talked much about its war games, and when it's been forced to, it's tended to spin them hard. Some of the exercises, it has maintained, may have actually helped air defenders. Two days after 9/11, NEADS's commander Col. Robert Marr claimed that because of the exercises "we had the fighters with a little more gas on board. A few more weapons on board" (ABC 9/13/02).

If there were benefits, they manifested in higher states of alertness among some air-defense personnel and first responders. While some of the ongoing exercises may have improved response times, most produced confusion, distraction, and paralysis. Taken together, these exercises significantly degraded air defenses on 9/11 (M. Ruppert *Crossing the Rubicon* pp. 333-348).

### New Threats, New Precautions

In 1994, terrorists attempted to fly an Air France airliner into the Eiffel Tower and a demented, apparently apolitical pilot tried to slam a Cessna into the White House (*Time* 9/26/94). Then in 1995, following arrest for his part in the Philippines Bojinka Plot, Abdul Hakim Murad revealed that he, Khalid Sheikh Mohammed (KSM), and others had already selected pilots to fly airliners into American landmarks, including the WTC and the Pentagon (P. Lance *1000 Years for Revenge* pp. 303-04).

For years before 9/11, preparations for National Special Security Events (NSSEs) had included the prospect of attackers using planes as weapons of mass destruction. NSSEs included the 1996 Summer Olympics, the national party conventions of 2000, the presidential inauguration of 2001, and the Genoa G-8 Summit that July. For each event, air security provisions involved restricted no-fly zones, fighter aircraft patrols, and surface-to-air missiles (Secret Service 2002).

The Secret Service, the FBI, NORAD, and FEMA all participated in planning and coordination for NSSEs. The training regimen included simulated attacks. Louis Freeh, FBI director from 1993 to 2001, acknowledged that "planes as weapons" were a concern for Special Events— that "resources were actually designated to deal with that particular threat," and that potential "use of airplanes, either packed with explosives or otherwise, in suicide missions" were "part of the planning" for security at NSSEs (Hearing 4/13/04). Use of hijacked planes as weapons wasn't just foreseen; for years, the Feds had been taking measures to prevent just such attacks.

### Exercises Respond to Threats of Terrorist Attacks from the Air

In the years before 9/11, several military and disaster exercises anticipated the 9/11 attacks. NORAD conducted four major, headquarters-level exercises each year, many including a simulated hijack (*USA Today* 4/18/04). During this period, several US government agencies had simulated terrorist attacks, including scenarios calling for multiple-plane hijackings. The Amalgam Virgo exercises of 2000 and 2001, for instance, each called for two *simultaneous* hijackings of commercial airliners *within* US airspace (*New Yorker* 9/24/01); Amalgam Virgo II, which was planned for 2001, involved interception of hijacked planes (Ruppert *Crossing the Rubicon* p. 345).

Most of these hijacking scenarios were not "traditional" ones in which someone takes over a plane and demands that it land in a given place. Accordingly, the simulated responses were not traditional; they weren't about fighters simply trailing the plane. Vigilant Guardian's 1999 exercise, for instance, involved both a hijacked Boeing 747 on a suicide mission; the plan was to intercept it decisively, possibly "with extreme prejudice." Similarly, Vigilant Guardian 01 also involved positioning fighters to shoot down a hijacked airliner. Amalgam Virgo 01 went further; it had simulated *multiple terrorist hijackings* and even depicted Osama bin Laden on the cover of its manual. The clincher, though, came just days before September 11: NORAD planned a simulation in which terrorists hijacked a flight and set off explosives over New York. To stage this multi-agency exercise, NORAD even provided scripts to FAA air traffic controllers, as they typically did (www.scribd.com/doc/16411947/NORAD-Exercises-Hijack-Summary).

Thus single traditional hijackings couldn't have reigned as the only possibility for air defenders on 9/11. Multiple terrorist hijackings couldn't have come as a total surprise on 9/11 and couldn't have "slipped beneath the radar."

**Military Professionals Contradict the Evidence**
All these facts challenged accounts given by NORAD personnel. Gen. Ralph Eberhart, NORAD's top commander on 9/11, claimed that "regrettably, the tragic events of 9/11 were never anticipated or exercised" (*USA Today* 4/18/04). Once their superiors had spoken, few NORAD and FAA professionals broke rank. In their depositions, the great majority agreed that all their live-fly exercises, including those simulating hijackings, had taken place *off*shore. NORAD's Ken Merchant acknowledged that, yes, hijackings were "gamed," but that "NORAD did not project shooting down a hijacked aircraft" (http://visibility911.com/eriklarson/?p=101). But as we've

just seen, NORAD *was* gaming suicide hijackings in which fighters were scripted to do more than tail the target aircraft.

However, cracks began to appear in the monolith. A few well-respected military professionals advanced very different perspectives: Prof. John Arquilla of the Naval Postgraduate School stated that "the idea of such an attack was well known [and] had been war-gamed as a possibility in exercises before September 11" (*Monterey Co. Herald* 7/18/02). Later NORAD's spokespersons acknowledged that before 9/11, it normally conducted four major exercises each year—and that most of them included a hijacking scenario closely resembling the actual attacks (CNN 4/19/04).

### Drills Closely Anticipate Actual Events

Not surprisingly, given the 1993 WTC bombing and the 1994 threats to bomb iconic American landmarks, several drills had involved hijackings aimed at these symbols of corporate capitalism, globalization, and military domination. *USA Today* reported "one of the imagined targets was the World Trade Center (WTC). In another exercise, jets performed a mock shootdown ... of a jet supposedly laden with chemical poisons ..." (*USA Today* 4/18/04). These exercises tested procedures for dealing with hijacks, with "detection and identification" on radar screens, and with "scramble and interception" by fighter jets.

In fact, several exercises anticipated attacks on the WTC. Trey Murphy, a former NORAD weapons controller, was struck by the similarity between what he'd been told and what he saw on 9/11. Glancing at the burning Towers, he instantly flashed back to the briefing: "What if a terrorist flies an airplane with a weapon of mass destruction into the World Trade Center? It had always been one of the military's big fears" (Spencer *Touching History* p. 179). In the two years prior to the attacks, NORAD staged several exercises with suicide pilots flying planes into the WTC (*USA Today* 4/18/04). All told, more than a dozen drills foretold the actual 9/11 attacks—except for the failure to intercept the hijacked aircraft.

### War Games at the Pentagon

In another striking coincidence, exercises also simulated plane-into-Pentagon attacks. In the twelve months before the actual attacks, three exercises followed this very scenario. These include a mass casualty (MASCAL) exercise in the fall of 2000. A description of this simulated impact closely resembled the 9/11 attacks (MDW News 11/3/00). A few months later, another medical drill was scripted around the crash of a Boeing 757, the same model that hit the Pentagon. After 9/11, the writers of the DoD's official history went out of their way to emphasize that the airliners in these simulations had hit the Pentagon by accident (A. Goldberg *Pentagon 9/11* p. 107). In some instances, perhaps, this was the actual idea. But how often do airliners accidentally fly into buildings?

In an uncanny preview of things to come, military planners actually considered a scenario in which terrorists hijacked a commercial airliner and crashed it into the Pentagon (Project on Government Oversight 4/13/04). In April of 2001, the Joint Chiefs conducted Positive Force 01, an exercise designed to test military "mobilization and force deployment in response to multiple crises." NORAD participated in the drill (*Air Force Times* 4/13/04).

A "continuity of operations exercise," Positive Force sought to test government plans for continued functioning after a serious attack. To this end, NORAD's planners had included "an event having a terrorist group hijack a commercial airliner and fly it into the Pentagon." However, the Joint Chiefs decided to scrap this plan as "too unrealistic" (*The Guardian* [UK] 4/15/04). But the "continued functioning" of government was the most important piece. Continuity of Government (COG), had long been a prospect of keen, almost obsessive interest among arch-neocons, including Dick Cheney, Donald Rumsfeld, and Paul Wolfowitz. COG involved plans to suspend the Constitution, declare martial law, and herd dissidents into detention camps. By affording an opportunity for top officials, many of them neocons, to execute partial COG the 9/11 attacks allowed them to implement plans for shadow government in exile (P. D. Scott *Road to 9/11* pp. 183-87, 234-38).

### Exercises Belie Statements by Bush and Rice

Together, then, these exercises exposed Bush's famous fabrication, stated just five days in the aftermath: "Never ... did we ever think that the evildoers would fly not one but four commercial aircraft into precious US targets ... never" (CBS 9/16/01). And so much for Condoleezza Rice's sworn testimony that nobody "could have predicted that these people ... would try to use an airplane as a missile" (P. Shenon *The Commission* p. 238).

Although government authorities claimed they'd received just a few warnings, most of which had gone unheeded, the record suggests that *many* alerts about terrorist attacks *were* received, that some *were* heeded, and some were even used as scripts for exercises. In fact, NORAD personnel conducted military exercises that actually replicated dire scenarios derived from these warnings. In the months and years prior to 9/11, American and Canadian air defenders had staged several exercises to prepare for possible suicide hijackings. In fact, one such drill was scheduled that very morning. How, when simulated hijackings complete with medical drills were going on that morning, could the Pentagon credibly claim that it was caught completely off guard? (Office of Med. Hist. *Soldiers to the Rescue* pp. 7, 39). Given all these preparations for handling hijacked airliners, why didn't air defenders perform better on 9/11?

The answers are complex, but comprehensible.

## Six Simultaneous Exercises, Near and Far

On 9/11, various agencies and institutions, including the Pentagon, NORAD, the FAA, FEMA, and the CIA's National Reconnaissance Office (NRO) were all involved with ongoing drills. Some of these exercises rehearsed emergency responses to aircraft slamming into a government building or to an act of bioterrorism in New York. Others involved practicing how to defend against conventional or terrorist air attacks.

These exercises are documented. Just because most American and Canadian news outlets haven't covered them doesn't mean they weren't real. When either the press or the powerful want to submerge an issue, it becomes all the more intriguing to truth seekers; but when *both* press and power suppress an issue, it becomes irresistible.

### 1. Pentagon Medical Drills Exhibit Uncanny Parallels

Well before 9/11, the Pentagon had staged several medical-emergency or mass casualty (MASCAL) exercises based on impacts by aircraft. Several of these drills bore a striking resemblance to the actual attack on the Pentagon. In the twelve months prior to 9/11, at least three separate exercises were conducted (*U.S. Medicine* 10/01). In May, medical personnel rehearsed a crashed airliner. In August, only a month before 9/11, a similar MASCAL exercise was staged; its scenario also included a plane hitting the building followed by an evacuation. Doctors remarked that these exercises prepared them for the actual attack (*U.S. Medicine* 10/01). One military newspaper's report on an exercise "read like an account of what actually happened on September 11" (*Daily Mirror* 5/24/02).

On that fateful morning, Pentagon medical personnel were getting ready to conduct yet another mass-casualty exercise. Anticipating a plane-as-missile strike, personnel were already making preparations before the building was hit. Maj. Lorie Brown, a nurse at a clinic, recalled how "we actually had our MASCAL equipment out.... So there were many pieces that just fell into place and worked so well on that day" (Office of Med. Hist. *Soldiers to the Rescue* pp. 39, 7). While these drills improved medical-emergency responses, they also raised a troubling question: Did someone have reason to suspect that something might strike the Pentagon?

The Commission's *Report* made no mention of the curious parallels between exercises and actual events.

## 2. Simulated Crash into NRO Headquarters

Jointly run by the CIA and the Air Force, the National Reconnaissance Office (NRO) operates many of the nation's spy satellites and tracks aircraft within the country (AP 9/21/02). On the morning of 9/11, the NRO was running a drill involving an errant plane. During this exercise, the real-life plots to crash planes into real buildings were rapidly unfolding: two airliners had struck, and two more were racing toward Washington. In the simulation, an off-course corporate jet was to "crash" into the NRO's headquarters just after 9:30. The CIA had scheduled an evacuation drill to follow this simulated crash. Although the simulation was canceled once the real attacks became known, the NRO's evacuation went forward.

After canceling the exercise, managers sent most of the NRO's staff home, including the techies who controlled surveillance satellites for the entire military-intelligence establishment. Since most of them couldn't perform their tasks from home, the CIA's ability to track off-course aircraft from spy satellites was seriously impaired. The NRO has never explained why, at a time of great urgency, someone ordered a complete evacuation that crippled aerial surveillance (www.911truth.org/article. php?story=20050830185334880).

On top of the other war games, the NRO exercise likely contributed to distraction and confusion among air defenders. The NRO's official statements failed to allay suspicions. Spokesman Art Haubold hastened to claim "it was just an incredible coincidence that this happened to involve an aircraft crashing into our facility" (AP 8/21/02). However, Haubold didn't comment on why the NRO's evacuation took place or whether the exercise could have distracted its staff from tracking the actual aircraft. It's possible the NRO wasn't involved in domestic surveillance, making its evacuation less consequential; if this was the case, though, why wouldn't they have said so?

These issues take on added importance when one considers that NORAD repeatedly pleaded difficulty in tracking the hijacked planes. These, readers will recall, included the "phantom" Flight 11, which NORAD believed was still heading south after the plane had actually crashed, and Flight 77, which it claimed had disappeared from military radar screens for half an hour (*Vanity Fair* 8/06).

## 3. Operation TRIPOD II in New York City

Another major exercise was coming together that morning, this one in New York City. Scheduled for 9/12/01, Trail Point of Dispensing Drill (TRIPOD) involved a simulated biochemical attack. To ready themselves for TRIPOD II, hundreds of emergency responders from federal, state, and city agencies were assembling in Manhattan. Participants from the State Emergency Management Office, the city Health Department, the Red Cross, FDNY, NYPD, the mayor's Office of Emergency Management (OEM), and the Federal Emergency Management Agency (FEMA) were gathering "to test how quickly staff could administer treatments at medical centers that would be set up ... in the event of an actual attack" (*NY Magazine* 9/15/01).

TRIPOD II was a revealing and consequential exercise. A pet project of former NYC Mayor Rudy Giuliani, the drill was to be run from both Pier 92 on the Hudson River and Giuliani's new Emergency Operations Center (EOC) in WTC Building 7.

The circumstances of the EOC evacuation were peculiar. In a move that's received little media attention, about 8:50 that morning Giuliani decided to close down his much-touted emergency communications hub and evacuate WTC-7 (NBC 9/11/01). Moments later, the mayor told NBC anchor Tom Brokaw that he'd heard the Towers would be coming down (NBC 9/11/01). This was only a few minutes after the first impact, and more than an hour before the first of the Towers fell (NBC 9/11/01).

However, the talkative Giuliani didn't talk about when and why he ordered the evacuation. Clearly the decision was made when the second impact screamed "terrorist attack." Describing the TRIPOD II exercise to the Commission, the mayor was allowed to steer away from several key questions (Hearing 5/19/04). It was probably true that the pre-assembled emergency-response teams contributed to the City's ability to cope with the disaster. But was the peculiar timing of the TRIPOD exercise just another odd coincidence, or did the assembly of so many responders possibly hint at foreknowledge?

## 4. Operation Northern Vigilance

Several days before the 9/11 attacks, as part of "live-fly" training exercises over Alaska and northern Canada, NORAD had sent fighters to monitor a Russian exercise over the Arctic (BBC *Day That Shook the World* p. 161). On September 9, NORAD had began to conduct Northern Vigilance, scheduled to run from the tenth through the fourteenth of September. Despite the shroud of secrecy covering most war games, Northern Vigilance was announced in a press release. That morning it was no secret to the FAA, as controllers' references to the exercise made clear.

Much about Northern Vigilance still remains classified; however, it's still not known, for instance, which NORAD bases sent fighters or exactly how many personnel and planes were involved. Clearly the numbers were substantial, even for the amply provisioned US Air Force. A similar drill in 2000 involved more than 350 American and Canadian military personnel (NORAD 9/9/01); this number would imply dozens of aircraft. It's reasonable to assume that, come September 2001, roughly this many were also involved, most of them from bases in the Lower Forty-Eight. Because of this lack of information, it's difficult to appraise how much this diversion of people and planes affected the performance of defenders in the northeast section. But it would be nice to know, one way or another.

## 5. Operation Vigilant Guardian: The Big Game
Like Northern Vigilance, Vigilant Guardian was one of NORAD's four major annual exercises. An actual flying drill, Vigilant Guardian responded to a potential Russian attack across the Arctic, with virtually all of NORAD participating on 9/11 (*Aviation Week* 6/3/02). However, much as the Commission had ignored the other exercises, it also disregarded this one. Devoting only a single footnote to all the exercises, its *Report* acknowledged only that Vigilant Guardian was a Cold War-style exercise (*Report* Ch. 1 Note 116).

By defining this war game so narrowly, the Commission didn't need to deal with diverted aircraft or distracted commanders. Vigilant Guardian deployed aircraft off the coasts of Canada and Alaska, and diverted planes from Langley AFB to Iceland (*Air Combat Command News* 6/3/02). Since Langley, one of the two on-alert bases on the East coast, came up short on both pilots and planes, the consequences of distant deployments can't be summarily dismissed.

***Problems with a War-Games Psychology*** NEADS was deeply involved in Vigilant Guardian, as was its commander, Col. Robert Marr. Preparing for a likely confrontation with Russian aircraft, Col. Marr had ordered that NORAD's on-alert fighters be loaded with additional fuel and live missiles. That morning, Colonel Marr was excited about strategizing to counter the "surprises" he anticipated planners having in store for him (Spencer *Touch. Hist.* p. 5). In a few pages, we'll see how Vigilant Guardian delivered additional surprises as they continued to toss wild-card simulations into the game over an hour after the attacks had begun.

His passion for war games activated, Col. Marr proceeded to lead NORAD's responses on 9/11. That day, Vigilant Guardian included something highly unusual in far-north simulations: a hijacking. In this exercise, traditional hijackers were to commandeer an aircraft "for political purposes, directing it to an island in order to seek asylum" (Spencer *Touch. Hist.* p. 24). This conception seems odd, since "traditional" hijackings of this sort had become rare in recent decades while "terrorist" hijackers had become far more common. In fact, the 1999 Hart-Rudman Commission on National Security for the Twenty-First Century had found that the greatest threat would come from terrorist attacks "on our homeland, and our military superiority will not entirely protect us" (www.au.af.mil/au/awc/awcgate/nssg/nwc.pdf).

Though Vigilant Guardian was conceived in conventional terms, it was hardly just another far-north maneuver with a hijacking added. Far broader in scope, Vigilant Guardian involved all of NORAD's command headquarters, including the Air National Guard unit at Atlantic City, New Jersey (Bamford *Pretext for War* p. 4). Since it also involved radar sites and command centers in Florida and upstate New York, it necessarily impacted NORAD's crucial Northeast Sector. Former LAPD detective Michael Ruppert, one of the first to probe the cumulative impact of the games, wondered "whether NORAD's attention was drawn in one direction—toward the North Pole—while the hijackings came from an entirely different direction" (Ruppert *Crossing the Rubicon* pp. 337-38).

Vigilant Guardian also placed its commanders in a mindset that left them more vulnerable to confusion and denial. When a colleague informed Col. Marr that Boston had "a hijacking, and this is real life, not part of the exercise," Marr reportedly thought "this 'real-world' [stuff] … will keep [my staff members] on their toes" (Spencer *Touch. Hist.* p. 26). When Maj. Kevin Nasypany, who'd helped design the exercise, was told of the actual hijacking, he protested that "the hijack's not supposed to be for another hour" (*Vanity Fair* 8/06). As FAA air-security personnel attempted to report the hijackings to NORAD, many had to insist that their calls for help were "real world," not exercise.

If we were to assume sinister intent in the planning of Vigilant Guardian, it's unclear whether this hijacking exercise was more about diverting resources, distracting defenders, or giving NORAD an excuse for failure. Perhaps a bit of each. Initially at least, the war games weren't something NORAD personnel wanted to talk about.

## 6. Global Guardian: The Drill of Drills

The most comprehensive exercise, Global Guardian, was an annual nuclear war game. Though normally scheduled for October or November, in 2001 the drill was inexplicably moved to the second Tuesday in September (*Space Observer* 3/21/01).

That memorable morning, Global Guardian was getting underway. For its master war game, the Strategic Command (Stratcom) at Offutt AFB in Nebraska had gone on full alert, dispatching warplanes in a dress rehearsal for nuclear war. Stratcom's underground command center served as an information hub for collecting and assessing data from high-tech "eyes and ears" around the globe. Since Operation Global Guardian was interlinked with other systems—including NORAD and the CIA's NRO—several interrelated air-defense "war games" proceeded under its command (W. Arkin *Code Names* p. 59).

As Stratcom "gamed" an attack with nuclear missiles, Global Guardian also had to seem like a grainy Cold-War replay. In 2001, the probability of a nuclear attack on or by the US was remote. Nevertheless, Global Guardian was one of several "practice Armageddons" the US military was still staging to determine its readiness to launch or respond to a nuclear attack.

Journalistic coverage suggested broader patterns. In its account of this "drill of drills," the *Omaha World Herald* made an intriguing observation: "that the exercise was, according to briefers, 'in full swing' at the time the United States came under attack is at least an odd coincidence" (*OWH* 2/27/02). The hint about an "odd coincidence" did invite questions, but it was as far as the journalists would go. Beyond the secrecy that shrouds military—and particularly nuclear—maneuvers, this meager coverage revealed how few journalists seem willing to source their reportage beyond official "briefers," let alone to pursue the implications of their news stories.

***Lingering over Breakfast*** Adm. Richard Mies, Stratcom's commander-in-chief, was in charge of Global Guardian and the Strategic Command on 9/11. At Offutt AFB, Adm. Mies was meeting with business leaders at a fundraising breakfast sponsored by multibillionaire Warren Buffett (*OWH* 2/27/02). Minutes after the first impact at 8:46, smoke and flames were dominating TV screens. An air-defense commander in charge of a major exercise surely must have received word that a plane had struck the World

Trade Center, yet Adm. Mies lingered at the fundraiser. Only after he'd learned about the second hit at 9:03 did he return to his post to suspend Global Guardian (*San Fran. Bus. Times* 2/1/02).

Yet no one, journalists included, seemed to wonder why the commander-in-chief and his staff were attending a fundraiser and absent from their posts during Stratcom's biggest exercise of the year. Nor did anyone make much of the fact that by keeping himself out of the loop, Adm. Mies joined the list of officials holding key positions in the chain of command who, at a moment of urgent need, absented themselves or remained absent from their decision-making duties. As usual, though, career consequences didn't ensue. In a move that illustrates the "revolving door" between the top brass and military contractors, Stratcom's Commander-in-Chief has since become the CEO of Hicks & Associates, a "strategic consultant" to the Pentagon dealing in "military transformation" (*OWH* 2/27/02).

***"Doomsday Planes" Scan the Skies*** On 9/11, the Global Guardian exercise involved military command aircraft fully loaded with sophisticated communications equipment. As noted previously, these E-4B National Airborne Operations Center aircraft (or "Doomsday planes") are alternative command posts to direct bombers or missiles, execute attack orders, and coordinate responses in a national emergency. Their highly advanced electronics and high operating altitude allow the Doomsday planes' ultra-powerful radars to surveil most of North America (www.fas.org/programs/ssp/man/uswpns/air/special/e4b.html).

At the moment of the attacks, in addition to the two argus-eyed Doomsday Planes over the Great Plains, a third and a fourth took off from Andrews AFB. One of these was spotted circling low over the White House on 9/11 and reported by CNN (www.airliners.net/aviation-forums/military/read.main/72653). E-4Bs typically maintain stratospheric altitudes to exploit their stunning radar and satellite-communications capabilities: Why was this one flying so *low* over Washington? Although military authorities canceled the master exercise between 9:04 and 9:40, all the E-4Bs remained in the sky (*USAF Weather Observer* 7/02).

The fact that at least *four* E-4Bs were aloft during the attacks has to challenge claims about a lack of radar visibility. Since E-4Bs are loaded with state-of-the-art radar, their presence in the skies made it all the more improbable that Flight 77, which allegedly struck the Pentagon, was "lost" on military radar screens for half an hour (Griffin *New Pearl Harbor* pp. 41-42).

## Diversion, Distraction, Confusion, and Delays

How could these ongoing drills possibly disrupt multi-trillion-dollar air defenses? The answer lies with three features of the exercises: "live-fly" drills pulled fighters far from their home bases, some commanders went into a war-game mentality, and "command-post" exercises injected "false blips" onto both military and civilian radar screens (R. Clarke *Against All Enemies* pp. 4-5). As a result, war games both denied air defenders the resources they needed and led some commanders and air controllers to confuse simulations with realities. The result was impaired responses.

Distant deployments frequently involved diversions of resources. Some of NORAD's jets were cruising near the Arctic Circle, hundreds or even thousands of miles from the East Coast. According to NORAD, this left only fourteen "on-alert" fighters to cover the entire continental United States, only eight to patrol the entire East Coast, and only four to defend the North East Air Defense Sector (NEADS), where the hijackings occurred (www.norad.mil.11Sept). Two cases involving odd displacements and distant deployments serve to illustrate this tendency.

## Operation Red Flag: Another War Game with Consequences

Other exercises weren't running on 9/11, but nevertheless affected the events of that day. Starting in late August, personnel and planes from Langley AFB's Seventy-First Fighter Squadron had been participating in Operation Red Flag, a regular exercise held at Nellis AFB in Nevada. The unit's 25 pilots were training for an expected deployment over Iraq (*Milwaukee Journal Sentinel* 10/19/01).

Although Red Flag had begun in August and ended on September 7, the unit's F-15s hadn't returned to Langley (*Virginian-Pilot* 9/24/01). The commander of the Seventy-First Fighter Squadron at Langley complained that "we had most of our F-15s at Nellis" for the exercise (Langley AFB 9/15/06). Although Langley was one of two "on-alert" sites upon which

NEADS could call for rapid responses, these distant deployments left Langley seriously under-resourced that morning. As a result, the three fighters Langley scrambled on 9/11 didn't belong to Langley, so they were parked across the runway, less ready to launch (Spencer *Touch. Hist.* p. 114). Resources reduced by military exercises—and especially by the absence of fighter aircraft involved in Red Flag—hampered not only Langley's response but those of other installations, including Andrews.

While "live-fly" drills drew personnel, pilots, and aircraft away from their home bases, "command-post" exercises preoccupied hundreds, of personnel at their regular workstations. Throughout NORAD, commanders in charge of regional air defenses were deeply involved in distant war games. Recall, for instance, Col. Marr's significant mental involvement in an exercise taking place hundreds of miles from NEADS's headquarters in Rome, New York, and the inevitable distraction from his primary responsibilities in the northeast sector, where the hijackings occurred.

Live-fly drills like Northern Vigilance and Vigilant Guardian weren't simply far-north battle simulations; they generated turbulence throughout much of NORAD's network—especially in the northeast. This, after all, is where most of the dysfunction occurred. In one memorably revealing instance, even Gen. Myers allowed that air defenses might have been slowed because NORAD was "in the middle of Vigilant Warrior" (Clarke *Against All Enemies* pp. 4-5). With hijacked airliners bearing down on New York and Washington, it was hardly helpful to find commanders distracted by, let alone preoccupied with exercises.

The games didn't just divert resources and distract personnel, however; they also produced a confusion of simulation versus reality. Several of the games involved radar "injects" or false blips that dotted radar scopes—and these didn't go away when the games were reportedly terminated.

**Delays in Shutting Down Two Major Exercises**
When Gen. Eberhart claimed that "it took about 30 seconds" to close out the war games and return to the impending real-world situation (*Report* p. 458), surely he didn't mean *all* of the games. That would have been highly

unlikely, even impossible, since different government agencies staged different exercises.

Moreover, recently discovered evidence has shown that although NORAD claimed it shut down its exercises as soon as it recognized the actual hijackings, its operations centers continued receiving simulated radar "injects" for at least another crucial hour afterward. NORAD's Northeast Air Defense Sector (NEADS) was still receiving simulated "injects" (or "inputs") around 9:37, when the Pentagon was hit. NORAD's Operations Center in Colorado continued receiving them even after the fourth hijacking, Flight 93, had crashed in Pennsylvania at 10:06 (http://911blogger.com/news/2010-08-12/lets-get-rid-goddamn-sim).

Thus military personnel had false simulations of nonexistant aircraft cluttering their radar screens throughout the attacks. Annoyed with the distraction, personnel attempted to clear their screens: "Let's get rid of this goddamn sim," one exclaimed, "let's get rid of that crap." But the technicians couldn't end the simulations: their surveillance scopes still displayed "injects" of simulated aircraft. Amazingly, this was an hour after the FAA had first called NEADS and a half hour after the fireball had engulfed the South Tower. Since false injects hindered the ability of personnel to deal with actual air attacks, remarked researcher Matt Everett, they "should have been terminated at the first sign of an actual emergency" (http://911blogger.com/news/2010-08-12/lets-get-rid-goddamn-sim).

### *Vigilant Guardian Continues Two Hours after First Calls for Help*

Recall that Vigilant Guardian was a major exercise, "a simulated air war" against a significant enemy (W. Arkin *Code Names* p. 545). According to accounts endorsed by the military, Vigilant Guardian was called off "shortly after" 9:03, when TV screens began to scream that a second Tower was hit (Filson *Air War* p. 59). In fact, however, the exercise continued long after that. False "injects" continued appearing on military radar screens, and Vigilant Guardian was not "formally terminated" until 10:44 (*The Bombardier* 9/8/06). This was more than half an hour after the attacks had ended and more than two hours after the FAA first sounded the alarm about a hijacking. Nor was this continuance of Vigilant Guardian the only instance.

Yet once again the military's reports minimized the duration of the exercise. At NORAD's headquarters in Colorado, battle staff technicians had been transmitting simulated radar tracks. Like NEADS, NORAD claimed that "any simulated information" was scrubbed from screens in response to the breaking news of real-world events, i. e., just after 9:03 (*Toronto Star* 12/9/01). But again the reality was quite different. Global Guardian, "the master exercise," continued to run past 10:06, when Flight 93 took its final dive. It was apparently not until 10:12 that NORAD called Capt. Brian Nagel, the chief of exercises, telling him that "what we need you to do right now is to terminate all exercise inputs ..." (NEADS Audio File Sr. Dir. Pos. Chan. 20 9/11/01). How long it actually took after 10:12 to clear all the simulations is not clear.

Why, once NORAD commanders recognized that they did face a real-world emergency, did they wait so long to terminate? Who decided to continue the simulations after it had become obvious that the country was under attack? Did this continuance stem from inattention, institutional inertia, or what?

### How Much Difference Did False Blips Make?

This is an open question. The answer given by most analysts goes like this. By about 8:40, as the FAA's warnings were finally getting through to defenders, "injects" cluttered its screens. Suddenly confronted with so many problem planes at once, some air traffic controllers became unable to distinguish the virtual from the actual hijacks (*Toronto Star* 12/9/01). Although NORAD claimed that the "injects" were removed from screens right after the hijackings were detected, both FAA administrator Jane Garvey and White House counterterrorism expert Richard Clarke complained about trying to track what looked like as many as *eleven* out-of-contact aircraft (Clarke *Against All Enemies* pp. 4-5). The confusion contributed to hesitation and delay (*Vanity Fair* 8/06).

Puzzling questions still linger. On 9/11, assuming that the military expunged its blips as quickly as it claimed, how do we account for NEADS's suddenly impaired vision along the Boston/New York/Washington corridor? And why, when "injects" would have helped NORAD explain its failures to find the intruders, did it choose to deny their ongoing presence? Nor did the American news media question NORAD's account. Despite coverage of "injects" in the Canadian and British press, observed Michael Ruppert, no American news outlets "mentioned that false radar blips had been inserted onto radar screens." Significant omissions from the standard accounts "had been officially ignored" (Ruppert *Crossing the Rubicon* p. 339).

While the Canadians reported the "injects," the Brits covered possible computer manipulation. Although some confusion caused by the "injects" was inevitable, technical intervention, argues British researcher Nafeez Mosaddeq Ahmed, may have intensified it. Due to the privatization of the US national security apparatus, Ahmed argues, corporations such as Ptech received high-level security clearances for the FAA and NORAD. Hence the company had access to some of the most sensitive computer systems within the federal government. Financed by indicted Saudi al Qaeda sympathizer and bin Laden supporter Yassin al Qadi, Ptech's links to these security nodes on the computer network could have been exploited on 9/11. The FBI investigated the company for possible involvement in 9/11 but made no indictments (Ahmed *Independent* [UK] 2/7/10).

### Problems with a Common "Simulation Mentality"

The confusion caused by the illusory "injects" wasn't the only problem. The false blips could have been readily removed, but a simulation mentality couldn't be switched off. When the first actual hijacking was reported, NORAD was on alert because of the war games going on (*Aviation Week* 6/3/02). Soon enough, however, ensuing interactions between NORAD personnel and FAA air-traffic controllers illustrated the disruptive consequences of the "games." Recall how the Commission highlighted the air controller's question, "Is this real world or exercise?" (*Report* p. 20). FAA personnel often had to waste precious time explaining that their calls for help were indeed "real world."

The many statements from personnel indicating confusion serve to belie NORAD's non- or late-notification defense, its contention that "we weren't notified in time." The question, however, wasn't simply *when* FAA controllers notified NORAD's commanders, but *how long* it took them to realize the hijackings were for real.

As one might expect, the Commission's *Report* glossed over questions about the full extent and consequences of the training drills. The Commission mentioned only one of the six exercises (*Report* p. 43) and drew totally unrealistic conclusions about their probable effects. Where NORAD's testimony was full of holes, the Commission papered them over. It's not surprising that the Pentagon and the White House would have been secretive about the exercises—especially those simulating the use of hijacked airliners to attack important buildings, which posed a direct challenge to the "caught-by-surprise" defense. Again, the more officialdom has tried to keep an issue in the shadows, the more it should come into the light.

## McKinney Hearings Elicit Admissions

After the Commission failed to investigate the war games, a few members of the House Armed Services Committee made another go at it. In 2005, Rep. Cynthia McKinney (D/Green-Ga.) convened hearings on 9/11. She evoked a grudging concession from Gen. Richard Myers, Chair of the Joint Chiefs. Along with Rumsfeld, Myers finally acknowledged that, yes, NORAD was actually staging *several* different exercises on 9/11 (www.911truth.org/downloads/McKinney-911Commission-OneYearLater.pdf). Faced with sharper jabs than he'd faced before, Gen. Myers bobbed and weaved. First he conceded that, okay, two exercises were going on.

Then Gen. Myers started to get more real, admitting that there were three, even four of them—and that several did, come to think of it, involve real aircraft. Although Myers recalled that there was "an actual operation ongoing because there was some Russian bomber activity up near Alaska ..." he quickly veered off topic when asked about who planned and ran the exercises (www.youtube.com/watch?v=4CnIy9W_IFQ). As Rep. McKinney pressed, Myers reiterated that the war games had actually *enhanced* defenders' responses (www.copvcia.com/free/ww3/031505_mckinney_transcript.shtml).

## Games Possibly Provided Cover for Plotters

Given the odd coincidence of so many disruptive drills running at the same time, a troubling question arises: Could the simultaneous exercises have offered cover for planners or perpetrators? Historian and analyst Webster

Tarpley has provided relevant background. He's observed that mirror-image drills can provide perfect cover for "a rogue network that is forced to conduct its operations using the same communications and computer systems used by other officers who are not necessarily a party to the illegal operation, coup, or provocation" (Tarpley *9/11 Synthetic Terror* pp. 204-05).

A rogue officer, Tarpley explained, can thus work alongside one who's not aware of the plot "and who might indeed oppose it if he knew about it." War games can generate smokescreens for unauthorized behavior. Stalling, distracting colleagues or diverting resources can receive less attention during an exercise, so suspicions are more apt to be allayed (Tarpley *9/11 Synthetic Terror* pp. 204-05).

## Cheney Commands Powers of Secret Service

When pressed, NORAD's Maj. Don Arias confirmed that a "maestro" coordinated *each* of the war games. After talking with Arias, Ruppert wondered, "If there were multiple maestros, how did they communicate with each other and who supervised them?" (Ruppert *Crossing the Rubicon* p. 367). Were presidential powers to make national security decisions usurped, or was the White House involved in making them?

Once it became clear that the nation was under attack, the Secret Service reportedly lifted Cheney out of his chair and rushed him into the tunnel leading to the White House bunker. Counterterrorism expert Richard Clarke informed Cheney that "we're putting together a secure teleconference to manage the crisis." However, Cheney chose to set up one of his own in the Presidential Emergency Operations Center (PEOC) (Clarke *Against All Enemies* pp. 1-2). His wife, Lynne, who held no position in the administration, immediately joined Cheney in the bunker. She must have walked fast to arrive so early.

Both of these accounts suggest that the Secret Service was already in the loop at the time of the second impact. If, as the Commission says, the chain of command on 9/11 was a somewhat tangled web, this should not obscure the fact that Cheney, who commanded the Secret Service, was literally calling the shots on 9/11. The Secret Service had the ability (if not the authority) to communicate orders directly to air defenders. Recall that the three fighter pilots from Langley AFB received orders from the Secret Service, not the Pentagon (*NYT* 10/16/01).

It's also important to recall that the Secret Service possessed the best communication systems of any federal agency, and it was especially well wired to the FAA, allowing it "to see what FAA's radar was seeing" (Clarke *Against All Enemies* pp. 6-7). Since the FAA's radar was better than NORAD's, the Secret Service had better access to information. And since Secret Service personnel always accompany both the president and vice president, it can take the lead in a crisis. By commanding the Secret Service, Cheney ran the country's defenses from the White House bunker (CNN 9/11/02).

Cheney also exercised some control over the war games. In May of 2001, a presidential mandate placed Cheney directly in charge of managing the "seamless integration" of all training exercises throughout the federal government, including military agencies (White House 4/13/01). In May 2001, a presidential mandate put Cheney in charge of the "seamless integration" of all training exercises throughout the federal establishment (*Wash. Post* 5/23/01). This assignment also gave Cheney theoretical (if not operational) control over FEMA, the lead agency for implementing Continuity of Government. Moreover, Cheney was among the top government officials to decide that the military exercises would continue as scheduled, despite intelligence warnings that terrorists were likely to hijack planes during the week of September 9 (P. Zarembka *Hidden History of 9/11* pp. 135-36).

## Stretching the Laws of Probability

As we've seen, US air defenses were running at least six drills on the day of the attacks. Since most were once-a-year events, it's reasonable to ask:

- Who planned or approved so many exercises for the same day?
- If the clustering of exercises was only an unusual coincidence, why did the officials, investigations, and the news media avoid explaining this unusual occurrence?
- Why, after months of increased warnings about imminent terrorist attacks, would the military have nevertheless planned war games likely to increase the country's vulnerability to such attacks?

Short of a real investigation with the power to both subpoena and interrogate witnesses under oath, we'll probably never get the answers.

The war games on 9/11 clearly expose contradictions in the official narrative. Since several exercises both before and on 9/11 involved domestic suicide hijackings, they debunk the Official Story's contention that "nobody could have possibly imagined terrorists using passenger planes as weapons of mass destruction." You can't "game" what you've never imagined. If someone were looking to cripple air defenses, then highly competent, dedicated air-security professionals had to be hamstrung. Multiple war games might seem like one way to effect a military slow down, if not a full stand down.

# 15.  Islamists, al Qaeda, and the Saudi Factor in 9/11

*It's proved to be a devil's game. The United States spent decades cultivating Islamists, manipulating and double-crossing them, cynically using and misusing them as Cold War allies, only to find that it spawned a force that turned against its sponsor, and with a vengeance ....*

—Robert Dreyfuss, *The Devil's Game*

I t's past time to examine how the United States has pursued the practice, formerly employed by the imperialist British, French, Italians, and Germans, of using Muslims for the purposes of power-projection. Right after the 9/11 attacks, the FBI announced that fifteen of the nineteen alleged hijackers were Saudis (ABC 9/13/01). Press coverage did not, however, consider this disclosure in relation to a long relationship between the US and Saudi Arabia, one that has included not just oil, banking, and military interconnections, but shared involvement in the rise of Islamist terrorism. Both countries, for instance, were crucial to the funding, training, and equipping of the *mujahedeen*, or "holy warriors" fighting the Soviets in Afghanistan.

## The "Great Game" on the Grand Chessboard
Used as proxies, ultraconservative Islamists have served as foot soldiers for American intervention. "For decades," Columbia scholar Rashid Khalidi has argued, "the United States was in fact a major patron, indeed in some respects *the* major patron" of extremist Islam (*The Progressive* 9/09). Obsessed with the threat of communism, the US utilized these *jihadis*: Cold Warriors

failed to perceive the possibility that, with the fall of the Soviet Union, they might themselves become dangerous.

In 1977, Zbigniew Brzezinski, Jimmy Carter's national security advisor, urged the president to consider a devious scheme to "give the USSR its own Vietnam War" (J. Cooley *Unholy Wars* p. 19). Washington began to see Islamist fundamentalism as a crescent-shaped scimitar it could thrust at the underbelly of the Soviet Union (R. Dreyfuss *The Devil's Game* p. 4).

In a grave miscalculation with long-term implications, Carter decided to implement Brzezinski's scheme. The gambit involved a new foray into one that British imperial novelist Rudyard Kipling called "the Great Game": the contest to control south-central Asia. In the early twentieth century, after two disastrous attempts to subdue Afghanistan, the Brits had fallen back on the idea of using Muslims—for whom they'd developed a very healthy respect—to repel any Russian designs on the country (Unger *House of Bush* p. 98). American planners resorted to this same tactic, ignoring the fact that Afghanistan had a very long history as "the graveyard of empires."

## The Saudi Prince and the Texas Oilmen

In the 1970s, Saudi Prince Bandar (bin Sultan bin Abdul Aziz) started hobnobbing with Texas corporate lawyer James Baker III (later secretary of state under Reagan). A quest for big profits and an antipathy toward communism united the Saudis and the Texans. Soon Bandar met Texas oilman G. H. W. Bush, and the two became longtime friends. Since Bush had worked for the CIA since 1956 (R. Baker *Family of Secrets* pp. 7-17), an alliance between Saudi Oil and Texas Oil was established, with the CIA linked to both sides. As Saudi princes conveyed an impression of Muslim piety, many partied like the playboys of the Western World.

## Secret Support for the *Mujahedeen*

By the late 1970s, Baker had coaxed a colorful congressman from Texas into leading the charge for "Charlie Wilson's War." As an opening volley in this Cold-War crusade, the CIA began to fund Gulbuddin Hekmatyar, a drug kingpin who trained and equipped the *mujahedeen*, the mostly Arab "holy warriors" who'd come so far to wage *jihad*.

One of the most controversial *mujahedeen* leaders, Hekmatyar was accused of spending more time fighting other *jihadis* than battling Soviet tanks (L. Wright *Looming Tower* p. 127). Other *jihadis*, however, were decidedly more effective. They often committed acts of sabotage within the Soviet Union, but Washington never called them "terrorists." Despite the often-barbaric tactics favored by these "holy warriors," Reagan applauded them as "freedom fighters," "the moral equivalent of the Founding Fathers" (www.youtube.com/watch?v=ipszh14WPFY).

As the Soviets battled *mujahedeen* guerrillas during the early 1980s, Washington escalated its Cold War crusade. This not only became the CIA's biggest operation, it was the most massive covert intervention by any nation in history. It included financing, training, and supplying high-tech weapons—including American Stinger missiles that took out hundreds of Soviet aircraft (Wright *Looming Tower* p. 127). Conversely, the fact that the crusade was clandestine and that Islamists could be deployed kept Washington's political costs low. Previewing so much that was to come, Washington opted to pass the huge costs to future generations and let foreigners do the fighting—and the dying.

## Proxy War Proves Deadly, Destructive, and Very Expensive

The CIA funneled massive amounts of money through its Pakistani counterpart, the Inter-Services Intelligence Directorate, or ISI (AP 11/13/09). As the second in command at the CIA, Robert Gates helped channel covert funds and weapons through the ISI (*NYT* 1/24/10). Trainees learned secret surveillance, placement of explosives, and recruitment of fighters (Cooley *Unholy Wars* pp. 70-72).

To share the increasing burden, the American officials got Saudi sheiks to help finance the *mujahedeen*, whose numbers included many Saudis, including the young Osama bin Laden. Saudi bankers became a conduit for cash intended for Islamist guerrillas. As the US diverted vast amounts of money into Saudi accounts, it became an open secret that "the Saudi royal family had taken over intelligence financing for the United States" (*WS Journal* 12/31/04). Tens of millions of dollars were transferred from CIA operational accounts to "those controlled by Saudi companies and the Saudi

Embassy itself" (J. Trento *Prelude to Terror* pp. 102-03). Even more blatant was the newly formed Bank of Credit and Commerce International (BCCI). Sometimes called the "the Bank of Corporate Crooks Incorrigible," the BCCI played a prominent role in Islamist financing. Among its Saudi financiers was Salem bin Laden, older brother of Osama.

## Bush Sr. and bin Laden Launch Shadow Support Group

In 1981, Washington began to fund Makhtab al Khidmat (MAK), the *mujahedeen's* "Support Services." From inside the White House, former CIA director G. H. W. Bush supervised MAK's covert operations. MAK was co-founded by Osama bin Laden, who served as its financier and logistics expert (Scott *Oil, Drugs, and War* p. 32).

Several shadow groups received funding from rich Saudis and Pakistan's ISI as they enlisted conservative Muslims in the Islamist cause. Bin Laden had served as the Saudi kingdom's personal emissary in Afghanistan, helping to recruit, train, and equip Arab fighters for the Afghan war. Not surprisingly, after the USSR pulled out in 1989 and the US abandoned Afghanistan, the *mujahedeen* evolved into the Taliban and al Qaeda, emerging from the interaction of three intelligence agencies—the CIA, the ISI, and the Saudis (World Socialist Web Site 6/26/09).

The ensuing decade-long war proved disastrous to Afghanistan, the Soviet Union, and, years later, the United States. A million Afghans died and six million were driven into exile. Along with Soviet soldiers, Islamists from various countries did most of the dying. While the costs remained low in American lives, they ran high in national treasure: $3 billion in the 1980s (Unger *House of Bush* p. 97). In a bitter historical irony, the USA would later spend many years, many lives, and much treasure fighting very similar Islamic insurgents in the very same country, oblivious to the symbolism of crumbling British forts and rusting Soviet tanks.

## Islamists Continue to Receive Help from CIA and ISI

After the flood of dollars flowing into Pakistan had subsided, the ISI continued to support Islamist militants (AP 11/13/09). The CIA also continued to fund, train, and arm the Islamists, for it had other deployments in mind.

After finding the "freedom fighters" so useful, the US wouldn't abandon its efforts to use these militants as potent proxies in conflict areas such as Bosnia, where Islamists fought the Serbs during the mid 1990s (*Christ. Sci. Mon.* 9/07/04). This was indeed a dangerous "devil's game." Pakistan's Prime Minister Benazir Bhutto warned President G. H. W. Bush outright: "you are creating a veritable Frankenstein" (*Newsweek Online* 10/1/01). However, her warning went unheeded in Washington, which continued to imagine it could keep the monster on a leash.

After the *mujahedeen* had emerged triumphant in Afghanistan, it didn't take long for the blowback to begin. Hardened "holy warriors," their confidence inflated by defeating one Superpower, turned their sights toward the other. Hard-core Islamists found it easy to enter the new target country. The State Department's Visa Express Program allowed known-to-be-dangerous operatives such as the "Blind Sheikh" Omar Abdul-Rahman and Ali Mohamed "the American" (MTA) to enter the US (P. Lance *1000 Years for Revenge* p. 42).

## Former US Visa Official Tells All

Michael Springman, formerly with the State Department's Visa Bureau in Jeddah, Saudi Arabia, has exposed what went on in the late 1980s (CBC 7/3/02). At this time, the CIA was recruiting fighters for the Afghan war against the Soviets; bin Laden, long a CIA asset, was fast becoming a useful legend. From the CIA's several recruiting offices in Saudi Arabia, it would send new recruits to Jeddah for their visas. When Springman complained to administrators in the consulate, he was told "to keep quiet, that there were reasons for doing this." (CBC 7/3/02).

Springman's concerns were hardly without basis; many of these visitors entered for the purpose of inflicting mass casualties. "Blind Sheikh" Omar Abdul-Rahman, who'd received his visa from a CIA case officer in Sudan, entered the US twice in 1990 despite being on the official Watch List (*Wash. Post* 7/13/93). He and other veterans of the Afghanistan conflict soon became involved with the Refugee Center (and Farooq Mosque) in Brooklyn, where US government agencies had recruited American Muslims for that war. It was there that "Blind Sheik" Abdul-Rahman first plotted the 1990 murder of Rabbi Meir Kahane and then helped mastermind the 1993 bombing of the World Trade Center (D. Benjamin and S. Simon *Age of Sacred Terror* p. 103). The Islamist cleric was finally convicted for helping plan the 1993 "Landmarks Plot," which hoped to blow up five New York City monuments, including the Lincoln Tunnel and the UN building (*NYT* 1/18/96).

## Islamist Militants and US Intelligence Agencies

During the early 1990s, the US left Afghanistan to the tribal warlords, and the *mujahedeen* morphed into the Taliban and al Qaeda. Many warlords who'd fought the Soviets turned their guns on the Taliban, shelling Kabul into rubble in a devastating civil war.

After the Taliban finally took control, drug lord Gulbuddin Hekmatyar nevertheless held posts high in the new government. In 1979, when the CIA began to back the *mujahedeen*, it wasn't much concerned that some of their leaders were deep into hard drugs. One leading CIA/ISI client was Hekmatyar, the notorious drug trafficker with his own heroin refineries. Despite these negotiations, Hekmatyar received fully 20 percent of the billions of dollars the CIA provided (NPR 12/2/09). Come 2003, though, former friend was declared an arch foe. Although once lavishly funded by the CIA, Hekmatyar was designated an "international terrorist" and since that time has continued to attack Western forces (www.state.gov/s/ct/rls/crt/2005/65275.htm). The State Department has neglected to mention that Washington had subsidized most of the holy warrior's worst crimes—including his wanton killing of civilians.

Although the CIA's interdependence with Islamists and drug kingpins is well documented, it still isn't widely known. As the CIA allowed Afghan drug lords to intercept huge sums, it became involved in the heroin trade, much as it had in Indochina fifteen years earlier. A network of connections linked CIA and Islamist militants, suggesting that the interests of the two weren't so different as one might assume. Not only were both anti-communist and interested in controlling resources, but both trafficked in drugs to raise funds (Scott *Drugs, Oil, and War* pp. 28-34). While the operation in Afghanistan allowed both the CIA and the ISI to vastly enlarge their budgets, it also allowed the Afghan and Pakistani drug lords to vastly increase operations and their profits. Little consideration was given to the tens of thousands of American lives that were lost or shortened due to the influx of Afghan heroin—unreported casualties that must be added to the full costs of that war.

## Proxy Soldiers in Foreign Wars

Looking for new places to wage *jihad,* many of the *mujahedeen* who fought the Soviets in Afghanistan in the 1980s gravitated toward fighting Serbs in Bosnia or Russians (again) in Chechnya in the 1990s. Al Qaeda operatives gained additional experience as America's proxies in Bosnia, where they fought the Christian Serbs, and later in Chechnya, where they fought Christian Russians. In a rare moment of candor, CIA Director George Tenet acknowledged that suspected hijackers had fought alongside the CIA in Chechnya (*LA Times* 9/1/02). In Chechnya, the Agency ran another large covert operation intended not only to weaken Russian influence in the region, but mainly to insure access to the massive oil deposits around the Caspian Sea (*Business Week Online* 12/24/01).

## Eavesdropping on a Very Confident bin Laden

The exposure of warrantless electronic eavesdropping has made more Americans aware of the National Security Agency (NSA), the largest of US intelligence-gathering agencies. This ultra-high-tech "puzzle palace" intercepts, translates, or decodes hundreds of thousands of electronic communications every day. NSA electronic monitoring of bin Laden had originated years before the 9/11 attacks. On numerous occasions, the NSA had recorded bin Laden's satellite-phone conversations from Afghanistan (*LA Times* 9/21/01).

Passed on to the CIA and the Pentagon, these intercepts helped pinpoint bin Laden's location, exposing him to cruise missile attacks. Somehow undaunted, the al Qaeda leader continued using unsecured phones. From 1996 to 1998, bin Laden used a traced satellite phone to call the safe house in Yemen dozens of times (*Times* [UK] 3/24/02). As further evidence of his confidence (laxity, recklessness, or boldness?), just before the 9/11 attacks, the al Qaeda leader reportedly called his mother, brazenly boasting that "in two days you're going to hear big news, and [then] you're not going to hear from me for a while" (*Toronto Globe* 10/5/01).

All this suggested that either al Qaeda wasn't the world's most savvy terrorist group or they weren't too worried about having their plans detected. Their schemes had included major strikes on two US embassies in Africa, a warship in Yemen, and three iconic buildings on the East Coast. If bin Laden were really worried about someone foiling al Qaeda's elaborate plan for 9/11, why would he have risked the whole operation by bragging on a bugged phone? Egyptian security specialist Mohammed Heikal expressed disbelief that al Qaeda could have launched the complex 9/11 attacks without risking that its plans would be revealed to US intelligence: "al Qaeda was penetrated by American intelligence.... They could not have kept secret an operation that required such a degree of organization and sophistication" (*Guardian* [UK] 10/10/01).

### FBI Involvement with Islamist Operatives

Investigation of the alleged hijackers inevitably led not only to the CIA but also to the FBI. While the CIA was supporting Islamist "holy warriors," the FBI was watching radical Islamists on the home front. In 1989, it even tracked major militants to where they took target practice and took extensive surveillance photos of key al Qaeda figures as they fired AK-47s at a range on Long Island. Investigative journalist Peter Lance noted that the FBI's thick albums of surveillance photos "offered a kind of class yearbook of the terrorist cell that would threaten the United States throughout the next twelve years." For no apparent reason, the FBI suddenly terminated its surveillance of the suspicious shooters and failed to make use of its extensive documentation (Lance *Cover Up* p. 25).

Nine years later, in 1998, the FBI obtained the phone number for the group's message center. Located in Sana, Yemen, the "safe house" was owned by hijacker al Khalid al Mihdhar's father-in-law. When the NSA tapped the line, it learned that this was al Qaeda's "logistics center," its hub for planning their attacks. Top leaders, including bin Laden himself, used the "switchboard" to coordinate the group's operations. Toward the end of 1999, intercepted phone calls made the CIA and FBI aware of an al Qaeda summit meeting in Malaysia (*Newsweek* 6/2/02). Over the two years before 9/11, at both the CIA and FBI, information poured in but action seldom followed.

## Al Qaeda Summit Finalizes Plans

In January 2000, American intelligence was well positioned to surveil the al Qaeda summit in Kuala Lumpur, Malaysia. This closely watched, amply photographed four-day meeting brought together East and West—the planners of the Bojinka Plot in the Philippines with leaders from the Hamburg cell. Their mission was to finalize plans for the attacks on the *USS Cole* (CNN 8/30/02) and on the US homeland (*NYT* 11/6/01).

A dozen big players managed to show. Hosting the al Qaeda summit was Riduan Isamuddin, an Indonesian also known as Hambali. Five years before, he'd been the moneyman behind the Bojinka Plot, the Islamist scheme that included plans to crash hijacked airliners into iconic American buildings. After 1995, Hambali had become one of the most important al Qaeda's figures in Asia (CNN 8/30/02). With these two associations alone, he surely would have attracted the attention of American intelligence.

In addition to Hambali, Khalid Sheikh Mohammed [KSM], the "mastermind" behind 9/11, also attended the summit. Surveillance of the summit was unusually close. At the request of the CIA, Malaysia's security service tracked and photographed the visitors: it "took pictures of the men sightseeing and ducking into cybercafés to check Arabic websites" (*Newsweek* 6/2/02). The CIA "indicated that the behavior of the individuals was consistent with clandestine activity ... they used public telephones exclusively" (JCI 10/17/02). Strangely, given the lead-time and the preparations to document the summit, no wiretapping or lip-reading translation technology was used (PBS "Frontline" 10/3/02).

## CIA Blocks Sharing of Information

By early 2000, as al Mihdhar and al Hazmi came off the summit, the CIA had assembled bulging dossiers on them. Of the nineteen alleged hijackers, Mihdhar and Hazmi were not only the most experienced *jihadis*; they also had the most obvious ties to militant Islamist groups (*Wash. Post* 9/25/01). Yet the CIA failed to share information about Mihdhar, Hazmi, and other attendees with either US immigration officials or the FBI, even at a face-to-face meeting with the latter (*NYT* 4/11/04).

After the summit, alleged hijackers Khalid al Mihdhar and Nawaf al Hazmi entered the US. When Mihdhar's flight made a stopover, the CIA ordered a search of his documents. The search uncovered the al Qaeda operative's full name, established his Saudi passport number, and found a multiple-entry visa (Copley News 10/17/02). After this revelation, the CIA must have understood that unless it intervened, Mihdhar could enter the country at will. FBI agent Ali Soufan, who led the investigation of the *Cole* bombing, documented how CIA officers "had repeatedly and criminally obstructed investigations that could have prevented the attacks on 9/11." Agent Soufan demonstrated that, following the summit, he made repeated requests for information about Mihdhar and Hazmi, but the CIA refused to furnish it (National Press Club 9/11/08).

So why didn't the CIA share the ample information it had gathered? The CIA is an agency whose purposes include internal control and external power projection: whether at home or abroad, protecting Islamist militants was apparently seen as a way to advance these ends.

### The Non-Informing Informant

After the summit meeting, Mihdhar and Hazmi entered the US using visas issued by consular authorities in Saudi Arabia. After landing in Los Angeles in January 2000, the deadly duo was met by Omar al Bayoumi, an employee of the Saudi civil aviation authority and also a Saudi agent (World Socialist Web Site 6/26/09).

Amazingly, while Mihdhar and Hazmi lived in San Diego they rented from and later even lived with an FBI counterterrorism informant, Abdussattar Shaikh. But the informant didn't inform. Shaikh wouldn't provide his FBI contact with even the most basic information, not even received surnames for the deadly duo (*Newsweek* 9/9/02). The lack of surnames wasn't because Mihdhar and Hazmi were hyper-secretive, though. To the contrary, Hazmi was even listed in the phone book—a detail that challenges the official claim that the hijackers cunningly covered their tracks.

Tellingly, the White House blocked the Joint Congressional Inquiry (JCI) from interviewing either the FBI "handler" or the informant (*NYT* 9/27/02). These blockages suggest a concern that they would reveal that elements within the FBI knew about preparations for the impending attacks and allowed them to go forward.

Even though Mihdhar and Hazmi's movements were monitored by the FBI, they were allowed to leave and enter the US throughout 2000 and 2001. Agent Soufan reported that on August 22, 2001, the CIA finally "discovered" that both operatives were living in the country and suspected they were planning a terrorist attack. However, the CIA's bin Laden Unit and the FBI's HQ took minimal action, again missing a chance—one of the very last—to prevent attacks that occurred twenty days later (National Press Club 9/11/08). It wasn't until August that the pair finally appeared on the federal Watch List. Yet even after this listing, both were able to buy one-way tickets for American Airlines Flight 77. Much more than US espionage and law enforcement agencies have ever let on, information about the alleged hijackers was amply available. Yet they too were allowed to go about their deadly business.

## The Anwar al Aulaqi Connection

As soon as Mihdhar and Hazmi arrived in San Diego, they hooked up with Anwar al Aulaqi (Awlaki), the Islamist cleric later strongly suspected of involvement in the 9/11 plot. Born a Saudi, al Aulaqi had become an American citizen.

Since 1999, the Bureau had been investigating Aulaqi's close connection to "charities" known to raise funds for *jihadis* in several countries (J. M. Burr and J. Collins *Alms for Jihad* p. 243). Al Aulaqi served as "spiritual leader" to several of the alleged hijackers. In February of 2000, imam Aulaqi received several calls from Omar al Bayoumi, the Saudi agent who'd been under investigation for his links to Islamist fundraising. Even though Aulaqi was under investigation at the time, and even though he'd received these calls from a Saudi under investigation, the FBI shut down its probe a month later (*Wash. Post* 2/27/08).

## Imam Moves Closer to Action, Then Leaves Country

In January 2001, al Aulaqi moved to Falls Church, Virginia, just outside Washington. There, several of the alleged hijackers attended his sermons at the elegant Dar al Hijrah mosque (*Report* p. 230). In early August 2001, Aulaqi told a neighbor he was leaving for Kuwait, "that something very big" was going to happen and he had "to be out of the country when it happened" (*Newsweek* 7/28/03).

Despite all these connections and many more, the FBI denied its active investigations and its knowledge of many alleged hijackers. In 2002, FBI Director Robert Mueller made outlandish disclaimers to the Joint Congressional Inquiry (JCI): "While here, the hijackers effectively operated without suspicion, triggering nothing that would have alerted law enforcement and doing nothing that exposed them to domestic coverage. As far as we know, they contacted no known terrorist sympathizers in the United States" (AP 9/26/02). CIA Director Tenet made similarly non-credible denials. The Inquiry itself understood full well that these were false testimonials: It had uncovered an FBI internal document stating that leading hijackers had "maintained a web of contacts both in the United States and abroad" (P. Thompson *Terror Timeline* p. 230).

## Aulaqi: From Special Treatment to the CIA's Hit List

In October 2002, al Aulaqi returned to the US. Since his name was on the Terrorist Watch List, customs agents notified the FBI, only to learn that, just the day before, his name was removed from the Watch List. Who took al Aulaqi's name off the list? Throughout 2002, a US Customs investigation into money laundering tracked Aulaqi, but he was not arrested for his dubious deeds (World Net Daily 8/16/03). Only much later, years after the attacks, did the FBI acknowledge that Aulaqi was definitely connected to al Qaeda and probably involved in 9/11. One detective believed Aulaqi "was at the center of the 9/11 story" (*NYT* 5/8/10).

But if Washington had under-reacted earlier, it over-reacted to this realization. Bypassing legal channels, the Obama administration approved the imam as a target for assassination. For the first time, so far as we know, the CIA's Counterterrorism Unit received permission to assassinate an American citizen

(*Wash. Post* 4/7/10). In doing so, the administration crossed a most significant line, one surely well known to a former professor of constitutional law.

## Other Suspected Operatives Also Enter Country

Several other al Qaeda operatives well known to American intelligence also breezed through customs. Ziad Samir Jarrah, a former member of the closely watched Hamburg cell, was permitted to enter and enroll in flight school (AP 9/9/02). Jarrah's tuition money had come from Ramzi bin al Shibh, co-organizer of al Qaeda's American cell (*Baltimore Sun* 12/14/01). Like Mihdhar, Hazmi, Jarrah, and Mohamed Atta, al Shibh had been under surveillance; cameras also caught him at the summit in Kuala Lumpur (CNN 8/30/02).

Despite all these suspicious involvements, Jarrah didn't even make the State Department's Watch List. Just two days before the attacks, he was stopped and released by the Maryland State Police—who probably ran his name through their database. FBI and CIA officials later admitted that neither agency had placed Jarrah's name on any domestic watch list (*Chicago Tribune* 12/14/01). At several points, Jarrah could have been apprehended. However, he allegedly went on to pilot UA Flight 93.

Nor were Mihdhar, Hazmi, Aulaqi and Jarrah the only ones allowed to continue because of missed opportunities. The claim that these were the only alleged hijackers pre-identified as terrorist suspects was proven false by the revelations of Able Danger, which had gathered extensive data on several other prominent operatives (*Gov. Security News* 9/05).

Why didn't all this suspicious behavior set warning lights flashing? Any time several leading Islamists attend a summit linking the major branches of a terrorist network, any time someone under surveillance receives phone calls or money from someone else under surveillance, surely intelligence agents are trained to move beyond just gathering information. Surely they must also share the information with law enforcement, yet the CIA and FBI apparently took no lawful action to protect the country.

## Alleged Hijackers Train at Military Flight Schools

But the US government involvement with al Qaeda operatives didn't stop with the CIA and FBI; it also involved the military. During the 1990s, as many as seven of the alleged hijackers had received flight training at supposedly secure US military bases. Al Qaeda operatives trained at different military flight schools. "Ringleader" Mohamed Atta trained at the Air War College on Maxwell Air Force Base in Alabama; alleged hijacker Abdulaziz al Omari reportedly took flight training at Brooks AFB in Texas. Accused hijackers Saeed al Ghamdi and his brother, Ahmed, were also among the Saudis to receive training at US military installations (Knight Ridder 9/27/01). Three accused hijackers provided addresses at Pensacola Naval Air Station, "the cradle of US Navy aviation" and home to the Navy's Blue Angels. Beneath the media radar, for many years Pensacola had trained foreign aviators, including many from Saudi Arabia and other US client states; thus it became easier for Saudi militants to enroll there without attracting attention (*Newsweek* 9/15/01).

Beyond Atta, the al Ghamdi brothers, and the Saudi pilots in training, other alleged hijackers attended the Defense Language Institute. Located in Monterey, California, the Institute was the military's premier language facility. Its vice chancellor for student affairs, Col. Steve Butler, confirmed the connection. He added that President Bush "did nothing to warn the American people because he needed this war on terrorism" (*Monterey Co. Herald* 5/26/02). The Pentagon threatened Col. Butler with court martial for his inappropriate remarks.

The alleged hijackers didn't only train at military installations, however. They also congregated at commercial flight schools, starting in 1993 at the Airman Flight School near Norman, Oklahoma. Most of the commercial flight schools, though, were located in Florida. In the fall of 2000, while Bush and Gore were crisscrossing the state, Mohamed Atta and Marwan al Shehhi were flying Cessnas up and down the coast. Many of the alleged 9/11 hijackers had taken flying lessons, and at least 44 of the individuals sought for questioning by the FBI had received flight instruction. Nor was this pattern of taking flying lessons anything unique for 9/11: one important paper confirmed that "federal authorities have been aware for years that suspected terrorists with ties to Osama bin Laden were receiving flight training at schools in the United States" (*Wash. Post* 9/23/01).

In fact, a high percentage of the alleged hijackers attended two flight schools in Venice, Florida, along the Gulf Coast. Flight training offered "cover" for Islamists who sought a purpose for entering the country. But according to investigative journalist Dan Hopsicker, "the terrorists ... were funneled through only a few 'special' schools." These particular schools provided both a place for US intelligence agencies to recruit spies and a "front" for the drug smuggling that's made Florida justly infamous (Hopsicker *Welcome To Terrorland* p. 182).

## Defense Department on the Defensive

Right after 9/11, following the disclosures about flight training at military flight schools, the corporate media dropped the story when the Air Force issued a statement aimed at preempting further inquiry. It tried to deny that hijackers had trained at military bases—claiming that the names might be the same, but due to discrepancies in their data, they must refer to different individuals (Hopsicker *Welcome to Terrorland* pp. 137-39). At some point, such logic faces the laws of probability. One case of confused identity, okay. Two, perhaps. Three, well, possibly. But seven? Yes, it could have been coincidental that two airliners hit the WTC within fifteen minutes, but few among us believed that, even in a state of shock.

When the military furnished flight training and language instruction to these individuals, did it also provide knowledge with a still more devastating potential: strategy, tactics, and insider acquaintance with American air defenses? All this, and especially the fact that some of the hijackers had entered the country or remained there with unusual help from federal agencies, was acutely embarrassing. It had to be covered up.

## Connections among Hijackers, Corporate Crooks, Underworld Figures, and the FBI

While it's obvious that 9/11 was mass murder—arguably the crime of the century—it's less understood that the criminality extended well beyond al Qaeda. Former FBI translator Sibel Edmonds spoke tough words about the underworld's role in 9/11: "you have money-laundering activities, drug-related activities, and terrorist-support activities converging at certain points and becoming one" (*Baltimore Chronicle* 5/7/04).

Since deals that erode the credibility of the legal system don't receive much ink in most newspapers, many educated people remain unaware of situations in which known criminals are allowed to become intelligence "assets." Rudi Dekkers, owner of Huffman Aviation in Venice, Florida, provides an intriguing case study. Over several years, Dekkers had become the target of several lawsuits and developed a reputation as a shady character and con man (*St. Petersburg Times* 7/25/04). However, Dekkers and his cronies in crime had become most notorious for their "milk runs" to the Caribbean. When Dekkers drove flashy new cars into the parking lot, coworkers began to suspect that he wasn't running milk.

Following 9/11, Dekkers became an instant media sensation. Someone who'd once smuggled drugs and apparently chummed with some of the alleged hijackers appeared before Congress. After crowing "I'm always on television," Dekkers presumed to offer House members "tips on preventing future terrorist attacks" (US Congress 3/19/02). As the "honcho of Huffman" spoke before the TV cameras, he became a contributing author of the Official Story. Dekkers's pronouncements to Congress and the media, investigative reporter Dan Hopsicker has observed, helped fashion a public image of the hijackers: "in the dozens of sound bites he fed to the world's media ... he lied ... for the [government] for whom he worked. They even coached him on what to say," much as they'd groomed the owner of another flight school in Venice (Hopsicker *Welcome to Terrorland* p. 205). Although Dekkers delivered different accounts, no one questioned the contradictions.

In his media appearances, Dekkers made it seem that all the Arabic students, including the alleged hijackers, had simply walked onto Huffman's tarmac. This was hardly the case. Speaking off the record because of fears for his life, one former Huffman executive told a different story: "Early on I gleaned that these guys had government protection. We heard that sixteen of the nineteen terrorists had been on Interpol's Most Wanted list. They were let into this country for a specific purpose" (Hopsicker *Welcome to Terrorland* p. 254).

Dekkers disguised not only his own involvement in the flight students' entry into the country but that of government agencies which supposedly oversaw aviation security and drug enforcement. As he did so, he previewed one of the most characteristic patterns exhibited in the aftermath of 9/11: people with obvious conflicts of interest—including likely suspects—were allowed and even encouraged to present themselves as expert witnesses.

While US intelligence agencies have played down their pre-9/11 surveillance of the alleged hijackers, clearly the FBI was spying closely enough to arrive at the flight schools just hours after the attacks. Rather than asking questions, however, agents often attempted to intimidate employees into silence, much as they did in Shanksville, Pennsylvania, and in lower Manhattan. The FBI arrived within minutes of the impact at parking lots, hotels, and gas stations around the Pentagon to seize all surveillance camera tapes (*Richmond Times-Dispatch* 12/11/01). Although at least eighty-five videos were impounded, none became available for nearly five years. Most of these tapes have never been seen again.

Despite its knowledge over many months of what was going on at the schools, the Bureau did little to intervene. Yet when questioned about FBI knowledge of al Qaeda students at American flight schools, FBI Director Robert Mueller asked the public to believe "if we had understood that to be the case, we would have … averted this" (*Newsweek* 9/22/01). Despite these disclaimers, much evidence suggests the FBI *did* understand. The Bureau may have bungled its surveillance of Mihdhar and Hazmi in San Diego, but, possibly with help from Dekkers, it kept close track of Atta while he was living in Venice, Florida. This shouldn't surprise us, for Spanish, German, and American intelligence had been watching Atta since 1995 (*NYT* 11/20/01).

## Hijacker Behavior Suggests Legal Impunity

When we consider what went on in Florida, we're forced to ponder another suspicious link between al Qaeda operatives and the US government. The operatives' apparent sense of legal impunity was often remarkable. If a foreigner leading a terrorist mission were concerned about getting caught and wrecking the plan, would he violate immigration protocols, try to purchase a crop duster plane, buy cocaine at his flight school, and carouse with strippers at nightclubs? (Hicks *Big Wedding* p. 37). Lead operative Mohamed Atta indulged in all of these imprudent behaviors. Furthermore, just days before the attacks, Atta got sloshed in a bar and shouted curses in Arabic, even blaspheming Allah. When the manager confronted him, Atta bellowed, "You think I can't pay? I'm a pilot for American Airlines. I can pay my fucking bill" (*Sunday Herald* [Scotland] 9/16/01). A few days later, Atta reportedly piloted a Boeing owned by American Airlines.

These Islamists just weren't worried about consequences. On July 5, 2001, just nine weeks before the attacks, Atta was pulled over for speeding in Delray Beach, Florida. However, the officer failed to notice a warrant for his arrest and simply issued a warning (*St. Petersburg Times* 12/14/01). If the police had checked Atta's immigration status, they'd have found that Atta had overstayed his visa (*GOVEXEC* 3/16/04).

Again, we have to wonder why the primary players in the attacks would run such risks. Former Sen. Bob Graham asked such questions not only about law enforcement's failure to red flag Atta, but also Ziad Jarrah who was also stopped for speeding just two days before the attacks (Graham and J. Nussbaum *Intelligence Matters* p. 37). All this seems hard to fathom—unless, of course, one is willing to entertain the notion that the alleged hijackers believed they wouldn't be detained.

### The Grand Bargain: A US/Saudi Relationship That's Lasted

It's crucial to understand that a long-standing relationship between American and Saudi elites also contributed the events of 9/11. The Saudis and the Americans go even further back than the Bushes and the bin Ladens. In the waning days of World War II, the two countries struck a grand bargain: Saudi oil in exchange for American weapons and training. As petrodollars poured in, rich Saudis deposited tens of billions in American banks.

Like the British and the Germans, the US long had cast a lustful eye on the oil fields of the Middle East. If this conclusion seems farsighted, recall that oil had already been driving US foreign policy for many years. A State Department memo written during World War II emphasized that "petroleum has historically played a larger part in the external relations of the United States than any other commodity" (Zinn *People's History* p. 413). In 1944, the US sent a delegation to talk business with the Saudis. One member of the group, which was led by Dallas oilmen, was very clear about the stakes: "the oil in this region is the greatest single prize in all history" (Baker *Family of Secrets* p. 288).

The following year, on the way home from the Yalta Conference, a dying FDR sailed out of his way to meet King Ibn Saud on a Navy ship in the Suez Canal. After FDR's death, President Truman went further by certifying the kingdom's eligibility for military training and equipment (Unger *House of Bush* p. 45).

Finalized during the evolving Cold War, the deal has remained straightforward: the Americans would provide security, external and internal, to the Saudi royals, and they would sell inexpensive oil to the Americans. The Americans not only helped the Saudis assemble a state-of-the-art air force and a modern army, it helped them create the repressive Saudi Arabian National Guard responsible for internal security—for protection of the royal family (M. Klare *Blood and Oil* p. 41).

Many have noted how the American/British decision to establish the state of Israel as a bastion against communism has contributed mightily to the rise of Islamic fundamentalism (AssociatedContent.com 4/26/10). Fewer, however, have understood that, from its inception, Islamic fundamentalists perceived the House of Saud as a den of moral decadence. American support for Saudi Arabia had everything to do with the US becoming the primary target of Islamist terrorism. In 1991, as the US military established bases in Saudi Arabia, bin Laden regarded the stationing of American troops in his native land as a violation against Islam and he turned against his former benefactors (C. Johnson *Blowback* p. 11). The "infidel" bases in the Muslim Holy Land became a rallying point for Islamists (PBS "Frontline" 2/8/05).

During the 1970s, 80s, and 90s, the bond between American and Saudi elites intensified, often centering on Saudi royals and bankers plus the Bush family. These clans share a long history. In his book *House of Bush, House of Saud: The Secret Relationship Between the World's Two Most Powerful Dynasties,* investigative journalist Craig Unger argued that 9/11 can be understood in the context of ties between these two dominant families.

## After the Attacks: Royal Treatment for the Saudis

Prince Bandar, the Saudi ambassador, epitomized the politically incestuous liaisons between the Saudi royals and the Bush clan. Bandar, noted insider journalist Bob Woodward, had long been "virtually a member of the Bush family" (CBS *60 Minutes* 4/17/04). Former FBI Director Louis Freeh disclosed that "Prince Bandar practically has his own key to the Oval Office" (Freeh *My FBI* p. 8). Bandar's extraordinary access to power became even more evident immediately following 9/11.

On September 13, 2001, Bandar had dinner with Bush (M. Moore PBS "Charlie Rose" 7/05/04). While the prince and president sat smoking cigars on the Truman balcony, sleep-deprived first responders in New York were frantically digging in the rubble, hoping to find survivors (Unger *House of Bush* pp. 254-55). Bush had already decided to attack Afghanistan. "Regime change" had been planned since July, two months before 9/11, and "military action against Afghanistan would go ahead ... before the snows started falling in Afghanistan, by the middle of October at the latest" (BBC 9/18/01). The very next day, just three days after the tragedy, Bush was on the phone with Tony Blair. The topic was a second war—the one they *really* wanted—this one on Iraq (BBC 11/30/09).

### Secret Charter Flights for Elite Saudis

Many have wondered why Bush entertained the Saudi ambassador and approved the special flights for Saudis. True, the president owed the prince some favors. Or did some Saudis also know things Bush didn't want known? The decision to approve the airlift wasn't Bush's alone. Prince Bandar had a personal relationship with FBI Director Freeh, who quickly approved the flights (W. Simpson *The Prince* pp. 314-16).

In the thirteen days following the attacks, at least 140 Saudi nationals—including twenty bin Laden family members—boarded private jets that flew them home (D. R. Griffin *9/11 Comm. Report* p. 71). The first of these secret charters operated outside of the no-fly rules still in effect at the time. When the flights began, hundreds of thousands of American citizens were still languishing in overcrowded airports and overbooked motels (Baker *Family of Secrets* p. 282). After gathering at secret assembly points in Florida and Texas, most Saudis flew to Boston and on to Europe. The State Department and the FAA were both involved, and FBI agents provided personal escorts for prominent Saudis fleeing the United States (CNN 3/19/02). Most importantly, most of the elite Saudis left the country before they could be interrogated (Pacifica "Democracy Now!" 3/29/05). The FBI repeatedly declined to interrogate or conduct extended interviews with the Saudis, causing Craig Unger to wonder, "in the context of the global manhunt and the War on Terror, didn't it make sense to at least interview Osama bin Laden's relatives …?" (Unger *House of Bush* pp. 256-57).

### Bin Laden Flights and Mass Roundups of Muslims

Especially problematic was the secret flight for members of the immediate bin Laden family. Ibrahim bin Laden was among twelve "Saudi businessmen" watched by intelligence law-enforcement agencies of the United States, Canada, Australia, and several European countries. Even less discussed was Osama's half brother Khalil, who lived on a twenty-acre estate outside Orlando: he was listed among the top twenty sources of finance for al Qaeda (*Vanity Fair* 12/02). The press blackout was near complete.

Not only did these secret charters start flying while 200,000 planes throughout the country were still grounded, but elite Saudi businessmen and members of the bin Laden clan were whisked out of country while law enforcement was rounding up ordinary Muslims. In a massive international crackdown, thousands of Muslims, especially male immigrants, were subjected to searches, interrogations, and arrests (Huffington Post 10/15/07).

If the "evacuation" of the bin Ladens raised eyebrows, that of Prince Ahmed bin Salman would eventually raise more questions. One of the richest among the royals, Prince bin Salman had worked closely with Osama bin Laden and his "Afghan Arabs" during the 1980s. The "bluegrass" prince boarded a lavishly refurbished Boeing 727 in Lexington, Kentucky, on September 15 (Unger *House of Bush* pp. 255-58). Bin Salman would later be implicated when, under interrogation, al Qaeda leader Abu Zubaydah provided the names of prominent Saudi financiers for al Qaeda.

# Did Captured al Qaeda Operative Expose Saudi Money Men?

In 2002, US intelligence captured Abu Zubaydah, describing him as the first high-ranking al Qaeda leader apprehended after 9/11. Zubaydah, a senior al Qaeda talent scout, had vetted foreign recruits before sending them on to training camps in Afghanistan. In doing this work, he cooperated closely with Pakistan's spy agency, the ISI (A. Rashid *Descent Into Chaos* p. 48).

Bullets flew during the capture. Although wounded three times, Zubaydah survived the shootout (R. Suskind *One Percent Doctrine* pp. 84-89). When he woke in a Lahore, Pakistan, hospital, he came face-to-face with CIA agent John Kiriakou. Desperate, the prisoner begged the agent to smother him with a pillow. Kiriakou retorted, "No, no. We have plans for you" (*NY Review of Books* 3/15/09).

The CIA had reason to believe that the prisoner might possess valuable information. Its famous President's Daily Brief (PDB) of August 6, 2001, had made two mentions of Zubaydah, describing him as the coordinator of attacks on the US—including the bombing of the high-tech *USS Cole* (http://hnn.us/articles/1680.html). And Zubaydah had worked al Qaeda's "Yemen switchboard," where he'd have processed important communications.

At first, interrogators used only "standard interview techniques" (*NY Rev. of Books* 3/15/09).

## "Enhanced Interrogation Techniques": Drugging and Waterboarding Prisoners

Soon enough, interrogation techniques were "enhanced." Under the influence of "truth serum" (sodium pentothal), Zubaydah reportedly told interrogators to just call Prince Ahmed bin Salman, the "Kentucky bluegrass" sheik and a nephew of King Fahd. Zubaydah not only revealed his ties with prominent Saudi and Pakistani officials: he even provided their phone numbers. The captive expressed relief that he wouldn't face Saudi interrogators (G. Posner *Why America Slept* pp. 189-94). Why would Zubaydah have been so deathly afraid of the Saudis—and why might they have been fearful of what he might tell the Americans?

After these increasingly inhumane interrogations, Zubaydah faced "extraordinary rendition," a euphemism for "being taken to a secret prison, often after being kidnapped." The CIA took him to "black sites": first to a secret holding tank in Thailand and then to Bagram Air Base in Afghanistan (*Observer* [UK] 6/13/04). Justice Department memos later revealed that his captors waterboarded Zubaydah 83 times in a month or two. Throughout Zubaydah's detention and torture, members of the National Security Council and senior Bush administration officials were briefed about his ongoing mistreatment. Rice and Rumsfeld were in the loop, and Cheney personally approved the waterboarding (Sen. Intell. Comm. 4/22/09).

While the CIA was extracting information from Abu Zubaydah, the FBI went through his journals, seized from the al Qaeda "safe house" in Yemen. Counterterrorist agent Dan Coleman concluded that "Zubaydah was like a receptionist, like the guy at the front desk.... There's nothing in there that refers to ... any al Qaeda attack, not even 9/11" (*Vanity Fair* 12/16/08). His journals held special significance, though. Zubaydah began keeping them in 1992, after he suffered a severe head injury while fighting in Afghanistan, significantly impairing his long- and short-term memory (*Guardian* [UK] 3/30/09).

## Prisoner with Amnesia Issues Conjures Vivid Memories

Despite his severe memory impairment, Zubaydah supposedly disclosed secrets about bin Laden, al Qaeda, Saudi financial support for the attacks, and, above all, a "protection" deal bin Laden cut with elite Saudis. Zubaydah apparently recalled a meeting in which prominent Saudi and Pakistani officials each cut deals with the bearded leader: the Saudis would continue to aid the Taliban, and the Pakistanis would offer al Qaeda sanctuary and provide him with arms and money. As if all this weren't enough, Zubaydah reportedly claimed that the Pakistani and Saudi governments were warned the US would be attacked on 9/11/01, though not given details as to when or where (G. Posner *Why America Slept* pp. 189-90).

These revelations were mostly conceptual, not detailed; but without consulting his journal, how could a guy with acute memory problem recall these phone numbers?

## Sudden Deaths of Four Officials Named by Zubaydah

After 9/11, the Saudi royals were surely enraged at fifteen Saudis whom the world believed had committed mass murder. But since they couldn't direct their full fury at al Qaeda, which they'd paid well to stay out of the kingdom, the royals may have turned their wrath on the money men who had been underwriting al Qaeda. At any rate four individuals, three Saudis and a Pakistani, died mysteriously in a short time.

After fleeing the US in his luxury airliner, "bluegrass" Prince Ahmed bin Sultan returned to pursue his passion for racing thoroughbreds. Having just purchased War Emblem for a huge sum, bin Sultan entered his new horse in the Kentucky Derby. When War Emblem won the Derby, the prince strode to the winner's circle and thrust the cup high, proud to become the first Arab to win the fabled race (*Newsday* 5/7/02). Just ten months after 9/11 and two months after his new thoroughbred won the Derby, bin Sultan died at 43, ostensibly of a heart attack (*Sports Network* 7/22/02).

If the Prince bin Sultan, the king's nephew, were the only sudden death among those Zubaydah named, we might consider his early demise as simply unfortunate. But his was *not* the only sudden death: two other Saudi royals also died suddenly in mysterious circumstances. The next day, Prince Sultan bin Faisal, the prince's cousin and another nephew of the king, died in a car crash. A week later, Prince Fahd bin Turki, another royal and the kingdom's longtime intelligence minister, was found dead in the desert (*World Markets Analysis* 7/30/02). A few months later, Pakistani air marshal Mushaf Ali Mir was killed in plane crash widely suspected of involving sabotage. Ali Mir had been closely allied to Islamic fundamentalists in the military intelligence (ISI) (Unger *House of Bush* p. 269).

Of the five officials Zubaydah named as intermediaries funneling funds to al Qaeda, four met sudden deaths in mysterious circumstances. In the US, the corporate news media stayed strangely silent. With the notable exception of an article in *Time* (8/31/03), few news outlets gave much coverage to a story that, in the aftermath of 9/11, would surely have piqued keen public interest.

All these deaths were puzzling, to be sure. *New York Times* correspondent James Risen affirmed that "the United States had obtained other evidence suggesting connections between al Qaeda operatives and telephone numbers associated with Saudi officials." Confirming the suspicions of many, Risen added that "there is no evidence that a thorough examination of [Zubaydah's] claims of ties to powerful Saudis was ever conducted" (Risen *State of War* p. 187).

The legal treatment of Zubaydah seems to suggest Washington's fear that detainees would have their day in open court. As the Supreme Court approached making a decision to affirm the legal rights of detainees, federal authorities put Zubaydah on a "black [secret] flight" and whisked away to another "black site" (*San Fran. Chron.* 8/7/10). Then in 2009, the Justice Department quietly recanted nearly every major claim the Bush administration had made about Zubaydah, by then a detainee at Guantánamo (*Guardian* [UK] 3/30/09).

A media blackout not only avoided embarrassment for the US, it suppressed the obvious Saudi involvement in 9/11. Addressing this conspiracy of silence and tacit denial, foreign policy expert James Risen observed that "the Saudis' influence on American politics is pervasive. It is an issue only slightly less sensitive to discuss … in Washington than that of Israeli political influence" (B. Woodward *State of War* p. 177).

**Ongoing Protection for Saudis**

In contrast to the Bush dynasties, the Obama administration didn't arrive with active connections to the House of Saud. Nevertheless, it too has sided with royals to suppress public scrutiny of Saudi funding for Islamist groups. In 2009, less than a week before the president was to meet with King Abdullah, the Obama's Solicitor General Elena Kagan filed a brief urging the Supreme Court to throw out a suit filed by families of 9/11 victims against the Saudi royal family (World Net Daily 5/12/10). Signed by more than 7,630 Americans, the suit accused Saudi Arabia of helping finance al Qaeda prior to attacks. Unimpressed, the Justice Department steadfastly upheld the Saudi's claim of "sovereign immunity" (Pacifica "Democracy Now!" 6/1/09).

American policies toward the Saudis also cast a blind eye toward their secret sympathies for terrorism at home. In several attacks occurring in Saudi Arabia from 2003 through 2004, al Qaeda terrorists were surrounded, only to somehow escape (*NYT* 11/13/04). Did al Qaeda have friends in the king's court? These odd escapes suggested that the US government has coddled a Saudi regime which has not only funded terrorists but had become infiltrated by them. The US, its economy long held hostage by the sheiks of Aramco (American Arabian Oil Company), had to deal with a monarchy influenced by Wahhabi fundamentalists and al Qaeda sympathizers.

As long as the US economy remains addicted to both Saudi oil and Saudi money, and as long as Washington clings to its traditional power-projection points, little is likely to change.

# 16.  Al Qaeda Operatives with Special Protection

*The confrontation that we are calling for with the apostate regimes does not know Socratic debates ... Platonic ideals ... nor Aristotelian diplomacy. But it knows the dialogue of bullets, the ideals of assassination, bombing, and destruction, and the diplomacy of the cannon and machine gun.*

—Ali Mohamed "the American"

This chapter will look at how three of al Qaeda's highest-ranking operatives—Ali Mohamed "the American" (MTA), Khalid Sheikh Mohammed (KSM), and Mohamed Atta—received astounding privileges and support from American government agencies. It's well known that, during the 1980s, Osama bin Laden received extensive help from the CIA while leading the *mujahedeen* fighting the Soviets in Afghanistan. It's far less known, though, that three of his top lieutenants were receiving "sweetheart deals"—legal immunity, reduced charges, inappropriate visas, sponsorship as double agents, and other support—right up to 9/11.

## Mohamed the American (MTA): Spy, Trainer, and Terrorist

In 1997, Deputy US Attorney Patrick Fitzgerald met face-to-face with MTA, who'd escaped prosecution for his involvement in the 1993 World Trade Center bombing and the New York Landmarks plot. Over dinner, MTA bragged about his false passports, his involvements with militant groups, and his love for bin Laden. He informed Fitzgerald, one of the country's top prosecutors, that he didn't need a *fatwa* to attack America. Though Fitzgerald had let MTA off the hook before, he emerged from the meeting stunned by what he'd heard: "He's the most dangerous man I've ever met. We cannot let this man out on the street." But the Feds did let him go, and within a year MTA had gone on to help bomb two US embassies. "In the annals of espionage," remarked Emmy-award-winning investigative reporter Peter Lance, "few men have moved between the hunters and the hunted with as much audacity as Ali Mohamed" (www. peterlance.com/Peter_Lance/Ali_Mohamed.html).

## A Double Agent with Immunity to Legal Consequences

Compared to Osama bin Laden's other top lieutenants, the double agent MTA, the "mastermind" KSM, and the "ringleader" Atta, MTA displayed greater understanding of American culture and the English language. All spoke several languages, and this helped them to evade capture by—or to work closely with—intelligence agencies from several countries, especially Pakistan and the United States. Capable as these leaders were, crucial as they were to the attacks on 9/11, they didn't do everything by themselves. If these bright boys were able to game US government agencies, it helped that the agencies were often willing to play along.

MTA cut a striking figure. An exceptionally fit martial artist, he stood six feet one and weighed a muscular 200 pounds. MTA was fluent in four languages, including Arabic, English, and Hebrew. According to reports, MTA was highly committed, competitive, and disciplined. He was, notes historian Lawrence Wright, "the kind of man who was going to get to the top of any organization" (L. Wright *Looming Tower* p. 204). MTA's knowledge of military techniques and command of languages qualified him for Islamist terrorism and espionage work—and not just for one side.

MTA was a gifted sociopath who planned dozens of terrorist schemes. Over two decades, he worked with his mentor, Dr. Ayman al Zawahiri (aka "Dr. Death"); with the notorious "Blind Sheikh" Abdul-Rahman; and finally with Osama bin Laden. MTA took part in several murderous plots; some were effective, others abortive. By 9/11, when the dramatic attacks put his efforts and expertise on full display, MTA was behind bars—though only in "custodial witness protection" (P. Lance *Triple Cross* pp. 320-23). Hardly his just desserts.

Although his involvements in terrorism were often obvious, only twice did MTA enter a courtroom. Even in these two instances, he didn't face charges anywhere near commensurate with his crimes. Without covert connections to the intelligence apparatus, he could neither have operated for so long without legal consequences nor exerted such crucial influence. Nor was MTA alone in enjoying such connections. As we'll see, KSM and Atta were also connected to the ISI, Pakistan's secret military intelligence (UPI 9/30/02), which was connected by charter to the CIA. As a master of terror techniques, MTA clearly illustrated an ongoing symbiotic relationship between US intelligence/law enforcement and Islamic-fundamentalist movements such as the Taliban, al Qaeda, Hezbollah, and Islamic Jihad.

Born in Egypt, Ali Mohamed's involvement in terrorism began in 1981 when army officers from his unit assassinated Egypt's semi-secular president, Anwar Sadat. MTA kept his distance from those who planned the killing, but because he'd joined Dr. Zawahiri's al Jihad, an extreme Islamist cell, Egyptian intelligence suspected him as a conspirator. When the Egyptian army forced MTA to resign in 1984, "Dr. Death" gave him a new challenge: to penetrate American intelligence (Wright *Looming Tower* p. 204).

Although MTA got off to a bad start with the CIA, he still went to work for them. Completely undaunted, MTA strode right into the CIA's Cairo Station and offered to spy on Islamic extremist groups. Although the desk officer suspected that Ali was a "plant" for Egyptian intelligence, he did assign MTA to the Frankfurt Station, which presented opportunities to spy on Iran. MTA got off to a bad start, however. He entered a mosque and informed the imam that he was "a CIA agent" assigned to infiltrate the Muslim community. Since the CIA already had a mole in the mosque, it not only fired MTA but also sent out cables warning that he wasn't a reliable asset (Wright *Looming Tower* pp. 204-5).

## MTA Comes to America, Becomes a Double or Triple Agent

Later, MTA was recruited and trained by the US Army, CIA, and FBI. Ali Mohamed first joined the US Army Special Forces and in turn helped train and equip hundreds of al Qaeda operatives—including some of the alleged hijackers (Wright *Looming Tower* pp. 204-206). Although MTA was a big success in the Special Forces, his real interest lay in training the soldiers of a very different army.

However, American intelligence failed to heed its own warnings to shun or detain Ali Mohamed. In 1985, after the CIA claimed it had put MTA's name on the Watch List to block his entrance to the country, he received a US visa under a special program run by the CIA (*Boston Globe* 2/3/95). Nor was MTA the only operative to pull this off, as indicated in the last chapter (CBC 7/3/02). Despite being flagged as a terror suspect on the Watch List, the Blind Sheikh was allowed to seek refuge in the US (Wright *Looming Tower* p. 201). Despite the CIA's blunt all-points bulletin, MTA not only remained connected to the Agency but also operated as an FBI informant: in fact, he became a triple agent. While posing as a CIA asset and an FBI informant, the master spy also served bin Laden and his second in command, Dr. al Zawahiri.

While ordinary double agents are devious infiltrators motivated by double wages, others operate within a symbiotic relationship, one in which two unlike entities work together for mutual advantage. Here the symbiosis—which will also become evident in the antics of Khalid Sheikh Mohammed (KSM) and Mohamed Atta—occurred between militant Islamic groups, especially al Qaeda, and government agencies, especially the FBI and the CIA.

But in addition to pay, double (and triple) agents often also receive legal cover or even immunity from prosecution from the one side—in this case from the United States. Between 1990 and 1997, MTA furnished some of al Qaeda's secrets to the FBI (CNN 10/30/98); in return, he received legal impunity which he fully exploited. Double agents make more effective terrorists because they're allowed to get away with more than ordinary mortals—much more. Rather than receiving enhanced security from its massive intelligence/military establishment, the American public was placed in greater danger when MTA's offenses went unpunished and he remained at large, free to commit additional crimes.

## American Bride, al Qaeda "Switchboard," and Army Special Forces

In 1985, MTA married an American woman. With a new bride and better prospects for American citizenship, Ali Mohamed became "Mohamed the American." After he joined his bride in Santa Clara, California, his neighbors remarked that "everyone knew he was working as a liaison between the CIA and the Afghan cause ..." (*WS Journal* 11/26/01).

Also during the early 1990s, as a personal assistant to Osama bin Laden, MTA helped the leader move his whole al Qaeda operation from Afghanistan to Sudan (Lance *Triple Cross* p. 174). Once bin Laden had located, MTA trained his bodyguards and taught al Qaeda trainees how to set up cells. In this period, he became a close associate of Dr. Zawahiri, the Egyptian-born founder of Islamic Jihad (W. Tarpley *9/11 Synthetic Terror* p. 165). Readers will recall videos with Dr. Death seated at bin Laden's side, threatening that terrorist attacks would continue until the US changed its policies toward Muslim countries (*LA Times* 9/18/08). In 1994, Zawahiri entered the US. Despite a well documented record of terrorism, al Zawahiri was granted residence in the US (Ahmed *War on Truth* p. 46). Since the Blind Sheikh's Islamist cell was on trial in New York, Zawahiri's easy entry was especially surprising.

Back home in Santa Clara, MTA set up a "jihadi switchboard" to connect calls from operatives throughout the Islamist world (*San Fran. Chron.* 10/11/01). Although this phone hub made MTA more visible to the CIA and FBI, he worked the phones hard, applying his talents to recruiting and fund raising. Despite his increased visibility to the Feds, Ali landed a job with Northrop Grumman, a major government contractor. By this time the Feds had mounds of evidence that MTA was seeking still better penetration of US intelligence (Wright *Looming Tower* pp. 206-207).

**Weapons Training for *Both* Special Forces and al Qaeda**
Not long after he arrived in the US, MTA enlisted in the Army's Special Forces. His training included instruction in sabotage, special reconnaissance, and counterinsurgency operations. After four months, proudly sporting a Green Beret, Ali received a diploma (*N. C. News Observer* 10/21/01). From 1986-89, while on active duty in the Army, MTA attended Blind Sheikh Rahman's sermons in New York. Full of fury at "the Satanic foes of Islam," these rants helped recruit *mujahedeen* for the CIA-sponsored campaign in Afghanistan. In response, MTA wanted to help the Islamist

cause by training fighters—and to further infiltrate American intelligence. While on extended leave, he traveled to Afghanistan where he first met bin Laden, who'd been receiving recruits, weapons, and huge amounts of money from the CIA (Tarpley *9/11 Synthetic Terror* pp. 163-64).

From 1987 through 1990, MTA taught Special Forces recruits at Ft. Bragg and received a "secret" security clearance. In the late 1980s, however, MTA turned his teaching talents in a different direction: he began to train Islamic militants on American soil. Still stationed at Fort Bragg, he frequently spent weekends with Islamic militants at the Al Kifah Refugee Center in Brooklyn. The Center was a branch of Makhtab al Khidmat (MAK), a "charity" front closely connected to the CIA's "Operation Cyclone" in Afghanistan. Both the Pakistani government and the CIA cast a blind eye on the expanding opium operations run by Islamist fighters and drug lords (P. D. Scott *Oil, Drugs, and War* pp. 32, 28-29).

Both at home and abroad, Ali Mohamed trained Islamic militants. Ever a man of action, MTA soon expanded his efforts, training Islamists at shooting ranges (Lance *Triple Cross* pp. 47-49). In 1989, the FBI took extensive surveillance photos of key al Qaeda figures shooting AK-47s. Later, the FBI's thick files of photos offered a rogue's gallery of Islamist operatives, most of whom would go on to commit murderous crimes. Strangely, though, the FBI suddenly terminated its surveillance of the Blind Sheikh's mosque, the nexus for his Jersey City/Brooklyn cell. A couple of years later, the Bureau placed a "worm" in the cell but again pulled him just as he was bringing in information that would have exposed those plotting to bomb the WTC (Lance *Cover Up* pp. 25, 28-31).

## MTA Violates Army Regulations but Faces Few Consequences

By 1988, MTA had become a highly regarded instructor at the Army's Special Warfare School. Flouting regulations, MTA proposed to use his leave time to train *mujahedeen* and "kill Russians" in Afghanistan. When MTA announced his plans, however, they didn't play well at Ft. Bragg. MTA's commanding officer, Col. Robert Anderson, warned him that it was illegal for an active-duty soldier to freelance in a foreign war. In a report to the Army brass, Col. Anderson expressed concerns that, if captured, MTA could expose the CIA's covert action and embarrass the United States. Anderson also pointed out that MTA could face court martial if he fought in Afghanistan (Lance *Triple Cross* pp. 42-44).

Imagine Col. Anderson's surprise when no attempt was made to keep MTA from breaking Army regulations (*NYT* 12/1/01). When the ever-audacious Ali returned, he bragged of combat exploits, brandishing belt buckles from Soviet officers. Actually, he'd spent his time training *mujahedeen* in the techniques of "unconventional warfare"—notably kidnapping and assassination—that he'd learned with the Special Forces (Wright *Looming Tower* p. 206). But the command structure at Ft. Bragg showed no interest in disciplinary action. MTA, remarked astute observer Peter Lance, "seemed to operate at Ft. Bragg under some sort of protection" (Lance *Triple Cross* p. 42).

## Commanding Officer Reaches Troubling Conclusions

Wondering who might have sponsored Ali's unauthorized actions, Col. Anderson reviewed the many coincidences in the Egyptian's career. Puzzled by these, he concluded that "you or I would have a better chance of winning Powerball [lottery] than an Egyptian major in the unit that assassinated Sadat would have [of] … getting assigned to a Special Forces unit. That just doesn't happen" (*San. Fran. Chron.* 11/4/01).

Col. Anderson realized that all this "didn't happen without support from an outside agency…. It would have to be the CIA getting him into the United States. And then once in the United States, the FBI" (Lance *Triple Cross* p. 34). MTA was frequently quite open about his double identity. In a later trial, court documents revealed conversations with FBI officials in which MTA made "alarming admissions about his links to al Qaeda terrorists, seemingly without fear of being arrested" (*San Fran. Chron.* 11/14/01).

Over several years, Ali taught Islamic fighters how to hijack aircraft, use firearms, and plant explosives (Y. Bodansky *Bin Laden* p. 106). On weekends, MTA frequently stayed with El Sayyid Nosair, who later assassinated Rabbi Meir Kahane, a right-wing Zionist. The FBI monitored and photographed MTA teaching future members of the 1993 WTC bomb plot how to use automatic weapons, but then dropped its surveillance (Lance *Cover Up* p. 25).

Toward the end of his stint at Ft. Bragg, MTA was openly informing his superiors that he'd renewed his collaboration with Blind Sheikh Rahman, leader of the militant Jersey City/Brooklyn cell.

Just *how* involved Ali had become would soon become apparent. From 1990 on, MTA became more and more closely associated with the Blind Sheikh (J. Miller *The Cell* pp. 143-144). Not surprisingly, MTA soon became more involved with violent crimes. In 1990, working with the Sheikh, MTA helped assassinate the speaker of the Egyptian Parliament. In 1993, he helped plan and prepare for both the WTC bombing and the equally murderous Landmarks Plot. In 1995, MTA helped Egyptian Islamic Jihad plot an ambush of President Hosni Mubarak (Wright *Looming Tower* pp. 242-44).

### Evidence Incriminates MTA, but Charges Don't Follow

Throughout the late 1980s, Ali Mohamed had been stealing classified documents from Ft. Bragg and furnishing them to militants in New York. MTA stole maps and training manuals from the base, provided them to Islamist trainees, and used them to write a terrorist training guide that became al Qaeda's playbook (Wright *Looming Tower* p. 205). The tactics presented in Army manuals were readily transferable to terrorists.

In 1990, MTA's abuse of these sensitive materials was exposed: investigators tracking the assassins of Rabbi Kahane uncovered a trove of highly incriminating evidence. At the residence of El Sayyid Nosair, police collected tapes of talks MTA had delivered at the Special Warfare Center, Special Forces training manuals, and even classified documents belonging to the Joint Chiefs of Staff. Especially ominous was a classified pamphlet on "How to Destroy Tall Buildings," complete with notes and commentary by MTA. Any of this evidence could have led to indictments on charges of espionage and treason (Lance *1000 Years for Revenge* pp. 34-35). Surely the time had come for the FBI to pull the bacon and fry the faker.

These top-secret documents comprised only a miniscule part of the evidence seized. Equally troubling were the instructions for making bombs and the receipts for thousands of rounds of ammunition. Most prophetic, however, were the Blind Sheikh Rahman's sermons exhorting his faithful to "mount steeds of war" for the *jihad,* to "destroy the edifices of capitalism" and their "high world buildings." These sermons were found with maps of New York City landmarks and floor plans for the WTC (Lance *1000 Years* pp. 34-35). Moreover, the abundant evidence pointed to a wider conspiracy (*Village Voice* 3/30/93).

**Ignoring Evidence of Collusion, Promoting a Lone-Gunman Theory**
Despite all this highly incriminating evidence found in Nosair's house, authorities refused to acknowledge that plotters had aided his assassination of Rabbi Kahane. Powerful players were moving the pieces on the chessboard, and again they shielded MTA.

In a reprise of the JFK, MLK, and RFK assassinations, government and media rushed to blame a single perpetrator. Ignoring reams of evidence, NYPD chief detective Joe Borelli concluded that the assassination was the work of a "lone deranged gunman." Nosair was charged with murder, but famed attorney William Kunstler helped him beat the charge. When the defendant got off with "assault and possession of an illegal firearm," Nosair literally got away with murder (*Village Voice* 3/30/93). The Blind Sheikh's cell was protected and most of its members escaped prosecution. Two years later, they'd go on to bomb the WTC.

**The 1993 WTC Bombing: More Impunity for MTA**
Now the Blind Sheik's cell had the target, the plan, and the personnel, but it needed more funding, greater technical expertise, and protection from the FBI. Both KSM and bin Laden helped fund the cell, and "master bomber" Ramzi Yousef joined the conspiracy. MTA, the Army demolitions expert, worked with Yousef, the brilliant chemist. Because it had an informant in the cell, the FBI knew about the plans for the bombing (Lance *Cover Up* pp. 28-31).

The '93 bombing was a close call with catastrophe. The plan was to concoct a urea-nitrate-fuel-oil "device" large enough to shatter the supporting pillars of the North Tower, toppling it onto its twin so both would come crashing down. The sinister intent was to kill 50,000 office workers.

Yousef didn't miss by much. Had he placed his bomb a few feet from where it went off, it might have felled the North Tower (MSNBC 9/11/01). "If they had found the exact architectural Achilles' heel, or if the bomb had been a little bit bigger," an FBI explosives expert stated, "it would have brought her down" (Congr. Hearings 2/24/98). The plotters issued a prophetic warning: "next time, it will be very precise" (AP 9/30/01). Yousef went to prison, but his uncle, Khalid Shaikh Mohammed (KSM), allegedly went on to mastermind 9/11 (*LA Times* 9/1/02).

### The Informer Reveals His Involvement

After the blast had rocked Lower Manhattan, Emad "the Mole" Salem claimed that he'd informed the FBI about the plot in February 1992, a *year* before the bombing (P. Thompson *Terror Timeline* p. 11). Then came the aftershock. Salem disclosed that the FBI's plan was for him to supply the plotters with a harmless powder instead of an actual explosive—but that the FBI chose not to furnish the powder, allowing Yousef to build the actual high-explosive bomb. But when the agents canceled the sting operation, Emad Salem got stung: the FBI dismissed him (Lance *Cover Up* pp. 30-32).

Salem pushed back, to no avail. When he presented recordings of more than a hundred telephone conversations with his FBI handlers, he surely should have gained credibility (*NYT* 10/28/93). The tapes not only offered evidence of the plot; they revealed how much the FBI knew and failed to act upon. Not only had it bungled the powder switch; it had also (in effect) fired Salem just when he was becoming most essential (Pacifica "Democracy Now!" 11/23/03).

After the deadly blast, the FBI not only dismissed Emad Salem, the informant who'd told the truth; it also disciplined and defamed his handler, Agent Nancy Floyd, subjecting her to a five-year internal investigation (Lance *Cover Up* pp. 184-85). Even worse, it turned to MTA, the very CIA/FBI/al Qaeda double agent who'd trained the perpetrators, furnished the manuals, and conspired with them to topple the Towers. If MTA's fingerprints weren't all over the crime, his footprints were all around it.

### After Release by Canadian Police, MTA Escapes Prosecution by Americans

Shortly after the WTC bombing, while much of North America was still jittery about Islamist terrorism, the FBI pulled strings for its informant at the US/Canadian border. MTA and a highly placed aide to bin Laden were detained by Royal Canadian Mounties after the aide was nabbed with MTA's driver's license and a false passport. MTA came right out and told the Mounties that, working for al Qaeda and the FBI, he was trying to smuggle an operative into the United States (*San Fran. Chron.* 11/4/01). Although all these disclosures likely perturbed border authorities, MTA had no problem blowing off the Mounties. Acting like a diplomat with a parking ticket, he told the Canadians to call his FBI handler in California. Prompt intervention secured his immediate release (*Toronto Globe* 11/22/01). Protected operatives could get away with becoming very brazen and cavalier.

In 1993, the plotters faced a tough federal prosecutor in a high-profile trial. Assistant US Attorney Patrick Fitzgerald had assisted in the successful prosecution of John Gambino, boss of a major Mafia crime syndicate. Years later, Patrick Fitzgerald would come to national attention in the case of Valerie Plame, the CIA officer who was "outed" through the actions of Lewis "Scooter" Libby, Chief of Staff for Dick Cheney. Fitzgerald, readers will recall, convicted Libby of perjury. In these cases, Fitzgerald pushed vigorously for conviction (NPR 3/6/07).

In 1994, Fitzgerald led the prosecution against Blind Sheikh Rahman and eleven others charged in the WTC bombing (*Observer* [UK] 2/12/06). However, while the Blind Sheikh and others—including El Sayyid Nosair, who'd remained behind bars since 1990—were convicted of the crime, MTA wasn't even *charged*. The Special Forces maps and manuals received consideration as evidence, but little attention was paid to their source. While Patrick Fitzgerald had the opportunity to charge MTA for his key roles in the WTC bombing and the Landmarks Plot, the federal prosecutor failed to do so. The "protected asset" was allowed to "walk," and he didn't walk away from a life of terrorism.

## The 1993 Landmarks Plot: Destruction on a Grander Scale

Hardly discouraged by the failure to bring down the Towers, the Blind Sheikh's cell pursued its far more ambitious "Landmarks Plot" (or "Day of Terror"). This new scheme targeted twelve prominent New York buildings (including synagogues) as well as two iconic bridges and two major tunnels. Again, the intent was to kill 50,000 people, most of them at the Twin Towers. After the plot was thwarted in 1993, five of the cell's members (including the Blind Sheikh) were convicted of attempted murder and other terrorist crimes (*NYT* 10/2/95).

But MTA, the explosives expert who'd trained those directly responsible, once again wasn't charged (*NYT* 1/18/96). As the Landmarks trial began, the court received a confidential Justice Department document listing MTA along with bin Laden and scores of other possible coconspirators in the plot. This document confirmed that investigators were well aware of MTA's involvement in al Qaeda's sinister schemes (*Report* p. 472). However, Prosecutor Fitzgerald simply named Ali as an unindicted coconspirator; he did not, in exchange for this leniency, demand that MTA serve as a state's witness (Lance *Triple Cross* p. 171).

The FBI called MTA in Kenya, where he was sharing an al Qaeda safe house with an operative who'd later help plan the 1998 US embassy bombings. MTA returned to Santa Clara, California, where he'd set up the al Qaeda "switchboard." But when the court didn't issue a subpoena, Ali didn't show at the trial. Apparently the Feds didn't want him on the stand in front of the national media—that could have blown his cover and exposed the FBI (Lance *Triple Cross* pp. 172-73, 77).

Despite abundant evidence of his role in the Landmarks Plot, MTA had once again escaped prosecution and exposure. MTA was allowed to preserve his double identity. He must have figured he enjoyed "unofficial immunity from the Feds," concluded investigative journalist Peter Lance, "so he decided to ratchet up his espionage efforts for *jihad*" (Lance *Triple Cross* pp. 205, 206, 208).

### The Politicalization of Key Government Agencies

When the Justice Department compromised its own case against dangerous terrorists, its explanation for this shortfall was revealing. Deputy Attorney General (and, later, 9/11 commissioner) Jamie Gorelick issued a memo limiting prosecutors' access to intelligence information generated in the 1993 WTC bombing cases. As indicated in Chapter 7, Gorelick's "Wall Memo" extended the so-called "wall" between FBI information gathered for immediate law enforcement from that gathered for long-range espionage (DOJ *Review* p. 28).

Although the new "wall" didn't help matters, the real problem was the politicalization of the Justice Department and intelligence agencies. According to analyst Peter Dale Scott, the prosecution allowed MTA to go free "because, as Fitzgerald knew, Ali Mohamed was an FBI informant" (Global Research 10/8/06). Instead of prosecuting MTA for aiding and abetting terrorist crimes, the FBI had preferred to cover its tracks and protect its asset (Lance *1000 Years* p. 38). MTA had become a man who knew too much: knowing about the FBI and CIA afforded him an additional layer of protection. Virtually until his arrest in 1998, MTA continued to work for both US intelligence and al Qaeda (*NYT* 10/30/98 &10/31/98).

## The Embassy Bombings: MTA Evades Justice Yet Again

Ali Mohamed collaborated closely with bin Laden on the 1998 bombings of US embassies in Kenya and Tanzania. He even took the photos of the targets so he could provide bin Laden with exact locations for the truck bombs. In these vicious attacks, 234 people were killed and more than 4,500 wounded (*NYT* 9/15/98).

But business as usual continued at FBI headquarters, where Thomas Pickard, head of the criminal division, calculated the Bureau's response. Ignoring pleas from Attorney General Janet Reno and counterterrorism czar Richard Clarke, Pickard blocked legendary special agent John O'Neill from leading the investigation into the bombings (Wright *Looming Tower* pp. 309-10). Was this decision mostly about ego conflicts, or did it provide another instance of the Bureau's shielding its longtime "asset" as a means of protecting itself from exposure? Either way, the FBI made a choice that compromised public safety.

Giving MTA another pass, the Justice Department charged bin Laden and Mohamed Atef, his "defense minister" plus eleven others with the embassy bombings (CNN 11/4/98). Soon after the bombings of the embassies, however, MTA was taken into custody. The Feds picked him up on a John Doe warrant and booked him under a fictitious name, "under a cloak of secrecy rarely seen in public courts" (*NYT* 5/18/99). The name of the al

Qaeda operative most responsible for the planning wasn't divulged. "The potential scandal the Feds faced if word got out about the years that he'd played them meant that Ali still controlled the play" (Lance *Triple Cross* pp. 301, 317-18).

Much as MTA had toyed with the Feds for years, he also gamed them outside the courtroom. In "proffer sessions" Ali was encouraged to provide truthful information which couldn't be used against him; but over several months MTA told prosecutors nothing but lies. His brilliance and arrogance showed when Ali looked up at color-coded computer wires and declared them to be hooked up wrong. He even offered to fix the computer: "I can probably crack the password and get into it." This dance went on for several months. Since the Feds had so much to hide, neither negotiation nor prosecution of the FBI informant/al Qaeda operative went anywhere (Lance *Triple Cross* p. 319).

## The Final Charade

When MTA's impunity finally ran out, he was never charged with the bombings, let alone convicted and sentenced for the mass murders. Although several other defendants faced charges carrying the death penalty, MTA was allowed to plead guilty to conspiracy charges, a lesser offense (*WS Journal* 1/3/01). As in the earlier trials, MTA wasn't even tapped to testify against other perpetrators in exchange for the astonishing degree of leniency he'd received. Compelling him to testify would have exposed him to cross examination, and this would have risked "outing" him as a double (likely triple) agent and possible *agent provocateur.*

MTA was never sentenced. Dates were set, but sentencing never happened—or at least no sentencing was ever publicly revealed (*WS Journal* 11/26/01). After 9/11, it was widely believed that MTA was cooperating with the US intelligence, providing information to the Feds "in hopes of winning his release from prison" or possibly a lighter sentence (*San. Fran. Chron.* 9/21/01). Despite intense public interest in al Qaeda operatives, almost nothing was reported about MTA. In 2006, MTA's wife, Linda Sanchez, lamented that "without him being sentenced, I really can't say much.... They have Ali pretty secretive" (Lance *Triple Cross* pp. 23-24). As of 2011, MTA's whereabouts remain unknown. Is he detained without a sentence at a federal prison, held in a hole at Guantánamo, or in "witness protection" somewhere?

No one seems to know, and the press doesn't ask.

## Khalid Sheikh Mohammed (KSM): Alleged "Mastermind" of 9/11

Called "the mastermind" behind 9/11, Khalid Sheikh Mohammed (KSM) deserved that tag: one of bin Laden's lieutenants, he apparently became the brilliant operational master planner of the attacks (APN News 11/20/02). KSM possessed a background in engineering, displayed a gift for organizing, spoke several languages, and bore a strong antipathy toward the US. To the extent that KSM, like MTA, was able to avoid getting caught, he doesn't deserve all the credit.

Born to parents from Pakistan, KSM spent his formative years in Kuwait. Like many *jihadis*, he joined the Muslim Brotherhood in his late teens (BBC 3/16/07). After secondary school in Kuwait, KSM attended Chowan College, a Baptist school in North Carolina. A Muslim fundamentalist at a Christian fundamentalist college, KSM improved his English at a remarkable pace. Later he transferred to North Carolina Agricultural and Technical State University, earning a mechanical engineering degree in 1986 (CNN 12/19/02).

After graduation, KSM traveled to Afghanistan to join the *mujahedeen* fighters who were receiving hundreds of millions of dollars from the CIA to fight the Soviets. From 1987 through 1991, KSM worked for Abdul Rasul Sayyaf, a prominent Afghan warlord much favored by CIA (*Playboy* 6/1/05). While he was in Afghanistan, KSM first met Osama bin Laden (*Financial Times* 12/15/03).

The Afghanistan experience immersed KSM in a cause that would consume his life (*NYT* 11/14/09). Although he worked for a warlord awash in American dollars, the war experience apparently heightened KSM's feelings against American actions abroad. The Commission contended that "KSM's animus toward the United States stemmed not from his experiences there as a student, but rather from his violent disagreement with US foreign policy favoring Israel" (*Report* p. 147).

## KSM's Involvement in 1993 WTC Bombing

The truck bombing of the World Trade Center was planned by a group of conspirators including "master bomber" Ramzi Yousef, and Blind Sheikh Abdul Rahman. Since Yousef had studied electrical engineering and refined his bomb-building skills at an al Qaeda training camp, the demonic genius was drafted to become the lead bomb builder (CBS "60 Minutes" 5/31/02). Working with Yousef, KSM became deeply involved in the planning and financing of the attack (GlobalSecurity.org 8/10/06).

The year after the WTC bombing and the Landmarks Plot, again working closely with "mad bomber" Yousef, "mastermind" KSM became the lead planner of the foiled Bojinka Plot.

## KSM's Defining Role in the Bojinka Plot

In 1994, KSM traveled to the Philippines to join Ramzi Yousef and Abdul Hakim Murad, another inventive bomb builder. Together they conceived the three-part Bojinka Plot: it included bold plans for assassinations of world leaders, midair bombings of airliners bound for the United States, and simultaneous suicide hijackings within the US. These guys could hardly be accused of thinking small.

For starters, Yousef, Murad, and KSM hatched plots to assassinate Pakistani Prime Minister Bhutto, President Bill Clinton, and Pope John Paul II (Lance *Cover Up* pp. 23-24). When these initial plans didn't work out, the Bojinka trio moved toward more technically challenging acts of mass destruction. The second phase drew on the considerable technical ingenuity and expertise of Yousef, and Murad, "the chemist." Together they devised a liquid-based bomb whose components could pass easily through security checks; once aboard the plane, an operative could assemble the bomb (Lance *Cover Up* pp. 185-86). For this second phase, which involved blowing up twelve commercial airliners in the air, KSM and "master bomber" Yousef intended not just to cause thousands of deaths but a disruption of major airlines worldwide lasting several months (*LA Times* 8/11/06). Catastrophe was averted when the Bojinka plot was uncovered in January 1995; Murad was captured when chemicals in the home laboratory caught fire, and Yousef was arrested in February. But

KSM would remain at large until 2003, eluding capture under peculiar circumstances.

## Bojinka's Final Phase: A Blueprint for 9/11

Except for a few details, the third and final phase of Bojinka offered a startling preview of 9/11. Its planners had identified at least seven targets, including the World Trade Center, the Pentagon, CIA headquarters, the Sears Tower in Chicago, the Transamerica Tower in San Francisco, and a nuclear power plant. This third phase, observed investigative journalist Lance, represented "a virtual blueprint of the 9/11 attacks" (Lance *1000 Years* pp. 278-80).

The similarities are indeed striking: though several of the specific final-stage targets were different, all but one came from categories also prevalent on 9/11: iconic tall buildings and centers of US military or economic power. Had the Commission covered this third phase, it would have inevitably faced a troubling question: If for six years US officials had known about the Bojinka plotters, about their plans to hijack airliners and crash them into iconic buildings, why weren't they able to prevent one of the very same plotters, KSM, from masterminding very similar attacks on 9/11?

## Flying Suicide Squad Chills Investigators

By the time the police intervened, preparations for Bojinka's final phase were already under way. Ten Islamists were training at flight schools in the United States—especially at Richmor Aviation in Schenectady, New York. A decade later, Richmor was exposed as a contractor working on "extraordinary renditions" for the CIA (http://intelwire.egoplex.com/unlocking911-1-ali-mohamed-wtc.html). As noted earlier, several al Qaeda pilots later trained at Huffman Aviation in Florida, which was also linked to the CIA (S. Hicks *Big Wedding* pp. 93-94). Coming from Saudi Arabia, Sudan, and Pakistan, these pilots in training were taking instruction as early as 1994; this, too, contradicts the usual story about 9/11 coming out of the blue, completely without precedent.

## Funding for Flight School, Informing the Feds

If *jihadis* were taking pilot training, then who was paying the bill? One of the leading funders was the Islamist Humbali, aka Riduan Isamuddin, "the

Osama bin Laden of Indonesia" (http://en.wikipedia.org/wiki/Riduan_Isamuddin). As the main "money man" behind the Bojinka Plot, Humbali provided cash through a front company (CNN 3/14/02). Although US intelligence knew of Humbali's financing for Bojinka, it didn't inform Malaysian officials, thereby squandering an opportunity to arrest the funder. Additional funders included Osama bin Laden and his brother in law, Mohammed Jamal Khalifa. Like Humbali, Khalifa was wealthy businessman deeply invested in the jihadist cause (Lance *1000 Years* pp. 234, 303-04).

Not long after they broke up the Bojinka Plot, Philippine authorities shared these findings but US intelligence failed to make use of them. Mohammed Khalifa, for instance, was arrested in California but released and allowed to leave the country (Thompson *Terror Timeline* p. 14). Moreover, since both Yousef and KSM were centrally involved in the Bojinka Plot, one would have expected that US authorities would have made every effort to track down *both*. Yet as we'll see, this didn't happen.

### Evasions and Scant Coverage of Bojinka

Although coverage in the American press was sketchy in 1995, it became even more limited after 9/11, when Bojinka surely should have merited full discussion. The Bojinka Plot received scant mention in the Commission's Official Story. Most revealingly, the Commission failed to even mention the *final* phase of Bojinka, which so closely resembled the hijack/suicide attacks on 9/11. Avoiding any connections between plans for earlier attacks and those on 9/11, its *Report* claimed this airplane bombing plot was hatched in 1996, not 1994, and that "this marked the first time KSM took part in the actual planning of a terrorist operation" (*Report* pp. 147-49). Well, not exactly.

Although the plotters' chemistry lab may have seemed amateurish, they were hardly hurting for money. While KSM wasn't plotting and helping mix up the medicine, he lived a lavish, flamboyant lifestyle, throwing wild parties, dating go-go dancers, and even renting a helicopter to buzz a girlfriend's office window (*LA Times* 6/24/02). Such reports obviously contradict the *Report*'s contention that these Islamist operatives were puritanical religious fanatics.

## Very Different Patterns of Pursuit

After the Landmarks and Bojinka plots were exposed, Yousef fled to Pakistan and received sanctuary in al Qaeda's House of Martyrs in Peshawar (*Financial Times* 8/15/03). It's widely believed that Yousef and KSM had strong connections to Pakistan's Inter-Services Intelligence (ISI), which almost certainly protected them and other Islamist operatives. In 1995, US law enforcement arrested Yousef. This hardly daunted KSM, who brazenly granted a brazenly defiant interview to *Time* describing Yousef's capture (Lance *1000 Years* p. 328).

By 1996, US intelligence had uncovered KSM's ties to both the 1993 bombing and the 1995 Bojinka Plot, two plans seriously threatening the American homeland. Immediately after each of these plots was exposed, the FBI cast a worldwide dragnet for Ramzi Yousef. Yet they did nothing comparable for his uncle, KSM, who was even more deeply involved. Whereas Yousef was openly indicted for his alleged involvement in the Bojinka plot, KSM was *secretly* charged fully a *year later*. Not until 1998, three years after Yousef was apprehended, did the FBI finally offer a $2 million reward for KSM. While Yousef's picture was distributed widely on free matchboxes, the same was not done for Mohammed (Thompson *Terror Timeline* p. 206).

Until 2003, KSM had also found sanctuary in Pakistan. There he became associated with supporters of the country's future (three-time) prime minister, Nawaz Sharif. The head of the Pakistan Muslim League, Sharif was a leading Islamist. When KSM also supported the attempt to assassinate Benazir Bhutto, leader of a more secular People's Party, his involvement ingratiated him to Islamists in the ISI (*Guardian* [UK] 3/3/03). Ascendant Islamists had not only come to power that year, but had also cemented their control over the increasingly powerful ISI (*Financial Times* 2/19/03). History Commons researcher Paul Thompson has asked, "If Mohammed had some relationship with the ISI, when—if ever—did this relationship end? When he was plotting the various al Qaeda attacks in the 1990s, did he have ISI backing?" (Thompson *Terror Timeline* p. 206). Perhaps the point is moot. The ISI has long received money from the CIA, and CIA money was apparently reaching KSM through other channels.

Ramzi Yousef was hardly chastened by his capture and imprisonment. As he was extradited, the "master bomber" became defiantly clear about al Qaeda's intentions. When the plane bringing him back descended over New York Harbor, a burly FBI agent lifted the prisoner's blindfold and gestured toward the Twin Towers. "See, you didn't get them after all." Yousef retorted: "They wouldn't be if I had enough money and enough explosives" (J. Miller, M. Stone, and C. Mitchell *The Cell* p. 135). Nor did prison subdue the al Qaeda operative. Yousef told a gangster imprisoned in an adjacent cell that, using hijacked aircraft, his partners in crime would "bring New York to its knees" by blowing up the WTC with "flying massive bombs." This disturbing information reached Assistant US Attorney Patrick Fitzgerald and FBI Counsel Valerie Caproni, but neither took action (S. Harmon *Mafia Son* pp. 187-188,199-201).

**Plans for the Big One**

The boastful, calculating, and fiercely independent KSM didn't always mesh with his al Qaeda chieftain. At KSM's first meeting with bin Laden in the 1980s, very different personalities had become evident. However, these opposite tendencies did seem to complement each other. KSM delivered the perspiration so essential for implementing complex plans; bin Laden offered the inspiration necessary for recruiting *jihadis*. In fact, KSM was impatient with the *fatwas* and theological diatribes of bin Laden and followers. As a result, KSM was likely considered too practical to be completely accepted by the network's senior leaders. Jarret Brachman, author of *Global Jihadism*, has remarked that "as opposed to the rest of these guys who sit around and talk, KSM actually got the job done. That's what ... made him so scary" (*NYT* 11/14/09).

In 1996, just a year after the Bojinka airplanes scheme had to be abandoned, KSM met with bin Laden in the mountains of Tora Bora, Afghanistan. There he sketched a plan strikingly similar to third phase of the Bojinka plot. This new scenario called for hijacking several planes on both East and West coasts and flying them into targets (BBC 9/22/03). One notable change, though, was that the hijacked airliners were to be *domestic* flights; this implied confidence that the operatives flying them could enter the US.

## Bin Laden Adapts KSM's One-Man Extravaganza

In late 1998 or early 1999, well over two years after KSM had first proposed his planes-as-missiles plan, he made a daring, self-aggrandizing second proposal. The alleged "mastermind" envisioned commandeering ten planes, with one group hitting targets on the West coast, the other striking the East. Nine of ten would slam into familiar targets: the WTC, the Transamerica Building, CIA headquarters, FBI headquarters, and a nuclear power plant. Casting himself as hero, KSM proposed to pilot the tenth airliner himself. Once the plane was hijacked and all the adult male passengers were killed, MTA proposed to broadcast a condemnation of American policy in the Middle East. Finally, in a grandiose *coup de theatre*, he would land the plane and release the women and children (Wright *Looming Tower* p. 347).

When the top leaders met again a few months later, bin Laden required some changes. After rejecting the targets on the West coast, he added the Pentagon, the White House, and the US Capitol to the list and nixed the "condemnation-from-on-high" grandstanding (*Wash. Times* 3/30/04). While Bin Laden provided leadership and financial support for the plot, KSM provided operational leadership, securing funding, calling meetings, and arranging travel (*Report* p. 145).

## Choosing Players for the Team

More than ever before, al Qaeda had to train personnel. Not surprisingly, bin Laden was directly involved in selecting pilots and hijackers (P. Bergen *Osama bin Laden I Know* p. 283). Mohamed Atta was selected as lead pilot and team leader; Ziad Jarrah, Marwan al Shehhi, and Hani Hanjour would also apply to US flight schools. Two other Saudis, Nawaf al Hazmi and his boyhood friend, Khalid al Mihdhar, were also selected as "muscle" hijackers (Wright *Looming Tower* pp. 345, 350).

After 9/11, many Western commentators would assume that the alleged hijackers were poor and infer that poverty was a root cause of the attacks. Although exploitation and poverty were issues for Islamists, the leaders of al Qaeda were typically educated middle-class professionals from fairly comfortable backgrounds (*Sunday Times* 4/3/05). *Al Watan*, a

Saudi paper, characterized the group as "middle-class adventurers" rather than fundamentalist ideologues (*Boston Globe* 3/3/02). "Adventurers"? Perhaps something was lost in translation.

Like KSM, most of the al Qaeda operatives shared a near-fanatical determination to *make* history after centuries of humiliation beneath the wheels of European, American, and Israeli colonial dominion. This implies an attempt to avenge or transcend the shame associated with domination, whether by foreign or domestic oppressors Many seemed to exhibit what Matthew Carr, British historian of terrorism and author of *The Infernal Machine*, has called "the ethos of heroic martyrdom" characterizing many, even most Islamist terrorist groups (Pacifica/KPFA Radio 12/30/09).

## Connecting with the Hamburg Cell

If the US intelligence apparatus failed to apprehend KSM, it wasn't because he'd fled to a cave. Using forged passports, throughout 1999 KSM visited al Qaeda's Hamburg cell to formulate plans for 9/11. Since German, Spanish, and American intelligence had been shriveling the cell, Hamburg was hardly a safe haven for a wanted man. However, even though KSM had a $2 million reward on his head, US intelligence apparently failed to inform its German counterparts about the "mastermind" (*Newsweek* 9/4/02).

In Hamburg, alleged "ringleader" Mohamed Atta was KSM's primary contact. Together they finalized the plans to attack inside the US (R. Gunaratna *Inside al Qaeda* p. xxx). The other members of the cell were nearly as auspicious: Ziad Jarrah would allegedly fly Flight 93; Marwan al Shehhi would become a pilot-trained hijacker on Flight 175; and Ramzi bin al Shibh would have became the "twentieth hijacker," had he not failed to obtain a US visa. In November 1999, the four began terrorist training at Khaldan Camp in Afghanistan (Wright *Looming Tower* pp. 346-47).

## Finalizing Plans for "Holy Tuesday"

According to KSM, bin Laden was pushing to advance the attack date. In 2000, an event brought bin Laden from a simmer to a boil. Israeli Likud

Party leader Ariel Sharon incited violence in the Middle East by visiting the Temple Mount, a holy site in Jerusalem sacred to both Muslims and Jews (Knight Ridder 9/28/00). Outraged, bin Laden demanded a strike as soon as possible. Although he recognized that Atta and the other pilots hadn't completed their flight training, the al Qaeda leader wanted to punish the US for enabling Israeli aggression. Bin Laden reportedly told KSM it would be sufficient simply to down the airliners and forget about specific targets (PBS "NewsHour" 6/16/04).

By 1999, following the embassy bombings of the previous year, bin Laden finally made the FBI's Wanted List. Nevertheless, FBI Director Louis Freeh continued to insist that terrorists didn't pose a threat to "domestic civil aviation" (www.fas.org/irp/congress/2002_hr/091802hill.html). Special Agent John O'Neill, the Bureau's ace on terrorism, thought otherwise. "We're due," he told friends. Aware of bin Laden's interest in cultural symbols and his apocalyptic leanings, O'Neill was particularly nervous about the millennial celebrations at the end of the 1999. No attacks occurred, but within a few months, al Qaeda had attempted to strike the USS *The Sullivans* and had struck the USS *Cole* in the port of Aden, Yemen, killing seventeen sailors (Wright *Looming Tower* pp. 336, 339).

## KSM under Intense Electronic Surveillance

Although the Commission claimed US intelligence was late to identify KSM as key player—let alone the "mastermind"—much evidence suggests otherwise. In response to activity near the Indian Ocean, no expense was spared; Agent O'Neill had his I-49 squad build an enormous antenna on Madagascar designed to intercept KSM's calls.

As a marked man and operational leader, KSM rightly suspected electronic eavesdropping. In June 2001, he made three calls from Pakistan to an Iraqi opponent of Saddam Hussein, who passed on the messages to contacts in Belgium. When the Iraqi was imprisoned for five years for relaying KSM's calls, his suspicions were apparently proven right (*Arab News* 9/15/04). Thus it's fair to conclude that by mid-2001—and probably much earlier—US intelligence was intercepting KSM's calls. If so, why didn't it *act* on what it was learning?

## The Final Intercepts

In 2001, just months before 9/11, US intelligence intercepted communications between the "mastermind" KSM and "ringleader" Atta. In June, US intelligence learned that KSM was keen on "sending terrorists to the United States" and assisting their activities once they entered the country (*USA Today* 12/12/01). Despite the fact the FBI was offering a huge reward for the "mastermind," NSA claimed it didn't get around to translating the intercept (Knight Ridder 6/6/02).

Even more remarkably, KSM's final go-head was also intercepted. On September 10, the NSA recorded a call in which KSM gave Atta the green light. For several years, NSA had monitored KSM's messages but claimed it didn't translate this intercept in time (*Independent* [UK] 9/15/02). The *Los Angeles Times* later observed it "would seem odd ... that NSA could not have been translating intercepts from KSM immediately, given the fact that ... US intelligence had learned that KSM was interested in 'sending terrorists to the United States'" (*LA Times* 12/12/03). Yes, all this does stretch credulity. "Given the knowledge of [KSM's] participation in previous major terrorist plots," Thompson has rightly asked, "why did these intercepts not lead to the detection of the 9/11 plot?" (Thompson *Terror Timeline* p. 206).

## Evidence Implicates Pakistan's Military Intelligence (ISI)

When, early in 2003, KSM was finally apprehended, he was discovered hiding near ISI headquarters in Rawalpindi, Pakistan. Reports on the capture indicated the Pakistanis allowed the Americans to capture KSM. These facts have led thoughtful observers in the news media to wonder whether the fugitive had been hiding with the previous approval of the ISI. Investigative journalist Robert Fisk drew logical conclusions: "Mohammed was an ISI asset; indeed, anyone who is 'handed over' by the ISI these days is almost certainly a former (or present) employee of the Pakistani agency whose control of Taliban operatives amazed even the Pakistan government" (*Toronto Star* 3/3/03). Many reports, notably the ability of Osama bin Laden to find refuge in a neighborhood with many ISI officers (*New Yorker* 5/16/11), suggest this pattern of sponsorship hasn't changed.

KSM was not only a key figure in al Qaeda but also closely associated with Gen. Mahmood Ahmad, Director of Pakistan's ISI. Thus KSM was connected to the ISI, itself closely linked to the CIA (UPI 9/30/02). The Commission's *Report* ignored key pieces of the puzzle. Though KSM was mentioned in 272 paragraphs, not a single one explored his links to General Ahmad, the ISI, or its close linkage to the CIA (D. R. Griffin *9/11 Commission Report* p. 112). Once again, omissions can speak volumes.

This ISI/CIA connection has received little attention in the American media, of course, because Washington's goal has long been to shore up Afghanistan's and Pakistan's military and police to fight the ISI's traditional proxies, the Taliban (*NYT* 7/20/08). During the Bush years alone, Washington showered Islamabad with more than $10 billion in military aid. (By 2009, US aid had risen to $1.7 billion per year.) (*NYT* 8/16/08 & 1/3/10). Since the ISI is a prominent branch of the Pakistani military, it's logical to conclude that the ISI received a hefty share of these billions. To acknowledge ISI sponsorship of the Taliban is to admit the US has been bankrolling its sworn enemy.

All this will receive more attention in Chapter 18, which further details the involvement of Pakistan's ISI in 9/11.

**Strange Impunity for "Ringleader" Atta and Others**
An Egyptian with a master's degree in city planning, Mohamed Atta first became the team leader of al Qaeda's notorious Hamburg cell and later the alleged ringleader of the American operation. Not surprisingly, Atta had long appeared on the FBI's list of suspected terrorists (*Daily Telegraph* [UK] 9/13/01). Although he'd also come under surveillance by Israeli, German, and American espionage, he bobbed and weaved around spy agencies, and they repeatedly failed to land a punch.

For years, Atta committed petty crimes in Germany but seldom faced consequences. As the 9/11 attacks approached, however, Atta's actions became more political: on one occasion, he attempted to buy large quantities of chemicals to make explosives. Although US agents trailed Atta, they failed to share their findings with German intelligence. Throughout 1999, 2000, and early 2001, Pentagon intelligence, the CIA, and the FBI all monitored Atta's movements and phone calls (German Channel ARD 11/23/03). A British newspaper remarked "the disclosure that Atta was being trailed by police long before 11 September raises the question [of] why the attacks could not have been prevented with the man's arrest" (*Observer* [UK] 9/30/01). The BBC concluded "the international intelligence community may have known more about Atta before September 11 than was previously thought, but failed to act" (BBC 11/26/01).

In addition to the other suspicious behavior, Atta visited Yemen and Afghanistan several times during the late 1990s. Despite all these signs, and just weeks after he was caught trying to purchase the chemicals, the State Department issued Atta a visa (CBC 9/14/01). In January 2001, despite being in violation of his visa, Atta was allowed to reenter the US. Supremely confident, Atta even told customs inspectors he'd be taking advanced flying lessons—something the visa in their hands didn't permit him to do. The recipient of this indulgent treatment, the reader will recall, was already under surveillance, running a terrorist cell, networking with other operatives, and making trips to countries associated with Islamic terrorism (*Wash. Post* 10/28/01).

Once inside the country, Atta continued to behave like someone above and beyond the law. He partied flamboyantly and was often surly with employees at flight schools, including his flight instructors. Atta moved in highly visible circles, sometimes hobnobbing with Saudi royals (D. Hopsicker *Welcome to Terrorland* p. 141). In early 2001, Atta had applied for a security job with Lufthansa Airlines (*Newsday* 1/24/02); since he didn't seem to need the money, did he hope to learn about how airline security worked?

A sometimes charming but always deceitful sociopath, Atta exhibited a taste for cocaine, marijuana, alcohol, and women. To maintain his high roller's lifestyle, pursue flight training, and continue to organize the al Qaeda mission, "the Boss" was well supported in both Germany and the United States (*Chicago Tribune* 3/7/03). Despite these vices, Atta became a good aviator and helped train other alleged 9/11 pilots.

In early 2000, after spending several months in New Jersey, Atta moved to Punta Gorda, Florida, an exclusive enclave frequented by the Bush family, and then to nearby Venice, Florida (*Bergen Record* 6/20/03). Three of the four pilots who allegedly flew the airliners trained in Venice.

Although he already held a private pilot's license, Atta returned to flight school. Along with other operatives from al Qaeda's Hamburg cell, Atta took instruction at Huffman Aviation, the school where two of the four alleged 9/11 pilots trained. Ziad Jarrah, the likely pilot of Flight 93, trained at the Florida Flight Training Center, also in Venice (J. Longman *Among the Heroes* p. 91).

In late 2000, Atta and al Shehhi passed their commercial pilot's license tests; Atta scored 93, al Shehhi 73, just above the FAA's minimal passing score (*Report* p. 17). Less than a year later, would Shehhi have developed the skill needed to fly Flight 175 into the World Trade Center? To enter a professional flight-training program, Atta and al Shehhi needed student visas allowing a longer stay in the country. After some hassles with the INS, their new visas were approved (*Charlotte Sun* 3/13/02).

## Dekkers's Quick Turnaround

Huffman Aviation, it turned out, had connections to organized crime (drug running) and the CIA (Hicks *Big Wedding* pp. 93-94). While attending the flight school, Atta got to know the company's owner, Rudi Dekkers, the Dutch immigrant introduced in the last chapter. Dekkers's background included several hostile lawsuits, one for sexual harassment, plus allegations of real estate fraud and drug smuggling. Intriguingly, Dekkers apparently benefited from the same manipulation of visa requirements (often by the CIA) that allowed several alleged hijackers to enter the country (*St. Petersburg Times* 7/5/04).

Like several of the al Qaeda operatives, Dekkers apparently received special treatment. So when the feds caught him smuggling drugs in the 1990s, they never charged him with the crime. Instead, they apparently insisted that he serve as a "confidential informant" who'd help catch other smugglers and possibly help recruit Arab-speaking agents (Hopsicker *Welcome to Terrorland* p. 205). After 9/11, Dekkers faced the potential embarrassment of having several alleged hijackers attend his flight school. But, enabled by politicians and media executives, Dekkers managed to present himself as a media personality and an expert on terrorism (US Congress 3/19/02).

**The Arabic Students, the Front Company Running Drugs, and the CIA**

As though these troubles weren't enough, Huffman Aviation faced several others. In fact, the CIA had encouraged Arabic flight students to study in Florida prior to 9/11 (*Sarasota Herald-Tribune* 7/11/05). Was the CIA trying to penetrate al Qaeda, hoping to make a move on its top leadership?

And if all this weren't enough, a CIA "front" company had not only kindled suspicions the Agency was trying to infiltrate al Qaeda, but also raised other questions. Former British intelligence officer John Hughes-Wilson disclosed that while alleged hijacker pilots Atta and Marwan al Shehhi were attending Huffman, Air Caribe, a CIA front company, was operating from the same hangar: "this highly curious coincidence must inevitably raise some suspicions about just how much the CIA really did know before 9/11" (Hughes-Wilson *Military Intelligence Blunders and Coverups* p. 391). Moreover, a significant drug smuggling operation was run out of Venice airport while Atta and al Shehhi were studying at Huffman (*Sarasota Herald-Trib.* 7/11/05). Or, by doing nothing with the information it was gathering, was the CIA allowing the cell to achieve its objectives?

**Pakistan's ISI "Ringleader" Receives Big Money**

Just as Atta's lifestyle was often highly visible, he wasn't cautious about receiving large payments that could be traced. In the year before 9/11, the "ringleader" twice received transfers of $100,000 from Saeed Sheikh, who worked for the ISI. Its director, Gen. Ahmad, had authorized the funding for the alleged hijackers (*Times of India* 10/11/01). In short, the head of Pakistan's military intelligence had ordered Saeed, who was both a British MI6 asset and a top assistant to bin Laden, to send large sums to Atta, the leader of the alleged hijackers (CNN 10/28/01).

Like MTA, paymaster Saeed Sheikh was a triple agent working for British and Pakistani intelligence (*London Times* 9/26/06) as well as al Qaeda. Along with KSM, Saeed was behind the 2002 kidnapping and murder of *Wall Street Journal* reporter Daniel Pearl (CNN 1/30/06). Pearl's investigative digging, it was widely reported, had taken him into "sensitive" areas—especially the ISI's role in financing for Islamist terrorism and illicit nuclear weapons (*New Yorker* 3/01/04). Though Saeed Sheikh was convicted for masterminding the Daniel Pearl kidnapping/murder, alleged 9/11 "mastermind" KSM was accused of responsibility for the crime (CNN 1/30/03). In fact, some of the captured perpetrators divulged that it was KSM who had cut Pearl's throat (MSNBC 9/17/02).

## What Was Going On Inside These Agencies?

As researchers discovered more about al Qaeda operatives before 9/11, the CIA and FBI faced more and more questions. While the CIA hid beneath its usual cloak of secrecy, the FBI made some attempt to explain. In discussing the Bureau's apparent failures to stop al Qaeda, however, FBI Director Robert Mueller made outlandish claims. He contended, for instance, that somehow "the Bureau had not been able to identify anyone who had prior knowledge of the plot" (*NYT* 4/11/04). Such statements eroded the FBI's credibility and, worse, diverted attention from much more crucial questions:

- How much did federal agencies know about al Qaeda's lead operatives?
- Which agencies knew what, and when did they know it?
- Why wasn't what was known acted upon?

Clearly the CIA, FBI, and other national-security agencies not only squandered opportunities to apprehend known terrorists, they sometimes seemed to help them along.

As their bios show, many al Qaeda operatives were well protected. Why they received such help, often in the form of legal impunity, is an open question. It's true that double or triple agents are often allowed to get away with crimes because it's assumed they have to commit them in order to validate themselves with their "other" employer. When Mohamed the American broke Army regulations and went to Afghanistan, for example, perhaps he was demonstrating his loyalty to the Islamist cause. Yet no one in the agencies seemed to ask, How good is the information we're getting, and does it justify the risks, the damage this guy could do? Did these agencies exercise incredibly bad judgment, did their priorities lie more with projecting power than with protecting the public, or did elements within them actually want the terrorists to strike?

Lance has provided ample evidence that in the 1990s, federal agencies—especially the FBI—had "begun intentionally *dis*connecting the dots" (Lance *Triple Cross* p. 210). Evidence now suggests that the unthinkable may be true—that contrary to the Commission's claims, US intelligence-gathering agencies may not simply have "failed" but, at least in some quarters, *intended* to "fail." Here we're looking at the role of "actors" who may have "stood down," passively letting attacks happen or even actively helping make them happen. After considering the evidence, it's difficult to dismiss the conclusion that, directly or indirectly, much Islamist terrorism has been state supported.

There's an even darker possibility. Were MTA, KSM, and Atta allowed—or even encouraged—to function as agents provocateurs whose terrorist crimes would eventually stampede American popular opinion? For many of us, this is an unsettling prospect; it's one thing to consider that the federal government, which is supposed to protect us, might have failed; it's another to consider that the very agencies most entrusted to do so might have betrayed that trust.

When we ask *cui bono?*—"who benefited?"—possible answers arise. The 9/11 attacks have had the predictable effect of enlarging the budgets or the profits of powerful intelligence, military, paramilitary, and corporate institutions. The espionage apparatus has expanded beyond anyone's understanding or control (*Wash. Post* 7/19/10). With this vast expansion of military and intelligence budgets, plus the establishment of whole new agencies such as the Department of Homeland Security, the 9/11 attacks have demonstrably led to a bloating of the national security state. All this helps us understand why, as we've seen, important figures in the US national security establishment might have longed for "a new Pearl Harbor" (PNAC *Restoring America's Defenses* p. 51).

All this has led to further concentration of power in Washington, a development most of the Founders had worked hard to avoid.

# 17.  Osama bin Laden: The Man, the Myth, and the Mythmaking

*There's an old poster out West, I recall, that says, 'Wanted: Dead or Alive.'*

—George W. Bush

While the name of Osama bin Laden will forever be associated with 9/11, the similarities between 9/11 and his killing have gone underreported. Much as different stories were told after the attacks in 2001, different narratives of bin Laden's death were presented in the wake of the killing on May 1, 2011.

In both cases, the White House presented different accounts of events. At first, the Obama administration indicated that the commandos had "engaged in a firefight," that bin Laden himself had fired at members of the elite Navy Seal Team, and that he'd tried to use a woman as a human shield. This first account had bin Laden living in a "mansion" and implied that he had forcefully attempted to resist arrest. Counterterrorism Advisor John Brennan even mocked the al Qaeda leader's final moments, claiming that bin Laden cowered behind his wife (*Wash. Post* 5/5/11).

The very next day, however, the administration changed its story. It claimed that rather than facing an intense "firefight," the commandos quickly killed the *one* guard who'd opposed them before shooting other residents, who were unarmed. These included bin Laden and one of his wives, who was wounded but not killed (AP 5/6/11). Whether or not the earlier account was designed for propaganda purposes, it did furnish "red meat" to right-wing talk radio, which seized the opportunity to mock the alleged hypocrisy of bin Laden living in a "mansion" and to underscore the alleged backwardness of subservient Islamic women (Fox Monday 5/2/11).

Earlier chapters have tracked bin Laden's involvement with the CIA as a *jihadi* leader fighting against the Soviets, his founding of al Qaeda after the Soviet retreat, and his increasingly prominent involvement in plots—some aborted, some successful—against the World Trade Center, New York landmarks, Khyber Towers in Saudi Arabia, two US embassies in Africa, and the *USS Cole*. Bin Laden's involvement in 9/11, however, is much less certain.

## Bin Laden and the Attack on Afghanistan: The Lingering Questions

Today, a decade into the war in Afghanistan, more and more Americans are raising questions about the lead up to and the early conduct of that campaign:

- Why, if the main objective was to extradite, capture, or kill Osama bin Laden, didn't any of these happen?
- Did the US negotiate in good faith to bring the alleged architect of 9/11 to justice?
- Did it either not have a case or not want to try bin Laden in open court?
- Why was US air power so often not used effectively, even when commanders received very current intelligence on high-ranking al Qaeda and Taliban leaders?
- Why were airlifts and convoys allowed to carry Islamist fighters back to Pakistan, where they could regroup and recruit more jihadi to fight the United States?

Officials offered many excuses but few real answers. Instead, government and media seemed most interested in magnifying and then maintaining the Big Threat allegedly posed by bin Laden.

# A Long List of Lost Opportunities

The strange failures to capture bin Laden in Afghanistan extended a longstanding pattern. For years, Pakistan and the Taliban in Afghanistan had protected bin Laden. The United States tolerated this, perhaps because both al Qaeda and the CIA had become deeply enmeshed in the black-market trade for weapons and narcotics (P. D Scott *Oil, Drugs and War* pp. 28-29, 32). As if this weren't enough, during this same time—the 1990s—the United States refused masses of intelligence on bin Laden and al Qaeda from Sudan, France, Israel, and Russia.

In 1995, Sudan offered the CIA its extensive files on bin Laden, who'd lived in that country since 1991. During this time, Sudanese spies collected a huge intelligence database on at least 200 members of his al Qaeda network. Nevertheless, the United States declined the Sudanese offer as well as Saudi intelligence on bin Laden (*Guardian* [UK] 9/30/01). About this same time, French intelligence offered a thick dossier on Zacarias Moussaoui, the al Qaeda operative apprehended just a month before 9/11. This, too, the US declined (*LA Times* 3/21/06).

In addition to these offers, the US rejected a treasure trove assembled by the Russians. In early 2001, when Moscow submitted a detailed report on al Qaeda's infrastructure in Afghanistan, Washington again refused a "breathtaking" intelligence bonanza (*Jane's Intelligence Digest* 10/91). Turning down this package seemed especially surprising, since Washington had so often complained about the ISI's training of *jihadis* in Afghanistan. But this Russian intelligence might have embarrassed Washington, for it likely revealed how the CIA had helped build the ISI into a formidable force which had also become involved in running heroin and funding Pakistan's illicit nuclear program (A. Rashid *Descent into Chaos* pp. 38, 41). It also played a significant role in 9/11.

## Why Was the Information Declined?

Long before Bush declared the War on Terror, American and British intelligence had tracked bin Laden and al Qaeda. CIA veteran Michael Scheuer, a specialist on bin Laden, told the 9/11 Commission that by 1997, the CIA was well informed on bin Laden (P. Shenon *The Commission* pp. 188-89). To get much of this information, spies had to infiltrate the target group. But since doing this required recruiting native speakers of, say, Arabic, Urdu, or Pashtu, American spy agencies themselves were easily infiltrated. It's tempting to collect two paychecks by spying for both sides.

But this enmeshment wasn't just a problem among spies and operatives; it was often a policy. It's fair to conclude, along with British researcher Nafiz Mosaddeq Ahmed, that to a surprising degree "US and Western interests have systematically melded with … international terrorism" (Ahmed *War on Truth* p. 87). This "melding" can produce evidence of politically embarrassing collusion—such as the one which had so long protected Mohammed the American (MTA). Avoidance of such exposure might help explain why Washington refused these caches of information.

The ongoing pattern didn't just involve turning down offers of information on al Qaeda, however; it also included turning down offers to get bin Laden himself.

## Protecting bin Laden, al Qaeda, and the Saudis

In 1995, bin Laden was named among the unindicted conspirators in the plots to blow up the World Trade Center and twelve New York landmarks (*Jane's Intell. Rev.* 10/1/05). The following year, bin Laden took up residence in Khartoum, Sudan. When that country's security services offered to hand him over, Washington cavalierly advised Khartoum to "let him go" (*Wash. Post* 10/03/01). Many intelligence professionals in Africa were aghast. One official commented "the State Department may have blocked bin Laden's arrest to placate a part of the Saudi Arabian government that supported bin Laden" (*Village Voice* 10/31-11/6/01).

In 1998, the CIA learned that the Saudis were harboring an al Qaeda cell. But when the CIA offered information on known Islamist militants in the country, the Saudis refused it. In another instance, the Saudi defense minister, Prince Sultan, refused to accept a list of operatives active throughout the Middle East (Ahmed *The War on Truth* p. 90). And when the FBI tried to arrest several operatives inside the US, the Saudi government issued them alias passports (*Financial Times* 1/12/02).

However, the CIA was involved in systematic obstructions of its own. In the late 1990s, the Agency turned down the Taliban's repeated offers to deal with bin Laden. Leili Helms, the niece of former CIA director Richard Helms, served as a clandestine liaison between the Agency and the Taliban during negotiations for the much-discussed oil pipeline through Afghanistan. (Cheney's Halliburton was poised to become a lead contractor.) Ms. Helms later reported that the State Department declined the Taliban's repeated offers to extradite or assassinate bin Laden (*Village Voice* 1/2-8/02). In addition to imperial power projection, commercial considerations had driven US foreign policy over many decades, with the CIA often functioning as a lead prong on the imperial pitchfork.

### Shielding al Qaeda and Saudis after the *Cole* Bombing

In October 2000, al Qaeda struck the *USS Cole*, a Navy destroyer moored in Aden, Yemen. Seventeen American sailors were killed (NPR 10/14/00). The Clinton administration tried to undertake a full investigation into the bombing. The legendary John O'Neill, the dedicated, relentless investigator who was one of "the FBI's brightest stars," led the investigation. However, US ambassador Barbara Bodine blocked O'Neill's team of FBI "rambos" from entering the country (*NYT* 8/19/01).

Known for his Irish temper, O'Neill was outraged. His previous investigatory work had already led him to conclude that bin Laden was responsible for the hit on the *Cole*—and that "all the answers, everything needed to dismantle Osama bin Laden's organization, can be found in Saudi Arabia." The State Department, however, stymied the investigation, fearful of offending the Saudis (J.C. Brisard and G. Dasquie *Forbidden Truth* p. xix). After the Bush administration assumed power, pressures to protect the Kingdom intensified. The BBC's Greg Palast reported that while it had always been difficult to investigate Saudi Arabia, under Bush investigators were directly ordered to "back off the Saudis" (Palast *Best Democracy Money Can Buy* p. 99).

But the inhibitions went well beyond the Saudis and the White House; sometimes they came from the CIA. In late 2000, chief of counterterrorism Richard Clarke urged that Predator drone flights over

Afghanistan be resumed in order to kill bin Laden. Clarke complained, however, that "every time we were ready to use [the drone], the CIA would change its mind." In a cabinet meeting held just a week before 9/11, CIA Director George Tenet blustered that the Agency would operate Predators "over my dead body" (*New Yorker* 8/4/03). If one has any illusions about the CIA often functioning as a "shadow government," beyond the control of policy makers and the public, this blunt refusal should dispel them.

## Bin Laden and the Attack on Afghanistan, 2001

In another curious and revealing incident, a CIA station chief visited bin Laden in the hospital. In July 2001, bin Laden underwent surgery in an American hospital in Dubai. Although he was a wanted man, indicted for the 1998 bombing of US embassies, bin Laden met with the local CIA station chief, who treated him as a VIP guest (*Le Figaro* 10/11/01). Accompanied by his personal physician, a nurse, and four bodyguards, the al Qaeda leader reportedly welcomed members of his large family and Saudi officials. Bin Laden's Saudi guests included Prince Turki al Faisal, then head of Saudi intelligence (*The Guardian* [UK] 11/1/01). If this reportage is accurate, bin Laden may have remained both a Saudi and an American intelligence "asset" right up until the morning of 9/11.

### A Pattern of Delays and Blockages

In the fall of 2001, following the 9/11 attacks, Bush officials and conservative pundits vilified bin Laden as a near-satanic nemesis. Bush himself proclaimed that "the most important thing is for us to find Osama bin Laden" (UPI 9/13/01). All but thumping his chest, the president famously bellowed that he wanted bin Laden "dead or alive" (CNN 9/17/01). Yet despite the tough talk, effective action didn't follow. Time after time, the United States failed to strike the al Qaeda leader, even when the timing was most opportune. One little-publicized opportunity to kill bin Laden came before the bombardment of Afghanistan began: US intelligence had pinpointed bin Laden, but the Pentagon wouldn't approve a missile strike (J. Risen *State of War* p. 185).

Even the CIA, "the first boots on the ground," showed surprisingly little interest. Despite the trauma of 9/11 and Washington's declarations that al Qaeda and the Taliban were involved in the attacks, US intelligence seemed lukewarm about locating either al Qaeda leaders or Mullah Mohammed Omar, leader of the Taliban in Afghanistan. The problem was hardly a lack of information: the CIA had a relationship with al Qaeda and bin Laden extending back to the 1980s (*Time* 2/25/02).

Right after 9/11, the US publicized its "negotiations" with the Taliban, ostensibly hoping to get custody of bin Laden. First the US demanded that if the Taliban wanted to avoid a crushing attack, they had to either turn bin Laden over for prosecution or stand aside and let the US hunt him down (G. Tenet *At the Center of the Storm* pp. 182-183). In response, the Taliban agreed to hand over bin Laden, but only if the US provided proof of his complicity in 9/11 (CNN 9/21/01). Next the Taliban offered to extradite bin Laden "to a neutral Islamic country for trial if the US presented them with evidence that he was responsible" (*Guardian* [UK] 11/11/03). Preferring a war for vengeance and strategic position, the US rejected the offer

The US also met with Islamic parties in Pakistan, which also attempted to negotiate bin Laden's extradition. Under the Pakistani proposal, bin Laden would have faced an international tribunal that would decide whether to try him or hand him over to the US. Surprisingly, this proposal was approved by both bin Laden and Mullah Omar (*Mirror* [UK] 7/8/02). Even the usually supportive *Washington Post* indicated that since the administration apparently didn't have a case, it was surely absurd that "State Department officials refused to soften their demand that bin Laden face trial in the US justice system" (*Wash. Post* 10/29/01).

Since Bush had just cited bin Laden as a primary object of his War on Terror, many observers expected the president to welcome the proposal for extradition. But Pervez Musharraf, Pakistan's president and Bush's newfound ally, also rejected the plan. Washington wanted to avoid risking "a premature collapse of the international effort" (to overthrow the Taliban) (*Mirror* [UK] 7/8/02). And much more than it wanted bin Laden, Washington wanted Pakistan's support for its war.

## Little Evidence Against bin Laden Was Available

It wasn't just a matter of wanting a pretext for war; it was also that little evidence was available—then or even later. The FBI confirmed the alleged lack of evidence eight months later. After the most intense international manhunt in history, Director Robert Mueller revealed "that the FBI believed that the plot may have been hatched in Afghanistan, but was probably implemented in the United Arab Emirates and Germany" (www. presstv.ir/detail/149520.html). To this day, many skeptics wonder: Did American intelligence agencies really lack evidence against bin Laden, or did they just not want to reveal it, for fear of self incrimination?

The negotiations never had a chance. If the tribunal found that the US lacked solid evidence of bin Laden's complicity or if the evidence was too "sensitive," Washington could have faced acute embarrassment. Always wary of terrorism trials in open court, Washington likely also refused the offers to extradite bin Laden because it wanted to avoid the exposure of "sensitive" information in a court of law. A trial might have exposed Washington's having given billions to the ISI and the *mujahedeen* in the 1980s or facilitating the nuclear and drug trafficking by its new ally, Pakistan (Scott *Drugs, Oil and War* pp. 27-29). This aversion to courtrooms has also driven the use of military tribunals for nearly all terrorism suspects.

Besides, the snows were coming, and America's war machine was gearing up: the juggernaut couldn't wait.

## US Already Planning to Attack Afghanistan and Iraq

What if the campaign in Afghanistan, like so many others, wasn't really about bin Laden? What if the negotiations with the Taliban were just polite formalities while the US was actually forging ahead with its plans for "regime change"?

Unknown to the public, attack plans were already in place. Frustrated by the Taliban's resistance to the oil pipeline, two months before 9/11 the Bush administration had issued a blunt ultimatum: "either you accept our offer for a carpet of gold, or we bury you under a carpet of bombs" (Inter Press Service 11/16/01). When neither the carrot nor the stick moved the Taliban,

Washington decided that "military action against Afghanistan would go ahead … before the snows started falling, by the middle of October at the latest" (BBC 9/18/01). This statement of intent, one of several made by Bush officials in the months *before* 9/11, raised a troubling question: Was a national trauma deemed necessary to galvanize public opinion for the attacks on Afghanistan and Iraq? (R. Baker *Family of Secrets* pp. 423-25). As we've seen, several top policy makers thought so.

The challenge was to somehow find pretexts for attacking both Afghanistan and Iraq. The 9/11 attacks not only solved the first problem; they helped to deal with the second: offering opportunities for fabricating connections between Osama bin Laden and Saddam Hussein. As part of the attempt to gather evidence that could somehow link 9/11 to Saddam, former CIA Director James Woolsey had contacted the Taliban. Always hawkish, even for a neocon, Woolsey sought out Mansoor Ijaz, a multimillionaire Pakistani businessman, a lobbyist for his country in the USA, and a Fox News commentator. Ijaz and Woolsey, who also sat on the board of Ijaz's company, worked with a friend of bin Laden who also served as a Pakistani intelligence operative. The extensive and ongoing links between al Qaeda and Pakistan's military intelligence (ISI) will be developed fully in the next chapter.

Woolsey and Ijaz met with the Taliban's Mullah Omar in Kandahar, Afghanistan. The Taliban had promised to provide details about an alleged meeting between al Qaeda leaders and Iraqi officials several years before. Set for October 8, the appointment was canceled when the bombing began (*Financial Times* 3/6/03). Thus even before it attacked Afghanistan, the US was trying to link bin Laden to Saddam Hussein so it could "justify" an invasion of Iraq (*New Yorker* 3/25/02).

## Massive Bombing Begins: Strange Reversals Soon Follow

On October 7, 2001, the bombardment began. Flying at night to maximize "shock and awe," waves of USAF bombers pounded a country already ravaged by two decades of war. As the dark, acrid smoke lifted, British special forces moved against Taliban fighters (*NYT* 10/8/01), and the CIA launched commando attacks. Cofer Black, former head of its

Counterterrorism Center, described Operation Jawbreaker, the Agency's commando mission: "to put their heads on pikes with flies crawling over their eyes ... we went in to kick ass and we did" (PBS "Frontline" 3/24/08). It wasn't clear whether this operation was mainly about ousting the Taliban, satisfying desires for revenge, increasing American power in south-central Asia, accessing Khazak and Caspian Basin oil, building that trans-Afghan pipeline, or restoring the opium trade, which the Taliban had quashed. All were demonstrably more important than getting Osama bin Laden.

Once the bombing had begun, the Pentagon suddenly downplayed bin Laden. At central command, Gen. Tommy Franks reconfigured the war's objectives: "we have not said that Osama bin Laden is a target of this effort. What we are about is the destruction of the al Qaeda network, as well as the ... Taliban that provide harbor to bin Laden and al Qaeda" (*USA Today* 10/8/01). Later that month, Rumsfeld released similar qualifiers about the United States' commitment to getting bin Laden (*USA Today* 10/24/01). One military expert underscored the "disconnect between what the US military was engaged in trying to do—which was to destroy al Qaeda and the Taliban—and the earlier rhetoric of President Bush, which had focused on getting bin Laden" (*Christian Sci. Mon.* 3/4/02).

### Refusing to Act, Aiding the Escape of Enemies

From the outset, the campaign wasn't focused on locating Taliban or al Qaeda leaders. The morning after the bombing began, a CIA Predator drone spotted a convoy fleeing Kabul. When the CIA determined that one of the trucks carried Taliban leader Mullah Omar, it insisted that its unmanned plane attack the vehicles. When the CIA sought clearance from commanders in Florida, however, Gen. Tommy Franks decided not to strike either the convoy or the building where Omar had taken shelter. Baffled by this failure to act, one senior official later bellowed "it's not a fuckup, it's an outrage" (*New Yorker* 10/16/01).

This was hardly the only such instance. In October and November, the Air Force was denied permission to bomb al Qaeda and Taliban leaders. On several occasions, American commanders had top leaders in their bombsights but had to seek permission from Gen. Franks or even Secretary Rumsfeld. When the commanders complained, they never received a response (*Wash. Post* 11/18/01). Throughout the whole campaign in Afghanistan, only *one* al Qaeda leader, Mohammed Atef, was killed by a bomb—and *no* major Taliban leaders were killed. Given all the rockets, cruise missiles, "smart" bombs, cluster bombs, "daisy cutters," and two-ton bunker busters the US dropped extensively (Knight Ridder 10/11/01), this was an astonishing shortfall.

## The Decision Not to Seal the Border

Less than a week into the campaign against the Taliban, the White House and Pentagon decided against attempting to seal the Afghanistan-Pakistan border (B. Woodward *Bush at War* p. 205). Declined by the Americans, the task of sealing the border fell to the Pakistanis, who were well paid but ill equipped for do the job.

In exchange for a billion dollars in new aid, Pakistan agreed to seal off routes from the Tora Bora Mountains in Afghanistan, where Taliban and al Qaeda *jihadi* were expected to gather. CNN terrorism expert Peter Bergen has affirmed that not only did the US fail to deploy enough troops to seal the border, but the Pakistani military and ISI made little effort to capture fleeing al Qaeda terrorists (NPR 5/2-3/05). When Pakistan, whether by intention or ineptitude, failed to seal the border, most of al Qaeda's leaders and fighters escaped (R. Suskind *One Percent Solution* p. 58). Bin Laden was almost certainly among the thousands who slipped across the border, ready to fight again.

If bin Laden was allowed to escape, he'd have been only one among thousands who'd been fighting coalition forces. After another deal was struck between the US and Pakistan, the Air Force secretly allowed cargo planes to fly though a designated corridor to reach the besieged Taliban stronghold of Kunduz (BBC 11/25/01). The mission was to rescue elite al Qaeda *jihadi* and Pakistanis fighting with the Taliban and airlift them to Pakistan. Dozens of senior officers, including two generals, received safe passage home (P. Thompson *Terror Timeline* p. 476). Of the 8,000 Pakistani, Taliban, and al Qaeda fighters trapped at Kunduz, 5,000 were airlifted out and 3,000 surrendered (*New Yorker* 1/21/02). Even more amazingly, "even some of bin Laden's immediate family were flown out" (PBS "NOW with Bill Moyers" 2/21/03). In addition to these flights, which had received US permission to fly in and out, 50 trucks packed with *jihadi* were allowed to escape from Kunduz alone (*NYT* 11/24/01).

Since the US Air Force completely ruled the skies, someone must have ordered a stand-down. Was this lenient arrangement part of the billion-dollar deal to close the border? It's true Pakistan's President Pervez Musharraf had extorted US support by warning that to do otherwise would "jeopardize his political survival" (PBS "NOW" 2/21/03). What Musharraf *didn't* acknowledge was that powerful elements within his own government had long supported Islamist extremism and weren't about to abandon their pet project next door. In effect, Musharraf apparently got the Bush administration not just to leave open an escape route for Islamists, but also to airlift them out of Afghanistan.

As part of the deal, the Taliban in that country had received word from their longtime sponsors in Pakistan not to resist the Americans, but to fall back and fight another day. It's still not well understood that "the Taliban had been organized and controlled by the Pakistani intelligence service, [the] ISI, since the very beginning.... Thus the ISI effectively controlled Afghanistan (A. Cockburn *Rumsfeld* pp. 126-27). The ISI loyalties to Islamists shouldn't come as a surprise for, as demonstrated earlier, it was the head of Pakistan's ISI who sent $100,000 to alleged 9/11 ringleader Mohamed Atta (*Times of India* 10/9/01).

Newsworthy as the failures to intercept convoys and the tacit sponsorship of airlifts would surely have seemed, the US media enforced a blackout. Although some news outlets reported that airlifts were occurring, very few disclosed Washington's secret cooperation with them. Later, when the United States and Pakistani governments denied the airlifts ever occurred, celebrated investigative reporter Seymour Hersh presented evidence demonstrating that Rumsfeld must have approved them (PBS 2/21/03).

## US Fails to Attack al Qaeda Convoys

In late October, US intelligence tracked bin Laden and al Qaeda fighters heading for Tora Bora and Pakistan (Knight Ridder 10/20/02). In early

November, locals in Afghanistan witnessed al Qaeda *jihadi* fleeing in long convoys from Kabul to Jalalabad, the largest city in eastern Afghanistan. From eight in the evening until three in the morning, their vehicles jammed the main road. One shopkeeper remarked that "we don't understand how they weren't all killed the night before because they came in a convoy of at least 1,000 cars and trucks. It must have been easy for American pilots to see the headlights" (*London Times* 7/22/02). Bin Laden was riding in one of the vehicles. US bombers passed right over the convoy and struck the Jalalabad airport instead (*Christian Sci. Mon.* 3/4/02). In November, throngs of bedraggled al Qaeda and Taliban fighters escaped from Jalalabad; after many hours of driving and walking, they finally reached the mountain village of Tora Bora.

## Tora Bora: More Signs of a Military Stand Down

Counterterrorism expert Richard Clarke recalled that "we knew from day one … Tora Bora was the place where he would be likely to go" (PBS "Frontline" 6/20/06). "All of this was known," remarked one intelligence official, "and frankly we were amazed that nothing was done" (Knight Ridder 10/20/02). Nevertheless, the US Central Command failed to act on ample intelligence to block escape routes. It tracked bin Laden to Tora Bora but bombed only one trail out of the village, leaving another wide open (*Newsweek* 8/18/02).

In late November, the CIA intercepted bin Laden's radio transmissions to his *jihadis*. An Arabic-speaking agent, the foremost expert on bin Laden's voice, overheard the leader's attempts to rally his troops. To Gary Berntsen, the CIA agent heading an undercover team charged with tracking bin Laden, "it was very clear that bin Laden was there on the mountain." The US command enlisted villagers familiar with the terrain, gave them GPS devices, and told them to push a button wherever they saw Islamist fighters. "The coordinates were then sent to American military spotters to call in air strikes" (*NYT* 11/28/09). The bombing was destructive but ineffective. For no discernible military purpose, the United States dropped massive amounts of depleted-uranium ordinance that would irradiate the area for decades, even centuries (DVD *War Promises*).

## Direct and Indirect Stand-Downs?

While the mountains towering above Tora Bora trembled beneath the B-52s, few feet crunched on the snowy trails. Lead agent Berntsen joined those urging Gen. Franks to seal the border but Franks refused, even though thousands of US troops were available and British marines were aching for action. Only 1,300 American troops were on the ground throughout Afghanistan, and only 1,000 were deployed in the climactic battle of the campaign (A. Rashid *Descent Into Chaos* p. 99). In fact, only 36 US soldiers assembled at Tora Bora, along with 100 journalists (*NYT* 9/11/05). Coupled with everything else, this does seem strange.

When US forces took another shot at bin Laden, it too was oddly ineffectual. Task Force Sword, comprised of more than 2,000 Special Forces, was ordered to "cut off al Qaeda troops attempting to flee into Pakistan." British signals intelligence pinpointed bin Laden near a labyrinth of caves. A team of British commandos was just 20 minutes behind him, but they were pulled off the trail to allow US troops to move in for the kill. However, "it took several hours for the Americans to get there, by which time he had escaped" (*Sunday Times* [UK] 2/12/06). To this day, this delay hasn't been satisfactorily explained.

## Viable Plans Are Rejected; Delta Force Is Held at Gunpoint

Using a colorful pseudonym, "Dalton Fury" told CBS of leading a secret Delta Force unit that "had hoped to come in over the mountain with oxygen, coming from the Pakistan side ... to get a drop on bin Laden from behind." But Delta Force didn't execute the mission because it couldn't get approval. A second plan was to drop hundreds of land mines in the mountain passes leading to Pakistan, but, he claimed, that plan was also disapproved. When Scott Pelley of CBS asked how often such tactical plans get rejected, Fury replied, "in my five years at Delta, never before" (CBS "60 Minutes" 10/2/08).

But this wasn't the most bizarre of the delays to beset the elite force. As Fury's team located bin Laden on a ridge top, Delta Force's supposed Afghan allies announced they'd negotiated a cease-fire with al Qaeda, a deal that astounded the Americans. When Fury's team tried to push on and pursue the *jihadi*, the Afghans drew their weapons on the Americans, holding them at gunpoint. It took twelve hours to end the bogus cease-fire, time enough for the al Qaeda fighters to slip away (CBS "60 Minutes" 10/2/08).

## What Was CIA Director Tenet Thinking?

When the CIA hired Pashtun warlords to direct the Afghan effort to contain al Qaeda in Tora Bora, Gen. Franks was warned that warlords could not be trusted. Former CIA administrator Michael Scheuer, the CIA's expert on bin Laden, recalled that "everyone who was cognizant of how Afghan operations worked would have told Mr. Tenet that [his plan to rely on Afghan warlords] was nuts.... The people we bought, the people Mr. Tenet said we would own, let Osama bin Laden escape ..." (PBS "Frontline" 6/20/06). If anyone should have known how unreliable tribal warlords would be, it was Tenet. For years, the CIA had been paying them to kill or capture bin Laden, but the tribesmen never got around to it. A *Time* news story concluded "the agency attempted to recruit tribal leaders in Afghanistan who might be persuaded to take on bin Laden.... But the tribal groups' loyalty was always in doubt. Despite the occasional abortive raid, they never seemed to get close to bin Laden" (*Time* 8/12/02).

Given the puzzlingly paltry numbers of troops in the field, the many missed opportunities to strike al Qaeda, the orders the US command failed to approve, the active enabling of airlifts for *jihadi*, and the failure to control key mountain passes, it's hard not to conclude that the US never intended to kill or capture bin Laden.

## Conduct of Campaign Raises Huge Credibility Issues

Whether or not bin Laden escaped from Tora Bora, thousands of other Islamist fighters were allowed to do so. Summing up the campaign, one military expert remarked that "there appears to be a real disconnect between what the US military was engaged in ... and the earlier rhetoric of President Bush, which had focused on getting bin Laden" (*Christian Sci. Mon.* 3/4/02). Thoughtful observers began to wonder, If bin Laden wasn't the goal, why did Washington issue an ultimatum to the Taliban government demanding, in effect, to "hand him over or we invade your country" (*Mirror* [UK] 7/8/02).

Several top officials did complete reversals on bin Laden's relation to the war. After these flip-flops, spin machines shifted into high gear.

- Gen. Tommy Franks, the ranking combat commander, suddenly claimed that capturing bin Laden wasn't one of the missions of the campaign (*USA Today* 11/8/01).
- While Bush had initially thundered about "moving heaven and Earth" to find the al Qaeda leader, only six months he later he'd quieted down: "I don't know where bin Laden is.... It's not that important" (White House 3/13/02).
- Rumsfeld also threw up his hands, joking evasively, "we are pretty sure he's either dead or alive" (DoD 4/26/02). Rumsfeld's subscript seemed to be, "so we didn't get our man; hey, it never mattered anyway." Unwilling to admit failure, yet equally unwilling to bury the personified threat needed to justify another war, the defense secretary contrived to create *uncertainty*—much as those who dispute that climate change is human induced have endeavored to foster public doubts (*SF Chron.* 7/27/10).

## The Uses of Confusion

Bush, Rumsfeld and others apparently wanted to have it both ways. On one hand, they wanted to shrug off an embarrassing failure to accomplish a stated mission; on the other, they apparently wanted to keep bin Laden around as a threat. The ambiguity of the dead-or-alive question also served as a distraction from much more relevant issues—most notably, Is it credible that bin Laden and al Qaeda were solely responsible for the 9/11 attacks?

Promoting contradiction, confusion, and ambiguity is central to almost any "psychological operation" (PSYOP). The technique is to so muddy the waters that researchers and intellectuals can't get clarity and the general public gets so confused and frustrated that they don't want to think about the issue. Incomplete or contradictory information also encourages speculation within "the chattering class" and especially on the Internet. Soon the public suffers from "speculation fatigue," which has a much longer history: Were one, two, or three shots fired at Daly Plaza? Did Kennedy's head jerk forward or backward? Is the Federal Reserve Bank a government entity or a private institution?

9/11 itself has provided a host of additional examples of induced confusion. Did a plane hit the Pentagon? Was the WTC defectively designed, or was it competently engineered, even over-engineered? In several of these cases, government has stubbornly withheld information from the public, quite possibly to intensify the confusion and the public turnoff that often follows it. Surveillance camera footage seized immediately after the impact would probably confirm that an airliner hit the Pentagon, but the Feds won't release it. The evidence available to the Warren Commission still remains unavailable to the public. Confused and frustrated, thoughtful citizens may conclude, "we'll probably never know; they've locked up the evidence. Who cares, anyway? Let's move on."

## Excuses for Not Finding bin Laden

Within just a few months, a Superpower's vast national security apparatus had suffered two remarkable setbacks: first it had failed to stop nineteen hijackers; then it had failed to kill or capture the enemy fugitive touted as the reason for invading Afghanistan. September 11 was seen as the biggest "intelligence failure" in American history, and Tora Bora looked like the anticlimax to an inconclusive campaign. Whereas 9/11 had been "explained" in an evolving Official Story, the escape of bin Laden required additional "explanations":

- *"That Impregnable Mountain Hideout"*

Thanks to politicians and the press, the idea that bin Laden and his followers had holed up in an unassailable fortress under a mountain immediately embedded itself into the American imagination. The story reached millions on NBC's "Meet the Press" when host Tim Russert provided Secretary of Defense Rumsfeld with an artist's rendering of the Tora Bora cave complex:

Russert: "It's a very sophisticated operation."
Rumsfeld: "Oh, you bet. This is serious business. And there's not [just] one of those" (NBC 12/2/01).

Exaggerating both the technology and the extent of the caves, Rumsfeld demonstrated a gift for getting his excuses lined up. A few weeks later, US and Afghan forces occupied Tora Bora. When they searched the mountains, they found labyrinthine caves but no vast underground fortress at all (www.edwardjayepstein.com/nether_fictoid3.htm).

• *"Forces Were Prematurely Diverted to Iraq"*
In 2002 Gen. Franks offered what would become the standard excuse: that following the invasion of Afghanistan, Predator drones and other resources were repositioned for the invasion of Iraq (*San Fran. Chron.* 9/5/04). While there's truth to the claim of prematurely diverted resources, the time frame is false. In making the claim, Franks ignored several key facts: that the Afghan campaign was over several months before the final buildup for Iraq ever began—and that bin Laden, if alive, had slipped away long *before* the diversions to Iraq.

• *"We Know Where He Is, But We Can't Go After Him"*
In 2005, CIA Director Porter Goss said he had an "excellent idea" where bin Laden was hiding, but that the al Qaeda chief won't be caught until "weak links" in the War on Terrorism are strengthened. Goss clearly meant Pakistan; he implied bin Laden wouldn't be "brought to justice" until Pakistan stopped harboring Taliban and al Qaeda leaders—which was to say "no time in the foreseeable future" (CNN 6/22/05).

## Bin Laden: The Man Becomes the Media Myth

Beyond the actual threat he posed, Osama bin Laden was transformed into a mythic Public Enemy Number One. This overblown stature was ironic, since many of the tapes attributed to bin Laden are obvious fakes. The tapes illustrate broader patterns of propaganda and mass-media manipulation.

While some of these tapes are probably authentic, many others are highly, even comically suspect.

## Why This Fabrication at this Moment?

In the lead up to the war, the absence of proof implicating bin Laden was already influencing media portrayals. When the BBC reported that there was "no direct evidence in the public domain linking Osama bin Laden to the 11 September attacks" (BBC 10/5/01), the absence of proof posed a challenge. The US and the UK were trying to assemble a "coalition of the willing" to attack Afghanistan, ostensibly to kill or capture bin Laden. Failure to produce proof of his involvement had become a political problem. Media involvement with "bin Laden" tapes seemed to offer a solution. Managers of media outlets likely felt increased pressure to sway public opinion—so if no one could come up with a "smoking gun," at least someone could spin the scripts and paint scary pictures.

The centers of power have become increasingly able to script the news. Nick Davies, author of *Flat Earth News* has exposed "a new machinery of propaganda which has been created by the United States and its allies since the terrorist attacks of September 2001." Davies noted "a concerted strategy to manipulate global perception. And the mass media are operating as its compliant assistants, failing both to resist it and to expose it" (*Independent* [UK] 2/11/08).

## The Blurry "Confession Video" of 2001: An Amateurish Fake

This tape, also known as "fatty bin Laden," was ostensibly found by US troops in Afghanistan. It showed bin Laden gloating over the success of the 9/11 attacks before followers. Exploiting this "evidence," Bush blustered— seeming to project his own shadow stuff—that "not only is [bin Laden] guilty of incredible murder, but he has no conscience and no soul" (CNN 12/10/01). The irony wasn't lost on this president; it just ran away.

The discrepancies between the tape released by the Pentagon and previous authenticated tapes of bin Laden were indeed striking:

- the bearded man wearing a turban in this video was much heavier and darker than the bin Laden appearing in other tapes.

- the speaker looked much healthier than he did in a tape made only six days earlier (*Telegraph* [UK] 12/27/01).

- this man had fatter hands and shorter fingers plus a shorter, fatter nose.

- this man was shown writing with his right hand, whereas bin Laden was left handed.

Researchers Victoria Ashley and Jim Hoffman have remarked, "in fairness, the producers of the confession video are due some credit for doing a good job with the beard and turban" (http://911research.wtc7.net/disinfo/deceptions/binladinvideo.html).

How could intelligent Brits and Americans accept such obvious hoaxes? The answers lay mainly with a wartime psychology of conformity and obedience plus implicit endorsement by media outlets. The BBC swiftly produced a completely uncritical, now infamous story, "Tape Proves Bin Laden's Guilt": "The tape is being seen by America's allies as vindicating the US-led military campaign in Afghanistan. The White House hopes the video will bolster international support for the war on terrorism" (BBC 12/14/01).

In America, the commercial media intensified the trauma, anxiety, and paranoia, noted Steve Coll, staff writer for the *New Yorker*: "The televised imagery of the attacks and their aftermath—the helpless office workers leaping to their deaths from the Twin Towers, the tear-streaked, dust-covered faces of the wounded; the shards of paper and debris; the impromptu bulletin boards covered by photos of the missing—still pulsed through the country like a crackling current" (Coll *Bin Ladens* p. 519).

It's not clear whether the news media were consciously contributing to a PSYOP or whether they simply furthered one while pursuing their everyday agenda of sensationalism. In any event, a shaken population shut down its already-limited critical acumen. With troops in the field, expressing doubts would have seemed disloyal, even treasonous. A week after the attacks, comedian/commentator Bill Maher had been pulled off the air for joking about 9/11 on "Politically Incorrect" (Salon 12/11/02). Even more than most, this was a tough time to be a critical thinker or a peace activist.

The bin Laden fakery and fear mongering apparently continued with a message delivered to al Jazeera in the fall of 2002. When this tape received close acoustic scrutiny from researchers at the Swiss Institute for Perceptual Artificial Intelligence, they concluded the message was recorded by an impostor. . ." (*Guardian* [UK] 11/30/02).

## The Fake "October Surprise" Video of 2004

Obviously fabricated too was the "October Surprise" video that first appeared on October 29, 2004, just four days before the presidential election. It was opportunely timed to help Bush and Cheney. In this video, the "bin Laden" figure addressed the American public directly. Oddly, though, he did so in Arabic, even though the real bin Laden was fluent in English (N. bin Laden *Growing Up bin Laden* p. 19). The strange-sounding language and ominous image thrust the threat home, further heightening the discomfort of many viewers. Going beyond the earlier "confession," this tape had "bin Laden" reveal "for the first time" that he'd *ordered* the attacks (AP 10/29/04).

Once again, the new message received wide acceptance but almost no critique or analysis, forensic or otherwise. Corporate outlets hastened to run it before the election and give it the widest possible exposure (CBS 10/29/04). When this "bin Laden" suddenly reappeared, he embodied a danger that a president who'd waged a War on Terror seemed best qualified to combat. When Deputy CIA Director John McLaughlin remarked that "bin Laden did a nice favor today for the president," he "got nods from CIA officers around the table" (Susskind *One Percent Doctrine* p. 336). McLaughlin didn't say whether any winks accompanied the nods.

How many voters did this last-minute injection of anxiety drive toward Bush/Cheney, whose campaign was explicitly based around offering protection from terrorism? Could this late-October "surprise" have influenced just enough voters in swing states to affect the outcome? Or could its impact, coming as it did just before the election, have pre-scripted a "frightened-voter" story that provided cover or what Robert F. Kennedy Jr. called a "stolen election"? (*Rolling Stone* 6/1/06). Whether by illegally disenfranchising voters, unusually long lines at the polls, rigged electric voting machines, or well-timed fear mongering, it's much easier to steal a *close* election.

**Incongruence with Earlier Tapes**

Aside from its timing, other clues that this video was a fraud included the speaker's implausible mode of thinking. Even government sources observed that bin Laden's earlier undoubtedly authentic talks had made frequent references to Allah and the Prophet Mohammed. But in the "October Surprise" video, Griffin has pointed out, Allah was mentioned infrequently, the prophet not at all. And whereas the authentic messages had portrayed events as caused by Allah, here the speaker attributed them to secular causes (Griffin *Osama bin Laden* pp. 49-50). Other incongruities struck many around the world, including one former Indian official: "How come OBL seems to be growing younger and healthier when … he should be growing older and weaker, particularly when he is being relentlessly hunted…" (South Asia Analysis Group 11/1/04).

The "October Surprise" video seemed to lay bare the ongoing government/media use of the "bin Laden" tapes. As PSYOPs, or psychological operations, these tapes insured that "big bad bin Laden" continued to haunt the public psyche.

**The 2007 "Repeat-Performance" Video**

Perhaps the most obviously faked video was one that appeared in 2007, years after the release of the "October Surprise." For three years there were no new videos, only three audiotapes. In this video, the bin Laden figure looked much as he had in 2004, except that he now sported a completely black beard (ABC 11/7/07). Again it's impossible to ignore the similarities to the government's daily presentation of Public Enemy Number One in *1984* (www.online-literature.com/orwell/1984/2).

The beard was hardly the only peculiarity, though. Computer expert Dr. Neal Krawetz pointed out that bin Laden was filmed "in the same clothing, [the] same studio, [with the] same studio setup and [the] same desk three years later." The papers he reads "are moved between the exact same stacks." The clincher, though, was that fewer than four of the tape's 25 minutes were moving footage and allusions to current events were "*only* made during the frozen-frame portions and only after splices in the audio track." Although the tape seemed barely "good enough for government work," the networks treated it as genuine, validated by "a senior US intelligence official" (MSNBC 10/29/07).

Nearly all of the validations for the tapes came from *unnamed* authorities, many within the national security establishment, yet validity was never an issue. ABC heavies weighed in on lightweight issues. Celebrity reporter Brian Ross reminded anchor Charles Gibson that "in [bin Laden's] last appearance, in October 2004, he had a very gray beard." Despite these anomalies, corporate media headlines were quick to trumpet "Al Qaeda's No. 1 Still Alive" (ABC 9/7/07) and "Bin Laden Slams Global Capitalism in New Video" (AP 9/6/07).

Former CIA officer Robert Baer pointed out that "experts will tell you that off-the-shelf digital-editing software could manipulate old bin Laden voice recordings to make it sound if he were discussing current events" (*Time* 11/18/08). A forensic specialist confirmed that today "it's possible to edit or fabricate in ways that completely defy forensic detections (BBC 12/14/01). Although major media outlets typically told the public that intelligence agencies had authenticated the latest item, they didn't mention that it's virtually impossible for *anyone* to fully authenticate audiotapes.

The bogus tapes seemed to reveal a larger pattern of mind manipulation. Griffin reminds us that "these fake bin Laden tapes appear to be simply one part of an extensive propaganda operation, in which the US military intelligence is using tax dollars—illegally—to propagandize the American public, with the aim of furthering the militarization of America and its foreign policy" (http://globalresearch.ca/index.php?context=va&aid=15601).

**FBI Produces No Evidence of bin Laden's Involvement in 9/11**
In the weeks immediately following 9/11, many Americans wanted the villain's head, but the FBI had to inform the populace that it would take time for criminal proceedings to commence against al Qaeda (Wired News 9/27/01). In early 2002, however, FBI Director Robert Mueller made a revelation: "In our investigation, we have not uncovered a single piece of paper either here in the United States or in the treasure trove of information that has turned up in Afghanistan and elsewhere that mentioned any aspect of the September 11 plot" (SF Commonwealth Club 4/19/02).

Nearly five years later, the FBI admitted it still had "no hard evidence" connecting bin Laden to the attacks. The Bureau explained that its Most Wanted posting was based on bin Laden's alleged involvement in the 1988 embassy bombings, not in 9/11 (*Wash. Post* 8/28/06). Had the FBI considered just the 2001 "confession video" or "the October Surprise" to be genuine, it wouldn't have lacked evidence against bin Laden. Evidently the FBI didn't want to present the tapes as evidence in court (Griffin *Osama bin Laden* pp. 35-36). Apparently counting on a short collective memory, Dick Cheney even denied that bin Laden had *ever* been a suspect (Fox 4/15/09), contradicting an Official Story he'd helped the Commission present—one that insists that *al Qaeda alone* was behind the attacks.

The tough questions went unanswered:

- If Osama bin Laden were such a prominent player, why wasn't more evidence available (*Independent* [UK] 2/7/10)?
- If there's never been a case against the guy, why did Washington put out a $25 million reward?
- If the FBI lacked "hard evidence" against bin Laden, why was the Justice Department continuing to prosecute his driver, cook, and media specialist (AP 8/10/10)?
- How could the FBI fail to muster evidence when its files—as well as the CIA's—were bursting with it?
- Do governments have a right to assassinate people whom they don't want to prosecute?
- If bin Laden and al Qaeda didn't do 9/11, then who did?

**Was the FBI Covering Its Own Past Involvement with al Qaeda?**
Moreover, how could the FBI claim it had no proof of bin Laden's involvement when, as we saw in the last chapter, it knew so much about him and several of his personally chosen lieutenants, notably Khalid Sheikh Mohamed (KSM) and Mohamed Atta? Not only had the FBI itself tracked, tapped or collaborated with every top al Qaeda leader, but additional evidence was available from other sources, such as the NSA intercepts of bin Laden's satellite phone calls and from the Yemeni "safe house" switchboard (Wright *Looming Tower* pp. 387-88). Yet the FBI seemingly

didn't want to reveal either the extent of its information or how it was collected. To acknowledge that it had lots of information—some of it from informants—would have raised vexing questions: How was it that you were so close to important al Qaeda operatives? Why didn't you *act* on the information, thereby saving thousands of lives?

The FBI's decision to remove bin Laden from its list was a big story, but it wasn't treated that way. One of the few mainstream stories to appear attempted to claim that the FBI's deletion had only occurred "because the connection to al Qaeda is uncertain." It expressed concern about what "conspiracy theorists" might conclude from the disclosure (*Wash. Post* 9/28/06). According to Project Censored, the fact that Osama bin Laden hadn't been formally charged has long ranked among the top 25 censored news stories (P. Phillips & A. Roth *Censored 2008* pp. 93-96). The trajectory of American depictions of bin Laden conforms to a common pattern which includes the creation, reinforcement and eventual replacement of government-designated enemies. During the first years of national mourning and trauma, release of a new tape practically guaranteed a jump in the threat level to Code Orange. Over time, though, bin Laden's impact began to wane. In response, the supposed threat shifted from suicide flights to nuclear weapons (CBS 11/14/04).

## That Mushroom Cloud Again

One of the CIA's foremost experts on bin Laden emerged from the shadows to discuss past mistakes, future strategies, and the dangers he and al Qaeda still posed. Former CIA employee Michael Scheuer had helped establish Alec Station, the Agency's secret unit charged with tracking and "neutralizing" bin Laden. Initially, Scheuer challenged the premises underlying the War on Terror. He argued that, ironically enough, America's military interventions were insuring "the radicalization of the Islamic world" (Scheuer [Anonymous] *Imperial Hubris* p. xv).

Scheuer pointed out that wars in Iraq and Afghanistan, plus continued lavish support for Israel, were advancing the agendas not just of military contractors and neocons, but also of Islamists. While these statements inflamed the powerful pro-Israel lobby, the former intelligence analyst also stated that the US needed to pay more attention to "the Saudi lobby, which is probably more dangerous to the United States than the Israeli lobby" (NPR 4/21/06). Scheuer implied that the US shouldn't treat bin Laden as a threat incarnate: its own policies were breeding new enemies every day. Given Scheuer's credentials and ongoing CIA connections, such statements initially endeared him to many in the peace movement. Within a few months, though, Scheuer moved from thoughtful analysis toward threats that seemed improbable at the time.

Having emphasized the rising anger among many Muslims, Scheuer released a shocker: bin Laden's alleged interest in nuclear weapons. "That growing hatred is going to yield growing violence," claimed the CIA's former bin Laden specialist. "Yes," Scheuer told "60 Minutes," "it's probably a near thing" (CBS 11/14/04). While the prospect of terrorists obtaining a nuclear weapon is decidedly daunting, in 2004 the chances of al Qaeda obtaining and delivering one had to seem remote.

Further upping the ante, Scheuer dropped a bomb himself: "the only chance we have as a country right now is for Osama bin Laden to deploy and detonate a major weapon in the United States … only Osama bin Laden can execute an attack which will force Americans to demand that their government protect them effectively, consistently and with as much violence as necessary" (*Extra!* 9/09). Continuing to assume that bin Laden was responsible for 9/11 and that he still posed a mortal threat, the former CIA officer invoked the Shock Doctrine: Scheuer all but called for a nuclear explosion to escalate the War on Terror. In so doing, he echoed the neocons' longing for a "new Pearl Harbor" to jolt the public into accepting their plans to invade countries in the Middle East (PNAC *Rebuilding America's Defenses* pp. 51ff).

## Purposes Served by Osama bin Laden

While we aren't sure to what degree bin Laden was involved in 9/11, we do know that he long remained a vivid presence in the American psyche. Reinforced by video and audiotapes, the specter of an Islamic Supervillain has resonated within popular culture. In bin Laden, the national security establishment has found an embodiment of the Terrorist Enemy. The bogeyman was tall, but mythmakers soon made him larger than life.

More than ever before, we're coming to understand the political role of the Arch Enemy. Coming to the fore in the years just after the Soviet Union had disintegrated and as Communist China was becoming part of capitalist economy, bin Laden filled a void. Neocons yearned for a new enemy, preferably one who personified the clash of Islamic and Christian civilizations. For the national security establishment, bin Laden and 9/11 were godsends. Since the attacks, military spending has more than doubled and the Pentagon bureaucracy has burgeoned (*Newsweek* 9/20/10).

As Osama bin Laden rose to prominence as a global menace, he received help from American politicians, journalists, and espionage agencies—plus the foreign policies they'd pursued. Although the United States has never charged bin Laden with the 9/11 attacks, this hasn't slowed the ongoing campaign, led by government and corporate media, to vilify him as Public Enemy Number One.

Exaggerated threats are a controlling feature of the national security state. Andrew Bacevich, author of *Washington Rules: America's Path to Permanent War*, has amply documented how "a permanent enemy" is required to maintain "a condition of permanent national-security crisis" (*NYT Book Rev.* 9/5/10). Orwell understood this requirement when he included "the two minutes of Hate" as a daily ritual in his *1984*. When images of Public Enemy Number One were broadcast on all TV screens each day, the message was clear: without the protection of the State, the Enemy will get you (www.online-literature.com/orwell/1984/2). A titanic struggle against evil personified has justified both sacrifices of personal freedom and ruinous wars.

As fear and anger build, a constant state of alarm produces the permanent "crisis" required for ongoing repression and perpetual war. External threats must constantly be manufactured to "justify" the costs of a huge military and its interventions. Thus war industries and the national security state require new mega-threats of almost mythic dimensions.

After spending well over a decade and hundreds of billions of dollars, the military finally "got its man." When one recalls the role of the US in the birth and growth of bin Laden and al Qaeda, the assassination might seem akin to Frankenstein killing the monster he created.

# 18.  Islamists, Pakistan, and Its ISI

*It seems to me quite plausible that Pakistan was quite involved in [9/11] … it's hard to say the ISI knew something the CIA had no knowledge of.*

—Daniel Ellsberg, "Pentagon Papers" whistleblower

Relations between the United States and Pakistan, especially between the spy agencies run by these two countries and the Islamist militants of south Asia, reveal much not only about *what* happened on 9/11 but *why*. Drawing on years of extensive, careful research, Paul Thompson of History Commons cited Pakistani involvement—especially that of Gen. Mahmood Ahmad, director of Pakistan's secret spy agency (ISI)—and Omer Saeed Sheikh, known for sending cash to the alleged hijackers. Both "the money man" Ahmad and "the paymaster" Saeed were deeply involved in 9/11. Their actions, Thompson has observed, "may explain many mysteries of 9/11, including solid evidence of foreign government involvement in the attacks …" (www.historycommons.org/essay.jsp?article=essaysaeed).

What follows illustrates the support al Qaeda was receiving, the group's close associations with US and Pakistani spy agencies, and the attempts by American journalists and politicians to hush up these connections.

For many years, Pakistan had supported al Qaeda and bin Laden. In 1996, Osama bin Laden struck a deal with Mushaf Ali Mir, a prominent Pakistani army officer connected to Islamist elements in Pakistan's Inter-Service Intelligence Directorate, its infamous ISI. Over the ensuing years, this cozy arrangement "provided bin Laden and al Qaeda [with] protection, arms, and supplies." Five years later, Mir was among those

393

who knew that al Qaeda planned to target the American homeland on 9/11/01 (G. Posner *Why America Slept* pp. 189, 191-93). As we'll see, though, bin Laden sought *additional* arms, including nuclear weapons, that Pakistani military intelligence wouldn't deliver. Since, as Daniel Ellsberg pointed out, the CIA typically knew what the ISI knew, one can assume shared foreknowledge of the attacks.

### "Those Towers Are Coming Down"

In 1999, ISI operative Gulum Abbas met illicit arms dealers in a restaurant within view of the WTC. FBI informant Randy Glass sat at the table (MSNBC 8/2/02) as Abbas inquired about purchasing black-market US weapons for bin Laden. After a deal was struck, Abbas gestured toward the WTC: "those Towers are coming down" FBI agents posing as customers sat nearby, recording the conversation (*Palm Beach Post* 10/17/02).

Because the agents witnessed the arms deal, one concludes the Feds must have known that bin Laden wanted weapons, that Pakistan was supplying them to him, and that the Towers were primary targets. Yet rather than acknowledge all this, plus the unsettling involvement of Pakistan, a nuclear-armed, supposedly friendly country, the Commission suppressed and even actively denied both Saudi or Pakistani involvement (*Report* p. 172). Long before this, though, truth had become a casualty in the War on Terror.

### Pakistan: Long a Blighted Democracy

A nation of 200 million, Pakistan is the second most populous Islamic state. The seeds of its past and present problems were sown at its creation. When the British pulled out of India in 1947, they broke off the Muslim areas of their former colony, forming a new and literally divided country based on its religion (A. Rashid *Descent into Chaos* pp. 33-34). Pakistan's proximity to a much more populous and more powerful Hindu country plus its sense that India was suppressing fellow Muslims in Kashmir have led to intense concerns with military confrontation.

Many past and present conflicts in south Asia have roots in decisions made by the British. As they pulled out, the Brits gave India control of the northern province of Kashmir even though its population was 90 percent Muslim. Other egregious examples of "British boundary drawing" include carving Israel out of Palestine and cutting Kuwait out of Iraq, creating a client state with a rich oil supply and a port of the Persian Gulf. Historical conflicts over religion, boundaries, and resources provide relevant background for understanding the present.

Pakistan has remained a stunted democracy, always in the shadow of the military and never allowed to develop (PBS "Charlie Rose" 6/1/11). The history of Pakistan is one of military coups supported or orchestrated from outside by the US and UK and from inside by tribal landowners, a greedy urban elite, and, above all, by the Army and the ISI. Not surprisingly, the country has also exhibited an exceptionally high degree of corruption: "Pakistan's rich have traditionally not paid much tax on the income or their property—and the country's collection rates are among the lowest in the world" (AP 9/17/10).

## The ISI: Pakistan's "Invisible Government"

The ISI is part of the Army, which has controlled Pakistan throughout half of its 64-year history (*NYT* 9/12/10). Pakistan's ISI plays a much more significant role in the Pakistan than do its counterparts in other countries. "Even by the shadowy standards of spy agencies," *Time* has noted, "the ISI is notorious. It is commonly branded 'a state within the state,' or Pakistan's 'invisible government'" (*Time* 5/6/02).

Although governments in Islamabad have regularly exaggerated the actual dangers posed by India for their political gain, the perceived peril has nevertheless loomed large. Created in response to these threats from the East, the ISI has a long history of spearheading opposition to India. In ways that a conventional military could not, the ISI has perfected the practice of using Islamist extremists for power projection, national defense, and subversion of Indian rule in largely Islamic Kashmir.

Pakistan soon learned that it could enlist Islamists, many of them mis-educated in its *madrassas* (fundamentalist schools), and deploy them as both defenders of the faith and liberators of Kashmir. Like Saudi Arabia and Egypt, Pakistan (through its ISI) has played a double game: controlling Islamists *internally* by using them *externally* as citizen combatants (*mujahedeen* and *jihadi*) not only against India but also for power projection in Afghanistan. This seems natural enough, for several tribes, including the Pashtuns, reside in both Pakistan and Afghanistan. Pakistan created the Taliban, or "students," and has continued to support them "in the hope of establishing an anti-Indian client state in Kabul" (*The Nation* 1/11-18/10).

State patronage of Islamist groups began in the 1980s with US/CIA and Pakistan/ISI sponsorship of the "holy warriors," the *mujahedeen*. During this period, the ISI worked closely with US, French, and British intelligence and "played a central role in arming and training the *mujahedeen* and later infiltrating the Taliban into Pakistan" (T. Ali *The Duel* pp. 12,145). From the Pakistani perspective, the assumption is that when (not if) the Americans leave Afghanistan, they want to be positioned with the Islamists who will likely take over. This is why, according to Lawrence Wright, paying Pakistan a billion or two a year to help fight the Taliban is futile, a complete waste of taxpayer dollars (*New Yorker* 5/16/11).

## US Sponsorship of Pakistan's ISI

The interconnections between militant Islamists, Pakistan's ISI, and the CIA reach *way* back. In 1979, even before the Soviet invasion of Afghanistan, the ISI had put the CIA in contact with Gulbuddin Hekmatyar, the ISI protégé who would soon lead *mujahedeen* drug trafficking. Pakistan offered its ISI to act as a conduit for the arms and funds the CIA wanted to provide for militants in Afghanistan. In the next few years the Americans built up the ISI to fight the Soviets and control political dynamics inside Pakistan. Widespread corruption within the ISI, plus its involvement in the heroin trade and the CIA arms pipeline, enriched many ISI generals. These sources also funded Pakistan's covert nuclear program and ISI-backed Islamic insurgencies in Kashmir and Central Asia (Rashid *Descent into Chaos* p 38). Created and financed by the CIA, the ISI came to resemble its creator.

The CIA has promoted ISI involvement in the drug trade and acts of state terrorism. Control of the opium trade became part of the ISI/CIA strategy. Pushed by CIA director William Casey, the former plan called for supplying heroin to Soviet troops; once addicted, their fighting capacity was assumed to be seriously compromised (P. D. Scott *Drugs, Oil and War* p. 59). Drugs were also a way to raise funds. During the 1980s, the ISI partnered with bin Laden and split annual drug profits of up to $100 million a year (Posner *Why America Slept* p. 29). But this wasn't the only scheme proposed by the CIA: during the mid-1980s, ISI commandos also began to undertake cross-border raids and sabotage missions into the Soviet Union itself (Rashid *Jihad* p. 43). Thus, the US waged a proxy war against the USSR on the cheap—with no casualties and little visibility, using the tactics of state-sponsored terrorism. More recently, Noam Chomsky and others have pointed to the increasing US acts of state terrorism (Predator drone strikes, commando raids) against Pakistan (Reader Supported News 5/21/11).

## 1990: Arms and Drug Sales Allow ISI to Sponsor Islamist Uprisings

Flush from its involvement in a growing regional illegal drug trade, the ISI had become a self-funding operation, a hidden government that wielded more power and independence than possibly any other country's intelligence agency (P. Thompson *Terror Timeline* p. 239). Not only did Pakistan's ISI help launch the Taliban, it facilitated connections between the Taliban and al Qaeda to help the Taliban prevail in Afghanistan (R. Clark *Against All Enemies* p. 53).

After 1995, Pakistan's intelligence agency continued its covert support of Islamist extremism. When one cabinet minister resigned in 2000, he lamented "the lack of reforms, the control of policy and decision making by the ISI and a few [hard-line] generals, the Army's pandering to the fundamentalists, the refusal to change direction in foreign policy—all this has sickened me." In 2001, the ISI funded an international conference and rally near Peshawar. A message from Osama bin Laden praised Taliban leader Mullah Omar, and hundreds of thousands of *jihadi* shouted their support for the Taliban (Rashid *Descent Into Chaos* pp. 51-54).

Because of the ISI's involvement in training Kashmiri insurgents, in 1993 Bill Clinton placed Pakistan on a watch list of state sponsors of terrorism (Rashid *Descent Into Chaos* pp. 38, 41). Clinton wasn't wrong about Pakistan's sponsorship of Islamist extremism, which extended far beyond building *madrasses* and selling opium. Steve Coll, Pulitzer Prize-winning journalist with the *New Yorker*, has noted that ISI elements frequently "tipped off" high-ranking al Qaeda leaders (PBS "NewsHour" 9/7/08). It's widely suspected that Clinton's 1998 cruise-missile strikes on al Qaeda training in camps fizzled because someone warned al Qaeda to vacate (Rashid *Descent Into Chaos* pp. 16, 18, 61).

## Pakistan Ignores Washington's Demands

In 1999, when Gen. Pervez Musharraf seized power, terrorism was already "on the agenda": soon enough, his regime became a state sponsor of terrorism. Falling back on this old tactic, Pakistan's new president sought to use Islamists against the Indians in Kashmir. In 2000, Washington delivered a blunt message urging Musharraf to capture bin Laden and other *jihadi*. But of course the president wouldn't rein in al Qaeda—let alone extradite its leaders—because its operatives were training militants fighting in Kashmir.

In the late 1990s, US intelligence discovered that Abu Zubaydah, the al Qaeda operative later tortured by the CIA, was vetting recruits for training in Afghanistan. When the State Department demanded that Musharraf hand over the recruiter, "the Pakistanis said they couldn't find him and the ISI just turned a blind eye" (Rashid *Descent Into Chaos* pp. 47-48). This shouldn't have come as a surprise. Pakistan had—and still has—a keen interest in Afghanistan, particularly one controlled by the Taliban.

Since the CIA needed the ISI, Musharraf could blow off the State Department. In 2001, attempting to escalate the War on Terror, counterterrorism czar Richard Clarke saw a need to "destroy terrorist camps, develop Uzbekistan's ability to attack Islamists, and send in Special Forces to collect intelligence" (*NYT* 2/11/05). However, the CIA station chief in Islamabad refused "because it would have infuriated the ISI." In similar fashion, Secretary of State Colin Powell insisted the CIA do nothing without consulting the ISI (Rashid *Descent Into Chaos* pp. 56, 88). Why would the CIA have been so solicitous of the ISI, a major sponsor of terrorism? Was this mostly about projecting power, making money from the drug trade, or protecting CIA contacts among Islamists?

## Pakistanis Remove Themselves from the Official Story

Matters hadn't changed much by 2003, when the Commission was working on its narrative. Someone on the Commission told Pakistan's lobbyists about potentially damaging revelations of their country's role in 9/11. According to one Indian paper, the lobbyists "contacted the panel members and asked them to go soft on the country. A lot of money was used to silence these members." When this didn't entirely quash the "damaging information," Pakistanis reportedly bribed some commissioners and paid tens of thousands of dollars to Washington lobbyists "to ensure that unfavorable references to Pakistan were dropped from the Commission's *Report*.... The disclosure sheds doubt on the integrity and honesty of the members of the 9/11 inquiry and, above all, [on] the authenticity of the information in their final *Report*" (*The Telegraph* [India] 3/13/06).

"After-the-event" circumstantial evidence can be quite instructive. Even if no conspiracy (other than that of al Qaeda) was responsible for 9/11, the cover-ups were themselves conspiracies. If, as some still contend, high-ranking Pakistanis weren't involved in planning and delivering the attacks, why would they have spent so much money and run serious political risks to insure that the Commission's *Report* didn't reveal "damaging information"?

Pakistan's ISI had plenty to hide.

## Pakistani Players: KSM, ISI Director Ahmad, and Saeed Sheikh

Again, one should acknowledge that Khalid Shaikh Mohammed (KSM), the alleged "mastermind" of the attacks, received ample discussion in the *Report*. This figures, since the Commission sought to hold Islamic terrorists wholly responsible, and it needed a prominent individual to represent the conspirators.

However, the Commission mentioned neither the ISI nor KSM's connections to that espionage agency nor the ISI "paymaster" Saeed Sheikh— who somehow wasn't mentioned at all. The Commission mentioned the ISI's director, Gen. Mahmood Ahmad, but only in connection with his visit to Washington (*Report* pp. 331, 333). Many of these omissions were likely "lobbied out" of the *Report*. It certainly said nothing about the ISI director ordering that $100,000 be sent to the alleged hijackers. Since when can a foreign country censor another country's official "blue-ribbon" inquiry?

It wasn't as if connections between the ISI and Islamists hadn't been well documented. By 2002, Yosef Bodansky, formerly director of the Congressional Task Force on Terrorism and Unconventional Warfare, had already detailed this linkage (UPI 9/30/02). Once again the Commission counted on the short memories of the public, legislature, and journalists.

## Saeed Sheikh: The Privileged "Paymaster"

In terms of financing, the Commission didn't just ignore evidence about key players; it also came up with the absurd conclusion that "we have seen no evidence that any foreign government—or foreign government official—supplied any funding" (*Report* p. 172). Like many others, this denial suggests that the Commission knew about all this plotting and scheming, but rather than just ignore it, they apparently felt it necessary to actively dismiss any such "speculation." In fact, much compelling evidence points toward the major "money men," ISI Gen. Ahmad and Saeed Sheikh.

Born in Britain to a wealthy Pakistani manufacturer, Omer Saeed Sheikh grew up in London and attended elite private schools. A speaker of five languages, the prodigy attended the London School of Economics (*South Asian Outlook* 3/02). At first glance, Saeed might seem an unlikely candidate for terrorism; he certainly did not fit the model of the young militant embittered by poverty and powerlessness.

Nevertheless, Saeed would eventually become deeply involved in the world of al Qaeda and the ISI. In 1992, he volunteered for charity work in Bosnia; there he witnessed atrocities committed by Christian Serbs against Bosnian Muslims. This experience likely intensified resentments Saeed had developed as a Muslim living in a Christian country. His impressive abilities, especially his fluency in English and understanding of Western ways, made him an invaluable asset to the Islamist cause (www.historycommons. org/essay.jsp?article=essaysaeed). While Saeed didn't fly an airliner into a building, he did send large sums to Mohamed Atta, who flew Flight 11. In this case, the money trail was the shortest distance between two points.

**Saeed Enjoys Special Protections from Three Intelligence Agencies**

Saeed Sheikh was likely recruited by MI6, the British CIA. Pakistani President Musharraf concluded that Saeed "probably became a rogue or double agent" (*London Times* 9/26/06). The president did not, however, explain Saeed's role on the Pakistani side of the "double," his own ISI. While Musharraf was likely trying to reduce suspicion of the ISI and deflect blame onto British intelligence, these motives don't necessarily invalidate his allegations about Saeed.

The scholarly looking son of privilege, Saeed was accumulating experience that validated him as a leader of Islamists. In 1993 he joined Pakistani militants attempting to liberate Kashmir from India. In 1994, Saeed began training at a camp in Afghanistan—and before long, he was teaching the classes (*LA Times* 2/9/02). While there, the young operative forged close bonds with bin Laden, who called him "my special son" (*London Times* 4/21/02).

In 1994, while attempting to kidnap tourists who could be traded for Kashmiri separatists, Saeed Sheikh was arrested. Indian courts sentenced Saeed to a long prison term (*London Times* 8/21/02). In 1999, British intelligence reportedly offered Saeed amnesty if he'd provide information about al Qaeda (*Daily Mail* [UK] 7/16/02). Al Qaeda, which also placed a high value on Saeed, eventually forced his release. In 1999, al Qaeda operatives hijacked an Indian airliner. Hostages were released in exchange for Saeed and two other operatives (BBC 12/31/99). After his release, Saeed met with bin Laden and Taliban leader Mullah Omar; then an ISI officer escorted him to a safe house in Pakistan (*Vanity Fair* 8/02).

For the two years before 9/11 and the six months following it, Saeed was all over the map. He was able to return to the UK just as if he'd accepted the secret offer of amnesty from MI6. British citizens kidnapped by Saeed called their government's decisions to grant him entry and not to press charges a "disgrace" and "scandalous" (Press Trust of India 1/3/00). Back in Pakistan, Saeed attended lavish parties thrown by Pakistani politicos and made little effort to hide his connection to terrorism. As a result, Washington assumed Saeed was a "protected asset" of the ISI (*Newsweek*

3/13/02). That was no doubt true. Other investigators, however, concluded "there are many in [Pervez] Musharraf's government who believe that Saeed Sheikh's power comes not from the ISI but from his connections with our own CIA" (*Pittsburgh Tribune-Review* 3/3/02). Like Mohamed the American (MTA), Saeed exploited the protections that came with working for two and probably three spy agencies.

A new whiz kid with skills fully as impressive as those of KSM and MTA, Saeed performed an array of services for al Qaeda. At camps in Afghanistan, he helped train several of the alleged hijackers (*NYT* 2/25/02). In Dubai, he provided al Qaeda operatives with credit cards and helped them open bank accounts (*Wash. Post* 12/13/01). During this period, Saeed continued to work for the ISI (*Guardian* [UK] 7/16/02).

How much of Saeed's work for al Qaeda was done on the orders of—or at least with the knowledge of—the ISI? As we'll see, Saeed did take direction from its director.

### Gen. Ahmad Orders Saeed to Send Money

By mid-2000, the 9/11 plot was moving forward. As we connect the dots, several facts are related. From Dubai, United Arab Emirates, Saeed made repeated calls to ISI director Gen. Mahmood Ahmad that summer. In the summer of 2000, using a variety of aliases, someone in Dubai sent alleged hijackers Mohamed Atta and Marwan al Shehhi more than $100,000 (MSNBC 12/11/01). The next summer, again from Dubai, someone made another large cash transfer (CNN 10/8/01).

Both cash transfers likely involved Gen. Ahmad, Saeed Sheikh, and Mohamed Atta (B. H. Levy *Who Killed Daniel Pearl?* pp. 320-324). Saeed had received a request to make the transfer from his boss, Gen. Ahmad. Apparently unaffected by his five years in prison, Saeed soon became involved in a criminal fund-raising scheme. Also based in Dubai, Indian gangster Aftab Ansari had ties to both Saeed and the ISI. After Ansari instigated a kidnapping of a wealthy Indian businessman, a ransom of $830,000 was paid to Saeed, who'd provided training and weapons to the kidnappers (*India Today* 2/25/02). Drawing on his share of the ransom, Saeed sent Atta the first $100,000 (CNN 10/8/01).

## ISI Director Finds Fundamentalist Religion

As we trace the actions of Gen. Mahmood Ahmad, ISI involvement in 9/11 becomes even more apparent. An imposing military figure in the mode of Chile's Gen. Augusto Pinochet, Gen. Ahmad had helped Gen. Musharraf seize power through a military coup. Musharraf—himself an Army general—took control of the country; the new president returned the favor by appointing Ahmad to head the ISI (Coll *Ghost Wars* pp. 504-05).

Soon Gen. Ahmad underwent a religious conversion. When he took control of the ISI in 1999, he wasn't especially devout. Soon after assuming the post, however, the director began to tell colleagues he'd become a "born-again Muslim." Whether the general's new piety was personal or political, only Allah knows. After the conversion, though, Ahmad became less cooperative with his CIA contacts. Noting these changes, US intelligence wondered about their potential impact on the ISI, especially the spy agency's relationship with the Islamist militants (Coll *Ghost Wars* pp. 510-511).

## The Director Receives Red-Carpet Treatment in Washington

In the two years he held the ISI directorship, Gen. Ahmad visited Washington twice. When he visited in 2000, the Clinton administration urged him to tell the Taliban not to harbor bin Laden (Coll *Ghost Wars* pp. 508-510).

Gen. Ahmad returned to the US just days before 9/11. While "mastermind" KSM was giving the green light to "ringleader" Atta, the ISI director was meeting with prominent American officials. The ten-day visit started with high-level meetings and ended with threats that the US could bomb Pakistan back to "the stone age" (AP 9/22/06). Despite the ISI's well-known links to al Qaeda, the Taliban, nuclear proliferation, and human rights violations, Gen. Ahmad received VIP treatment. His aviator glasses reflecting a gunpowder-gray moustache, the ISI director met with CIA Director George Tenet and Secretary of State Colin Powell.

On 9/11, Gen. Ahmad was attending a breakfast meeting at the Capitol with Sen. Bob Graham (D-Fla.) and Rep. Porter Goss (R-Fla), chairmen of the House and Senate Intelligence Committees. Both were former CIA operatives (*Wash. Post* 5/18/02). With them was Sen. John Kyl (R-Az). When the attacks began, the attendees were discussing al Qaeda and bin Laden (Salon 9/14/01). Readers will recall that Graham and Goss later co-chaired the superficial Joint Congressional Inquiry (JCI) into 9/11. Still later, Bush nominated Porter Goss to head the CIA (*Global Outlook* Spr./Sum. 05).

Were these just ironic coincidences?

## US and Others Threaten Pakistan with "the Stone Age"

Later on 9/11 and again the day afterward, Gen. Ahmad was summoned to less cordial meetings. But rather than questioning the director about possible Pakistani involvement, administration officials demanded Pakistan's cooperation against Islamic terrorism. And rather than relying on diplomatic niceties, Deputy Secretary Richard Armitage jabbed the point home and offered the ISI director a stark choice: "Help us breathe in the twenty-first century along with the international community or be prepared to live in the Stone Age" (*LA Weekly* 11/9/01). Armitage, a former Navy Seal and covert operative, was never the most diplomatic of diplomats, but his especially blunt threats may have belied a suspicion that Pakistan was involved.

Two days after 9/11, Pakistan was dealing with specific threats against its nuclear arsenal. On September 13 the airport in Islamabad, the country's capital, was closed because of threats made against "strategic assets." The next day, after Pakistan declared "unstinting" support for the US, the airport reopened. It was later suggested that Israel and India threatened to attack Pakistan and take control of its nuclear weapons if Pakistan did not side with the US and acquiesce to its other demands (*LA Weekly* 11/9/2001).

If, as would seem highly likely, Gen. Ahmad knew the 9/11 attacks were coming, why would he be hobnobbing with high officials in Washington at the exact moment they took place? By being so available to "take the heat," Gen. Ahmad's presence in Washington may have made it possible for Pakistan to participate in a heinous criminal act while avoiding retribution. Once it agreed to cooperate with the US, Pakistan faced no punishments. Much to the contrary, it received lavish rewards, including billions in cancelled or postponed debt (*Daily Times* 7/20/04), plus an additional $11 billion in US military aid over eight years (*NYT* 11/13/09). Instead of strongly sanctioning Pakistan, the US implemented its plans to attack Afghanistan.

As soon as Gen. Ahmad returned, Pres. Musharraf met with senior officers to respond to the situation. Possibly giving additional credence to the alleged "national security threats," Musharraf stated that "the fate of millions of people and the future of Pakistan" rested on the decision. But the president also saw a chance to manipulate the situation for Pakistan's benefit. He believed that for Pakistan "it was 1979 all over again"—that just as at the start of the Soviet-Afghan war, siding with the US could bring in billions of dollars in aid (A. Levy and C. Scott-Clark *Deception* pp. 313-14). Pakistani elites would be the big winners, American taxpayers the big losers.

### Unchastened, ISI Director Gives Military Advice to Taliban

While in Washington immediately after 9/11, Gen. Ahmad had promised Pakistan's complete support in defeating the Taliban. Initially, he kept his word; he did try to convince the Taliban's Mullah Omar to extradite bin Laden to avoid an imminent attack by the US (*London Times* 9/18/01). Just days after his return, though, the ISI director broke the agreement when he offered Omar and other Taliban leaders advice on how to resist the US (K. Gannon *I, Is for Infidel* pp. 93-94).

Soon enough, Gen. Ahmad was advising a key Taliban leader to fight on. Jalaluddin Haqqani, a Taliban warlord close to bin Laden, controlled the Khost region of eastern Afghanistan. Haqqani had worked with the CIA during the 1980s and had extensive ties to the ISI. Associated Press correspondent Kathy Gannon underscored his importance: "Had he wanted to, Haqqani could have handed the United States the entire al Qaeda network." But after Gen. Ahmad advised Haqqani *not* to defect, he continued to fight against the US long after the Taliban had lost control of Afghanistan (Gannon *I, Is for Infidel* p. 94). Late in 2010, the Haqqani network was still a virulent faction based in Pakistan's North Waziristan tribal area presenting "one of the greatest threats to foreign forces" (AP 9/26/10). A decade later, the Haqqani faction was still closely allied with the ISI (*Wash. Post* 10/6/10).

## ISI Director Forced to Retire After 9/11

Less than a month after 9/11, after links were discovered between Gen. Ahmad, Saeed Sheikh, and funding for the attacks, the ISI director suddenly had to retire. Two other ISI generals were also sacked on the same day (*Times of India* 10/9/01). While Musharraf claimed that ousting the generals would purge the ISI of its fundamentalists, one Pakistani diplomat remarked that "to remove the top two or three doesn't matter at all.... [The ISI is] a parallel government of its own. If you go through the officer list, almost all of the ISI regulars would say of the Taliban, 'They are my boys'" (*New Yorker* 10/29/01).

Although revelations of ISI funding pointed to a major role in the plot, they barely appeared in the Euro-American press. In the US, the only mention came in the *Wall Street Journal*: "authorities ... confirm[ed] the fact that $100,000 [was] wired to WTC hijacker Mohamed Atta from Pakistan by Ahmad Umar [Saeed] Sheikh at the insistence of General Mahmood [Ahmad]" (*WS Journal* 10/10/01). This wasn't Watergate, and Western journalists were less apt to "follow the money" than to spike the story, however important. The media blackout not only suggested a lack of commitment to understanding a pivotal event; it pointed to another pattern—a great reluctance to present any evidence that Pakistan was involved.

## Journalists Deliberately Confuse Paymaster's Identity

Because of the many aliases Saeed used, the "paymaster's" identity was initially difficult to establish. Initially, it took fully three weeks after the attacks for a British paper to determine that "the man at the center of the financial web is believed to be Sheikh Saeed, also known as Mustafa Mohamed Ahmad" (*Guardian* [UK] 10/1/01). A week later CNN elaborated, revealing that "Sheik Syed [sic], using the alias Mustafa Muhammad Ahmad, sent more than $100,000 from Pakistan to Mohamed Atta." The network also confirmed that this was the same Saeed Sheikh who'd been released from an Indian prison in 1999 (CNN 10/6, 7, & 8/01).

Then the curtain descended and the house went dark. The American press presented an extended catalogue of common, closely related Muslim names, so the "9/11 paymaster" story soon disappeared behind a cloud of confusion. As corporate news media reported on the paymaster, his names continually changed: "Mustafa Ahmed al Hisawi," "Mustafa Ahmed," "Ahamad Mustafa," and other aliases produced information overload, much like the "injects" on NORAD's radar screens. Spelling variations and multiple aliases obscured the paymaster's identity. Adding to the confusion, the FBI provided names similar to "Mustafa Ahmed" or "Saeed Sheikh"; these too obscured deeper issues of responsibility, both individual and institutional (Thompson *Terror Timeline* pp. 257-58). Among the various ways in which press and power have hidden the truth about 9/11, this one was admittedly creative—albeit indicative of compromised integrity and contempt for the public's right to know.

Since the initial revelations, the news media have rarely made the obvious connection that Gen. Ahmad, director of the ISI, ordered the payments and that "the paymaster" was Saeed Sheikh—the versatile operative who made frequent trips to Dubai, trained some of the alleged hijackers, and twice wired the big bucks to Atta. In the absence of meaningful press coverage, making these connections often defaulted to pundits and politicians, right and left. Michael Meacher, a former member of Parliament and British cabinet minister, found it "extraordinary that neither Ahmad nor Sheikh have been charged and brought to trial on this count" (*Guardian* [UK] 7/22/04).

As the corporate media puffed out a smoke screen of names, serving as a megaphone for "official sources," they could avoid presenting evidence that linked Saeed to 9/11 funding. To do so would have meant confronting Saeed's ties to the ISI and al Qaeda, as well as the prospect that he was acting on orders not just from Gen. Ahmad but also from the director's close associate, Gen. Pervez Musharraf. Since Musharaff was the leader of a nuclear power that had suddenly become a key US ally, revelations of involvement would have caused problems for both Washington and Islamabad.

## Reporter Daniel Pearl Kidnapped and Killed While Investigating ISI

In early 2002, after writing stories about the ISI, *Wall Street Journal* reporter Daniel Pearl was kidnapped and killed (BBC 7/5/02). Apparently, Pearl's triggering disclosure was that Jaish-e-Mohammed, an al Qaeda spin-off, still had its office and bank accounts. This contradicted Musharraf's assurances that they'd been shut down. At the time of his abduction, Pearl was indeed digging in perilous places. He was likely investigating the ISI's connection to Islamist militants as well as ISI/Islamist links to the US military and intelligence. As if all this wasn't dangerous enough, Pearl was, according to former CIA agent Robert Baer, also working on an investigation of the 9/11 "mastermind" Khalid Sheikh Mohammed (KSM) (Thompson *Terror Timeline* p. 262).

During those final months, the young reporter was almost certainly under ISI surveillance. Western journalists visiting Pakistan were routinely followed, so Pearl, who was looking into the ISI and making contacts with extremist groups, must have been watched—and probably stalked (*Guardian* [UK] 4/5/02). Evidence suggested the ISI and Islamists were behind his kidnapping and murder. Saeed Sheikh, someone well connected to both, was convicted for planning the crime, although KSM was accused with its overall conception (CNN 1/30/03). Some of the captured perpetrators fingered KSM as the one who administered the *coup de grace*, cutting the reporter's throat (MSNBC 9/17/02).

Saeed turned himself in, but not to the police. In February 2002, after the Pakistani police determined that Saeed was behind the kidnapping, they threatened his family. To protect then, Saeed did turn himself in, though not to the police (*Boston Globe* 2/7/02). Instead, he went to his friends at the ISI—and they held him without telling anybody. After a week in their custody, the ISI finally delivered Saeed to the police. This "missing week" became a source of speculation: it most likely involved negotiating a deal on what story Saeed would tell the police and the press (*Newsweek* 3/11/02). Overconfident, even cocky, Saeed confessed to his involvement in Pearl's kidnapping and murder, apparently assuming he'd receive a light sentence (*Newsweek* 3/11/02). Instead, he was sentenced to a long prison term (*Guardian* [UK] 7/16/02).

### Secret Trials Go Largely Unreported

The secret trials of Saeed revealed a growing anxiety about what information might emerge, especially in a US court (*Wash. Post* 3/28/02). MSNBC reported the obvious: that "some in Pakistan's government also are very concerned about what [the defendant] Saeed might say in court.... There are concerns he could try to implicate that government agency [the ISI] in the Pearl case, or [reveal] other questionable dealings that could be at the very least embarrassing ..." (MSNBC 4/5/02). The *London Times* concluded the real truth about Saeed Sheikh will not come out because he "is no ordinary terrorist but a man who has connections that reach high into Pakistan's military and intelligence elite and into the innermost circles of bin Laden and al Qaeda" (*London Times* 4/21/02).

As Musharraf tried to spin the aftermath of the Pearl tragedy, he all but blamed the victim as he warned against journalistic digging into "sensitive" places: "Perhaps Daniel Pearl was over-intrusive. A media person should be aware of the dangers of getting into dangerous areas" (*Hindu* 3/8/02) and suggested that the young reporter had gotten caught up in "intelligence games" (*Wash. Post* 5/3/02). This sounded like code for "he was spying for the Americans."

Neither American nor British news media raised the obvious question about Saeed: If he had reportedly helped finance attacks that killed 3,000 Americans, and the Justice Department had charged him for the murder of an American citizen, why wasn't the US interrogating him? It fell to an Indian newspaper to make the obvious suggestion that if the US were to pressure Pakistan, its close ally, to allow the FBI to interrogate Saeed in prison, it could quite possibly learn more not only about the financing of 9/11 but also about Islamist militants (*Indian Express* 7/19/02).

## Western Media Ignore Links between Saeed, ISI, and 9/11

The kidnapping/murder of an American reporter made a huge media splash, but the trial and the back story were drastically underreported. Following news that Saeed faced charges for the crime, the American media remained in a disconnect-the-dots mode. While the police named Saeed as the murder suspect and connected him to "an Islamist militant group," Western media didn't make connections beyond this. In 2003, French philosopher Bernard-Henri Levy published *Who Killed Daniel Pearl?* The book argued that Pearl was uncovering links between Pakistan's ISI, rogue nuclear scientists, and al Qaeda. Predictably, though, American interviewers avoided the full implications of Levy's exposé (PBS "Charlie Rose" 9/5/03).

While foreign sources were covering Saeed's multiple involvements, their American counterparts failed to mention these linkages. Virtually none reported that Saeed was simultaneously connected to *both* al Qaeda and the ISI *and* also involved in the financing of 9/11 (Thompson *Terror Timeline* pp. 265-66). Revealing Washington's aversion to disclosure, Secretary of State Powell denied any links between "elements of the ISI" and the murderers of Pearl (*Dawn* [Pak.] 3/3/02). The *Guardian* later called Powell's comment "shocking," given that Saeed was "widely believed in Pakistan to be an experienced ISI 'asset'" (*Guardian* [UK] 4/5/02).

In 2006, however, the HBO documentary "The Journalist and the Jihadi" did imply that Daniel Pearl's murder resulted from ISI complicity with al Qaeda. Narrated by CNN's Christiane Amanpour, the film depicted "a passionate journalist and a shrewd terrorist"; it focused on Pearl's kidnapping while he was on the 9/11 money trail. Most importantly, it suggested that Pearl might be alive today had al Qaeda not been sponsored by elements within the ISI (*NYT* 10/10/06).

But such reporting was decidedly the exception. Most journalists collaborated in a conspiracy of silence, reinforced by conventional wisdom about what the public did or didn't need to know. But can the near-universal corporate media avoidances (such as the obscuring of Saeed's name or his links to the ISI) be attributed solely to professional "group think" or even to individual editors—or could more systemic factors also be operative?

### Operation Mockingbird, the CIA, and Manipulation of the News

How do we account for this pervasive, nearly across-the-networks media blackout? This is a complex question, but the CIA, despite its charge to deal only with foreign situations, has to be an institution of interest. Starting in 1948, the year after it was founded, the CIA undertook Operation Mockingbird, a program to insinuate itself and place "assets" in major domestic media outlets. Its purpose was influence, even control the news and promulgate propaganda. Within just a few years, the program had grown to several thousand paid employees (H. Wilford *Mighty Wurlitzer* p. 7).

Attesting to the success of this infiltration, the public learned almost nothing about it for nearly three decades. In 1976 the Senate's Church Committee studying espionage agencies concluded that the CIA was attempting "to influence opinion though the use of covert propaganda" (D. R. Griffin *Cognitive Infiltration* p. 13). The Church Committee's report, however, was at best a "limited hang out." In an important and courageous expose, reporter Carl Bernstein (of Watergate renown) identified several of the country's most influential publishers and editors who were collaborating with the CIA. Among others, Bernstein cited C. L. Sulzberger, an influential columnist and close relative of two former publishers at the *New York Times*. It was telling that Bernstein's own paper, the *Washington Post*, wouldn't publish his story (*Rolling Stone* 10/20/77).

## Pampering Pakistan Before and After 9/11

Occasional gruff language not withstanding, the US has long pampered Pakistan. A story in the *Times of India* drew the logical conclusions: "A direct link between the ISI and the WTC attack could have enormous repercussions. The United States could not but suspect whether or not other senior Pakistani army commanders were in the know.... Evidence of a larger conspiracy could shake US confidence in Pakistan's ability to participate in the anti-terrorism coalition" (*Times of India* 10/9/01).

Rather then reviewing its established policies toward its new partner in the War on Terror, Washington extended the ongoing pattern of ignoring Pakistani "bad behavior." Recall the convoys and airlifts of Pakistani *jihadi*—both al Qaeda and Taliban—that the American command allowed to escape from Afghanistan in 2001. However, going easy on the Pakistanis had started long before "the great escape." It typically involved astonishing inattention to double-dealing typically by the Pakistani military and ISI. Taking American military aid and using it to build and sell nuclear weapons (*New Yorker* 5/16/11) was *very* bad behavior. But to this day, how many Americans are aware they may pay dearly for such sociopathic criminality?

Far beyond a few "bad apples," the ISI was rotten to the core. It had long trafficked in drugs and was reaping lavish profits from an opium economy worth $15 billion a year. The ISI had become so used to operating on its own that even its honest agents frequently resisted outside control (*Christian Sci. Mon.* 2/22/02). The US didn't even insist on reductions as a condition for its billions in aid for Pakistan (*Vanity Fair* 3/1/02). If, as seems undeniable, ISI "rogue elements" were involved in supporting Islamic militants, then such revelations also raise questions about CIA "black operations"—including those done by its Counterterrorist Pursuit Team. Described by Bob Woodward in *Obama's Wars*, this paramilitary force consists of 3,000 CIA-trained Afghan operatives (AP 9/23/10). How many of these fighters are advancing US objectives, and how many are ISI or Islamist infiltrators?

While this is a relevant question, the inquiry must return to the role of the ISI, and with it the CIA, in the planning and financing of 9/11. These are questions that only a fully independent investigation can answer.

# 19. Flight 77 and the Pentagon

*They told us to turn and follow that aircraft—in twenty-plus years of flying, I've never been asked to do something like that.*

—Col. Steve O'Brien, Captain of the C-130 cargo plane

More than most areas of 9/11, American Airlines Flight 77 and the Pentagon have frequently led researchers into a maze of controversies. Recently, though, researchers with scientific backgrounds have found new threads leading out of the labyrinth. But while scientific analysts have tracked the clues, affording many new perspectives, many questions still remain.

Along with researchers David Chandler, Jim Hoffman, Frank Legge, and Kevin Ryan, David Ray Griffin has emphasized the importance of rigorous adherence to the scientific method (Griffin *Mysterious Collapse of World Trade Center 7* pp. 13-26). In this scientific spirit, analysts wield Occam's Razor, which basically says the most logical answer is often best. Here the approach will rely not only on the principles of simplicity and logic, but also on empirical evidence: if it looks like a duck, waddles like a duck, and quacks like a duck, it's probably a duck. So this inquiry will stay near the evidence, following it where it leads.

Once again, it pays to look at what's implied by the stories people tell.

## Significantly Different Stories Regarding Flight 77

There are two basic narratives. One is based on the 9/11 Commission's *Report* (pp. 24-27) plus the Flight Path Study released belatedly by the National Transportation Safety Board (NTSB). The second main narrative reflects a wider spectrum of evidence, much of it from journalistic sources.

***Once again, we're back to the centrality of story: here's the official version:*** American Flight 77 departed from Washington Dulles at 8:20 and reached its cruising altitude of 35,000 feet. The Boeing 757 made its last routine radio transmission at 8:50 as it approached the West Virginia/Ohio border (*Boston Globe* 11/23/01). Minutes later, at 8:56, hijackers commandeered the airliner, which immediately deviated from its flight path, went out of radio contact, and turned off its transponder. Just after 8:56, the FAA's Indianapolis Center tried three times to make radio contact (www.gwu. edu/~nsarchiv/NSAEBB/NSAEBB196/doc02.pdf). Minutes later, it concluded the flight was "gone," "missing and possibly had crashed" (*Report* p. 24).

By 9:00, the plane had completed its U-turn and was heading back east: according to the NTSB, "the autopilot remained engaged during the initial descent from 35,000 feet." At 9:07, over northern West Virginia, the autopilot went off for about three minutes and the plane lost significant altitude, about 3,000 feet (NTSB Flight Path Report). After the autopilot came back on, the airliner stayed on a straight course at extremely high speed (J. Longman *Among the Heroes* p. 208). At 9:29, "when the airliner was approximately 35 miles west of the Pentagon," the autopilot was disconnected again "as the aircraft leveled near 7,000 feet." At 9:30, the airliner continued toward Washington over Fairfax, Va., maintaining this same altitude. At 9:34, Flight 77 began its now-famous "descending turn to the right." At 9:37, the plane came out of the turn and leveled off "at about 2,000 feet about 4 miles southwest of Pentagon." In the final 30 seconds, "the power was increased to near maximum . . ." as the airliner continued to descend. The plane had accelerated to about 530 miles mph when it struck the building's West Block. The time of impact was 9:37:45 (NTSB *Report*).

Short though this account is, it tends to affirm the idea, so central to the Official Story, that Flight 77 struck like a bolt from the blue. In the standard narrative, the airliner turned off its transponder, went out of radio contact, and disappeared from radar screens most of the way to its target. Moreover, in this account, Flight 77 sped directly toward the Pentagon until it made its downward loop turn, allegedly diminishing opportunities for detection, interception, or tracking by radar or action by anti-aircraft defenses.

While the NTSB report had Flight 77 heading straight toward its target before swooping down three and a half minutes before impact, the alternative narrative has the plane meandering over Arlington, Virginia, flying along the Potomac River and right past the Pentagon before doing its famous downward loop and final descent. In short, while the Flight Path Study may be largely factual until the airliner approached Washington, its rendering of events is often incomplete, and its final fifteen minutes don't square with much additional evidence.

On the other hand, the NTSB Report contains useful and apparently accurate information, particularly about the seemingly amateurish manner in which the plane was flown, with the autopilot turned off and then on again.

***A More Probable Narrative with a Different Flight Path*** When Flight 77 departs from Washington Dulles at 8:20, it's ten minutes late. Nevertheless, the alleged hijackers wait more than half an hour to make their move; this delay lengthens their time in the air—thereby increasing their possible exposure to passenger revolt or air defenses.

At 8:56, they hijack Flight 77: the tragic fate of passengers and crew is sealed. Moments after the takeover, the plane's transponder and radio go dead as it swings wide into a U-turn, abandoning its approved flight path to Los Angeles (*USA Today* 8/13/02). Controllers tracking the flight from the FAA's Indianapolis Center receive all three telltale signs of a hijacking: no radio response, no transponder signal, and departure from flight path. Given what has been going on that morning, these signs should have shot red flags up the pole. Somehow, though, the controllers working Flight 77 fail to track the U-turn and continue to conclude it is "lost" (*Report* p. 25).

For terrified passengers, the eastward flight is rough because of the high speed and abrupt changes in altitude. Yet for some reason, very few passengers make phone calls. Had they known, some might have derived some comfort from the fact that starting at 9:17, the FAA has ordered all of New York's airports to close. In Washington, though, the FAA is slower to react. It won't close Washington's airports until 9:40, three minutes after the plane has slammed into the Pentagon (*NYT* 9/12/01).

### Controllers in Washington Finally Become Aware

In Washington, air traffic controllers are seeing more. Just before 9:20, the FAA's Herndon Command Center informs the Dulles Airport Control that the FAA has lost track of American 77 and desperately needs help locating it. Dulles is located in Chantilly, Virginia, 26 miles west of the capital and 22 miles west of the Pentagon (www.metwashairports.com/dulles/dulles.htm). It's well positioned to spot an airliner coming in from the west. Dulles tells its controllers that a commercial aircraft is missing and asks them to look for "primary targets"—the radar tracks made by planes that aren't sending out a transponder signal (*USA Today* 9/13/01). This greatly reduces the number of likely suspects on their screens, but since most primary radar tracks indicate only speed and location, the controllers must work from partial information (*Wash. Post* 9/11/01).

### Starting at 9:20, FAA Reports Sighting Flight 77

Since erratic or extreme speed characterizes most hijacked aircraft, it's not surprising that Dulles controllers soon get a "bingo." At about 9:20, the FAA notifies FBI's Washington field office that American Flight 77 has been hijacked shortly after takeoff from Dulles. The FBI dispatches a team of 50 agents to investigate the hijacking and provide additional security to prevent another. Nevertheless, NORAD/NEADS learns of the hijacked flight at 9:21 and knows it's heading for Washington (Scott *Road to 9/11* p. 202).

After the Dulles controllers first identify a large plane at 9:20, Flight 77 will remain over the Washington area for another *seventeen minutes*. This stands in sharp contrast to the NTSB narrative, which has the plane entering the outskirts of the area about twelve minutes later. About 9:25, perhaps slightly afterward, Dulles controller Danielle O'Brien notices a strange blip to the southwest, now only twelve to fourteen miles away. A minute or two later, other controllers' radar scopes also show this plane just to the southwest, heading at high speed and "within 30 miles of

Washington" (CBS 9/21/01). Dulles controllers continue to feed updates into a teleconference at the FAA's Washington headquarters (FAA 9/17/01).

### Information about Flight 77 Reaches Cheney at White House

Several Dulles controllers observe a "primary target" streaking eastbound toward Washington at almost 500 miles per hour (*USA Today* 9/13/01). The FAA is sharing what it's seeing with the Secret Service—and specifically with Cheney, who's calling the shots from the White House bunker. This is evident in the famous testimony of Transportation Secretary Mineta: that at 9:26, a "young lieutenant" warned the vice president of an incoming plane only 50, 40, and then 10 miles out, but Cheney ordered the military to hold back any defensive action (www.youtube.com/watch?v=bDfdOwt2v3Y).

### Dulles Controllers Cooperate with Colleagues at Reagan

From Dulles, controllers immediately contact their counterparts at Washington's Reagan National Airport. They inform them that an unidentified aircraft is not just heading toward the nation's capital, but rapidly approaching the P-56 prohibited airspace over the city (FAA 9/28/01): "Hey! Untracked target fifteen [miles] west of you. Primary target eastbound! Heading toward P-56!" (L. Spencer *Touching History* pp. 145-146). Encompassing the airspace above the Capitol building and the White House, the P-56 zone is highly restricted; private and commercial aircraft are prohibited, and any plane entering it must beep a military transponder signal (Dept. of Transport. 8/4/05). At Reagan, located less than a mile from the Pentagon, controller Dan Creedon sees the incoming aircraft about ten miles west of the White House. Its radar blip is untagged, primary track only (FAA 9/14/01). This has to be the "lost" flight, but he'd rather be sure.

### The Divergence, the Flyover, and the Final Descent: The Last Nine Minutes

In this version, the route is hardly a straight shot. As the airliner approaches Washington, it completes its main descent and the autopilot is switched off. At 9:28, over western Fairfax County, Virginia, just south of Dulles Airport, Flight 77 is now about 25 miles from Washington. Although visibility is good and the target is likely visible in the distance, the airliner seems in no hurry to strike it. During most of this nine-minute period, the plane's speed averages about 375 mph, sometimes dropping below 350. The airliner veers off the NTSB's direct flight path and meanders around for five of the next nine minutes before swooping down for the hit. Over these five minutes, the altitude ranges between about 7,500 feet and 8,500 feet as the airliner makes sudden climbs, exhibits wide fluctuations in banking angles, and shows erratic variations in engine power. Dr. Frank Legge, who analyzed the Flight Data Recorder (FDR), suggests that all this reveals the difficulties of an inept pilot attempting to hand fly a Boeing 757 (Pers. Corresp.).

Now heading northeast, the airliner enters the urban area several miles north of the Pentagon; it's now heading directly for the White House, where staffers are starting to run for the doors (Wash. Post 9/11/01). But when the plane approaches the Potomac, it suddenly banks right, reportedly flying the river southward toward the Pentagon (Aviation Security International 10/2). Coming from the north, the airliner passes by the building's East Block, which houses the offices of the top brass and the secretary of defense. To strike the Pentagon, it must now circle back and lose altitude quickly (http://911research.wtc7.net/talks/pentagon/approach.html).

At 9:30, another FAA controller, noting that a C-130 cargo plane is ascending from nearby Andrews Air Force Base, asks pilot Col. Steve O'Brien to identify the rogue plane. Col. O'Brien radios back that a large airliner has turned sharply "moving right in front of us, a mile and a half, two miles away." Then the controller tells O'Brien to follow the airliner as it plunges into a steep descent (*Minnesota Star-Tribune* 9/12/02).

## Pentagon Receives Warning but Does Not Evacuate

Within the Pentagon, the National Military Command Center (NMCC) receives warnings that a hijacked airliner is now heading toward central Washington. The time is 9:31, six minutes before impact. Yet commanders at the Pentagon do nothing to alert or evacuate the 24,000 people, military and civilian, who are working in the huge building (S. Vogel *The Pentagon* p. 429).

With only one exception, no evacuations take place (*Newsday* 9/23/01). Worthy as it is, the exception is accomplished by civilian contractors, not the military command, and the warning comes off network TV, not from the vast information-gathering apparatus of the military. After three years of renovation on this wing of the Pentagon, a crew is applying the finishing touches. At 9:35 the crew leader learns of these attacks; he instructs workers to forget about renovations. Two minutes later, they feel a huge explosion, followed by a fireball above the exact area they've just vacated (P. Freni *Ground Stop* pp. 43-44).

## That Famous Downward Loop

At 9:34, the standard version tells us, the airliner "started a 330-degree descending turn to the right." The plane banks steeply and arcs downward, doing a loop three miles across as it drops about 6,000 feet. During this descent the speed remains about 350 mph, rarely exceeding 400, and the airliner even does a couple of short ascents (NTSB Flight Data Recorder). The sweeping loop takes fewer than three minutes. Since commercial airliners don't make moves like this, controllers are amazed (*Boston Globe* 11/23/01). When Flight 77 pulls out of the steep descent at 2,000 feet, it's over Alexandria, Virginia, four miles west of the Pentagon.

The airliner revs its engines as it begins its descending final approach, which takes it near the Sheraton Hotel, over the Navy Annex, and by a Citgo gas station. Six hundred feet from its target, the airliner blasts down five lamp posts at a cloverleaf. Then, at near-ground level, it slams into the concrete-and-limestone facade of the Pentagon. FEMA's Building Performance Report on the Pentagon crash had the 757 slamming into the building eight feet off the ground at 532 mph (*Civil Engineering* 2/03).

Among the hundreds of observers, if one counts the amazed motorists, are many military personnel. Donald Bouchoux, a retired Naval officer, is driving on Washington Boulevard when he sees the aircraft streak by and dissolve into the building: "There was an enormous fireball, followed about two seconds later by debris raining down" (*Wash. Post* 11/20/01). Many other motorists also report confetti-like shards of metal falling on their vehicles.

Moments after the impact, Col. O'Brien peers down from his C-130. He too reports seeing an enormous fireball and billowing black smoke (*NYT* 6/18/04). Ten minutes later, three F-16s from Langley AFB finally arrive, too late to protect the capital. As Maj. Dean Eckmann flies over the burning building, he reports extensive damage to its two outer rings. When Maj. Eckmann sees the black smoke and surmises that the conflagration is "a big fuel tanker truck because of the amount of smoke and flames coming up …" (L. Filson *Air War Over America* p. 6).

The next day, after the fires are extinguished, Army Sgt. Mark Williams reports seeing the charred bodies of passengers still strapped in their seats (*USA Today* 9/13/01). End of story.

## Questions Raised by These Narratives

This second account is not that one that's usually told, but it's grounded in solid sources and corroborated by Frank Legge's recent and meticulous analysis of the Flight Data Recorder (FDR). If this narrative provides a more accurate account, it challenges the accuracy of the first, the Official Story. Since this new narrative involves a longer flight path with sudden turns, it raises questions about both the piloting of the plane—human or autopilot—and the intentions of those who chose a longer route that might have put their mission at greater risk. It also raises a much-posed question: Even if assisted by autopilot, could a pilot who's never flown a big Boeing before have pulled off these maneuvers?

With a fuller, more accurate flight-path narrative, it's possible to look more closely into several key issues:

- At the alleged failure of civilian controllers and military air defenders to locate Flight 77 on their radar scopes for half an hour;
- At the implications of a jetliner flying unimpeded toward the White House, along the Potomac, and right by the Pentagon—especially after other jetliners had already hit the WTC Towers;
- At why an E-4B "flying communications center" was circling over Washington at the same time;

- And at the still-impounded evidence—airplane parts and debris, passenger remains and belongings, plus videotapes—that would, if released, help researchers address additional questions about the Pentagon impact.

## Radar "Blind Spots" Too Big to Believe

The Commission's claim that Flight 77 was lost to both civilian and military radar for more than half an hour raises many additional questions. Citing poor thinking and inadequate equipment at the FAA Indianapolis Center, the Commission concluded that "American 77 traveled undetected for 36 minutes on a course heading due east for Washington DC" (*Report* p. 25).

Now *that*'s one to ponder. How, for 36 minutes—i.e., for most of the time Flight 77 was in the air after the hijacking—could the FAA and NORAD have failed to detect a large airliner as it sped across West Virginia and Virginia? Why didn't the FAA notify NORAD, as its operating procedures required? In addition, the Air Force had an Airborne Warning And Control System (AWACS) E-3 Sentry plane over Pennsylvania; its radar could see for hundreds of miles (www.stthomas.edu/aquin/archive/041202/anaconda.html).

If, as reported, Flight 77 was known to be flying without a transponder signal, the airliner would have stood out as one of the very few radar tracks without an identifying tag. If, as reported, Dulles controllers had identified and even marked the "unidentified" flight, why were flight controllers along the plane's route unable to identify it?

## The FAA's Sighting at 9:20

By all accounts, the controllers at Dulles detected an incoming, unidentified plane as soon as it appeared on their screens at 9:20 (FAA 9/17/01). A minute later, this rogue airliner was ten, nine, and then eight miles west of Dulles, flying at 500 mph toward the White House (*St. Petersburg Times* 9/12/01). Since Flight 77 was first spotted at 9:20, this left seventeen minutes for defenders to act before the airliner struck its target at 9:37. What happened?

The plane's high speed and lack of transponder signal have sometimes served as excuses for not identifying Flight 77. One flight controller at

Dulles remarked that "nobody knew it was a commercial airliner; it was moving too fast" (CBS 9/21/01). Yes, Flight 77 reportedly did approach Washington at 500 mph (J. Longman *Among the Heroes* p. 208). But since Boeing airliners routinely cruise at 550-570 mph (http://hypertextbook.com/facts/2002/ JobyJosekutty.shtml), such claims don't explain FAA failures to locate, identify, and intercept Flight 77. Moreover, private and commercial jets are required to have "squawking" transponders and military aircraft typically fly with their transponders on when they're not on combat missions (I. L. Peppler *From The Ground Up*). Thus, a no-transponder radar track at any speed should definitely have grabbed controllers' attention. If the plane's lack of a transponder didn't make it jump off the screen, its speed and erratic flight should have sounded a very loud alarm.

### Why Were Air Defenses Not Activated?

The NTSB Report had the airliner heading straight toward its target, not reaching the Potomac, and never seeming to threaten the White House. But the actual path, as we've seen, took the plane on a quite different trajectory.

The White House felt threatened, and not without reason. Two sources, Bush's Chief of Staff Ari Fleischer (CBS 9/21/01) and a reputable British newspaper, both claimed that Flight 77 crossed the River, entering the P-56 prohibited air space, and approached the White House, thereby inviting obliteration: "If the airliner had approached much nearer to the White House it might have been shot down by the Secret Service, who are believed to have a battery of ground-to-air Stinger missiles ready to defend the president's home" (*Daily Telegraph* [UK] 9/16/01).

If Secretary of Transportation Mineta's testimony is accurate, the incoming flight was already in the crosshairs of air defenders—and not only at the White House. Several sources have stated that the Pentagon itself had no anti-aircraft defenses, but this is not the same as claiming the headquarters of the US military was completely undefended. A "day-of" (less guarded) news report stated that Washington "is ringed with Air Force bases, and the ability to get defensive planes in the air is very, very high" (Fox 9/11/01). The defensive perimeters against air attack had to extend well beyond Washington for the "young lieutenant" to burst into the White House bunker and tell Cheney that an incoming aircraft was "50 miles out."

Recall that Secretary Mineta placed the ultimate "crosshairs moment," when the lieutenant came in a third time to update Cheney, at 9:26 (BBC 9/1/02). If this was correct, then Flight 77 roared around just west of Washington for ten minutes more before it finally made impact. If the plane's distance from the capital and the estimated time are even roughly correct, then the official NTSB's direct flight path has to be incorrect.

At what point did the plane veer away from the White House?

## The Over-Arlington, Along-the-River, By-the-Pentagon Route

Today the Flight Data Recorder evidence suggests that Flight 77 banked to the right before reaching the Potomac, followed the river south, flew right by the Pentagon, and did its tight 330-degree downward turn over Alexandria, Va. (CBS 9/21/01). Former Secretary of Transportation Norman Mineta confirmed that "it was following pretty much the ... down-river approach, and it had not crossed over toward the White House or toward the Capitol" (*Aviation Security International* 10/02). Mineta was apparently drawing on sources at the FAA, which had done a radar-track analysis of the hijacked airliners.

If we assume Flight 77 flew along the Potomac, it would seemingly have missed a perfect opportunity to swoop down and strike the Pentagon. The plane passed by the building's East Block, whose walls weren't reinforced—over the logical easy target, where it could have inflicted more damage and killed more high-ranking personnel. The offices of the secretary of defense, the chairman of the joint chiefs, and many generals and admirals lined the outer E Ring on this east side. Instead, Flight 77 struck a recently reinforced section where it could do the *least* damage (Griffin *New Pearl Harbor* p. 40).

If the attackers were targeting senior government officials, they could easily have figured out exactly where to strike (P. Creed and R. Newman *Firefight* pp. 171-72). That the alleged hijackers did want to inflict maximum casualties seems clear from the fact that "ringleader" Mohamed Atta planned the attacks for "after the first week in September, when Congress reconvened" (J. Bamford *Shadow Factory* p. 71). Why, then, would the alleged hijackers have passed up an opportunity to take out the big shots?

One answer is that they may not have intended to fly right by, speculated Australian analyst Frank Legge, PhD. It's easy to use a GPS, he's pointed out, and it's easy to steer a plane, but it would also be easy for an inexperienced pilot flying at speeds far exceeding those on simulators to over fly his target: "It would be no trouble to turn in the right direction, head for the target and look for it by eye—these were huge buildings, easily recognized. But then you have to descend. Clearly they waited too long at the Pentagon and had to do a spiral to get down low enough for the attack" (Legge Pers. Corresp.). If the errant airliner did over fly the Pentagon, it had to loop back several miles to strike Wedge 1 of the West Block. This section was still under renovation, so it was sparsely occupied. Although 125 workers were killed in the attack, no high-level military officials were among them (http://911research.wtc7.net/talks/pentagon/approach.html).

**Three Tough Questions**

Circling over Arlington, heading toward the White House, flying over the river past the Pentagon, and doing the downward dive all had to involve additional time in the air and thus additional exposure to interception.

If we assume that whomever was piloting Flight 77 must have anticipated activating formidable air defenses, why would they have taken a circuitous route that kept them in the air longer than necessary and therefore run additional risks? (Griffin *New Pearl Harbor Revisited* p. 77).

- Why might whomever was piloting the plane have come anywhere near the P-56 restricted airspace? Even if the plane didn't skirt the P-56 restricted zone, why would the pilots/planners have chosen a route where they must have been highly conspicuous to controllers at nearby Reagan Airport? Flight 77 would have been.
- Flying *against* the air traffic flow at an unassigned altitude seems unnecessarily provocative. Or did whomever was controlling the

plane *knowingly* take chances, confident they'd sail right though the defenses?

### C-130 Pilot Reportedly Shadows Flight 77 during Final Moments

About 9:30, as Flight 77 was zeroing in on the Pentagon, a C-130 cargo plane had just taken off from nearby Andrews Air Force Base, nine miles east/southeast of the Pentagon. As noted, an FAA controller asked pilot Col. O'Brien to locate, identify, and follow the plane.

When the controller asked the pilot if he had the other plane in sight, O'Brien told him "that was an understatement"—that by then, a large airliner "had pretty much filled our windscreen. Then he made a pretty aggressive turn so he was moving right in front of us, a mile and a half, two miles away" (*Minn. Star-Trib.* 9/12/02). But viewed from two miles away, would an airliner have filled the windshield? This exaggeration, if that's indeed what it was, does cast some doubt on O'Brien's narrative.

After Colonel O'Brien reported that he had the airliner in sight, "the controller asked me what kind of plane it was." O'Brien told the FAA that "the plane is either a 757 or 767 and its silver fuselage means it is probably an American Airlines plane" (*NYT* 6/18/04). Next, the FAA instructed the C-130 to follow the Boeing. O'Brien later remarked that in twenty-plus years of flying, "I've never been asked to do something like that" (*NYT* 6/18/04). "The next thing I saw was the fireball" (*Minn. Star-Trib.* 9/12/02).

### Observers Make Troubling Revelations

Startling as it was, Col. O'Brien's account didn't tell the whole story. According to several eyewitnesses, O'Brien's cargo plane not only followed Flight 77 into its downward loop and its final descent to treetop level; it may have done so much more *closely* than he let on. But how would a turboprop cargo plane have been able to keep up with a jetliner reaching 530 miles an hour? That Boeing was a tough act to follow.

Curiously, O'Brien's statements didn't highlight another relevant detail: that his turboprop plane, once back on its way to Minnesota, showed up half an hour later just seventeen miles from where UA Flight 93 crashed in rural Pennsylvania. Moreover, O'Brien's C-130 was one of several aircraft spotted near that crash site.

On-the-ground observers, including military professionals, have added additional, often vivid recollections about the C-130 and the Boeing:

- Air Force officer Allen Cleveland indicated that when he first saw Flight 77, a military plane was flying right behind it. Within 30 seconds of the crash, Cleveland recalled, "I witnessed a military cargo plane (possibly a C-130) fly over the crash site and circle the mushroom cloud. My brother-in-law also witnessed the same plane following the jet …" (http://911research.wtc7.net/pentagon/evidence/witnesses/other.html).

- Pam Young and her brother Keith Wheelhouse were attending a funeral in Arlington National Cemetery when they witnessed two aircraft: "The second plane looked similar to a C-130 transport plane," Wheelhouse told a reporter. "It flew directly above the American Airlines jet, as if to prevent two planes from appearing on radar while at the same time guiding the jet toward the Pentagon" (*Daily Press* [Newport News, Va.] 9/15/01).

This last testimonial is intriguing, since it correctly states that the Pentagon has outfitted its C-130s for electronic warfare (*Independent* [UK] 9/13/02). It also provides a possible answer to the question, Why did O'Brien pursue the airliner after he'd identified it? Was the C-130 possibly controlling its trajectory toward the target? Did the cargo plane's military transponder possibly inhibit air defenses near the Pentagon, providing Flight 77 with radar cover? The role of the C-130 remains yet another enigma.

Whatever the C-130's role, it's hard to miss the irony that a lumbering prop-driven cargo plane actually reached Flight 77—and later, unbelievably, also Flight 93—while supersonic fighters were supposedly unable to reach *any* of the hijacked airliners. If Andrews AFB could launch a C-130 at 9:30, why couldn't it have launched one of its F-16s?

## The Unmistakable Mystery Plane

The C-130, however, wasn't the only plane shrouded in mystery. As noted in Chapter 14, the annual Global Guardian exercise had been moved up to September 11; it put several E-4B "Doomsday planes" into the skies that morning. When a strange plane was filmed crisscrossing the sky above the White House, it wasn't that difficult to identify. With four engines, a white fuselage with a blue "dot," and a telltale "bump" behind a bulging cockpit, these flying command centers are unmistakable. E-4Bs, which are modified Boeing 747-200s, serve as ultra-high-tech flying command centers with extraordinary range of radar vision. According to an Air Force fact sheet, its E-4B is "the world's most advanced electronic war machine" (www.af.mil/factsheets/factsheet.asp?fsID=99).

Just after 9:30 on 9/11, an E-4B was observed circling over central Washington. These sightings accord with the recollections of former counterterrorism expert Richard Clarke, who indicated that reports of a large unidentified aircraft had prompted him to order an evacuation of the White House (Clarke *Against All Enemies* p. 7). CNN reporter John King—one of the journalists who'd seen the mysterious plane on 9/11—explained that because the E-4B was designed "to keep the government running no matter what, even in the event of a nuclear war," it was "nicknamed the Doomsday Plane" (CNN 9/12/07).

Minutes after the Pentagon impact at 9:37, the large, white, stealth jet was captured on videos, including one shot for CNN (www.youtube.com/watch?v=xFNY8r_lrIs). Shot from Lafayette Park, right in front of the White House, the CNN footage contradicts the Pentagon's denial that military aircraft were within the P-56 prohibited area. If this *wasn't* a military plane, how could it have escaped being intercepted or even shot down?

Retired Marine officer Dan Verton claimed that the E-4B had in fact been launched from an airfield near Washington to "conduct a previously scheduled Defense Department exercise." Since NORAD was, as we've seen, conducting the Global Guardian exercise, Verton reasonably surmised "the E-4B may have quit the exercise and become the actual national airborne operations center" (Verton *Black Ice* pp. 143-44). That definitely seems possible, but why, according to many observers, did the flying command center fly off while Fight 93 was still bearing down on the nation's capital?

## Possible Use of E-4B for Continuity of Government (COG)?

What everyone failed to mention, though, was that the E-4B was also designed to serve "as the National Airborne Operations Center for the president, secretary of defense, and the Joint Chiefs of Staff" (www.af.mil/ factsheets/factsheet.asp?fsID=99) after Continuity of Government (COG) was invoked—and that on 9/11, Cheney had ordered its partial implementation (Scott *Road to 9/11* pp. 236-238). Was this state-of-the-art electronic command post deployed, at least in part, to help implement COG?

If most of the public still hasn't heard of COG, that's because the public isn't supposed to know about it: it's still classified. Not surprisingly, the Commission made no mention of the E-4B, of COG, or of Cheney's partial implementation of it (Scott *Road to 9/11* pp. 236-238). Among the possible reasons for the dogged denials by the DoD and Department of Homeland Security, one readily comes to mind: if the Feds had admitted that an E-4B was circling over central Washington, just a few miles from the Pentagon, it would have become much harder for them to claim that Flight 77 wasn't detected long before it reached the capital. If there was more than one E-4B over the mid-Atlantic states—and a similarly Argus-eyed AWACS plane was reported over central Pennsylvania—then it would become even more unlikely that Flight 77 was ever "lost" to military radar.

In addition, any admission that the mystery plane was an E-4B could have presented official storytellers with an even more glaring problem. Griffin has astutely observed "if there was a military plane over Washington at the time, there would have been no need to employ the C-130H cargo plane to identify the aircraft that was approaching the Pentagon"; thus questions would arise about the true purpose of the C-130's diversion to follow Flight 77 (Griffin *9/11 Contradictions* p. 223). But what if the FAA controllers—who, it would seem, opportunistically asked O'Brien to find the plane—didn't have access to the E-4B's data? Then they'd still have needed to identify that fast-moving big blip.

## Massive Amounts of Evidence Impounded at the Pentagon

Researchers have often objected to ongoing government impoundment of Flight 77's cockpit voice recorder, its initial impoundment of the Flight Data Recorders found in the "black boxes," plus many of the FAA and NORAD audiotapes of conversations regarding Flight 77. But the unavailable evidence goes far beyond these impoundments.

Photos taken immediately following the impact depict lawns littered with small pieces of debris as well as pieces of aircraft wreckage. As we've noted, one larger piece with American Airlines markings was documented on the lawn a few hundred feet from the point of impact. These just-after-the-crash photographs also show men in dark slacks and white shirts rapidly removing pieces of wreckage and debris from the lawn: "a column of 50 FBI officers walked shoulder to shoulder across the South grounds of the Pentagon, picking up debris" (*Wash. Post* 9/12/01). How were they able to gather at the impact site and get to work so quickly? If this wasn't a full "Bureau special" operation, it had to come close.

Not only did these "cleanup workers" arrive on the scene with astonishing speed, they moved into violation of federal law prohibiting disturbance of a crime scene. Why were they literally "cleaning up" instead of treating the Pentagon lawn as the crime scene that it was, taking photographs and possibly laying down a grid to help catalog the evidence? Instead of cordoning off the area, as federal law required, they seemed oblivious to protocols for both crash sites and crime scenes. Photographs show them making no attempt to record the positions of objects they're picking up; instead, they appear much like a litter crew along a highway (http://911research.wtc7.net/pentagon/evidence/missing.html).

Much like the other 9/11 crime scenes, authorities immediately seized control of the Pentagon site, destroying or suppressing physical evidence and preventing close, systematic photography by onlookers. Although individual FEMA officials were allowed brief visits starting on September 15, FEMA's full investigative team wasn't allowed on site until all the debris was removed (www.fema.gov/news/newsrelease.fema?id=5679). This was unbelievable, yet the same prohibitions on photography and access also happened at Ground Zero (*Atlantic Monthly* 9/02).

To make matters worse, the NTSB, which ordinarily investigates all US plane crashes, was never allowed to perform a full analysis at the Pentagon. In fact, the NTSB didn't even release the serial number of the plane's Flight Data Recorder, something it ordinarily does as a matter of course. Just to get a sense of how much suppression of evidence has surrounded 9/11, consider that between 1991 and 2006, the NTSB's non-release of reports on the four airliners were the *only* exceptions to this policy (Griffin *New Pearl Harbor Revisited* p. 69). What were the authorities trying to hide? Was the NTSB kept away by others who were orchestrating a cover-up, or was the NTSB itself participating in the cover-up?

Nor was the lawn cleanup the only near-instant intervention that conflicted with standard investigative procedures. Within minutes of the crash, the FBI visited businesses along the plane's flight path which had installed surveillance cameras. At a Citgo station just across the street from the Pentagon, the FBI confiscated a camera that had probably filmed the ill-fated airliner (*Richmond-Times Dispatch* 12/11/01). At the Doubletree Hotel, the FBI seized videotapes from surveillance cameras (*Wash. Times* 9/21/01). And at the Sheraton National Hotel, the FBI impounded a video employees had already replayed in horror (*Inside the Ring* 9/21/01). Nevertheless, the FBI denied the footage had captured the attacking aircraft. Several public-interest groups, including Judicial Watch, have brought Freedom of Information Act suits demanding that federal authorities release these and other confiscated tapes (Judicial Watch 9/15/06).

The military and FBI have shown similar resistance to allowing public access to tapes from the Pentagon's own surveillance cameras, not to mention other evidence. Of an estimated 85 videos, the Feds have released only a few short clips (M. Gaffney *9/11 Mystery Plane* p. 24). When challenged, Federal authorities have evoked the logic of Catch 22, altering their rationale to claim that only the released videos show what was requested, so others need not be released. In short, the issue is not only *what* was impounded, but *how quickly* so much of it disappeared, never to be seen again.

## The Olson-to-Olson Disconnection

While this inquiry tries to avoid dwelling on personalities, putting the spotlight on individuals is sometime unavoidable. The only person who reported receiving a call from Flight 77 was Solicitor General Ted Olson at the Justice Department. Olson, a prominent Washington lawyer, jumped a flight to Florida immediately following the November 2000 election. A couple of weeks later, Olson worked feverishly to bring the Bush versus Gore case before the Supreme Court (*NYT* 11/21/10). Still later, as a member of the Bush administration, Olson led legal efforts to block release of papers from Cheney's Energy Task Force to a committee investigating the Enron scandal. Olson's wife, Barbara, was a conservative commentator on Fox and CNN (Griffin *New Pearl Harbor* pp. 27-28).

Solicitor General Olson's stories changed twice in three days. Olson initially reported that, at about 9:25 and 9:30, his wife Barbara had used her cell phone to call him from Flight 77 (CNN 9/11/01). But three days later he claimed that she'd called him collect, using a seatback phone because she didn't have her purse (Fox 9/14/01). Later that day, Olson told Larry King the second call from Barbara wasn't completed because "the signals coming from cell phones from planes don't work that well" (CNN 9/14/01).

All of these reports seem highly unlikely if not factually impossible, since until the very last four minutes, Flight 77 was too high for cell phones to function and seatback phones required a credit card (Griffin *New Pearl Harbor Revisited* p. 60). Olson had already indicated that the second call had "gone dead": ergo, he'd received no completed calls. The FBI agreed. Five years later, at the trial of "twentieth hijacker" Zacariah Moussaoui, the FBI attributed only *one* call to Barbara Olson: it lasted "zero seconds" (US v. Moussaoui Exhibit P200054).

According to the Official Story, the alleged hijackers reportedly told the passengers that they were going to die and that they should call their families (*Aviation Week* 6/3/02). But researcher Paul Thompson wondered why, "Given this announcement, why are there no phone calls from this flight except for Barbara Olson's?" (Griffin *New Pearl Harbor* p. 28). Assuming her calls did not go through, how could anyone have known the hijackers made such an announcement? What was Olson trying to accomplish? Was he attempting to legitimize the calls made from the airliners or assure that they'd receive maximum media coverage?

## The Convergence: Neocon Background, Aviation Technology, and "Misplaced" Money at Pentagon

Dov Zakheim, a friend of Donald Rumsfeld, was also an old Texas sidekick whom Bush appointed assistant secretary of defense and comptroller for the Pentagon. Zakheim placed himself at the center of several areas of concern and suspicion: neoconservative militarism and contrived provocations for it, remote control technology, and hundreds of billions in accounting "irregularities" among expenditures at the Pentagon. That figure is conservative; on the day before 9/11, Rumsfeld announced that $3.2 *trillion* could not be accounted for (CBS 1/29/02).

## Zakheim's Membership in Neoconservative Pressure Groups

In 1998, two ironically named neocon pressure groups—the Committee for Peace and Security in the Gulf (CPSG); and the Project for the New American Century (PNAC)—sent an "open letter" urging Bill Clinton to overthrow Saddam Hussein. Led by Richard Perle, a former assistant secretary of defense, the group included Elliott Abrams, Richard Armitage, John Bolton, Douglas Feith, William Kristol, Bernard Lewis, Donald Rumsfeld, Casper Weinberger, and Paul Wolfowitz. Dov Zakheim was also a CPSG signatory (CNN 2/20/98).

Less than a year later, Zakheim again emerged as a hard-liner when he joined PNAC. In addition to the names listed just above, PNAC's roster of prominent neocons included Dick Cheney, "Scooter" Libby, and Jeb Bush. PNAC published a "blueprint" for the "creation of a 'global Pax Americana,'" by which it meant global military domination, including the control of space (PNAC *Rebuilding America's Defenses* p. iv). In 1999, Zakheim was among the neocons urging Clinton to end diplomatic efforts in the Balkans. Instead, they argued, the US should take "decisive action" against the Serbs (PNAC 9/11/98). The result was Operation Noble Anvil, 76 days of "shock and awe" courtesy of the USAF (on behalf of NATO) (CNN 6/10/99).

Zakheim also helped author *Rebuilding America's Defenses: Strategy, Forces, and Resources for a New Century*. Published a year before 9/11, this think-tank treatise included that infamous statement: "the process of transformation ... is likely to be a long one, absent some catastrophic and catalyzing event—like a new Pearl Harbor" (PNAC *Rebuilding America's Defenses* p. 51). Since 9/11 became the "catalyzing event" that allowed the neocons to effect "regime change" in Iraq, they've often been suspected of having some role in the attacks. People ask, "Who talked about 'a new Pearl Harbor'?" and "Who benefited?" To the latter query, five answers come to mind: the neocons, the military/industrial complex, the intelligence apparatus, the Bush administration, and Israeli conservatives. Since the 1980s, when he was a hard-liner in Reagan's Pentagon, Zakheim had ties to most of these entities (http://en.wikipedia.org/wiki/Dov_Zakheim).

Just two years later, these same neocons—led by Cheney—would control the Bush administration's national-security machinery.

## Zakheim Deeply Involved in Advanced Aviation Technology

Prior to his appointment by Bush to a high position at the Pentagon, Dov Zakheim was CEO of System Planning Corporation International, a company dealing in advanced technologies that enable aircraft to fly by remote control. System Planning International had marketed the technology needed to take over the controls of a plane already in flight and land it safely. The firm was also involved in high-tech DoD war games (M. Ruppert *Crossing the Rubicon* p. 584). If any of the hijacked airliners did receive high-tech guidance, System Planning might have served as a ready source of the requisite technology.

In 2001, George Bush appointed Zakheim undersecretary of defense and comptroller for the DoD, where he controlled the Pentagon's convoluted, seemingly bottomless accounts. The very day before the attacks, Secretary of Defense Rumsfeld had announced that $2.3 *trillion* had gone "missing" or "unaccounted for" from the Pentagon's budget (DoD 9/10/01). Later, the "misplaced" amount was reported as "only" $700 billion.

## Impact of Airliner Destroyed Important Records

When the smoke cleared, it became clear that one of the most heavily damaged areas of the Pentagon's West Block contained the Army's Office of Financial Management and Records, where auditors were investigating this staggering loss of DoD funds (CBS 1/29/02). If the Pentagon strike destroyed the accounting department, it's surprising that accountants were so quickly able to resolve two thirds of the $2.3 trillion shortfall (Vogel *The Pentagon* p. 431, 449). As Comptroller, Zakheim was tasked with locating the lost $700 billion, but neither he nor anyone else ever made any public accounting of it—except to acknowledge that it was still missing (Ruppert *Crossing the Rubicon* p. 587).

Rumsfeld's disclosure "might have resulted in serious questions from Congress and the press," David Ray Griffin has observed, "if it had been announced at some other time. But it was quickly forgotten the next morning." When 9/11 researcher Barbara Honnegger asked the civilian auditor for the Army whether he believed his office might have been targeted because vast sums had gone missing, he replied in the affirmative—and added that yes, records had been destroyed in the explosion and fire (Griffin *New Pearl Harbor Revisited* pp. 293-94, 104).

## Understanding How Flight 77 Was Flown

Ground observation, radar tracking, and the Flight Data Recorder have indicated that although the airliner was sometimes flown competently, it was more often flown incompetently. How might we determine whether the jetliner was flown by a suicidal amateur pilot, a sophisticated remote control device, or by some combination of the two?

Is it probable that Hani Hanjour, who'd never flown an airliner before, could have taken a Boeing 757 into a 270-degree, 6,000-foot downward loop and zoomed in at 530 mph for a direct hit? This has been one of the great unanswered questions about 9/11. While the Commission made no attempt to resolve this conundrum, looking at Hanjour's biography, technology, and the Flight Data Recorder can help to resolve it.

When we review Hanjour's experience in pilot training, we see a mixed picture. From 1996 through 1999, Hanjour took flying lessons. His instructors frequently found his piloting skills "shoddy" (*NYT* 4/4/01) and one described him as a "terrible pilot" (*Report* p. 520n). While many skeptics have dismissed Hanjour as a complete incompetent, he did take flight training over several years and did qualify for pilot's licenses. Most significantly, perhaps, he was awarded a certificate after completing 60 hours of advanced airliner simulation training (J. Bamford *Shadow Factory* pp. 40, 49).

## FBI Spies on Hanjour

In 1998, FBI informant Aukai Collins, an American and Caucasian Muslim, returned from Afghanistan, where he'd achieved deep penetration of al Qaeda and even received an invitation to meet Osama bin Laden (AP 5/24/02). Back stateside, the FBI assigned Collins to spy on Hani Hanjour and other Arab flight students. Later, Collins disclosed that the FBI "knew everything about the guy," even what car he drove. In 1998, Collins recalled, Hanjour "wasn't even moderately religious, let alone fanatically religious"; he was a "hanky-panky" hijacker who "couldn't even spell *jihad* in Arabic" (A. Collins *My Jihad* p. 343). The FBI has denied that it knew anything about Hanjour before 9/11 (ABC 5/23/02). That denial wouldn't pass the sniff test.

After 9/11, Collins claimed that based on his experience with the FBI and also the CIA, he was very sure that administrators in those agencies knew about the 9/11 attacks in advance and let them happen. To make this accusation, Collins posed a rhetorical question: How, without detection, "could a group of people plan such a big operation full of so many logistics and probably countless e-mails ... plus phone calls and messages? And you're telling me that, through all of that, the CIA never caught wind of it?" (Salon 10/17/02). Since the FBI failed to intervene, the militants—including Hanjour—were able to continue their training.

Hanjour did earn his FAA commercial pilot certificate in 1999 (*NYT* 6/19/02). He returned to Saudi Arabia but was rejected by a civil aviation school. Frustrated, Hanjour "turned his attention toward religious texts and cassette tapes of militant Islamic preachers" (*Boston Globe* 3/3/02). He seemingly fit the profile of the young man who, thwarted in his aspirations, turns to fundamentalism and holy war to find meaning.

When Hanjour returned to the US in 2000, he began training for multi-engine aircraft on a Boeing 737 simulator. According to intelligence expert James Bamford, Hanjour strapped himself in his pilot's seat, "perfected his turns, his control, and his stabilization ... as he prepared for his first multi-engine solo, and his last" (Bamford *Shadow Factory* p. 40). Paying $250 an hour, the pilot-in-training underwent long sessions on the simulator. Revealing a specialized orientation to flying, Hanjour's performance log indicated much practice on "steep turns." Hanjour ordered training videos, but given his special requirements didn't spend much time on "How an Airline Captain Should Look and Act" (Bamford *Shadow Factory* p. 48).

### *Agent Ken Williams Cautions FBI Bosses*

From Phoenix, FBI agent Ken Williams warned superiors about suspicious activities on the part of a group of Middle-Eastern men taking flight training (*Arizona Republic* 7/24/03). In a now-infamous "Phoenix Memo," Williams named nine suspect flight students, including two associates of Hanjour plus others connected to bin Laden (*Wash. Post* 7/25/03). Aware that many of these students were suspiciously well informed about security procedures at American airports, Williams also warned that bin Laden was sending militants to the US to hijack aircraft (*Die Zeit* 10/1/02). The Phoenix Memo alerted eight key FBI supervisors, including Dave Frasca, chief of the Radical Fundamentalist Unit at FBI headquarters, and Jack Cloonan, special agent on the New York FBI's bin Laden unit. In another case of resistance from FBI higher-ups, Williams's repeated pleas for intervention were ignored (JCI *Report* p. 135).

### Hanjour's Last Months as a Flight Student

Starting in the late spring of 2001, Hanjour did a lot of flying. At that time he flew the Hudson River Corridor with a trainer who "declined a second request because of what he considered Hanjour's poor piloting skills." Undaunted, the young Saudi undertook more flight training (*Report* p. 242). When instructors took Hanjour on test runs, they found he had trouble controlling the Cessna 172 (*Newsday* 9/23/01). This was less than a month before Hanjour was slated to fly a "great silver bird." Judging by the difficulties he was continuing to experience, it seems unlikely that Hani Hanjour, unaided, could have flown a Boeing 757. Much would depend on Hanjour's command of the autopilot.

## The Autopilot: Its Navigational and Targeting Capabilities

If Hanjour and other al Qaeda pilots had developed competence on the autopilot, which includes GPS navigational features, the odds for a hijacker pilot do change. Expert researcher Frank Legge suggests that the alleged al Qaeda pilots may have developed specialized expertise: "they could have become reasonably proficient in operating the autopilot, especially if they had focused on the intuitive autopilot mode called Control Wheel Steering (CWS), with which the 757 is equipped" (*Journal of 911 Studies* 9/09).

The NTSB's Flight Path Study established that Flight 77 was flown on autopilot all of the time from takeoff until the hijacking and much of the time during its return to Washington (NTSB Report). As we'd expect, the flight data shows the plane performing very smoothly on autopilot until 8:56. According to Legge, an expert on the Flight Data Recorder (FDR) tape, on the flight back "the autopilot was going in and out of use and [also] being used in a partial manner." In fact, this data showed the airliner making extreme movements: in one instance, it suddenly lost 3,000 feet when the autopilot went off; in another, the airliner held its altitude but lost speed. Questioning the autopilot hypothesis, Legge concludes "this is all very hard to explain as a result of a preprogrammed autopilot function" (Legge Pers. Corresp).

In fact, the FDR tape doesn't suggest programmed control during Flight 77's final eleven minutes in the air. According to Legge, who's studied the tape in minute detail, the data suggests *human* control during this time, with possible autopilot assistance only during the final 90 seconds. As we've seen, Flight 77 approached the Pentagon's West Block from the southwest, taking a three-mile descending arc that carried it into the building. Challenging though it apparently was, this final descent didn't involve reliance on the autopilot (F. Legge and W. Stutt *J. of 911 Studies* 1/11).

If the autopilot were engaged during the final 90 seconds, it was probably in Control Wheel Steering (CWS) Mode. This mode doesn't require setting a course; it simply keeps the plane flying in its current direction and pitch, thereby allowing the pilot to keep his eyes on the scene ahead as he uses controls on the "yoke" to alter heading or pitch (www.gaavionics.com/Autopilots3.htm).

Aviation experts might object, however, and say that you can't "push the envelope" too hard; autopilots include alarms that would *not* allow flying the way Flight 77 did. According to journalist and author Jere Longman, an alarm is set off when the autopilot is disconnected ..." (Longman *Among the Heroes* p. 208). Legge points out, however, that alarms could have been turned off, assuming the pilot knew how to do so. (Legge Pers. Corresp.). So we're back to the toughest riddle to solve: Did Hani Hanjour or some other hijacker pilot fly Flight 77? A tentative answer is a qualified "yes, though possibly not without outside assistance." If the cockpit voice recorder were released, this and many other issues could be resolved.

- Citing one of his mentors, the great Alfred North Whitehead, Griffin reminded us that "the moral temperament required for the pursuit of truth [is] an unflinching determination to take the whole evidence into account" (Whitehead *Science in the Modern World* p. 167). In this case, as in so much about 9/11, the "whole evidence" is simply not available. Nor, apparently, was it intended to be. We're left, then, with that array of unanswered questions:
- How was it possible an hour and twenty minutes after the attacks first began and seventeen minutes after the "lost" airliner, Flight 77, had appeared on radar screens at Dulles, that no defenses were activated?
- Why have the official accounts misrepresented both the actual flight path and the amount of time that Flight 77 flew around the Washington area?
- Why was there no fighter response from Andrews Air Force Base, located just ten miles from the Pentagon, home to Air National Guard units charged with defending the nation's capital?
- What was an E-4B doing in restricted airspace over the White House at the time of the Pentagon attack? Why were this plane's extraordinary radar capabilities apparently not used to observe intruders and protect Washington?
- What was the actual role, if any, of the C-130 in the final moments of Flight 77?

- Above all, as scientific researchers David Chandler and Jon Cole aptly ask, "How could the Pentagon, the hub of the US military, have been so poorly defended that it could be hit in the first place, [especially] after the buildings in New York had already been hit and other hijacked planes were known to still be in the air?" (http://911blogger.com/news/2011-01-01/joint-statement-pentagon-david-chandler-and-jon-cole#new)

Along with many others, these are questions that only a genuine, fully resourced international investigation will be able to answer.

Much as no one hypothesis can explain all the evidence, no one chapter can cover all facets of an issue as complex as Flight 77 and the Pentagon. For further information, readers are referred to the timelines prepared by Paul Thompson (http://www.historycommons.org/entity.jsp?entity=pentagon) and the presentation of crash-site evidence ably assembled by Jim Hoffman (http://911research.wtc7.net/pentagon/official/index.html).

Like WTC Building 7, much about Flight 77 and the Pentagon remain a mystery, a riddle wrapped in an enigma.

# 20. Flight 93: Legends and Realities

*The news media are very reluctant to challenge a story they love so much.*

—Will Bunch, *Philadelphia Daily News* reporter
who did onsite investigation into Flight 93

Even more than in most other areas of 9/11, discrepancies divide the Official Story of UA Flight 93 from a more fact-based account. Whereas the standard narrative emphasizes cell phone calls from passengers and the utter failures of air defenders to respond, fuller accounting tells a different story. Additional evidence also invites us to reexamine the time of impact, physical evidence at the crash site, real-time eyewitness testimonials, reports of shoot-down orders, and FBI mishandling of the crime scene.

As a springboard into these issues, let's summarize the familiar Official Story.

## The Commission's Account: A Short Version

United Airlines Flight 93, headed for San Francisco, took off from Newark at 8:42 am, 25 minutes late. The Boeing 757 flew west for 46 minutes, reaching a cruising altitude of 35,000 feet. At 9:24, the pilots made their last regular radio communication. Two minutes later, the pilots received a warning to lock the cabin doors and to "beware of any cockpit intrusion." Then at 9:28, over northeastern Ohio, the hijackers attacked. As the plane suddenly dropped 700 feet, air traffic controllers heard a voice crying "Mayday" along with sounds of "physical struggle in the cockpit." Three times the first officer shouted "Hey, get out of here," followed by more screaming and scuffling. Although teams of five did the other alleged hijackings, here there were only four (*Report* p. 11).

Just west of Cleveland, Flight 93 suddenly veered south, making a 180-degree turn, and began to streak southeast toward the nation's capital. Four minutes later, at 9:32, air-traffic controllers overheard someone announcing "we have a bomb on board" and commanding passengers to "remain seated." Pilot Ziad Jarrah inadvertently broadcast his message because he "did not know how to operate the radio and the intercom" (*Report* p. 12).

By 9:34, a passenger had called his wife, and a flight attendant had notified United Airlines that its Flight 93 was hijacked. A United employee contacted the company's errant airliner, but did not notify NORAD. At 9:41, the hijackers turned off the plane's transponder beacon. At 9:56, the FAA changed the plane's flight plan, entering a new destination: Reagan National Airport in Washington (*St. Petersburg Times* 9/12/01). In the half hour following the takeover, at least ten passengers and crew members made phone calls, most of them from cell phones, along with some GTE Airfones, that shared crucial information with friends and families on the ground (*Report* pp. 12-13).

At 9:57, the Official Story told us, passenger Todd Beamer shouted, "Are you guys ready? Let's roll" (J. Longman *Among the Heroes* p. 118); then Beamer and others led the revolt against the hijackers. As passengers beat against the cockpit door, pilot Jarrah "immediately began to roll the airplane to the left and right, attempting to knock the passengers off balance." After urging another hijacker to block the door, Jarrah pitched the nose of the plane up and down and finally flew it upside down. Discouraged, the hijackers decided to "pull it down" and Jarrah threw the airliner into a towering nosedive. At 10:03, according to the Commission, Flight 93 "hit the ground nearly vertically from about 30,000 feet, traveling at 580 mph." The Boeing cratered into an empty field near Shanksville in Somerset County, Pennsylvania (*Report* p. 14).

At 10:07, so the Official Story goes, the FAA finally informed NORAD of the hijacking, too late for military intervention. And at 10:15, the FAA advised NORAD that Flight 93 had crashed.

When the Commission told this lively tale, it presented a mixture of fact and fiction. This isn't surprising, for as Chomsky and others have pointed out, the most engaging fictions often include some facts. The Commission's account focused on the actions of the passengers when the most important issues lay elsewhere.

**Controlling the Narrative: What the Official Story Didn't Say**

Media popularizers found well-known meanings in the passenger revolt: that heroic "regular" Americans rose up and thwarted a terrorist attack, saved the lives of their leaders in Washington, and had begun to fight the War on Terror before the president had declared it.

When the official narrative recounted the signs of trouble aboard, it typically ignored the lack of response to them. It indicates that flight controllers had overheard sounds of an In Flight Emergency (*Report* p. 12) and had noted radio silence, a transponder turnoff, and a wide deviation from the airliner's assigned flight path. This latter departure alone should have grabbed attention. Only a slight change of direction alarms flight controllers: "If a plane deviates by fifteen degrees," reported one corporate new outlet, "the controllers will hit the panic button" (MSNBC 9/12/01). Why, then, didn't Flight 93's 180-degree turn set red lights blinking? How could controllers have received all these blatant signs of a hijacking and *not* have realized they were dealing with an emergency?

The Commission's answer was to paint a picture of complete incompetence at the FAA. It cited one FAA functionary sighing, "Uh, do we want to think, uh, about scrambling aircraft?" (*Report* p. 29). "To accept this account," remarked Canadian media critic Barrie Zwicker, "we must believe that, on a day on which there had already been attacks by hijacked airliners, officials at FAA headquarters had to debate whether a hijacked airliner with a bomb on board was important enough to disturb the military" (Zwicker *Towers of Deception* p. 87). By highlighting such unprofessional, indifferent responses, the Commission made the FAA "take the fall," exonerated the military, and avoided implicating Bush administration officials.

**FAA Accepts New Flight Plan for Hijacked Airliner**

Although the Commission usually portrayed the FAA as bunglers, it made no mention of a bizarre request for—and the FAA's odd acceptance of—a new flight plan for the hijacked United 93. At 9:36, as the plane began its 180-degree turn and began to streak for Washington, one of the hijacker pilots asked the FAA for a new flight plan. The new destination? Reagan National Airport near Washington (ABC 9/13/01).

This request for change of destination occurred after planes had already hit the Twin Towers, after FAA controllers had declared Flight 77 "lost," and while that airliner was zeroing in on the Pentagon, tracked by the Secret Service and Cheney in the bunker. It also came ten minutes after the FAA had called for a "national ground stop" (*Time* 9/14/01) and was about to order all nonmilitary aircraft to "land at nearest appropriate airport" (*Newsday* 9/10/02). Why would hijackers request an unusual change in destination, thereby revealing a short list of likely targets? Flight Explorer, a software company that works from FAA data, also found the request odd. The company's CEO remarked, "we hardly ever get a plan change. Very unusual" (*Wash. Business Journal* 9/11/01). Somehow, the FAA's entry of the new flight path rarely made the news.

**Eyewitness Reports on a Desperate Final Descent**

When the Official Story talked of a terminal dive from 30,000 feet, it didn't jibe with most eyewitness reports. Most suggested that the low-flying, faltering airliner descended gradually and sputtered or spun out of control before taking a downturn:

- Just before 10:00, from the tower at the Jamestown-Cambria Airport, Dennis Fritz received a call from the FAA's Cleveland Center asking him to look for a large aircraft "descending below 6,000 feet" (*Pitts. Post-Gazette* 9/12/01). This radar coverage challenged not only the Commission's assertion of a high-altitude plunge but also its claim that "dead spots" over rural areas contributed to FAA difficulties tracking Flight 77 on its way toward the Pentagon.

- Ten miles from Shanksville, Rodney Peterson and Brandon Leventry observed Flight 93 as its wings "dipped sharply to the left, then to the right" (*Pitts. Post-Gazette* 9/12/01). Reinforcing this observation, the National Transportation Safety Board (NTSB) found that at 9:59, "the airplane was at 5,000 feet when about two minutes of rapid full left and right control inputs resulted in multiple 30-degree rolls left and right" (NTSB Flight Path Study).
- From a scrap yard a quarter mile from the crash site, Lee Purbaugh lifted his welder's mask to glimpse the stricken plane: "there it was, right there, right above my head ..." (*Independent* [UK] 8/13/02). "It was coming down in a 45-degree angle and rocking from side to side" (*Daily* [UK] *Mirror* 8/13/02).

Most observers saw an airliner faltering, rocking, or flying upside down, all at low altitudes; no one reported a nosedive from 30,000 feet. But altering the account of the plane's final demise was far from the most important of the omissions.

While the Official Story told of fighter aircraft scrambled from two NORAD bases, it placed them mostly over the Atlantic Ocean, New York, and Washington. Although it didn't talk about interceptors over Pennsylvania, several credible reports have placed them there.

**Pilot Receives Order to Shoot Down Airliner**
Although few Air Force flyers have talked about what went on over Pennsylvania, Lt. Anthony Kuczynski did make an explosive revelation. Lt. Kuczynski disclosed that on the morning of 9/11, he'd flown E-3 Sentry Airborne Warning and Control System (AWACS), a "flying radar platform" loaded with advanced electronics equipment. Like the E-4B spotted over the White House, the E-3 is a flying command and control center: its radar has a range of at least 250 miles (www.af.mil/factsheets/factsheet. asp?fsID=98).

That morning, Lt. Kuczynski and his crew were directing two F-16s: "I was given direct orders to shoot down an airliner" (*Aquin* 4/12/02). Among the many implications of this statement, none is more important than its serious challenge to the Commission's claim that the military had no notification on Flight 93 until 10:07, after it crashed (*Report* p. 30). This disclosure raised a myriad of additional questions: Was the E-3 AWACS on a regular mission over Pennsylvania, or was it ordered there on 9/11? What other purpose did the E-3 pursue as it cruised over southern Pennsylvania? Were its immense radar-tracking capabilities engaged? Who issued a shoot-down order?

Nor was Lt. Kuczynski's recollection the only report of F-16 activity over Pennsylvania. Shortly before the crash, two F-16s reportedly tailed Flight 93 before it went down at 10:06 (CBS 9/11/01). News sources featured local eyewitnesses who spoke of seeing both the airliner and interceptor jets (Reuters 9/13/01). One flight controller, ignoring an FBI order not to talk to the media, indicated that FAA employees "learned from controllers at other facilities that an F-16 'stayed in hot pursuit' of the Boeing 757 ..." (AP 9/13/01). If true, these reports contradict the official narrative; they verify that fighters *were* trailing the hijacked airliner, and they strongly suggest that the FAA *was* in fact able to track the flight.

**Officials First Acknowledge, Then Deny F-16s in Area**
In the first few days after 9/11, the authorities waffled back and forth, uncertain of their story. The day after 9/11, Maj. Gen. Paul Weaver, director of the Air National Guard, denied that planes were ever scrambled to go after Flight 93 (*Seattle Times* 9/16/01). Two days after the crash, the FBI initially confirmed the fighter sightings, albeit vaguely: "Agent [Andrew] Crowley confirmed that there were *two other aircraft* within 25 miles of the United flight [93] that were heading *east* when it crashed ..." (*Pitts. Tribune Review* 9/14/01) (Italics mine). These could have been F-16s which, since they reportedly trailed Flight 93, would also have been heading east.

At the highest levels, the Defense Department also affirmed that, yes, fighters *were* active in the area. Trying to pin a smile button on the biggest military failure in US history, Deputy Defense Secretary Paul Wolfowitz reminded the public that "we responded awfully quickly..." but "I think it was the heroism of the passengers on board that brought it down" (PBS "NewsHour" 9/14/01). Wolfowitz' statements not only suggest how quickly the saga of heroic passengers bringing down the plane had taken shape but also how badly the Pentagon wanted to deny a shoot down while claiming that its defenders made a robust response.

Within a week, though, Pentagon spokespersons would pull the F-16s farther and farther back from the doomed airliner, completely out of range. When military sources reported that two F-16s had tailed Flight 93, they insisted that the fighters were 60 miles away when it went down (CBS 9/16/01). Two days later, NORAD has its jets remaining 100 miles away (NORAD 9/18/01). Validating the fighter reports could only feed lingering suspicions that a missile had struck Flight 93—thereby making the valiant passenger revolt seem futile. Few saw that it was the *act* of rebellion, not the outcome, that mattered most.

## Other Mysterious Players in the Sky

Although the FAA's "national ground stop" was an immense success, three planes were reported flying near Flight 93 well after the FAA's command to clear the skies. The first two provide insight into what controllers were trying to do, but the last remains an enigma.

### Piper Arrow and C-130 Also Asked to Locate Flight 93

Still aloft over Youngwood, Pennsylvania, Bill Wright was piloting a Piper Arrow. Just minutes before 10:00, he received a call from FAA flight controllers. But instead of insisting that he land, as Wright expected, the controllers asked him to look out his window for UA Flight 93. The puzzled pilot did spot the airliner three miles away, noting its blue-and-white United Airlines colors as it rocked back and forth three or four times (WTAE-TV 9/19/01). The controllers first inquired about the airliner's altitude, then told Wright "to get as far away from it as fast as he could" (WTAE-TV 9/19/01).

Readers will recall that at 9:32 air traffic controllers in Washington had asked Col. Steve O'Brien's unarmed C-130 cargo plane to identify Flight 77 as it began its downward turn before slamming into the Pentagon (*Report* p. 30). In one of many coincidences that took place on 9/11, this same C-130 showed up for the final moments of *another* hijacked airliner, Flight 93, which crashed a half hour later and 125 miles away. In a replay of the order O'Brien received to inspect the damage at the Pentagon, a controller asked Col. O'Brien to circle Flight 93's crash site (*Report* p. 30). What are the odds that the same cargo plane, on the same morning, would show up where two hijacked airliners were going down, and then be tasked with locating both and surveying their crash sites?

### The Phantom White Jet's Flyover

If the requests going to the Piper Arrow and the C-130 strike us as bizarre, the presence of a white jet was even more so. In one of the most mysterious, most suspicious episodes in 9/11 lore, a still-unidentified white jet swooped low, crisscrossing the area around the crash site. At least a dozen eyewitnesses reported seeing this phantom plane before and after the crash. According to one reputable British paper, observers "described this plane as a small white jet with rear engines and no discernible markings" (*Independent* [UK] 8/13/02).

Many eyewitnesses saw the phantom white jet. Lee Purbaugh, who'd raced to the crash site, recalled that "it was white and it circled the area about twice and then it flew off" (*Mirror* [UK] 9/13/02). Jim Brant also noticed a white plane "circling the wreckage." Another witness, Tom Spinelli, "saw the white plane ... flying around all over the place like it was looking for something.... The plane had no markings on it, either civilian or military" (Morgan *Flight 93 Revealed* p. 144). Bob Page spotted a white jet above the crash site before it shot almost vertically into the sky. He knew immediately that "it sure wasn't no puddle jumper" (*Pitts. Tribune-Review* 9/12/01).

Finally, eyewitness Susan McElwain recalled that just before the concussion thundered through the hills, a white jet without discernible markings "swooped low ... and disappeared over a hilltop" (*Bergen* [NJ] *Record* 9/14/01). "It was white with no markings but it was definitely military." When FBI agents came to question McElwain, they "did not want my story—nobody here did." One agent even told her she'd seen no such plane; another informed her she must have seen a plane taking pictures from 3,000 feet (*Mirror* [UK] 9/13/02).

The phantom white jet didn't fit the story the Feds had decided to tell.

## Other Outlandish Explanations for the White "Business Jet"

This was not the only bizarre behavior at the FBI. At 9:58, an emergency call (apparently from passenger Edward Felt) reported that hijackers had taken over Flight 93—and that he'd heard an explosion and seen smoke. Judging by its response, the FBI had monitored this call. In near real time, at a field office near Pittsburgh, Special Agent Wells Morrison learned that a large plane had crashed in Somerset County (*Pitts. Tribune-Review* 4/13/03); the crash, however, wasn't his top priority. Agent Morrison first sent another agent to impound the tape of Felt's 911 call; next he called the FBI's Johnstown office, commanding agents there to rush to the airport (G. Kashurba *Courage After the Crash* pp. 109-10). Then, after dispatching other agents to the crash site, Morrison sped there himself (*Wash. Post* 9/12/01).

Patrick Madigan, a commander with the State Police, also arrived at the crash scene about 10:20. As Madigan looked up, a white jet was "circling the crash site very low." The commander was left scratching his head until an FBI agent informed him that a Fairchild Falcon 20 business jet was allowing United Airlines executives to view the disaster before landing at nearby Johnstown Airport (Kashurba *Courage After the Crash* pp. 60, 110, 63). How, one has to wonder, would this agent know that it was a *United* flight that crashed a few minutes before? And how could he possibly have known who was inside the "business jet"?

Afterward, the FBI dropped the United executives but clung to its claim that the white jet was a Fairfield Falcon (*Independent* [UK] 9/13/02). Contradicting the FBI field agent, the Pentagon claimed that it could "neither confirm nor deny" any of these mysterious nearby planes (*Pitts. Tribune-Review* 9/14/01). "Neither confirm nor deny" is Pentagonese, code language for "we're not going to tell you because Pentagon business is none of yours." But it can also mean, "yeah, it's true, but we don't talk about that."

Neither the FAA, the Pentagon, nor the FBI has ever identified the white jet, its pilot, or its actual mission (*Daily Mirror* [UK] 8/1/02).

## Commission Changes Time of Impact

In another strategic switch, the Commission manipulated the time of Flight 93's final plunge. Until the Commission's *Report* came out in 2004, the time of the crash had rarely been listed as earlier than 10:06, though one source did have it later. FAA controllers in Cleveland had indicated that the plane disappeared from their screens at this time (*Pitts. Post-Gazette* 12/28/01). In 2002 a seismic study sponsored by the Army, Columbia University, and the Maryland Geological Survey pinpointed the crash at 10:06:05 (Griffin *New Pearl Harbor Revisited* p. 121).

The Commission probably changed the time of impact for one or more of the following reasons. When it moved the time of impact forward to 10:03 (*Report* pp. 13-14), its apparent intent was to bring its official narrative into compliance with the cockpit voice recording, which the FBI claimed had cut off at 10:03. While some journalists had reported a "three-minute discrepancy in the tape" (*Phila. Daily News* 9/16/02), the Commission's account implied that the tape ran right up to the moment of impact. By leaving this impression, the Commission may have sought to quash questions about what happened in the plane's ultimate moments.

### Avoidance of the Shoot-Down Issue

Faced with persistent reports of a shoot down, the Commission finally had to put any such suspicions to rest. Judging by the changes it made for the Official Story, the Commission felt it important not just to deny that a shoot down had occurred, but to rearrange the times of preceding events so that one would seem completely impossible. It may have needed, above all, to tell a story making it seem impossible that the Secret Service, commanded by Cheney, could have ordered a shoot down.

To do all this, the Commission needed to avoid the fact that the Secret Service was receiving FAA reports on aircraft in *real time*. Dick Cheney, who ran the Secret Service from the White House bunker that morning, would seem like the last person to talk about this special arrangement. Yet he too revealed this special hookup, however inadvertently, on "Meet the Press": "The Secret Service has an arrangement with the FAA. They had open lines after the World Trade Center was—" The vice president stopped midsentence, and interviewer Tim Russert fumbled the opportunity for a follow-up (NBC 10/16/01). Cheney apparently preferred to avoid discussing the fact that, as acting commander in chief, he was receiving real-time information from the FAA—and that this info could have allowed him to order action (or inaction) in response to incoming aircraft.

So even if the FAA didn't formally notify the military in time for it to scramble interceptors, the Secret Service would have learned about hijacked aircraft as soon as the FAA detected them. Moreover, the Secret Service was able to order military interventions, as Cheney nearly did until he waved off the young lieutenant (www.youtube.com/watch?v=bDfdOwt2v3Y). The key question was, *When* did this incident take place—before or after Flight 93 went down?

The sensitivity of the real-time tracking and shoot-down issues—particularly Cheney's possible involvement in them—may have also driven the Commission's new timetable. Finally, we're told, air defenders at NEADS didn't learn that Flight 93 had been hijacked until 10:07, after its crash, so its jets couldn't have tracked it (*Report* p. 30), let alone shot it down. But the claim that NEADS couldn't have tracked Flight 93 doesn't square with proof that the military received information about Flight 93 well before it crashed, possibly even before it was hijacked (Griffin *New Pearl Harbor Revisited* pp. 123-26).

Again we return to the crucial testimony of Transportation Secretary Norman Mineta (www.youtube.com/watch?v=bDfdOwt2v3Y), which the Commission tried so hard to suppress. Mineta opened the intriguing probability that the Secret Service (Cheney) was notified about hijacked aircraft before NORAD. If this was the case, then another question arose: Did Cheney and the Secret Service command the fighters—and possibly authorize military action—*directly*, without authorization from NORAD?

It might be objected that the Secret Service could only give orders to Andrews AFB, home to Air Force One. That morning, however, the Secret Service intervened to command the F-16s from Langley AFB. Capt. "Borgy" Borgstrom, the lead F-16 pilot from Langley, stated that he received "garbled orders" to "protect the White House at all costs by order of the vice president" (*NYT* 11/15/01). If "Borgy" was telling the truth, then Cheney had seemingly exceeded his authority. And if those fighters received "shootdown authority directly from the Secret Service, bypassing the military" (Spencer *Touching History* p. 223), then Cheney was possibly twice in breach. He was neither authorized to command NORAD's jets nor to initiate stand-down or shoot-down orders.

**White House Pressures Commission to Accept Cheney's Account**

If the question of Cheney possibly ordering a stand down or a shoot down weren't sensitive enough, the question of whether he received presidential authorization became a hypersensitive issue. As the 9/11 Commission went about finishing its business, "Cheney's version of events" wasn't playing well. Some of the Commission's staffers believed Cheney ordered a shoot down before he had authorization from the president. To its credit, *Newsweek* was courageous enough to report "some on the Commission staff [are], in fact, highly skeptical of the vice president's account...." Some were skeptical about the widely discussed phone call from Bush to Cheney; others "flat out didn't believe the call ever took place" (*Newsweek* 6/20/04).

When an early draft of the *Report* circulated among top administration officials, it provoked a strong reaction. Surprisingly, though, a White House spokesman didn't deny the allegation; he just claimed it didn't accord with the official version of events: "We didn't think it was written in a way that clearly reflected the accounting the president and vice president had given to the Commission." When the White House forcefully lobbied the Commission to change the language, Kean and Hamilton caved: "the chairman and vice chair of the Commission ... agreed to remove some of the offending language. The *Report* 'was watered down,' groused one staffer" (*Newsweek* 6/20/04).

# Shanksville: An Initially Puzzling Impact Site

Alerted by roaring engines, a loud boom, a fireball, and a column of smoke, first responders and locals arrived at the crash site in the minutes after impact. Most reported finding a smoldering crater. Estimates of the hole's size ranged from 15 to 30 feet wide and 30 to 35 feet deep. This does seem small, to be sure, though the plane's wings also left imprints in the soft Earth (MSNBC 9/11/01).

**Big Plane, Small Crater, Little Observable Debris**

Many of those first on the scene commented on seeing surprisingly little aircraft wreckage or debris. Since Somerset County Coroner Wallace Miller expected to find dismembered bodies, he was baffled by the absence of remains: "you would have thought no one was on the plane" (Longman *Among the Heroes* p. 217). However, in the following weeks, several hundred pounds of human remains were retrieved from the surrounding area (*Wash. Post* 5/12/02).

In part, this was about preconceptions. While the coroner was looking through his professional lens and seeing no bodies, he was far from alone in bringing preconceptions. Immersed as we are in a culture of visual media, most of us have absorbed mental images about what a crash scene looks like. Since sites with big hunks of fuselage get covered in the media more fully than those that lack them, we expect to see large pieces at a crash site. Journalists working in visual media also carry these images. Jon Meyer, a reporter with WJAC-TV, recalled "all I saw was a crater filled with small, charred plane parts. Nothing that would even tell you that it was the plane ... no suitcases, no recognizable plane parts, no body parts" (C. Trost *Running Toward Danger* p. 148).

Jetliner impact sites do vary, however. At the Shanksville site, Frank Monaco of the State Police reported "there's nothing but tiny pieces of debris" (*Pitts. Post-Gazette* 9/12/01). Yet Continental Flight 3407, which crashed near Buffalo, left little to see beyond a pile of smoldering debris. One first responder exclaimed, "there was nothing there, only part of a wing and a landing gear jutting toward the sky" (*NYT* 2/14/09). Other high-speed crashes of airliners, including that of Flight 77 at the Pentagon, have also largely reduced the aircraft to "confetti" fragments. While the Continental crash seems roughly equivalent to the Pentagon in terms of visible aircraft debris, other sites have exhibited even less (http://911research.wtc7.net/pentagon/official/index.html).

It's fair to ask why Flight 93 didn't follow the typical pattern and leave more wreckage around its crash site. The short answers are, the earth at the crash site was exceptionally soft, and the aircraft clearly wasn't intact when it hit.

### Debris and Remains Scattered over Vast Area

Although little debris other than fragmented metal was found near the charred crater, important evidence dropped over many square miles. Right at the crash site, Shanksville Fire Chief Rick King saw only small fires. But farther from the point of impact, he also noticed "small chunks of yellow honeycomb insulation dangling like ornaments from some of the trees" plus "some shirts, pants, and loose papers scattered among the branches" (Thomas *Days of Deception* pp. 192-93). Local residents collected shopping bags of "clothing, books, papers, and what appeared to be human remains," all of which they turned over to federal authorities (*Pitts. Post-Gazette* 9/13/01).

An investigative program on 9/11 by Japanese Asahi TV indicated ten locations where locals had found aircraft parts. A photo made public five years after the crash shows "metallic debris found a mile from the impact crater" (Morgan *Flight 93 Revealed* pp. 127-28, 135). Although the fallout from Flight 93 was spread over at least five square miles (Zwicker *Towers of Deception* pp. 86-87) it was concentrated in several debris fields. The first of these was a mile from the crater; a second centered around Indian Lake, three miles away; and a third was situated near New Baltimore, eight miles east of the crash site (CNN 9/13/01).

Nearly a mile away, a half-ton piece of engine was found (*Pitts. Tribune-Review* 9/11/02). "This was the single heaviest piece recovered from the crash," reported one British paper, "and the biggest, apart from a piece of fuselage the size of a dining-room table" (*Independent* [UK] 8/13/02). Once again, the official theorizing didn't explain the physical evidence. Although the ground at the site was a reclaimed strip mine and therefore demonstrably soft, and although the massive plane's engines weighed six tons each, the FBI maintained that this piece must have "bounced," landing a mile away—and that paper debris must have wafted on the wind for eight miles (*Independent* [UK] 9/13/02). That's a big, big stretch.

More distant debris fields presented an even greater challenge to the received narrative. Moments after hearing an explosion, workers at Indian Lake Marina saw a cloud of flaming confetti-like debris dropping on the lake and nearby farms (*Pitts. Post-Gazette* 9/13/01). John Fleegle, who operated the marina, reported "a piece of fuselage the size of a table [including two windows] dropped into the lake, about three miles from the crater" (*Independent* [UK] 8/13/02). Still farther from the crash site, witnesses found more human remains plus another chunk from a jet engine. State Police

Maj. Lyle Szupinka reported that searchers located the jet turbine fully eight miles away from the crash scene (CBS 5/23/02). Indeed, much of the evidence, both anecdotal and forensic, pointed to an airliner that had broken up in flight.

## No Crime Scene Investigation (CSI)

If ever a crime scene called for a professional investigation, this was it. The news media emphasized how little wreckage was visible and how small the crater was; but some also reported that "the debris here is spread over a three to four mile radius, which has now been completely sealed off and is being treated, according to the FBI, as a crime scene" (NBC/Fox 9/11/01). For thirteen days, 150 FBI agents searched the crater, and supported by the National Guard, fanned out over the large debris fields. Agents moved with great haste to seize evidence and intimidate locals into not talking to the news media (A. Lappe *True Lies*).

Just as the crash site wasn't treated as a crime scene, the debris fields weren't treated forensically either. While the FBI did seal off the immediate area, the purpose was hardly to ensure scientific analysis of clues. Professional protocols weren't followed. Claiming it would be too time-consuming, the Bureau discarded a plan to map the area and mark the positions of debris to determine how the flight crashed (Longman *Among the Heroes* p. 262). Most of the evidence collected was never seen again, and no report ever appeared. The reason for this unprofessionalism, it's long seemed, was simple: the scattered debris strongly suggested that the Boeing which made the small crater couldn't have been *intact*.

In no way did this resemble the thorough crime scene investigations of past. In 1996, TWA Flight 800 crashed off Long Island, killing 230 people. Following the disaster, navy divers did extensive salvage work to retrieve pieces of the ill-fated airliner, and FBI boats trolled the ocean floor, dredging up 96 percent of the wreckage (www.navy.mil/navydata/navy_legacy_hr.asp?id=284). For Flight 800, federal agencies had conducted a thorough investigation; for Flight 93, nothing of the sort took place. The FBI didn't undertake a probe even remotely resembling the one that it, the NTSB, and the Navy had done five years earlier. Nor did the Bureau follow the strict "yellow-ribbon" forensics protocol it had enforced at other terrorist crime scenes, such as the 1996 bomb blast area at Khobar Towers in Saudi Arabia (L. Freeh *My FBI* p. 4).

## A Focus on Hijacker Personal Effects

While the FBI silenced witnesses and suppressed evidence, it immediately publicized the retrieval of politically charged personal effects allegedly found at the crash site. Such evidence kept the focus on the alleged hijackers, diverting attention from the pieces of the plane and the question of what happened to it.

At the site itself, the FBI was thorough, even enterprising, and its findings included some odd items. Despite the disintegration of the plane, the scorched earth, and charred wreckage, the FBI announced that it had recovered personal effects belonging to the alleged hijackers. Most notably, these included a red bandana and a slightly burned passport issued to the alleged pilot, Ziad Jarrah (*Athens Banner-Herald* 9/10/04). Other objects found reportedly included a Saudi passport belonging to alleged hijacker Saeed al Ghamdi plus a Saudi ID card and a Florida driver's license belonging to alleged hijacker Ahmed al Nami (*US v. Z. Moussaoui* 2006). The address on the license was 10 Radford Blvd., Pensacola, Florida—that of a base famous for Navy aviation (Morgan *Flight 93 Revealed* p. 48). Was al Nami among the al Qaeda operatives who took flight training at US military bases? If so, and finders or fabricators of the ID didn't know recognize the address, that's a good chuckle.

Since all these items apparently belonged to alleged hijackers, most of whom were presumably situated in the nose of the plane, their bodies must have been crushed beyond recognition when the plane nose-dived into the earth. So, we're told, was nearly everything else at the site. Whatever was left of the plane apparently disintegrated or buried itself in the soft earth; everything around the crater was charred and smoldering. Given that so little else survived amid the fragmented metal, pulverized debris, and pulped flesh, how could so many of the hijackers' possessions have come through nearly intact (Morgan *Flight 93 Revealed* pp. 126-27)?

Given all these improbabilities, could someone have planted some of these items? Civil rights lawyers have long protested the practice of planting evidence on suspects, and such malfeasance possibly also occurred at the WTC crash site.

### Top Brass Waffle about Shoot-Down Approval and Interception

During the first few days, officials did talk about—or at least hint at—a shoot down. When Gen. Richard Myers, Chairman of the Joint Chiefs on 9/11, came before a Senate hearing, Sen. Carl Levin (D-Mich.) observed "there have been statements that the aircraft that crashed in Pennsylvania was shot down," and "those stories continue to exist." Moving toward a cautious but categorical denial, Gen. Myers stated that fighters were scrambled "on the [airliner] that eventually crashed in Pennsylvania.… [W]e had gotten somebody close to it." Without explaining why the stories persisted among insiders, Gen. Myers emphasized that "the armed forces did not shoot down any aircraft" (Sen. Armed Services Comm. 9/13/01).

Within a few days, though, military commanders got on the same page, claiming that starting about 9:36, though perhaps earlier, NORAD was tracking Flight 93 and getting ready to shoot it down, if necessary.

- **Gen. Larry Arnold**, NORAD's commander for the continental United States, indicated that he had been "anxious to see what 93 was going to do, and our intent was to intercept it.… I had every intention of shooting down United 93 if it continued to progress toward Washington DC." General Arnold added that NORAD was all ready to "take lives in the air to save lives on the ground" (L. Filson *Air War* p. 73).
- **Col. Robert Marr**, Commander of NEADS, similarly insisted that "Flight 93 would not have hit Washington DC. [The hijacker pilot] would have been engaged and shot down before he got there." Reporting that NEADS received timely shoot-down authorization, Col. Marr said "we received the clearance to kill if need be" (Filson *Air War* p. 73). In fact, both Arnold and Marr maintained that they were tracking Flight 93 early on—possibly even before it was hijacked— and had received shoot-down approval by around 9:40 (Comm. Staff Statement #17). Flight 93 was in the air for another 23 to 26 min.

- **Gen. David Wherley**, who commanded the DC Air National Guard, recalled that "within a half-hour" of the hijacking, probably about 10:00, he received "oral instructions from the White House [of Cheney] giving pilots extraordinary discretion to shoot down any threatening aircraft" (*Wash. Post* 4/8/02). This revelation is important. Since Gen. Wherley was base commander at Andrews AFB and the fighters there were under the direct command of the Secret Service, this meant, as we've seen, that Cheney ordered military action outside the chain of command. Secondly, Cheney's order strongly implied that, contrary to government claims, Andrews *did* have fighters available that morning (www.andrews.af.mil/units/index.asp).

- **Gen. Montague Winfield Reveals Even More** While Arnold and Marr had hinted at early notification for Flight 93, Gen. Montague Winfield was more explicit. He recalled that the Pentagon's National Military Command Center (NMCC) had "received the report from the FAA that Flight 93 had turned off its transponder, had turned, and was now heading toward Washington DC." At that point, he added, "the decision was made to go intercept Flight 93.… The vice president [said] that the president had given us permission to shoot down innocent civilian aircraft.… We started receiving reports from the fighters that were heading to … intercept" (ABC 9/11/02).

This is a striking statement. Since Flight 93 turned off its transponder and deviated from its flight path about 9:36, Gen. Winfield was strongly implying that NORAD and the FAA *were* able to track the flight on primary radar and that fighters *were* closing in on it. This didn't play well at the top of the pyramid. Gen. Richard Myers, chief of the entire US military on 9/11, claimed Flight 93 "had switched off its transponder, making it much harder if not impossible to track on ground radar" (Myers *Eyes on the Horizon* p. 152). This was a silly claim for an Air Force general to make; if it were true, then attackers could just turn off their transponders and become invisible to radar.

**Commission Contradicts Military Commanders**

Nevertheless, the Commission was adamant on the questions of NORAD's responses, even to the point of insisting that Gen. Arnold change his testimony so as to allow for the ostensible distraction presented by "phantom Flight 11" (Hearing 6/17/04). Its *Report*, as we've seen, claimed that NORAD had never heard about Flight 93 until 10:07, after it crashed. Yet despite all the statements from top commanders that NORAD had fighters tracking Flight 93 and permission to shoot down the airliner, the Commission claimed that Bush and Cheney didn't authorize a shoot down until 10:18. Therefore, it insisted, NORAD couldn't have intercepted the flight: its fighters got nowhere near it, and besides, they lacked permission to fire. Lest anyone miss the point, the Commission made it repeatedly (*Report* pp. 30-31, 34, 37, 42). Above all, no one could suspect Cheney of ordering the shoot down of an airliner, and no one could suspect the military of executing such an order.

If the Commission insisted on the bigger lies, that doesn't mean that top brass were telling the whole truth. If we accept these pronouncements from the military brass, then we'd want to ask some questions: Did you possibly enjoy the advantage of having defenses *already* on high alert because of the three earlier hijackings? If your air defenders were watching Flight 93 early on, perhaps even before it was hijacked, and only 35 minutes were needed for fighters to reach the airliner, how could they have failed to intercept it?

This was another question the Commission didn't want raised.

**Problems Surrounding "The Cell Phone Flight"**

Since much of the Official Story for Flight 93 is predicated on calls allegedly made from cell phones, let's consider the technology available at the time. In 2001, how many of these reported cell phone calls actually went through? To examine these questions is not to discount the heroism of the passengers but to follow the facts where they take us.

While few of us would willingly want to question last calls to loved ones, technical limitations, at least to some degree, do challenge the cell-phone reports. Both scientific and industry sources indicate that at high altitudes and high speeds, cell phones could not make viable connections with cell sites on the ground (www.avweb.com/other/avma9910.html). Canadian mathematician and computer scientist A. K. Dewdney tested cell phones in light aircraft and found that service deteriorated in correlation with increased altitude and engine mass. Dewdney demonstrated that in 2001, cell phones functioned consistently only below 2,000 feet, that only about 10 percent of cell phones could make a connection above 7,000 feet, and that none could connect above 8,000 feet (http://physics911.net/cellphoneflight93). In addition, airline sources have also confirmed that cell phones were inoperable in the air (*Travel Technologist* 9/19/01) and, later, that high-altitude capabilities only became available in 2006 (www.qualcomm.com/press/releases/2004).

Since most of UA 93's flight time was at altitudes above 25,000 feet, alleged cell-phone calls placed while the plane was at such altitudes could not have made a connection. Working from this technical impossibility, the FBI reported that of the 37 calls reportedly made from Flight 93 only two could likely have been made from cell phones. Both of these were made at about 9:58, when the airliner had likely descended to about 5,000 feet (*US v. Moussaoui* P200054). The Commission knew of the FBI findings but didn't incorporate them into its *Report*. As a result, it allowed the news media to "continue reporting that passengers had reached loved ones by means of cell phone calls" (Griffin *New Pea~l Harbor Revisited* pp. 115-16).

### Possible Explanations for Contradictions among Reports from Call Recipients

The findings from Dewdney, the airline industry, and the FBI all affirmed the altitude limitations for cell phones in; these conflicted with the recollections of individuals who received calls. Deena Burnett reported receiving four calls from her husband, Tom, and recalled that she had recognized his cell phone number on her caller ID (*Sacramento Bee* 9/11/02). Other recipients had similar recollections.

To make sense of such conflicts, we can entertain five possibilities:

- some recipients were mistaken about the number and/or time of calls they received;

- some recipients of the calls from Flight 93 were lying;
- some recipients were mistaken about the calls originating from cell phones;
- more calls were made from seat-back Airfones than recipients believed;
- or some special device allowed cell phone calls to go through at higher altitudes.

These last two hypotheses would seem most likely, but to imagine all that 35 calls which went through were made from seat-back phones contradicts the reports of too many recipients. The seat-back hypothesis could reasonably account for *some* of the 35 calls, but surely not all. If, as reported, the hijackers forced all the passengers to the back of the plane, then only a few seatback phones would have been available for calls. This leaves us with the "special-device" hypothesis to account for at least some of the calls. Although some of us are skeptical about "sci-fi," "gee-whiz" explanations, the "special-device" hypothesis does help to explain known data—and not just the 35 cell phone calls.

### The Cell-Phone Repeater Hypothesis

If we entertain the "special device" hypothesis, we do so in the spirit of Sir Arthur Conan Doyle and his famous creation, Sherlock Holmes: "When you have eliminated the impossible, whatever remains, however improbable, must be the truth" (www.quoteworld.org/quotes/3856). According to this theory, "the impossible" includes the near impossibility that *all* of the calls attributed to cell phones—by both callers and recipients—were actually made from seatback Airfones. Applying Holmes's logic of elimination, we're left with the "cell-phone repeater" hypothesis. This idea comes from one of our most reliable and rational researchers, Jim Hoffman.

To explain the 35 calls, Hoffman has hypothesized that in order to give cell phones the greater range they'd have needed, a powerful "repeater" box may have been planted on board the plane: A self-powered cell phone repeater the size of a shoe box was placed on board Flight 93 within a piece of luggage. The repeater is sufficiently powerful to establish reliable connections with ground stations for several minutes at a time and forwards all the communications between the cell phones aboard the plane and ground stations (http://911research.wtc7.net/planes/analysis/phonecalls. html). Besides being technically simple, this method would have afforded the attack planners—whether al Qaeda or others—considerable benefits with little risk of exposure. Hijackers could have possibly communicated with other operatives on the ground, and other parties, if responsible for planting the power box, would have been assured of stirring accounts from passengers. By placing the box on the *last* of the four flights, completed calls would inform passengers that the airliner was not going "back to the airport." Thus the calls could provide vivid descriptions not only of small men wearing red headbands but also of a passenger revolt that would become legend (http://911research.wtc7.net/planes/analysis/phonecalls.html).

In addition, the cell phone repeater hypothesis helps to explain other events. The uncanny *immediacy* of media coverage for the calls from Flight 93 has struck some analysts as peculiar. How many of us, reeling in shock from four hijackings of airliners, the disintegration of the Towers, and the death of a loved one, would have in a few hours mustered the composure to contact the news media? Conversely, in such a short time how would the news media have known whom to contact? How many of us would have picked up a call from a strange number and talked to a reporter under such circumstances of shock and grief? Nevertheless, many alleged recipients of calls from Flight 93 did receive both immediate (day-of) coverage and also extended media attention (CBS 9/11/01). Thus the instant legend of "the cell-phone flight" and the passenger revolt was able to take shape exceptionally quickly and possibly beyond the usual criteria for what's newsworthy.

## The Emergency Call from the Bathroom

At 9:58, as Flight 93 passed over Mt. Pleasant Township, Pennsylvania, passenger Edward Felt reportedly called 911 operator John Shaw and talked for 70 seconds. This time, the caller was anything but calm. Digits possibly quaking as he dialed, Felt told the operator that he'd locked himself in the bathroom (*Pitts. Tribune Review* 9/8/02). If Felt called from a bathroom, where seatback GTE Airfones weren't available, then he must have called from a cell phone.

If the operator's report is accurate, Felt's call had several implications, all of them starkly contradicting the Official Story. The operator recalled that Felt "was very distraught" because he "believed the plane was going down" (*Mirror* [UK] 9/13/02). Were there any calls other than Felt's made during those last few minutes of flight, when the plane was low enough for cell calls to go through? Wouldn't one expect other passengers to make calls, possibly to report on the passengers' assault on the cockpit?

As we noted earlier, the FBI immediately seized the tape of Felt's automatically recorded emergency call. Furthermore, the FBI also blocked the 911 operator from talking with the news media. A year later the Bureau included another emergency operator, Glenn Cramer, who was also restrained by a gag order (*Mirror* [UK] 9/13/02). Can there be any doubt that the FBI, while likely involved in enabling 9/11, clearly also became a lead agency in what looks like a cover-up?

## The Passengers' Revolt, Plus a Shoot Down?

If, as we've seen, considerable evidence debunks the claim that NORAD and the Secret Service didn't know about Flight 93 until after it crashed, the proof becomes even more positive when we probe its final moments in the air.

As we've seen, the core question about Flight 93 has been, What happened to Flight 93 in its final minutes? The public was initially told, Griffin has noted, "that the heroic passengers brought it down after storming the cabin and wresting control from the hijackers. It was later said that the hijackers, fearing that the passengers would gain control, brought it down themselves. But there have been, from the first, rumors the plane was shot down by the US military" (Griffin *9/11 Contradictions* p. 109). In truth, those final moments may have involved a bit of each. Even though the passenger revolt very likely reached the cockpit, and even though the alleged hijackers may well have decided to terminate their mission, these narratives may have crowded out a key question: What else might have caused Flight 93 to go down?

## A Stricken Airliner: What Eyewitnesses Saw and Heard

Eyewitnesses on the ground recounted don't all agree—in part because they weren't observing at the same time or from the same place—but telling patterns do emerge, nevertheless:

- Several witnesses observed—and a major news outlet reported—jet fighters tailing or attacking the airliner (CBS 9/11/01). In addition, one news story called finding the engine part far from the crater "intriguing" because "the heat seeking, air-to-air Sidewinder missiles aboard an F-16 would likely target one of the Boeing 757's two large engines" (*Phila. Daily News* 11/15/06).

- Laura Temyer reported hearing "a boom," "a loud thump that echoed off the hills and then I heard the plane's engine. I heard two more loud thumps and didn't hear the plane's engine any more." Temyer also recalled that when she asked why the widely scattered debris contained so many personal possessions, law-enforcement professionals "privately told her that the plane was shot down and decompression sucked objects from the aircraft ..." (*Phila. Daily News* 11/15/01).

Several observers reported explosions followed by either strange noises from jet engines or just atypical silence. Of these testimonials, Laura Temyer's most closely matched what one would expect from an air-to-air missile attack: one missile takes out one engine; another missile takes out the other. Corroborating Temyer's recollections, another eyewitness reported an F-16 firing two missiles, one of which hit an engine (CBS 9/11/01).

Skeptics have objected that a plane hit by a missile couldn't continue flying as long as Flight 93 did after it apparently started to disintegrate. In fact, however, Korean Airlines Flight 7 took hits from Soviet missiles in 1983 yet continued to fly for two additional minutes (Thompson *Terror Timeline* p. 449), and KAL Flight 902 flew on for 40 minutes after being hit by Soviet missiles (D. Eric *KAL 007: The Cover-up* p. 110).

## Government Officials Talk about a Shoot Down

As we've seen, insiders like Sen. Carl Levin (D-Mich.) had heard about a possible shoot down. Just after the attacks, NORAD and the Pentagon were buzzing with chatter about such an intervention. Maj. David Nash, one of the fighter pilots sent from Otis AFB toward New York City revealed that immediately after he returned to base he was told that "an F-16 had shot down a fourth airliner in Pennsylvania" (*Aviation Week & Space Tech.* 6/3/02). FAA flight controllers were forbidden from talking to the media—including those in Cleveland who'd tracked the final minutes of Flight 93 on their screens (*Independent* [UK] 9/13/02). But at least one controller, defying this gag order, spoke about how "an F-16 fighter closely pursued Flight 93" (CBS 9/11/01).

Within a few days though, top officials stopped any references to a possible a shoot down. Acknowledging that F-16s were tracking the target and ready to act might have salved the Pentagon's pride, but someone in power had perhaps decided that such reports should be squelched. Snippets did slip out, nonetheless. Although Rumsfeld had likely influenced any decision to sing the same tune, that didn't prevent him from sounding some sour notes—touting the people who "shot down the plane over Pennsylvania" (CNN 12/24/01).

Working, no doubt, from the fact that government officials and military officers had spoken about shoot-down authorization complete with rules of engagement, reporters Dan Balz and Bob Woodward expressed concern that the military had shot down Flight 93 (*Wash. Post* 1/27/02). Their concerns must have deepened when they learned Lt. Kuczynski had reported that, while flying an E-3 Sentry over Pennsylvania, he directed two F-16s after receiving "direct orders to shoot down an airliner" (*Aquin* 4/12/02).

So the evidence for a shoot down is circumstantial but hardly insubstantial. Considering all the evidence, researcher Hoffman has concluded "the cause of the crash was apparently trauma to the aircraft—such as a missile strike—rather than the actions of whoever was in the cockpit" (http://911research.wtc7.net/planes/analysis/flight93/index.html). If this part of the Official Story is false, then other strands of the yarn may also unravel.

Ultimately, it's not a matter of how heroic the passengers were or what they did; similarly, it's not primarily a matter of how many cellphone calls were actually completed by passengers. Instead, it's a matter of how the standard story was fashioned into an emotionally affecting but oversimplified patriotic narrative.

A real investigation could, via subpoena and sworn testimony, uncover evidence and interview witnesses under oath, taking us much closer to the elusive truth.

# 21. The Fall of the Twin Towers

*As a structural engineer, I believe in the laws of physics and rely on them every day.*

—Ron Brookman

The destruction of the World Trade Center furnished the most horrific, iconic images of 9/11: the hand-in-hand jumpers, the fireballs, the crowds running from the dust clouds, the firemen drenched in grime, and the jagged remains of the Towers jutting from the rubble at Ground Zero. Clips of these symbols of American power coming down were played and replayed on TV, well into the cleanup. All this repetition etched these images even more deeply into the psyche, imprinting the stock footage of nightmares.

However, the destruction at the WTC also provides one of the best sources of insight into 9/11. Using a variety of methods, researchers have generated detailed knowledge about the design and construction of the buildings, the extent of the damage and intensity of the fires, the gross mishandling of the crime scene, and the molten steel beneath the "pile." To address these issues, we'll look at the extensive suppression of evidence, track the official investigations, and expose the shoddy science presented to explain the Towers' demise.

## Suppression of "Inconvenient" Truths

Restriction of evidence began immediately after the catastrophic events. Early reports sometimes stated the obvious—that the disintegration of the buildings resembled planned demolitions. Two network anchors made such statements: Peter Jennings reported that "anybody who's ever watched a building being demolished on purpose knows … that if you're going to do this you have to get at the … infrastructure of a building and bring it down" (ABC 9/11/01). Dan Rather told viewers "for the third time today—it's reminiscent of those pictures we've all seen too much on television before when a building was deliberately destroyed by well placed dynamite …" (CBS 9/11/01). Neither the striking similarities to demolition nor footage of a third skyscraper coming down received mass media exposure again.

Even worse was the suppression of medical hazards. Denying the "toxic soup" that covered Lower Manhattan, the Feds issued an "all clear" just days after the attacks. Under pressure from the White House, EPA administrator Christine Todd Whitman declared on September 18th that the smoke, dust, asbestos, lead, and mercury hanging over Manhattan were "not a health problem." Rather than warning the public of the hazards, she recommended that New Yorkers "vacuum everything and wipe all surfaces with a damp cloth" (*Newsweek* 9/14/01). It didn't take long for hundreds of victims, especially among first responders, to start suing the city, the EPA, and Whitman (AP 1/10/02).

The city was also deeply involved in the suppression of evidence. Starting right after 9/11, New York's Fire Department recorded more than 500 interviews with firefighters and emergency medical workers (*NYT* 8/12/05). While politicians were exploiting the nation's infatuation with firemen, they were also suppressing the actual first-responder testimonials. As Mayor Rudy Giuliani praised the bravery of first responders, he impounded their testimonials, citing possible use as evidence in federal trials. Only after the *New York Times*, joined by several families of 9/11 victims, filed suit—and then only after a long legal battle—did the New York Court of Appeals order the city to release the oral histories. More than three years after the attacks, the public finally gained access. Although the *Times* made the accounts publicly available as "The Sept. 11 Records," it made little effort to determine their significance.

When suppression didn't suffice, the offending party was apparently pressured to relent. Dr. Van Romero, a prominent explosives expert at New Mexico Institute of Mining and Technology, illustrated this tendency. After viewing replays of the Towers' demise, Prof. Romero stated that the "collapses" must have been caused by "some explosive devices inside the buildings" because they were "too methodical" to have been simply the results of the airplane impacts (*Albuquerque Journal* 9/11/01). Ten days later, the explosives expert suddenly changed his professional opinion.

## Design Specs of Towers are Conveniently Forgotten

Early on, official sources emphasized that the destruction was caused not simply by fire but by raging fires combined with plane crashes (CNN 9/13/01). Other networks soon reinforced this basic theory of fire plus structural damage. Initially, both government and media exaggerated the extent, duration, and intensity of the fires; later they emphasized design flaws, structural damage, and fluke events.

However, the design specs for the Towers cast doubts on the official explanations. Conceived in the mid 1960s, the Towers were designed and built to handle extreme hazards. Their welded exterior supports, according to the engineers' calculations, were so strong that all the columns on one side of a tower could be cut and the building could still withstand "a 100-mile-per-hour wind." A structural analysis of the Towers found them able to resist the impact of "a fully loaded large jet airliner [Boeing 707 or DC-8] at 600 miles per hour": "such a collision would result in only local damage which could not cause collapse" (J. Glanz and E. Lipton *City in the Sky* pp. 133, 17).

Many design and construction professionals concurred. Leslie Robertson, a member of the firm responsible for designing the Towers, also affirmed that they were designed to take a hit from the largest airliner of that time (1966) (BBC 3/7/02). Going even further, Frank De Martini, a construction manager at the WTC, declared that they could "probably sustain multiple impacts from airliners" (*Report* pp. 21-23). Excellent construction shots showing the massive steel superstructure are available courtesy of Architects and Engineers for 9/11Truth: http://www2.ae911truth.org/docs/wtcconst.php. These photos show how even the "small" peripheral columns were actually fourteen inches on a side and tightly spaced.

Investigating agencies, however, paid little attention to all this. The Federal Emergency Management Agency (FEMA) just ignored these special design capabilities; the National Institute for Standards and Technology (NIST) even claimed the Towers were not constructed to withstand the impact of a plane as large as a Boeing 767 (NIST *Exec. Summary* p. xlvii). If NIST's investigators had done their math, they'd have found that yes, the contemporary Boeing 767s weighed slightly more, but those that hit the Towers were flying at speeds well under 600 mph. Also, 707s had four engines instead of just two. A four-engine plane would impact in two additional zones and thus have a significantly greater chance of inflicting serious damage. So the potential for inflicting damage was actually *less* for the airliners that struck the buildings.

### False Claims from Bogus Authorities

Soon after the attacks, the public was told that "very intense" fires "burned for a long time" (CNN 9/24/01). However, evidence of several types now indicates the fires were both less intense and less enduring than networks and questionable experts had initially reported.

NBC anchorman Tom Brokaw interviewed Hyman Brown, whom he introduced as the "architect" of the Twin Towers (NBC 9/11/01). Two days later, Brown was falsely introduced as the "chief engineer" of the Towers (BBC 9/13/01). Neither an architect nor the chief engineer, the University of Colorado professor of construction engineering nevertheless helped impart the standard explanation. Prof. Brown told BBC "steel melts, and 24,000 gallons of aviation fluid melted the steel." (In fact, each plane was carrying about 10,000 gallons of fuel, most of which burned off very rapidly.) Another expert proclaimed "there's nothing on Earth that could survive those temperatures with that amount of fuel burning.... The columns would have melted" (BBC 9/13/01). On what basis did corporate networks and a federal investigating panel select these authorities?

These claims were blatantly false. Even under ideal conditions open fires fueled by jet fuel rarely exceed 1,700°F, nowhere near steel's 2,800° melting point (www.uniweld.com/catalog/alloys_melting.htm). Furthermore, fires fueled by jet fuel (mostly kerosene) reach nowhere near the melting point of steel. Even under ideal conditions, they rarely exceed 1,700°F, fully 1,100° degrees below the requisite 2,800°.

Dr. Thomas Eagar, metals and materials engineering expert at MIT, came much closer to the mark when he stated that although open hydrocarbon fires could possibly reach 1,700° (PBS "NOVA" 4/30/02), they typically range from 930 to 1,200°F. Steel begins to soften at 800°F, Eager added, and loses half its strength at 1,200°F. However, even if high temperatures had halved the strength of the steel, it could still have supported two or three times the additional stresses (*J. of the Minerals, Metals & Materials Society* 12/01: 8-11).

Other estimates for the WTC office fires fell in the 800-900°F range—not only less than *one third* of the extreme temperature needed to *melt* steel but also several hundred degrees below the point of causing it to lose half its strength.

## Blatant Disturbance of the Crime Scene

As we've seen at the Pentagon and in Pennsylvania, the FBI failed to follow its own regulations for crime scenes. The FBI didn't even roll out yellow plastic ribbon; the logic seemed to be, if we don't call it a crime scene, then it's not a federal offense to disturb it. Granted, Ground Zero was a disaster area whose magnitude far exceeded the typical crime scene. But this did not justify sealing it off from journalists and photographers—and then ordering it to be deliberately and systematically disturbed before evidence could be tagged, photographed, and studied (AP 9/27/01).

The cleanup effort was immense, almost unprecedented. Thousands took part—including police, firefighters, and iron workers, many of whom came to New York voluntarily from all over the country (*Guardian* [UK] 9/11/09). Despite their heroic efforts and good intentions, the use of heavy machinery to remove debris caused human remains to end up at Fresh Kills landfill (*NYT* 9/21/08). Hundreds of firefighters protested strongly against Giuliani's hasty "industrial" methods: "There had been as many as 300 firefighters at a time involved in search and recovery, but Giuliani cut that number to no more than 25 … Giuliani also made a conscious decision to institute a 'scoop-and-dump' operation to expedite the clean-up of Ground Zero in lieu of the more time-consuming, but [more] respectful process of removing debris piece by piece …" (*FireFighting News* 3/9/07).

In violation of federal law, most of the twisted steel was summarily cut up, shipped off, and melted down. In a remarkably short time, trucks and barges were readied to receive the steel. Just two weeks after the collapses, the City of New York had contracted to sell much of the wrecked steel to China. How many complex international business deals are completed in two weeks? The hasty removal soon produced a "cold" crime scene (*NYT* 12/25/01). Although the steel was supposedly of no value to investigators, someone considered it important enough to equip trucks hauling it with GPS locators at $1,000 each. Trucks' locations were individually tracked, and drivers were instructed neither to deviate from approved routes nor to stop along the way (http://securitysolutions.com/ar/security_gps_job_massive).

This wholesale destruction of evidence also ignored the National Fire Protection Association's broadly accepted guidelines for investigations. Engineer Dick Scar has pointed out that "Mayor Rudy Giuliani, a former prosecutor, surely knew the importance of securing evidence—and that the law in fact requires it. Yet, of the 200,000 tons of structural steel contained in the Twin Towers, only a few hundred pieces were saved" (www. ae911truth.org/en/news/41-articles/350-evidence-destroyed-is-justice-denied.html).

## Both FEMA and Public Blocked from WTC Site

FEMA personnel, backed by American Society of Civil Engineers (ASCE) investigators, operated without subpoena power, with limited funding, and under ridiculous constraints. Three months after 9/11, investigators still hadn't received blueprints for the buildings.

Except for one walkthrough tour, FEMA was blocked from Ground Zero until the cleanup was completed (*Fire Engineering* 1/02). Its only hands-on study of the debris took place in salvage yards. Investigators had access to less than one percent of the steel from the collapsed buildings. Investigators complained of "bureaucratic restrictions that prevented them from interviewing witnesses, examining the disaster site, and requesting crucial information" (*NYT* 12/25/01).

However, lest we conclude that FEMA was fully committed, consider that the American Society for Civil Engineers wanted to issue a call to the public for photos and videos of the attacks, yet "for reasons that would remain known only to FEMA," the Agency wouldn't let them do it (Glanz and Lipton *City in the Sky* p. 330).

Even though work at "the pile" received daily media attention, few protested the massive disturbance of the crime scene or removal of evidence. Corporate and alternative journalists; city, state, and federal politicians; law-enforcement officials; civil liberties groups and even most of the families of victims raised few objections.

### Muted Protest, Except for Firefighters and One Gutsy Editor

It was Bill Manning, a national leader of the firefighting profession, who called for immediate cessation of disturbance to the crime scene. From the editor's chair at a trade journal, Manning bellowed "structural steel from the World Trade Center has been and continues to be cut up and sold for scrap. Crucial evidence that could answer many questions … is on a slow boat to China" (*Fire Engineering* 1/02).

Even more vehemently, Manning maintained that a growing number of fire-protection specialists were coming to suspect that "the structural damage from the planes and the explosive ignition of jet fuel in themselves were not enough to bring down the Towers." The editor added that "*Fire Engineering* has good reason to believe that the 'official investigation' blessed by FEMA … is a half-baked farce that may already have been commandeered by political forces whose primary interests, to put it mildly, lie far afield of full disclosure" (*Fire Engineering* 1/02). These statements proved prophetic. "Half-baked farce" might seem harsh, but as we'll see, Manning may have actually *understated* the glaring flaws in both federal investigations. He was certainly among the few to protest. In New York, the highly politicized international hub for news outlets, it fell to the editor of a small-circulation journal to protest the removal of evidence and wonder whether it might be politically motivated.

## Molten Steel Lingers, "Flowing Like Lava"

As proponents of the Official Story emphasized the heat of the fires, some scientists initially validated and others attempted to rationalize the melted and molten steel. Berkeley's Dr. Abolhassan Astaneh-Asl described a "charred

I-beam" whose "steel flanges had been reduced from an inch thick to paper thin" (http://berkeley.edu/news/berkeleyan/2001/10/03_grou.html). Prof. Astaneh-Asl's findings were no doubt accurate, but he's rarely affirmed them since 2001. While Prof. Thomas Eager was pointing out that jet-fuel fires couldn't melt steel, other scientific authorities were attempting to validate this very misconception. Fellow MIT professor Eduardo Kausel claimed the fires' "intense heat softened or melted the structural elements" (*Scientific American* 10/09/01).

In similar fashion, several scientists initially reported that both Towers came down at virtual free-fall speed but suddenly stopped making these claims, which implied that explosives must have enabled such rapid disintegration. Just days after the catastrophe, MIT's Dr. Oral Buyukozturk determined that "the towers crashed into the ground with an almost free-fall velocity (http://web.mit.edu/newsoffice/2001/skyscrapers.html). Other scientists, including Eduardo Kausel, made this same determination of near freefall, only to go silent when it became evident that this fact subverted an emerging Official Story.

Among many others, Bertrand Russell, Aldous Huxley and George Orwell have warned against state control of science. But with MIT professors stating falsehoods, and *Scientific American* supporting a specious scenario, scientists strangely going silent or reversing themselves, how different was this?

While much of the scientific establishment rapidly came to condone falsehoods, observers on the ground consistently told a different story. Over many months, observers from different backgrounds also reported molten steel. Rescue personnel, ironworkers, and firefighters regularly reported finding "rivers of molten steel in the pile" (*NY Post* 3/3/04). The heat was hellish; boots were literally burned off workers' feet. Several months afterward, FDNY Capt. Philip Ruvolo remarked "you'd see molten steel, *molten* steel, running down the channel rails like you're in a foundry, like lava" (Infowars.net 11/17/06). Despite rains, frigid winter weather, and constant dousing with fire hoses, melted steel persisted in the rubble for *five* months (Knight Ridder 5/29/02).

A few official observers filed similar reports. William Langewiesche, the only journalist allowed unrestricted access to Ground Zero, reported "streams of molten metal" that "flowed down broken walls inside the foundation hole" (Langewiesche *American Ground* p. 32). Three weeks after 9/11, Leslie Robertson, a prominent partner in the engineering firm which designed the Towers, also affirmed that molten steel was present (SEAU 10/01). Later, however, Robertson denied he'd said so, likely disavowing his statement in order to support the Official Story (www.youtube.com/ watch?v=DF4C6qtU_Fc&amp). This remarkable five-minute video supports many contentions presented in this chapter.

As it became more apparent that jet fuel fires couldn't have melted structural steel, the scientific and journalistic establishments had to either ignore the molten metal or deny its presence. To this day, few Americans have any idea how much smoldered beneath "the pile," how long it stayed red hot, or what might have caused it to melt.

## Orange Molten Metal Pours from South Tower

Since steel had to stay above 2800°F to remain molten, troubling questions arose: If some of the steel was still a red- or orange-hot liquid five months after the attacks, then how *extremely* hot was it when it melted? What could have possibly generated and sustained those super-hot temperatures? These were questions that no one in government or media asked, let alone tried to answer.

The evidence of molten steel didn't square with the theory of hydrocarbon fires. Physics expert David Chandler underscored this contradiction: government investigators had placed themselves "in the untenable position of arguing that the buildings of the World Trade Center were brought down by office fires started by jet fuel (kerosene) which burn 1,000°F cooler than the melting point of iron while denying the evidence that temperatures hot enough to melt iron were present" (http://911speakout.org).

The government account failed to explain vivid photographic evidence of melting significantly before the buildings started to fall (www.youtube.com/ watch?v=OmuzyWC60eE). About seven minutes before the South Tower came down, a yellow and orange liquid suddenly began to pour from the building, dripping showers of sparks (http://911research.wtc7.net/wtc/evidence/orangespout. html). In fewer than 50 minutes, then, *something* had superheated this steel beyond red-hot and caused it to liquefy. This fact helps us understand how it might still be red-hot fully five months later.

## Steel Not Melted, Just Softened

Even if no molten steel had been found, temperature issues would have arisen when FEMA, NIST, and the 9/11 Commission all asked the public to believe that hydrocarbon fires had fatally weakened the buildings' structural steel. Soon the public was told that the steel in the buildings didn't melt; it just softened and buckled. Changing his earlier estimate, MIT's Thomas Eagar contended that steel would lose *80 percent* of its strength when heated to 1,300°F and that this loss of strength had caused the disintegrations. At the same time, Prof. Eagar insisted the fires were probably "only about 1,200 or 1,300°F" (PBS "NOVA" 4/30/02), at the high end for all but the hottest hydrocarbon fires. So Eagar essentially matched the estimated temperature supposedly reached by the fires to 1,200°—the point where, according to his later estimate, steel loses most of its strength. He offered no proof for these contentions.

Following NIST's lead, some proponents of the Official Story have claimed that the biggest fires were very big indeed—that they turned the buildings into "towering infernos." Again, the evidence counters this claim.

## The Intensity and Duration of the Fires

Because it came down in the shortest time, the South Tower might have been expected to experience the hottest fires. Since the South Tower was struck between floors 78 and 84, that's where the fires likely burned the hottest. Surprisingly, though, FDNY Chief Orio Palmer and firefighter Ronald Bucca reached the building's 78th floor. Palmer's radio call reported only a couple of isolated pockets of fire; Palmer wanted to run hoses and "knock them down" (CNN 9/4/02). While one might argue that the fires above floor 78 were more severe, survivor Brian Clark recalled that when he walked down from floor 84, he saw "not a roaring inferno, just quiet flames licking up and smoke sort of eking through the wall" (PBS "NOVA" 4/30/02). At the North Tower, a woman stood right in the huge hole left by the airliner (http://911research.wtc7.net/wtc/evidence/photos/wtc1hole1.html).

The improbability of the "melting" or "softening" theories showed clearly in the photographic record. According to fire professionals, after the enormous fireballs subsided, most of the kerosene had burned off within ten minutes (*Firehouse* 2/04). True, temperatures near the ceilings likely spiked temporarily in a "flashover." After this, though, the flames died down and many fires burned out. Photographs of the Towers fifteen minutes after they were struck show few flames but much sooty black smoke, a sign the fires were starved for oxygen and hence not very hot (http://911research.wtc7.net/wtc/evidence/photos/wtc1hole1.html).

The Official Story didn't factor in the *duration* of the fires, which obviously affected their ability to heat and soften massive steel columns. For fires to weaken these, they would have needed to be not only *very* big and *very* hot but also much longer lasting than they were. This just didn't happen. The South Tower collapsed after only 56 minutes, and the North Tower collapsed an hour and 42 minutes after it was struck (http://911review.com/articles/griffin/nyc1.html). For all of these conditions to have occurred in both Towers, the laws of probability would be stretched way beyond the betting point.

### FEMA's Theory of "Pancaking" Floors

In 2002, FEMA floated a theory that reigned for several years. Its "pancake theory" held that when floors above the impact cavity fell upon the floors below it, this started a chain reaction, "a pancake type of collapse of successive floors." In a "domino effect," the floors allegedly "pancaked all the way down." In FEMA's pancake theory, the steel floor supports broke free from the 236 exterior columns (FEMA *Report*). Trouble was, the floors weren't stacked like pancakes on "the Pile." And although "pancaking" should have left most of the 47 massive core columns standing, all these columns also came down, inexplicably reduced to twisted wreckage.

While these were objections that FEMA couldn't explain away, the Commission came up with a bold solution to this problem: it simply denied the existence of the 47 core columns: "The interior core of the buildings was a hollow steel shaft, in which elevators and stairwells were grouped" (*Report* p. 541). Eliminate those troublesome core columns, and none would be expected to remain standing.

## FEMA to NIST: From Bad Science to Worse

Whereas FEMA and the Commission promoted the "pancake theory," NIST resurrected the "pile-driver effect," adding several planks to that creaky platform (NIST *Report* p. 146). NIST needed a way to explain the symmetry of the disintegrations. Whereas FEMA's "pancake" theory had proposed that the floors fell when they disconnected from the outer columns, NIST's theory had the floors stay connected to the outer columns, which they allegedly pulled inward (Griffin *New Pearl Harbor Revisited* p. 21). If that happened, however, why didn't the buildings show more signs that their outer walls were pulled inward? While photos do show *slight* inward deformation (NIST NCSTAR 1 Fig. 2-2), it seems insufficient to support NIST's "pile-driver" theory.

### NIST's Main Contentions

1.  The planes shattered several exterior and core columns and stripped the insulation from many more.
2.  The subsequent very hot fires weakened these suddenly vulnerable steel columns.
3.  These fires caused the floors to sag, pulling the exterior columns inward and reducing their ability to provide support.
4.  The upper sections of the buildings (those above the points of impact) dropped on the lower portions, slamming down so hard that lower portions collapsed "essentially in freefall" (NIST NCSTAR *Report* pp. xxxvii-xl, 144, 146).

In short, the NIST Report claimed that when floors collapsed, they increased the load on outer core columns already weakened by very hot fires. This combination of factors, NIST claimed, somehow produced "global collapse." This was NIST's favorite abstraction, but one it never fully defined; NIST's analyses focused on conditions leading up to "global collapse," not on what came *after* collapse initiation (NCSTAR *Report* pp. 145-46, 151-52).

Whereas a sound theory logically explains particulars, those based heavily on computer models either ignored pesky particulars or failed to explain them. These include the fact that the top 300 feet of the South Tower broke off at the point of impact and tilted 22 degrees before straightening up and seeming to dissolve into the remaining base of the building (http://911research. wtc7.net/wtc/attack/wtc2.html). What accounts for the fact that this huge tilting block could have stopped its twisting rotation, started to drop straight down, and turned into dust? If this breakaway section were regarded as the "pile driver," then what was its counterpart at the North Tower? When one theory attempts to explain two very different events such as the disintegrations of the Twin Towers, it's very likely to run into logical inconsistencies.

## NIST: Hot Temperatures, Lost Insulation, Column Damage

Moreover, no evidence backs NIST's claims of extremely hot fires. NIST asserted that the fires raged out of control in the core and even reached 1,300°F, the temperature needed to soften steel. This was hardly credible, either. Jim Hoffman has challenged NIST's emphasis on extraordinarily hot fires in the core, citing three cogent objections:

- Any jet fuel that reached the cores would have either burned off rapidly or (as NIST itself claimed) trickled down stairways and utility shafts;
- The cores contained comparatively little fuel for fires;
- And the cores' huge steel columns wicked away heat.

In their attempts to explain the Towers' fall, NIST's investigators downplayed the considerable conductivity of structural steel (http://911research. wtc7.net/essays/nist/index.html#conduction).

In fact, NIST's own studies failed to find evidence that any of the core columns had reached temperatures of even 482°F—thus NIST's theory involved a huge discrepancy; it required a leap of nearly 900°F to reach the loss-of-strength point for the steel. Even if fires in the cores had somehow reached and sustained such extreme high temperatures, NIST never showed how they could have led to "global collapse" (NCSTAR *Report* pp. 88, 96, 176-180).

The closest NIST would come to an explanation was to eventually claim that the aircraft impacts knocked the fireproofing off many floor trusses and core columns. The Towers, it said, "would have remained standing were it not for the dislodged insulation" (NCSTAR *Report* pp. xliii, 68,171). Insulation was no doubt dislodged in a *few* areas of both buildings. Yet in order to support its theory, NIST had to claim, based on no evidence, that a great many columns which weren't struck by aircraft debris had their insulation knocked off (Griffin *New Pearl Harbor Revisited* pp. 16-17). How could NIST explain the loss of fireproofing on steel supports that were located either nowhere near the (five or six) floors which absorbed the impact or on the opposite side of the core?

## Same Theory for Both Buildings

In putting forth a generic theory for the buildings, NIST had to play down differences in point and angle of impact. NIST did mention that Flight 175 hit the South Tower on an angle at the right side of the building (NCSTAR *Report* Fig. 1-4) but didn't address the full implications of this fact.

The damage to the South Tower's core was likely more limited because of the off-center, oblique-angle, and lower impact of the airliner. The building swayed several feet in response to the crash, but "a large portion" of the 10,000 gallons of jet fuel was consumed in the fireball seen outside the Tower. One engine tore right through the building, exited, and fell to the street; this would suggest that one of the most potentially damaging parts of the airliner didn't strike many interior columns. Because of the angle, some researchers have wondered whether the fuselage, decidedly the most damaging part of a plane, missed the core completely (http://911research. wtc7.net/wtc/attack/wtc2.html). NIST, however, somehow concluded ten of the South Tower's core columns were severed (NCSTAR1 *Report* p. 40). Even if that were true, though, 37 others would have remained to pick up the load.

Moreover, the South Tower was struck lower (80th floor) than the North (95th floor), and this meant that at the point of impact the core columns were thicker, designed to carry the weight of fifteen additional floors (Griffin *New Pearl Harbor Revisited* p. 14). Finally, the South Tower came down after a significantly shorter exposure to fires (46 min.) than the North (1 hr. 42 min.).

NIST didn't credibly explain how the South Tower, which had likely suffered less structural and fire damage, had come down so much sooner.

To "explain" these anomalies, NIST had to theorize that damaged core columns in the South Tower buckled because some were directly exposed to kerosene-and-office-furnishing fires for just 56 minutes, max—and the weakening of a few columns brought down the entire building (NCSTAR *Report* pp. 88, 180). That does stretch credulity.

## No Precedent for Steel-Framed Buildings Destroyed by Fire

Moreover, when FEMA and NIST emphasized the factor of fire, they neglected to present the historical record of fires in tall steel-framed buildings. High-rise buildings with much larger, much hotter, and much longer-lasting fires have never collapsed.

Even though the news media thrive on spectacular fires, they acted as though there were no precedents for those at the WTC. If they'd looked in their own files, they'd have found that although no steel-framed skyscraper had ever come down due to fire before, suddenly three had fallen on a single day. David Ray Griffin underscores this incongruity, calling the Official Story "essentially a fire theory, so it cannot be emphasized too much that fire has never caused large steel-frame buildings to collapse—never ..." (http://911review.com/articles/griffin/nyc1.html). These facts are well articulated by Architects and Engineers for 9/11 Truth, comprised of over 1,500 professionals from these fields (www.ae911truth.org).

The steel in the following examples faced direct exposure to *more intense heat* for *much longer periods*. Yet the steel frameworks endured.

### Parallel Cases That Stand in Contrast to the Three WTC Buildings

- In 1988, at the 62-story Interstate Bank Building in Los Angeles, fires lasting several hours gutted five floors. Yet there was little structural damage and the building stood fast (www.iklimnet.com/hotelfires/interstatebank.html).

- In 1991, at the 38-story One Meridian Plaza Hotel in Philadelphia, a twelve-alarm fire erupted and blazed for *eighteen hours*, utterly destroying eight floors. Although "beams and girders sagged and twisted ..., the columns continued to support their loads" (FEMA 1991). Importantly, considered in relation to World Trade Center Building 7 (WTC-7), the Meridian Plaza lacked sprinklers on all but one floor; yet unlike WTC-7, the Plaza Hotel remained standing (*NYT* 4/28/91).

- In 2004, at the 56-story Caracas Tower in Venezuela, a fire raged for *seventeen hours* over 26 stories, ravaging the top 20 floors (http://venezuelanalysis.com 10/18/04). Two floors did collapse, but the underlying floors did not—and the Tower itself did not fall (CBS 10/18/04).

- In 2009, the 522-foot Television Cultural Center Tower (TVCC) (and Mandarin Hotel) in Beijing burst into flames. A conflagration ensued, with ferocious fires reaching the top of the complex. Yet the steel structure of the building "looked to be remarkably unscathed" (*Guardian* [UK] 2/11/09). In many respects, the Cultural Center Tower closely resembled WTC-7, the third skyscraper that come down on 9/11.

### British Study Also Illustrates Steel's Resistance to Fire

The Cardington experiments run in Great Britain in the mid-1990s afford another illuminating contrast. By subjecting steel-framed buildings to extremely hot fires that lasted for many hours, experimenters sought to determine what damage the fires would do. After reviewing the results, FEMA had to conclude that "despite the temperature of the steel beams reaching 800-900°C (1,500-1,700°F) in three of the tests ... no collapse was observed in any of the six experiments" (FEMA 1998 Appendix A).

The only *three* steel-framed buildings in history to come down mainly because of fire all fell on the same day. While fire has never—either prior to or after 9/11—caused steel-framed high-rise buildings to collapse, proponents of the Official Story rarely mention this fact. Indeed, the supposedly definitive NIST *Report* even implied that fire-induced collapses of large steel-framed buildings are *normal* events. This is among the many defects cited in ace researcher Jim Hoffman's devastating critique, "Building a Better Mirage: NIST's Three-Year

$20,000,000 Cover-Up of the Crime of the Century" (http://911research. wtc7.net/essays/nist/index.html).

## NIST Makes Another Attempt to Explain

As steel weakened by fire became a less tenable explanation, NIST shifted toward greater emphasis on structural flaws and improbable events. In 2005, NIST characterized the disintegrations as instances of "progressive collapse"—events (albeit unprecedented) that might occur when "a building collapses due to disproportionate spread of an initial local failure" (NCSTAR *Report* p. 200). Clearly NIST didn't intend to abandon the house-of-cards theory, just to redesign it.

Again, public ignorance afforded NIST room to maneuver. Few recalled that the Towers were over-designed to both absorb a hit from a large airliner and withstand a full-force hurricane (BBC 3/7/02). The public was largely unaware of how designers had installed huge core girders and closely spaced exterior columns to assure redundancy of support (*Engineering News-Record* 1/1/70).

When NIST did mention the safety features, it was to sigh, "alas, on this one day, these systems all failed": NIST talked about "a system of interdependent fire protection features, including suppression systems" (NCSTAR *Report* 2.2.1). First NIST dishonestly conflated other fire suppression systems with sprinklers; then it reported that in both Towers, debris from the crashes ruptured the sprinklers' supply lines. Given the fact that both buildings had water tanks on their upper floors, that the airliners struck many floors below, and that water flows downward, it's difficult to track the logic of two complete sprinkler failures.

## NIST Neglects Conduction and Resiliency Factors

Even if some fires had reached 1,300°F, during the limited time they burned they couldn't have heated massive steel columns to that temperature. Moreover, conduction would have dispersed much of the heat (http://911review.com/articles/griffin/nyc1.html). After all, steel and its main component, iron, are good conductors. Grab a crow bar that's had one end in a fire, and you'll drop it fast. Apply a blowtorch to a girder that's connected to a steel structure, and some of the heat will quickly diffuse. Yet as widely understood as the principle of conduction is, NIST acted as if this basic fact of materials science had gone AWOL that morning.

Emphasizing the allegedly weakened steel, NIST continued to exaggerate fire temperatures and their alleged consequences. Kevin Ryan, a chemist working for Underwriters Laboratories, the product-safety testing giant, blew the whistle on the distortions of scientific fact. In a well known letter, Ryan reminded NIST of what it should have known all along:

> We know that the steel components were certified to ASTM E119. The time temperature curves for this standard require the samples to be exposed to temperatures around 2,000°F for several hours. And as we all agree, the steel met those specifications. Additionally, I think we can all agree that even un-fireproofed steel will not melt until reaching red-hot temperatures of nearly 3,000°F"
> (www.septembereleventh.org/newsarchive/2004-11-11-ryan.php).

NIST had talked up heat but didn't like having to take it. Soon after Ryan made his letter public, he was fired by Underwriters (*South Bend Tribune* 11/22/04).

Nor was the structural damage severe. MIT materials engineering professor Thomas Eagar, who supports the Official Story, concluded "the impact of the airplanes would not have been significant" because "the number of columns lost on the initial impact was not large and the loads were shifted to remaining columns in this highly redundant structure" (*J. of the Minerals, Metals & Materials Society* Vol. 53 12/01: 8-11).

## The WTC Impacts: An Arboreal Analogy

While commentators have compared the disintegration of the Towers to tall trees that were ground into sawdust as they were coming down (*The Nation* 2/5/07), it's instructive to consider a different arboreal analogy for the impact of an airliner to the core of the Towers.

Imagine a grove of redwoods with smaller trees to the outside surrounding a tight clump of 47 mature redwoods. A fast-flying Cessna slams into the redwood grove. As the plane crashes into the smaller outer trees, it's mostly torn apart. Its fuselage and two engines do, however, strike several of the interior, more massive trunks. Aircraft parts snap the first trunks they hit, knocking the fireproof bark off a few others. The aircraft's fuel immediately ignites fires, which cause significant damage. But the older trunks are still protected by their thick bark—so the fires, although initially intense, burn themselves out in less than a half hour. Though some are damaged, all but a few of the 47 rugged-barked redwoods remain standing. And if, like the giant columns in those buildings, the trunks were interconnected with cross beams, even fewer would fall.

While analogies aren't proof, this one does suggest that aircraft impact plus fire damage couldn't have brought down the solidly engineered, massively constructed Trade Towers.

## Evidence for the Controlled Demolition Hypothesis

When Hypothesis A doesn't fit the facts, one has to consider Hypothesis B. Since fire has never caused modern steel-framed skyscrapers to collapse, and since the government hypothesis doesn't explain the data, one looks at another alternative. Granted, controlled demolition is not a pleasant prospect.

Controlled demolition involves positioning explosives capable of cutting steel in crucial places and then setting them off in a carefully calculated sequence. Then, according to Controlled Demolition, Inc., the company that did the cleanup at Ground Zero, the building "collapses like a house of cards, crumbling in on itself—a waterfall of well-fractured steel and concrete debris" (www.controlled-demolition.com/about-us). Does that description evoke familiar images?

Let's compare the criteria for controlled demolition to what happened at Ground Zero.

### Six Primary Characteristics of Planned Demolition

The National Fire Protection Association's *Guide for Fire and Explosion Investigations* lists the characteristics:

1.  The onset of the collapse is sudden.

2. The building accelerates to near free-fall speed.
3. The building comes down straight and symmetrically.
4. The building implodes and drops into its own footprint.
5. The collapse is total, with very little left standing.
6. Much of the nonmetallic material is pulverized, resulting in large dust clouds (Griffin *Mysterious Collapse* p. 28).

According to the standard National Fire Protection Association (NPFA) *Guide*, "damage is characterized by shattering of the structure, producing small, pulverized debris. Walls, roofs, and structural members are splintered or shattered, with the building completely demolished." (*Guide for Fire and Explosion Investigations* Sect. 18.3.2). If explosives were used, the characteristics of controlled demolitions would be expected—and in fact were widely observed at the WTC:

### 1. The Onset of the Collapse Is Sudden.

In controlled demolition, the onset of the collapse is typically sudden. One moment the building stands motionless; the next moment it suddenly begins to fall. This we can observe in videos of the WTC "collapses." But buildings which have suffered structural damage from fire don't suddenly drop. Instead, horizontal beams and trusses begin to buckle, bend, and sag, frequently dropping fragments and sparks.

Unlike fire-induced collapses, the WTC buildings showed few signs of tilting, bending, or sagging, not even on floors just above the impact points. Aside from the inward distortion of perimeter columns, the Twin Towers stayed remarkably still until they began to explode at the top and dropped precipitously (http://911research.wtc7.net/essays/nist/index.html).

### 2. The Building Accelerates to Near Free-Fall Speed.

As we've seen, buildings brought down by controlled demolition drop at near free-fall velocity because lower stories are blown out: upper floors fall without resistance, as if through thin air. The 1,363-foot Towers would take about 10 seconds at freefall; this is close to the actual time. The Commission reported that the "South Tower collapsed in 10 seconds" (*Report* p. 305).

The authors of the *Report* evidently assumed that the rapidity of this disintegration didn't conflict with their favored pancake theory. But if the floors had pancaked all the way down, each lower floor, comprised of steel supporting a slab of concrete, would have offered resistance. As physicist Steven Jones has pointed out, the upper floors could not have fallen through the lower ones the way they'd free fall through air (www.wtc7.net/articles/stevenjones_b7.html#current). Near-free-fall speed indicates a nearly complete absence of resistance: something had to suddenly remove all support for the floors.

### 3. The Building Comes Straight Down with Striking Symmetry.

Any controlled demolition of a tall building close to other properties is rigged to drop into its own "footprint" so it doesn't damage other buildings (www.controlled-demolition.com/about-us). Demolition experts joke about "oops, there goes the neighborhood"; their goal is to make buildings drop straight down. For both Towers, once the initial blowouts at the tops were over, it was hard not to feel amazement at the unusual symmetry of the descending ice-cream-cone-shaped debris clouds.

The aircraft-damage plus fire-damage hypothesis doesn't fit the evidence. To precipitate a disintegration that began suddenly, fell at near free-fall speed, displayed a symmetrical shape, and fell straight down, fires would have needed to weaken *all* the supports simultaneously—even though the fires weren't spread at all evenly throughout either Tower. As researcher Hoffman has noted, "all 287 columns would have to have weakened to the point of collapse at the same instant" (http://911review.com/articles/griffin/nyc1.html). The TV antenna atop the North Tower also illustrates these characteristics: without a simultaneous and symmetrical failure of the top floor trusses, the antenna would have toppled, not dropped straight down.

Ascribing all this to fire damage requires a significant suspension of disbelief.

### 4. The Building Implodes and Drops into Its Own Footprint.

Of the various features of controlled demolition, these two might seem to apply least to the Trade Towers. As we'll soon see, they do apply more completely to World Trade Center Building 7.

That said, the Towers did exhibit telltale signs of implosion. Videos show the TV antenna beginning to drop just before the exterior of the building. This implies internal destruction of the core columns timed just a split second ahead, pulling the outside columns inward. Noting the telltale implosion, Deputy Fire Commissioner Thomas Fitzpatrick remarked "my initial reaction was that this was exactly the way it looks when they show you those implosions on TV" (*NYT* "Sept. 11 Records" pp. 13-14).

At first glance, the Ground Zero debris field might not seem to indicate that the Towers fell into their foundations. The debris field was considerably larger than the two-acre footprints of the towers, with debris thrown outward as far as 600 feet. But given the Towers' height and atypical top-to-bottom demolitions, it's amazing how much did fall into a small area.

### 5. The Collapse Is Total, with Little Left Standing.

Not only did these 110-story towers drop around their own foundations, they fell into piles only a few stories high. Very few of the steel columns remained standing, although sections of the aluminum cladding jutted like desperate fingers into a smoldering, angry sky. This reduction to rubble was astonishing when we consider the enormous mass of concrete and heavy-duty steel in each Tower. The core of each building contained 47 massive steel box columns; at the base sixteen of these measured 54" x 22," with 4" thick steel (http://911research.wtc7.net/wtc/arch/core.html).

### 6. Much of the Nonmetallic Material Is Pulverized, Resulting in Enormous Dust Clouds.

Cutter charges can slice steel, and potent explosives can blow apart structural assemblies and pulverize nonmetallic components: at the WTC, hundreds of thousands of tons of concrete, plasterboard, glass, and asbestos were rapidly reduced to a fine powder (History Channel 9/8/02). This was especially true at the WTC. The disintegration produced a vast amount of highly toxic dust laced not only with asbestos but also with lead, mercury and other toxins from plastics, phones and computers. The results include an epidemic of cancers, especially among those who worked the huge cleanup operation (*Guardian* [UK] 11/11/09) or lived in the area (www.wtceo.org).

Among the many horrific scenes of the tragedy, few were more memorable than those of New Yorkers running frantically from huge, fast-moving dust clouds. Comprised mostly of pulverized concrete, these enormous, rapidly expanding clouds resembled the "pyroclastic" clouds generated from volcanoes. According to Richard Gage, AIA, founder of Architects and Engineers for 911 Truth, these massive clouds are yet another telltale sign of planned demolition (DVD "Blueprint for Truth").

## The Physics of Pulverization

These huge dust clouds not only endangered public health; they also posed a serious challenge to the Official Story. Since the standard account insists on gravity as the only available source of energy, the massive pulverization must, according to this hypothesis, have resulted from gravitationally driven impacts. Strangely, though, little intact concrete was found in "the pile"; most of it was pulverized on the way down. This immediate, mid-air creation of dust clouds is especially evident in videos of the North Tower (www.youtube.com/watch?v=SYUx5zJ3yss).

Granted, gravitational energy might have sufficed to break some of the concrete into small pieces. Yet to break apart something requires considerable energy, as anyone who's taken a sledgehammer to concrete can attest; and to reduce something to dust requires much more energy. Therefore, as Griffin has cogently pointed out, gravity "would not have come anywhere close to [supplying] the amount of energy needed to turn the concrete and nonmetallic contents of the buildings into tiny particles of dust" (http://911review.com/articles/griffin/nyc1.html).

The energy required just for pulverization exceeded, perhaps by at least a factor of ten, the available *gravitational* energy. This imbalance was pronounced at the moment of inception, when the gravitational energy available was minimal but the explosive outward ejections were most dramatic. In fact, as Hoffman has noted, "you can see thick clouds of pulverized concrete being ejected within the first two seconds. That's when the motion of the top of the tower relative to the intact portion was only a few feet per second" (http://911research.wtc7.net/papers/dustvolume/volume.html).

NIST's Official Story, then, seems to ignore the laws of physics. When one considers the energy required to pulverize concrete and other nonmetallic materials, break structural steel, propel large chunks of metal, and generate roaring dust clouds of near-volcanic proportions, the standard account doesn't compute. The energy required just isn't there.

### Analysis of WTC Dust Raises More Suspicions

Though not intended to determine what happened to the Towers, an early study generated revealing results. The RJ Lee Group's "Dust Signature Study" (2003) found unexpected spherical particles in the characteristic dust. One type, which comprised about 6 percent of the samples, was spherical iron and silicate particles that indicated *very* high temperatures ("WTC Dust Signature Study" pp. 4, 24, 17). Although it's possible that the microspheres were fly ash used in lightweight concrete, these spherical particles may also imply that metals in the Towers melted and then condensed as droplets.

It's intriguing to note that the original Lee Report strongly implied the possibility that *extremely* high temperatures—far above those generated by the hydrocarbon fires observed at the Towers—had produced the particles. A later version of the Report, however, avoided words like "melt," apparently in order to play down any implication of extreme temperatures (Griffin *Mysterious Collapse* pp. 40-42).

The presence of the microspheres, suggested physicist Steven Jones, chemist Kevin Ryan, and other researchers, revealed that the iron had first boiled and evaporated and then was "sprayed into the air so that the surface tension draws the droplets into near spherical shapes." In 2008, using electron microscope and X-ray spectroscopy to study very fine particles, these researchers came out with a report, "Extremely High Temperatures during the World Trade Center Destruction." Going beyond iron, the study also pointed to a microsphere rich in molybdenum. The presence of this metal implied a high temperature of 4,753°F (*J. of 9/11 Studies* 1/08). What could have generated such extreme heat?

In recent years, scientific studies and papers have focused on the WTC destruction. Led by Jones, Ryan, Dr. Frank Legge and other scientists, these researchers have moved beyond establishing extreme temperatures into establishing the chemical content of whatever produced these temperatures. This will be part of our discussion in the next chapter on WTC-7.

Several additional features of planned demolitions are readily observable at the WTC.

## 1. Outward Ejections from the Buildings.

One characteristic is the outward and even upward ejection of materials from the building. Photos and videos of the Towers reveal that huge, four-to twenty-ton pieces of steel were ejected in several directions for distances up to 500 feet (www2.ae911truth.org/twintowers.php). Sections of aluminum cladding were blown even farther, up to 700 feet away (D. Paul and J. Hoffman *Waking Up from Our Nightmare* p. 7). Since gravity's pull is essentially vertical, gravity alone can't account for these horizontal ejections.

## 2. Sounds of Explosions.

Explosives used to demolish a building produce loud sounds. Many witnesses reported hearing explosions before and during the collapses of the Towers. Several persons on site reported hearing an explosion just before one of the Towers came down: NYPD Battalion Chief John Sudnik remembered that "we heard … what sounded like a loud explosion and looked up and I saw Tower Two start coming down" (*NYT* "The Sept. 11 Records" p. 4).

Many other fire professionals reported not only multiple explosions, but also successive flashes. FDNY firefighter Edward Cachia watched as the titanic Tower gave way "at a lower floor, not the floor where the plane hit … explosions went in succession, boom, boom, boom, boom, and then the Tower came down." Firefighter James Curran recalled that "every floor went chu-chu-chu … from the pressure everything was getting blown out before it actually collapsed" ("Sept. 11 Records" pp. 5, 10-11). Windows in buildings up to 400 feet away from the Towers were also blown out. FDNY Captain Karin Deshore recalled that "with each popping sound it was initially an orange and then a red flash came out of the building and then it would just go all around the building …" ("Sept. 11 Records" p. 15).

All told, 118 first responders reported either sounds of explosions or flashes of light, mostly as the buildings began to come down.

### 3. Explosive Evidence of Demolition "Squibs."

A characteristic of demolition, "squibs" refer to the puffs or jets of dust shooting outward from buildings during destruction. Chemist Kevin Ryan has defined them as "high velocity bursts of debris ejected from point-like sources …." They can occur "at levels twenty to thirty floors below a 'collapse' front " (*J. of 9/11 Studies* 9/07). Squibs often seem unsynchronized, isolated, and infrequent, like explosive shells striking a building. But a closer look, such as the one of the North Tower afforded by physicist David Chandler, reveals that many of the squibs are hidden behind the descending debris and dust clouds, and most are not random but carefully timed (www.youtube.com/watch?v=EgN080yySe0).

### 4. Synchronized Demolition Rings.

Common characteristics of induced collapses also include demolition rings, the series of small, synchronized explosions that run rapidly around a building. Far below the scars from aircraft impacts, these "strings of fireworks" were visible in the disintegrations of both Towers (http://911research. wtc7.net/index.html).

Again, credible testimonials speak of demolition rings:

- Firefighter Joseph Meola reported, "it looked like the building was blowing out on all four sides. We actually heard the pops" ("Sept. 11 Records" p. 5).
- Firefighter Kenneth Rogers recalled that "Floor after floor after floor…. It looked like a synchronized, deliberate kind of thing" ("Sept. 11 Records" pp. 3-4).
- Paramedic Daniel Rivera also heard the "pops" just before the South Tower came down: "At first I thought it was—do you ever see professional demolition where they set the charges on certain floors and then you hear 'pop, pop, pop, pop, pop'? … I thought it was that" ("Sept. 11 Records" p. 9).

Horizontal lines of explosions are well illustrated in still shots of the South Tower's disintegration (http://911research.wtc7.net/wtc/evidence/videos/stc_frames.html).

For any of us, it's difficult to think the unthinkable. In many of these interviews with firefighters, we sense a tentative tone, an implication that "at the time I thought ..." When first responders vividly recalled events that didn't square with rapidly emerging official narratives, many may have experienced difficulty maintaining their original hypothesis, even though it accorded with the horrors they'd experienced.

It was Teresa Veliz, employee in the North Tower, who went beyond reportage to picture other possibilities: "There were explosions going off everywhere. I was convinced that there were bombs planted all over the place and someone was sitting at a control panel pushing detonator buttons" (Griffin *New Pearl Harbor Revisited* p. 29). She paints a horrifying picture—yet its implications, though chilling, must be considered.

## How Could Explosives Have Found Their Way into Those Buildings?

That's a fair question. While it's not one that anyone can answer definitively with the evidence currently available, this evidence may guide a future investigation.

Over the years, researchers have received many reports of incidents that, in retrospect, struck people who worked in the Towers as suspicious. According to several employees, during the last few weeks and days, an exceptional number of power outages occurred, raising questions about whether security systems were compromised during their duration. In addition, elevators in entire areas of the buildings were isolated. Nancy Cass, who worked on the forty-fourth floor of the North Tower, recalled that on 9/11 "passenger elevators on the west side of the building had been out of order for the past five or six weeks and the elevator company had a crew working at the scene" (D. DiMarco *Tower Stories* p. 59).

### Elevator Renovations Continue Right Up to 9/11

Such reports were hardly idle speculation. Since 2000, major renovations to the Towers had been ongoing. The Port Authority of New York and

New Jersey, the owners of the WTC, had commissioned ACE Elevator Company to undertake a complete modernization of the 198 elevators (*USA Today* 9/11/02). By early 2001, ACE announced a "towering" achievement: it had completed installation of the first six of its "elite Shuttle Fleet" (*Elevator World* 3/01). The ongoing renovations meant that ACE employees worked extended hours and received special security clearances. In early September 2001, from an office located on the 35th floor in the South Tower, ACE was still working on renovation (*Elevator World* 9/01).

Could someone have exploited the relaxed security or the unprecedented access to the huge core columns that surrounded the elevator shafts—or the buildings more broadly? On the morning of 9/11, 80 elevator mechanics were on duty in the Towers—many, in fact, were just a few steps from passengers trapped in elevators. For decades, firefighters had relied on elevator mechanics with specialized tools to help with rescues. Yet "fearing for their own safety," the mechanics "evacuated on their own initiative when the South Tower was struck." Before the South Tower came down, a supervisor from the Port Authority radioed the mechanics "to say [that] firefighters needed their help. The South Tower collapsed as two supervisors were on their way back" (*USA Today* 9/11/02).

If the mechanics were particularly eager to leave, what might have intensified fears for their own safety?

## Other Possible Factors in Compromised Security?

Moreover, who was responsible for security at the WTC? President G. W. Bush's younger brother, Marvin, and distant relative, Wirt Walker III, were executives with Stratesec (formerly Securacom), the company in charge of security. Walker, in fact, was CEO. In the years and months leading up to 9/11, Stratesec was developing security systems for the WTC buildings. Neither the president's relatives nor Stratesec were mentioned in the Commission's *Report*.

The company provided security services for both federal facilities and foreign governments linked to the 9/11 attacks. It had, for instance, run security for Los Alamos National Laboratories, where scientists were developing super-thermite explosives like those found in the WTC dust (*Open Chemical Physics Journal* 7/09). And in the years leading up to 9/11, Stratesec had security contracts with the Kuwaiti and Saudi elites. Marvin Bush joined Securacom when it was capitalized by the Kuwait-American (KuwAm) Corporation, which became the company's major investor. Ever since the Gulf War, KuwAm had cultivated close financial ties to the Bush family. One member of the Kuwaiti royal family, Mishal Yousef Saud al Sabah, served on the board of Stratesec (*Prince George's Journal* [Md.] 2/4/03).

The interconnections to the Bush dynasty are particularly instructive. Wirt Walker III, the managing director at KuwAm, headed up Stratesec. Marvin Bush's last year on the board at Stratesec coincided with his first year on that of HCC Insurance, formerly Houston Casualty Company, one of the insurance carriers for the WTC (www.commondreams.org/views03/0204-06. htm). Stratesec's Chief Operating Officer, Barry McDaniel, came to the company from BDM International, a subsidiary of the Carlyle Group which specialized in "black projects" (D. Briody *Iron Triangle* p. 35). The Carlyle Group was virtually a Bush family project; it was managed by several Bush insiders, including White House former chief of staff James Baker and former CIA deputy director Frank Carluccci.

Interconnections with the Bush dynasty are particularly instructive. Wirt Walker III, the managing director at KuwAm, headed up Stratesec. Marvin Bush's last year on the board at Stratesec coincided with his first year on that of HCC Insurance, formerly Houston Casualty Company, one of the insurance carriers for the WTC (www.commondreams.org/views03/0204-06. htm). Stratesec's Chief Operating Officer, Barry McDaniel, came to the company from BDM International, a subsidiary of the Carlyle Investment Group which specialized in "black projects" (D. Briody *Iron Triangle* p. 35). The Carlyle Group was virtually a Bush family project; it was managed by several Bush insiders, including White House former chief of staff James Baker and former CIA deputy director Frank Carluccci.

**House of Bush, House of Saud**

The connections between the Bushes and Saudis—especially the bin Laden family—are equally intriguing. As several researchers have shown,

Carlyle was funded by investors from both Bush and bin Laden families. In 1998, former President G. H. W. Bush himself met with bin Laden family members on behalf of Carlyle, which described itself as "one of the world's largest global private equity investment firms" (*Sunday Herald* [Glascow] 10/7/01). And on the morning of 9/11, the former president appeared at a Carlyle Group meeting also attended by Shafig bin Laden, half brother to Osama. Given the evidence that both Washington insiders and wealthy Arabs were possibly involved in the 9/11 attacks, these connections are important (K. Ryan 911Blogger 9/3/10).

Exactly what to draw from these connections isn't clear; it is evident, though, that Securacom illustrated problems with American and Arabic elites exploiting political influence for mutual enrichment. If compromised security at the WTC complex remains a possibility, so does foreknowledge of the attacks.

**Possible Foreknowledge in High Places?**
That morning, Mayor Rudy Giuliani made a startling statement to NBC's Peter Jennings: "we set up headquarters at 75 Barclay Street, which was right there with the police commissioner, the fire commissioner ... when we were told that the World Trade Center was going to collapse" (NBC 9/11/01). Sadly, Jennings neglected to ask the obvious follow-up question: "If you 'were told,' then who told you?"

Later Giuliani changed his story, claiming he didn't mean the Towers were coming down right away, only "over a seven-, eight-, nine-, ten-hour period." But as Griffin has remarked, since no steel-framed buildings had ever come down before, one has to wonder "how Giuliani's people— possibly among the police or fire commissioners—could have known that the Towers were going to collapse ..." (Griffin *New Pearl Harbor Revisited* p. 40).

If much of this strikes the reader as circumstantial evidence, that's a fair take on it. In examining WTC-7, we'll not only learn more about the involvement of city officials and investors but about other startling instances of foreknowledge within the news media before the skyscraper came down. Above all, though, we'll examine hard scientific evidence on WTC-7, the "smoking gun" of 9/11.

# 22. "Building What?"
## The Strange Fall of WTC-7

*When you have eliminated the impossible, whatever remains,*
*however improbable, must be the truth.*

—Sir Arthur Conan Doyle, *A Study in Scarlet*

In September 2009, Judge Edward Lehner was hearing arguments on whether to allow New Yorkers to vote on a proposal to investigate the attacks on the World Trade Center. Sponsored by NYC CAN, the petition included the signatures of 52,000 residents (*Villager* 8/4/09). When Judge Lehner remarked that the 9/11 Commission had already completed an investigation, the group's attorney, Dennis McMahon, replied that the Commission had left many questions unanswered. "One of the biggest questions," the lawyer noted, "is why did Building 7 come down?" Puzzled, Judge Lehner asked "Building what?" McMahon informed the judge that a *third* World Trade Center skyscraper, Building 7, also came down on 9/11.

## A Little-Known Event

Such public ignorance is widespread. One national poll found that 43 percent of Americans weren't aware that three buildings had fallen (Zogby Intl. 5/24/06); of this number, only a small percentage had any idea about the circumstances. Even among those who were more knowledgeable, the disintegration of this third skyscraper has remained an enigma.

WTC-7's relative obscurity is itself puzzling. This high-rise building wasn't hit by an airliner, and at 47 stories it would have stood as the tallest skyscraper in 30 states. When *New York Times* reporter James

Glanz characterized the fall of WTC-7 as "a mystery that under normal circumstances would probably have captured the attention of the city and the world" (*NYT* 11/29/01), he was factoring in media environment right after 9/11. But it wasn't just a *tsunami* of shocking news that has caused WTC-7 to go underreported; it also posed big challenges to the Official Story.

The fall of WTC-7 should have been a bigger story because the circumstances of its demise were anything but "normal." While the standard narrative says the skyscraper disintegrated because of fire damage, this seemingly simple hypothesis introduces more ambiguity than it dispels. Was fire really a sufficient cause, especially when one recalls that, before 9/11, no steel-framed high rise had ever come down because of fire?

### The WTC-7 Fires: Location, Time, Fuel, Size, and Damage

The fire reports ranged widely. While no one has talked about a towering inferno or even a huge conflagration, Fire Capt. Brenda Berkman did affirm "fire on every floor" (S. Hagan and M. Carouba *Women at Ground Zero* p. 213). But perceptions do differ, even among professionals, and it would be easy to confuse a lot of smoke with a lot of fire. Mark Jacobson, a journalist who'd reported large fires, recalled "the whole building wasn't on fire"; instead, he wrote, "there was a lot of fire coming out of a few floors" (*NY Magazine* 3/37/06). The photographic record also supports the conclusion that the building experienced *medium to hot* fires on a *few* floors.

Even those promoting the hypothesis of destruction from fire damage have come in way under Capt. Berkman's estimate. According to NIST, itself a prime defender of this theory, fires burned on only ten of the building's 47 floors—and only on six did they grow and burn out of control (NCSTAR1A p. xxxvi). Moreover, officials with Consolidated Edison (Con Ed) of New York who entered WTC-7 said "there was a fire, but they did not think the building would collapse" (http://media.nara.gov/9-11/MFR/t-0148-911MFR-00174.pdf). Thus Con Ed personnel apparently felt the building was safe to enter, reporting only "a fire," not the "large fires" claimed by many proponents of the fire theory.

It was the Fire Department, then, that predicted the building was going to collapse. Granted, a walkthrough is not an inspection of a tall building. But if in fact the fires were small, on what basis did building security personnel and the FDNY chiefs make a different determination?

### When Did Fires in WTC-7 First Become Visible?

The question of when the fires first broke out is also controversial. The standard analysis of WTC-7 asserts that when the North Tower came down at 10:28, flying debris ignited the fires. Although WTC-7 stood 325 feet away, tremendous mushrooming explosions at the top of the Tower propelled large chunks of metal, some of them likely superheated, hundreds of feet outward (www.youtube.com/watch?v=EgN080yySe0).

For the first two or three hours, the blazes were scattered and not immediately visible. NIST also acknowledged that the first photographs or videos of WTC-7 fires were taken at about 12:10 a.m., and that two other photos were taken at 12:28. This meant, as David Ray Griffin has noted, that the first fires were photographed between one and two hours after the flying debris hit the building (Griffin *Mysterious Collapse* pp. 160-61). These times pose a plausibility challenge to the standard narrative; they ask us "to believe," remarked Griffin, "that, although the fires were supposedly started near the building's south and southwest faces, and hence near the windows, they remained invisible from outside the building for all that time." And "the fact that fires first became visible on the eleventh and twelfth floors at 2:00 [also] makes it very difficult to believe NIST's claim that the fires began at 10:28" (Griffin *Mysterious Collapse* pp. 160-61).

### Did Fires Start Even Before the North Tower Fell?

Although some of the fires apparently started later than claimed, others may have actually started *earlier*—up to an hour before the North Tower came down, supposedly starting all the WTC-7 fires. Although structural engineer Matthys Levy supported the Official Story about the Towers, he too indicated "the initial fires started around 9:30 in the morning, so the building was allowed to burn for eight hours" (Griffin *Mysterious Collapse* pp. 168-69). About this same time, City staffers Michael Hess and Barry Jennings also reported smoke on the eighth floor when they were forced to wait for rescue there. "It was dark," Jennings told BBC. "It was also hot—*very* hot" (www.youtube.com/watch?v=VQY-ksiuwKU). So the fires may have started up to an hour *before* the first Tower came down.

These incongruities led physical chemist Dr. Frank H. Greening to remark that one of the most important problems with the official account "is the question of where and how fires started in the building" (wtc.nist. gov/comments08). The official account depends on fires burning long enough and hot enough to cause a floor beam to expand and break a column loose, leading to "sudden and global collapse." Thus it's not surprising that proponents of the Official Story speculated about what might have fueled such hot, long-burning fires.

**Early Fuel-Oil Hypotheses**

Early speculation claimed the impact of debris ignited thousands of gallons of diesel fuel stored in fire-resistant containers. Three small storage tanks located on floors five, seven, and eight were fed from "larger tanks near ground level" (*NYT* 3/20/02). In addition, FEMA reported one 6,000-gallon tank between floors two and three, plus one 6,000-gallon and two 12,000-gallon tanks under a loading dock (*Report* 2002). However, FEMA later found the latter subterranean containers intact, still containing 20,000 gallons of oil (www.wtc7.net/articles/FEMA/WTC_ch5.htm).

Most photos show fires in only a few windows, primarily on the seventh and twelfth floors. The seventh had an oil tank, but the twelfth did not. Since fires broke out on floors where *no* storage tanks were located but not on all the floors where tanks were present, it's reasonable to conclude that diesel wasn't the major fuel for most of the fires. If oil had been a major source, some fires would have grown *much* larger on floors with storage tanks.

**FEMA Looks Toward Other Causes for Fires**

FEMA, the first federal agency to investigate, was rightly skeptical about the fuel-oil hypothesis. Its investigators reported that "on the north face, photographs and videos show that the fires were located on approximately the seventh, eighth, eleventh, twelfth, and thirteenth floors." However, many photos and videos also show little fire or smoke on the north side, leading some to speculate that the fires remained mostly on the southern side of the building, where the debris had hit. From this evidence, FEMA theorized that these blazes might have somehow warped the steel on the southern side to the point where the whole building collapsed.

But if this scenario were correct, then why didn't WTC-7 sag, list, or topple toward its south side? In one of its most useful observations, FEMA concluded "the facade came straight down, suggesting an internal collapse.… The building imploded, with collapse initiating at an interior location" (www.fema.gov/pdf/library/fema403_ch5.pdf).

Although the FEMA investigation was under funded, poorly managed, denied access to most of the physical evidence, and sometimes self-contradictory, FEMA did draw valid conclusions. Its 2002 WTC Building Performance Study allowed that even its best guess, even its "best hypothesis has only a low probability of occurrence" (FEMA *Report* Appendix C). Nevertheless, most officials and media commentators clung to an improbable story: after the building's sprinkler system failed and additional water was not available, the fires spread, fueled by diesel oil, and eventually burned so hot they caused the steel support structure to weaken, resulting in a collapse. This scenario was highly improbable, as even NIST would later acknowledge.

### How Much Damage Did the Debris Inflict?

Observers have also disagreed about how much WTC-7 was damaged by debris blown outward from the North Tower. Some witnesses and many proponents of a damage-plus-fire hypothesis have claimed *very* substantial damage. EMT Mercedes Rivera said that the building "had no face and it was ready to collapse" (Hagan and Carouba *Women at Ground Zero* p. 29). It's highly unlikely, though, that WTC-7 received damage anywhere near a "great gash scooped deeply," as *Popular Mechanics* once claimed (*Pop. Mech.* 3/05). The photo and video record just doesn't show any structural damage of this magnitude.

Although NIST initially promoted the notion that the south side of WTC-7 was scooped out, it ultimately conceded that structural damage had *no part* in the collapse initiation (*Final Report*). If serious structural damage—

whether caused by large fires or flying debris or some combination of the two—was the main cause for the demise of WTC-7, then why would the building have stood looking just fine—without significant slumping, sagging, or listing—and then suddenly drop straight down?

### Early Evacuation and Explosions at WTC-7

WTC-7's twenty-third floor housed Mayor Rudy Giuliani's new command center, the Office for Emergency Management (OEM), which had cost the city $13 million. After the first plane hit the North Tower at 8:46 a.m., the mayor, an aide, and two bodyguards drove down to the WTC (W. Barrett and D. Collins *Grand Illusion* pp. 3-5). According to his testimony, Giuliani was still in the car when the second plane hit. When he met with Police Commissioner Bernie Kerik, the commissioner told him they'd already evacuated WTC-7 and were setting up a command center at 75 Barclay Street. Then Giuliani dashed over to FDNY Chief Peter Ganci's command post on West Street (Comm. Hearing 5/19/04). Because several OEM officials and their deputies had gone the North Tower lobby, not to the OEM, the command center was dysfunctional from the outset. New Yorkers had scoffed at the mayor's decision to locate his command center in the World Trade Center, long the top target for terrorists. Later they were vindicated when Giuliani chose to abandon his new emergency-management center before its first big emergency (Barrett and Collins *Grand Illusion* pp. 31, 34).

While it's not clear whether the departure from Giuliani's command center came before or after 9:03, when the second airliner hit, some office workers have reported that WTC-7 itself was evacuated *before* that time (*Ft. Detrick Standard* 10/18/01). Since most people—both in the city and around the country—had not realized that the Towers were under attack until the second impact, one does wonder who initiated the evacuation order for the OEM and why they might have deemed it necessary.

### Stranded Aides Make Unsettling Reports

Despite the evacuation order and the police presence that must have accompanied it, the mayor's staffers did enter the WTC-7 just after 9:00. Michael Hess, corporation counsel for the city and a close friend of

Giuliani; and Barry Jennings, the Director of Emergency Services for the City Housing Authority, made it up to the OEM (*Independent* [UK] 9/13/01). Expecting to find Giuliani at the command center, they were amazed to find "everybody was gone." Since evacuations take time, these reports imply an evacuation order was given before 9:03.

Puzzled, Jennings called other staffers, one of whom told him "to leave and leave right away." A superior also commanded him to "get out of there now." But the elevators didn't work because the power had gone out (BBC 9/6/08). Do these warnings suggest foreknowledge that "seven is coming down," or do they convey caution about a possible third hit on a building that housed many government offices, including the SEC, DoD, and CIA?

In characteristic fashion, the 9/11 Commission claimed that the OEM wasn't fully evacuated until after 9:30: "After the South Tower was hit [at 9:03], OEM senior leadership decided to remain in its 'bunker' and continue conducting operations, even though all civilians had been evacuated from 7 WTC" (*Report* p. 305). This contradicted Giuliani's claim that he arrived at the improvised command center on 75 Barclay St. *before* 9:30 (ABC 9/11/01). In an apparent attempt to make Giuliani look good, the Commission's *Report* overrode his testimony, much as it had done with Rumsfeld and Cheney.

## Mayor's Staffers Report Explosions and Smoke

After receiving orders to leave the building, Hess and Jennings reportedly headed down the stairs until they got to the sixth floor. There, according to Jennings, "the landing that we were standing on gave way" because of a "big explosion" from below. They retreated to the eighth floor, broke a window, and called to firefighters for help: "They came twice. Why? I was trapped in there when both buildings [Towers] came down. All this time I was hearing explosions" (www.youtube.com/watch?v=kxUj6UgPODo). Hess largely corroborated Jennings's story, adding "we were trapped on the eighth floor with smoke, thick smoke, all around us, for about an hour and a half (www.youtube.com/watch?v=BUfiLbXMa64).

Giuliani claimed the sounds of explosions and the smoke hadn't come from within WTC-7; instead, they'd come from the stricken Towers.

502

But the power outage surely didn't come from another building, and since WTC-7's windows remained intact, it was highly unlikely that the reported smoke and heat had come from one of the Towers. Although the fires at WTC-7 were reportedly ignited when the North Tower came down at 10:28, this was an hour *after* the staffers reported that an explosion blew away the stairwell. Griffin points out that "the testimony of Michael Hess and Barry Jennings was threatening to the official account of WTC-7, according to which its collapse was not caused or even aided by explosives" (Griffin *Mysterious Collapse* pp. 85-92). While Hess changed his testimony, Jennings continued to contradict the standard account.

This challenge may have contributed to an odd coincidence. On August 19, 2008, just two days before the National Institute of Standards and Technology (NIST) was due to release the draft of its Final Report on WTC-7, Jennings died after spending several days in a hospital. Filmmaker Dylan Avery, who was among the last to interview Jennings, hired a well-regarded private investigator to look into Jennings's death. Within 24 hours, Avery received a terse message back: "Due to some of the information I have uncovered, I have determined that this is a job for the police. I have refunded your credit card. Please do not contact me again about this individual" (Griffin *Mysterious Collapse* pp. 98-99).

**Reports of Later Explosions**

There were also reports of explosions in the late afternoon, as WTC-7 came down at 5:21 p.m. Reporter Peter Demarco of the *New York Daily News* recalled, "there was a rumble. The building's top row of windows popped out. Then all the windows on the thirty-ninth floor popped out. Then the thirty-eighth floor. Pop! Pop! Pop! was all you heard until the building sunk into a rising cloud of gray" (C. Bull and S. Erman *At Ground Zero* p. 97).

Beyond Demarco, NYPD officer Craig Bartmer also reported "I was real close to Building 7 when it fell down.... There's a lot of eyewitness testimony down there of hearing explosions ... all of a sudden I looked up, and ... the thing started peeling in on itself.... I started running ... and the whole time you're hearing 'boom, boom, boom, boom, boom.'" Another eyewitness, a New York University medical student who'd served as an emergency medic that day, provided a similar account: "we heard this sound that sounded like a clap of thunder... it looked like there was a shock wave ripping through the building and the windows all busted out.... About a second later the bottom floor caved out and the building followed after that" (www.911truth.org/article.php?story=20100527162010811).

### Likely Foreknowledge WTC-7 Would Come Down

As reported in the previous chapter, Mayor Giuliani told Peter Jennings he'd received word that the World Trade Center was going to collapse (NBC 9/11/01). But Mayor Giuliani was hardly the only one who apparently had foreknowledge.

On July 24, 2001, just six weeks before 9/11, a private consortium headed by Silverstein Properties acquired a 99-year lease on the World Trade Center complex. The price? A cool $3.2 billion. Larry Silverstein, the new owner, took out insurance policies that included special provisions for loss due to terrorist attacks. In the wake of the 9/11 debacle, these details initially received little media scrutiny, even in an otherwise politically savvy town like New York.

A year after the unprecedented collapses of the three skyscrapers, the mystery surrounding WTC-7 took a new twist. Larry Silverstein seemingly revealed he'd thought it best to demolish one of his own properties. "I remember getting a call from the fire department commander telling me that they weren't sure they were gonna be able to contain the fire, and I said, 'We've had such terrible loss of life: maybe the smartest thing to do is pull it.' And they made that decision to pull and we watched the building collapse" (PBS "America Rebuilds" 9/02).

While one can fully appreciate Mr. Silverstein's concern for loss of life, the building in question had *already* been evacuated for several hours and the fire department had *already* pulled back. No one had fought the fires. Mr. Silverstein implied that soon after he'd decided to "pull it," he watched his 47-story skyscraper dissolve into a neat pile of rubble. Later, Silverstein Properties insisted in a formal statement that its owner only meant to "pull" "the contingent of firefighters" (Letter to NIST 3/24/06). However, since "pull" is an industry term for "demolish," it's difficult to imagine what "pull it" might have meant other than "demolish it." And because of the preparations necessary for a demolition, it's hard to see how Silverstein simply decided to finish off a property that, because of fire damage, had possibly lost its value.

### Questions Surround Highly Favorable Insurance Settlement

Since the insurance policies on the WTC included coverage against terrorist attacks, Silverstein successfully received a settlement not just for his losses, but based on "two occurrences" of terrorism, for *twice* the value of the lost property. This meant that Silverstein sought to collect $7 billion (*NYT* 9/30/02). In December 2004, a federal jury awarded "only" $4.6 billion in damages to Silverstein. It did seem true that in just three and a half years, the real estate magnate had realized a huge profit on his investment (*Forbes* 12/06/04). But to be fair, that wasn't all profit. Silverstein continued to owe the Port Authority $100 million a year for rent, had lost $300 million a year in rent revenues, and had to rebuild the WTC (*NYT* 03/27/08).

Even with these requirements, how did the apparently outsized insurance settlement come about? How could someone collect on a property he'd approved for demolition? Attorney Bill Veale has remarked that "you are dancing with one of the most perplexing conundrums of 9/11." Veale made an important legal distinction: "Silverstein never made a statement of intent to demolish. He made, legally, what is called an 'admission,' a statement that can be used against him, but is less than a confession" (Pers. Corresp.). Still, the case for planned demolition, it does seem, would have been a fairly easy one to make, so one has to wonder why the insurer's attorneys didn't argue it.

Answering this conundrum will likely merit the attention of a full and genuine inquiry into "Building What?"

### Questions Surrounding the Apparent Foreknowledge

Skeptics have sometimes been too quick to conclude that Silverstein's statement solves the mystery of WTC-7. In reality, though, it underscores more questions than it answers.

Why did the fire department decide not to fight the fires? The answer, at least after 10:28, might be that flying debris had inflicted major structural damage to the building, as the various chiefs reported. Several regular firefighters claimed the building was leaning (www.youtube. com/watch?v=WnYBX6QT0R4). Once the fires and structural damage were observed, firefighters were reportedly pulled back because the building was considered dangerous, whether because of structural damage or the possibility of explosives inside, and because no water was available after the Towers water mains ruptured. Nevertheless, many firefighters reported frustration when they were ordered to stand back and not fight the fires (http://911research.wtc7.net/wtc/attack/wtc7.html).

After receiving reports of explosions at the Twin Towers, the fire department may have suspected that explosives might also be present in WTC-7. If these reports reached the middle and higher levels of the FDNY, the commanders may have decided that it would be irresponsible to risk entering a building which might contain explosives. But of course they couldn't say this publicly because of its implications regarding the demise of all three buildings. So the top officials may have felt it necessary to rely on exaggerations of the size of the fires and the degree of the damage inflicted on WTC-7.

It should be emphasized that seeming foreknowledge of an event is not the same as involvement in its planning. In a hierarchical organization like a fire department, predictive statements can be made and passed along without discussion, especially in a catastrophic emergency.

### First Responder Testimonials of Foreboding or Foreknowledge

Dozens of first responders and firefighters have agreed that they were ordered not to fight the fires in WTC-7 and were told the building was coming down. Researcher Matt Everett has compiled these statements (http://911blogger.com/node/6195).

First responder Indira Singh, a volunteer EMT, recalled "there was another panic around 4 o'clock because *they were bringing the building down* and people seemed to know this ahead of time" (Pacifica KPFA Radio 4/27/05). Fire Capt. Brenda Berkman stated that "we no sooner got going on something there when a chief came along and said, 'Everybody's got to leave the area. We're afraid Seven WTC is going to fall down" (Hagan and Carouba *Women at Ground Zero* p. 213). This comes as close to a recollection of actually fighting fires in the building as any in the testimonials. While the higher-ups claimed that they couldn't get water to WTC-7, this alleged problem doesn't appear in statements made by the people who would have fought the fires.

While only a few of the firefighters questioned the orders, some did murmur, wondering what was going on: Deputy Fire Chief Nick Visconti recalled that "World Trade Center 7 was burning and I was thinking to myself, *how come they're not trying to put this fire out?* … At some point, [FDNY Assistant Chief] Frank Fellini said, now we've got hundreds of guys out there.… He said to me, Nick, you've got to get those people out of there.… One comment was, oh, that building is never coming down, it didn't get hit by a plane, why isn't somebody in there putting the fire out?" (*Firehouse* 8/02).

As one reads these statements, questions arise once again: Who made the decision that the fires couldn't be fought and the building couldn't be saved? When was that decision first made? And at that time, what was the basis for making it? These too are tough questions to answer.

However, a *New York Times* story may offer some help: "By 11:30 a.m., the fire commander in charge of that area, Assistant Chief Frank Fellini, ordered firefighters away from [WTC-7] for safety reasons" (*NYT* 11/29/01). Yet since most observers have claimed that the fires in the building were *not* visible for an hour or even two after 11:30, NIST stated that "visual evidence of fires in the building was not available until around noon" (NIST NCSTAR1A p. 18). Thus it's difficult to understand why anyone would make the decision not to fight the fires so early on. Perhaps Chief Fellini inspected the interior of the building or otherwise worked from information not available to most observers. His concern for firefighters' safety was commendable.

## Networks Also Anticipate Fall of WTC-7
Moments after the building came down, MSNBC's Brian Williams asked David Restuccio, an FDNY lieutenant, about the fall of the skyscraper: "You guys knew this was coming all day?" Lt. Restuccio replied "we had

heard reports that the building was unstable, and that it would eventually need to come down on its own, or it would be taken down. I would imagine it came down on its own." Lt. Restuccio didn't explain what he meant by "it would be taken down," nor did anyone at the network ask (MSNBC 9/11/01). While one can understand why an FDNY lieutenant would report what he did, one does have to wonder where in the chain of command the terminal prognosis about the building might have originated.

Adding to suspicions that prominent individuals did seem to have foreknowledge, fully *four* major news outlets anticipated the disintegration of WTC-7. A Fox News Channel 5 crew was all set up to film well before the 47-story building ever began to drop (Fox 9/11/01). CNN aired a story about the "collapse" of WTC-7 over an hour *before* it happened. About 4:10, CNN announced that WTC-7 "was incredibly structurally damaged" (www.youtube.com/watch?v=58h0LjdMry0). On what basis did Fox make that determination?

Then, fully 23 minutes *before* the building actually came down, BBC reporter Jane Standley announced that WTC-7 had fallen while in the video it still stood serenely behind her. She explained that "this was not a result of a new attack; it was because the building had been weakened during this morning's attacks" (BBC 9/11/01). Next, and no less laughably, MSNBC got into the act. With the building visible behind her, the network's Ashleigh Banfield announced "that is the building that is going to go down next … there's no way they can stabilize it." Startled by an explosion, Banfield turned toward WTC-7, which was still fully standing, and cried out "Oh my God! This is it!" (www.youtube.com/watch?v=ERhoNYj9_fg). Banfield's outcry indicated that she'd been informed beforehand that the building would be coming down. No one asked the question: since no plane had hit this skyscraper and its fires were far smaller than those in the Towers, how could anyone seem so sure of its demise?

**Instant Media Imprinting of the Official Story**
Much as CNN told viewers that the building was "incredibly structurally damaged," other networks reported on "the building that is going down next … we heard earlier that it was structurally unstable." Still others

described the demise of WTC-7 as "part of the ancillary damage from the other two," ruined by falling debris from the Twin Towers. Thus major mass-media outlets—including Fox, CNN, BBC, and NBC, and MSNBC (twice)—had begun to introduce and even inculcate an official narrative before the last WTC building had come down (www.youtube.com/watch?v=ERhoNYj9_fg). The twist, though, was that NIST quietly changed the story in 2006 when it finally discarded structural damage as a factor in the fall of WTC-7.

## Scientifically Embarrassing FEMA and NIST Reports

As the discussion so far has shown, WTC-7 became the subject of government investigations—and both, considered as science, were national disasters.

After the American Society of Civil Engineers had assembled a team of volunteers, FEMA took over and led the investigation. Handicapped by insufficient funding, a small staff (many of them volunteers), and a lack of access to both witnesses and evidence, FEMA's 2002 *WTC Building Performance Study* was by its own admission inconclusive.

FEMA's work was doomed from the outset. In the months following the attacks, FEMA investigators, backed by civil engineers, operated under ridiculous limitations. Except for one brief walkthrough tour of Ground Zero, the FEMA team had to work from small samples of wreckage. Only about one percent of the structural steel was available for them to examine. Astoundingly, more than three months after 9/11 the investigators hadn't even received the blueprints for the buildings (*NYT* 12/25/01). The hasty disposal of wreckage and the destruction of evidence were inexcusable. WTC-7 had been evacuated, so bodies of victims weren't a concern. Its disintegration, however, was of keen interest to architecture, engineering and insurance professionals.

When the cleanup routine blatantly ignored FBI crime-scene protocol, it moved into violations of federal law. Surely, the Bureau itself must have known that it was enabling a completely unprofessional and demonstrably illegal disturbance of the site. In complete contrast to what went on at Ground Zero, former FBI Director Louis Freeh described what FBI protocol seeks to avoid: "Crime scenes can grow stale in a hurry. Evidence is lost, or it decays beyond useful capacity. Well-meaning efforts to clear the site of a human disaster can destroy vital information about angles of impact, the size of an explosion, and the nature of the explosive materials themselves" (Freeh *My FBI* p. 4). Did the FBI really want to *solve* the crime of the century, or did it prefer to issue a list of nineteen Islamic names and, in effect, declare the case closed?

As noted earlier, FEMA did have the humility to admit that even its best guess had "only a low probability of occurrence" (www.fema.gov/library/wtcstudy.shtm). And FEMA did discard some scientifically untenable theories. Within hours of the tragedy, Stanford Professor Steven Block had rushed to compare the airliner attacks to the nuclear bomb dropped on Hiroshima, claiming "you don't design buildings to withstand nuclear attacks." Prof. Block was among the first academics to falsely claim that the fires actually melted the structural steel (www.stanford.edu/dept/news/pr/01/block911.html). Others would follow.

FEMA, however, enlisted MIT engineering professor Thomas Eagar, who talked much better physics. Prof. Eagar challenged the idea, advanced by several other experts (including some on PBS) that the fires had *melted* the steel support beams. Since temperatures must approach 2,800°F to melt steel, and since only a special device such as an oxyacetylene torch will sustain those temperatures, the meltdown theory was easy to debunk. Once Professor Eagar pointed out that the maximum temperature from open hydrocarbon fires is 1,700°F, the belief that fires fueled by kerosene, paper, and office furniture could melt the steel became untenable (PBS "NOVA" 4/30/02).

But to replace the discredited melted-steel theory, FEMA fell back on a softened-steel hypothesis and also popularized the "domino" or "pancaking" theory to explain the collapses. According to FEMA, fires weakened the structural steel so that floors dropped upon those below, "pancaking" all the way down. This was a hypothesis that the 9/11 Commission would later appropriate—making it a centerpiece of the Official Story—but also one that a legion of critics would deconstruct.

Even if the Towers had "pancaked," this would have been an inadequate explanation for the demise of WTC-7, a very different building that wasn't hit by an airliner. Rather than pursuing the building's disintegration as the unique event it was, FEMA displayed little interest in visiting the WTC-7 site, neglected to ask anyone to take photos, and failed to interview cleanup workers. So far as researchers can tell, FEMA didn't even ask whether the building's massive (22" x 22") transfer trusses were broken or still standing.

### The "Deepest Mystery": The "Swiss-Cheese" Steel

FEMA's researchers made some startling discoveries, but their assumptions kept them from drawing the logical conclusions. Within a few months of 9/11, three professors from Worcester Polytechnic Institute (WPI) had issued their report about a remarkably deformed piece of steel from Building 7.

This "Swiss-cheese" specimen came from a thick I-beam whose "steel flanges had been reduced from an inch thick to paper thin" (www.berkeley.edu/news/berkeleyan/2001/10/03_grou.html). In places this fragment was "extremely thin," indicating that the steel had melted away even though no fire in any of the buildings was hot enough to melt steel outright. Both this thinning and the holes suggested that some of the steel "had vaporized, partly evaporated in extraordinarily high temperatures." To compound the riddle, the WPI researchers found that iron atoms in the steel had combined with sulfur to form compounds causing the steel to melt at lower temperatures (*WPI Transformations* Sp. 02). Despite evidence that some of the steel had vaporized and partly evaporated at extraordinarily high temperatures, the researchers were unwilling or unable to determine the source of the sulfur.

The Worcester Polytechnic findings made it clear that "this Swiss cheese appearance [had] shocked all of the fire-wise professors, who expected to see distortion and bending—but not holes." These cavities, some as large as a silver dollar, were caused by a "eutectic mixture" containing iron, oxygen and sulfur that could lower the melting point, causing "inter-granular melting capable of turning a solid steel girder into Swiss cheese" (*WPI Transformations* Sp. 02). Perplexed by the presence of sulfur as well as the piece itself, *New York Times* reporters James Glanz and Eric Lipton characterized this piece of ruined steel as "perhaps the deepest mystery uncovered in the investigation" (*NYT* 2/2/02).

FEMA's Report also revealed that the WTC steel appeared to have encountered "severe high-temperature erosion" and been "rapidly corroded by sulfidation." Investigators were puzzled because "the severe corrosion and subsequent erosion ... are a very unusual event. No clear explanation for the source of the sulfur has been identified" (FEMA *WTC Building Performance Study* Appendix C).

Some researchers speculated that the sulfur might have come from gypsum found in building materials. In the years that followed, scientists—including Dr. Steven Jones—had called on government investigators to conduct experiments to see whether the sulfur could have come from inside the buildings—especially from drywall. When investigators refused to run the tests, freelance experimenters such as engineer Jonathan Cole ran them—and proved that the reactive sulfur came from neither the building materials nor the aluminum nor the jet fuel (www.youtube.com/watch?v=VvQD FV1HINw&feature=player_embedded#!). All this made sense, since the calcium sulfate in drywall is inert; that's why they use it for fireproofing.

FEMA was equally puzzled by the three collapses, asserting "the sequence of events leading to the collapse of each Tower could not be definitively determined." While FEMA did have the integrity to admit that none of its theories made much sense, it also kicked the can of worms down the road. Although the phrase "sequence of events leading to the collapse" sounded innocuous enough, NIST investigators would later find this before-the-tumble focus useful for their own purposes.

**Losses at WTC-7 Are Under Acknowledged**

FEMA took criticism from many directions. Media critic Scott Loughrey cited not only FEMA's nonchalance about WTC-7's demise but a curious silence among the tenants of the building. *What kind of society,* he wondered, *treats such an unprecedented disaster as though it were an everyday event?* In addition to the mayor's Office of Emergency Management (OEM), tenants at WTC-7 included the CIA, the IRS, the Defense Department, and the Securities and Exchange Commission (SEC). However, few heads of these departments were at all vocal in demanding to know why the building had collapsed (http://globalresearch.ca/articles/LOU308A.html).

Beyond life and private property, the press scarcely noticed how the losses of public property affected the legal system. Few in the news media raised any outcry when it became evident that thousands of SEC documents crucial to ongoing federal cases against WorldCom, Global Crossing, and Enron were lost. SEC investigations also included huge corporate banking firms such as Citicorp and others spun off from the Bank of Credit and Commerce International (BCCI) (*National Law Review* 9/17/01), otherwise known as "the Bank for Crooks and Criminals Incorporated." After BCCI closed in 1991, the network was largely rebuilt by the bin Ladens (*Wash. Post* 2/17/01). American and British governments had known all about the bank but had allowed it to operate for many years, in part because the CIA and Pakistani ISI had major accounts with BCCI (P. Thompson *Terror Timeline* p. 242).

Underreactions can be revealing, however. They bring to mind Sherlock Holmes puffing on his pipe and thinking it odd that the guard dog had failed to bark at the intruder.

## NIST: A Pattern of Evasion, Denial, and Dishonesty

Possibly taking a cue from the fact that FEMA had thrown up its hands, the National Institute of Standards and Technology (NIST) repeatedly delayed its report on WTC-7. NIST initially promised to cover WTC-7 along with the Towers in its Report of late 2004, but devoted only 56 pages to it. When the full Report finally came out in 2005, WTC-7 received only 42 pages. Next, NIST promised to complete a separate report on WTC-7 in 2006; then it promised a draft report for early 2007. But the draft didn't appear until August 2008, and the Final Report came out three months later, just after the elections. Explaining WTC-7 to an increasingly skeptical public wasn't a challenge NIST's investigators approached with great enthusiasm.

Understandably, for NIST faced big problems. Since no modern steel-framed high-rise had ever before come down mainly due to fire, NIST's investigators had much to explain. NIST faced two challenges the Towers didn't pose: WTC-7 didn't suffer structural damage from an airplane, and no jet fuel could have ignited fires.

**The Breakaway Column Theory** Attempting to assemble a scenario, NIST offered an elaborate theory: as fire-induced thermal expansion of steel beams on the thirteenth floor expanded, they broke a girder loose from a major interior support, column 79 (Griffin *Mysterious Collapse* pp. 150-55). This scenario not only sounds quirky, it also, in describing WTC-7 as a house of cards, overlooks the principle of redundancy in structural engineering: i.e., if one support should fail, others pick up its load (http://www.nd.edu/~tallbldg/rr_panel.htm). As the previous chapter demonstrated, notable redundancy was built into the WTC.

The building's external support system of closely spaced columns tied together with welded spandrel plates was exceptionally resilient. Structural engineers had raved about the design. The exterior structure tied the columns together in a very solid matrix. Like the Trade Towers, WTC-7 was built to withstand extreme challenges (Glanz and Lipton *City in the Sky* pp. 133-36).

Rather than building on FEMA's findings and doing the research it recommended, NIST moved into abstraction, computer modeling, and just plain bad science. To avoid troubling truths, the investigators consistently denied evidence, manipulated data, and made things up, making a travesty of the scientific method (Griffin *Mysterious Collapse* pp. 13-31). So when NIST refused to do serious scientific investigation, independent researchers once again undertook the task.

## Better Sleuthing Through Chemistry and Physics

By 2006, drawing on the work of the RJ Lee group, analysts led by chemist Kevin Ryan and physicist Steven Jones moved into analysis of the signature WTC dust. Making effective use of the Freedom of Information Act (FOIA), Ryan and his team discovered that soon after the buildings came down, the EPA had monitored "volatile organic chemicals" (VOCs) rising from lingering fires around Ground Zero. Once the researchers had obtained the EPA's long-suppressed reports, they learned that these toxic VOCs were measured "at levels *thousands* of times higher than seen in other structure fires." This suggested "extremely violent but short-lived fire events." Something burning in the debris had continued to emit toxic chemicals for several months (K. Ryan *The Environmentalist* 8/08).

**Looking into Self-Sustaining Combustion** Trying to find out why the debris could burn for so long, the researchers considered "chemical energetic materials which provide their own fuel and oxidant and are not deterred by water, dust, or chemical suppressants." This took them into "nanoenergetics," the study of ways to manipulate the flow of energy between molecules, and finally into "nanothermites," the explosives which contain finely particulate iron and aluminum. Nanoparticles, because they have such a great surface-to-volume ratio, can react very rapidly (www. technologyreview.com/computing/14105/page1).

Using spectrographic and electron-microscope technology, these researchers began finding both aluminosilicate and iron-rich microspheres (formed from droplets of molten metal) in the dust. For these particles to have formed, temperatures had to reach at least 2652°F and 2800°F respectively (Jones *J. of 9/11 Studies* 1/08). While the nanoenergetics/nanothermite hypothesis doesn't answer all questions, it does help explain the very long-burning, intensely hot fires at Ground Zero (Knight Ridder 5/29/02).

Also pertinent was the data that Dr. Jones obtained through a Freedom of Information Act request: the full results of an earlier but suppressed USGS study. Jones and his colleagues found that the USGS had discovered far more than their published results let on: in the dust they'd found a microsphere rich in molybdenum, an uncommon element. Since the melting point for metallic molybdenum is an amazing 4753°F, the presence of this microsphere implied that combustion in the buildings had generated temperatures over three times those reached by even the hottest hydrocarbon/office fires (Jones *J. of 9/11 Studies* 1/08). Whereas office fires peaking at 1400°F obviously don't generate the 2700°F needed to melt steel, nanothermite reaches 4500°F or more.

### International Scientific Analysis of the Red/Gray Chips

Since scientists improve their credibility when they work in teams and publish their findings in peer-reviewed journals, this was the way to go. This time, Prof. Niels Harrit, a chemist at the University of Copenhagen, was the lead researcher, backed by Steven Jones, Kevin Ryan, and six others.

Also present in the WTC dust were microscopic two-sided, red/gray chips. So the question seemed simple enough: What were these chips found in the WTC dust made of, and what might they reveal about what went on during the buildings' ultimate moments? The methods were impressively scientific; researchers worked from several samples of WTC dust gathered in different places, and "controlled" their experiment by testing the dust from conventional demolitions as well. Using state-of-the-art instrumentation, the researchers found that while the gray sides of the chips consisted of rhomboidal crystals with "high iron and oxygen content" along with carbon, the red sides were comprised mainly of "aluminum, iron, oxygen, silicon and carbon." When heated to about 830°F, this red side burned intensely, pointing to the presence of "highly energetic thermitic material" in the dust (*Open Chemical Physics Journal* 1/09).

While the researchers were less certain about the gray side of the chips, they found compelling evidence that the red side was unreacted nanothermite, an explosive. Later, larger fragments of unignited thermite were discovered in the dust. Professor Harrit was careful, however, not to dismiss other possibilities: "we found nanothermite in the rubble; we are not saying that only nanothermite was used" (*Open Chemical Physics Journal* 1/09). This was an important qualifier, since thermite lacks sulfur—and sulfur, after all, was the mystery element that puzzled the Worcester Polytechnic researchers, as they noted in FEMA's Report.

Most of the criticism of the nanothermite paper has focused on surrounding issues, not the science itself. So although the *Open Chemical Physics Journal* wasn't the most prestigious in its field, it *was* juried. Enhanced by the use of high-tech instruments, the design and methodology seem logically tight and sufficiently solid. It's the study itself that counts most; the nanothermite paper has made an important contribution. If other researchers haven't yet replicated its experiments, thereby validating its results, that's not the fault of those who did the original work.

In summary, evidence of strange substances has been found by government investigators, environmental firms, academics, and three different sets of independent scientists. According to Griffin, all of their research has shown that destruction of the steel must have involved "extremely high temperatures" that hydrocarbon fires simply could not have produced (Griffin *Mysterious Collapse* p. 45).

**NIST Delivers Draft Report: David Confronts Government Goliath**
After repeatedly missing deadlines to complete its report on WTC-7, the Draft for Public Comment finally appeared in August 2008. Making no mention of NIST's four-year delay, Shyam Sunder, the agency's lead investigator for its WTC projects, announced with bravado that "the reason for the collapse of World Trade Center 7 is no longer a mystery. WTC-7 collapsed because of fires fueled by office furnishings. It did not collapse from explosives." The corporate media trumpeted Sunder's pronouncement (AP 9/21/08). Three times in this Draft Report, NIST insisted that its findings were "consistent with physical principles."

Soon enough, though, Sunder and NIST had to eat humble pie. High school physics teacher David Chandler was fond of quipping "two planes, three buildings: do the math." But Chandler was dead serious about Building 7, and he'd done the math. He'd made a video, "WTC-7 in Freefall" (www.youtube.com/watch?v=rVCDpL4Ax7I), which furnished evidence of the building's observable near-free-fall for 2.5 seconds, implying that after it dropped behind another building, it completed its fall in 6.6 seconds. Chandler might have cited Yogi Berra, who famously remarked "you can observe a lot just by watching."

At the public hearing, Chandler pointed out that video evidence showed WTC-7 coming down at a near free-fall speed and that, if one accepted NIST's theory of successive column failure, this speed was hardly consistent with "physical principles." Chandler asked why, when videos show the top of WTC-7 dropping at near free-fall speed, NIST was claiming a fall speed 40 percent slower than that. "How," he asked, "can such a publicly visible, easily measurable quantity be set aside?" It was almost painful to watch Sunder stumble around. NIST's leader lectured on universal gravity (which "applies to everybody; every—all bodies on, uh, on, uh, on this particular—on this planet, not just, uh, in Ground Zero") rather than dealing with the evidence of near free-fall speed of WTC-7 (www.youtube.com/watch?v=eDvNS9iMjzA&p=206C1F5EDFC83824).

Soon after the August events, videos of both the "Questions and Answers" and "Technical Briefing" sessions were removed from NIST's website.

### NIST Comes Up with Entirely New Theory

Responding to the sharp critique it had encountered at its August meetings, NIST released a Final Report that revealed more about NIST than about WTC-7. Come November, NIST presented a whole new theory for the fall of WTC-7. This one involved three stages: a slow initial descent, a freefall descent for 2.25 seconds, and a decreasing velocity as the building met with "resistance from the structure below" (*Final Report* p. 607). This was inventive, but was it science or science fiction? NIST also had removed its claim that its findings were "consistent with physical principles."

It was NIST's first stage, that of slow initial descent, that most bothered Chandler, Jones, and other scientific skeptics. Referring to the photographic record, Chandler pointed out that virtually no movement was observed during NIST's first stage; that NIST was working from an artificially early start time set to agree with a computer model and that its first stage contradicted the videographic evidence, which showed the building starting to fall suddenly and then dropping precipitously, accelerating like those balls Galileo dropped from the Leaning Tower of Pisa (www.youtube.com/watch?v=rVCDpL4Ax7I).

Perhaps NIST tossed a bone to its critics, hoping that they'd be so hungry for some concession that they'd quit howling about the contradictions. Yet when NIST acknowledged free-fall speed, however briefly, it tacitly admitted that its theory of successive collapse could not be true. Put another way, in a free-fall descent all 82 columns had to fail simultaneously, and this was just the opposite of NIST's fire-damage theory, which involved much slower progressive collapse of the columns. Thus when NIST affirmed near free-fall speed, even for a moment, it came very close to implicitly acknowledging that WTC-7 was intentionally demolished.

**Revisiting the Primary Characteristics of Planned Demolition**

Adapted from the National Fire Protection Association's *Guide for Fire and Explosion Investigations* (Sect. 18.3.2), here are the characteristics of planned demolition:

1. The onset of the collapse was sudden.
2. The building fell at near freefall velocity.
3. The building dropped straight down and fell symmetrically.
4. The building imploded and dropped mostly into its own footprint.
5. The collapse was total, with very little left standing.
6. Much of the nonmetallic material was pulverized, resulting in large dust clouds (Griffin *Mysterious Collapse* p. 28).

In the aftermath of WTC-7's destruction, additional signs of demolition were evident:

- Hot spots of molten metal were reported by numerous highly qualified witnesses, including Mark Loizeaux, president of Controlled Demolition, Inc. (Griffin *Mysterious Collapse* p. 36).
- FEMA found rapid oxidation and intergranular melting on structural steel samples.
- The chemical signature of the explosive thermite was found in solidified molten metal and dust samples.
- Ample evidence suggests foreknowledge of the "collapse" by the news media, city officials, NYPD, and FDNY (http://911blogger.com/node/6195).
- Eyewitnesses observed that the collapse started at the bottom, and sounds of explosions were heard at ground level just seconds before inception.
- Puffs of smoke called "squibs" shot out of the falling building in synchronization.
- A "kink" or slight dip in the roof was evident (www.youtube.com/watch?v=Zv7BimVvEyk).

## Beyond Just Criteria for Demolition

Thunder-like rumbles were heard just *before* the penthouse began to disintegrate (http://www.youtube.com/watch?v=ERhoNYj9_fg), and its disintegration was virtually complete several seconds before the whole building started to descend. The early sag in the penthouse parallels the early drop of the broadcast antenna on top of the North Tower. Kinks in the roof occur when charges have shattered the inner structure of the building, which is an essential task of controlled demolition so the building will implode on itself, avoiding damage to surrounding structures. Thus kinks are one of the surest signs of implosion—and therefore, like near free-fall speed and near perfect symmetry during disintegration, of planned demolition.

At WTC-7, though, the evidence extends beyond the physical and forensic. When one considers the scattered fires, the limited accessibility of fuel to stoke them, and the apparent foreknowledge by officials, first responders, and media figures, one has to raise the issue of access to the building. Unlike the Towers, WTC-7 wasn't undergoing elevator renovations. Since both physical phenomena and human behavior require explanation, questions about them would be standard fare on *Crime Scene Investigation*. They'll no doubt be pursued in a well-funded investigation, but in the meantime they'll continue to engage excellent independent researchers.

Since no opportunity for access comparable to the ACE Elevator renovation is known to have gone on at WTC-7, the question of how someone could have planted explosives can provoke a "whistleblower objection." Journalist Robert Parry has underscored the absence of anyone among dozens of technicians who must have worked, possibly over several weeks, to "wire" the buildings (Consortium News 1/5/11). Chemist Kevin Ryan retorted that "demolition of a building does not require wiring each of the floors" and that contemporary technology relies instead on remote detonators. Moreover, Ryan pointed out that "claiming that a deceptive demolition event could not happen because those who placed the charges have not come forward to boast of their handiwork is absurd. Who's going to admit killing nearly 3,000 people? … are you asking that all investigators throw out their evidence until they get a confession?" (Consortium/blogspot).

Since the whistleblower objection to the demolition hypothesis is a valid one to raise, the debate will receive more coverage in the Conclusion.

**Why Is Building 7 So Little Known?**

It's fun to smile at a judge's ignorance of "building what?" but lack of awareness about WTC-7 is no laughing matter. When one asks why this ignorance has existed, four reasons come to mind. One is circumstantial— that the fall of this very tall building was literally overshadowed by the fall of two much taller, more iconic ones. Clearly the scale of the death and destruction, the symbolic absence from the skyline, and the psychological trauma, were all far greater for the Towers. James Glanz seemed to have these factors in mind when he wrote that WTC-7 "was a mystery that under normal circumstances would probably have captured the attention of the city and the world" (*NYT* 11/29/01). In the fall of 2001, Americans didn't want to deal with mysteries. New Yorkers were dealing with the stench of death and a smoldering "pile"; they didn't need to hear about a "smoking gun."

Despite the relevance of these factors, they don't tell the full story. It's also true that information about WTC-7 was deliberately suppressed, as Griffin has suggested. Recall that immediately after 9/11, American TV networks played horrific clips of the Towers being hit by planes, set afire, and falling down. While they played and replayed these, they rarely if ever aired footage of the fires or fall of WTC-7. Moreover, the Commission's *Report* didn't so much as mention that a third building had come down. Plus NIST's reports, some of which were supposed to include coverage of Building 7, were repeatedly delayed, further diminishing public interest (www.911truth.org/article.php?story=20100527162010811).

Above all, though, WTC-7 has likely been the most completely ignored and thoroughly suppressed of the buildings because it poses a special challenge to the Official Story. Since it wasn't hit by a hijacked airliner, since its fires were smaller, and since its fall most clearly exhibits the hallmarks of controlled demolition, it's more difficult to explain, let alone to blame on al Qaeda hijackers.

## Creative Attempts to Raise Public Awareness

For some time, Richard Gage and others at Architects and Engineers for 9/11 Truth have highlighted the fact that real scientific investigation "casts grave doubt upon the media stories and the official report by the 9/11 Commission, FEMA, and NIST." In 2010, the group dramatically called attention to the fact that a third building had come down by adding a *third* searchlight beam to the two generated by the city at the WTC site (www. ae911truth.org). In the fall of that year, "Building What?," a newer group led by dedicated family members of 9/11 victims, ran very effective TV ads that led to an appearance on Geraldo Rivera's talk show (http://buildingwhat.org).

With WTC-7 as the entering wedge, the 9/11 truth movement is pressing forward, ever closer to its goal of a new investigation. And much as the WTC buildings offer a scientifically solid way into other facets of the 9/11 issue, a fuller understanding of that issue offers a way into understanding many other related areas: civil rights, media mythmaking, power and the press, access to government information, the role of intelligence agencies, and the consequences of American foreign policy.

Just as we've spent significant time unraveling a cloak of secrecy, we'll also weave a layered tapestry of new meaning. The Conclusion suggests places to start.

# Conclusion: ´ The Need for a New Investigation

*We still can speak, and the question for us now is,*
*What do we say with our voice?*

—Daniel Ellsberg, Interview with Studs Terkel, 1972.

The reviews are in: the 9/11 Commission produced a bad movie. Starting with the opening credits, the production was tightly directed. Having already scripted the story line, the White House picked a "dependable" cast and kept curious reporters off the set. Lest any "independent" actors stray from the script, the producers limited their time on camera or edited out their performances. Dramatic moments, such as the soliloquy of Transportation Secretary Mineta, ended up on the cutting room floor. Rather than receiving extensive big-screen exposure, this B movie should have gone straight to DVD, shelved under "fiction" or "docudrama."

It's not as if nobody warned us. As he resigned from the Commission, Sen. Max Cleland charged "Americans are being scammed.... This government knew a whole lot more about these terrorists than it has ever admitted" (CNN 11/13/03). From inside the Commission, Cleland came to realize that truth doesn't wear the trappings of august authority.

Even after all these pages, the book on 9/11 isn't closed. On one hand, it's important to acknowledge that even with all the evidence presented here, we've still got still a lot to uncover. On the other, it's crucial to realize that we've got enough evidence to demand accountability.

## History Suggests New Narrative

Etched into our memories by endlessly repeated horrific images, 9/11 is still an unsettling event. But when Americans understand how many contrived provocations have characterized their history—especially as springboards into wars—they're able to take a more rational overview. When Americans become more aware of their history, they can see 9/11 within patterns, not as a complete aberration.

Historically minded analyst Noam Chomsky has reminded Americans that in the 1950s, President Eisenhower wondered why Arabic peoples in the Middle East disliked Americans. The National Security Council (NSC) looked into the matter and told the president that most Arabs resented US support for oppressive regimes in the region. NSC advisors told the president that such oppression was not necessarily a bad thing; that as long as these dictators controlled their people, "we can control the oil." The advisors added that dissidents in those countries "should direct their anger elsewhere" (Pacifica "Democracy Now!" 2/16/11).

This idea that Arab dissidents should "direct their anger elsewhere," toward foreign enemies rather than domestic despots, guided US policy for decades. The Saudis encouraged dissidents like Osama bin Laden to fight "godless communist infidels," and the CIA trained and equipped these *mujahedeen* to fight the Soviets in Afghanistan. Over a dozen years the *mujahedeen*, the precursors of al Qaeda, received $10 billion from the Saudis and Americans (A. Rashid *Taliban* p. 18). During the 1980s, then, the Saudi monarchy gladly sent its militants to fight elsewhere, and Washington was only too happy to have *jihadi* do the dying in a secret war. Neither government gave much thought to how cozy relationships among al Qaeda, the CIA, and Pakistan's ISI might bode danger.

## Blowback from American Policies

Washington took little notice of the fact that its policies were breeding deep resentments—that Islamists might come to hate the United States for supporting Arabic dictators and enabling Israeli aggression. Novelist Gore Vidal insisted that "our policies were such that we were going to have a lot of crazy people out there in the Arab world who were going to try to blow us up, because of crimes they feel we committed against them. Any fool could see it coming" (*Independent* [UK] 2/7/10).

Long before 9/11, then, blowback had become evident when Islamists began to target the US. When they bombed the WTC in 1993, decades of Israeli violence against the Palestinians came home to rock Manhattan. The bombers—including several of the very Islamists who went on to mastermind 9/11—said they were returning "the terrorism that Israel practices, which is supported by America." Attempting to justify their attacks on civilians, the perpetrators added "the American people are responsible for … the crimes that their government is committing …" (J. Bamford *Pretext for War* pp. 101-02).

Between 1993 and 2001, bin Laden repeatedly pointed to American policies—especially supporting Israel and stationing US troops on Saudi soil—as the reasons he was targeting America. But the Clinton and Bush administrations, both of them committed to advancing the Global Domination Project, didn't pay much attention to Islamist militants unless they could used them as proxies for power projection. If Washington didn't completely ignore warnings of a gathering storm, it certainly didn't consider changing the policies (C. Johnson *Blowback* pp. 9-12). Ever since Islamist terrorism became a problem, Washington officialdom, Beltway pundits, and radio shouters have refused to see it as a response to US foreign policy.

In the wake of 9/11, the few bold Americans who talked about blowback or backlash were widely reviled as "unpatriotic." When fellow Americans asked "why do they hate us?' the standard answer was simple: "they hate our freedoms," Bush and others insisted. This was doubly misleading, for it both reduced justified resentments to simple envy and also affirmed domestic freedoms at the very time these same leaders were curtailing them. However, the recent pro-democracy protests in Tunisia, Egypt, and Libya have shown how false this claim was. The citizens of these countries clearly don't "hate our freedoms": they want what we want—freedom and democracy. It's not America they hate, but its policy of supporting the corrupt dictators who've denied them freedom and democracy (NPR 2/24/11).

## Other Patterns: SCADs and Shock Doctrine Events

In recent years, even mainstream commentators have come to see that American society has, over the past decades, become increasingly corporatist, undemocratic, and economically unjust. However, these commentators have less often discussed the likelihood that these disturbing trends in American life have often been engineered by some ranking civilian, intelligence, and military officials. The transgressions include State Crimes Against Democracy (SCADs) (http://abs.sagepub.com/content/53/6.toc). SCADs include political assassinations, contrived incidents, and stolen elections that can be exploited under the Shock Doctrine.

In this century, the Shock Doctrine has become an especially operative factor. Skeptics have rightly emphasized how neocon longings for a "new Pearl Harbor" were expressed in 2000 and how, after many neocons had come to power, the trauma of 9/11 came less than a year later. This allowed the Bush administration to curtail civil right through the Patriot Act and to declare a War on Terror that enabled it to start major wars. In this way, peace activist Norman Solomon has observed, "9/11 still serves as a blank check for endless war" (Pacifica Radio 3/17/10).

More recently, the world has also experienced "the Great Recession." In response, filmmaker Charles Ferguson has contributed the Academy Award-winning *Inside Job*, a superb film that documents how big financial players and predatory lenders knew full well their actions were likely to wreak economic disaster. The results have included huge profits for Wall Street, for the biggest banks, and for real estate speculators who've snatched up foreclosed properties (M. Moore *Capitalism: A Love Story*). Even more recently, Naomi Klein, the author of *The Shock Doctrine*, has pointed out how widely publicized perceptions of a government budget crisis (another shock) have provided pretexts for "austerity measures." Instead of looking at ways to increase income through fair taxation of billionaires or plugging tax loopholes for the rich, politicians make massive cuts to services essential not only to the poor, but for most people of limited means (www.commondreams. org/video/2011/03/09-0).

Deeply based on fear, the Shock Doctrine is simple: while "regular people" are in shock, it's much easier to push through changes most citizens would otherwise oppose. Passing the Patriot Act and declaring the War on Terror right after 9/11 are pertinent examples.

## Questions of Collaboration

It's tempting to assume that just because many parts of the Official Story are demonstrably false, *all* parts are false. Here we need to recall that most successful propaganda contains elements of truth. As Chapters 15-18 have shown, it seems highly likely that al Qaeda Islamists *did* exist, *did* take flying lessons, and *did* fly those airliners. But this doesn't mean they didn't receive help, past or present, passive or active.

So as previous chapters have shown, 9/11 was less about *either* al Qaeda *or* other actors as about *both/and*. "Much of the debate over 9/11," Prof. Peter Dale Scott has noted, "has been focused on … a false dilemma: whether it was Islamists or the US government who were responsible for the disaster. We should at least contemplate the possibility that it was a global meta-group … that had the various resources and far-reaching connections necessary for the successful plot" (Scott *Road to 9/11* p. 179). That may sound vague, but Scott certainly didn't intend, like the 9/11 Commission, to say that "everybody's responsible, so nobody's responsible." Not at all. His "meta-group" suggested collaboration among al Qaeda, Pakistan's ISI, the CIA, the FBI, drug lords, rich Saudis, and corrupt financial institutions like the Bank of Credit and Commerce International (BCCI). The key relationships, however, likely involved al Qaeda operatives: Pakistan's ISI, the CIA, and the FBI.

By the early 1990s, and possibly before, the FBI was supporting double agents such as Ali Mohammed "the American." By the late 1990s, high-ranking FBI officials were blocking investigations of al Qaeda operatives within the United States. Blockages went way beyond Agent Ken Williams's memos from Phoenix, which repeatedly warned FBI bosses that suspicious young Arabs were taking flying lessons. In another instance, regular FBI agents and military intelligence officials revealed how they were prevented from carrying out investigations into members of the bin Laden family (*Guardian* [UK] 11/7/01).

When the CIA first established collaborative links to Islamic militants, most of its personnel were probably doing so for officially approved (if not lawful) purposes. But by the late 1990s, after years of cooperating to oppose Soviet expansion, to reduce Russian influence in Chechyna, or to block Serbian aggression in the Balkans, these collaborative efforts apparently shifted toward more sinister intent. How else can one explain a CIA agent visiting Osama bin Laden while the latter was in the hospital? (*Le Figaro* [Fr.] 10/11/01).

Could "rogue elements" in a spy agency which had long financed and directed al Qaeda operations have shifted its targets to the US homeland? When one considers that the CIA has a long history of doing assassinations, conducting "black operations," PSYOPs, and planning false-flag operations, Agency involvement in the 9/11 attacks wouldn't seem out of the question. If the CIA is seen as an instrument designed to project US power and influence, and the 9/11 attacks are seen as a way to generate public support for those goals, then CIA involvement in the 9/11 attacks, while in clear violation of its charter, wouldn't seem completely "off mission." If the corporate news media have long censored their coverage of FBI and CIA actions, since 9/11 they've even more strenuously resisted covering most of the research findings about that event. They certainly don't place the debacle in meaningful contexts.

## Consequences of Compromised News Media

Once a country's news media have taken part in government distortions or cover-ups, their credibility is in jeopardy if they reverse themselves. The longer they suppress the truth, the more they risk being eventually suspected as failing to do their job—or worse, as actively censoring the news. Their first defense is typically to continue suppressing evidence that challenges the official accounts. Then, if that doesn't seem sufficient, they'll often move into dismissal or ridicule of those who challenge the Official Story as "extremists" or "conspiracy theorists." For most editors and publishers, among the most dreaded questions are these: Why didn't you report all this years ago? Who exercises editorial control there, anyway?

As noted in Chapter 1, SCADs that damage democracy are usually connected to the Global Domination Project. Since the corporate news media typically haven't reported these events, they're invested in preventing the truth about such crimes from coming out. "The problem," observed Prof. Scott, "is a global dominance mindset that prevails not only inside the Washington Beltway but also in the mainstream media…, one which has come to accept recent inroads on constitutional liberties, and stigmatizes, or at least responds with silence to, those who are alarmed by them … " (Global Research 6/11/08).

Thus rather than providing a check on centralized power, the corporate media have come to protect it while suppressing dissent. Anyone who's attended a peace rally and then read a newspaper account of it knows that journalists are apt to seriously underestimate the numbers attending demonstrations. This, of course, assumes the demonstration was covered at all.

### Why Haven't We Had More Whistleblowers?

In response to someone who suspects foul play on 9/11, it's often objected that "surely by now someone involved would have come forth." This is a fair point, but it may overlook all that's involved. For someone to become a whistleblower, he or she must have knowledge to report, sufficient motivation to report it, and the means for it to reach the public. If we assume that more actors were involved in the 9/11 attacks than just the al Qaeda operatives, then the existence of people with things to say wouldn't seem to be the problem.

In fact, several whistleblowers have come forth, but they've paid a high price for doing so. Former FBI translator Sibel Edmonds spoke out, but after she appeared on "60 Minutes" in 2002, she faced a gag order from the Justice Department (Huffington Post 2/4/08). Someone's motivation to disclose usually involves perceived rewards and punishments, and frequently the probable punishments considerably outweigh the possible rewards.

### Going to the Media—and Then What?

Media coverage is another crucial issue, and few corporate programs are anything like "60 Minutes." Beyond a very few programs, revelations have seldom received much coverage in the corporate media. Therefore, the well documented revelations of Sibel Edmonds haven't seen much daylight. When Edmonds couldn't find a major US outlet that would run her exposé on black-market nuclear arms dealing, she went to the *London Times* (1/6/08). Given the typical media blackout on challenges to the Official Story, if someone did speak out, would the public ever hear about it through the corporate media? Today many of us would be apt to say, "forget the news media; we have the internet." But mass-exposure sites such as Huffington Post, Common Dreams, and Alternet also enforce boundaries on what they cover. And some disturbing coverage, such as the video of the US forces gunning down unarmed civilians in Baghdad (www. collateralmurder.com) released in 2010 by Pvt. Bradley Manning, tend to be inaccessible on such sites. Confined to a solitary cell 23 hours a day, mostly without clothing, the mistreatment of Pvt. Manning illustrated what can happen to whistleblowers (*Guardian* [UK] 3/11/11).

In his excellent article "Where Are the Whistleblowers?" (911research. wtc7.net/essays/roberts/index.htm) writer and researcher Gregg Roberts lists four questions facing a whistleblower who wants to make a difference:

1. Is the whistleblowing exposé likely to be published by a reputable news outlet or website?
2. Will the story be picked up by other mainstream news organizations?
3. Does the exposé seem likely to be deemed credible, or is it more likely to face ridicule by talk show hosts, pundits, and editorialists?
4. If the exposé does receive media coverage, will it be widely accepted and become part of the conversation?

If at least some of these outcomes didn't seem likely, how many of us would risk blowing the whistle? Beyond these considerations, potential whistleblowers naturally weigh threats to their careers, their families, and even their lives.

## How Long Can a Secret Be Kept?

Historical examples of how long and how well some secrets have been kept are surprising and instructive. To this day, few Americans know that FDR provoked Imperial Japan and that Pearl Harbor was less a surprise than a setup. This is fully documented in Chapter 2. Hundreds of potential whistleblowers were around for decades, but very few came forth. The Manhattan Project offers another example of a very well kept secret. Though more than 100,000 people were involved in the Project, the secret never leaked out; despite their spy networks, the Germans and Japanese never learned about the Bomb.

Israel's 1967 strike on the US Navy's *USS Liberty* provides another example. In this deadly attack, 43 Americans were killed, yet Navy commanders threatened survivors with fines, imprisonment, and even death if they talked about what they'd experienced. Largely because of these government threats and the power of pro-Israel lobbies, the attack remains almost completely omitted from American history (DVD *The Loss of Liberty*).

## Whistleblowing More Broadly Considered

For 9/11, the stakes are much higher. Disclosures about 9/11 threaten far more than just policies toward one country; they could expose many prominent figures, both in office and out, and also invite the public to further question the nature of the federal government. Thus enormous pressures come down on those who might consider speaking out. This said, though, one does wonder, Why hasn't just one of those demolition technicians who helped rig the buildings come forth? Perhaps some have, and perhaps others are dead. It could be very dangerous to do so.

Perhaps looking for *individual* truth tellers is limiting. It's worth looking at a model in which a larger number of people with *some* knowledge tell *some* of what they know. If we include this model of "whistleblowing," then one can note several limited revelations. Such revelations—e.g., Richard Clarke's *Against All Enemies*, Philip Shenon's *The Commission*, James Bamford's *Body of Secrets*, Anthony Shaffer's *Dark Heart, and* Peter Lance in several books, especially *Triple Cross*—may not accept the controlled demolition hypothesis or frame the 9/11 attacks as state terrorism. If questioned, most such writers would probably say they support the Official Story. Yet, read carefully, their books frequently undermine it.

Nevertheless, several writers have contributed knowledge useful to researchers entertaining more drastic conclusions.

## Pursuing the Truth about 9/11

Calls to continue the press for truth continue to come from many quarters. Speaking after the death of Beverly Eckert, a 9/11 widow and member of the Families Steering Committee, Robert F. Kennedy Jr. lamented the activist's passing but affirmed that "we must move forward in our search for the truth. We must honor her by continuing to demand real answers and accountability from our government officials.… That's all Beverly was saying: that the most patriotic thing we as Americans can do is to raise legitimate questions and expect honest answers" (2/13/09).

The "Building What?" campaign in New York has extended the legacy of Beverly Eckert. As widows and other members of the families continue their work, progressive academics have joined their call for justice. As the evidence mounts, remarked Harvard Professor Elaine Scarry, "a weight is on the population's shoulders: does our already existing knowledge … obligate us to press for legal redress?" (*Boston Review* Sept./Oct 08).

## Actual Investigations, Near and Far

In the fifteen years following World War I, many Americans suspected that elite interests might have misled their country into that conflict. In 1933, the Senate's Nye Report made headlines by drawing connections between wartime profits of the banking and munitions industries and America's involvement in World War I (B. Tuchman *March of Folly* p. 382). And in the 1970s, in the wake of Watergate, the Senate's Church Committee probed the CIA in ways that made insiders uncomfortable. These investigations were successful in promoting greater public understanding of how their government worked—or didn't.

Today, as many among us have lamented, we live in a culture that's apt to ignore the importance of accountability. This became particularly evident in early 2009 when Sen. Patrick Leahy (D-Vt.) called for a "truth commission" to look into the Bush administration. Reacting strongly, Sen. Arlen Specter (R/D Penn.) responded with a prejudicial dismissal of truth seeking: "going after a prior administration sounds like something they do in Latin American banana republics" (*San Fran. Chron.* 4/23/09). Sen. Specter was wrong on several counts. Citizens in many countries have realized that it's never too late to face unfinished business from the past.

## Cultures Exorcise Their Ghosts

On the "Latin" side of Specter's snide dismissal, consider Spain. More than 70 years after the atrocities of the Spanish Civil War, resistance to excavating the country's repressed memories had ossified. Yet in 2007, Spain's Socialist government enacted a Law of Historical Memory which, for the first time, acknowledged the victims of Gen. Franco's fascist dictatorship. The subscript was simple: we're not going to "pretend" about these crimes any longer.

On the "America" side, several South American countries have shown remarkable integrity as they've dealt with the demons of the past. In Chile, citizens have made courageous efforts to address the crimes of Gen. Pinochet's military dictatorship. An independent judiciary has recently gained the citizen support allowing it to file charges in hundreds of cases. Recently President Sebastian Pinera requested CIA documents revealing the Chilean agents responsible for more than 12,000 civil rights violations committed during the Pinochet police state (*San Fran. Chron.* 3/23/11).

In Argentina, several films, one titled *The Official Story,* have examined the troubled past. Investigations into the crimes of the country's infamous military junta ensued and in recent years, these have led to more than 500 trials (www. laverdadyjusticia.net). Years after crimes are committed, justice can still be done.

## Four Focus Areas for a Real Inquiry into 9/11

When it comes to the crime or our century, so many questions remain:

1. Why didn't the intelligence agencies identify the growing threats and head off the attacks in the first place?
2. How do we account for the spectacular failures of air defenders to intervene, despite the billions spent on state-of-the-art equipment, supersonic aircraft, and highly trained pilots?

3. What would explain the unprecedented structural failures of not two but three World Trade Center buildings?

4. The FBI has acknowledged that it has "no hard evidence" to hold Osama bin Laden responsible for the attacks; so if bin Laden didn't do it, then who was responsible for the deaths of 3,000 Americans that day?

## Outer Work and Inner Work

Crucial as it is that Americans as a society understand the huge *tsunami* that hit them, we must also attend to their personal growth. Retired Air Force Col. Karen Kwiatkowski speaks of her personal quest to understand what the country was doing with its national security and foreign policies: "I spent months and years after 9/11 reading and watching and questioning, trying to learn more ... [but] this effort at self-education was marred by the insistent drumbeat of the 'one true path'" (Griffin and Scott *9/11 and the American Empire* p. 21).

Such personal commitment to learning is crucial, both to us as individuals and to our collective enterprise, a vibrant American democracy. A combination of savvy political analysis and self-reflection offer us the best protection against an increasingly manipulative power structure. Above all, argues scientist and activist Kevin Ryan, 9/11 issues illustrate not just how we've been deceived, but how we've deceived ourselves—and how the powerful "exploit that fact of human nature. Our best chance at avoiding such exploitation is to notice the self-deceptive tendencies in ourselves." If we do this, Ryan has observed, we can tap a "powerful potential to effect real change in our society" (www.911blogger.com/node/18673).

As the ultimate mass murder mystery, 9/11 demands unflinching investigation. By facing the truth, Americans will show themselves and the world that they are both resilient and courageous—and that they can reverse the decline of their democracy. Those of us who've seen threads break loose bear a responsibility to help unravel the whole tangle of deceit.

Restorative truth is out there: a truly independent inquiry will bring it to light.

# About the Author

A longtime student of American culture, Paul W. Rea, PhD, has tried to live his commitments to good government, participatory democracy, and a passionate love of nature. He is also a longtime peace and environmental activist. Dr. Rea is a former professor of humanities and the author of *Still Seeking the Truth about 9/11* (2005). Drawing on the specialized expertise of many other researchers, *Mounting Evidence* is a thorough but readable introduction to the complex issues surrounding 9/11. An avid reader, traveler, gardener, and naturalist, Paul Rea is also the author of *Canyon Interludes*, a collection of natural history essays about the American Southwest. He lives with his beloved Sandy in the San Francisco Bay area.

# Recommended Resources:
## Films, Websites, and Readings

(*Asterisks signify especially well respected sources).

**Involved and Supportive Groups, Based on Profession or Calling**
–Actors and Artists for 9/11 Truth: www.AA911truth.com
*Architects and Engineers for 9/11 Truth: www.ae911truth.org
–Family Steering Committee: http://www.911independentcommission.org
    (or http://911independentcommission.org)
*Firefighters for 9/11 Truth: www.firefightersfor911truth.org
*Intelligence Officers for 9/11 Truth: www.IO911truth.org
–Journalists and other Media Professionals for 9/11 Truth:
    http://mediafor911truth.org
–Lawyers for 9/11 Truth: www.l911truth.com
*Patriots Question 9/11: http://patriotsquestion911.com
–Political Leaders for 9/11 Truth: www.pl911t.org
–Professors Question 9/11: http://patriotsquestion911.com/professors.html
–Religious Leaders for 911truth: www.rl911truth.org
–Scholars for 911 Truth: http://911scholars.org
*Scholars for 911 Truth and Justice: http://stj911.org
–Veterans for 911/Truth: www.V911t.com

## Research Opportunities

*www.911researchWTC7.org High quality research ably supervised and accessibly presented by ace researcher Jim Hoffman

*www.911truth.org High quality, well presented research under the careful tutelage of Janice Matthews and Michael Berger

*Center for Cooperative Research/History Commons: www.cooperativeresearch.org/ Organized by Paul Thompson and other researchers, this is a very useful, reliable site for information on historical and current events.

* "The 9/11 Complete Timeline": www.historycommons.org/project. jsp?project=911_project. A constantly updated extension of Thompson's book *The CompleteTerror Timeline*, truly massive, responsibly sourced site is essential for many facets of 9/11; it's especially strong on foreknowledge of the attacks.

*Centre for Research on Globalization: *http://www.globalresearch.ca The project of Michel Chossudovsky, a well known Canadian economist and professor of economics at the University of Ottawa, this site is not limited to 9/11 issues. Posts articles by important researchers, including Sibel Edmonds and Peter Dale Scott.

*www.visibility911.com – topical and ably run by Scott Ford

## Research on WTC-7

*http://wtc7.net A definitive but accessible site on the fall of WTC-7, run by Jim Hoffman.

*www.911review.com - very current, well organized site run by Jim Hoffman; addresses "internal" controversies.

*www.7problemswithbuilding7.info - created and maintained by former NASA aerospace research engineer Dwain Deets; current and scientific.

–http://investigatebuilding7.org Useful site run by the "Building What?" campaign calling for a new investigation of WTC-7.

–www.911ReadingRoom.org

–www.rememberbuilding7.com – run by Rev. Frank Morales, families of the victims, and others.

## Science-Oriented Sites/Sources

*www.scienceof911.com.au Excellent research done by Australian scientist Dr. Frank Legge

*Journal of 9/11 Studies: www.journalof91studies.com A peer-reviewed, open-access, electronic-only journal covering the whole of research related to 9/11/01. Edited by topflight researchers Steven Jones, Ph.D., and Kevin Ryan.

*http://911TruthNews.org Exhibits a strong commitment to the best evidence. Editors are Victoria Ashley, Cosmos, Scott Ford, and Julian Ware. Jon Gold contributes frequently.

## Activism Sites

*www.911.Blogger.com

–911truthaction: http://groups.yahoo.com/group/911TruthAction/?tab=s

–www.truthaction.org

–Family Steering Committee/ or http://911independentcommission.org/

–Community Calendar for Social Change Events:
www.communitycalender.org

–Citizens 9/11 Commission sponsoring state referenda calling for a new investigation: http://citizens911commission.com

–www.911speakout.org

–www.justicefor911.org

*http://9-11cc.org – updates on referendum campaigns for a new investigation

# Recommended Films/Videos Dealing with 9/11

## Documentaries for Viewers New to 9/11 Issues

–*9/11: Press for Truth* (2005) 95 min. Produced by Kyle Hence and
directed by young filmmakers Ray Nowosielski and John Duffy,
this award-winning, critically acclaimed film is based on the
Paul Thompson's *Complete Terror Timeline* and features three
of "the Jersey Girls." Still among the very best films on 9/11.
www.911pressfortruth.org

–*Loose Change 9/11: An American Coup?* (2009) 90 min.
Directed by Dylan Avery, narrated by Daniel Sunjata. The latest in
the "Loose Change" series of widely viewed films.
http://www.loosechange911.com/loose-change-911-an-american-coup/

–*9/11: Blueprint for Truth* (2008) 30 min., 60 min., and 120 min. versions
- Features Richard Gage, A.I.A., of Architects and Engineers for
9/11 Truth. Directed and Produced by Ken Jenkins. http://www.
ae911truth.net/store/product_info.php?cPath=27&products_id=96&os
Csid=9bf3ee3cdb1ea38d76469b5acf2351f1

## Documentaries for More Specialized Study

–*The Elephant in the Room* (2008) 92 min. Produced, directed, edited
and shot by Dean Puckett, *The Elephant in the Room* was deemed
the Best Documentary at the 2008 London Independent Film
Festival. It features Rep. Cynthia McKinney and architect Richard
Gage. This film delivers a peace message and examines the 9/11
truth movement
http://www.moviesfoundonline.com/elephant_in_the_room.php/

–*Hypothesis* (2010, 2011) 40 min. Directed by Brett Smith. This
documentary follows physics professor Steven Jones after he went
public with a theory about 9/11 so controversial that it resulted in
threats and even bribery to end his research. Despite the outside

pressures, Jones vowed to never give up on his pursuit of the truth. http://www.hypothesisfilm.com/index.php/about/

—*Kill the Messenger: A Documentary on State Secrets Privilege and US Whisteblowers* (France, 2005) Directed by Mathieu Verboud and Jean Robert Viallet, this focus of this excellent documentary is Sibel Edmonds, the former FBI translator turned whistleblower. http://video.google.com/videoplay?docid=6063340745569143497/

—*9/11 and Nationalist Faith* (2008) 63 min. Directed by Ken Jenkins, this informative, insightful film features Dr. David Ray Griffin discussing emotional blocks, intensified by the national faith in "American exceptionalism," to understanding the truth about 9/11. http://communitycurrency.org/911TV/detailnationalistfaith2.html/

—*War Promises* (Germany, 2009) 75 min. Directed by Frank Höfer, this film shows the growing importance of the international 9/11 truth movement as a gateway to reaching a more peaceful world. *War Promises* is visually arresting and substantive but not well subtitled. http://www.youtube.com/watch?v=_mAQVQtLSK8/

—*Zero* (Italy, 2008) Directed by Italian journalist and Europarliamentarian Giulietto Chiesa, *Zero* features very powerful clips plus interviews with novelist Gore Vidal, Nobel laureate Dario Fo, Dr. David Ray Griffin, Dr. Steven Jones, and others. *Zero* shows that official version of events cannot be true. The film has shown in many countries, but some sections may seem dated. No website in English. Available from Netflix.

# Recommended Readings
## (Full Bibliography appears at www.mountingevidence.org).

Ahmed, Nafeez Mosaddeq. *The War on Freedom: How and Why America was Attacked September 11, 2001.* Joshua Tree, Calif.: Tree of Life Publications, 2002.

_____. *The War on Truth: 9/11, Disinformation, and the Anatomy of Terrorism.* Northampton, Mass.: Olive Branch Press, 2005.

Bamford, James. *Body of Secrets: Anatomy of the Ultra-Secret National Security Agency.* New York: Anchor, 2002.

_____. *A Pretext for War: 9/11, Iraq, and the Abuse of America's Intelligence Agencies.* New York: Doubleday, 2004.

_____. *The Shadow Factory: The Ultra-Secret NSA from 9/11 to the Eavesdropping on America.* New York: Doubleday, 2008.

Clarke, Richard. *Against All Enemies.* New York: Free Press, 2004.

Griffin, David Ray. *The Mysterious Collapse of World Trade Center 7: Why the Final Official Report About 9/11 Is Unscientific and False.* Northampton, Mass.: Olive Branch Press, 2009.

_____. *The New Pearl Harbor Revisited: 9/11, the Cover-Up, and the Exposé.* Northampton, Mass: Olive Branch Press, 2008.

_____. *The 9/11 Commission Report: Omissions and Distortions.* Northampton, Mass.: Olive Branch Press, 2004.

Griffin, David Ray, and Peter Dale Scott, eds. *9/11 and the American Empire: The Intellectuals Speak Out.* Vol. 1. Northhampton, Mass: Olive Branch Press, 2007.

Hoffman, Jim. "Building a Better Mirage: NIST's Three-Year $20,000,000 Cover-Up of the Crime of the Century." http://911research.wtc7.net/essays/nist/index.html

Lance, Peter. *Cover Up: What the Government Is Still Hiding About the War on Terror.* New York: Regan Books, 2004.

_____. *Triple Cross: How bin Laden's Master Spy Penetrated the CIA, the Green Berets, and the FBI-And Why Patrick Fitzgerald Failed To Stop Him*. New York: William Morrow, 2006.

Ryan, Kevin R., James R. Gourley, and Steven A. Jones. "Environmental Anomalies at the World Trade Center: Evidence of Energetic Materials." *The Environmentalist* (9/08): 56-63. http://911reports.wordpress.com/2008/09/17/environmental-anomalies-at-the-world-trade-center-evidence-for-energetic-materials-by-kevin-r-ryan-james-r-gourley-and-steven-e-jones

Ruppert, Michael C. *Crossing the Rubicon: The Decline of the American Empire at the End of the Age of Oil*.Gabriola Island, BC: New Society Publishers, 2004.

Scott, Peter Dale. *Drugs, Oil, and War: The United States in Afghanistan, Colombia, and Indochina*. Lanham, Md.: Rowman and Littlefield, 2003.

_____. *The Road to 9/11: Wealth, Empire and the Future of America*. Berkeley: University of California Press, 2007.

Unger, Craig. *The Fall of the House of Bush: The Untold Story of How a Band of True Believers Seized the Executive Branch, Started the Iraq War, and Still Imperils America's Future*. New York, Scribner: 2004.

Wright, Lawrence. "The Double Game: The Unintended Consequences of American Funding in Pakistan." *The New Yorker* 5/16/11. http://www.newyorker.com/reporting/2011/05/16/110516fa_fact_wright#ixzz1M51iAT1q

*For a well- researched overview of 9/11 evidence, go to:
*http://www.911truth.org/article.php?story=20050204132153814/ or go to 911truth.org and click on "A Short Course"

# Index

Bold page numbers indicate an important and extensive discussion.